THE

AMERICAN PAGEANT

THE
American Pageant

A History of the Republic

TWELFTH EDITION

VOLUME II
SINCE 1865

David M. Kennedy
Stanford University

Lizabeth Cohen
Harvard University

Thomas A. Bailey

Houghton Mifflin Company   New York   Boston

Editor-in-Chief: Jean L. Woy
Sponsoring Editor: Colleen Shanley Kyle
Basic Book Editor: Ann West
Editorial Associate: Michael A. Kerns
Senior Project Editor: Rosemary R. Jaffe
Senior Designer: Henry Rachlin
Senior Production/Design Coordinator: Jill Haber
Senior Manufacturing Coordinator: Marie Barnes
Senior Marketing Manager: Sandra McGuire

Cover Image: *Armistice Day,* by Gifford Beal. Indiana Art Museum, William Lowe Bryan Memorial.

Credits for photographs are found following the Appendix at the end of the book.

Library of Congress Control Number: 2001131391

Printed in the U.S.A.

ISBN: 0-618-10354-6

2   3   4   5   6   7   8   9-VH-05   04   03   02

About the Authors

David M. Kennedy is the Donald J. McLachlan Professor of History at Stanford University, where he has taught for more than three decades. Born and raised in Seattle, he received his undergraduate education at Stanford and did his graduate training at Yale in American Studies, combining the fields of history, econom- ics, and literature. His first book, *Birth Control in America: The Career of Margaret Sanger* (1970) was honored with both the Bancroft Prize and the John Gilmary Shea Prize. His study of World War I, *Over Here: The First World War and American Society* (1980) was a Pulitzer Prize finalist. In 1999 he published *Freedom from Fear: The American People in Depression and War, 1929–1945*, which won the Pulitzer Prize for History, as well as the Francis Parkman Prize, the English-Speaking Union's Ambassador's Prize, and the Commonwealth Club of California's Gold Medal for Literature. At Stanford he teaches courses in American political, diplomatic, intellectual, and social history, and in American literature. He has received several teaching awards, including the Dean's Award for Distinguished Teaching. He has been a visiting professor at the University of Florence, Italy, and in 1995–1996 served as the Harmsworth Professor of American History at Oxford University. He has also served on the Advisory Board for the PBS television series, *The American Experience,* and as a consultant to several documentary films, including *The Great War, Cadillac Desert,* and *Woodrow Wilson.* From 1990 to 1995 he chaired the Test Development Committee for the Advanced Placement United States History examination. He is an elected Fellow of the American Academy of Arts and Sciences and of the American Philosophical Society. Married and the father of two sons and a daughter, in his leisure time he enjoys hiking, bicycling, river-rafting, and fly-fishing.

Lizabeth Cohen is the Howard Mumford Jones Professor of American Studies in the history department of Harvard University. Previously she taught at New York University (1992–1997) and Carnegie Mellon University (1986–1992). Born and raised in the New York metropolitan area, she received her A.B. from Princeton University and her M.A. and Ph.D. from the University of California at Berkeley. Her book, *Making a New Deal: Industrial Workers in Chicago, 1919–1939* (1990) won the Bancroft Prize in American History and the Philip Taft Labor History Award, and was a finalist for the Pulitzer Prize. Her article, "Encountering Mass Culture at the Grassroots: The Experience of Chicago Workers in the 1920s," (1989) was awarded the Constance Roarke Prize of the American Studies Association. She is currently finishing a book entitled *A Consumers' Republic: The Politics of Mass Consumption in Postwar America* about how an economy and culture built around mass consumption have shaped social life and politics in post–World War II America. An article related to this book, "From Town Center to Shopping Center: The Reconfiguration of Community Marketplaces in Postwar America," (1996) was honored with the ABC-CLIO, *America: History and Life* Award for the journal article that most advances new perspectives on accepted interpretations or previously unconsidered topics. At Harvard, she teaches courses in twentieth-century America, material and popular culture, and gender, urban, and working-class history and directs the undergraduate program in history. Before attending graduate school, she taught history at the secondary level and worked in history and art museums. She continues to help develop public history programs for general audiences through museums and documentary films. At present she also serves as president of the Urban History Association. She is married to an historian of modern France, with whom she has two daughters. For leisure, she enjoys swimming and bicycling with her family, and reading fiction.

Thomas A. Bailey (1903–1983) taught history for nearly forty years at Stanford University, his alma mater. Long regarded as one of the nation's leading historians of American diplomacy, he was honored by his colleagues in 1968 with election to the presidencies of both the Organization of American Historians and the Society for Historians of American Foreign Relations. He was the author, editor, or co-editor of some twenty books, but the work in which he took most pride was *The American Pageant*, through which, he liked to say, he had taught American history to several million students.

Contents

PART FOUR
Forging an Industrial Society   1865–1899
500

PART SIX
Creating Modern America   1945 to the Present
856

Maps

Charts and Tables

Preface

For this twelfth edition of *The American Pageant,* we have worked together closely to incorporate the most recent scholarship about American history, and to preserve the readability that has long been the *Pageant's* hallmark. We are often told that the *Pageant* is the sole American history text that has a distinctive personality—defined by clarity, concreteness, a consistent chronological narrative, strong emphasis on major themes, avoidance of clutter, access to a variety of interpretive perspectives, and a colorful writing style leavened, as appropriate, with wit. That personality, we strongly believe, is what has made the *Pageant* both appealing and useful to countless students for more than four decades.

Our collaboration on the *Pageant* reflects our respective scholarly interests, which are complementary to a remarkable degree. David Kennedy is primarily a political and economic historian, while Lizabeth Cohen's work emphasizes social and cultural history. Together, we have revised the *Pageant* chapter by chapter, even paragraph by paragraph, guided by our shared commitment to tell the story of the American past as vividly and clearly as possible, without sacrificing a sense of the often sobering seriousness of history, and of its sometimes challenging complexity.

Changes in the Twelfth Edition

The eleventh edition of the *Pageant* introduced essays designed to encourage students to think coherently about six eras in American history. Those essays, revised for this edition, seek to demonstrate that the study of history is not just a matter of piling up mountains of facts, but is principally concerned with discovering complex patterns of change over time, and organizing seemingly disparate events, actions, and ideas into meaningful chains of cause and consequence. This twelfth edition introduces an additional feature, "Examining the Evidence." It is intended to deepen students' understanding of the historical craft in another way, by conveying how historians develop interpretations of the past through research in many kinds of primary sources.

To acquaint students with the various sorts of evidence that underlie all historical accounts, new "Examining the Evidence" inserts in twenty-two chapters offer examples of the diverse materials from which historical interpretations are constructed. Students will learn about the insights historians derive from a wide range of historical artifacts: what an indentured servant's contract can teach about colonial labor relations, for example, or how an early sewing machine contains clues to changes in technology and manufacturing; why the Gettysburg Address sheds light not only on President Lincoln's brilliant oratory but also his vision of the American nation; what the manuscript census reveals about immigrant households on the Lower East Side of New York in 1900; and how a magazine advertisement for a Ford car has much to tell about gender norms in the post–World War II period. Other sources showcased include maps, furniture, architecture, private correspondence, travelogues, paintings and photographs, court decisions, political broadsides and cartoons, novels, motion pictures, newspapers, and transcripts of important diplomatic conferences and political meetings.

This edition also contains two new "Makers of America" essays, one on the environmentalists who pioneered the conservation of American natural resources in the early twentieth century, and the other on feminists during the nineteenth and twentieth centuries who founded movements committed to securing equal rights for women. We seek with these additions to show that Americans have forged group identities through their shared political commitments as much as through their ethnicity and neighborhoods. Along with the twenty-seven existing "Makers" essays, these additions help constitute a comprehensive mosaic of the diverse peoples and groups that have composed our strikingly pluralistic society.

Readers will find other new features in this edition of the *Pageant* as well: enriched discussion at many points on the experiences and contributions of women; expanded treatment of the environment, the West, and Indians; deeper analysis of the ideological origins of the American Revolution and the enduring commitment to republicanism after it; updated discussion of the War of 1812; and exploration of how the market revolution in the antebellum period transformed American life. We are deeply indebted to the wise counsel of several professional colleagues as we undertook these revisions: Drew R. McCoy, Jack Rakove, Rosalind Rosenberg, and Richard White.

All chapters in the twelfth edition now begin with new introductory paragraphs to help readers grasp the major topics and themes to follow. In addition, new box-quotes bring more varied perspectives to the events chronicled in the *Pageant's* historical narrative. We have also compressed and reorganized the material concerning the period from 1824 to 1840 into a single Chapter 13, covering the whole of Jacksonian Democracy. The discussion of Populism has also been integrated into two other chapters (Chapters 24 and 26) in order to better situate the critically important Populist episode in the contexts of late-nineteenth-century political and economic history. The twelfth edition also features many new and revised maps and charts, as well as fresh illustrations. Completely updated bibliographies are now located at the end of the book, along with a revised Appendix, containing abundant statistical data on many aspects of the American historical experience.

Goals of *The American Pageant*

Like its predecessors, this edition of *The American Pageant* tries to cultivate in its readers the capacity for balanced judgment and informed understanding about American society by holding up to the present the mirror and measuring rod that is the past. The book's goal is not to teach the art of prophecy but the much subtler and more difficult arts of seeing things in context, of understanding the roots and direction and pace of change, and of distinguishing what is truly new under the sun from what is not. The study of history, it has been rightly said, does not make one smart for the next time, but wise forever.

We hope that the *Pageant* will help to develop those intellectual assets in its readers, and that those who use the book will take from it both a fresh appreciation of what has gone before and a seasoned perspective on what is to come. And we hope,

too, that readers will take as much pleasure in reading *The American Pageant* as we have had in writing it.

Supplements Available with *The American Pageant,* Twelfth Edition

FOR STUDENTS:

- **The American Spirit, Tenth Edition, Volumes I and II:** primary-source readers
- **Complete Guidebook:** study guide without answers to exercises
- **Guidebook, Volumes I and II:** study guides with answers to exercises
- **Rand McNally Atlas of American History**
- **The American Pageant @history CD-ROM:** Student's Version
- **Student Resource Web Site,** featuring:
  ACE self-quizzes
  Online primary sources with activities
  Annotated guide to history sites
  "Examining the Evidence" activities
- **American History GeoQuest:** A CD-ROM with thirty interactive historical maps

FOR INSTRUCTORS:

- **ClassPrep CD-ROM:** A complete instructor resource
- **Instructor's Resource Guide**
- **Quizbook:** printed test item file
- **Instructor's Resource Web Site,** featuring:
  Teaching tips and assignment suggestions
  Online primary sources with instructor notes
  "Examining the Evidence" activities
  Bibliobase: customized coursepacks
- **Computerized Test Bank:** for Macintosh and Windows
- **American History Map Transparency Set:** Volumes I and II

A correlation from the text to the Advanced Placement course description ("acorn book") is available from your McDougal Littell representative.

Acknowledgments

Many people have contributed to this revision of *The American Pageant*. Foremost among them are the countless students and teachers who have written unsolicited letters of comment or inquiry. We have learned from every one of them, and encourage all readers to offer us suggestions for improving future editions. Several colleagues have also given us the benefit of their assistance, including:

Matthew Booker, *Stanford University*
Henry F. Buhl, *Harrisonburg High School, Harrisonburg, Virginia*
Ted Dickson, *Providence Day School, Charlotte, North Carolina*
Kurk Dorsey, *University of New Hampshire*
Michael C. Erickson, *Bella Vista High School, Fair Oaks, California*

JuNelle Harris, *Harvard University*
Robert Henry, *Skyline College*
Donna Kumler, *Grayson County College*
Sean Malloy, *Stanford University*
Drew R. McCoy, *Clark University*
Robert MacDougall, *Harvard University*
G. Kay Pulley, *Trinity Valley Community College*
Jack Rakove, *Stanford University*
Rosalind Rosenberg, *Barnard College*
Shirley Teresa Wajda, *Kent State University*
Richard White, *Stanford University*

Our warm thanks to each of them.

David M. Kennedy

Lizabeth Cohen

Sail, sail thy best, ship of Democracy,
Of value is thy freight, 'tis not the Present only,
The Past is also stored in thee,
Thou holdest not the venture of thyself alone, not of
  the Western continent alone,
Earth's résumé entire floats on thy keel, O ship, is
  steadied by thy spars,
With thee Time voyages in trust, the antecedent
  nations sink or swim with thee,
With all their ancient struggles, martyrs, heroes, epics,
  wars, thou bear'st the other continents,
Theirs, theirs as much as thine, the destination-port
  triumphant. . . .

Walt Whitman
Thou Mother with Thy Equal Brood, 1872

The Ordeal of Reconstruction

1865–1877

With malice toward none, with charity for all, with firmness in the right as God gives us to see the right, let us strive on to finish the work we are in, to bind up the nation's wounds, to care for him who shall have borne the battle and for his widow and orphan, to do all which may achieve and cherish a just and lasting peace among ourselves and with all nations.

ABRAHAM LINCOLN, SECOND INAUGURAL, MARCH 4, 1865

The battle was done, the buglers silent. Bone-weary and bloodied, the American people, North and South, now faced the staggering challenges of peace. Four questions loomed large. How would the South, physically devastated by war and socially revolutionized by emancipation, be rebuilt? How would the liberated blacks fare as free men and women? How would the Southern states be reintegrated into the Union? And who would direct the process of Reconstruction—the Southern states themselves, the president, or Congress?

The Problems of Peace

Other questions also clamored for answers. What should be done with the captured Confederate ringleaders, all of whom were liable to charges of treason? During the war a popular Northern song had been "Hang Jeff Davis to a Sour Apple Tree," and even innocent children had lisped it. Davis was temporarily clapped into irons during the early days of his two-year imprisonment. But he and his fellow

Richmond Devastated   Charleston, Atlanta, and other Southern cities looked much the same, resembling bombed-out Berlin and Dresden in 1945.

"conspirators" were finally released, partly because the odds were that no Virginia jury would convict them. All rebel leaders were finally pardoned by President Johnson as sort of a Christmas present in 1868. But Congress did not remove all remaining civil disabilities until thirty years later and only posthumously restored Davis's citizenship more than a century later.

Dismal indeed was the picture presented by the war-racked South when the rattle of musketry faded. Not only had an age perished, but a civilization had collapsed, in both its economic and its social structure. The moonlight-and-magnolia Old South, largely imaginary in any case, had forever gone with the wind.

Handsome cities of yesteryear, such as Charleston and Richmond, were rubble-strewn and weed-choked. An Atlantan returned to his once-fair hometown and remarked, "Hell has laid her egg, and right here it hatched."

Economic life had creaked to a halt. Banks and business houses had locked their doors, ruined by runaway inflation. Factories were smokeless, silent, dismantled. The transportation system had broken down completely. Before the war five different rail-road lines had converged on Columbia, South Carolina; now the nearest connected track was twenty-nine miles away. Efforts to untwist the rails corkscrewed by Sherman's soldiers proved bumpily unsatisfactory.

Agriculture—the economic lifeblood of the South—was almost hopelessly crippled. Once-white cotton fields now yielded a lush harvest of nothing but green weeds. The slave-labor system had collapsed, seed was scarce, and livestock had been driven off by plundering Yankees. Pathetic instances were reported of men hitching themselves to plows, while women and children gripped the handles. Not until 1870 did the seceded states produce as large a cotton crop as that of the fateful year 1860, and much of that yield came from new acreage in the Southwest.

The princely planter aristocrats were humbled by the war—at least temporarily. Reduced to proud poverty, they faced charred and gutted mansions, lost investments, and almost worthless land. Their investments of more than $2 billion in slaves, their primary form of wealth, had evaporated with emancipation.

Beaten but unbent, many high-spirited white Southerners remained dangerously defiant. They cursed the "damnyankees" and spoke of "your government" in Washington, instead of "our government." One Southern bishop refused to pray for President Andrew Johnson, though Johnson proved to be in sore need of divine guidance. Conscious of no crime, these former Confederates continued to believe that their view of secession was correct and that the "lost cause" was still a just war. One popular anti-Union song ran,

> *I'm glad I fought agin her, I only wish we'd won,*
> *And I ain't axed any pardon for anything I've*
> *done.*

Such attitudes boded ill for the prospects of painlessly binding up the Republic's wounds.

Freedmen Define Freedom

Confusion abounded in the still-smoldering South about the precise meaning of "freedom" for blacks. Emancipation took effect haltingly and unevenly in different parts of the conquered Confederacy. As Union armies marched in and out of various localities, many blacks found themselves emancipated and then re-enslaved. A North Carolina slave estimated that he had celebrated freedom about twelve times. Blacks from one Texas county fleeing to the free soil of the liberated county next door were attacked by slaveowners as they swam across the river that marked the county line. The next day, trees along the riverbank were bent with swinging corpses—a grisly warning to others dreaming of liberty. Other planters resisted emancipation more legalistically, stubbornly protesting that slavery was lawful until state legislatures or the Supreme Court declared otherwise. For many slaves the shackles of bondage were not struck off in a single mighty blow; long-suffering blacks often had to wrench free of their chains link by link.

The variety of responses to emancipation, by whites as well as blacks, illustrated the sometimes startling complexity of the master-slave relationship. Loyalty to the plantation master prompted some slaves to resist the liberating Union armies, while other slaves' pent-up bitterness burst forth violently on the day of liberation. Many newly emancipated slaves, for example, joined Union troops in pillaging their master's possessions. In one instance a group of Virginia slaves laid twenty lashes on the back of their former master—a painful dose of his own favorite medicine.

Prodded by the bayonets of Yankee armies of occupation, all masters were eventually forced to recognize their slaves' permanent freedom. The once-commanding planter would assemble his former human chattels in front of the porch of the "big

Commemorating Emancipation Day
These African-Americans in Richmond, Virginia, in 1888, commemorated the twenty-fifth anniversary of the Emancipation Proclamation by paying their respects to the "Great Emancipator," Abraham Lincoln.

house" and announce their liberty. Though some blacks initially responded to news of their emancipation with suspicion and uncertainty, they soon celebrated their newfound freedom. Many took new names in place of the ones given by their masters and demanded that whites formally address them as "Mr." or "Mrs." Others abandoned the coarse cottons that had been their only clothing as slaves and sought silks, satins, and other finery. Though many whites perceived such behavior as insubordinate, they were forced to recognize the realities of emancipation. "Never before had I a word of impudence from any of our black folk," wrote one white Southerner, "but they are not ours any longer."

Tens of thousands of emancipated blacks took to the roads, some to test their freedom, others to search for long-lost spouses, parents, and children. Emancipation thus strengthened the black family, and many newly freed men and women formalized "slave marriages" for personal and pragmatic reasons, including the desire to make their children legal heirs. Other blacks left their former masters to work in towns and cities, where existing black communities provided protection and mutual assistance. Whole communities sometimes moved together in search of opportunity. From 1878 to 1880, some twenty-five thousand blacks from Louisiana, Texas, and Mississippi surged in a mass exodus to Kansas. The westward flood of these "Exodusters" was stemmed only when steamboat cap-

tains refused to transport more black migrants across the Mississippi River.

The church became the focus of black community life in the years following emancipation. As slaves, blacks had worshiped alongside whites, but now they formed their own churches pastored by their own ministers. The black churches grew robustly. The 150,000-member black Baptist Church of 1850 reached 500,000 by 1870, while the African Methodist Episcopal Church quadrupled in size from 100,000 to 400,000 in the first decade after emancipation. These churches formed the bedrock of black community life, and they soon gave rise to other benevolent, fraternal, and mutual aid societies. All these organizations helped blacks protect their newly won freedom.

Emancipation also meant education for many blacks. Learning to read and write had been a privilege generally denied to them under slavery. Freedmen wasted no time establishing societies for self-improvement, which undertook to raise funds to purchase land, build schoolhouses, and hire teachers. One member of a North Carolina education society asserted that "a schoolhouse would be the first proof of their *independence*." Southern blacks soon found, however, that the demand outstripped the supply of qualified black teachers. They accepted the aid of Northern white women sent by the American Missionary Association, who volunteered their services as teachers. They also turned to the federal government for help. The freed blacks were going to need all the friends—and the power—they could muster in Washington.

Houston H. Holloway, age twenty at the time of his emancipation, recalled his feelings upon hearing of his freedom:

"I felt like a bird out of a cage. Amen. Amen. Amen. I could hardly ask to feel any better than I did that day. . . . The week passed off in a blaze of glory."

The reunion of long-lost relatives also inspired joy; one Union officer wrote home,

"Men are taking their wives and children, families which had been for a long time broken up are united and oh! such happiness. I am glad I am here."

The Freedmen's Bureau

Abolitionists had long preached that slavery was a degrading institution. Now the emancipators were faced with the brutal reality that the freedmen were overwhelmingly unskilled, unlettered, without property or money, and with scant knowledge of how to survive as free people. To cope with this problem throughout the conquered South, Congress created the Freedmen's Bureau on March 3, 1865.

On paper at least, the bureau was intended to be a kind of primitive welfare agency. It was to provide food, clothing, medical care, and education both to freedmen and to white refugees. Heading

The Faculty of a Freedmen's Bureau School near Norfolk, Virginia Note the racial diversity—but the gender homogeneity—of the teaching staff.

gap between themselves and the whites and partly because they longed to read the Word of God. In one elementary class in North Carolina sat four generations of the same family, ranging from a six-year-old child to a seventy-five-year-old grandmother.

But in other areas, the bureau's accomplishments were meager—or even mischievous. Although the bureau was authorized to settle former slaves on forty-acre tracts confiscated from the Confederates, little land actually made it into blacks' hands. Instead local administrators often collaborated with planters in expelling blacks from towns and cajoling them into signing labor contracts to work for their former masters. Still, the white South resented the bureau as a meddlesome federal interloper that threatened to upset white racial dominance. President Andrew Johnson, who shared the white-supremacist views of most white Southerners, repeatedly tried to kill it, and it expired in 1872.

the bureau was a warmly sympathetic friend of the blacks, Union general Oliver O. Howard, who later founded and served as president of Howard University in Washington, D.C.

The bureau achieved its greatest successes in education. It taught an estimated 200,000 blacks how to read. Many former slaves had a passion for learning, partly because they wanted to close the

> *Women from the North enthusiastically embraced the opportunity to go south and teach in Freedmen's Bureau schools for emancipated blacks. One volunteer explained her motives:*
>
> "I thought I *must* do something, not having money at my command, what could I do but give *myself* to the work. . . . I would go to them, and give them my life if necessary."

Johnson: The Tailor President

Few presidents have ever been faced with a more perplexing sea of troubles than that confronting Andrew Johnson. What manner of man was this medium-built, dark-eyed, black-haired Tennessean, now chief executive by virtue of the bullet that killed Lincoln?

No citizen, not even Lincoln, has ever reached the White House from humbler beginnings. Born to impoverished parents in North Carolina and early orphaned, Johnson never attended school but was apprenticed to a tailor at age ten. Ambitious to get ahead, he taught himself to read, and later his wife taught him to write and do simple arithmetic. Like many another self-made man, he was inclined to overpraise his maker.

Johnson early became active in politics in Tennessee, where he had moved when seventeen years old. He shone as an impassioned champion of the poor whites against the planter aristocrats, although he himself ultimately owned a few slaves. He excelled as a two-fisted stump speaker before angry and heckling crowds, who on occasion greeted his political oratory with cocked pistols, not just cocked ears. Elected to Congress, he attracted much favorable attention in the North (but not the South) when he refused to secede with his own state. After Tennessee was partially "redeemed" by Union armies,

President Andrew Johnson (1808–1875), by Arthur Stumpf An "accidental president," Andrew Johnson was the only chief executive to be impeached by the House until 1998, though he was narrowly acquitted by the Senate. A former U.S. senator from Tennessee, he was reelected in 1875 to the Senate that had formally tried him seven years earlier. As Johnson said in a public speech in 1866, "I love my country. Every public act of my life testifies that is so. Where is the man who can put his finger upon one act of mine . . . to prove the contrary?"

he was appointed war governor and served courageously in an atmosphere of danger.

Political exigency next thrust Johnson into the vice presidency. Lincoln's Union party in 1864 needed to attract support from the War Democrats and other pro-Southern elements, and Johnson, a Democrat, seemed to be the ideal man. Unfortunately, he appeared at the vice-presidential inaugural ceremonies the following March in a scandalous condition. He had recently been afflicted with typhoid fever, and although not known as a heavy drinker, he was urged by his friends to take a stiff bracer of whiskey. This he did—with unfortunate results.

"Old Andy" Johnson was no doubt a man of parts—unpolished parts. He was intelligent, able, forceful, and gifted with homespun honesty. Steadfastly devoted to duty and to the people, he was a dogmatic champion of states' rights and the Constitution. He would often present a copy of the document to visitors, and he was buried with one as a pillow.

Crushed by the Constitution President Andrew Johnson revered the U.S. Constitution but eventually felt its awesome weight in his impeachment trial.

Yet the man who had raised himself from the tailor's bench to the president's chair was a misfit. A Southerner who did not understand the North, a Tennessean who had earned the distrust of the South, a Democrat who had never been accepted by the Republicans, a president who had never been elected to the office, he was not at home in a Republican White House. Hotheaded, contentious, and stubborn, he was the wrong man in the wrong place at the wrong time. A Reconstruction policy devised by angels might well have failed in his tactless hands.

Presidential Reconstruction

Even before the shooting war had ended, the political war over Reconstruction had begun. Abraham Lincoln believed that the Southern states had never legally withdrawn from the Union. Their formal restoration to the Union would therefore be relatively simple. Accordingly, Lincoln in 1863 proclaimed his "10 percent" Reconstruction plan. It decreed that a state could be reintegrated into the Union when 10 percent of its voters in the presidential election of 1860 had taken an oath of allegiance to the United States and pledged to abide by emancipation. The next step would be formal erection of a state government. Lincoln would then recognize the purified regime.

Lincoln's proclamation provoked a sharp reaction in Congress, where Republicans feared the restoration of the planter aristocracy to power and the possible re-enslavement of the blacks. Republicans therefore rammed through Congress in 1864 the Wade-Davis Bill. It required that 50 percent of a state's voters take the oath of allegiance and demanded stronger safeguards for emancipation than Lincoln's as the price of readmission. Lincoln "pocket-vetoed" this bill by refusing to sign it after Congress had adjourned. Republicans were outraged. They refused to seat delegates from Louisiana after that state had reorganized its government in accordance with Lincoln's 10 percent plan in 1864.

The controversy surrounding the Wade-Davis Bill had revealed deep differences between the president and Congress. Unlike Lincoln, many in Congress insisted that the seceders had indeed left the Union—had "committed suicide" as republican states—and

had therefore forfeited all their rights. They could be readmitted only as "conquered provinces" on such conditions as Congress should decree.

This episode further revealed differences among Republicans. Two factions were emerging. The majority moderate group tended to agree with Lincoln that the seceded states should be restored to the Union as simply and swiftly as reasonable—though on Congress's terms, not the president's. The minority radical group believed that the South should atone more painfully for its sins. Before the South should be restored, the radicals wanted its social structure uprooted, the haughty planters punished, and the newly emancipated blacks protected by federal power.

Some of the radicals were secretly pleased when the assassin's bullet felled Lincoln, for the martyred president had shown tenderness toward the South. Spiteful "Andy" Johnson, who shared their hatred for the planter aristocrats, would presumably also share their desire to reconstruct the South with a rod of iron.

Johnson soon disillusioned them. He agreed with Lincoln that the seceded states had never legally been outside the Union. Thus he quickly recognized several of Lincoln's 10 percent governments, and on May 29, 1865, he issued his own Reconstruction proclamation. It disfranchised

Before President Andrew Johnson (1808–1875) softened his Southern policy, his views were radical. Speaking on April 21, 1865, he declared,

"It is not promulgating anything that I have not heretofore said to say that traitors must be made odious, that treason must be made odious, that traitors must be punished and impoverished. They must not only be punished, but their social power must be destroyed. If not, they will still maintain an ascendancy, and may again become numerous and powerful; for, in the words of a former Senator of the United States, 'When traitors become numerous enough, treason becomes respectable.'"

certain leading Confederates, including those with taxable property worth more than $20,000, though they might petition him for personal pardons. It called for special state conventions, which were required to repeal the ordinances of secession, repudiate all Confederate debts, and ratify the slave-freeing Thirteenth Amendment. States that complied with these conditions, Johnson declared, would be swiftly readmitted to the Union.

Johnson, savoring his dominance over the high-toned aristocrats who now begged his favor, granted pardons in abundance. Bolstered by the political resurrection of the planter elite, the recently rebellious states moved rapidly in the second half of 1865 to organize governments. But as the pattern of the new governments became clear, Republicans of all stripes grew furious.

The Baleful Black Codes

Among the first acts of the new Southern regimes sanctioned by Johnson was the passage of the iron-toothed Black Codes. These laws were designed to regulate the affairs of the emancipated blacks, much as the slave statutes had done in pre–Civil War days. Mississippi passed the first such law in November 1865, and other Southern states soon followed suit. The Black Codes varied in severity from state to state (Mississippi's was the harshest and Georgia's the most lenient), but they had much in common. The Black Codes aimed, first of all, to ensure a stable and subservient labor force. The crushed Cotton Kingdom could not rise from its weeds until the fields were once again put under hoe and plow—and many whites wanted to make sure that they retained the tight control they had exercised over black field hands and plow drivers in the days of slavery.

Dire penalties were therefore imposed by the codes on blacks who "jumped" their labor contracts, which usually committed them to work for the same employer for one year, and generally at pittance wages. Violators could be made to forfeit back wages or could be forcibly dragged back to work by a paid "Negro-catcher." In Mississippi the captured freedmen could be fined and then hired out to pay their fines—an arrangement that closely resembled slavery itself.

The codes also sought to restore as nearly as possible the pre-emancipation system of race relations. Freedom was legally recognized, as were some other privileges, such as the right to marry. But all the codes forbade a black to serve on a jury; some even barred blacks from renting or leasing land. A black could be punished for "idleness" by being sentenced to work on a chain gang. Nowhere were blacks allowed to vote.

These oppressive laws mocked the ideal of freedom, so recently purchased by buckets of blood. The Black Codes imposed terrible burdens on the unfettered blacks, struggling against mistreatment and poverty to make their way as free people. The worst features of the Black Codes would eventually be repealed, but their revocation could not by itself lift the liberated blacks into economic independence. Lacking capital, and with little to offer but their labor, thousands of impoverished former slaves slipped into the status of sharecropper farmers, as did many landless whites. Luckless sharecroppers gradually sank into a morass of virtual peonage and remained there for generations. Formerly slaves to masters, countless blacks as well as poorer whites in effect became slaves to the soil and to their creditors. Yet the dethroned planter aristocracy resented even this pitiful concession to freedom. Sharecropping was the "wrong policy," said one planter. "It makes the laborer too independent; he becomes a partner, and has a right to be consulted."

Early in 1866 one congressman quoted a Georgian:

"The blacks eat, sleep, move, live, only by the tolerance of the whites, who hate them. The blacks own absolutely nothing but their bodies; their former masters own everything, and will sell them nothing. If a black man draws even a bucket of water from a well, he must first get the permission of a white man, his enemy. . . . If he asks for work to earn his living, he must ask it of a white man; and the whites are determined to give him no work, except on such terms as will make him a serf and impair his liberty."

A Family of Sharecroppers at the End of the Civil War
They were free at last, but most African-Americans would have to wait a century or more to escape slavery's cruel legacy of poverty, ignorance, and discrimination.

The Black Codes made an ugly impression in the North. If the former slaves were being re-enslaved, people asked one another, had not the Boys in Blue spilled their blood in vain? Had the North really won the war?

Congressional Reconstruction

These questions grew more insistent when the congressional delegations from the newly reconstituted Southern states presented themselves in the Capitol in December 1865. To the shock and disgust of the Republicans, many former Confederate leaders were on hand to claim their seats.

The appearance of these ex-rebels was a natural but costly blunder. Voters of the South, seeking able representatives, had turned instinctively to their experienced statesmen. But most of the Southern leaders were tainted by active association with the "lost cause." Among them were four former Confederate generals, five colonels, and various members of the Richmond cabinet and Congress. Worst of all, there was the shrimpy but brainy Alexander Stephens, ex–vice president of the Confederacy, still under indictment for treason.

The presence of these "whitewashed rebels" infuriated the Republicans in Congress. The war had been fought to restore the Union, but not on these kinds of terms. The Republicans were in no hurry to embrace their former enemies—virtually all of them Democrats —in the chambers of the Capitol. While the South had been "out" from 1861 to 1865, the Republicans in Congress had enjoyed a relatively free hand. They had passed much legislation that favored the North, such as the Morrill Tariff, the Pacific Railroad Act, and the Homestead Act. Now many Republicans balked at giving up this political advantage. On the first day of the congressional session, December 4, 1865, they banged shut the door in the face of the newly elected Southern delegations.

Looking to the future, the Republicans were alarmed to realize that a restored South would be stronger than ever in national politics. Before the war a black slave had counted as three-fifths of a person in apportioning congressional representation. Now the slave was five-fifths of a person. Eleven Southern states had seceded and been subdued by force of arms. But now, owing to full counting of free blacks, the rebel states were entitled to twelve more votes in Congress, and twelve more presidential electoral votes, than they had previously enjoyed. Again, angry voices in the North raised the cry, Who won the war?

Republicans had good reason to fear that ultimately they might be elbowed aside. Southerners might join hands with Democrats in the North and win control of Congress or maybe even the White House. If this happened, they could perpetuate the Black Codes, virtually re-enslaving the blacks. They could dismantle the economic program of the Republican party by lowering tariffs, rerouting the transcontinental railroad, repealing the free-farm Homestead Act, possibly even repudiating the national debt. President Johnson thus deeply disturbed the congressional Republicans when he announced on December 6, 1865, that the recently rebellious states had satisfied his conditions and that in his view the Union was now restored.

Andrew Johnson Pictured as a Tyrant
President Andrew Johnson's repeated clashes with Congress over Reconstruction policies outraged many Northerners who thought he abused the power of the presidency to shelter the defeated Confederacy from the consequences of defeat.

Johnson Clashes with Congress

A clash between president and Congress was now inevitable. It exploded into the open in February 1866, when the president vetoed a bill (later repassed) extending the life of the controversial Freedmen's Bureau.

Aroused, the Republicans swiftly struck back. In March 1866 they passed the Civil Rights Bill, which conferred on blacks the privilege of American citizenship and struck at the Black Codes. President Johnson resolutely vetoed this forward-looking measure on constitutional grounds, but in April congressmen steamrollered it over his veto—some-

thing they repeatedly did henceforth. The hapless president, dubbed "Sir Veto" and "Andy Veto," had his presidential wings clipped, as Congress increasingly assumed the dominant role in running the government. One critic called Johnson "the dead dog of the White House."

The Republicans now undertook to rivet the principles of the Civil Rights Bill into the Constitution as the Fourteenth Amendment. They feared that the Southerners might one day win control of Congress and repeal the hated law. The proposed amendment, as approved by Congress and sent to the states in June 1866, was sweeping. It (1) conferred civil rights, including citizenship but excluding the franchise, on the freedmen; (2) reduced proportionately the representation of a state in Congress and in the Electoral College if it denied blacks the ballot; (3) disqualified from federal and state office former Confederates who as federal officeholders had once sworn "to support the Constitution of the United States"; and (4) guaranteed the federal debt, while repudiating all Confederate debts. (See text of Fourteenth Amendment in the Appendix.)

The radical faction was disappointed that the Fourteenth Amendment did not grant the right to vote, but all Republicans were agreed that no state should be welcomed back into the Union fold without first ratifying the Fourteenth Amendment. Yet President Johnson advised the Southern states to reject it, and all of the "sinful eleven," except Tennessee, defiantly spurned the amendment. Their spirit was reflected in a Southern song:

> *And I don't want no pardon for what I was or am,*
> *I won't be reconstructed and I don't give a damn.*

Swinging 'Round the Circle with Johnson

As 1866 lengthened, the battle grew between the Congress and the president. The root of the controversy was Johnson's "10 percent" governments that had passed the most stringent Black Codes. Congress had tried to temper the worst features of the codes by extending the life of the embattled Freedmen's Bureau and passing the Civil Rights Bill. Both measures Johnson had vetoed. Now the issue was whether Reconstruction was to be carried on with or without the Fourteenth Amendment. The Republicans would settle for nothing less.

The crucial congressional elections of 1866—more crucial than some presidential elections—were fast approaching. Johnson was naturally eager to escape from the clutch of Congress by securing a

An Inflexible President, 1866 This Republican cartoon shows Johnson knocking blacks out of the Freedmen's Bureau by his veto.

majority favorable to his soft-on-the-South policy. Invited to dedicate a Chicago monument to Stephen A. Douglas, he undertook to speak at various cities en route in support of his views.

Johnson's famous "swing 'round the circle," beginning in the late summer of 1866, was a serio-

Principal Reconstruction Proposals and Plans

Year	Proposal or Plan
1864–1865	Lincoln's 10 percent proposal
1865–1866	Johnson's version of Lincoln's proposal
1866–1867	Congressional plan: 10 percent plan with Fourteenth Amendment
1867–1877	Congressional plan of military Reconstruction: Fourteenth Amendment plus black suffrage, later established nationwide by Fifteenth Amendment

comedy of errors. The president delivered a series of "give 'em hell" speeches, in which he accused the radicals in Congress of having planned large-scale antiblack riots and murder in the South. As he spoke, hecklers hurled insults at him. Reverting to his stump-speaking days in Tennessee, he shouted back angry retorts, amid cries of "You be damned" and "Don't get mad, Andy." The dignity of his high office sank to a new low, as the old charges of drunkenness were revived.

As a vote-getter, Johnson was highly successful—for the opposition. His inept speechmaking heightened the cry "Stand by Congress" against the "Tailor of the Potomac." When the ballots were counted, the Republicans had rolled up more than a two-thirds majority in both houses of Congress.

Republican Principles and Programs

The Republicans now had a veto-proof Congress and virtually unlimited control of Reconstruction policy. But moderates and radicals still disagreed over the best course to pursue in the South.

The radicals in the Senate were led by the courtly and principled idealist Charles Sumner, long since recovered from his prewar caning on the Senate floor, who tirelessly labored not only for black freedom but for racial equality. In the House the most powerful radical was Thaddeus Stevens, crusty and vindictive congressman from Pennsylvania. Seventy-four years old in 1866, he was a curious figure, with a protruding lower lip, a heavy black wig

covering his bald head, and a deformed foot. An unswerving friend of blacks, he had defended runaway slaves in court without fee and, before dying, insisted on burial in a black cemetery. His affectionate devotion to blacks was matched by his vitriolic hatred of rebellious white Southerners. A masterly parliamentarian with a razor-sharp mind and withering wit, Stevens was a leading figure on the Joint (House-Senate) Committee on Reconstruction.

Still opposed to rapid restoration of the Southern states, the radicals wanted to keep them out as long as possible and apply federal power to bring about a drastic social and economic transformation in the South. But moderate Republicans, more attuned to time-honored principles of states' rights and self-government, recoiled from the full implications of the radical program. They preferred policies that restrained the states from abridging citizens' rights, rather than policies that directly involved the

Thaddeus Stevens (1792–1868) Stevens, who regarded the seceded states as "conquered provinces," promoted much of the major Reconstruction legislation, including the Fourteenth (civil rights) Amendment. Reconstruction, he said, must "revolutionize Southern institutions, habits, and manners. . . . The foundation of their institutions . . . must be broken up and relaid, or all our blood and treasure have been spent in vain."

Representative Thaddeus Stevens (1792–1868), in a congressional speech on January 3, 1867, urged the ballot for blacks out of concern for them and out of bitterness against the whites:

"I am for Negro suffrage in every rebel state. If it be just, it should not be denied; if it be necessary, it should be adopted; if it be a punishment to traitors, they deserve it."

federal government in individual lives. The actual policies adopted by Congress showed the influence of both these schools of thought, though the moderates, as the majority faction, had the upper hand. And one thing both groups had come to agree on by 1867 was the necessity to enfranchise black voters, even if it took federal troops to do it.

Reconstruction by the Sword

Against a backdrop of vicious and bloody race riots that had erupted in several Southern cities, Congress passed the Reconstruction Act on March 2, 1867. Supplemented by later measures, this drastic legislation divided the South into five military districts, each commanded by a Union general and policed by blue-clad soldiers, about twenty thousand all told. The act also temporarily disfranchised tens of thousands of former Confederates.

Congress additionally laid down stringent conditions for the readmission of the seceded states. The wayward states were required to ratify the Fourteenth Amendment, giving the former slaves their rights as citizens. The bitterest pill of all to white Southerners was the stipulation that they guarantee in their state constitutions full suffrage for their former adult male slaves. Yet the act, reflecting moderate sentiment, stopped short of giving the freedmen land or education at federal expense. The overriding purpose of the moderates was to create an electorate in Southern states that would vote those states back into the Union on acceptable terms and thus free the federal government from direct responsibility for the protection of black rights. As later events would demonstrate, this approach proved woefully inadequate to the cause of justice for blacks.

The radical Republicans were still worried. The danger loomed that once the unrepentant states were readmitted, they would amend their constitutions so as to withdraw the ballot from the blacks. The only ironclad safeguard was to incorporate black suffrage in the federal Constitution. This goal was finally achieved by the Fifteenth Amendment, passed by Congress in 1869 and ratified by the required number of states in 1870. (For text, see the Appendix.)

Military Reconstruction of the South not only usurped certain functions of the president as commander in chief but set up a martial regime of dubious legality. The Supreme Court had already ruled, in the case *Ex parte Milligan* (1866), that military tribunals could not try civilians, even during wartime, in areas where the civil courts were open. Peacetime military rule seemed starkly contrary to the spirit of the Constitution. But the circumstances were extraordinary in the Republic's history, and for the time being the Supreme Court avoided offending the Republican Congress.

Prodded into line by federal bayonets, the Southern states got on with the task of constitution making. By 1870 all of them had reorganized their governments and had been accorded full rights. The hated "bluebellies" remained until the new Republican regimes—usually called "radical" regimes—appeared to be firmly entrenched. Yet when the federal troops finally left a state, its government swiftly passed back into the hands of white "Redeemers," or "Home Rule" regimes, which were inevitably Democratic. Finally, in 1877, the last federal muskets were removed from state politics, and the "solid" Democratic South congealed.

No Women Voters

The passage of the three Reconstruction-era Amendments—the Thirteenth, Fourteenth, and Fifteenth—delighted former abolitionists but deeply disappointed advocates of women's rights. Women had played a prominent part in the prewar abolitionist movement and had often pointed out that both women and blacks lacked basic civil rights, especially the crucial right to vote. The struggle for black freedom and the crusade for women's rights, therefore, were one and the same in the eyes of many women. Yet during the war, feminist leaders such as Elizabeth Cady Stanton and Susan B. Anthony had temporarily suspended their own demands and worked wholeheartedly for the cause of black emancipation. The Woman's Loyal League had gathered nearly 400,000 signatures on petitions asking Congress to pass a constitutional amendment prohibiting slavery.

Now, with the war ended and the Thirteenth Amendment passed, feminist leaders believed that their time had come. They reeled with shock, however, when the wording of the Fourteenth Amendment, which defined equal national citizenship, for

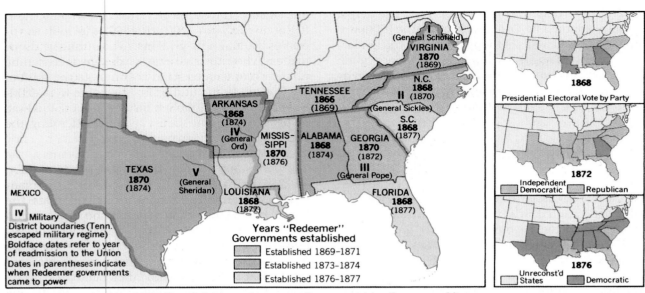

Military Reconstruction, 1867 (five districts and commanding generals)   For many white Southerners, military Reconstruction amounted to turning the knife in the wound of defeat. An often-repeated story of later years had a Southerner remark, "I was sixteen years old before I discovered that damnyankee was two words."

Southern Reconstruction by State

State	Readmitted to Representation in Congress	Home Rule (Democratic or "Redeemer" Regime) Reestablished	Comments
Tennessee	July 24, 1866		Ratified Fourteenth Amendment in 1866 and hence avoided military Reconstruction*
Arkansas	June 22, 1868	1874	
North Carolina	June 25, 1868	1870	
Alabama	June 25, 1868	1874	
Florida	June 25, 1868	1877	Federal troops restationed in 1877, as result of Hayes-Tilden electoral bargain
Louisiana	June 25, 1868	1877	Same as Florida
South Carolina	June 25, 1868	1877	Same as Florida
Virginia	January 26, 1870	1869	
Mississippi	February 23, 1870	1876	
Texas	March 30, 1870	1874	
Georgia	[June 25, 1868] July 15, 1870	1872	Readmitted June 25, 1868, but returned to military control after expulsion of blacks from legislature

*For many years Tennessee was the only state of the secession to observe Lincoln's birthday as a legal holiday. Many southern states still observe the birthdays of Jefferson Davis and Robert E. Lee.

The prominent suffragist and abolitionist Susan B. Anthony (1820–1906) was outraged over the proposed exclusion of women from the Fourteenth Amendment. In a conversation with her former male allies Wendell Phillips and Theodore Tilton, she reportedly held out her arm and declared,

"Look at this, all of you. And hear me swear that I will cut off this right arm of mine before I will ever work for or demand the ballot for the negro and not the woman."

the first time inserted the word *male* into the Constitution in referring to a citizen's right to vote. Both Stanton and Anthony campaigned actively against the Fourteenth Amendment despite the pleas of Frederick Douglass, who had long supported woman suffrage but believed that this was "the Negro's hour." When the Fifteenth Amendment proposed to prohibit denial of the vote on the basis of "race, color, or previous condition of servitude," Stanton and Anthony wanted the word *sex* added to the list. They lost this battle, too. Fifty years would pass before the Constitution granted women the right to vote.

The Realities of Radical Reconstruction in the South

The blacks now had freedom, of a sort. Their friends in Congress had only haltingly and somewhat belatedly secured the franchise for them. Both Presidents Lincoln and Johnson had proposed to give the ballot gradually to selected blacks who qualified for it through education, property ownership, or military service. Moderate Republicans and even many radicals at first hesitated to bestow suffrage on the freedmen. The Fourteenth Amendment, in many ways the heart of the Republican program for Reconstruction, had fallen short of guaranteeing the right to vote. (It envisioned for blacks the same status as women—citizenship without voting rights.)

But by 1867 hesitation had given way to a hard determination to enfranchise the former slaves wholesale and immediately, while thousands of white Southerners were being denied the vote. By glaring contrast most of the Northern states, before ratification of the Fifteenth Amendment in 1870, withheld the ballot from their tiny black minorities. White Southerners naturally concluded that the Republicans were hypocritical in insisting that blacks in the South be allowed to vote.

Having gained their right to suffrage, Southern black men seized the initiative and began to organize politically. Their primary vehicle became the Union League, originally a pro-Union organization based in the North. Assisted by Northern blacks, freedmen turned the League into a network of political clubs that educated members in their civic duties and campaigned for Republican candidates. The league's mission soon expanded to include building black churches and schools, representing black grievances before local employers and government, and recruiting militias to protect black communities from white retaliation.

Though African-American women did not obtain the right to vote, they too assumed new political roles. Black women faithfully attended the parades and rallies common in black communities during the early years of Reconstruction and helped assemble mass meetings in the newly constructed black churches. They even showed up at the constitutional conventions held throughout the South in 1867, monitoring the proceedings and participating in informal votes outside the convention halls.

But black men elected as delegates to the state constitutional conventions held the greater political authority. They formed the backbone of the black political community. At the conventions, they sat down with whites to hammer out new state constitutions, which most importantly provided for universal male suffrage. Though the subsequent elections produced no black governors or majorities in state senates, black political participation expanded exponentially during Reconstruction. Between 1868 and 1876, fourteen black congressmen and two black senators, Hiram Revels and Blanche K. Bruce, both of Mississippi, served in Washington, D.C. Blacks also served in state governments as lieutenant governors and representatives, and in local governments as mayors, magistrates, sheriffs, and justices of the peace.

The sight of former slaves holding office deeply offended their onetime masters, who lashed out with particular fury at the freedmen's white allies, labeling them "scalawags" and "carpetbaggers." The so-called scalawags were Southerners, often former Unionists and Whigs. The former Confederates accused them, often with wild exaggeration, of plundering the treasuries of the Southern states through their political influence in the radical governments. The carpetbaggers, on the other hand, were supposedly sleazy Northerners who had packed all their worldly goods into a carpetbag suitcase at war's end and had come South to seek personal power and profit. In fact, most were former Union soldiers and Northern businessmen and professionals who wanted to play a role in modernizing the "New South."

How well did the radical regimes rule? The radical legislatures passed much desirable legislation and introduced many badly needed reforms. For the first time in Southern history, steps were taken toward establishing adequate public schools. Tax systems were streamlined; public works were launched; and property rights were guaranteed to women. Many welcome reforms were retained by

At a constitutional convention in Alabama, freed people affirmed their rights in the following declaration:

"We claim exactly the same rights, privileges and immunities as are enjoyed by white men—we ask nothing more and will be content with nothing less. . . . The law no longer knows white nor black, but simply men, and consequently we are entitled to ride in public conveyances, hold office, sit on juries and do everything else which we have in the past been prevented from doing solely on the ground of color."

the all-white "Redeemer" governments that later returned to power.

Despite these achievements, graft ran rampant in many "radical" governments. This was especially true in South Carolina and Louisiana, where con-

Freedmen Voting, Richmond, Virginia, 1871 The exercise of democratic rights by former slaves constituted a political and social revolution in the South and was bitterly resented by whites.

Black Reconstruction
A composite portrait of the first black senators and representatives in the Forty-first and Forty-second Congresses. Senator Hiram Revels, on the left, was elected in 1870 to the seat that had been occupied by Jefferson Davis when the South seceded.

scienceless promoters and other pocket-padders used politically inexperienced blacks as pawns. The worst "black-and-white" legislatures purchased, as "legislative supplies," such "stationery" as hams, perfumes, suspenders, bonnets, corsets, champagne, and a coffin. One "thrifty" carpetbag governor in a single year "saved" $100,000 from a salary of $8,000. Yet this sort of corruption was by no means confined to the South in these postwar years. The crimes of the Reconstruction governments were no more outrageous than the scams and felonies being perpetrated in the North at the same time, especially in Boss Tweed's New York.

The Ku Klux Klan

Deeply embittered, some Southern whites resorted to savage measures against "radical" rule. Many whites resented the success and ability of black legislators as much as they resented alleged "corruption." A number of secret organizations mushroomed forth, the most notorious of which was the "Invisible Empire of the South," or Ku Klux Klan, founded in Tennessee in 1866. Besheeted nightrid-

ers, their horses' hoofs muffled, would approach the cabin of an "upstart" black and hammer on the door. In ghoulish tones one thirsty horseman would demand a bucket of water. Then, under pretense of drinking, he would pour it into a rubber attachment concealed beneath his mask and gown, smack his lips, and declare that this was the first water he had tasted since he was killed at the Battle of Shiloh. If fright did not produce the desired effect, force was employed.

Such tomfoolery and terror proved partially effective. Many ex-bondsmen and white "carpet-baggers," quick to take a hint, shunned the polls. Those stubborn souls who persisted in their "upstart" ways were flogged, mutilated, or even murdered. In one Louisiana parish in 1868, the whites in two days killed or wounded two hundred victims; a pile of twenty-five bodies was found half-buried in the woods. By such atrocious practices were blacks "kept in their place"—that is, down. The Klan became a refuge for numerous bandits and cutthroats. Any scoundrel could don a sheet.

Congress, outraged by this night-riding lawlessness, passed the harsh Force Acts of 1870 and 1871. Federal troops were able to stamp out much of the "lash law," but by this time the Invisible Empire had

The following excerpt is part of a heartrending appeal to Congress in 1871 by a group of Kentucky blacks:

"We believe you are not familiar with the description of the Ku Klux Klans riding nightly over the country, going from county to county, and in the county towns, spreading terror wherever they go by robbing, whipping, ravishing, and killing our people without provocation, compelling colored people to break the ice and bathe in the chilly waters of the Kentucky River.

"The [state] legislature has adjourned. They refused to enact any laws to suppress Ku-Klux disorder. We regard them [the Ku-Kluxers] as now being licensed to continue their dark and bloody deeds under cover of the dark night. They refuse to allow us to testify in the state courts where a white man is concerned. We find their deeds are perpetrated only upon colored men and white Republicans. We also find that for our services to the government and our race we have become the special object of hatred and persecution at the hands of the Democratic Party. Our people are driven from their homes in great numbers, having no redress only [except] the United States court, which is in many cases unable to reach them."

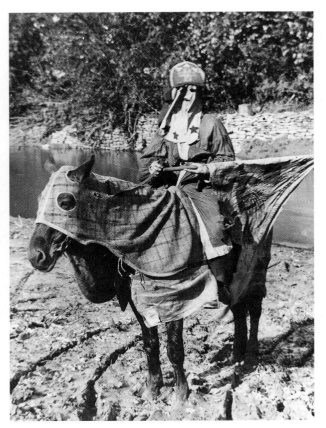

The Ku Klux Klan, Tennessee, 1868   This night-riding terrorist has even masked the identity of his horse.

already done its work of intimidation. Many of the outlawed groups continued their tactics in the guise of "dancing clubs," "missionary societies," and "rifle clubs."

White resistance undermined attempts to empower the blacks politically. The white South, for many decades, openly flouted the Fourteenth and Fifteenth Amendments. Wholesale disfranchisement of the blacks, starting conspicuously about 1890, was achieved by intimidation, fraud, and trickery. Among various underhanded schemes were the literacy tests, unfairly administered by whites to the advantage of illiterate whites. In the eyes of the white Southerners, the goal of white supremacy fully justified these dishonorable devices.

Johnson Walks the Impeachment Plank

Radicals meanwhile had been sharpening their hatchets for President Johnson. Annoyed by the obstruction of the "drunken tailor" in the White House, they falsely accused him of maintaining there a harem of "dissolute women." Not content with curbing his authority, they decided to remove him altogether by constitutional processes.* Under

---

*For impeachment, see Art. I, Sec. II, para. 5; Art. I, Sec. III, paras. 6, 7; Art. II, Sec. IV, in the Appendix.

A black leader protested to whites in 1868,

"It is extraordinary that a race such as yours, professing gallantry, chivalry, education, and superiority, living in a land where ringing chimes call child and sire to the Gospel of God—that with all these advantages on your side, you can make war upon the poor defenseless black man."

existing law the president pro tempore of the Senate, the unscrupulous and rabidly radical "Bluff Ben" Wade of Ohio, would then become president.

As an initial step, Congress in 1867 passed the Tenure of Office Act—as usual, over Johnson's veto. Contrary to precedent, the new law required the president to secure the consent of the Senate before he could remove his appointees once they had been approved by that body. One purpose was to freeze into the cabinet the secretary of war, Edwin M. Stanton, a holdover from the Lincoln administration. Although outwardly loyal to Johnson, he was secretly serving as a spy and informer for the radicals.

Johnson provided the radicals with a pretext to begin impeachment proceedings when he abruptly dismissed Stanton early in 1868. The House of Representatives immediately voted 126 to 47 to impeach Johnson for "high crimes and misdemeanors," as required by the Constitution, charging him with various violations of the Tenure of Office Act. Two additional articles related to Johnson's verbal assaults on the Congress, involving "disgrace, ridicule, hatred, contempt, and reproach."

A Not-Guilty Verdict for Johnson

With evident zeal the radical-led Senate now sat as a court to try Johnson on the dubious impeachment charges. The House conducted the prosecution. The trial aroused intense public interest and, with one thousand tickets printed, proved to be the biggest show of 1868. Johnson kept his dignity and sobriety and maintained a discreet silence. His battery of attorneys argued that the president, convinced that the Tenure of Office Act was unconstitutional, had fired Stanton merely to put a test case before the Supreme Court. (That slow-moving tribunal finally ruled indirectly in Johnson's favor fifty-eight years later.) House prosecutors, including oily-tongued Benjamin F. Butler and embittered Thaddeus Stevens, had a harder time building a compelling case for impeachment.

On May 16, 1868, the day for the first voting in the Senate, the tension was electric, and heavy breathing could be heard in the galleries. By a margin of only one vote, the radicals failed to muster the two-thirds majority for Johnson's removal. Seven independent-minded Republican senators, courageously putting country above party, voted "not guilty."

Several factors shaped the outcome. Fears of creating a destabilizing precedent played a role, as did principled opposition to abusing the constitutional mechanism of checks and balances. Political considerations also figured conspicuously. As the vice presidency remained vacant under Johnson, his successor would have been radical Republican Ben Wade, the president pro tempore of the Senate. Wade was disliked by many members of the business community for his high-tariff, soft-money, prolabor views, and distrusted by moderate Republicans. Meanwhile, Johnson indicated through his attorney that he would stop obstructing Republican policies in return for remaining in office.

Die-hard radicals were infuriated by their failure to muster a two-thirds majority for Johnson's removal. "The Country is going to the Devil!" cried the crippled Stevens as he was carried from the hall. But the nation, though violently aroused, accepted the verdict with a good temper that did credit to its political maturity. In a less stable republic, an armed uprising might have erupted against the president.

The nation thus narrowly avoided a dangerous precedent that would have gravely weakened one of the three branches of the federal government. Johnson was clearly guilty of bad speeches, bad judgment, and bad temper, but not of "high crimes and misdemeanors." From the standpoint of the radicals, his greatest crime had been to stand inflexibly in their path.

The Purchase of Alaska

Johnson's administration, though largely reduced to a figurehead, achieved its most enduring success in the field of foreign relations.

The Russians by 1867 were in a mood to sell the vast and chilly expanse of land now known as Alaska. They had already overextended themselves in North America, and they saw that in the likely event of another war with Britain, they probably would lose their defenseless northern province to the sea-dominant British. Alaska, moreover, had been ruthlessly "furred out" and was a growing economic liability. The Russians were therefore quite eager to unload their "frozen asset" on the Americans, and they put out seductive feelers in Washington. They preferred the United States to any other purchaser, primarily because they wanted to strengthen further the Republic as a barrier against their ancient enemy, Britain.

In 1867 Secretary of State William Seward, an ardent expansionist, signed a treaty with Russia that transferred Alaska to the United States for the bargain price of $7.2 million. But Seward's enthusiasm for these frigid wastes was not shared by his ignorant or uninformed countrymen, who jeered at "Seward's Folly," "Seward's Icebox," "Frigidia," and "Walrussia." The American people, still preoccupied with Reconstruction and other internal vexations, were economy-minded and anti-expansionist.

Then why did Congress and the American public sanction the purchase? For one thing Russia, alone among the powers, had been conspicuously friendly to the North during the recent Civil War. Americans did not feel that they could offend their great and good friend, the tsar, by hurling his walrus-covered icebergs back into his face. Besides,

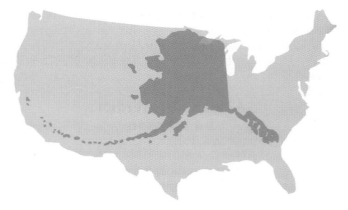

Alaska and the Lower Forty-eight States
(a size comparison)

the territory was rumored to be teeming with furs, fish, and gold, and it might yet "pan out" profitably—as it later did with natural resources, including oil and gas. So Congress and the country accepted "Seward's Polar Bear Garden," somewhat derisively but nevertheless hopefully.

The Heritage of Reconstruction

Many white Southerners regarded Reconstruction as a more grievous wound than the war itself. It left a festering scar that would take generations to heal. They resented the upending of their social and racial system, political empowerment of blacks, and the insult of federal intervention in their local affairs. Yet few rebellions have ended with the victors sitting down to a love feast with the vanquished. Given the explosiveness of the issues that had caused the war, and the bitterness of the fighting, the wonder is that Reconstruction was not far harsher than it was. The fact is that Lincoln, Johnson, and most Republicans had no clear picture at war's end of what federal policy toward the South should be. Policymakers groped for the right policies, influenced as much by Southern responses to defeat and emancipation as by any plans of their own to impose a specific program on the South.

The Republicans acted from a mixture of idealism and political expediency. They wanted both to protect the freed slaves and to promote the fortunes of the Republican party. In the end their efforts backfired badly. Reconstruction conferred only fleeting benefits on the blacks and virtually extinguished the Republican party in the South for nearly one hundred years.

Moderate Republicans never fully appreciated the extensive effort necessary to make the freed slaves completely independent citizens, nor the lengths to which Southern whites would go to pre-

The remarkable ex-slave Frederick Douglass (1817?–1895) wrote in 1882,

"Though slavery was abolished, the wrongs of my people were not ended. Though they were not slaves, they were not yet quite free. No man can be truly free whose liberty is dependent upon the thought, feeling, and action of others, and who has himself no means in his own hands for guarding, protecting, defending, and maintaining that liberty. Yet the Negro after his emancipation was precisely in this state of destitution. . . . He was free from the individual master, but the slave of society. He had neither money, property, nor friends. He was free from the old plantation, but he had nothing but the dusty road under his feet. He was free from the old quarter that once gave him shelter, but a slave to the rains of summer and the frosts of winter. He was, in a word, literally turned loose, naked, hungry, and destitute, to the open sky."

serve their system of racial dominance. Had Thaddeus Stevens's radical program of drastic economic reforms and heftier protection of political rights been enacted, things might well have been different. But deep-seated racism, ingrained American resistance to tampering with property rights, and rigid loyalty to the principle of local self-government, combined with spreading indifference in the North to the plight of the blacks, formed too formidable an obstacle. Despite good intentions by Republicans, the Old South was in many ways more resurrected than reconstructed.

Chronology

1863	Lincoln announces "10 percent" Reconstruction plan
1864	Lincoln vetoes Wade-Davis Bill
1865	Lincoln assassinated
	Johnson issues Reconstruction proclamation
	Congress refuses to seat Southern congressmen
	Freedmen's Bureau established
	Southern states pass Black Codes
1866	Congress passes Civil Rights Bill over Johnson's veto
	Congress passes Fourteenth Amendment
	Johnson-backed candidates lose congressional election
	Ex parte Milligan case
	Ku Klux Klan founded

1867	Reconstruction Act
	Tenure of Office Act
	United States purchases Alaska from Russia
1868	Johnson impeached and acquitted
	Johnson pardons Confederate leaders
1870	Fifteenth Amendment ratified
1870-1871	Force Acts
1872	Freedmen's Bureau ended
1877	Reconstruction ends

VARYING VIEWPOINTS

How Radical Was Reconstruction?

Few topics have triggered as much intellectual warfare as the "dark and bloody ground" of Reconstruction. The period provoked questions—sectional, racial, and constitutional—about which people felt deeply and remain deeply divided even today. Scholarly argument goes back conspicuously to a Columbia University historian, William A. Dunning, whose students, in the early 1900s, published a series of histories of the Reconstruction South. Dunning and his disciples were influenced by the turn-of-the-century spirit of sectional conciliation as well as by current theories about black racial inferiority. Sympathizing with the white South, they wrote about the Reconstruction period as a kind of national disgrace, foisted upon a prostrate region by vindictive and self-seeking radical Republican politicians. If the South had wronged the North by seceding, the North had wronged the South by reconstructing.

A second cycle of scholarship in the 1920s was impelled by a widespread suspicion that the Civil War itself had been a tragic and unnecessary blunder. Attention now shifted to Northern politicians. Scholars like Howard Beale further questioned the motives of the radical Republicans. To Beale and others, the radicals had masked a ruthless desire to exploit Southern labor and resources behind a false front of "concern" for the freed slaves. Moreover, Northern advocacy of black voting rights was merely a calculated attempt to ensure a Republican political presence in the defeated South. The unfortunate Andrew Johnson, in this view, had valiantly tried to uphold constitutional principles in the face of this cynical Northern onslaught.

Following World War II, Kenneth Stampp, among others, turned this view on its head. Influenced by the modern civil rights movement, he argued that Reconstruction had been a noble attempt to extend American principles of equity and justice. The radical Republicans and the carpetbaggers were now heroes, whereas Andrew Johnson was castigated for his obstinate racism. By the early 1970s, this view had become orthodoxy, and it generally holds sway today. Yet some scholars, such as Michael Benedict and Leon Litwack, disillusioned with the inability to achieve full racial justice in the 1960s, began once more to scrutinize the motives of Northern politicians immediately after the Civil War. They claimed to discover that Reconstruction had never been very radical and that the Freedmen's Bureau and other agencies had merely allowed the white planters to maintain their dominance over local politics as well as over the local economy.

More recently, Eric Foner has powerfully reasserted the argument that Reconstruction was a truly radical and noble attempt to establish an interracial democracy. Drawing upon the work of black scholar W. E. B. Du Bois, Foner emphasizes the comparative approach to American Reconstruction. Clearly, Foner admits, Reconstruction did not create full equality, but it did allow blacks to form political organizations and churches, to vote, and to establish some measure of economic independence. In South Africa, the Caribbean, and other areas once marked by slavery, the freed slaves never received these opportunities. Many of the benefits of Reconstruction were erased by white southerners during the Gilded Age, but in the twentieth century, the constitutional principles and organizations developed during Reconstruction provided the focus and foundation for the modern civil rights movement—which some have called the second Reconstruction.

For further reading, see page A16 of the Appendix. For web resources, go to **http://college.hmco.com.**

PART FOUR

FORGING AN INDUSTRIAL SOCIETY

~

1865–1899

A nation of farmers fought the Civil War in the 1860s. By the time the Spanish-American War broke out in 1898, America was an industrial nation. For generations Americans had plunged into the wilderness and plowed their fields. Now they settled in cities and toiled in factories. Between the Civil War and the century's end, economic and technological change came so swiftly and massively that it seemed to many Americans that a whole new civilization had emerged.

In some ways it had. The sheer scale of the new industrial civilization was dazzling. Transcontinental railroads knit the country together from sea to sea. New industries like oil and steel grew to staggering size—and made megamillionaires out of entrepreneurs like oilman John D. Rockefeller and steel maker Andrew Carnegie.

Drawn by the allure of industrial employment, Americans moved to the city. In 1860 only about 20 percent of the population were city dwellers. By 1900 that proportion doubled, as rural Americans and European immigrants alike flocked to mill town and metropolis in search of steady jobs.

These sweeping changes challenged the spirit of individualism that Americans had celebrated since the seventeenth century. Even on the western frontier, that historic bastion of rugged loners, the hand of government was increasingly felt, as large armies were dispatched to subdue the Plains Indians and federal authority was invoked to regulate the use of natural resources. The rise of powerful monopolies called into question the government's traditional hands-off policy toward business, and a growing band of reformers increasingly clamored for government regulation of private enterprise. The mushrooming cities, with their needs for transport systems, schools, hospitals, sanitation, and fire and police protection, required bigger governments and budgets than an earlier generation could have imagined. As never before, Americans struggled to adapt old ideals of private autonomy to the new realities of industrial civilization.

With economic change came social and political turmoil. Labor violence brought bloodshed to places such as Chicago and Homestead, Pennsylvania. Small farmers, squeezed by debt and foreign competition, rallied behind the People's, or "Populist," party, a radical movement of the 1880s and 1890s that attacked the power of Wall Street, big business, and the banks. Anti-immigrant sentiment swelled. Bitter disputes over tariffs and monetary policy deeply divided the country, setting debtors against lenders, farmers against manufacturers, the West and South against the Northeast. And in this unfamiliar era of big money and expanding government, corruption flourished, from town hall to Congress, fueling loud cries for political reform.

The bloodiest conflict of all pitted Plains Indians against the relentless push of westward expansion. As railroads drove their iron arrows through the heart of the West, the Indians lost their land and life-sustaining buffalo herds. By the 1890s, after three decades of fierce fighting with the U.S. Army, the Indians who had once roamed across the vast rolling prairies were struggling to preserve their shattered cultures within the confinement of reservations.

The South remained the one region largely untouched by the Industrial Revolution sweeping the rest of America. A few sleepy southern hamlets did become boomtowns, but for the most part, the South's rural way of life and its peculiar system of race relations were largely unperturbed by the changes happening elsewhere. On African-Americans, the vast majority of whom continued to live in the Old South, the post-emancipation era inflicted new forms of racial injustice. State legislatures systematically deprived black Americans of their politi-

cal rights, including the right to vote. Segregation of schools, housing, and all kinds of public facilities made a mockery of African-Americans' Reconstruction-era hopes for equality before the law.

The new wealth and power of industrial America nurtured a growing sense of national self-confidence. Literature flowered, and a golden age of philanthropy dawned. The reform spirit spread. So did a restless appetite for overseas expansion. In a brief war against Spain in 1898, the United States, born in a revolutionary war of independence and long the champion of colonial peoples yearning to breathe free, seized control of the Philippines and itself became an imperial power. Uncle Sam's venture into empire touched off a bitter national debate about America's role in the world and ushered in a long period of argument over the responsibilities, at home as well as abroad, of a modern industrial state.

Dearborn Street, Chicago Loop, Around 1900
"America is energetic, but Chicago is in a fever," marveled a visiting Englishman about turn-of-the-century Chicago. Street scenes like this were common in America's booming new cities, especially in the "Lord of the Midwest."

23

Political Paralysis in the Gilded Age

◆

1869–1896

*Grant . . . had no right to exist. He should have been extinct for ages.
. . . That, two thousand years after Alexander the Great and Julius
Caesar, a man like Grant should be called—and should actually and
truly be—the highest product of the most advanced evolution, made
evolution ludicrous. . . . The progress of evolution, from President
Washington to President Grant, was alone evidence enough to upset
Darwin. . . . Grant . . . should have lived in a cave and worn skins.*

HENRY ADAMS, THE EDUCATION OF HENRY ADAMS, 1907

The population of the post–Civil War Republic continued to vault upward by vigorous leaps, despite the awful bloodletting in both Union and Confederate ranks. Census takers reported over 39 million people in 1870, a gain of 26.6 percent over the preceding decade, as the immigrant tide surged again. The United States was now the third largest nation in the Western world, ranking behind Russia and France.

But the civic health of the United States did not keep pace with its physical growth. The Civil War and its aftermath spawned waste, extravagance, speculation, and graft. Disillusionment ran deep among idealistic Americans in the postwar era. They had spilled their blood for the Union, emancipation, and Abraham Lincoln, who had promised "a new birth of freedom." Instead they got a bitter dose of corruption and political stalemate—beginning with Ulysses S. Grant, a great soldier but an utterly inept politician.

The "Bloody Shirt" Elects Grant

Wrangling between Congress and President Andrew Johnson had soured the people on professional politicians in the Reconstruction era, and the notion still prevailed that a good general would make a good president. Stubbily bearded General Grant was by far the most popular Northern hero to emerge from the war. Grateful citizens of Philadelphia, Washington, and his hometown of Galena, Illinois,

502

passed the hat around and in each place presented him with a house. New Yorkers tendered him a check for $105,000. The general, silently puffing on his cigar, unapologetically accepted these gifts as his just deserts for having rescued the Union.

Grant was a hapless greenhorn in the political arena. His one presidential vote had been cast for the Democratic ticket in 1856. A better judge of horseflesh than of humans, his cultural background was breathtakingly narrow. He once reportedly remarked that Venice (Italy) would be a fine city if only it were drained.

The Republicans, freed from the Union party coalition of war days, enthusiastically nominated Grant for the presidency in 1868. The party's platform sounded a clarion call for continued Reconstruction of the South under the glinting steel of federal bayonets. Yet Grant, always a man of few words, struck a highly popular note in his letter of acceptance when he said, "Let us have peace." This noble sentiment became a leading campaign slogan and was later engraved on his tomb beside the Hudson River.

Expectant Democrats, meeting in their own nominating convention, denounced military Reconstruction but could agree on little else. Wealthy eastern delegates demanded a plank promising that federal war bonds be redeemed in gold—even though many of the bonds had been purchased with badly depreciated paper greenbacks. Poorer midwestern delegates answered with the "Ohio Idea," which called for redemption in greenbacks. Debt-burdened agrarian Democrats thus hoped to keep more money in circulation and keep interest rates lower. This dispute introduced a bitter contest over monetary policy that continued to convulse the Republic until the century's end.

Midwestern delegates got the platform but not the candidate. The nominee, former New York governor Horatio Seymour, scuttled the Democrats' faint hope for success by repudiating the Ohio Idea. Republicans whipped up enthusiasm for Grant by energetically "waving the bloody shirt"—that is, reviving gory memories of the Civil War—which became for the first time a prominent feature of a presidential campaign.* "Vote as You Shot" was a powerful Republican slogan aimed at Union army veterans.

---

*The expression is said to have derived from a speech by Representative Benjamin F. Butler of Massachusetts, who allegedly waved before the House the bloodstained nightshirt of a Klan-flogged carpetbagger.

Grant won, with 214 electoral votes to 80 for Seymour. But despite his great popularity, the former general scored a majority of only 300,000 in the popular vote (3,013,421 to 2,706,829). Most white voters apparently supported Seymour, and the ballots of three still-unreconstructed southern states (Mississippi, Texas, and Virginia) were not counted at all. An estimated 500,000 former slaves gave Grant his margin of victory. To remain in power, the Republican party somehow had to continue to control the South—and to keep the ballot in the hands of the grateful freedmen. Republicans could not take future victories "for Granted."

The Era of Good Stealings

A few skunks can pollute a large area. Although the great majority of businesspeople and government officials continued to conduct their affairs with decency and honor, the whole postwar atmosphere was fetid. The Man in the Moon, it was said, had to hold his nose when passing over America. Free-wheeling railroad promoters sometimes left gullible bond buyers with only "two streaks of rust and a right of way." Unscrupulous stock-market manipulators were a cinder in the public eye. Too many judges and legislators put their power up for hire. Cynics defined an honest politician as one who, when bought, would stay bought.

Notorious in the financial world were two millionaire partners, "Jubilee Jim" Fisk and Jay Gould. The corpulent and unscrupulous Fisk provided the "brass," while the undersized and cunning Gould provided the brains. The crafty pair concocted a plot in 1869 to corner the gold market. Their slippery game would work only if the federal Treasury refrained from selling gold. The conspirators worked on President Grant directly and also through his brother-in-law, who received $25,000 for his complicity. On "Black Friday" (September 24, 1869), Fisk and Gould madly bid the price of gold skyward, while scores of honest businesspeople were driven to the wall. The bubble finally broke when the Treasury, contrary to Grant's supposed assurances, was compelled to release gold. A congressional probe concluded that Grant had done nothing crooked, though he had acted stupidly and indiscreetly.

The infamous Tweed Ring in New York City vividly displayed the ethics (or lack of ethics) typical of the age. Burly "Boss" Tweed—240 pounds of rascality—employed bribery, graft, and fraudulent elections to milk the metropolis of as much as $200 million. Honest citizens were cowed into silence. Protesters found their tax assessments raised.

Tweed's luck finally ran out. The *New York Times* secured damning evidence in 1871 and courageously published it, though offered $5 million not to do so. Gifted cartoonist Thomas Nast pilloried Tweed mercilessly, after spurning a heavy bribe to desist. The portly thief reportedly complained that his illiterate followers could not help seeing "them damn pictures." New York attorney Samuel J. Tilden

headed the prosecution, gaining fame that later paved the path to his presidential nomination. Unbailed and unwept, Tweed died behind bars.

A Carnival of Corruption

More serious than Boss Tweed's peccadilloes were the misdeeds of the federal government. President Grant's cabinet was a rodent's nest of grafters and incompetents. Favor seekers haunted the White House, plying Grant himself with cigars, wines, and horses. His election was a godsend to his in-laws of the Dent family, several dozen of whom attached themselves to the public payroll.

The easygoing Grant was first tarred by the Crédit Mobilier scandal, which erupted in 1872. Union Pacific Railroad insiders had formed the Crédit Mobilier construction company and then cleverly hired themselves at inflated prices to build the railroad line, earning dividends as high as 348 percent. Fearing that Congress might blow the whistle, the company furtively distributed shares of its valuable stock to key congressmen. A newspaper exposé and congressional investigation of the scandal led to the formal censure of two congressmen and the revelation that the vice president of the United States had accepted payments from Crédit Mobilier.

The breath of scandal in Washington also reeked of alcohol. In 1874–1875 the sprawling Whiskey Ring robbed the Treasury of millions in excise-tax revenues. "Let no guilty man escape," declared President Grant. But when his own private secretary turned up among the culprits, he volunteered a written statement to the jury that helped exonerate the thief. Further rottenness in the Grant administration came to light in 1876, forcing Secretary of War William Belknap to resign after pocketing bribes from suppliers to the Indian reservations. Grant, ever loyal to his crooked cronies, accepted Belknap's resignation "with great regret."

The Liberal Republican Revolt of 1872

By 1872 a powerful wave of disgust with Grantism was beginning to build up throughout the nation, even before some of the worst scandals had been

Can the Law Reach Him? 1872
Cartoonist Thomas Nast attacked "Boss" Tweed in a series of cartoons like this one that appeared in *Harper's Weekly* in 1872. Here Nast depicts the corrupt Tweed as a powerful giant, towering over a puny law force.

In a famous series of newspaper interviews in 1905, George Washington Plunkitt (1842–1924), a political "boss" in the same Tammany Hall Democratic political "machine" that had spawned William Marcy ("Boss") Tweed, candidly described his ethical and political principles:

"Everybody is talkin' these days about Tammany men growin' rich on graft, but nobody thinks of drawin' the distinction between honest graft and dishonest graft. There's all the difference in the world between the two. Yes, many of our men have grown rich in politics. I have myself. I've made a big fortune out of the game, and I'm gettin' richer every day, but I've not gone in for dishonest graft—blackmailin' gamblers, saloonkeepers, disorderly people, etc.—and neither has any of the men who have made big fortunes in politics.

"There's an honest graft, and I'm an example of how it works. I might sum up the whole thing by sayin': 'I seen my opportunities and I took 'em.'

"Just let me explain by examples. My party's in power in the city, and it's goin' to undertake a lot of public improvements. Well, I'm tipped off, say, that they're going to lay out a new park at a certain place.

"I see my opportunity and I take it. I go to that place and I buy up all the land I can in the neighborhood. Then the board of this or that makes its plan public, and there is a rush to get my land, which nobody cared particular for before.

"Ain't it perfectly honest to charge a good price and make a profit on my investment and foresight? Of course, it is. Well, that's honest graft."

The Liberal Republicans muffed their chance when their Cincinnati nominating convention astounded the country by nominating the brilliant but erratic Horace Greeley for the presidency. Although Greeley was the fearless editor of the *New York Tribune,* he was dogmatic, emotional, petulant, and notoriously unsound in his political judgments.

More astonishing still was the action of the office-hungry Democrats, who foolishly proceeded to endorse Greeley's candidacy. In swallowing Greeley the Democrats "ate crow" in large gulps, for the eccentric editor had long blasted them as traitors, slave shippers, saloon keepers, horse thieves, and idiots. Yet Greeley pleased the Democrats, North and South, when he pleaded for clasping hands across "the bloody chasm." The Republicans dutifully renominated Grant. The voters were thus presented with a choice between two candidates who had made their careers in fields other than politics and who were both eminently unqualified, by temperament and lifelong training, for high political office.

Can Greeley and the Democrats "Swallow" Each Other, 1872   This cartoon by Thomas Nast is a Republican gibe at the forced alliance between these former foes. General W. T. Sherman wrote from Paris to his brother, "I feel amazed to see the turn things have taken. Grant who never was a Republican is your candidate; and Greeley who never was a Democrat, but quite the reverse, is the Democratic candidate."

exposed. Reform-minded citizens banded together to form the Liberal Republican party. Voicing the slogan "Turn the Rascals Out," they urged purification of the Washington administration as well as an end to military Reconstruction.

In the mud-spattered campaign that followed, regular Republicans denounced Greeley as an atheist, a communist, a free-lover, a vegetarian, a brown-bread eater, and a cosigner of Jefferson Davis's bail bond. Democrats derided Grant as an ignoramus, a drunkard, and a swindler. But the regular Republicans, chanting "Grant us another term," pulled the president through. The count in the electoral column was 286 to 66, in the popular column 3,596,745 to 2,843,446.

Liberal Republican agitation frightened the regular Republicans into cleaning their own house before they were thrown out of it. The Republican Congress in 1872 passed a general amnesty act, removing political disabilities from all but some five hundred former Confederate leaders. Congress also moved to reduce high Civil War tariffs and to fumigate the Grant administration with mild civil-service reform. Like many American third parties, the Liberal Republicans left some enduring footprints, even in defeat.

Depression, Deflation, and Inflation

Grant's woes deepened in the paralyzing economic panic that broke in 1873. Bursting with startling rapidity, the crash was one of those periodic plummets that roller-coastered the economy in this age of unbridled capitalist expansion. Overreaching promoters had laid more railroad track, sunk more mines, erected more factories, and sowed more grainfields than existing markets could bear. Bankers, in turn, had made too many imprudent loans to finance those enterprises. When profits failed to materialize, loans went unpaid, and the whole credit-based house of cards fluttered down.

Boom times became gloom times as more than fifteen thousand businesses went bankrupt. In New York City, an army of unemployed riotously battled police. Black Americans were hard hit. The Freedman's Savings and Trust Company had made unsecured loans to several companies that went under. Black depositors who had entrusted over $7 million to the bank lost their savings, and black economic development and black confidence in savings institutions went down with it.

Hard times inflicted the worst punishment on debtors, who intensified their clamor for inflationary policies. Proponents of inflation breathed new life into the issue of greenbacks. During the war $450 million of the "folding money" had been issued, but it had depreciated under a cloud of popular mistrust and dubious legality.* By 1868 the Treasury had already withdrawn $100 million of the "battle-born currency" from circulation, and "hard-money" people everywhere looked forward to its complete disappearance. But now afflicted agrarian and debtor groups—"cheap-money" supporters—clamored for a reissuance of the greenbacks. With a crude but essentially accurate grasp of monetary theory, they reasoned that more money meant cheaper money and, hence, rising prices and easier-to-pay debts. Creditors, of course, reasoning from the same premises, advocated precisely the opposite policy. They had no desire to see the money they had loaned repaid in depreciated dollars. They wanted deflation, not inflation.

The "hard-money" advocates carried the day. In 1874 they persuaded a confused Grant to veto a bill to print more paper money. They scored another victory in the Resumption Act of 1875, which pledged the government to the further withdrawal of greenbacks from circulation and to the redemption of all paper currency in gold at face value, beginning in 1879.

Down but not out, debtors now looked for relief to another precious metal, silver. The "sacred white metal," they claimed, had received a raw deal. In the early 1870s, the Treasury stubbornly and unrealistically maintained that an ounce of silver was worth only one-sixteenth as much as an ounce of gold, though open-market prices for silver were higher. Silver miners thus stopped offering their shiny product for sale to the federal mints. With no silver flowing into the federal coffers, Congress formally dropped the coinage of silver dollars in 1873. Fate then played a sly joke when new silver discoveries later in the 1870s shot production up and forced silver prices down. Westerners from silver-mining states joined with debtors in assailing the "Crime of '73," demanding a return to the "Dollar of Our Daddies." Like the demand for more greenbacks, the demand for the coinage of more silver was nothing

---

*The Supreme Court in 1870 declared the Civil War Legal Tender Act unconstitutional. With the concurrence of the Senate, Grant thereupon added to the bench two justices who could be counted on to help reverse that decision, which happened in 1871. This is how the Court grew to its current size of nine justices.

more nor less than another scheme to promote inflation.

Hard-money Republicans resisted this scheme and counted on Grant to hold the line against it. He did not disappoint them. The Treasury began to accumulate gold stocks against the appointed day for resumption of metallic-money payments. Coupled with the reduction of greenbacks, this policy was called "contraction." It had a noticeable deflationary effect—the amount of money per capita in circulation actually *decreased* between 1870 and 1880, from $19.42 to $19.37. Contraction probably worsened the impact of the depression. But the new policy did restore the government's credit rating, and it brought the embattled greenbacks up to their full face value. When Redemption Day came in 1879, few greenback holders bothered to exchange the lighter and more convenient bills for gold.

Republican hard-money policy had a political backlash. It helped elect a Democratic House of Representatives in 1874, and in 1878 it spawned the Greenback Labor party, which polled over a million votes and elected fourteen members of Congress. The contest over monetary policy was far from over.

Pallid Politics in the Gilded Age

The political seesaw was delicately balanced throughout most of the Gilded Age (a sarcastic name given to the three-decade-long post–Civil War era by Mark Twain in 1873). Even a slight nudge could tip the teeter-totter to the advantage of the opposition party. Every presidential election was a squeaker, and the majority party in the House of Representatives switched six times in the eleven sessions between 1869 and 1891. In only three sessions did the same party control the House, the Senate, and the White House. Wobbling in such shaky equilibrium, politicians tiptoed timidly, producing a political record that was often trivial and petty.

Few significant economic issues separated the major parties. Democrats and Republicans saw very nearly eye-to-eye on questions like the tariff and civil-service reform, and majorities in both parties substantially agreed even on the much-debated currency question. Yet despite their rough agreement on these national matters, the two parties were ferociously competitive with each other. They were tightly and efficiently organized, and they

commanded fierce loyalty from their members. Voter turnouts reached heights unmatched before or since. Nearly 80 percent of eligible voters cast their ballots in presidential elections in the three decades after the Civil War. On election days droves of the party faithful tramped behind marching bands to the polling places, and "ticket splitting," or failing to vote the straight party line, was as rare as a silver dollar.

How can this apparent paradox of political consensus and partisan fervor be explained? The answer lies in the sharp ethnic and cultural differences in the membership of the two parties—in distinctions of style and tone, and especially of religious sentiment. Republican voters tended to adhere to those creeds that traced their lineage to Puritanism. They stressed strict codes of personal morality and believed that government should play a role in regulating both the economic and the moral affairs of society. Democrats, among whom immigrant Lutherans and Roman Catholics figured heavily, were more likely to adhere to faiths that took a less stern view of human weakness. Their religions professed toleration of differences in an imperfect world, and they spurned government efforts to impose a single moral standard on the entire society. These differences in temperament and religious values often produced raucous political contests at the local level, where issues like prohibition and education loomed large.

Democrats had a solid electoral base in the South and in the northern industrial cities, teeming with immigrants and controlled by well-oiled political machines. Republican strength lay largely in the Midwest and the rural and small-town Northeast. Grateful freedmen in the South continued to vote Republican in significant numbers. Another important bloc of Republican ballots came from the members of the Grand Army of the Republic (GAR)—a politically potent fraternal organization of several hundred thousand Union veterans of the Civil War.

The lifeblood of both parties was patronage—disbursing jobs by the bucketful in return for votes, kickbacks, and party service. Boisterous infighting over patronage beset the Republican party in the 1870s and 1880s. A "Stalwart" faction, led by the handsome and imperious Roscoe ("Lord Roscoe") Conkling, U.S. senator from New York, unblushingly embraced the time-honored system of swapping civil-service jobs for votes. Opposed to the Conklingites were the so-called Half-Breeds, who flirted coyly with civil-service reform, but whose real quarrel with the Stalwarts was over who should grasp the ladle that dished out the spoils. The champion of the Half-Breeds was James G. Blaine of Maine, a radiantly personable congressman with an elastic conscience. But despite the color of their personalities, Conkling and Blaine succeeded only in stalemating each other and deadlocking their party.

The Hayes-Tilden Standoff, 1876

Hangers-on around Grant, like fleas urging their ailing dog to live, begged the "Old Man" to try for a third term in 1876. The general, blind to his own ineptitudes, showed a disquieting willingness. But the House, by a lopsided bipartisan vote of 233 to 18, derailed the third-term bandwagon. It passed a resolution that sternly reminded the country—and Grant—of the antidictator implications of the two-term tradition.

With Grant out of the running and with the Conklingites and Blaineites neutralizing each other, the Republicans turned to a compromise candidate, Rutherford B. Hayes, who was obscure enough to be dubbed "The Great Unknown." His foremost qualification was the fact that he hailed from the electorally doubtful but potent state of Ohio, where he had served three terms as governor. So crucial were the "swing" votes of Ohio in the cliffhanging presidential contests of the day that the state produced

more than its share of presidential candidates. A political saying of the 1870s paraphrased Shakespeare:

> Some are born great,
> Some achieve greatness,
> And some are born in Ohio.

Pitted against the humdrum Hayes was the Democratic nominee, Samuel J. Tilden, who had risen to fame as the man who bagged Boss Tweed in New York. Campaigning against Republican scandal, Tilden racked up 184 electoral votes of the needed 185, with 20 votes in four states—three of them in the South—doubtful because of irregular returns (see the map below). Surely Tilden could pick up at least one of these, especially in view of the fact that he had polled 247,448 more popular votes than Hayes, 4,284,020 to 4,036,572.

Both parties scurried to send "visiting statesmen" to the contested southern states of Louisiana, South Carolina, and Florida. All three disputed states submitted two sets of returns, one Democratic and one Republican. As the weeks drifted by, the paralysis tightened, generating a dramatic constitutional crisis. The Constitution merely specifies that the electoral returns from the states shall be sent to Congress, and in the presence of the House and Senate, they shall be opened by the president of the Senate (see the Twelfth Amendment). But who should count them? On this point the Constitution was silent. If counted by the president of the Senate (a Republican), the Republican returns would be

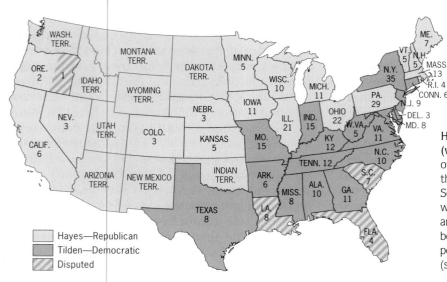

Hayes-Tilden Disputed Election of 1876 (with electoral vote by state) Nineteen of the twenty disputed votes composed the total electoral count of Louisiana, South Carolina, and Florida. The twentieth was one of Oregon's three votes, cast by an elector who turned out to be ineligible because he was a federal officeholder (a postmaster), contrary to the Constitution (see Art. II, Sec. I, para. 2).

selected. If counted by the Speaker of the House (a Democrat), the Democratic returns would be chosen. How could the impasse be resolved?

The Compromise of 1877 and the End of Reconstruction

Clash or compromise was the stark choice. The danger loomed that there would be no president on Inauguration Day, March 4, 1877. "Tilden or Blood!" cried Democratic hotheads, and some of their "Minute Men" began to drill with arms. But behind the scenes, frantically laboring statesmen gradually hammered out an agreement in the Henry Clay tradition—the Compromise of 1877.

The election deadlock itself was to be broken by the Electoral Count Act, which passed Congress early in 1877. It set up an electoral commission consisting of fifteen men selected from the Senate, the House, and the Supreme Court.

In February 1877, about a month before Inauguration Day, the Senate and House met together in an electric atmosphere to settle the dispute. The roll of the states was tolled off alphabetically. When Florida was reached—the first of the three southern states with two sets of returns—the disputed documents were referred to the electoral commission, which sat in a nearby chamber. After prolonged discussion the members agreed, by the partisan vote of eight Republicans to seven Democrats, to accept the Republican returns. Outraged Democrats in Congress, smelling defeat, undertook to launch a filibuster "until hell froze over."

Renewed deadlock was avoided by the rest of the complex Compromise of 1877, already partially concluded behind closed doors. The Democrats reluctantly agreed that Hayes might take office in return for his withdrawing intimidating federal troops from the two states in which they remained, Louisiana and South Carolina. Among various concessions, the Republicans assured the Democrats a place at the presidential patronage trough and support for a bill subsidizing the Texas and Pacific Railroad's construction of a southern transcontinental line. Not all of these promises were kept in later years, including the Texas and Pacific subsidy. But the deal held together long enough to break the dangerous electoral standoff. The Democrats permitted Hayes to receive the remainder of the disputed returns—all by the partisan vote of 8 to 7. So close was the margin of safety that the explosive issue was settled only three days before the new president was officially sworn into office. The nation breathed a collective sigh of relief.

The compromise bought peace at a price. Violence was averted by sacrificing the black freedmen in the South. With the Hayes-Tilden deal, the Republican party quietly abandoned its commitment to racial equality. That commitment had been weakening in any case. The Civil Rights Act of 1875 was in a sense the last feeble gasp of the congressional radical Republicans. The act supposedly guaranteed equal accommodations in public places and prohibited racial discrimination in jury selection, but the law was born toothless and stayed that way for nearly a century. The Supreme Court pronounced much of the act unconstitutional in the *Civil Rights Cases* (1883). The Court declared that the Fourteenth Amendment prohibited only *government* violations of civil rights, not the denial of civil rights by *individuals*. Hayes clinched the bargain by withdrawing the last federal troops that were propping up carpetbag governments. The bayonet-backed Republican regimes collapsed as the blue-clad soldiers departed.

Composition of the Electoral Commission, 1877

Members	Republicans	Democrats
Senate (Republican majority)	3	3
House (Democratic majority)	2	3
Supreme Court	3	2
TOTAL	8	7

The Birth of Jim Crow in the Post-Reconstruction South

The Democratic South speedily solidified and swiftly suppressed the now-friendless blacks. Reconstruction, for better or worse, was officially ended. Shamelessly relying on fraud and intimidation, white Democrats ("Redeemers") resumed political power in the South and exercised it ruth-

A Southern Plantation, Before and After the Civil War   The emancipated blacks moved out of the slave quarters and into humble cabins dispersed around the plantation. The master had now become the landlord and the employer, and the slaves had become tenant farmers and sharecroppers—but were they better off?

lessly. Blacks who tried to assert their rights faced unemployment, eviction, and physical harm.

Blacks (as well as poor whites) were forced into sharecropping and tenant farming. Former slaves often found themselves at the mercy of former masters who were now their landlords and creditors. Through the "crop-lien" system, storekeepers extended credit to small farmers for food and supplies and in return took a lien on their harvests. Shrewd merchants manipulated the system so that

farmers remained perpetually in debt to them. For generations to come, southern blacks were condemned to eke out a threadbare living under conditions scarcely better than slavery.

With white southerners back in the political saddle, daily discrimination against blacks grew increasingly oppressive. What had started as the informal separation of blacks and whites in the immediate postwar years developed by the 1890s into systematic state-level legal codes of segregation

Weighing Cotton   Cotton pickers who once toiled under the lash as slaves now worked for wages as sharecroppers, but they were still beholden to the plantation owner. At this "weigh up," the "Boss Man" carefully calculates his profit as each hamper is filled, while the sharecroppers await their meager payment.

known as Jim Crow laws. Southern states also enacted literacy requirements, voter-registration laws, and poll taxes to ensure full-scale disfranchisement of the South's black population. The Supreme Court validated the South's segregationist social order in the case of *Plessy* v. *Ferguson* (1896). It ruled that "separate but equal" facilities were constitutional under the "equal protection" clause of the Fourteenth Amendment.

But in reality the quality of African-American life was grotesquely unequal to that of whites. Segregated in inferior schools and separated from whites in virtually all public facilities, including railroad cars, theaters, and even restrooms, blacks were assaulted daily by galling reminders of their second-class citizenship. To ensure the stability of this political and economic "new order," southern whites dealt harshly with any black who dared to violate the South's racial code of conduct. A record number of blacks were lynched during the 1890s, most often for the "crime" of asserting themselves as equals (see the table below). It would take a second Reconstruction, nearly a century later, to redress the racist imbalance of southern society.

Persons in United States Lynched [by race], 1882–1970*

Year	Whites	Blacks	Total
1882	64	49	113
1885	110	74	184
1890	11	85	96
1895	66	113	179
1900	9	106	115
1905	5	57	62
1910	9	67	76
1915	13	56	69
1920	8	53	61
1925	0	17	17
1930	1	20	21
1935	2	18	20
1940	1	4	5
1945	0	1	1
1950	1	1	2
1965	0	0	0

*There were no lynchings in 1965–1970. In every year from 1882 (when records were first kept) to 1964, the number of lynchings corresponded roughly to the figures given here. The worst year was 1892, when 161 blacks and 69 whites were lynched (total 230); the next worst was 1884, when 164 whites and 51 blacks were lynched (total 215).

Class Conflicts and Ethnic Clashes

The year 1877 marked more than the end of Reconstruction. As the curtains officially closed on regional warfare, they opened on scenes of class warfare. The explosive atmosphere was largely a by-product of the long years of depression and deflation following the panic of 1873. Railroad workers faced particularly hard times. When the presidents of the nation's four largest railroads collectively decided in 1877 to cut employees' wages by 10 percent, the workers struck back. President Hayes's decision to call in federal troops to quell the unrest brought the striking laborers an outpouring of working-class support. Work stoppages spread like wildfire in cities from Baltimore to St. Louis. When the battling between workers and soldiers ended after several weeks, over one hundred people were dead.

The failure of the great railroad strike exposed the weakness of the labor movement. Racial and ethnic fissures among workers everywhere fractured labor unity and were particularly acute between the Irish and the Chinese in California (see "Makers of America: The Chinese," pp. 512–513). By 1880 the Golden State counted seventy-five thousand Asian newcomers, about 9 percent of its entire population. Mostly poor, uneducated, single males, they derived predominantly from the Taishan district of K'uang-t'ung (Guangdong) province in southern China. They had originally come to America to dig in the goldfields and to sledgehammer the tracks of the transcontinental railroads across the West. When the gold supply petered out and the tracks were laid, many—perhaps half of those who arrived before the 1880s—returned home to China with their meager savings.

Those who remained in America faced extraordinary hardships. They worked at the most menial jobs, often as cooks, laundrymen, or domestic servants. Without women or families, they were marooned in a land where they neither were wanted nor wanted to be. They lived lonely lives, bereft of the children who in other immigrant communities eased their parents' assimilation through their exposure to the English language and American customs in school. The phrase "not a Chinaman's chance" emerged in this era to describe the daunting odds against which they struggled.

In San Francisco Irish-born demagogue Denis Kearney incited his followers to violent abuse of the

The Chinese

In the late nineteenth century, the burgeoning industries and booming frontier towns of the United States' Pacific coast hungered for laborers to wrench minerals from stubborn rock, to lay down railroad track through untamed wastelands, and to transform dry expanses into fertile fields of fruit and vegetables. In faraway Asia the Chinese answered the call. Contributing their muscle to the building of the West, they dug in the gold mines and helped to lay the transcontinental railroads that stitched together the American nation.

The first Chinese had arrived in Spanish America as early as 1565. But few followed those earliest pioneers until the 1848 discovery of gold in California attracted people from all over the world to America's Pacific coast. Among them were many fortune-hungry Chinese who sailed into San Francisco, which Chinese immigrants named the "golden mountain."

The California boom coincided with the culmination of years of tumult and suffering in China. The once great Chinese Empire was disintegrating, while a few ruthless landlords, like looters, grabbed control of nearly every acre of farmland. In destructive complement to this internal disarray, the European imperial powers forced their way into the unstable country, seeking to unlock the riches of a nation that had been closed to outsiders for centuries.

Faced with economic hardship and political turmoil, more than 2 million Chinese left their homeland between 1840 and 1900, for destinations as diverse as Southeast Asia, Peru, Hawaii, and Cuba, with more than 300,000 entering the United States. Although their numbers included a few merchants and artisans, most were unskilled country folk. In some cases families pooled their money to send out a son, but most travelers, desperately poor, obtained their passage through Chinese middlemen, who advanced them ship fare in return for the emigrants' promise to work off their debts after they landed. This contracting sometimes led to conditions so cruel that the practice was ignominiously called pig selling.

The Chinese-America of the late-nineteenth-century West was overwhelmingly a bachelor society. Women of good repute rarely made the passage. Of the very few Chinese women who ventured to California at this time, most became prostitutes. Many of them had been deceived by the false promise of honest jobs.

Although a stream of workers returned to their homeland, many Chinese stayed. "Chinatowns" sprang up wherever economic opportunities presented themselves—in railroad towns, farming villages, and cities. Chinese in these settlements spoke their own language, enjoyed the fellowship of their own compatriots, and sought safety from prejudice and violence, never rare in American society. Many

Surviving Central Pacific Railroad Workers These men, posing in 1919, helped build the railroad during the 1860s.

Chinese Butcher Shop,
San Francisco, California, c. 1890

immigrant clubs, American adaptations of Chinese traditions of loyalty to clan or region, were established in these communities. Rivaling such clubs and associations were the secret societies known as tongs. The word *tong*—literally, "meeting hall"—acquired a sinister reputation among non-Chinese, for the tongs counted the poorest and shadiest immigrants among their members. These were people without ties to a clan, those individuals most alienated from traditional Chinese organizations and from American society as well.

After 1882 the Chinese Exclusion Act barred nearly all Chinese from the United States for six decades. Many of the bachelors who had made the long journey to America died or returned home. Slowly, however, those men and the few women who remained raised families and reared a new generation of Chinese Americans. Like their immigrant parents, this second generation suffered from discrimination. They had to eke out a living in jobs despised by Caucasian laborers or take daunting risks in small entrepreneurial ventures. Yet many hard-working Chinese did manage to open their own restaurants, laundries, and other small businesses. The enterprises formed a solid economic foundation for their small community and remain a source of livelihood for many Chinese-Americans even today.

Chinese Population in the Continental United States, 1850–1900

Year	Population	Males per One Female	Percentage U.S.-Born	Total Chinese Immigrants in Preceding Decade*
1850	4,018†	—	—	—
1860	34,933	19	—	41,397
1870	63,199	13	1	64,301
1880	105,465	21	1	123,201
1890	107,488	27	3	61,711
1900	89,863	19	10	14,799

*Includes Chinese immigrants in Hawaii after 1898.
†Estimated.

The First Blow at the Chinese Question, 1877   Caucasian workers, seething with economic anxiety and ethnic prejudice, savagely mistreated the Chinese in California in the 1870s.

hapless Chinese. The Kearneyites, many of whom were recently arrived immigrants from Europe, hotly resented the competition of cheap labor from the still more recently arrived Chinese. The beef-eater, they claimed, had no chance against the rice-eater in a life-and-death struggle for jobs and wages. The present tens of thousands of Chinese "coolies" were regarded as a menace, the prospective millions as a calamity. Taking to the streets, gangs of Kear-neyites terrorized the Chinese by shearing off their precious pigtails. Some victims were murdered outright.

Congress finally slammed the door on Chinese immigrant laborers when it passed the Chinese Exclusion Act in 1882, prohibiting all further immi-gration from China. The door stayed shut until 1943. Some exclusionists even tried to strip native-born Chinese-Americans of their citizenship, but the

Supreme Court ruled in *U.S.* v. *Wong Kim Ark* in 1898 that the Fourteenth Amendment guaranteed citizenship to all persons born in the United States. This doctrine of "birthright citizenship" (or *jus soli,* the "right of the soil," as contrasted with *jus sangui-nis,* the "right of blood-tie," which based citizenship on the parents' nationality) provided important pro-tections to Chinese-Americans as well as to other immigrant communities.

Garfield and Arthur

As the presidential campaign of 1880 approached, "Rutherfraud" Hayes was a man without a party, denounced and repudiated by the Republican Old Guard. The Republican party sought a new standard-bearer for 1880 and finally settled on a "dark-horse" candidate, James A. Garfield, from the electorally powerful state of Ohio. His vice-presidential running mate was a notorious Stalwart henchman, Chester A. Arthur of New York.

Energetically waving the bloody shirt, Garfield barely squeaked out a victory over the Democratic candidate and Civil War hero, Winfield Scott Han-cock. He polled only 39,213 more votes than Han-cock—4,453,295 to 4,414,082—but his margin in the electoral column was a comfortable 214 to 155.

The new president was energetic and able, but he was immediately ensnared in a political conflict between his secretary of state, James G. Blaine, and Blaine's Stalwart nemesis, Senator Roscoe Conkling. Then, as the Republican factions dueled, tragedy struck. A disappointed and mentally deranged office seeker, Charles J. Guiteau, shot President Garfield in the back in a Washington railroad sta-tion. Garfield lingered in agony for eleven weeks and died on September 19, 1881. Guiteau, when seized, reportedly cried, "I am a Stalwart. Arthur is now President of the United States." The implication was that now the Conklingites would all get good jobs. Guiteau's attorneys argued that he was not guilty because of his incapacity to distinguish right from wrong—an early instance of the "insanity defense." The defendant himself demonstrated his weak grip on reality when he asked all those who had benefited politically by the assassination to contribute to his defense fund. These tactics availed little. Guiteau was found guilty of murder and hanged.

The Office Makes the Man, 1881 Besieged by his former New York cronies, Arthur tries to assert the dignity of his new presidential office.

reform. It made compulsory campaign contributions from federal employees illegal, and it established the Civil Service Commission to make appointments to federal jobs on the basis of competitive examinations rather than "pull."

Although at first covering only about 10 percent of federal jobs, civil-service reform did rein in the most blatant abuses. Yet like many well-intentioned reforms, it bred unintended problems of its own. With the "plum" federal posts now beyond their

Garfield's death had one positive outcome: it shocked politicians into reforming the shameful spoils system. The unlikely instrument of reform was Chester Arthur. Observers at first underestimated him. His record of cronyism and his fondness for fine wines and elegant clothing (including eighty pairs of trousers) suggested that he was little more than a foppish dandy. But Arthur surprised his critics by prosecuting several fraud cases and giving his former Stalwart pals the cold shoulder.

Disgust with Garfield's murder gave the Republican party itself a previously undetected taste for reform. The medicine finally applied to the long-suffering federal government was the Pendleton Act of 1883—the so-called Magna Carta of civil-service

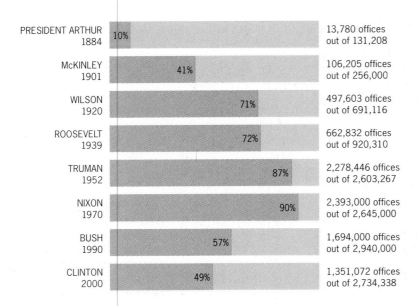

PRESIDENT ARTHUR 1884	10%	13,780 offices out of 131,208
McKINLEY 1901	41%	106,205 offices out of 256,000
WILSON 1920	71%	497,603 offices out of 691,116
ROOSEVELT 1939	72%	662,832 offices out of 920,310
TRUMAN 1952	87%	2,278,446 offices out of 2,603,267
NIXON 1970	90%	2,393,000 offices out of 2,645,000
BUSH 1990	57%	1,694,000 offices out of 2,940,000
CLINTON 2000	49%	1,351,072 offices out of 2,734,338

Growth of Classified Civil Service (subject to competitive requirements) The most recent numbers reflect the changes mandated by the Postal Reorganization Act of 1971, which moved U.S. Postal Service employees from competitive to excepted service.

reach, politicians were forced to look elsewhere for money, "the mother's milk of politics." Increasingly, they turned to the bulging coffers of the big corporations. A new breed of "boss" emerged—less skilled at mobilizing small armies of immigrants and other voters on election day, but more adept at milking dollars from manufacturers and lobbyists. The Pendleton Act partially divorced politics from patronage, but it helped drive politicians into "marriages of convenience" with big-business leaders.

President Arthur's surprising display of integrity offended too many powerful Republicans. His ungrateful party turned him out to pasture, and in 1886 he died of a cerebral hemorrhage.

The Blaine-Cleveland Mudslingers of 1884

James G. Blaine's persistence in pursuit of his party's presidential nomination finally paid off in 1884. The dashing Maine politician, blessed with almost every political asset except a reputation for honesty, was the clear choice of the Republican convention in Chicago. But many reform-minded Republicans gagged on Blaine's candidacy. Blaine's enemies publicized the fishy-smelling "Mulligan letters," written by Blaine to a Boston businessman and linking the powerful politician to a corrupt deal involving federal favors to a southern railroad. At least one of the

damning documents ended with the furtive warning "Burn this letter." Some reformers, unable to swallow Blaine, bolted to the Democrats. They were sneeringly dubbed Mugwumps, a word of Indian derivation meant to suggest that they were "sanctimonious" or "holier-than-thou."*

Victory-starved Democrats turned enthusiastically to a noted reformer, Grover Cleveland. A burly bachelor with a soup-straining mustache and a taste for chewing tobacco, Cleveland was a solid but not brilliant lawyer of forty-seven. He had rocketed from the mayor's office in Buffalo to the governorship of New York and the presidential nomination in three short years. Known as "Grover the Good" he enjoyed a well-deserved reputation for probity in office.

But Cleveland's admirers soon got a shock. Resolute Republicans, digging for dirt in the past of bachelor Cleveland, unearthed the report that he had been involved in an amorous affair with a Buffalo widow. She had an illegitimate son, now eight years old, for whom Cleveland had made financial provision. Democratic elders were demoralized. They hurried to Cleveland and urged him to lie like a gentleman, but their ruggedly honest candidate insisted, "Tell the truth."

---

*Latter-day punsters gibed that the Mugwumps were priggish politicians who sat on the fence with their "mugs" on one side and their "wumps" on the other.

**Little Lost Mugwumps
Who Had Gone Astray**
James G. Blaine, depicted as
Little Bo Peep, tries to woo
the errant Mugwump
reformers back into the
Republican fold in 1884.

The campaign of 1884 sank to perhaps the lowest level in American experience, as the two parties grunted and shoved for the hog trough of office. Few fundamental differences separated them. Even the bloody shirt had faded to a pale pink.* Personalities, not principles, claimed the headlines. Crowds of Democrats surged through city streets, chanting—to the rhythm of left, left, left, right, left—"Burn, burn, burn this letter!" Republicans taunted in return, "Ma, ma, where's my pa?" Defiant Democrats shouted back, "Gone to the White House, ha, ha, ha!"

The contest hinged on the state of New York, where Blaine blundered badly in the closing days of the campaign. A witless Republican clergyman damned the Democrats in a speech as the party of "Rum, Romanism, and Rebellion"—insulting with one swift stroke the race, the faith, and the patriotism of New York's numerous Irish-American voters. Blaine was present at the time but lacked the presence of mind to repudiate the statement immediately. The pungent phrase, shortened to "RRR," stung and stuck. Blaine's silence seemed to give assent, and the wavering Irishmen who deserted his

camp helped account for Cleveland's paper-thin plurality of about a thousand votes in New York State, enough to give him the presidency. Cleveland swept the solid South and squeaked into office with 219 to 182 electoral votes and 4,879,507 to 4,850,93 popular votes.

"**I Want My Pa!**"   Malicious anti-Cleveland cartoon.

---

*Neither candidate had served in the Civil War. Cleveland had hired a substitute to go in his stead while he supported his widowed mother and two sisters. Blaine was the only Republican presidential candidate from Grant through McKinley (1868 to 1900) who had not been a Civil War officer.

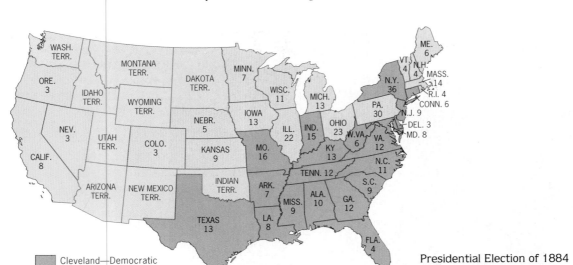

Presidential Election of 1884
(with electoral vote by state)

- ■ Cleveland—Democratic
- ☐ Blaine—Republican

"Old Grover" Takes Over

Bull-necked Cleveland in 1885 was the first Democrat to take the oath of presidential office since Buchanan, twenty-eight years earlier. Huge question marks hung over his ample frame (5 feet 11 inches, 250 pounds). Could the "party of disunion" be trusted to govern the Union? Would desperate Democrats, ravenously hungry after twenty-four years of exile, trample the frail sprouts of civil-service reform in a stampede to the patronage trough? Could Cleveland restore a measure of respect and power to the maligned and enfeebled presidency?

Cleveland was a man of principles, most of them safely orthodox by the standards of his day. A staunch apostle of the hands-off creed of laissez-faire, the new president caused the hearts of businesspeople and bankers to throb with contentment. He summed up his political philosophy in 1887 when he vetoed a bill to provide seeds for drought-ravaged Texas farmers. "Though the people support the government," he declared, "the government should not support the people." As tactless as a mirror and as direct as a bulldozer, he was outspoken, unbending, and profanely hot-tempered.

At the outset Cleveland narrowed the North-South chasm by naming to his cabinet two former Confederates. As for the civil service, Cleveland was whipsawed between the demands of the Democratic faithful for jobs and the demands of the Mug-wumps, who had helped elect him, for reform. Believing in the merit system, Cleveland at first favored the cause of the reformers, but he eventually caved in to the carpings of Democratic bosses and fired almost two-thirds of the 120,000 federal employees, including 40,000 incumbent (Republican) postmasters, to make room for "deserving Democrats."

Military pensions gave Cleveland some of his most painful political headaches. The politically powerful Grand Army of the Republic (GAR) routinely lobbied hundreds of private pension bills through a compliant Congress. Benefits were granted to deserters, to bounty jumpers, to men who never served, and to former soldiers who in later years had incurred disabilities in no way connected with war service. A Democrat and a nonveteran, Cleveland was in an awkward position when it came to fighting the pension-grabbers. But the conscience-driven president read each bill carefully, vetoed several hundred of them, and then laboriously penned individual veto messages for Congress.

Cleveland Battles for a Lower Tariff

Cleveland also risked his political neck by prodding the hornet's nest of the tariff issue. During the Civil War, tariff schedules had been jacked up to new

Grover Cleveland (1837–1908)
A strong supporter of civil-service reform and tariff reduction, President-elect Cleveland was also the country's most eligible bachelor. In this cartoon of 1884, he is shown struggling to avoid office seekers on the one side and potential mothers-in-law on the other.

high levels, partly to raise revenues for the insatiable military machine. American industry, which was preponderantly in Republican hands, had profited from this protection and hated to see the sheltering benefits reduced in peacetime. But the high duties continued to pile up revenue at the customshouses, and by 1881 the Treasury was running an annual surplus amounting to an embarrassing $145 million. Most of the government's income, in those pre–income tax days, came from the tariff.

Congress could reduce the vexatious surplus in two ways. One was to squander it on pensions and "pork-barrel" bills and thus curry favor with veterans and other self-seeking groups. The other was to lower the tariff—something the big industrialists vehemently opposed. Grover Cleveland, the rustic Buffalo attorney, had known little and cared less about the tariff before entering the White House. But as he studied the subject, he was much impressed by the arguments for downward revision of the tariff schedules. Lower barriers would mean lower prices for consumers and less protection for monopolies. Most important, they would mean an end to the Treasury surplus, a standing mockery of Cleveland's professed belief in fiscal orthodoxy and small-government frugality. After much hesitation Cleveland saw his duty and overdid it.

With his characteristic bluntness, Cleveland tossed an appeal for lower tariffs like a bombshell into the lap of Congress in late 1887. The response was electric. Cleveland succeeded admirably in smoking the issue out into the open. Democrats were deeply depressed at the obstinacy of their chief. Republicans rejoiced at his apparent recklessness. The old warrior Blaine gloated, "There's one more President for us in [tariff] protection." For the first time in years, a real issue divided the two parties as the 1888 presidential election loomed.

Weighing the Candidates, 1888
Novelties like this were widely distributed in late-nineteenth-century political campaigns. This toy scale evidently favored the corpulent Democratic candidate, Grover Cleveland.

> *On the night before the inauguration of Harrison, a crowd of jubilant Republicans tauntingly serenaded the darkened White House with a popular campaign ditty directed at Grover Cleveland:*
>
> Down in the cornfield
> Hear that mournful sound;
> All the Democrats are weeping—
> Grover's in the cold, cold ground!
>
> *But Grover was to rise again and serve as president for a second term of four more years.*

Dismayed Democrats, seeing no alternative, somewhat dejectedly nominated Grover Cleveland in their St. Louis convention. Eager Republicans turned to Benjamin Harrison, whose grandfather was former president William Henry ("Tippecanoe") Harrison. The tariff was the prime issue. The two parties flooded the country with some 10 million pamphlets on the subject.

The specter of a lowered tariff spurred the Republicans to frantic action. In an impressive demonstration of the post–Pendleton Act politics of alliances with big business, they raised a war chest of some $3 million—the heftiest yet—largely by "frying the fat" out of nervous industrialists. The money was widely used to line up corrupt "voting cattle" known as "repeaters" and "floaters." In Indiana, always a crucial "swing" state, votes were shamelessly purchased for as much as $20 each.

On election day Harrison nosed out Cleveland, 233 to 168 electoral votes. A change of about 7,000 ballots in New York would have reversed the outcome. Cleveland actually polled more popular votes, 5,537,857 to 5,447,129, but he nevertheless became the first sitting president to be voted out of his chair since Martin Van Buren in 1840.

The Billion-Dollar Congress

After a four-year famine, the Republicans under Harrison licked their lips hungrily for the bounty of federal offices. They yearned to lavish upon the party faithful the fat surpluses produced by the high tariffs. But in the House of Representatives, they had only three more votes than the necessary quorum of 163 members, and the Democrats were preparing to obstruct all House business by refusing to answer roll calls, demanding roll calls to determine the presence of a quorum, and employing other delaying tactics.

Into this tense cockpit stepped the new Republican Speaker of the House, Thomas B. Reed of Maine. A hulking figure who towered six feet three inches, he was renowned as a master debater. He spoke with a harsh nasal drawl and wielded a verbal harpoon of sarcasm. To one congressman who quoted Henry Clay that he would "rather be right than be president," Reed caustically retorted that he "would never be either." Opponents cringed at the crack of his quip.

Reed soon bent the intimidated House to his imperious will. He counted as present Democrats who had not answered the roll and who, rule book in hand, furiously denied that they were legally there. By such tactics "Czar" Reed utterly dominated the "Billion-Dollar" Congress—the first in history to

President Harrison Disposes of Surplus, 1892

BILLION-DOLLARISM HOLE

appropriate that sum. Congress showered pensions on Civil War veterans and increased government purchases of silver. To keep the revenues flowing in—and to protect Republican industrialists from foreign competition—the Billion-Dollar Congress also passed the McKinley Tariff Act of 1890, boosting rates to their highest peacetime level ever (an average of 48.4 percent on dutiable goods).

Sponsored in the House by rising Republican star William McKinley of Ohio, the new tariff act brought fresh woes to farmers. Debt-burdened farmers had no choice but to buy manufactured goods from high-priced protected American industrialists, but were compelled to sell their own agricultural products into highly competitive, unprotected world markets. Mounting discontent against the McKinley Tariff caused many rural voters to rise in wrath. In the congressional elections of 1890, the Republicans lost their precarious majority and were reduced to just 88 seats, as compared with 235 Democrats. Even the much-touted McKinley went down to defeat. Ominously for conservatives, the new Congress also included nine members of the Farmers' Alliance, a militant organization of southern and western farmers.

The Drumbeat of Discontent

Politics was no longer "as usual" in 1892, when the newly formed People's Party, or "Populists," burst upon the scene. Rooted in the Farmers' Alliance of frustrated farmers in the great agricultural belts of the West and South, the Populists met in Omaha and adopted a scorching platform that denounced "the prolific womb of governmental injustice." They demanded inflation through free and unlimited coinage of silver at the rate of sixteen ounces of silver to one ounce of gold. They further called for a graduated income tax; government ownership of the railroads, telegraph, and telephone; the direct election of U.S. senators; a one-term limit on the presidency; the adoption of the initiative and referendum to allow citizens to shape legislation more directly; a shorter workday; and immigration

Cornhusking
Hard-working farmers like the Krueger family, pictured in Wisconsin around the turn of the century, sought relief from their heavy debt burdens in the 1890s by clamoring for various inflationary schemes, including the monetization of silver.

> *A popular protest song of the 1890s among western farmers was titled "The Hayseed."* *One stanza ran,*
>
> I once was a tool of oppression,
> And as green as a sucker could be,
> And monopolies banded together
> To beat a poor hayseed like me.

restriction. As their presidential candidate, the Populists uproariously nominated the eloquent old Greenbacker, General James B. Weaver.

An epidemic of nationwide strikes in the summer of 1892 raised the prospect that the Populists

The Homestead Strike, 1892   Three hundred armed Pinkerton detectives floated on barges down the Monongahela River to the site of the Carnegie steel plant at Homestead. Met by a defiant and disciplined force of strikers, they were compelled to surrender. Here the Pinkerton men are shown disembarking from their barges after their capitulation, while the jeering strikers ashore exult in their victory.

could weld together a coalition of aggrieved workers and indebted farmers in a revolutionary joint assault on the capitalist order. At Andrew Carnegie's Homestead steel plant near Pittsburgh, company officials called in three hundred armed Pinkerton detectives in July to crush a strike by steelworkers angry over pay cuts. Defiant strikers, armed with rifles and dynamite, forced their assailants to surrender after a vicious battle that left ten people dead and some sixty wounded. Troops were eventually summoned, and both the strike and the union were broken. That same month, federal troops bloodily smashed a strike among silver miners in Idaho's fabled Coeur d'Alene district.

The Populists made a remarkable showing in the 1892 presidential election. Singing "Good-by, Party Bosses," they rolled up 1,029,846 popular votes and 22 electoral votes for General Weaver. They thus became one of the few third parties in U.S. history to break into the electoral column. But they fell far short of an electoral majority. Industrial laborers, especially in the urban East, did not rally to the Populist banner in appreciable numbers. Populist electoral votes came from only six midwestern and western states, four of which (Kansas, Colorado, Idaho, and Nevada) fell completely into the Populist basket.

The South, although a hotbed of agrarian agitation, proved especially unwilling to throw in its lot with the new party. Race was the reason. The more than one million southern black farmers organized in the Colored Farmers' National Alliance shared a host of complaints with poor white farmers, and for a time their common economic goals promised to overcome their racial differences. Recognizing the crucial edge that black votes could give them in the South, Populist leaders like Georgia's Tom Watson reached out to the black community. Watson was a wiry redhead who could "talk like the thrust of a Bowie knife." He declared, "There is no reason why the black man should not understand that the law that hurts me, as a farmer, hurts him, as a farmer." Many blacks were disillusioned enough with the Republican party to respond. Alarmed, the conservative white "Bourbon" elite in the South played cynically upon historic racial antagonisms to counter the Populists' appeal for interracial solidarity and woo back poor whites.

Southern blacks were heavy losers. The Populist-inspired reminder of potential black political strength led to the near-total extinction of what little

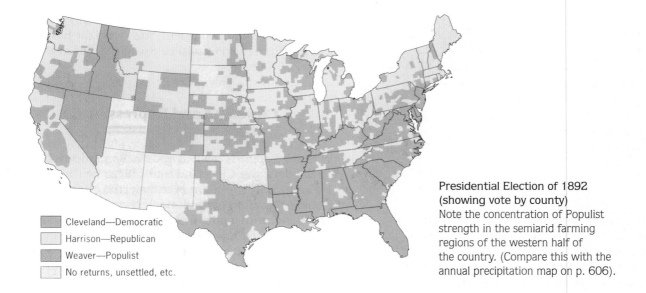

Cleveland—Democratic
Harrison—Republican
Weaver—Populist
No returns, unsettled, etc.

Presidential Election of 1892 (showing vote by county) Note the concentration of Populist strength in the semiarid farming regions of the western half of the country. (Compare this with the annual precipitation map on p. 606).

African-American suffrage remained in the South. White southerners more aggressively than ever used literacy tests and poll taxes to deny blacks the ballot. The notorious "grandfather clause" exempted from those requirements anyone whose forebear had voted in 1860—when, of course, black slaves had not voted at all. More than half a century would pass before southern blacks could again vote in considerable numbers. Accompanying this disfranchisement were more severe Jim Crow laws,

The Kansas Legislature, 1893 Rifle-bearing Populists seized the Kansas capitol after the election of 1892 to make good their claim that they had won at the polls. Republicans disagreed and eventually prevailed when sergeants at arms, shown here, restored order.

Thomas Edward Watson (1865–1922)
Populist leader Tom Watson of Georgia began his public career promoting interracial political cooperation, though he sometimes despaired that many poor white farmers preferred to "hug the chains of . . . wretchedness rather than do any experimenting on [the race] question." Watson himself eventually succumbed to racism. In 1913 he proclaimed that "The Negro has no comprehension of virtue, honesty, truth, gratitude, and principle. The South has to lynch him occasionally, and flog him, now and then, to keep him from blaspheming the Almighty by his conduct . . . and color."

designed to enforce racial segregation in public places, including hotels and restaurants, and backed up by atrocious lynchings and other forms of intimidation.

The conservative crusade to eliminate the black vote also had dire consequences for the Populist party itself. Even Tom Watson abandoned his interracial appeals and, in time, became a vociferous racist himself. After 1896 the Populist party lapsed

increasingly into vile racism and staunchly advocated black disfranchisement. Such were the bitterly ironic fruits of the Populist campaign in the South.

Cleveland and Depression

With the Populists divided and the Republicans discredited, Grover Cleveland took office once again in 1893, the only president ever reelected after defeat. He was the same old bull-necked and bull-headed Cleveland, with a little more weight, polish, conservatism, and self-assertiveness.

But though it was the same old Cleveland, it was not the same old country. Debtors were up in arms, workers were restless, and the advance shadows of panic were falling. Hardly had Cleveland seated himself in the presidential chair when the devastating depression of 1893 burst about his burly frame. Lasting for about four years, it was the most punishing economic downturn of the nineteenth century. Contributing causes were the splurge of overbuilding and speculation, labor disorders, and the ongoing agricultural depression. Free-silver agitation had also damaged American credit abroad, and the usual pinch on American finances had come when European banking houses began to call in loans from the United States.

Distress ran deep and far. About eight thousand American businesses collapsed in six months. Dozens of railroad lines went into the hands of receivers. Soup kitchens fed the unemployed, while gangs of hoboes ("tramps") wandered aimlessly about the country. Local charities did their feeble best, but the federal government, bound by the let-nature-take-its-course philosophy of the times, saw no legitimate way to relieve the suffering masses.

Cleveland, who had earlier been bothered by a surplus, was now burdened with a deepening deficit. The Treasury was required to issue legal tender notes for the silver bullion that it bought. Owners of the paper currency would then present it for gold, and by law the notes had to be reissued. New holders would repeat the process, thus draining away precious gold in an "endless-chain" operation.

Alarmingly, the gold reserve in the Treasury dropped below $100 million, which was popularly regarded as the safe minimum for supporting about

$350 million in outstanding paper money. Cleveland saw no alternative but to halt the bleeding away of gold by engineering a repeal of the Sherman Silver Purchase Act of 1890. For this purpose he summoned Congress into an extra session in the summer of 1893.

Unknown to the country, complications threatened from another quarter. A malignant growth had developed on the roof of Cleveland's mouth, and it had to be removed on a private yacht with extreme secrecy. If the president had died under the surgeon's knife, his place would have been taken by the "soft-money" vice president, Adlai E. Stevenson—an eventuality that would have deepened the crisis.

In Congress the debate over the repeal of the silver act was meanwhile running its heated course. A silver-tongued young Democratic congressman from Nebraska, thirty-three-year-old William Jennings Bryan, held the galleries spellbound for three hours as he championed the cause of free silver. The friends of silver announced that "hell would freeze over" before Congress would pass the repeal measure. But an angered Cleveland used his job-granting power to break the filibuster in the Senate. He thus alienated the Democratic silverites like Bryan and disrupted his party at the very outset of his administration.

Repeal of the Sherman Silver Purchase Act only partially stopped the hemorrhaging of gold from the Treasury. In February 1894 the gold reserve sank to a dismaying $41 million. The United States was now in grave danger of going off the gold standard—a move that would render the nation's currency volatile and unreliable as a measure of value and that would also mortally cripple America's international trade. Cleveland floated two Treasury bond issues in 1894, totaling over $100 million, but the "endless-chain" operations continued relentlessly.

Early in 1895 Cleveland turned in desperation to J. P. Morgan, "the bankers' banker" and the head of a Wall Street syndicate. After tense negotiations at the White House, the bankers agreed to lend the government $65 million in gold. They were obviously in business for profit, so they charged a commission amounting to about $7 million. But they did make a significant concession when they agreed to obtain one-half of the gold abroad and take the necessary steps to dam it up in the leaky Treasury. The loan, at least temporarily, helped restore confidence in the nation's finances.

Cleveland Breeds a Backlash

The bond deal stirred up a storm. The Wall Street ogre, especially in the eyes of the silverites and other debtors, symbolized all that was wicked and grasping in American politics. President Cleveland's secretive dealings with the mighty "Jupiter" Morgan were savagely condemned as a "sellout" of the national government. But Cleveland was certain that he had done no wrong. Sarcastically denying that he was "Morgan's errand boy," Cleveland asserted, "Without shame and without repentance I confess my share of the guilt."

Cleveland suffered further embarrassment with the passage of the Wilson-Gorman Tariff in 1894. The Democrats had pledged to lower tariffs, but by the time their tariff bill made it through Congress, it had been so loaded with special-interest protection that it made scarcely a dent in the high McKinley Tariff rates. An outraged Cleveland grudgingly allowed the bill, which also contained a 2 percent tax on incomes over $4,000, to become law without his signature. When the Supreme Court struck down the income-tax provision in 1895,* the Populists and other disaffected groups found proof that the courts were only the tools of the plutocrats.

Democratic political fortunes naturally suffered in the face of these several setbacks. The tariff dynamite that had blasted the Republicans out of the House in 1890 now dislodged the Democrats, with a strong helping hand from the depression. The revitalized Republicans, singing "Times Are Mighty Hard," won the congressional elections of 1894 in a landslide—244 seats to 105 for the Democrats. The Republicans began to look forward to the presidential race of 1896 with unconcealed glee.

Despite his gruff integrity and occasional courage, Grover Cleveland failed utterly to cope with the serious economic crisis that befell the country in 1893. He was tied down in office by the same threads that held all the politicians of the day to Lilliputian levels. Grant, Hayes, Garfield, Arthur, Harrison, and Cleveland are often referred to as the

---

*It violated the "direct tax" clause. See Art. I, Sec. IX, para. 4 in the Appendix. The Sixteenth Amendment to the Constitution, adopted in 1913, permitted an income tax.

"forgettable presidents." Bewhiskered and bland in person, they left mostly blanks—or blots—on the nation's political record, as issues like the tariff, the money question, and the rights of labor continued to fester. What little political vitality existed in Gilded Age America was to be found in local settings or in Congress, which overshadowed the White House for most of this period. But before the century ended, down-and-out debtors and disgruntled workers would make one last titanic effort to wring reform out of the political system—in the momentous election of 1896.

Chronology

1868   Grant defeats Seymour for the presidency

1869   Fisk and Gould corner the gold market

1871   Tweed scandal in New York

1872   Crédit Mobilier scandal exposed
Liberal Republicans break with Grant
Grant defeats Greeley for the presidency

1873   Panic of 1873

1875   Whiskey Ring scandal
Civil Rights Act of 1875
Resumption Act passed

1876   Hayes-Tilden election standoff and crisis

1877   Compromise of 1877
Reconstruction ends
Railroad strikes paralyze nation

1880   Garfield defeats Hancock for presidency

1881   Garfield assassinated; Arthur assumes presidency

1882   Chinese Exclusion Act

1883   *Civil Rights Cases*
Pendleton Act sets up Civil Service Commission

1884   Cleveland defeats Blaine for presidency

1888   Harrison defeats Cleveland for presidency

1889   Thomas B. "Czar" Reed becomes Speaker of the House of Representatives

1890   "Billion-Dollar" Congress
McKinley Tariff Act
Sherman Silver Purchase Act (repealed 1893)

1892   Homestead steel strike
Coeur d'Alene (Idaho) silver miners' strike
People's party candidate James B. Weaver wins twenty-two electoral votes
Cleveland defeats Harrison and Weaver to regain presidency

1893   Depression of 1893 begins

1894   Wilson-Gorman Tariff (contains income-tax provision, declared unconstitutional 1895)
Republicans regain House of Representatives

1895   J. P. Morgan's banking syndicate loans $65 million in gold to federal government

1896   *Plessy* v. *Ferguson* legitimizes "separate but equal" doctrine

VARYING VIEWPOINTS

The Populists: Radicals or Reactionaries?

Taking their cue from contemporary satirical commentaries like Mark Twain and Charles Dudley Warner's *The Gilded Age* (1873), the first historians who wrote about the post–Civil War era judged it harshly. They condemned its politicians as petty and corrupt, lamented the emergence of a new plutocratic class, and railed against the arrogance of corporate power. Such a view is conspicuous in Charles and Mary Beard's *The Rise of American Civilization* (4 vols., 1927–1942), perhaps the most influential American history textbook ever written. It is equally evident in Vernon Louis Parrington's classic literary history, *Main Currents of American Thought* (3 vols., 1927–1930), in which the entire post–Civil War period is contemptuously dismissed as the time of "the great barbecue."

The Beards and Parrington were leaders of the so-called progressive school of historical writing that flourished in the early years of the twentieth century. Progressive historians, many of whom grew up in the Gilded Age, shared in a widespread disillusionment that the Civil War had failed to generate a rebirth of American idealism. Their political sympathies were chillingly antibusiness and warmly pro-labor, pro-farmer, and pro-reform.

Historians of the progressive persuasion identified Populism as virtually the only organized opposition to the social, economic, and political order that took shape in the last decades of the nineteenth century. The Populists thus became heroes to several generations of writers who bemoaned that order and looked back longingly at Americans' agrarian past. John D. Hicks, *The Populist Revolt* (1931), is the classic portrayal of the Populists as embattled farmers hurling defiance at Wall Street and the robber barons in a last-ditch defense of their simple, honest way of life. Bowed but unbroken by the defeat of their great champion, William Jennings Bryan, in the presidential election of 1896,

the Populists, Hicks claimed, left a reforming legacy that flourished again in the progressive era and the New Deal.

Hicks's point of view was the dominant one until the 1950s, when it was sharply criticized by Richard Hofstadter in *The Age of Reform* (1955). Hofstadter charged that the progressive historians had romanticized the Populists, who were best understood not as picturesque protesters, but as "harassed little country businessmen" bristling with provincial prejudices. The city-born-and-bred Hofstadter argued that the Populist revolt was aimed not just at big business and the money power but also somewhat irrationally at urbanism, immigrants, the East, and modernity itself. Hofstadter thus exposed a "dark side" of Populism, which contained elements of backwoods anti-intellectualism, paranoia, and even anti-Semitism.

In the 1960s several scholars, inspired by the work of C. Vann Woodward, as well as by sympathy with the protest movements of that turbulent decade, began to rehabilitate the Populists as authentic reformers with genuine grievances. Especially notable in this vein was Lawrence Goodwyn's *Democratic Promise: The Populist Movement in America* (1976). Goodwyn depicted the Populists as reasonable radicals who were justifiably resentful of their eclipse by urban industrialism and finance capitalism. He also portrayed Populism as the last gasp of popular political participation, a democratic "moment" in American history that expired with the Populists' absorption into the Democratic party.

Two subsequent works, Edward L. Ayers's *Promise of the New South* (1992) and Robert C. McMath's *American Populism* (1993), synthesized many of the older perspectives and presented a balanced view of the Populists as radical in many ways but also limited by their nostalgia for a lost agrarian past.

For further reading, see page A16 of the Appendix. For web resources, go to **http://college.hmco.com.**

24

Industry Comes of Age

1865–1900

The wealthy class is becoming more wealthy; but the poorer class is becoming more dependent. The gulf between the employed and the employer is growing wider; social contrasts are becoming sharper; as liveried carriages appear; so do barefooted children.

HENRY GEORGE, 1879

As the nineteenth century drew to a close, observers were asking, "Why are the best men not in politics?" One answer was that they were being lured away from public life by the lusty attractions of the booming private economy. As America's Industrial Revolution slipped into high gear, talented men ached for profits, not the presidency. They dreamed of controlling corporations, not the Congress. What the nation lost in civic leadership, it gained in an astounding surge of economic growth. Although in many ways still a political dwarf, the United States was about to stand up before the world as an industrial colossus—and the lives of millions of working Americans would be transformed in the process.

The Iron Colt Becomes an Iron Horse

The government-business entanglements that increasingly shaped politics after the Civil War also undergirded the industrial development of the nation. The unparalleled outburst of railroad construction was a crucial case. When Lincoln was shot in 1865, there were only 35,000 miles of steam railways in the United States, mostly east of the Mississippi. By 1900 the figure had spurted up to 192,556 miles, or more than that for all of Europe combined, and much of the new trackage ran west of the Mississippi.

Transcontinental railroad building was so costly and risky as to require government subsidies. The extension of rails into thinly populated regions was unprofitable until the areas could be built up; and private promoters were unwilling to suffer heavy initial losses. Congress, impressed by arguments pleading military and postal needs, began to advance liberal money loans to two favored cross-continent companies in 1862 and added enormous donations of acreage paralleling the tracks. All told, Washington rewarded the railroads with 155,504,994 acres, and the western states contributed 49 million more—a total area larger than Texas.

Grasping railroads tied up even more land than this for a number of years. Land grants to railroads

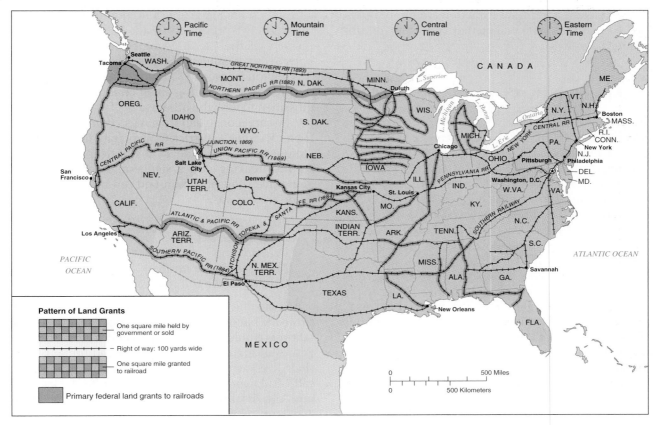

Federal Land Grants to Railroads
The heavy red lines indicate areas within which the railroads might be given specific parcels of land. As shown in the inset, lands were reserved in belts of various widths on either side of a railroad's right of way. Until the railroad selected the individual mile-square sections it chose to possess, *all* such sections within the belt were withdrawn from eligibility for settlement. The "time zones" were introduced in 1883 (see p. 534), and their boundaries have since been adjusted.

were made in broad belts along the proposed route. Within these belts the railroads were allowed to choose *alternate* mile-square sections in checkerboard fashion (see the map above). But until they determined the precise location of their tracks and decided which sections were the choicest selections, the railroads withheld *all* the land from other users. President Grover Cleveland put an end to this foot-dragging practice in 1887 and threw open to settlement the still-unclaimed public portions of the land-grant areas.

Noisy criticism, especially in later years, was leveled at the "giveaway" of so valuable a birthright to greedy corporations. But the government did receive beneficial returns, including long-term preferential rates for postal service and military traffic.

Granting land was also a "cheap" way to subsidize a much-desired transportation system, because it avoided new taxes for direct cash grants. The railroads could turn the land into gold by using it as collateral for loans from private bankers or, later, by selling it. This they often did, at an average price of $3 an acre. Critics were also prone to overlook the fact that the land did not have even that relatively modest value until the railroads had ribboned it with steel.

Frontier villages touched by the magic wand of the iron rail became flourishing cities; those that were bypassed often withered away and became "ghost towns." Little wonder that communities fought one another for the privilege of playing host to the railroads. Ambitious towns customarily held out monetary and other attractions to the builders, who sometimes blackmailed them into contributing more generously.

Spanning the Continent with Rails

Deadlock in the 1850s over the proposed transcontinental railroad was broken when the South seceded, leaving the field to the North. In 1862, the year after the guns first spoke at Fort Sumter, Congress made provision for starting the long-awaited line. One weighty argument for action was the urgency of bolstering the Union, already disrupted, by binding the Pacific Coast—especially gold-rich California—more securely to the rest of the Republic.

The Union Pacific Railroad—note the word *Union*—was thus commissioned by Congress to thrust westward from Omaha, Nebraska. For each mile of track constructed, the company was granted 20 square miles of land, alternating in 640-acre sections on either side of the track. For each mile the builders were also to receive a generous federal loan, ranging from $16,000 on the flat prairie land to $48,000 for mountainous country. The laying of rails began in earnest after the Civil War ended in 1865,

and with juicy loans and land grants available, the "groundhog" promoters made all possible haste. Insiders of the Crédit Mobilier construction company reaped fabulous profits. They slyly pocketed $73 million for some $50 million worth of breakneck construction, spending small change to bribe congressmen to look the other way.

Sweaty construction gangs, containing many Irish "Paddies" (Patricks) who had fought in the Union armies, worked at a frantic pace. On one record-breaking day, a sledge-and-shovel army of some five thousand men laid ten miles of track. A favorite song was,

> *Then drill, my Paddies, drill;*
> *Drill, my heroes, drill;*
> *Drill all day,*
> *No sugar in your tay* [tea]
> *Workin' on the U.P. Railway.*

When hostile Indians attacked in futile efforts to protect what once rightfully had been their land, the laborers would drop their picks and seize their rifles. Scores of men—railroad workers and Indians—lost their lives as the rails stretched ever westward. At rail's end, workers tried their best to find relaxation and conviviality in their tented towns, known as "hells on wheels," often teeming with as many as

Snow Sheds on the Central Pacific Railroad in the Sierra Nevada Mountains, by Joseph H. Becker, c. 1869 Formidable obstacles of climate and terrain confronted the builders of the Central Pacific Railroad in the mountainous heights of California. Note the Chinese laborers in the foreground.

Promoting the Union Pacific Railroad, 1869

The Central Pacific, which was granted the same princely subsidies as the Union Pacific, had the same incentive to haste. Some ten thousand Chinese laborers, sweating from dawn to dusk under their basket hats, proved to be cheap, efficient, and expendable (hundreds lost their lives in premature explosions and other mishaps). The towering Sierra Nevada presented a formidable barrier, and the nerves of the Big Four were strained when their workers could chip only a few inches a day tunneling through solid rock, while the Union Pacific was sledgehammering westward across the open plains.

A "wedding of the rails" was finally consummated near Ogden, Utah, in 1869, as two locomotives—"facing on a single track, half a world behind each back"—gently kissed cowcatchers. The colorful ceremony included the breaking of champagne bottles and the driving of a last ceremonial (golden) spike, with ex-governor Leland Stanford clumsily wielding a silver sledgehammer.* In all, the Union Pacific built 1,086 miles, the Central Pacific 689 miles.

Completion of the transcontinental line—a magnificent engineering feat for that day—was one of America's most impressive peacetime undertakings. It welded the West Coast more firmly to the Union and facilitated a flourishing trade with Asia. It penetrated the arid barrier of the deserts, paving the way for the phenomenal growth of the Great West. Americans compared this electrifying achievement with the Declaration of Independence and the emancipation of the slaves; jubilant Philadelphians again rang the cracked bell of Independence Hall.

Binding the Country with Railroad Ties

With the westward trail now blazed, four other transcontinental lines were completed before the century's end. None of them secured monetary loans from the federal government, as did the Union Pacific and the Central Pacific. But all of them except the Great Northern received generous grants of land.

ten thousand men and a sprinkling of painted prostitutes and performers.

Rail laying at the California end was undertaken by the Central Pacific Railroad. This line pushed boldly eastward from boomtown Sacramento, over and through the towering, snow-clogged Sierra Nevada. Four farseeing men—the so-called Big Four—were the chief financial backers of the enterprise. The quartet included the heavyset, enterprising ex-governor Leland Stanford of California, who had useful political connections, and the burly, energetic Collis P. Huntington, an adept lobbyist. The Big Four cleverly operated through two construction companies, and although they walked away with tens of millions in profits, they kept their hands relatively clean by not becoming involved in the bribery of congressmen.

---

*The spike was promptly removed and is now exhibited at the Stanford University Museum.

Grading for the Northern Pacific Railroad, 1879
This grading crew sliced a path through the Beaver Creek valley of western North Dakota in what became known as the "Big Cut." This first rail line to the Pacific Northwest opened in 1883. Railroad trackage grew prodigiously in the 1880s, when an average of more than seven thousand miles of new line was laid each year.

The Northern Pacific Railroad, stretching from Lake Superior to Puget Sound, reached its terminus in 1883. The Atchison, Topeka and Santa Fe, stretching through the southwestern deserts to California, was completed in 1884. The Southern Pacific ribboned from New Orleans to San Francisco and was consolidated in the same year.

In 1892 James Baird Weaver (1833–1912), nominee of the Populists, wrote regarding the railroad magnates,

"In their delirium of greed the managers of our transportation systems disregard both private right and the public welfare. Today they will combine and bankrupt their weak rivals, and by the expenditure of a trifling sum possess themselves of properties which cost the outlay of millions. Tomorrow they will capitalize their booty for five times the cost, issue their bonds, and proceed to levy tariffs upon the people to pay dividends upon the fraud."

The last spike of the last of the five transcontinental railroads of the nineteenth century was hammered home in 1893. The Great Northern, which ran from Duluth to Seattle north of the Northern Pacific, was the creation of a far-visioned Canadian-American, James J. Hill, a bearlike man who was probably the greatest railroad builder of all. Endowed with a high sense of public duty, he perceived that the prosperity of his railroad depended on the prosperity of the area that it served. He ran agricultural demonstration trains through the "Hill Country" and imported from England blooded bulls, which he distributed to the farmers. His enterprise was so soundly organized that it rode through later financial storms with flying colors.

Yet the romance of the rails was not without its sordid side. Pioneer builders were often guilty of gross overoptimism. Avidly seeking land bounties and pushing into areas that lacked enough potential population to support a railroad, they sometimes laid down rails that led "from nowhere to nothing." When prosperity failed to smile upon their coming, they went into bankruptcy, carrying down with them the savings of trusting investors. Many of the large railroads in the post–Civil War decades passed through seemingly endless bankruptcies, mergers, or reorganizations.

Cornelius Vanderbilt (1794–1877)
Vanderbilt established a shipping–land transit line across Nicaragua in response to the California gold rush. By the time of his death, his New York Central rail line ran from New York to Chicago and operated along more than forty-five hundred miles of track.

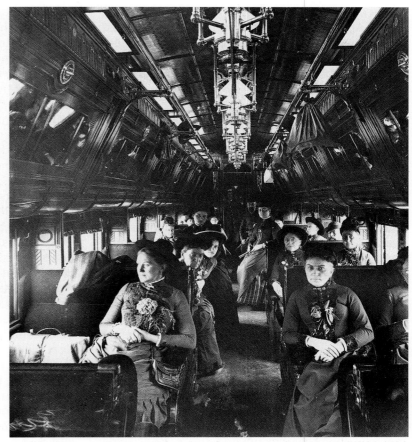

Traveling First Class   This sumptuously appointed Pullman Palace Car offered its prosperous passengers the comforts of home while they were far away from it.

Railroad Consolidation and Mechanization

The success of the western lines was facilitated by welding together and expanding the older eastern networks, notably the New York Central. The genius in this enterprise was "Commodore" Cornelius Vanderbilt—burly, boisterous, white-whiskered. Having made his millions in steamboating, he daringly turned, in his late sixties, to a new career in railroading. Though ill educated, ungrammatical, coarse, and ruthless, he was clear-visioned. Offering superior railway service at lower rates, he amassed a fortune of $100 million. His name is perhaps best remembered through his contribution of $1 million to the founding of Vanderbilt University in Tennessee.

Two significant new improvements proved a boon to the railroads. One was the steel rail, which Vanderbilt helped popularize when he replaced the old iron tracks of the New York Central with the tougher metal. Steel was safer and more economical because it could bear a heavier load. A standard gauge of track width likewise came into wide use during the postwar years, thus eliminating the expense and inconvenience of numerous changes from one line to another.

Other refinements played a vital role in railroading. The Westinghouse air brake, generally adopted in the 1870s, was a marvelous contribution to efficiency and safety. The Pullman Palace Cars, advertised as "gorgeous traveling hotels," were introduced on a considerable scale in the 1860s. Alarmists condemned them as "wheeled torture chambers" and potential funeral pyres, for the wooden cars were equipped with swaying kerosene lamps. Appalling accidents continued to be almost daily tragedies, despite safety devices like the telegraph ("talking wires"), double-tracking, and (later) the block signal.

Revolution by Railways

The metallic fingers of the railroads intimately touched countless phases of American life. For the first time, a sprawling nation became united in a physical sense, bound with ribs of iron and steel. By stitching North America together from ocean to ocean, the transcontinental lines created an enormous domestic market for American raw materials and manufactured goods—probably the largest integrated national market area in the world. This huge empire of commerce beckoned to foreign and domestic investors alike, as well as to businesspeople who could now dare to dream on a continental scale.

More than any other single factor, the railroad network spurred the amazing industrialization of the post–Civil War years. The puffing locomotives opened up fresh markets for manufactured goods and sped raw materials to factories. The forging of the rails themselves generated the largest single source of orders for the adolescent steel industry.

The screeching iron horse likewise stimulated mining and agriculture, especially in the West. It took farmers out to their land, carried the fruits of their toil to market, and brought them their manufactured necessities. Clusters of farm settlements paralleled the railroads, just as earlier they had followed the rivers.

Railways were a boon for cities and played a leading role in the great cityward movement of the last decades of the century. The iron monsters could carry food to enormous concentrations of people and at the same time ensure them a livelihood by providing both raw materials and markets.

Railroad companies also stimulated the mighty stream of immigration. Seeking settlers to whom their land grants might be sold at a profit, they advertised seductively in Europe and sometimes offered to transport the newcomers free to their farms.

The land also felt the impact of the railroad—especially the broad, ecologically fragile midsection of the continent that Thomas Jefferson had purchased from France in 1803. Settlers following the railroads plowed up the tallgrass prairies of Iowa, Illinois, Kansas, and Nebraska and planted well-drained, rectangular cornfields. On the shortgrass prairies of the high plains in the Dakotas and Montana, range-fed cattle rapidly displaced the buffalo, which were hunted to near-extinction. The white pine forests of Michigan, Wisconsin, and Minnesota disappeared into lumber that was rushed by rail to prairie farmers, who used it to build houses and fences.

Time itself was bent to the railroads' needs. Until the 1880s every town in the United States had its own "local" time, dictated by the sun's position. When it was noon in Chicago, it was 11:50 A.M. in St. Louis and 12:18 P.M. in Detroit. For railroad operators worried about keeping schedules and avoiding wrecks, this patchwork of local times was a nightmare. Thus on November 18, 1883, the major rail lines decreed that the continent would henceforth be divided into four "time zones." Most communities quickly adopted railroad "standard" time.

Finally, the railroad, more than any other single factor, was the maker of millionaires. A raw new aristocracy, consisting of "lords of the rail," replaced the old southern "lords of the lash." The multi-webbed lines became the playthings of Wall Street, and colossal wealth was amassed by stock speculators and railroad wreckers.

Wrongdoing in Railroading

Corruption lurks nearby when fabulous fortunes can materialize overnight. The fleecings administered by the railroad construction companies, such as the Crédit Mobilier, were but the first of the bunco games that the railroad promoters learned to play. Methods soon became more refined, as fast-fingered financiers executed multimillion-dollar maneuvers beneath the noses of a bedazzled public. Jay Gould was the most adept of these ringmasters of rapacity. For nearly thirty years, he boomed and busted the stocks of the Erie, the Kansas Pacific, the Union Pacific, and the Texas and Pacific in an incredible circus of speculative skullduggery.

One of the favorite devices of the moguls of manipulation was "stock watering." The term originally referred to the practice of making cattle thirsty by feeding them salt and then having them bloat themselves with water before they were weighed in for sale. Using a variation of this technique, railroad stock promoters grossly inflated their claims about a given line's assets and profitability and sold stocks and bonds far in excess of the railroad's actual value. "Promoters' profits" were often the tail that wagged the iron horse itself. Railroad managers were forced to charge extortionate rates and wage ruthless competitive battles in order to pay off the exaggerated financial obligations with which they were saddled.

The public interest was frequently trampled underfoot as the railroad titans waged their brutal wars. Crusty old Cornelius Vanderbilt, when told that the law stood in his way, reportedly exclaimed, "Law! What do I care about the law? Hain't I got the power?" On another occasion he supposedly threatened some associates: "I won't sue you, for the law is too slow. I'll ruin you." His son, William H. Vanderbilt, when asked in 1883 about the discontinuance of a fast mail train, reportedly snorted, "The public be damned!"

While abusing the public, the railroaders blandly bought and sold people in public life. They bribed judges and legislatures, employed arm-twisting lobbyists, and elected their own "creatures" to high office. They showered free passes on jour-nalists and politicians in profusion. One railroad man noted in 1885 that in the West "no man who has money, or official position, or influence thinks he ought to pay anything for riding on a railroad."

Railroad kings were, for a time, virtual industrial monarchs. As manipulators of a huge natural monopoly, they exercised more direct control over the lives of more people than did the president of the United States—and their terms were not limited to four years. They increasingly shunned the crude bloodletting of cutthroat competition and began to cooperate with one another to rule the railroad dominion. Sorely pressed to show at least some returns on their bloated investments, they entered into defensive alliances to protect precious profits.

The earliest form of combination was the "pool"—an agreement to divide the business in a given area and share the profits. Other rail barons granted secret rebates or kickbacks to powerful shippers in return for steady and assured traffic. Often they slashed their rates on competing lines, but they more than made up the difference on non-competing ones, where they might actually charge more for a short haul than for a long one.

Government Bridles the Iron Horse

William H. Vanderbilt, Robber Baron
This 1885 cartoon takes aim at Vanderbilt's notorious comment, "The public be damned!"

It was neither healthy nor politically acceptable that so many people should be at the mercy of so few. Impoverished farmers, especially in the Midwest, began to wonder if the nation had not escaped from the slavery power only to fall into the hands of the money power, as represented by the railroad plutocracy.

But the American people, though quick to respond to political injustice, were slow to combat economic injustice. Dedicated to free enterprise and to the principle that competition is the soul of trade, they cherished a traditionally keen pride in progress. They remembered that Jefferson's ideals were hostile to government interference with business. Above all, there shimmered the "American dream": the hope that in a catch-as-catch-can economic system, anyone might become a millionaire.

The depression of the 1870s finally goaded the farmers into protesting against being "rail-roaded" into bankruptcy. Under pressure from organized agrarian groups like the Grange (Patrons of

The Modern Colossus of Railroads, 1879
William H. Vanderbilt, flanked by Cyrus Field (left) and Jay Gould (right), towers over the scene. With the Interstate Commerce Act in 1887, the government began to weaken the magnates' grip on the nation's transportation system.

Husbandry), many midwestern legislatures tried to regulate the railroad monopoly.

The scattered state efforts screeched to a halt in 1886. The Supreme Court, in the famed *Wabash* case, decreed that individual states had no power to regulate *inter*state commerce. If the mechanical monster were to be corralled, the federal government would have to do the job.

Stiff-necked President Cleveland did not look kindly on effective regulation. But Congress ignored his grumbling indifference and passed the epochal Interstate Commerce Act in 1887. It prohibited rebates and pools and required the railroads to publish their rates openly. It also forbade unfair

discrimination against shippers and outlawed charging more for a short haul than for a long one over the same line. Most important, it set up the Interstate Commerce Commission (ICC) to administer and enforce the new legislation.

Despite acclaim, the Interstate Commerce Act emphatically did not represent a popular victory over corporate wealth. One of the leading corporation lawyers of the day, Richard Olney, shrewdly noted that the new commission "can be made of great use to the railroads. It satisfies the popular clamor for a government supervision of railroads, at the same time that such supervision is almost entirely nominal. . . . The part of wisdom is not to destroy the Commission, but to utilize it."

What the new legislation did do was to provide an orderly forum where competing business interests could resolve their conflicts in peaceable ways. The country could now avoid ruinous rate wars among the railroads and outraged, "confiscatory" attacks on the lines by pitchfork-prodded state legislatures. This was a modest accomplishment but by no means an unimportant one. The Interstate Commerce Act tended to stabilize, not revolutionize, the existing business system.

Yet the act still ranks as a red-letter law. It was the first large-scale attempt by Washington to regulate business in the interest of society at large. It heralded the arrival of a series of independent regulatory commissions in the next century, which would irrevocably commit the government to the daunting task of monitoring and guiding the private economy. It foreshadowed the doom of freewheeling, buccaneering business practices and served full notice that there was a public interest in private enterprise that the government was bound to protect.

Miracles of Mechanization

Postwar industrial expansion, partly a result of the railroad network, rapidly began to assume mammoth proportions. When Lincoln was elected in 1860, the Republic ranked only fourth among the manufacturing nations of the world. By 1894 it had bounded into first place. Why the sudden upsurge?

Liquid capital, previously scarce, was now becoming abundant. The word *millionaire* had not been coined until the 1840s, and in 1861 only a handful of individuals were eligible for this class.

But the Civil War, partly through profiteering, created immense fortunes, and these accumulations could now be combined with the customary borrowings from foreign capitalists.

The amazing natural resources of the nation were now about to be fully exploited, including coal, oil, and iron. For example, the Minnesota–Lake Superior region, which had yielded some iron ore by the 1850s, contributed the rich deposits of the Mesabi Range by the 1890s. This priceless bonanza, where mountains of red-rusted ore could be scooped up by steam shovels, ultimately became a cornerstone of a vast steel empire.

Massive immigration helped make unskilled labor cheap and plentiful. Steel, the keystone industry, built its strength largely on the sweat of low-priced immigrant labor from eastern and southern Europe, working in two twelve-hour shifts, seven days a week.

American ingenuity at the same time played a vital role in the second American industrial revolution. Techniques of mass production, pioneered by Eli Whitney, were being perfected by the captains of industry. American inventiveness flowered luxuriantly in the postwar years: between 1860 and 1890 some 440,000 patents were issued. Business operations were facilitated by such machines as the cash register, the stock ticker, and the typewriter ("literary piano"), which attracted women from the confines of home to industry. Urbanization was speeded by the refrigerator car, the electric dynamo, and the electric railway, which displaced animal-drawn cars.

One of the most ingenious inventions was the telephone, introduced by Alexander Graham Bell in 1876. A teacher of the deaf who was given a dead man's ear to experiment with, he remarked that if he could make the mute talk, he could make iron speak. America was speedily turned into a nation of "telephoniacs," as a gigantic communication network was built on his invention. The social impact of this instrument was further revealed when an additional army of "number please" women was attracted from the stove to the switchboard. Telephone boys were at first employed as operators, but their profanity shocked patrons.

The most versatile inventor of all was Thomas Alva Edison (1847–1931), who as a boy had been considered so dull-witted that he was taken out of school. His severe deafness enabled him to concentrate without distraction. Edison was a gifted tinkerer and a tireless worker, not a pure scientist. "Genius," he said, "is one percent inspiration and ninety-nine percent perspiration." Wondrous devices poured out of his "invention factory" in New Jersey—the phonograph, the mimeograph, the dictaphone, and the moving picture. He is probably best known for his perfection in 1879 of the electric light bulb, which he unveiled after experimenting with some six thousand different filaments. The electric light turned night into day and transformed ancient human habits as well. People had previously slept an average of nine hours a night; now they slept just a bit more than seven hours.

The Trust Titan Emerges

Despite pious protests to the contrary, competition was the bugbear of most business leaders of the day. Tycoons like Andrew Carnegie, the steel king; John D. Rockefeller, the oil baron; and J. Pierpont Morgan, the bankers' banker, exercised their genius in devising ways to circumvent competition. Carnegie integrated every phase of his steel-making operation. His miners scratched the ore from the earth in the Mesabi Range; Carnegie ships floated it across the Great Lakes; Carnegie railroads delivered it to the blast furnaces at Pittsburgh. When the molten metal finally poured from the glowing crucibles into the waiting ingot molds, no other hands but those in Carnegie's employ had touched the product. Carnegie thus pioneered the creative entrepreneurial tactic of "vertical integration," combining into one organization all phases of manufacturing from

> *Regarding the exploitation of immigrant labor, Ralph Waldo Emerson (1803–1882) wrote in 1860,*
>
> "The German and Irish millions, like the Negro, have a great deal of guano in their destiny. They are ferried over the Atlantic, and carted over America, to ditch and to drudge, to make corn cheap, and then to lie down prematurely to make a spot of green grass on the prairie."

The Octopus, 1904
This cartoon visually captures a feeling of widespread resentment against Standard Oil as a powerful, sprawling "octopus" whose tentacles controlled all branches of government.

mining to marketing. His goal was to improve efficiency by making supplies more reliable, controlling the quality of the product at all stages of production, and eliminating middlemen's fees.

Less justifiable on grounds of efficiency was the technique of "horizontal integration," which simply meant allying with competitors to monopolize a given market. Rockefeller was a master of this stratagem. He perfected a device for controlling bothersome rivals—the "trust." Stockholders in various smaller oil companies assigned their stock to the board of directors of his Standard Oil Company, formed in 1870. It then consolidated and concerted the operations of the previously competing enterprises. "Let us prey" was said to be Rockefeller's unwritten motto. Ruthlessly wielding vast power, Standard Oil soon cornered virtually the entire world petroleum market. Weaker competitors, left out of the trust agreement, were forced to the wall. Rockefeller's stunning success inspired many imitators, and the word *trust* came to be generally used to describe any large-scale business combination.

The imperial Morgan devised still other schemes for eliminating "wasteful" competition. The depression of the 1890s drove into his welcoming arms many bleeding businesspeople, wounded by cutthroat competition. His prescribed remedy was to consolidate rival enterprises and to ensure future harmony by placing officers of his own banking syndicate on their various boards of directors. These came to be known as "interlocking directorates."

The Supremacy of Steel

"Steel is king!" might well have been the exultant war cry of the new industrialized generation. The mighty metal ultimately held together the new steel civilization, from skyscrapers to coal scuttles, while providing it with food, shelter, and transportation. Steel making, notably rails for railroads, typified the dominance of "heavy industry," which concentrated on making "capital goods," as distinct from the production of "consumer goods" such as clothes and shoes.

Now taken for granted, steel was a scarce commodity in the wood-and-brick America of Abraham Lincoln. Considerable iron went into railroad rails and bridges, but steel was expensive and was used largely for products like cutlery. The early iron horse snorted exclusively (and dangerously) over iron rails. When in the 1870s "Commodore" Vanderbilt of the New York Central began to use steel rails, he was forced to import them from Britain.

Yet within an amazing twenty years, the United States had outdistanced all foreign competitors and was pouring out more than one-third of the world's supply of steel. By 1900 America was producing as much as Britain and Germany combined.

What wrought the transformation? Chiefly the invention in the 1850s of a method of making cheap steel—the Bessemer process. It was named after a derided British inventor, although an American had stumbled on it a few years earlier. William Kelly, a Kentucky manufacturer of iron kettles, discovered that cold air blown on red-hot iron caused the metal to become white-hot by igniting the carbon and thus eliminating impurities. He tried to apply the new "air boiling" technique to his own product, but his customers decried "Kelly's fool steel," and his business declined. Gradually the Bessemer-Kelly process won acceptance, and these two "crazy men" ultimately made possible the present steel civilization.

A revolutionary steel-fabricating process was not the whole story. America was one of the few places in the world where one could find relatively close together abundant coal for fuel, rich iron ore for smelting, and other essential ingredients for making steel. The nation also boasted an abundant labor supply, guided by industrial know-how of a high order. The stage was set for miracles of production.

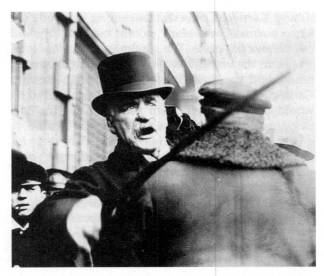

J. P. Morgan (1837–1913) As the most influential banker of his day, he symbolized to many people the power and arrogance of "finance capitalism." The chronic skin disorder on his nose inspired the taunt, "Johnny Morgan's nasal organ has a purple hue."

Carnegie and Other Sultans of Steel

Kingpin among steelmasters was Andrew Carnegie, an undersized, charming Scotsman. As a towheaded lad of thirteen, he was brought to America by his impoverished parents in 1848 and got a job as a bobbin boy at $1.20 a week. Mounting the ladder of success so fast that he was said to have scorched the rungs, he forged ahead by working hard, doing the extra chore, cheerfully assuming responsibility, and smoothly cultivating influential people.

After accumulating some capital, Carnegie entered the steel business in the Pittsburgh area. A gifted organizer and administrator, he succeeded by picking high-class associates and by eliminating many middlemen. Although inclined to be tough-

Andrew Carnegie (1835–1919) wrote in 1889,

"The man who dies leaving behind him millions of available wealth, which was his to administer during life, will pass away 'unwept, unhonored, and unsung,' no matter to what uses he leaves the dross which he cannot take with him. Of such as these the public verdict will then be: 'The man who dies thus rich dies disgraced.' "

fisted in business, he was not a monopolist and disliked monopolistic trusts. His remarkable organization was a partnership that involved, at its maximum, about forty "Pittsburgh millionaires." By 1900 he was producing one-fourth of the nation's Bessemer steel, and the partners were dividing profits of $40 million a year, with the "Napoleon of the Smokestacks" himself receiving a cool $25 million. These were the pre–income tax days, when millionaires made real money and profits represented take-home pay.

Into the picture now stepped the financial giant of the age, J. Pierpont Morgan. "Jupiter" Morgan had made a legendary reputation for himself and his Wall Street banking house by financing the reorganization of railroads, insurance companies, and banks. An impressive figure of a man, with massive shoulders, shaggy brows, piercing eyes, and a bulbous, acne-cursed red nose, he had established an enviable reputation for integrity. He did not believe that "money power" was dangerous, except when in dangerous hands—and he did not regard his own hands as dangerous.

The force of circumstances brought Morgan and Carnegie into collision. By 1900 the canny little Scotsman, weary of turning steel into gold, was eager to sell his holdings. Morgan had meanwhile plunged heavily into the manufacture of steel pipe tubing. Carnegie, cleverly threatening to invade the same business, was ready to ruin his rival if he did not receive his price. The steelmaster's agents haggled with the imperious Morgan for eight agonizing hours, and the financier finally agreed to buy out Carnegie for over $400 million. Fearing that he would die "disgraced" with so much wealth, Carnegie dedicated the remaining years of his life to giving away money for public libraries, pensions for professors, and other such philanthropic purposes—in all disposing of about $350 million.

Morgan moved rapidly to expand his new industrial empire. He took the Carnegie holdings, added others, "watered" the stock liberally, and in 1901 launched the enlarged United States Steel Corporation. Capitalized at $1.4 billion, it was America's first billion-dollar corporation—a larger sum than the total estimated wealth of the nation in 1800. The Industrial Revolution, with its hot Bessemer breath, had come into its own.

Rockefeller Grows an American Beauty Rose

The sudden emergence of the oil industry was one of the most striking developments of the years during and after the Civil War. Traces of oil found on streams had earlier been bottled for back-rub and other patent medicines, but not until 1859 did the first well in Pennsylvania—"Drake's Folly"—pour out its liquid "black gold." Almost overnight an industry was born that was to take more wealth from the earth, and more useful wealth at that, than all of the gold extracted by the forty-niners and their western successors. Kerosene, derived from petroleum, was the first major product of the infant oil industry. Burned from a cotton wick in a glass chimney lamp, kerosene produced a much brighter flame than whale oil. The oil business boomed; by the 1870s kerosene was America's fourth most valuable export. Whaling, in contrast, the lifeblood of ocean-roaming New Englanders since before the days of *Moby Dick,* swiftly became a sick industry.

But what technology gives, technology takes away. By 1885, 250,000 of Thomas Edison's electric light bulbs were in use; fifteen years later, perhaps 15 million. The new electrical industry rendered kerosene obsolete just as kerosene had rendered whale oil obsolete. Only in rural America and overseas did a market continue for oil-fired lamps.

Oil might thus have remained a modest, even a shrinking, industry but for yet another turn of the technological tide—the invention of the automobile. By 1900 the gasoline-burning internal combustion engine had clearly bested its rivals, steam and electricity, as the superior means of automobile propulsion. As the century of the automobile dawned, the oil business got a new, long-lasting, and hugely profitable lease on life.

Washington as Seen by the Trusts, 1900   "What a funny little government," John D. Rockefeller observes in this satirical cartoon. His own wealth and power are presumed to dwarf the resources of the federal government.

The Robber Barons of Today, 1889 This cartoon bitterly caricatures the alleged rapacity of the "Robber Barons." Here an intimidated people pay servile tribute to the lordly tycoons.

John D. Rockefeller—lanky, shrewd, ambitious, abstemious (he neither drank, smoked, nor swore) —came to dominate the oil industry. Born to a family of precarious income, he became a successful businessman at age nineteen. One upward stride led to another, and in 1870 he organized the Standard Oil Company of Ohio, nucleus of the great trust formed in 1882. Locating his refineries in Cleveland, he sought to eliminate the middlemen and squeeze out competitors.

Pious and parsimonious, Rockefeller flourished in an era of completely free enterprise. So-called piratical practices were employed by "corsairs of finance," and business ethics were distressingly low. Rockefeller, operating "just to the windward of the law," pursued a policy of rule or ruin. "Sell all the oil that is sold in your district" was the hard-boiled order that went out to his local agents. By 1877 Rockefeller controlled 95 percent of all the oil refineries in the country.

Rockefeller—"Reckafellow," as Carnegie had once called him—showed little mercy. A kind of primitive savagery prevailed in the jungle world of big business, where only the fittest survived. Or so Rockefeller believed. His son later explained that the giant American Beauty rose could be produced "only by sacrificing the early buds that grew up around it." His father pinched off the small buds with complete ruthlessness. Employing spies and extorting secret rebates from the railroads, he even

forced the lines to pay him rebates on the freight bills of his competitors!

Rockefeller thought he was simply obeying a law of nature. "The time was ripe" for aggressive consolidation, he later reflected. "It had to come, though all we saw at the moment was the need to save ourselves from wasteful conditions. . . . The day of combination is here to stay. Individualism has gone, never to return."

On the other side of the ledger, Rockefeller's oil monopoly did turn out a superior product at a relatively cheap price. It achieved important economies, both at home and abroad, by its large-scale methods of production and distribution. This, in truth, was the tale of the other trusts as well. The efficient use of expensive machinery called for bigness, and consolidation proved more profitable than ruinous price wars.

Other trusts blossomed along with the American Beauty of oil. These included the sugar trust, the tobacco trust, the leather trust, and the harvester trust, which amalgamated some two hundred competitors. The meat industry arose on the backs of bawling western herds, and meat kings like Gustavus F. Swift and Philip Armour took their place among the new royalty. Wealth was coming to dominate the commonwealth.

These untrustworthy trusts, and the "pirates" who captained them, were disturbingly new. They eclipsed an older American aristocracy of modestly successful merchants and professionals. An arrogant class of "new rich" was now elbowing aside the patrician families in the mad scramble for power and prestige. Not surprisingly, the ranks of the antitrust crusaders were frequently spearheaded by the "best men"—genteel old-family do-gooders who were not radicals but conservative defenders of their own vanishing influence.

The Gospel of Wealth

Monarchs of yore invoked the divine right of kings, and America's industrial plutocrats took a somewhat similar stance. Some candidly credited heavenly help. "Godliness is in league with riches," preached the Episcopal bishop of Massachusetts, and hardfisted John D. Rockefeller piously acknowledged that "the good Lord gave me my money." Steel baron Andrew Carnegie agreed that the wealthy, entrusted with society's riches, had to prove themselves morally responsible according to a "Gospel of Wealth." But most defenders of wide-open capitalism relied more heavily on the survival-of-the-fittest theories of Charles Darwin. "The millionaires are a product of natural selection," concluded Yale Professor and Social Darwinist William Graham Sumner. "They get high wages and live in luxury, but the bargain is a good one for society." Despite plutocracy and deepening class divisions, the captains of industry provided material progress.

Self-justification by the wealthy inevitably involved contempt for the poor. Many of the rich, especially the newly rich, had pulled themselves up by their own bootstraps; hence they concluded that those who stayed poor must be lazy and lacking in enterprise. The Reverend Russell Conwell of Philadelphia became rich by delivering his lecture "Acres of Diamonds" thousands of times. In it he charged, "There is not a poor person in the United States who was not made poor by his own shortcomings." Such attitudes were a formidable roadblock to social reform.

Plutocracy, like the earlier slavocracy, took its stand firmly on the Constitution. The clause that gave Congress sole jurisdiction over interstate commerce was a godsend to the monopolists; their high-priced lawyers used it time and again to thwart controls by

The New Rich and the New Immigrants
A well-to-do family plays chess at its parlor table (left), while a tenement family does "piecework" around its kitchen table—shelling nuts for commercial use (below). The young working girl seems to be "snitching" some nuts for herself. the apparently growing gulf between the rich and the poor deeply worried reformers in the late nineteenth century. They feared that democracy could not survive in the face of such gross inequality.

the state legislatures. Giant trusts likewise sought refuge behind the Fourteenth Amendment, which had been originally designed to protect the rights of the ex-slaves as persons. The courts ingeniously interpreted a corporation to be a legal "person" and decreed that, as such, it could not be deprived of its property by a state without "due process of law" (see Amendment XIV, para. 1). There is some questionable evidence that slippery corporation lawyers deliberately inserted this loophole when the Fourteenth Amendment was being fashioned in 1866.

Great industrialists likewise sought to incorporate in "easy states," like New Jersey, where the restrictions on big business were mild or nonexistent. For example, the Southern Pacific Railroad, with much of its trackage in California, was incorporated in Kentucky.

Government Tackles the Trust Evil

At long last the masses of the people began to mobilize against monopoly. They first tried to control the trusts through state legislation, as they had earlier attempted to curb the railroads. Failing here, as before, they were forced to appeal to Congress. After prolonged pulling and hauling, the Sherman Anti-Trust Act of 1890 was finally signed into law.

The Sherman Act flatly forbade combinations in restraint of trade, without any distinction between "good" trusts and "bad" trusts. Bigness, not badness, was the sin. The law proved ineffective, largely because it had only baby teeth or no teeth at all, and because it contained legal loopholes through which

clever corporation lawyers could wriggle. But it was unexpectedly effective in one respect. Contrary to its original intent, it was used to curb labor unions or labor combinations that were deemed to be restraining trade.

Early prosecutions of the trusts by the Justice Department under the Sherman Act of 1890, as it turned out, were neither vigorous nor successful. The decisions in seven of the first eight cases presented by the attorney general were adverse to the government. More new trusts were formed in the 1890s under President McKinley than during any other like period. Not until 1914 were the paper jaws of the Sherman Act fitted with reasonably sharp teeth. Until then, there was some question whether the government would control the trusts or the trusts the government.

But the iron grip of monopolistic corporations was being threatened. A revolutionary new principle had been written into the law books by the Sherman Anti-Trust Act of 1890, as well as by the Interstate Commerce Act of 1887. Private greed must henceforth be subordinated to public need.

The South in the Age of Industry

The industrial tidal wave that washed over the North after the Civil War caused only feeble ripples in the backwater of the South. As late as 1900, the South still produced a smaller percentage of the nation's manufactured goods than it had before the Civil War. The plantation system had degenerated into a pattern of absentee land ownership. White and black sharecroppers now tilled the soil for a share of the crop, or they became tenants, in bondage to their landlords, who controlled needed credit and supplies.

Southern agriculture received a welcome boost in the 1880s, when machine-made cigarettes replaced the roll-your-own variety and tobacco consumption shot up. James Buchanan Duke took full advantage of the new technology to mass-produce the dainty "coffin nails." In 1890, in what was becoming a familiar pattern, he absorbed his main competitors into the American Tobacco Company. The cigarette czar later showed such generosity to Trinity College, near his birthplace in Durham, North Carolina, that the trustees gratefully changed its name to Duke University.

A Virginia Tobacco Factory, c. 1880   The employment of women and children was a common practice in late-nineteenth-century American industry, north as well as south.

Industrialists tried to coax the agricultural South out of the fields and into the factories, but with only modest success. The region remained overwhelmingly rural. Prominent among the boosters of a "new South" was silver-tongued Henry W. Grady, editor of the *Atlanta Constitution.* He tirelessly exhorted the ex-Confederates to become "Georgia Yankees" and outplay the North at the commercial and industrial game.

Yet formidable obstacles lay in the path of southern industrialization. One was the paper barrier of regional rate-setting systems imposed by the northern-dominated railroad interests. Railroads gave preferential rates to manufactured goods moving southward from the north, but in the opposite direction they discriminated in favor of southern raw materials. The net effect was to keep the South in a kind of "Third World" servitude to the Northeast—as a supplier of raw materials to the manufacturing metropolis, unable to develop a substantial industrial base of its own.

A bitter example of this economic discrimination against the South was the "Pittsburgh plus" pricing system in the steel industry. Rich deposits of

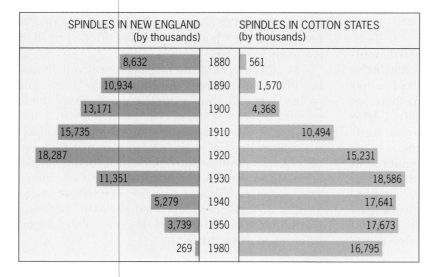

SPINDLES IN NEW ENGLAND (by thousands)		SPINDLES IN COTTON STATES (by thousands)
8,632	1880	561
10,934	1890	1,570
13,171	1900	4,368
15,735	1910	10,494
18,287	1920	15,231
11,351	1930	18,586
5,279	1940	17,641
3,739	1950	17,673
269	1980	16,795

Cotton Manufacturing Moves South, 1880–1980   Textile manufacturing usually looms large in the early stages of industrial development. In later stages it gives way to higher-technology businesses. This trend can be seen here, both in the migration of textile manufacturing to the southern United States and in the decline in the number of spindles in the United States as a whole since the 1930s, as developing Third World countries became major textile producers.

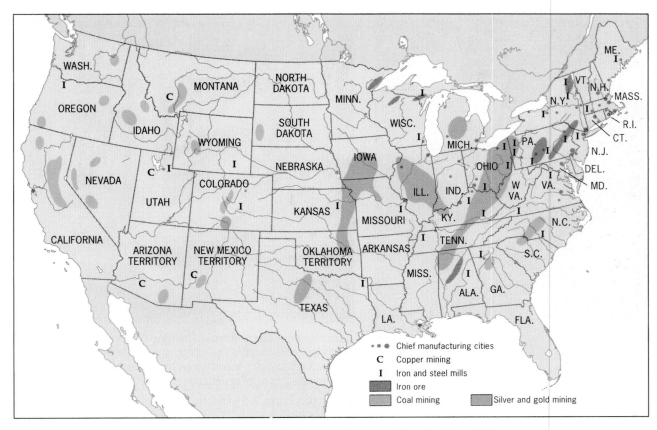

American Industry in 1900   By the end of the nineteenth century, once-rural America boasted the world's largest industrial output—a development with enormous consequences for politics, diplomacy, and family life.

coal and iron ore near Birmingham, Alabama, worked by low-wage southern labor, should have given steel manufacturers there a competitive edge, especially in southern markets. But the steel lords of Pittsburgh brought pressure to bear on the compliant railroads. As a result, Birmingham steel, no matter where it was delivered, was charged a fictional fee, as if it had been shipped from Pittsburgh. This stunting of the South's natural economic advantages throttled the growth of the Birmingham steel industry.

In manufacturing cotton textiles, the South fared considerably better. Southerners had long resented shipping their fiber to New England, and now their cry was "Bring the mills to the cotton." Beginning about 1880, northern capital began to erect cotton mills in the South, largely in response to tax benefits and the prospect of cheap and nonunionized labor. (See the chart at left.)

Henry W. Grady (1851–1889), editor of the Atlanta Constitution, *urged the new South to industrialize. In a Boston speech in 1889, he described the burial in Georgia of a Confederate veteran:*

"The South didn't furnish a thing on earth for that funeral but the corpse and the hole in the ground. . . . They buried him in a New York coat and a Boston pair of shoes and a pair of breeches from Chicago and a shirt from Cincinnati, leaving him nothing to carry into the next world with him to remind him of the country in which he lived, and for which he fought for four years, but the chill of blood in his veins and the marrow in his bones."

Assembly Line, Westinghouse Foundry, Pittsburgh, 1890
Technological innovations like this continuous assembly line created
abundant employment opportunities for semiskilled workers, many of
them immigrants from eastern and southern Europe.

**Breaker Boys at Woodward Coal Mining, Kingston,
Pennsylvania, c. 1900**   Photographer Lewis Hine captured the grimness of
these mine helpers' lives. For hours they sat on benches above a moving belt
kicking large pieces of coal with their feet, breaking the lumps to uniform size
for shipment. Photographs like this one became icons of the reform crusade
against child labor, a campaign crowned with success only with the passage of
the Fair Labor Standards Act in 1938.

The textile mills proved a mixed blessing to the
economically blighted South. They slowly wove an
industrial thread into the fabric of southern life, but
at a considerable human cost. Cheap labor was the
South's major attraction for potential investors, and
keeping labor cheap became almost a religion
among southern industrialists. The mills took root
in the chronically depressed piedmont region of
southern Appalachia and came to dominate utterly
the communities in which they were located.

Rural southerners—virtually all of them white,
for blacks were excluded from all but the most
menial jobs in the mills—poured out of the hills and
hollows to seek employment in the hastily erected
company mill towns. Entire families—often derided
as "hillbillies" or "lint-heads"—worked from dawn
to dusk amid the whirring spindles. They were paid
at half the rate of their northern counterparts and
often received their compensation in the form of
credit at a company store, to which they were habit-
ually in debt. But despite their depressed working
conditions and poor pay, many southerners saw
employment in the mills as a salvation, the first
steady jobs and wages they had ever known. With
many mills anxious to tap the cheap labor of
women and children, mill work often offered destitute farm-fugitive families their only chance to
remain together.

EXAMINING THE EVIDENCE

The Photography of Lewis W. Hine The pell-mell onrush of industrialization after the Civil War spawned countless human abuses, few more objectionable than the employment of children, often in hazardous jobs. For decades, reformers tried to arouse public outrage against child labor, and they made significant headway at last with the help of photography—especially the photographs of Lewis W. Hine (1874–1940). A native of Wisconsin, Hine in 1908 became the staff photographer for the National Child Labor Committee, an organization committed to ending child labor. This 1909 photo of young "doffers," whose job it was to remove fully wound bobbins from textile spinning machines, is typical of Hine's work. He shows the boys climbing dangerously on the whirling mechanism, and his own caption for the photo names the mill—"Bibb Mill No. 1, Macon, Georgia"—but not the boys, as if to underline the impersonal, dehumanizing nature of their work, and the specific responsibilities of their employer. His other subjects included child workers on Colorado beet farms, in Pennsylvania coal mines and Gulf Coast fish canneries, and in the glass, tobacco, and garment trades. Hine's images contributed heavily to the eventual success of the campaign to end child labor in the New Deal era. He is

also celebrated as one of the fathers of documentary photography. Why might Hine's graphic images have succeeded in stirring public opinion more powerfully than factual and statistical demonstrations of the evil of child labor? Given Hine's own reform objectives, can his photographs—or any so-called "documentary" images—be taken at face value as literal, accurate information about the past?

The Impact of the New Industrial Revolution on America

Economic miracles wrought during the decades after the Civil War enormously increased the wealth of the Republic. The standard of living rose sharply, and well-fed American workers enjoyed more physical comforts than their counterparts in any other industrial nation. Urban centers mushroomed as the insatiable factories demanded more American labor and as immigrants swarmed like honeybees to the new jobs (see "Makers of America: The Poles," pp. 734–735).

Early Jeffersonian ideals were withering before the smudgy blasts from the smokestacks. As agriculture declined in relation to manufacturing, America could no longer aspire to be a nation of small freehold farms. Jefferson's concepts of free enterprise, with neither help nor hindrance from Washington, were being thrown out the factory window. Tariffs had already provided assistance, but the long arm of federal authority was now committed to decades of corporation curbing and "trust-busting."

Older ways of life also wilted in the heat of the factory furnaces. The very concept of time was revolutionized. Rural American migrants and peasant European immigrants, used to living by the languid clock of nature, now had to regiment their lives by the factory whistle. The seemingly arbitrary discipline of industrial labor did not come easily and sometimes had to be forcibly taught. One large corporation simultaneously instructed its Polish immigrant workers in the English language and in the obligations of factory work schedules:

I hear the whistle. I must hurry.
I hear the five-minute whistle.
It is time to go into the shop. . . .
I change my clothes and get ready to work.
The starting whistle blows.
I eat my lunch.
It is forbidden to eat until then. . . .
I work until the whistle blows to quit.
I leave my place nice and clean.
I put all my clothes in the locker.
I must go home.

Probably no single group was more profoundly affected by the new industrial age than women. Propelled into industry by recent inventions, chiefly the typewriter and the telephone switchboard, millions of stenographers and "hello girls" discovered new economic and social opportunities. The "Gibson Girl," a magazine image of an independent and athletic "new woman" created in the 1890s by the artist Charles Dana Gibson, became the romantic ideal of the age. For middle-class women, careers often meant delayed marriages and smaller families. Most women workers, however, toiled neither for independence nor for glamour, but out of economic necessity. They faced the same long hours and dangerous working conditions as did their mates and brothers, and they earned less, as wages for "women's jobs" were usually set below those for men's.

The clattering machine age likewise accentuated class division. "Industrial buccaneers" flaunted bloated fortunes, and their rags-to-riches spouses displayed glittering diamonds. Such extravagances evoked bitter criticism. Some of it was envious, but much of it rose from a small but increasingly vocal group of socialists and other radicals, many of whom were recent European immigrants. The existence of an oligarchy of money was amply demonstrated by the fact that in 1900 about one-tenth of the people owned nine-tenths of the nation's wealth.

A nation of farmers and independent producers was becoming a nation of wage earners. In 1860 half of all workers were self-employed; by the century's end, two of every three working Americans depended on wages. Real wages were rising, and times were good for workers who were working. But with dependence on wages came vulnerability to the swings of the economy and the whims of the employer. The fear of unemployment was never distant. A breadwinner's illness could mean catastrophe for an entire family. Nothing more sharply defined the growing difference between working-class and middle-class conditions of life than the precariousness of the laborer's lot. Reformers struggled to introduce a measure of security—job and wage protection, and provision for temporary unemployment—into the lives of the working class.

Finally, strong pressures for foreign trade developed as the tireless industrial machine threatened to

Gibson Girl, 1899   Illustrator Charles Dana Gibson created a sensation with his drawings of healthy, athletic, young women. The image of the "Gibson Girl" inspired new standards of female fashion as the twentieth century opened, and came to symbolize women's growing independence and assertiveness.

saturate the domestic market. American products radiated out all over the world—notably the five-gallon kerosene can of the Standard Oil Company. The flag follows trade, and empire tends to follow the flag—a harsh lesson that America was soon to learn.

In Unions There Is Strength

Sweat of the laborer lubricated the vast new industrial machine. Yet the wage workers did not share proportionately with their employers in the benefits of the age of big business.

The worker, suggestive of the Roman galley slave, was becoming a lever-puller in a giant mechanism. Individual originality and creativity were being stifled, and less value than ever before was being placed on manual skills. Before the Civil War, the worker might have toiled in a small plant whose owner hailed the employee in the morning by first name and inquired after the family's health. But now the factory hand was employed by a corporation—depersonalized, bodiless, soulless, and often conscienceless. The directors knew the worker not; and in fairness to their stockholders they were not inclined to engage in large-scale private philanthropy.

New machines displaced employees, and though in the long run more jobs were created than destroyed, in the short run the manual worker was often hard hit. A glutted labor market, moreover, severely handicapped wage earners. Employers could take advantage of the vast new railroad network and bring in unemployed workers, from the four corners of the country and beyond, to beat down high wage levels. During the 1880s and 1890s, several hundred thousand unskilled workers a year poured into the country from Europe, creating a labor market more favorable to the boss than the worker.

Individual workers were powerless to battle single-handedly against giant industry. Forced to organize and fight for basic rights, they found the dice heavily loaded against them. The corporation could dispense with the individual worker much more easily than the worker could dispense with the corporation. Employers could pool vast wealth through thousands of stockholders, retain high-priced lawyers, buy up the local press, and put pressure on the politicians. They could import

strikebreakers ("scabs") and employ thugs to beat up labor organizers. In 1886 Jay Gould reputedly boasted, "I can hire one-half of the working class to kill the other half."

Corporations had still other weapons in their arsenals. They could call upon the federal courts—presided over by well-fed and conservative judges—to issue injunctions ordering the strikers to cease striking. If defiance and disorders ensued, the company could request the state and federal authorities to bring in troops. Employers could lock their doors against rebellious workers—a procedure called the "lockout"—and then starve them into submission. They could compel them to sign "ironclad oaths" or "yellow-dog contracts," both of which were solemn agreements not to join a labor union. They could put the names of agitators on a "black list" and circulate it among fellow employers. A corporation might even own the "company town," with its high-priced grocery stores and "easy" credit. Often the worker sank into perpetual debt—a status that strongly resembled serfdom. Countless thousands of blackened coal miners were born in a company house, nurtured by a (high-priced) company store, and buried in a company graveyard—prematurely dead.

The middle-class public, annoyed by recurrent strikes, grew deaf to the outcry of the worker. American wages were perhaps the highest in the world, although a dollar a day for pick-and-shovel labor does not now seem excessive. Carnegie and Rockefeller had battled their way to the top, and the view was common that the laborer could do likewise.

The Reverend Henry Ward Beecher (1813–1887) of Brooklyn, the most distinguished (and notorious) clergyman of the era after the Civil War, said,

"The trade union, which originated under the European system, destroys liberty. I do not say a dollar a day is enough to support a working man, but it is enough to support a man. Not enough to support a man and five children if a man insists on smoking and drinking beer."

The Strike, by Robert Koehler, 1886   Scenes like this were becoming more typical of American life in the late nineteenth century as industrialism advanced spectacularly and sometimes ruthlessly. Here Koehler (1850–1917) shows an entire community of men, women, and children—many of them apparently immigrant newcomers—challenging the power of the "boss." The scene is tense but orderly, though violence seems to be imminent as one striker reaches for a rock.

Somehow the strike seemed like a foreign importation—socialistic and hence unpatriotic. Big business might combine into trusts to raise prices, but the worker must not combine into unions to raise wages. Unemployment seemed to be an act of God, who somehow would take care of the laborer.

Labor Limps Along

Labor unions, which had been few and disorganized in 1861, were given a strong boost by the Civil War. This bloody conflict, with its drain on human resources, put more of a premium on labor; and the mounting cost of living provided an urgent incentive to unionization. By 1872 there were several hundred thousand organized workers and thirty-two national unions, representing such crafts as bricklayers, typesetters, and shoemakers.

The National Labor Union, organized in 1866, represented a giant bootstride by workers. The union lasted six years and attracted the impressive total of some 600,000 members, including the skilled, unskilled, and farmers, though in keeping with the times, it excluded the Chinese and made only nominal efforts to include women and blacks. Black workers organized their own Colored National Labor Union as an adjunct, but their support for the Republican party and the persistent racism of white unionists prevented the two national unions from working together. The National Labor Union agitated for the arbitration of industrial disputes and the eight-hour workday, and won the latter for government workers. But the devastating depression of the 1870s dealt it a knockout blow. Labor was generally rocked back on its heels during the tumultuous years of the depression, but it never completely toppled. Wage reductions in 1877 touched off such disruptive strikes on the railroads that nothing short of federal troops could restore order.

A new organization—the Knights of Labor—seized the torch dropped by the defunct National Labor Union (see "Makers of America: The Knights of Labor," pp. 552–553). Officially known as The Noble and Holy Order of the Knights of Labor, it began inauspiciously in 1869 as a secret society, with a private ritual, passwords, and a special handshake. Secrecy, which continued until 1881, would forestall possible reprisals by employers.

The Knights of Labor, like the National Labor Union, sought to include all workers in "one big union." Their slogan was "An injury to one is the concern of all." A welcome mat was rolled out for the skilled and unskilled, for men and women, for whites and underprivileged blacks, some ninety thousand of whom joined. The Knights barred only "nonproducers"—liquor dealers, professional gamblers, lawyers, bankers, and stockbrokers.

Setting up broad goals, the embattled Knights refused to thrust their lance into politics. Instead they campaigned for economic and social reform, including producers' cooperatives and codes for safety and health. Voicing the war cry "Labor is the only creator of values and capital," they frowned upon industrial warfare while fostering industrial arbitration. The ordinary workday was then ten hours or more, and the Knights waged a determined campaign for the eight-hour stint. A favorite song of these years ran,

> Hurrah, hurrah, for labor,
>   it is mustering all its powers,
> And shall march along to victory
>   with the banner of eight hours.

Under the eloquent but often erratic leadership of Terence V. Powderly, an Irish-American of nimble wit and fluent tongue, the Knights won a number of strikes for the eight-hour day. When the Knights staged a successful strike against Jay Gould's Wabash Railroad in 1885, membership mushroomed, to about three-quarters of a million workers.

Unhorsing the Knights of Labor

Despite their outward success, the Knights were riding for a fall. They became involved in a number of May Day strikes in 1886, about half of which failed. A focal point was Chicago, home to about eighty thousand Knights. The city was also honeycombed with a few hundred anarchists, many of them foreign-born, who were advocating a violent overthrow of the American government.

Tensions rapidly built up to the bloody Haymarket Square episode. Labor disorders had broken out, and on May 4, 1886, the Chicago police advanced on a meeting called to protest alleged brutalities by the authorities. Suddenly a dynamite bomb was thrown that killed or injured several dozen people, including police.

Hysteria swept the Windy City. Eight anarchists were rounded up, although nobody proved that they had anything to do directly with the bomb. But the judge and jury held that since they had preached incendiary doctrines, they could be charged with conspiracy. Five were sentenced to death, one of whom committed suicide, and the other three were given stiff prison terms.

Agitation for clemency mounted. In 1892, some six years later, John P. Altgeld, a German-born Democrat of strong liberal tendencies, was elected governor of Illinois. After studying the Haymarket case exhaustively, he pardoned the three survivors. Violent abuse was showered on him by conservatives, unstinted praise by those who thought the men innocent. He was defeated for reelection and died a few years later in relative obscurity, "The Eagle Forgotten." Whatever the merits of the case, Altgeld displayed courage in opposing what he regarded as a gross injustice.

The Haymarket Square bomb helped blow the props from under the Knights of Labor. They were associated in the public mind, though mistakenly, with the anarchists. The eight-hour movement suffered correspondingly, and subsequent strikes by the Knights met with scant success.

Another fatal handicap of the Knights was their inclusion of both skilled and unskilled workers. Unskilled labor could easily be replaced by strikebreaking "scabs." High-class craft unionists, who enjoyed a semimonopoly of skills, could not readily be supplanted and hence enjoyed a superior bargaining position. They finally wearied of sacrificing this advantage on the altar of solidarity with their unskilled coworkers and sought refuge in a federation of exclusively skilled craft unions—the American Federation of Labor. The desertion of the skilled craft unionists dealt the Knights a body blow. By the 1890s they had melted away to 100,000 members, and these gradually fused with other protest groups of that decade.

The Knights of Labor

It was 1875. The young worker was guided into a room, where his blindfold was removed. Surrounding him were a dozen men, their faces covered by hoods. One of the masked figures solemnly asked three questions: "Do you believe in God?" "Do you gain your bread by the sweat of your brow?" "Are you willing to take a solemn vow, binding you to secrecy, obedience, and mutual assistance?" Yes, came the reply. The men doffed their hoods and joined hands in a circle. Their leader, the Master Workman, declared, "On behalf of the toiling millions of earth, I welcome you to this Sanctuary, dedicated to the service of God, by serving humanity." Then the entire group burst into song:

> *Storm the fort, ye Knights of Labor,*
> *Battle for your cause;*
> *Equal rights for every neighbor,*
> *Down with tyrant laws!*

The carefully staged pageantry then drew to a close. The worker was now a full-fledged member of the Knights of Labor.

He had just joined a loose-knit organization of some 100,000 workingpeople, soon to swell to nearly one million after the Knights led several successful strikes in the 1880s. The first women Knights joined in 1881, when an all-female local was established in the shoe trade in Philadelphia, and one in ten members were women by 1885. They were organizers, too. Fiery Mary Harris ("Mother") Jones got her start agitating for the Knights in the Illinois coal fields. The first all-black local was founded among coal miners in Ottumwa, Iowa. The Knights preached tolerance and the solidarity of all working men and women, and they meant it, but even their inclusionary spirit had its limits. Chinese workers were barred from joining, and the Knights vigorously supported the Chinese Exclusion Act of 1882. They also championed the Contract Labor Law of 1885, which aimed to restrain competition from

"Mother Jones"

low-wage immigrant workers—though immigrants, especially the Irish, were themselves disproportionately represented among the Knights' membership.

Terence V. Powderly, born to Irish immigrant parents in Carbondale, Pennsylvania, in 1849, became the Grand Master Workman of the Knights in 1879. Slightly built, with mild blue eyes behind glasses, he had dropped out of school at age thirteen to take a job guarding railroad track switches and rose to mayor of Scranton, Pennsylvania, in the 1870s. In 1894 he became a lawyer—despite the fact that the Knights excluded lawyers from membership. A complex, colorful, and sometimes cynical man, he denounced the "multimillionaires [for] laying the foundation for their colossal fortunes on the bodies and souls of living men." In the eyes of Powderly and his Knights, only the economic and political independence of American workers could preserve republican traditions and institutions from corruption by monopolists and other "parasites."

Powderly denounced "wage-slavery" and dedicated the Knights to achieving the "cooperative commonwealth." Shunning socialism, which advocated government ownership of the means of production, Powderly urged laborers to save enough from their wages to purchase mines, factories, railroads, and stores. They would thereby create a kind of toilers' utopia; because labor would own and operate those enterprises, workers themselves would be owner-producers, and the conflict between labor and capital would evaporate. The Knights actually did operate a few businesses, including coal mines in Indiana, but all eventually failed.

Powderly's vision of the cooperative commonwealth reflected the persistent dream of many nineteenth-century American workers that they would all one day become producers. As expectant capitalists, they lacked "class consciousness"—that is, a sense of themselves as a permanent working class that must organize to coax what benefits it could out of the capitalist system. Samuel Gompers, by contrast, accepted the framework of American capitalism, and his American Federation of Labor sought to work within that framework, not to overturn it. Gompers's conservative strategy, not Powderly's utopian dream, eventually carried the day. The swift decline of the Knights in the 1890s underscored the obsolescence of their unrealistic, even naive, view that a bygone age of independent producers could be restored. Yet the Knights' commitment to unifying all workers in one union—regardless of race, gender, ethnicity, or skill level—provided a blueprint for the eventual success of

Machinist Frank J. Ferrell, Black Delegate of District Assembly No. 49, Introducing General Master Workman Terence Powderly to the 10th Annual Convention of the Knights of Labor, Held in Richmond, Virginia, 1886

similarly committed unions like the Congress of Industrial Organizations in the 1930s.

Women Delegates to the 1886 Convention of the Knights of Labor

Samuel Gompers (1850–1924) Gompers (second from the right in the first row) shown here marching in a labor demonstration in Washington, D.C, in 1919, once declared: "Show me the country in which there are no strikes and I'll show you that country in which there is no liberty."

The AF of L to the Fore

The elitist American Federation of Labor, born in 1886, was largely the brainchild of squat, square-jawed Samuel Gompers. This colorful Jewish cigar maker, born in a London tenement and removed from school at age ten, was brought to America when thirteen. Taking his turn at reading informative literature to fellow cigar makers in New York, he was pressed into overtime service because of his strong voice. Rising spectacularly in the labor ranks, he was elected president of the American Federation of Labor every year except one from 1886 to 1924.

Significantly, the American *Federation* of Labor was just what it called itself—a federation. It consisted of an association of self-governing national unions, each of which kept its independence, with the AF of L unifying overall strategy. No individual laborer as such could join the central organization.

Gompers adopted a down-to-earth approach, soft-pedaling attempts to engineer sweeping social reform. A bitter foe of socialism, he shunned politics for economic strategies and goals. Gompers had no quarrel with capitalism, but he demanded a fairer share for labor. All he wanted, he said, was "more." Promoting what he called a "pure and simple" unionism, he sought better wages, hours, and working conditions. Unlike the somewhat utopian Knights of Labor, he was not concerned with the sweet by-and-by, but with the bitter here and now. A major goal of Gompers was the "trade agreement" authorizing the "closed shop"—or all-union labor. His chief weapons were the walkout and the boycott, enforced by "We don't patronize" signs. The stronger craft unions of the federation, by pooling funds, were able to amass a war chest that would enable them to ride out prolonged strikes.

The AF of L thus established itself on solid but narrow foundations. Although attempting to speak for all workers, it fell far short of being representative of them. Composed of skilled craftsmen, like the carpenters and the bricklayers, it was willing to let unskilled laborers, including women and especially blacks, fend for themselves. Though hard-pressed by big industry, the federation was basically nonpolitical. But it did attempt to persuade members to reward friends and punish foes at the polls. The AF of L weathered the panic of 1893 reasonably well, and by 1900 it could boast a membership of 500,000. Critics referred to it, with questionable accuracy, as "the labor trust."

Labor disorders continued, peppering the years from 1881 to 1900 with an alarming total of over 23,000 strikes. These disturbances involved 6,610,000 workers, with a total loss to both employers and employees of $450 million. The strikers lost about half their strikes and won or compromised the remainder. Perhaps the gravest weakness of organized labor was that it still embraced only a small minority of all workingpeople—about 3 percent in 1900.

But attitudes toward labor had begun to change perceptibly by 1900. The public was beginning to concede the right of workers to organize, to bargain collectively, and to strike. As a sign of the times, Labor Day was made a legal holiday by act of Congress in 1894. A few enlightened industrialists had come to perceive the wisdom of avoiding costly economic warfare by bargaining with the unions and signing agreements. But the vast majority of employers continued to fight organized labor, which achieved its grudging gains only after recurrent strikes and frequent reverses. Nothing was handed to it on a silver platter. Management still held the whip hand, and several trouble-fraught decades were to pass before labor was to gain a position of relative equality with capital. If the age of big business had dawned, the age of big labor was still some distance over the horizon.

Chronology

1862	Congress authorizes a transcontinental railroad		**1879**	Edison invents the electric light
1866	National Labor Union organized		**1886**	Haymarket Square bombing *Wabash* case American Federation of Labor formed
1869	Transcontinental railroad joined near Ogden, Utah Knights of Labor organized		**1887**	Interstate Commerce Act
			1890	Sherman Anti-Trust Act
1870	Standard Oil Company organized		**1901**	United States Steel Corporation formed
1876	Bell invents the telephone			

VARYING VIEWPOINTS

Industrialization: Boon or Blight?

The capitalists who forged an industrial America in the late nineteenth century were once called captains of industry—a respectful title that bespoke the awe due their wondrous material accomplishments. But these economic innovators have never been universally admired. During the Great Depression of the 1930s, when the entire industrial order they had created seemed to have collapsed utterly, it was fashionable to speak of them as robber barons—a term implying scorn for their high-handed methods. This sneer often issued from the lips and pens of leftist critics like Matthew Joseph-son, who sympathized with the working classes that were allegedly brutalized by the factory system.

Criticism has also come from writers nostalgic for a preindustrial past. These critics believe that industrialization stripped away the traditions, values, and pride of native farmers and immigrant craftspeople. Conceding that economic development elevated the material standard of living for working Americans, this interpretation contends that the Industrial Revolution diminished their spiritual "quality of life." Accordingly, historians like Herbert Gutman and David Montgomery portray labor's struggle for control of the workplace as the central drama of industrial expansion.

Nevertheless, even these historians concede that class-based protest has never been as powerful a force in the United States as in certain European countries. Many historians believe that this is so because greater social mobility in America dampened class tensions. The French observer Alexis de Tocqueville noted in the 1830s that America had few huge inherited fortunes and that most of its wealthy men were self-made. For two centuries a majority of Americans have believed that greater opportunity distinguished the New World from the Old.

In the 1960s historians led by Stephan Thernstrom began to test this long-standing belief. Looking at such factors as occupation, wealth, and geographic mobility, they tried to gauge the nature and extent of social mobility in the United States. Most of these historians concluded that although relatively few Americans made rags-to-riches leaps like those heralded in the Horatio Alger stories, large numbers experienced small improvements in their economic and social status. Few sons of laborers became corporate tycoons, but many more became line bosses and white-collar clerks. These studies also have found that race and ethnicity often affected one's chances for success. For instance, the children and grandchildren of Jewish immigrants tended to rise faster in the professions than Americans of Italian and Irish descent. Throughout the nineteenth and early twentieth centuries, blacks lagged far behind other groups in almost every category.

In recent years such studies have been criticized by certain historians who point out the difficulties involved in defining social status. For instance, some white-collar clerical workers received lower wages than manual laborers did. Were they higher or lower on the social scale? Furthermore, James Henretta has pointed out that different groups defined success differently: whereas Jewish immigrants often struggled to give their sons professional educations, the Irish put more emphasis on acquiring land, and Italians on building small family-run businesses.

Meanwhile, leftist historians such as Michael Katz have argued that the degree of social mobility in America has been overrated. These historians argue that industrial capitalism created two classes: a working class that sold its labor, and a business class that controlled resources and bought labor. Although most Americans took small steps upward, they generally remained within the class in which they began. Thus, these historians argue, the inequality of a capitalistic class system persisted in America's seemingly fluid society.

For further reading, see page A17 of the Appendix. For web resources, go to **http://college.hmco.com.**

America Moves to the City

1865–1900

What shall we do with our great cities? What will our great cities do with us . . . ? [T]he question . . . does not concern the city alone. The whole country is affected . . . by the condition of its great cities.

LYMAN ABBOTT, 1891

B orn in the country, America moved to the city in the decades following the Civil War. By the year 1900, the United States' upsurging population nearly doubled from its level of some 40 million souls enumerated in the census of 1870. Yet in the very same period, the population of American cities *tripled.* By the end of the nineteenth century, four out of ten Americans were city dwellers, in striking contrast to the rustic population of stagecoach days.

This cityward drift affected not only the United States but most of the Western world. European peasants, pushed off the land in part by competition from cheap American foodstuffs, were pulled into cities—in both Europe and America—by the new lure of industrial jobs. A revolution in American agriculture thus fed the industrial and urban revolutions in Europe, as well as in the United States.

The Urban Frontier

The growth of American metropolises was spectacular. In 1860 no city in the United States could boast a million inhabitants; by 1890 New York, Chicago, and Philadelphia had vaulted past the million mark. By 1900 New York, with some 3.5 million people, was the second largest city in the world, outranked only by London.

Cities grew both up and out. The cloud-brushing skyscraper allowed more people and workplaces to be packed onto a parcel of land. Appearing first as a ten-story building in Chicago in 1885, the skyscraper was made usable by the perfecting of the electric elevator. An opinionated Chicago architect, Louis Sullivan (1856–1924), contributed formidably

Lower Broadway, 1875   Horses still abounded in New York and other cities when this lithograph was made, but they would soon be displaced by street railways and automobiles.

to the further development of the skyscraper with his famous principle that "form follows function." Nesting loftily above city streets in the new steel-skeleton high-rises that Sullivan helped to make popular, many Americans were becoming modern cliff dwellers.

Americans were also becoming commuters, carted daily between home and job on the mass-transit lines that radiated out from central cities to surrounding suburbs. Electric trolleys, powered by wagging antennae from overhead wires, propelled city limits explosively outward. The compact and communal "walking city," its boundaries fixed by the limits of leg-power, gave way to the immense and impersonal megalopolis, carved into distinctly different districts for business, industry, and residential neighborhoods—which were in turn segregated by race, ethnicity, and social class.

Rural America could not compete with the siren song of the city. Industrial jobs, above all, drew country folks off the farms and into factory centers.

But the urban lifestyle also held powerful attractions. The predawn milking of cows had little appeal when compared with the late-night glitter of city lights. Electricity, indoor plumbing, and telephones—whose numbers leapt from some 50,000 in 1880 to over 1 million in 1900—all made life in the big city more alluring. Engineering marvels like the skyscraper and New York's awesome Brooklyn Bridge, a harplike suspension span dedicated in 1883, further added to the seductive glamour of the gleaming cities.

Cavernous department stores such as Macy's in New York and Marshall Field's in Chicago attracted urban middle-class shoppers and provided urban working-class jobs, many of them for women. The bustling emporiums also heralded a dawning era of consumerism and accentuated widening class divisions. When Carrie Meeber, novelist Theodore Dreiser's fictional heroine in *Sister Carrie* (1900), escapes from rural boredom to Chicago just before the turn of the century, it is the spectacle of the city's

The Brooklyn Bridge, 1890
Completed in 1883, the bridge was an engineering marvel in its day and has inspired poets ever since. The twentieth-century poet Hart Crane called it "O harp and altar!"

dazzling department stores that awakens her fateful yearning for a richer, more elegant way of life—for entry into the privileged urban middle class, whose existence she had scarcely imagined in the rustic countryside.

The move to the city introduced Americans to new ways of living. Country dwellers produced little household waste. Domestic animals or scavenging pigs ate food scraps on the farm. Rural women mended and darned worn clothing rather than discard it. Household products were sold in bulk at the local store, without wrapping. Mail-order houses such as Sears and Montgomery Ward, which increasingly displaced the rural "general store" in the late nineteenth century, at first did not list trash barrels or garbage cans in their catalogues. In the city, however, goods came in throwaway bottles, boxes, bags, and cans. Apartment houses had no adjoining barnyards where residents might toss garbage to the hogs. Cheap ready-to-wear clothing

The Shift to the City   This chart shows the percentage of total population living in locales with a population of twenty-five hundred or more. Note the slowing of the cityward trend from 1970 on.

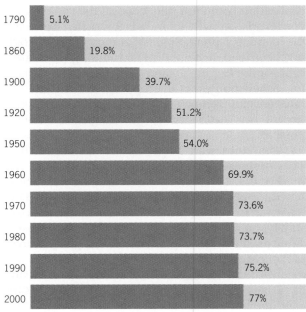

Year	Percentage
1790	5.1%
1860	19.8%
1900	39.7%
1920	51.2%
1950	54.0%
1960	69.9%
1970	73.6%
1980	73.7%
1990	75.2%
2000	77%

Dumbbell Tenement   This was the standard architectural plan for the human warehouses on New York's Lower East Side. Despite the innovation of an air shaft to bring light and ventilation to the middle of the building, only one room in each of the apartments was directly exposed to sunlight and open air. All families on a floor shared the toilet ("W.C.") in the hallway.

and swiftly changing fashions pushed old suits and dresses out of the closet and onto the trash heap. Waste disposal, in short, was an issue new to the urban age. And the mountains of waste that urbanites generated further testified to a cultural shift away from the virtues of thrift to the conveniences of consumerism.

The jagged skyline of America's perpendicular civilization could not fully conceal the canker sores of a feverish growth. Criminals flourished like lice in the teeming asphalt jungles. Sanitary facilities could not keep pace with the mushrooming population explosion. Impure water, uncollected garbage, unwashed bodies, and droppings from draft animals enveloped many cities in a satanic stench. Baltimore was described as smelling like a billion polecats.

The cities were monuments of contradiction. They represented "humanity compressed," remarked one observer, "the best and the worst combined, in a strangely composite community." They harbored merchant princes and miserable paupers, stately banks and sooty factories, green-grassed suburbs and treeless ghettos, towering skyscrapers and stinking tenements. The glaring contrasts that assaulted the eye in New York reminded one visitor of "a lady in ball costume, with diamonds in her ears, and her toes out at the boots."

Worst of all were the human pigsties known as slums. They seemed to grow ever more crowded, more filthy, and more rat-infested, especially after the perfection in 1879 of the "dumbbell" tenement. So named because of the outline of its floor plan, the dumbbell was usually seven or eight stories high, with shallow, sunless, and ill-smelling air shafts providing minimal ventilation. Several families were sardined onto each floor of the barracks-like structures, and they shared a malodorous toilet in the hall. In these fetid warrens, conspicuously in New York's "Lung Block," hundreds of unfortunate urbanites coughed away their lives. "Flophouses" abounded where the half-starved and unemployed might sleep for a few cents on verminous mattresses. Small wonder that slum dwellers strove mightily to escape their wretched surroundings—as many of them did. The slums remained foul places, inhabited by successive waves of newcomers. To a remarkable degree hard-working people moved up and out of them. But although they escaped the old ghetto, they generally resettled in other urban neighborhoods alongside people of the same ethnicity or religion. The wealthiest left the cities altogether and headed for the semirural suburbs. These leafy "bedroom communities" eventually ringed the brick-and-concrete cities with a greenbelt of affluence.

The New Immigration

The powerful pull of the American urban magnet was felt even in faraway Europe. A brightly colored stream of immigrants continued to pour in from the old "mother continent." In each of the three decades from the 1850s through the 1870s, more than 2 million migrants had stepped onto America's shores. By the 1880s the stream had swelled to a rushing torrent, as more than 5 million cascaded into the country. A new high for a single year was reached in 1882, when 788,992 arrived—or more than 2,100 a day.

Until the 1880s most immigrants had come from the British Isles and western Europe, chiefly Germany and Scandinavia. They were typically fair-skinned Anglo-Saxon and Teutonic types, and they were usually Protestant, except for the Catholic Irish and many Catholic Germans. Many of them boasted a comparatively high rate of literacy and were accustomed to some kind of representative government. Their Old Country ways of life were such that they fit-

ted relatively easily into American society, especially when they took up farming, as many did.

But in the 1880s, the character of the immigrant stream changed drastically. The so-called New Immigrants came from southern and eastern Europe. Among them were Italians, Croats, Slovaks, Greeks, and Poles; many of them worshiped in orthodox churches or synagogues. They came from countries with little history of democratic government, where people had grown accustomed to cringing before despotism and where opportunities for advancement were few. Largely illiterate and impoverished, most new immigrants preferred to seek industrial jobs in jam-packed cities rather than move out to farms (see "Makers of America: The Italians," pp. 566–567).

These new peoples totaled only 19 percent of the inpouring immigrants in the 1880s, but by the first decade of the twentieth century, they constituted an astonishing 66 percent of the total inflow. They hived together in cities like New York and Chicago, where the "Little Italys" and "Little

Annual Immigration, 1860–1997 The 1989 total includes 478,814 people granted permanent residence status under the "amnesty" provisions of the 1986 Immigration Reform and Control Act. The 1990 total includes 880,372 people granted permanent residence under these provisions. The peak came in 1991, when 1,123,162 people were affected. (Source: *Statistical Abstract of the United States,* relevant years.)

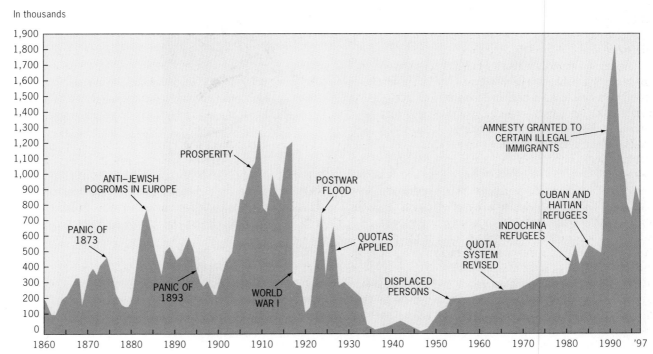

In thousands

Polands" soon claimed more inhabitants than many of the largest cities of the same nationality in the Old World. Some Americans feared that these New Immigrants would not—or could not—assimilate to life in their new land, and they began asking if the nation had become a melting pot or a dumping ground.

Southern Europe Uprooted

Why were these bright-shawled and quaint-jacketed strangers hammering on the gates? In part they left their native countries because Europe seemed to have no room for them. The population of the Old World was growing vigorously. It nearly doubled in the century after 1800, thanks in part to abundant supplies of fish and grain from America and to the widespread cultivation in Europe of that humble New World transplant, the potato. American food imports and the galloping pace of European indus-

trialization shook the peasantry loose from its ancient habitats and customary occupations, creating a vast, footloose army of the unemployed. Europeans by the millions drained out of the countryside and into European cities. Most stayed there, but some kept moving and left Europe altogether. About 60 million Europeans abandoned the Old Continent in the nineteenth and early twentieth centuries. More than half of them moved to the United States. But that striking fact should not obscure the important truth that masses of people were already in motion in Europe before they felt the tug of the American magnet. Immigration to America was, in many ways, a by-product of the urbanization of Europe.

"America fever" proved highly contagious in Europe. The United States was often painted as a land of fabulous opportunity in the "America letters" sent by friends and relatives already transplanted—letters that were soiled by the hands of many readers. "We eat here every day," wrote one jubilant Pole, "what we get only for Easter in our

Mulberry Street on New York City's Lower East Side, c. 1900   Population densities in early-twentieth-century American cities were among the highest in the world. Mulberry Street, shown in this photo, was at the heart of New York's "Little Italy" neighborhood.

EXAMINING THE EVIDENCE

Manuscript Census Data, 1900 Article I of the Constitution requires that a census of the American people be taken every ten years, in order to provide a reliable basis for congressional apportionment. Early censuses gathered little more than basic population numbers, but over the years, the census-takers have collected information on other matters as well, including occupational categories, educational levels, and citizenship status, yielding copious raw data for historical analysis. The census of 1890 was the first to use punch cards and electric tabulating machines, which greatly expanded the range of data that could be assembled and correlated—though the basic information was still hand-recorded by individual canvassers who went door-to-door to question household members and fill out the census forms. Those hand-written forms, as much as the aggregate numbers printed in the final census tally, can furnish invaluable insights to the historian. Despite its apparent bureaucratic formality, the form shown here richly details the lives of the residents of a tenement house on New York's Lower East Side in 1900. See in particular the entries for the Goldberg family. In what ways does this document reflect the great demographic changes that swept late-nineteenth-century America? What light does it shed on the character of immigrant "ghettoes?" What further use might historians make out of information like this?

[native] country." The land of the free was also blessed with freedom from military conscription and institutionalized religious persecution.

Profit-seeking Americans trumpeted throughout Europe the attractions of the new promised land. Industrialists wanted low-wage labor, railroads wanted buyers for their land grants, states wanted more population, and steamship lines wanted more human cargo for their holds. In fact, the ease and cheapness of steam-powered shipping greatly accelerated the transoceanic surge.

As the century lengthened, savage persecutions of minorities in Europe drove many shattered souls to American shores. In the 1880s the Russians turned violently upon their own Jews, chiefly in the Polish areas. Tens of thousands of these battered refugees, survivors of centuries of harassment as hated outcasts, fled their burning homes. They made their way to the seaboard cities of the Atlantic Coast, notably New York. Jews had experienced city life in Europe—a circumstance that made them virtually unique among the New Immigrants. Many of them brought their urban skills of tailoring or shopkeeping to American cities. Destitute and devout, eastern European Jews were frequently given a frosty reception not only by old-stock Americans but also by those German Jews who had arrived decades earlier and prospered in the United States, some as garment manufacturers who now conde-

Mary Antin (1881–1949), who came to America from Russian Poland in 1894 when thirteen years of age, later wrote in The Promised Land *(1912),*

"So at last I was going to America! Really, really going, at last! The boundaries burst. The arch of heaven soared. A million suns shone out for every star. The winds rushed in from outer space, roaring in my ears, 'America! America!'"

scendingly employed their coreligionists as cheap labor.

Many of the immigrants never intended to become Americans in any case. A large number of them were single men who worked in the United States for several months or years and then returned home with their hard-earned roll of American dollars. Some 25 percent of the nearly 20 million people who arrived between 1820 and 1900 were "birds of passage" who eventually returned to their country of origin. For them the grip of the American magnet was never strong.

Jewish Women Working in a Sweatshop, c. 1910 Countless immigrant women found their first American employment in shops like this.

Even those who stayed in America struggled heroically to preserve their traditional culture. Catholics expanded their parochial-school system and Jews established Hebrew schools. Foreign-language newspapers abounded. Yiddish theaters, kosher food stores, Polish parishes, Greek restaurants, and Italian social clubs all attested to the desire to keep old ways alive. Yet time took its toll on these efforts to conserve the customs of the Old World in the New. The children of the immigrants grew up speaking fluent English, sometimes mocking the broken grammar of their parents. They often rejected the Old Country manners of their mothers and fathers in their desire to plunge headlong into the mainstream of American life.

Reactions to the New Immigration

America's government system, nurtured in wide-open spaces, was ill suited to the cement forests of the great cities. Beyond minimal checking to weed out criminals and the insane, the federal government did virtually nothing to ease the assimilation of immigrants into American society. State governments, usually dominated by rural representatives, did even less. City governments, overwhelmed by the sheer scale of rampant urban growth, proved woefully inadequate to the task. By default, the business of ministering to the immigrants' needs fell to the unofficial "governments" of the urban political machines, led by "bosses" like New York's notorious Boss Tweed.

Taking care of the immigrants was big business, indeed. Trading jobs and services for votes, a powerful boss might claim the loyalty of thousands of followers. In return for their support at the polls, the boss provided jobs on the city's payroll, found housing for new arrivals, tided over the needy with gifts of food and clothing, patched up minor scrapes with the law, and helped get schools, parks, and hospitals built in immigrant neighborhoods. Reformers gagged at this cynical exploitation of the immigrant vote, but the political boss gave valuable assistance that was forthcoming from no other source.

The nation's social conscience, slumbering since the antislavery crusade, gradually awakened to the plight of the cities, and especially their immigrant masses. Prominent in this awakening were several Protestant clergymen, who sought to apply the lessons of Christianity to the slums and factories. Noteworthy among them was Walter Rauschenbusch, who in 1886 became pastor of a German Baptist church in New York City. Also conspicuous was Washington Gladden, who took over a Congregational church in Columbus, Ohio, in 1882. Preaching the "social gospel," they both insisted that the churches tackle the burning social issues of the day. The Sermon on the Mount, they declared, was the science of society, and many social gospelers predicted that socialism would be the logical outcome of Christianity. These "Christian socialists" did much to prick calloused middle-class consciences, thus preparing the path for the progressive reform movement after the turn of the century.

One middle-class woman who was deeply dedicated to uplifting the urban masses was Jane Addams (1860–1935). Born into a prosperous Illinois family, Addams was one of the first generation of college-educated women. Upon her graduation she sought other outlets for her large talents than could be found in teaching or charitable volunteer work, then the only permissible occupations for a young woman of her social class. Inspired by a visit to England, in 1889 she acquired the decaying Hull mansion in Chicago. There she established Hull House, the most prominent (though not the first) American settlement house.

Soft-spoken but tenacious, Jane Addams became a kind of urban American saint in the eyes of many admirers. The philosopher William James told her, "You utter instinctively the truth we others vainly seek." She was a broad-gauge reformer who courageously condemned war as well as poverty, and she eventually won the Nobel Peace Prize in 1931. But her pacifism also earned her the enmity of some Americans, including the Daughters of the American Revolution, who choked on her antiwar views and expelled her from membership in their august organization.

Located in a poor immigrant neighborhood of Greeks, Italians, Russians, and Germans, Hull House offered instruction in English, counseling to help newcomers cope with American big-city life, child-care services for working mothers, and cultural activities for neighborhood residents. Following Jane Addams's lead, women founded settlement houses in other cities as well. Conspicuous among the houses was Lillian Wald's Henry Street Settlement in New York, which opened its doors in 1893.

The Italians

Who were the "New Immigrants"? Who were these southern and eastern European birds of passage that flocked to the United States between 1880 and 1920? Prominent and typical among them were Italians, some 4 million of whom sailed to the United States during the four decades of the New Immigration.

They came from the southern provinces of their native land, the heel and toe of the Italian boot. These areas had lagged behind the prosperous, industrial region of northern Italy. The north had been the seat of earlier Italian glory, as well as the fountainhead of the successful movement to unify the country in 1860. There industry had been planted and agriculture modernized. Unification raised hopes of similar progress in the downtrodden south, but it was slow in coming. Southern Italian peasants tilled their fields without fertilizer or machinery, using hand plows and rickety hoes that had been passed down for generations.

From such disappointed and demeaned conditions, southern Italians set out for the New World. Almost all of them were young men who intended to spend only a few months in America, stuff their pockets with dollars, and return home. Almost half of Italian immigrants did indeed repatriate—as did comparable numbers of the other New Immigrants, with the conspicuous exception of the Jews, who had fled their native lands to escape religious persecution. Almost all Italian immigrants sailed through

Pietro Learning to Write on Jersey Street
"The sons shall teach the fathers," the old saying goes. Many immigrants learned English from their children who attended American schools, like this youngster and parent in early-twentieth-century New Jersey.

Italian Immigrants Arriving at Ellis Island, c. 1910

Italian Construction Workers, c. 1910

Italian Immigrant Women Doing Piecework at Home in New York, c. 1910

New York harbor, sighting the Statue of Liberty as they debarked from crowded ships. Many soon moved on to other large cities, but so many remained that in the early years of the twentieth century, more Italians resided in New York than in the Italian cities of Florence, Venice, and Genoa combined.

Since the immigrant Italians, with few exceptions, had been peasant farmers in the Old Country, the U.S. government encouraged them to practice their ancestral livelihood here, believing they would more rapidly assimilate in the countryside than in the ethnic enclaves of the cities. But almost all such ventures failed. The farmers lacked capital, and they were in any case more interested in earning quick money than in permanently sinking roots. Although they huddled in the cities, Italian immigrants did not abandon their rural upbringings entirely. Much to their neighbors' consternation, they often kept chickens in vacant lots and raised vegetables in small garden plots nestled between decaying tenement houses.

Those who bade a permanent farewell to Italy clustered in tightly knit communities that boasted opera clubs, Italian-language newspapers, and courts for playing bocci—a version of lawn bowling imported from the Old Country. Pizza emerged from the hot wood-burning ovens of these Little Italys, its aroma and flavor wafting their way into the hearts and stomachs of all Americans.

Italians typically earned their daily bread as industrial laborers—most famously as longshoremen and construction workers. They owed their prominence in the building trades to the "padrone system." The *padrone,* or labor boss, met immigrants upon arrival and secured jobs for them in New York, Chicago, or wherever there was an immediate demand for industrial labor. The padrone owed his power to his ability to speak both Italian and English, and he often found homes as well as jobs for the newcomers.

Lacking education, the Italians, as a group, remained in blue-collar jobs longer than some of their fellow New Immigrants. Many Italians, valuing vocation over schooling, sent their children off to work as early in their young lives as possible. Before World War I, less than 1 percent of Italian children enrolled in high school. Over the next fifty years, Italian-Americans and their offspring gradually prospered, moving out of the cities into the more affluent suburbs. Many served heroically in World War II and availed themselves of the GI Bill to finance the college educations and professional training their immigrant forebears had lacked.

Jane Addams (1860–1935)   Although Addams never married or bore children of her own, she "mothered" hundreds of youngsters like this one at Hull House, the Chicago settlement house she founded in 1889.

The settlement houses became centers of women's activism and of social reform. The women of Hull House successfully lobbied in 1893 for an Illinois antisweatshop law that protected women workers and prohibited child labor. They were led in this case by the black-clad Florence Kelley, a guerrilla warrior in the urban jungle. Armed with the insights of socialism and endowed with the voice of an actress, Kelley was a lifelong battler for the welfare of women, children, blacks, and consumers. She later moved to the Henry Street Settlement in New York and served for three decades as general secretary of the National Consumers League.

The pioneering work of Addams, Wald, and Kelley helped blaze the trail that many women—and some men—later followed into careers in the new profession of social work. These reformers vividly demonstrated the truth that the city was the frontier of opportunity for women, just as the wilderness had been for men.

The urban frontier opened new possibilities for women. More than a million women joined the work force in the single decade of the 1890s. Strict social codes prescribed which women might work and what jobs they might hold. Because employment for wives and mothers was considered taboo, the vast majority of working women were single. Their jobs depended on their race, ethnicity, and class. Black women had few opportunities beyond domestic service. White-collar jobs as social workers, secretaries, department store clerks, and telephone operators were largely reserved for native-born women. Immigrant women tended to cluster in particular industries, as Jewish women did in the garment trades. Although hours were often long, pay low, and advancement limited, a job still bought working women some economic and social independence. After contributing a large share of their earnings to their families, many women still had enough money in their pocketbooks to enter a new urban world of sociability—excursions to amusement parks with friends on days off, Saturday night dances with the "fellas."

Narrowing the Welcome Mat

Antiforeignism, or "nativism," earlier touched off by the Irish and German arrivals in the 1840s and 1850s, bared its ugly face in the 1880s with fresh ferocity. The New Immigrants had come for much the same reasons as the Old—to escape the poverty and squalor of Europe and to seek new opportunities in America. But "nativists" viewed the eastern and southern Europeans as culturally and religiously exotic hordes and often gave them a rude reception. The newest newcomers aroused widespread alarm. Their high birthrate, common among people with a low standard of living and sufficient youth and vigor to pull up stakes, raised worries that the original Anglo-Saxon stock would soon be outbred and outvoted. Still more horrifying was the prospect that it would be mongrelized by a mixture of "inferior" southern European blood and that the fairer Anglo-Saxon types would disappear. One New England writer cried out in anguish,

O Liberty, white Goddess! is it well
To leave the gates unguarded?

Looking Backward
Older immigrants, trying to keep their own humble arrival in America "in the shadows," sought to close the bridge that had carried them and their ancestors across the Atlantic.

Native born and nativist, sociologist E. A. Ross (1866–1951) condemned the new immigrants as despicable human specimens who threatened to drag down the American race:

"Observe immigrants . . . in their gatherings. You are struck by the fact that from ten to twenty per cent are hirsute, low-browed, big-faced persons of obviously low mentality. . . . They . . . clearly belong in skins, in wattled huts at the close of the Great Ice Age. These oxlike men are descendants of those who always stayed behind."

Taking a very different stance, Jewish immigrant playwright Israel Zangwill (1864–1926) celebrated the new superior American emerging out of what he called "the great melting pot" of European races:

"America is God's crucible, the great melting pot, where all the races of Europe are melting and re-forming! . . . Germans and Frenchmen, Irishmen and Englishmen, Jews and Russians—into the Crucible with you all! God is making the American!"

"Native" Americans voiced additional fears. They blamed the immigrants for the degradation of urban government. Trade unionists assailed the alien arrivals for their willingness to work for "starvation" wages that seemed to them like princely sums and for importing in their intellectual baggage such dangerous doctrines as socialism, communism, and anarchism. Many business leaders, who had welcomed the flood of cheap manual labor, began to fear that they had embraced a Frankenstein's monster.

Antiforeign organizations, reminiscent of the "Know-Nothings" of antebellum days, were now revived in a different guise. Notorious among them was the American Protective Association (APA), which was created in 1887 and soon claimed a million members. In pursuing its nativist goals, the APA urged voting against Roman Catholic candidates for office and sponsored the publication of lustful fantasies about runaway nuns.

Organized labor was quick to throw its growing weight behind the move to choke off the rising tide of foreigners. Frequently used as strikebreakers, the wage-depressing immigrants were hard to unionize because of the language barrier. Labor leaders argued, not illogically, that if American industry was entitled to protection from foreign goods, American workers were entitled to protection from foreign laborers.

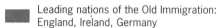

Million

6 ┤   5,789,000

5 ┤

4 ┤

3 ┤

2 ┤

1 ┤

0 ┤
   1871–1880 1881–1890 1891–1900 1901–1910 1911–1920

1,593,000 181,000 2,753,000 926,000 1,110,000 1,847,000 1,069,000 5,789,000 540,000 2,928,000

Old and New Immigration (by decade)
In the 1970s the sources of immigration to the United States shifted yet again. The largest number of immigrants came from Latin America (especially Mexico), the next largest from Asia. The old "mother continent" of Europe accounted for only 10 percent of immigrants to America as the twenty-first century opened. (See the chart on p. 1023.)

▮ Leading nations of the Old Immigration: England, Ireland, Germany

▮ Leading nations of the New Immigration: Italy, Austria– Hungary, Russia

Lady Liberty Being Readied for Travel   A centennial "birthday present" from the French people, the Statue of Liberty arrived from France in 1886.

Congress finally nailed up partial bars against the inpouring immigrants. The first restrictive law, passed in 1882, banged the gate shut in the faces of paupers, criminals, and convicts, all of whom had to be returned at the expense of the greedy or careless shipper. Congress further responded to pained outcries from organized labor when in 1885 it prohibited the importation of foreign workers under contract—usually for substandard wages.

In later years other federal laws lengthened the list of undesirables to include the insane, polygamists, prostitutes, alcoholics, anarchists, and people carrying contagious diseases. A proposed literacy test, long a favorite of nativists because it favored the Old Immigrants over the New, met vigorous opposition. It was not enacted until 1917, after three presidents had vetoed it on the grounds that literacy was more a measure of opportunity than of intelligence.

The year 1882, in addition to the first federal restrictions on immigration, brought forth a law to bar completely one ethnic group—the Chinese (see p. 514). Hitherto America, at least officially, had embraced the oppressed and underprivileged of all races and creeds. Hereafter the gates would be padlocked against defective undesirables—plus the Chinese.

Four years later, in 1886, the Statue of Liberty arose in New York harbor, a gift from the people of France. On its base were inscribed the words of Emma Lazarus:

Give me your tired, your poor
Your huddled masses yearning to breathe free,
The wretched refuse of your teeming shore.

To many nativists, those noble words described only too accurately the "scum" washed up by the New Immigrant tides. Yet the uprooted immigrants, unlike "natives" lucky enough to have had parents who caught an earlier ship, became American citizens the hard way. These new immigrants stepped off the boat, many of them full-grown and well muscled, ready to put their shoulders to the nation's industrial wheels. The Republic owes much to these latercomers—for their brawn, their brains, their courage, and the yeasty diversity they brought to American society.

Churches Confront the Urban Challenge

The swelling size and changing character of the urban population posed sharp challenges to American churches, which, like other national institutions, had grown up in the country. Protestant churches, in particular, suffered heavily from the shift to the city, where many of their traditional doctrines and pastoral approaches seemed irrelevant. Some of the larger houses of worship, with their stained-glass windows and thundering pipe organs, were tending to become merely sacred diversions or amusements. Reflecting the wealth of their prosperous parishioners, many of the old-line churches were distressingly slow to raise their voices against social and economic vices. John D. Rockefeller was a pillar of the Baptist Church, J. Pierpont Morgan of the Episcopal Church. Trinity Episcopal Church in New York actually owned some of the city's worst slum property. Cynics remarked that the Episcopal Church had become "the Republican party at prayer." Some religious leaders began to worry that in the age-old struggle between God and the Devil, the Wicked One was registering dismaying gains. The mounting emphasis was on materialism; too many devotees worshiped at the altar of avarice. Money was the accepted measure of achievement, and the new gospel of wealth proclaimed that God caused the righteous to prosper.

Into this spreading moral vacuum stepped a new generation of urban revivalists. Most conspicuous was a former Chicago shoe salesman, Dwight Lyman Moody. Like many of those to whom he preached, Moody was a country boy who had made good in the big city. Proclaiming a gospel of kindness and forgiveness, Moody was a modern urban circuit rider who took his message to countless American cities in the 1870s and 1880s. Clad in a dark business suit, the bearded and rotund Moody held huge audiences spellbound. When he preached in Brooklyn, special trolley tracks had to be laid to carry the crowds who wanted to hear him. Moody contributed powerfully to adapting the old-time religion to the facts of city life. The Moody Bible Institute founded in Chicago in 1889 continued to carry on his work after his death in 1899.

Simultaneously, the Roman Catholic and Jewish faiths were gaining enormous strength from the New Immigration. By 1900 the Roman Catholics had increased their lead as the largest single denomination, numbering nearly 9 million communicants. Roman Catholic and Jewish groups kept the common touch better than many of the leading Protestant churches. Cardinal Gibbons (1834–1921), an urban Catholic leader devoted to American unity, was immensely popular with Roman Catholics and Protestants alike. Acquainted with every president from Johnson to Harding, he employed his liberal sympathies to assist the American labor movement.

By 1890 the variety-loving Americans could choose from 150 religious denominations, 2 of them newcomers. One was the band-playing Salvation Army, whose soldiers without swords invaded America from England in 1879 and established a beachhead on the street corners. Appealing frankly to the down-and-outers, the boldly named Salvation Army did much practical good, especially with free soup.

Mary Baker Eddy (1821–1910)   The founder of the Christian Science Church declared in her *Science and Health,* "We classify disease as error, which nothing but Truth or Mind can heal, and this Mind must be divine, not human."

The other important new faith was the Church of Christ, Scientist (Christian Science), founded by Mary Baker Eddy in 1879, after she had suffered much ill health. Preaching that the true practice of Christianity heals sickness, she set forth her views in a book entitled *Science and Health with Key to the Scriptures* (1875), which sold an amazing 400,000 copies before her death. A fertile field for converts was found in America's hurried, nerve-racked, and urbanized civilization, to which Eddy held out the hope of relief from discords and diseases through prayer as taught by Christian Science. By the time she died in 1910, she had founded an influential church that embraced several hundred thousand devoted worshipers.

Urbanites also participated in a new kind of religious-affiliated organization, the Young Men's and Women's Christian Associations. The YMCA and the YWCA, established in the United States before the Civil War, grew by leaps and bounds. Combining physical and other kinds of education with religious instruction, the "Y's" appeared in virtually every major American city by the end of the nineteenth century.

Darwin Disrupts the Churches

The old-time religion received many blows from modern trends, including a booming sale of books on comparative religion and on historical criticism as applied to the Bible. Most unsettling of all was *On the Origin of Species,* a highly controversial volume published in 1859, on the eve of the Civil War, by the English naturalist Charles Darwin. He set forth in lucid form the sensational theory that humans had slowly evolved from lower forms of life—a theory that was soon summarized to mean "the survival of the fittest."

Evolution cast serious doubt on a literal interpretation of the Bible, which relates how God created the heaven and the earth in six days. The Conservatives, or "Fundamentalists," stood firmly on the Scripture as the inspired and infallible Word of God, and they condemned what they thought was the "bestial hypothesis" of the Darwinians. The "Modernists" parted company with the "Fundamentalists" and flatly refused to accept the Bible in its entirety as either history or science.

This furious battle over Darwinism created rifts in the churches and colleges of the post–Civil War era. "Modernist" clergymen were removed from their pulpits; teachers of biology who embraced evolution were dismissed from their chairs. But as time wore on, an increasing number of liberal thinkers were able to reconcile Darwinism with Christianity. They heralded the revolutionary theory as a newer and grander revelation of the ways of the Almighty. As one commentator observed,

> *Some call it Evolution,*
> *And others call it God.*

But Darwinism undoubtedly did much to loosen religious moorings and to promote unbelief among the gospel-glutted. The most bitterly denounced skeptic of the era was a golden-tongued orator, Colonel Robert G. Ingersoll, who lectured widely on "Some Mistakes of Moses" and "Why I Am an Agnostic." He might have gone far in public life if he had stuck to politics and refrained from attacking orthodox religion by "giving hell hell," as he put it.

The Lust for Learning

Public education continued its upward climb. The ideal of tax-supported elementary schools, adopted on a nationwide basis before the Civil War, was still gathering strength. Americans were accepting the truism that a free government cannot function successfully if the people are shackled by ignorance. Beginning about 1870, more and more states were making at least a grade-school education compulsory, and this gain, incidentally, helped check the frightful abuses of child labor.

Spectacular indeed was the spread of high schools, especially by the 1880s and 1890s. Before the Civil War, private academies at the secondary level were common, and tax-supported high schools were rare, numbering only a few hundred. But the concept was now gaining impressive support that a high-school education, as well as a grade-school education, was the birthright of every citizen. By 1900 there were some six thousand high schools. In addition, free textbooks were being provided in increasing quantities by the taxpayers of the states during the last two decades of the century.

Other trends were noteworthy. Teacher-training schools, then called "normal schools," experienced a striking expansion after the Civil War. In 1860 there were only twelve of them, in 1910 over three hundred. Kindergartens, earlier borrowed from Germany, also began to gain strong support. The New

Immigration in the 1880s and 1890s brought vast new strength to the private Catholic parochial schools, which were fast becoming a major pillar of the nation's educational structure.

Public schools, though showering benefits on children, excluded millions of adults. This deficiency was partially remedied by the Chautauqua movement, a successor to the lyceums, which was launched in 1874 on the shores of Lake Chautauqua, in New York. The organizers achieved gratifying success through nationwide public lectures, often held in tents and featuring well-known speakers, including the witty Mark Twain. In addition, there were extensive Chautauqua courses of home study, for which 100,000 people enrolled in 1892 alone.

Crowded cities, despite their cancers, generally provided better educational facilities than the old one-room, one-teacher red schoolhouse. The success of the public schools·is confirmed by the falling of the illiteracy rate from 20 percent in 1870 to 10.7 percent in 1900. Americans were developing a profound faith, often misplaced, in formal education as the sovereign remedy for their ills.

Booker T. Washington and Education for Black People

War-torn and impoverished, the South lagged far behind other regions in public education, and African-Americans suffered most severely. A staggering 44 percent of nonwhites were illiterate in 1900. Some help came from northern philanthropists, but the foremost champion of black education was an ex-slave, Booker T. Washington, who had slept under a board sidewalk to save pennies for his schooling. Called in 1881 to head the black normal and industrial school at Tuskegee, Alabama, he began with forty students in a tumbledown shanty. Undaunted, he taught black students useful trades so that they could gain self-respect and economic security. Washington's self-help approach to solving the nation's racial problems was labeled "accommodationist" because it stopped short of directly challenging white supremacy. Recognizing the depths of southern white racism, Washington avoided the issue of *social* equality. Instead he grudgingly acquiesced in segregation in return for the right to develop—however modestly and painstakingly—the economic and educational resources of the

Booker T. Washington (1856–1915) Addresses a New Orleans Audience In a famous speech in 1895, Washington acquiesced in social separateness for blacks. On that occasion, he told his largely white audience: "In all things that are purely social, we can be as separate as the fingers, yet one as the hand in all things essential to mutual progress."

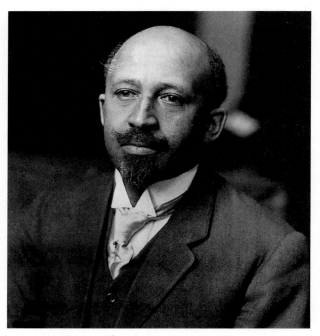

W. E. B. Du Bois (1868–1963) At the end of a long lifetime of struggle for racial justice in the United States, Du Bois renounced his American citizenship in 1961, at the age of ninety-three, and took up residence in the newly independent African state of Ghana.

black community. Economic independence would ultimately be the ticket, Washington believed, to black political and civil rights.

Washington's commitment to training young blacks in agriculture and the trades guided the curriculum at Tuskegee Institute and made it an ideal place for slave-born George Washington Carver to teach and research. After Carver joined the faculty in 1896, he became an internationally famous agricultural chemist who provided a much-needed boost to the southern economy by discovering hundreds of new uses for the lowly peanut (shampoo, axle grease), sweet potato (vinegar), and soybean (paint).

Other black leaders, notably Dr. W. E. B. Du Bois, assailed Booker T. Washington as an "Uncle Tom" who was condemning their race to manual labor and perpetual inferiority. Born in Massachusetts, Du Bois was a mixture of African, French, Dutch, and Indian blood ("Thank God, no Anglo-Saxon," he would add). After a determined struggle, he earned a Ph.D. at Harvard, the first of his race to

achieve this goal. ("The honor, I assure you, was Harvard's," he said.) He demanded complete equality for blacks, social as well as economic, and helped to found the National Association for the Advance-

> *W. E. B. Du Bois (1868–1963) wrote in his 1903 classic,* The Souls of Black Folk,
>
> "It is a peculiar sensation, this double-consciousness, this sense of always looking at one's self through the eyes of others, of measuring one's self through the eyes of others. . . . One ever feels his two-ness—an American, a Negro; two souls, two thoughts, two unreconciled strivings; two warring ideals in one dark body, whose dogged strength alone keeps it from being torn asunder."

ment of Colored People (NAACP) in 1910. Rejecting Washington's gradualism and separatism, he demanded that the "talented tenth" of the black community be given full and immediate access to the mainstream of American life. An exceptionally skilled historian, sociologist, and poet, he died as a self-exile in Africa in 1963, at the age of ninety-five. Many of Du Bois's differences with Washington reflected the contrasting life experiences of southern and northern blacks.

The Hallowed Halls of Ivy

Colleges and universities also shot up like lusty young saplings in the decades after the Civil War. A college education increasingly seemed indispensable in the scramble for the golden apple of success. The educational battle for women, only partially won before the war, now turned into a rout of the masculine diehards. Women's colleges such as Vassar were gaining ground, and universities open to both genders were blossoming, notably in the Midwest.

By 1900 every fourth college graduate was a woman. By the turn of the century as well, the black institutes and academies planted during Reconstruction had blossomed into a crop of southern black colleges. Howard University in Washington, D.C., Hampton Institute in Virginia, Atlanta University, and numerous others nurtured higher education for blacks until the civil rights movement of the 1960s made attendance at white institutions possible.

The truly phenomenal growth of higher education owed much to the Morrill Act of 1862. This enlightened law, passed after the South had seceded, provided a generous grant of the public lands to the states for support of education. "Land-grant colleges," most of which became state universities, in turn bound themselves to provide certain services, such as military training. The Hatch Act of 1887, extending the Morrill Act, provided federal funds for the establishment of agricultural experiment stations in connection with the land-grant colleges.

Private philanthropy richly supplemented federal grants to higher education. Many of the new industrial millionaires, developing tender social

Educational Levels, 1870–2000

Year	Number Graduating from High School	Number Graduating from College	Median School Years Completed Completed (Years)*	High School Graduates as a Percentage of 17-Year-Old Population
1870	16,000	9,371		2.0%
1880	24,000	12,896		2.5
1890	44,000	15,539		3.5
1900	95,000	27,410		6.4
1910	156,000	37,199	8.1[†]	8.8
1920	311,000	48,622	8.2[†]	16.8
1930	667,000	122,484	8.4[†]	29.0
1940	1,221,000	186,500	8.6	50.8
1950	1,199,700	432,058	9.3	59.0
1960	1,858,000	392,440	10.5	69.5
1970	2,889,000	792,656	12.2	76.9
1980	3,043,000	929,417	12.5	71.4
1990	2,503,000	1,048,631	12.7	74.2
2000	2,875,000 (est.)	1,173,000 (est.)	N.A.	N.A.

*People twenty-five years and over.
[†]1910–1930 based on retrogressions of 1940 data; 1940 was the first year measured (Folger and Nam, *Education of the American Population,* a 1960 Census Monograph).
(Sources: *Digest of Education Statistics,* 1992, a publication of the National Center for Education Statistics, and *Statistical Abstract of the United States,* relevant years.)

consciences, donated immense fortunes to educational enterprises. A philanthropist was cynically described as "one who steals privately and gives publicly." In the twenty years from 1878 to 1898, these money barons gave away about $150 million. Noteworthy among the new private universities of high quality to open were Cornell (1865) and Leland Stanford Junior (1891), the latter founded in memory of the deceased fifteen-year-old only child of a builder of the Central Pacific Railroad. The University of Chicago, opened in 1892, speedily forged into a front-rank position, owing largely to the lubricant of John D. Rockefeller's oil millions. Rockefeller died at ninety-seven, after having given some $550 million for philanthropic purposes.

Significant also was the sharp increase in professional and technical schools, where modern laboratories were replacing the solo experiments performed by instructors in front of their classes. Towering among the specialized institutions was Johns Hopkins University, opened in 1876, which maintained the nation's first high-grade graduate school. Several generations of American scholars, repelled by snobbish English cousins and attracted by painstaking Continental methods, had attended German universities. Johns Hopkins ably carried on the Germanic tradition of profusely footnoted tomes. Reputable scholars no longer had to go abroad for a gilt-edged graduate degree. Dr. Woodrow Wilson, among others, received his Ph.D. from Johns Hopkins.

The March of the Mind

Cut-and-dried, the old classical curriculum in the colleges was on the way out, as the new industrialization brought insistent demands for "practical" courses and specialized training in the sciences. The elective system, which permitted students to choose more courses in cafeteria fashion, was gaining popularity. It received a powerful boost in the 1870s when Dr. Charles W. Eliot, a vigorous young chemist, became president of Harvard College and embarked upon a lengthy career of educational statesmanship.

Medical schools and medical science after the Civil War were prospering. Despite the enormous sale of patent medicines and so-called Indian remedies—"good for man or beast"—the new scientific

gains were reflected in improved public health. Revolutionary discoveries abroad, such as those of the French scientist Louis Pasteur and the English physician Joseph Lister, left their imprint on America.* The popularity of heavy whiskers waned as the century ended; such hairy adornments were now coming to be regarded as germ traps. As a result of new health-promoting precautions, including campaigns against public spitting, life expectancy at birth was measurably increased.

One of America's most brilliant intellectuals, the slight and sickly William James (1842–1910), served for thirty-five years on the Harvard faculty. Through his numerous writings, he made a deep mark on many fields. His *Principles of Psychology* (1890) helped to establish the modern discipline of behavioral psychology. In *The Will to Believe* (1897) and *Varieties of Religious Experience* (1902), he explored the philosophy and psychology of religion. In his most famous work, *Pragmatism* (1907), he colorfully described America's greatest contribution to the history of philosophy. The concept of pragmatism held that truth was to be tested, above all, by the practical consequences of an idea, by action rather than theories. This kind of reasoning aptly expressed the philosophical temperament of a nation of doers.

The Appeal of the Press

Books continued to be a major source of edification and enjoyment, for both juveniles and adults. Bestsellers of the 1880s were generally old favorites like *David Copperfield* and *Ivanhoe*.

Well-stocked public libraries—the poor person's university—were making encouraging progress, especially in Boston and New York. The magnificent Library of Congress building, which opened its doors in 1897, provided thirteen acres of floor space in the largest and costliest edifice of its kind in the world. A new era was inaugurated by the generous gifts of Andrew Carnegie. This openhanded Scotsman, book-starved in his youth, contributed $60 million for the construction of public libraries all over the country. By 1900 there were about nine

---

*From Pasteur came the word *pasteurize;* from Lister came *Listerine.*

The "Penny Press"
The *Chicago Daily News* was but one of several cheap, mass-circulation newspapers that flourished in the new urban environment of Gilded Age America.

human-interest stories burst into the headlines, as a vulgarization of the press accompanied the growth of circulation. Critics now complained in vain of these "presstitutes."

Two new journalistic tycoons emerged. Joseph Pulitzer, Hungarian-born and near-blind, was a leader in the techniques of sensationalism in St. Louis and especially with the *New York World*. His use of the colored comic supplements, featuring the "Yellow Kid," gave the name *yellow journalism* to his lurid sheets. A close and ruthless competitor was youthful William Randolph Hearst, who had been expelled from Harvard College for a crude prank. Able to draw on his California father's mining millions, he ultimately built up a powerful chain of newspapers, beginning with the *San Francisco Examiner* in 1887.

Unfortunately, the overall influence of Pulitzer and Hearst was not altogether wholesome. Although both championed many worthy causes, both prostituted the press in their struggle for increased circulation; both "stooped, snooped, and scooped to conquer." Their flair for scandal and sensational rumor was happily somewhat offset by the introduction of syndicated material and by the strengthening of the news-gathering Associated Press, which had been founded in the 1840s.

Apostles of Reform

Magazines partially satisfied the public appetite for good reading, notably old standbys like *Harper's*, the *Atlantic Monthly*, and *Scribner's Monthly*. Possibly the most influential journal of all was the liberal and highly intellectual New York *Nation*, which was read largely by professors, preachers, and publicists as "the weekly Day of Judgment." Launched in 1865 by the Irish-born Edwin L. Godkin, a merciless critic, it crusaded militantly for civil-service reform, honesty in government, and a moderate tariff. The *Nation* attained only a modest circulation—about 10,000 in the nineteenth century—but Godkin believed that if he could reach the right 10,000 leaders, his ideas through them might reach the 10 millions.

Another journalist-author, Henry George, was an original thinker who left an enduring mark. Poor in formal schooling, he was rich in idealism and in the milk of human kindness. After seeing poverty at its worst in India and land-grabbing at its greediest

thousand free circulating libraries in America, each with at least three hundred books.

Roaring newspaper presses, spurred by the invention of the Linotype in 1885, more than kept pace with the demands of a word-hungry public. But the heavy investment in machinery and plant was accompanied by a growing fear of offending advertisers and subscribers. Bare-knuckle editorials were, to an increasing degree, being supplanted by feature articles and noncontroversial syndicated material. The day of slashing journalistic giants like Horace Greeley was passing.

Sensationalism, at the same time, was capturing the public taste. The semiliterate immigrants, combined with straphanging urban commuters, created a profitable market for news that was simply and punchily written. Sex, scandal, and other

Henry George (1839–1897) wrote in Progress and Poverty *(1879),*

"Our boasted freedom necessarily involves slavery, so long as we recognize private property in land. Until that is abolished, Declarations of Independence and Acts of Emancipation are in vain. So long as one man can claim the exclusive ownership of the land from which other men must live, slavery will exist, and as material progresses on, must grow and deepen!"

in California, he took pen in hand. His classic treatise *Progress and Poverty* undertook to solve "the great enigma of our times"—"the association of progress with poverty." According to George, the pressure of growing population on a fixed supply of land unjustifiably pushed up property values, showering unearned profits on owners of land. A single 100 percent tax on those windfall profits would eliminate unfair inequalities and stimulate economic growth.

George soon became a most controversial figure. His single-tax ideas were so horrifying to the propertied classes that his manuscript was rejected by numerous publishers. Finally brought out in 1879, the book gradually broke into the best-seller lists and ultimately sold some 3 million copies. George also lectured widely in America, where he influenced thinking about the maldistribution of wealth, and in Britain, where he left an indelible mark on English Fabian socialism.

Edward Bellamy, a quiet Massachusetts Yankee, was another journalist-reformer of remarkable power. In 1888 he published a socialistic novel, *Looking Backward,* in which the hero, falling into a hypnotic sleep, awakens in the year 2000. He "looks backward" and finds that the social and economic injustices of 1887 have melted away under an idyllic government, which has nationalized big business to serve the public interest. To a nation already alarmed by the trust evil, the book had a magnetic appeal and sold over a million copies. Scores of Bellamy Clubs sprang up to discuss this mild utopian socialism, and they heavily influenced American reform movements near the end of the century.

Postwar Writing

As literacy increased, so did book reading. Post–Civil War Americans devoured millions of "dime novels," usually depicting the wilds of the woolly West. Paint-bedaubed Indians and quick-triggered gunmen like "Deadwood Dick" shot off vast quantities of powder, and virtue invariably triumphed. These lurid "paperbacks" were frowned upon by parents, but goggle-eyed youths read them in haylofts or in schools behind the broad covers of geography books. The king of dime novelists was Harlan F. Halsey, who made a fortune by dashing off about 650 novels, often one in a day.

General Lewis Wallace—lawyer-soldier-author—was a colorful figure. Having fought with distinction in the Civil War, he sought to combat the prevailing wave of Darwinian skepticism with his novel *Ben Hur: A Tale of the Christ* (1880). A phenomenal success, the book sold an estimated 2 million copies in many languages, including Arabic and Chinese, and later appeared on stage and screen. It was the *Uncle Tom's Cabin* of the anti-Darwinists, who found in it support for the Holy Scriptures.

An even more popular writer was Horatio ("Holy Horatio") Alger, a Puritan-reared New Englander, who in 1866 forsook the pulpit for the pen. Deeply interested in New York newsboys, he wrote more than a hundred volumes of juvenile fiction that sold over 100 million copies. His stock formula was that virtue, honesty, and industry are rewarded by success, wealth, and honor—a kind of survival of the purest, especially nonsmokers, nondrinkers, nonswearers, and nonliars. Although Alger's own bachelor life was criticized, he implanted morality and the conviction that there is always room at the top (especially if one is lucky enough to save the life of the boss's daughter and marry her).

In poetry Walt Whitman was one of the few luminaries of yesteryear who remained active. Although shattered in health by service as a Civil War nurse, he brought out successive—and purified—revisions of his hardy perennial, *Leaves of Grass.* The assassination of Lincoln inspired him to write two of the most moving poems in American literature, "O Captain! My Captain!" and "When Lilacs Last in the Dooryard Bloom'd."

The curious figure of Emily Dickinson, one of America's most gifted lyric poets, did not emerge until 1886, when she died and her poems were dis-

Emily Dickinson (1830–1886)   A great American poet, she pursued intense intellectual relationships with several literary and cultural figures, including the abolitionist Thomas Wentworth Higginson.

Mark Twain (1835–1910)   Born Samuel Langhorne Clemens, he was not only America's most popular author but also a renowned platform lecturer.

covered. A Massachusetts recluse, she wrote over a thousand short lyrics on scraps of paper. Only two were published during her lifetime, and those without her consent. As she wrote,

> *How dreary to be somebody!*
> *How public, like a frog*
> *To tell your name the livelong June*
> *To an admiring bog!*

Among the lesser poetical lights was a tragic southerner, Sidney Lanier (1842–1881). He was oppressed by poverty and ill health, and torn between flute playing and poetry. Dying young of tuberculosis, he wrote some of his finest poems while afflicted with a temperature of 104 degrees. He is perhaps best known for "The Marshes of Glynn," a poem of faith inspired by the current clash between Darwinism and orthodox religion.

Literary Landmarks

In novel writing the romantic sentimentality of a youthful era was giving way to a rugged realism that reflected more faithfully the materialism of an industrial society. American authors now turned increasingly to the coarse human comedy and drama of the world around them to find their subjects.

Two Missouri-born authors with deep connections to the South brought altogether new voices to the late-nineteenth-century literary scene. The daring feminist author Kate Chopin (1851–1904) wrote candidly about adultery, suicide, and women's ambitions in *The Awakening* (1899). Largely ignored in her own day, Chopin was rediscovered by later readers, who cited her work as suggestive of the feminist yearnings that stirred beneath the surface of "respectability" in the Gilded Age.

Mustachioed Mark Twain (1835–1910) had leapt to fame with *The Celebrated Jumping Frog of Calaveras County* (1867) and *The Innocents Abroad* (1869). He teamed up with Charles Dudley Warner in 1873 to write *The Gilded Age*. An acid satire on post–Civil War politicians and speculators, the book gave a name to an era. With his scanty formal schooling in frontier Missouri, Twain typified a new breed of American authors in revolt against the elegant refinements of the old New England school of writing. Christened Samuel Langhorne Clemens, he had served for a time as a Mississippi riverboat pilot and later took his pen name, Mark Twain, from the boatman's cry that meant two fathoms. After a brief stint in the armed forces, Twain journeyed westward to California, a trip he described, with a mixture of truth and tall tales, in *Roughing It* (1872).

Many other books flowed from Twain's busy pen. *The Adventures of Tom Sawyer* (1876) and *The Adventures of Huckleberry Finn* (1884) rank among American masterpieces, though initially regarded as "trash" by snobbish Boston critics. His later years were soured by bankruptcy growing out of unwise investments, and he was forced to take to the lecture platform and amuse what he called "the damned human race." A great tribute was paid to his self-tutored genius—and to American letters—when England's Oxford University awarded him an honorary degree in 1907. Journalist, humorist, satirist, and foe of social injustice, he made his most enduring contribution in recapturing frontier realism and humor in the authentic American dialect.

Another author who wrote out of the West and achieved at least temporary fame and fortune was Bret Harte (1836–1902). A foppishly dressed New Yorker, Harte struck it rich in California with gold-rush stories, especially "The Luck of Roaring Camp" and "The Outcasts of Poker Flat." Catapulted suddenly into notoriety by those stories, he never again matched their excellence or their popularity. He lived out his final years in London as little more than a hack writer.

William Dean Howells (1837–1920), a printer's son from Ohio, could boast of little schoolhouse education, but his busy pen carried him high into the literary circles of the East. In 1871 he became the editor in chief of the prestigious Boston-based *Atlantic Monthly* and was subsequently presented with honorary degrees from six universities, including Oxford. He wrote about ordinary people and about contemporary and sometimes controversial social themes. *A Modern Instance* (1882) deals with the once-taboo subject of divorce; *The Rise of Silas Lapham* (1885) describes the trials of a newly rich paint manufacturer caught up in the caste system of Brahmin Boston. *A Hazard of New Fortunes* (1890) portrays the reformers, strikers, and Socialists in Gilded Age New York.

Stephen Crane (1871–1900), the fourteenth son of a Methodist minister, also wrote about the seamy underside of life in urban, industrial America. His *Maggie: A Girl of the Streets* (1893), a brutal tale about a poor prostitute driven to suicide, was too grim to find a publisher. Crane had to have it printed privately. He rose quickly to prominence with *The Red Badge of Courage* (1895), the stirring story of a bloodied young Civil War recruit ("fresh fish") under fire. Crane himself had never seen a battle and wrote entirely from the printed Civil War records. He died of tuberculosis in 1900, when only twenty-nine.

In 1935 Ernest Hemingway (1899–1961) wrote,

"All modern American literature comes from one book by Mark Twain called *Huckleberry Finn*. . . . All American writing comes from that. There was nothing before. There has been nothing as good since."

Jack London (1876–1916), the socialist who hated strikebreakers known as "scabs," said,

"No man has a right to scab so long as there is a pool of water to drown his carcass in, or a rope long enough to hang his body with. Judas Iscariot was a gentleman compared with a scab. For betraying his master, he had character enough to hang himself. A scab has not."

Henry James (1843–1916), brother of Harvard philosopher William James, was a New Yorker who turned from law to literature. Taking as his dominant theme the confrontation of innocent Americans with subtle Europeans, James penned a remarkable number of brilliant novels, including *Daisy Miller* (1879), *The Portrait of a Lady* (1881), and *The Wings of the Dove* (1902). His book *The Bostonians* (1886) was one of the first novels about the rising feminist movement. James frequently made women his central characters, exploring their inner reactions to complex situations with a deftness that marked him as a master of "psychological realism." Long resident in England, he became a British subject shortly before his death.

Candid portrayals of contemporary life and social problems were the literary order of the day by the turn of the century. Jack London (1876–1916), famous as a nature writer in such books as *The Call of the Wild* (1903), turned to depicting a possible fascistic revolution in *The Iron Heel* (1907). Frank Norris (1870–1902), like London a Californian, wrote *The Octopus* (1901), an earthy saga of the stranglehold of the railroad and corrupt politicians on California wheat ranchers. A sequel, *The Pit* (1903), dealt with the making and breaking of speculators on the Chicago wheat exchange.

Two black writers, Paul Laurence Dunbar (1872–1906) and Charles W. Chesnutt (1858–1932), brought another kind of realism to late-nineteenth-century literature. Dunbar through poetry—particularly his acclaimed *Lyrics of Lowly Life* (1896)—and Chesnutt through fiction—short stories in the *Atlantic Monthly* and *The Conjure Women* (1899)—embraced the use of black dialect and folklore, previously shunned by black authors, to capture the spontaneity and richness of southern black culture.

Conspicuous among the new "social novelists" rising in the literary firmament was Theodore Dreiser (1871–1945), a homely, gangling writer from Indiana. He burst upon the literary scene in 1900 with *Sister Carrie,* a graphically realistic narrative of a poor working girl in Chicago and New York. She becomes one man's mistress, then elopes with another, and finally strikes out on her own to make a career on the stage. The fictional Carrie's disregard for prevailing moral standards so offended Dreiser's publisher that the book was soon withdrawn from circulation, though it later reemerged as an acclaimed American classic.

The New Morality

Victoria Woodhull, who was real flesh and blood, also shook the pillars of conventional morality when she publicly proclaimed her belief in free love in 1871. Woodhull was a beautiful and eloquent divorcée, sometime stockbroker, and tireless femi-

Victoria Woodhull (1838–1927) Pleads for Woman Suffrage Before the House Judiciary Committee, 1871 A colorful and charismatic figure, Woodhull became the first woman to run for the presidency in 1872, as the candidate of the Equal Rights Party.

nist propagandist. Together with her sister, Tennessee Claflin, she published a far-out periodical, *Woodhull and Claflin's Weekly.* The sisters again shocked "respectable" society in 1872 when their journal struck a blow for the new morality by charging that Henry Ward Beecher, the most famous preacher of his day, had for years been carrying on an adulterous affair.

Pure-minded Americans sternly resisted these affronts to their moral principles. Their foremost champion was a portly crusader, Anthony Comstock, who made lifelong war on the "immoral." Armed after 1873 with a federal statute—the notorious "Comstock Law"—this self-appointed defender of sexual purity boasted that he had confiscated no fewer than 202,679 "obscene pictures and photos"; 4,185 "boxes of pills, powders, etc., used by abortionists"; and 26 "obscene pictures, framed on walls of saloons." His proud claim was that he had driven at least fifteen people to suicide.

The antics of the Woodhull sisters and Anthony Comstock exposed to daylight the battle going on in late-nineteenth-century America over sexual attitudes and the place of women. Switchboards and typewriters in the booming cities became increasingly the tools of women's liberation. Economic freedom encouraged sexual freedom, and the "new morality" began to be reflected in soaring divorce rates, the spreading practice of birth control, and increasingly frank discussion of sexual topics. By 1913, said one popular magazine, the chimes had struck "sex o'clock in America."

Families and Women in the City

The new urban environment was hard on families. Paradoxically, the crowded cities were emotionally isolating places. Urban families had to go it alone, separated from clan, kin, and village. As families increasingly became the virtually exclusive arena for intimate companionship and for emotional and psychological satisfaction, they were subjected to unprecedented stress. Many families cracked under the strain. The urban era launched the era of divorce. From the late nineteenth century dates the beginning of the "divorce revolution" that transformed the United States' social landscape in the twentieth century (see the table below).

Urban life also dictated changes in work habits and even in family size. Not only fathers but mothers and even children as young as ten years old often worked, and usually in widely scattered locations. On the farm having many children meant having more hands to help with hoeing and harvesting; but in the city more children meant more mouths to feed, more crowding in sardine-tin tenements, and more human baggage to carry in the uphill struggle for social mobility. Not surprisingly, birthrates were still dropping and family size continued to shrink as the nineteenth century lengthened. Marriages were being delayed, and more couples learned the techniques of birth control. The decline in family size in fact affected rural Americans as well as urban dwellers, and old-stock "natives" as well as new immigrant groups.

Marriages and Divorces, 1890–1997

Year	Marriages	Divorces	Ratio of Divorces to Marriages
1890	570,000	33,461	1 : 17
1900	709,000	55,751	1 : 12
1910	948,166	83,045	1 : 11
1920	1,274,476	170,505	1 : 7
1930	1,126,856	195,961	1 : 5
1940	1,595,879	264,000	1 : 6
1950	1,667,231	385,144	1 : 4.3
1960	1,523,381	393,000	1 : 3.8
1970	2,159,000	708,000	1 : 3
1980	2,390,000	1,189,000	1 : 2
1990	2,443,000	1,182,000	1 : 2
1995	2,336,000	1,169,000	1 : 2
1997	2,383,000	870,000	1 : 2.7

(Source: *Statistical Abstract of the United States,* relevant years.)

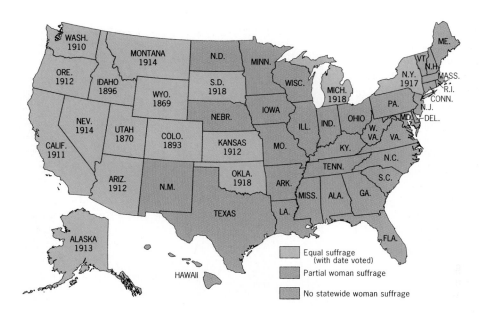

Woman Suffrage Before the Nineteenth Amendment
Dates show when a state or territory adopted woman suffrage. Note the concentration of woman-suffrage states in the West.

Legend:
- Equal suffrage (with date voted)
- Partial woman suffrage
- No statewide woman suffrage

Women were growing more independent in the urban environment, and in 1898 they heard the voice of a major feminist prophet, Charlotte Perkins Gilman. In that year the freethinking and original-minded Gilman published *Women and Economics,* a classic of feminist literature. A distant relative of Harriet Beecher Stowe and Catharine Beecher, Gilman displayed the restless temperament and reforming zeal characteristic of the remarkable Beecher clan. Strikingly handsome, she shunned traditional feminine frills and instead devoted herself to a vigorous regimen of physical exercise and philosophical meditation.

In her masterwork of 1898, Gilman called on women to abandon their dependent status and contribute to the larger life of the community through productive involvement in the economy. Rejecting all claims that biology gave women a fundamentally different character from men, she argued that "our highly specialized motherhood is not so advantageous as believed." She advocated centralized nurseries and cooperative kitchens to facilitate women's participation in the work force—anticipating by more than half a century the day-care centers and convenience-food services of a later day.

Fiery feminists also continued to insist on the ballot. They had been demanding the vote since before the Civil War, but many high-minded female reformers had temporarily shelved the cause of women to battle for the rights of blacks. In 1890 militant suffragists formed the National American

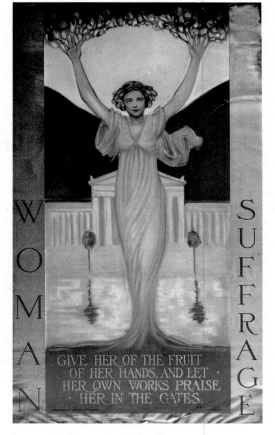

Woman Suffrage, by Evelyn Rumsey Cary
After a century of struggle, women finally won a constitutionally guaranteed right to vote in 1920.

In 1906 progressive reformer Jane Addams (1860–1935) argued that granting women the vote would improve the social and political condition of American cities:

"City housekeeping has failed partly because women, the traditional housekeepers, have not been consulted as to its multiform activities. The men have been carelessly indifferent to much of the civic housekeeping, as they have been indifferent to the details of the household. . . . City government demands the help of minds accustomed to detail and a variety of work, to a sense of obligation to the health and welfare of young children, and to a responsibility for the cleanliness and comfort of other people."

Ida B. Wells In 1892 Wells spearheaded a protest against the heinous lynching of three respected black businessmen in Memphis. Faced with threats on her life, Wells fled from the South, persevering with her tenacious antilynching campaign from the North and from England.

Woman Suffrage Association. Its founders included aging pioneers like Elizabeth Cady Stanton, who had helped organize the first women's rights convention in 1848, and her long-time comrade Susan B. Anthony, the radical Quaker spitfire who had courted jail by trying to cast a ballot in the 1872 presidential election.

By 1900 a new generation of women had taken command of the suffrage battle. Their most effective leader was Carrie Chapman Catt, a pragmatic and businesslike reformer of relentless dedication. Significantly, under Catt the suffragists de-emphasized the argument that women deserved the vote as a matter of right, because they were in all respects the equals of men. Instead Catt stressed the desirability of giving women the vote if they were to continue to discharge their traditional duties as homemakers and mothers in the increasingly public world of the city. Women had special responsibility for the health of the family and the education of children, the argument ran. On the farm, women could discharge these responsibilities in the separate sphere of the isolated homestead. But in the city, they needed a voice on boards of public health, police commissions, and school boards.

By thus linking the ballot to a traditional definition of women's role, suffragists registered encouraging gains as the new century opened, despite continuing showers of rotten eggs and the jeers of male critics who insisted that women were made for loving, not for vot-

ing. Women were increasingly permitted to vote in local elections, particularly on issues related to the schools. Wyoming Territory—later called "the Equality State"—granted the first unrestricted suffrage to women in 1869. This important breach in the dike once made, many states followed Wyoming's example. Paralleling these triumphs, most of the states by 1890 had passed laws to permit wives to own or control their property after marriage. City life also fostered the growth of a spate of women's organizations, including the General Federation of Women's Clubs, which counted some 200,000 members in 1900.

The reborn suffrage movement and other women's organizations excluded black women from their ranks. Fearful that an integrated campaign would compromise its efforts to get the vote, the

National American Woman Suffrage Association limited membership to whites. Black women, however, created their own associations. Journalist and teacher Ida B. Wells inspired black women to mount a nationwide antilynching crusade. She also helped launch the black women's club movement, which culminated in the establishment of the National Association of Colored Women in 1896.

Prohibition of Alcohol and Social Progress

Alarming gains by Demon Rum spurred the temperance reformers to redoubled zeal. Especially obnoxious to them was the shutter-doored corner saloon, appropriately called "the poor man's club." The barroom helped keep both him and his family poor.

Liquor consumption had increased during the nerve-racking days of the Civil War, and immigrant groups, accustomed to alcohol in the Old Country, were hostile to restraints. Whiskey-loving foreigners in Boston would rudely hiss temperance lecturers. Many tipplers charged, with some accuracy, that temperance reform amounted to a middle-class assault on working-class lifestyles.

The National Prohibition party, organized in 1869, polled a sprinkling of votes in some of the ensuing presidential elections. Among the favorite songs of these sober souls were "I'll Marry No Man If He Drinks," "Vote Down the Vile Traffic," and "The Drunkard's Doom." Typical was this:

> *Now, all young men, a warning take,*
> *And shun the poisoned bowl;*
> *'Twill lead you down to hell's dark gate,*
> *And ruin your own soul.*

Carrie Nation Advertised as a Lecturer
She holds her famous hatchet. Carrie Nation took her antidrink crusade to several universities, including Harvard and Yale, which she denounced as "hellholes." Predictably, the students greeted her with wild burlesque.

Clara Barton (1821–1912)
A shy Massachusetts schoolteacher, afflicted by nervous breakdowns in her early life, she was inspired by her nursing work during the Civil War to found the American Red Cross in 1881 and served as its president until 1904. She is shown here in an 1866 portrait by famed Civil War photographer Matthew Brady.

Militant women entered the alcoholic arena, notably when the Woman's Christian Temperance Union (WCTU) was organized in 1874. The white ribbon was its symbol of purity; the saintly Frances E. Willard—also a champion of planned parenthood—was its leading spirit. Less saintly was a muscular and mentally deranged "Kansas Cyclone," Carrie A. Nation, whose first husband had died of alcoholism. With her hatchet she boldly smashed saloon bottles and bars, and her "hatchetations" brought considerable disrepute to the prohibition movement because of the violence of her one-woman crusade.

But rum was now on the run. The potent Anti-Saloon League was formed in 1893, with its members singing "The Saloon Must Go" and "Vote for Cold Water, Boys." Female supporters sang "The Lips That Touch Liquor Must Never Touch Mine." Statewide prohibition, which had made surprising gains in Maine and elsewhere before the Civil War, was sweeping new states into the "dry" column. The great triumph—but only a temporary one—came in 1919, when the national prohibition amendment (Eighteenth) was attached to the Constitution.

Banners of other social crusaders were aloft. The American Society for the Prevention of Cruelty to Animals was created in 1866, after its founder had witnessed brutality to horses in Russia. The American Red Cross was launched in 1881, with the dynamic and diminutive five-foot-tall Clara Barton, an "angel" of Civil War battlefields, at the helm.

Artistic Triumphs

John Adams had anticipated that his generation's preoccupation with nation building would allow art to flourish in the future, but the results long proved unspectacular. Portrait painting continued to appeal, as it had since the colonial era, but many of America's finest painters made their living abroad. James Whistler (1834–1903) did much of his work, including the celebrated portrait of his mother, in England. This eccentric and quarrelsome Massachusetts Yankee had earlier been dropped from West Point after failing chemistry. "Had silicon been a gas," he later jested, "I would have been a major general." Another gifted portrait painter, likewise self-exiled in England, was John Singer Sargent (1856–1925). His flattering but somewhat superficial likenesses of the British nobility were highly prized. Mary Cassatt, an American in exile in Paris, painted sensitive portrayals of women and children that earned her a place in the pantheon of the French impressionist painters.

Other brush wielders, no less talented, brightened the artistic horizon. Self-taught George Inness (1825–1894), who looked like a fanatic with his long hair and piercing gaze, became America's leading landscapist. Thomas Eakins (1844–1916) attained a high degree of realism in his paintings, a quality not appreciated by portrait sitters who wanted their moles overlooked. Boston-born Winslow Homer (1836–1910), who as a youth had secretly drawn sketches in school, was perhaps the greatest painter of the group. Earthily American and largely resistant to foreign influences, he revealed rugged realism and boldness of conception. His canvases of the sea and of fisherfolk were masterly, and probably no American artist has excelled him in portraying the awesome power of the ocean.

Probably the most gifted sculptor yet produced by America was Augustus Saint-Gaudens (1848–1907). Born in Ireland of an Irish mother and a French father, he became an adopted American. Among his most moving works is the Robert Gould Shaw memorial, erected in Boston in 1897. It depicts Colonel Shaw, a young white "Boston Brahmin" officer, leading his black troops into battle in the Civil War.

Music, too, was gaining popularity. America of the 1880s and 1890s was assembling high-quality symphony orchestras, notably in Boston and Chicago. The famed Metropolitan Opera House of New York was erected in 1883. In its fabled "Diamond Horseshoe," the newly rich, often under the pretense of enjoying the imported singers, would flaunt their jewels, gowns, and furs. While symphonies and operas were devoted to bringing European music to elite American audiences, new strains of homegrown American music were sprouting in the South. Black folk traditions like spirituals and "ragged music" were evolving into the blues, ragtime, and jazz, which would transform American popular music in the twentieth century.

A marvelous discovery was the reproduction of music by mechanical means. The phonograph, though a squeakily imperfect instrument when invented by the deaf Edison, had by 1900 reached over 150,000 homes. Americans were rapidly being dosed with "canned music," as the "sitting room" piano increasingly gathered dust.

In addition to skyscraper builder Louis Sullivan, a famous American architect of the age was Henry H. Richardson. Born in Louisiana and educated at

Harvard and in Paris, Richardson settled in Boston and from there spread his immense influence throughout the eastern half of the United States. He popularized a distinctive, ornamental style that came to be known as "Richardsonian." High-vaulted arches, like those on Gothic churches, were his trademark. His masterpiece and most famous work was the Marshall Field Building (1885) in Chicago. Enjoying his success, Richardson was noted for his capacity for champagne, his love of laughter, and the bright yellow vests he sported.

A revival of classical architectural forms—and a setback for realism—came with the great Columbian Exposition. Held in Chicago in 1893, it honored the four-hundredth anniversary of Columbus's first voyage. This so-called dream of loveliness, which was visited by 27 million people, did much to raise American artistic standards and promote city planning, although many of the spectators were attracted primarily by the contortions of a hootchy-kootchy dancer, "Little Egypt."

> *Hamlin Garland (1860–1940), the well-known novelist and writer of short stories, was immensely impressed by the cultural value of Chicago's Columbian Exposition. He wrote to his aged parents on their Dakota farm,*
>
> "Sell the cook stove if necessary and come. You *must* see this fair."

The Business of Amusement

Fun and frolic were not neglected by the workaday American. The pursuit of happiness, heralded in the Declaration of Independence, had by century's end

Buffalo Bill's Wild West Show, c. 1907   By the late 1800s, the "Wild West" was already passing into the realm of myth—and popular entertainment. Famed frontiersman William F. ("Buffalo Bill") Cody made his fortune showing off his tame cowboys and Indians to urban audiences.

The New Woman, by Edward Lamson Henry, 1892 Bicycling appealed to young women eager to escape nineteenth-century strictures against female exercise and bodily exposure. This young female cyclist, pedaling on her own and free of corsets and elaborate clothing, both shocked and amused an older generation.

become a frenzied scramble. People sought their pleasures fiercely, as they had overrun their continent fiercely. And now they had more time to play.

Varied diversions beckoned. As a nation of "joiners" contemptuous of royalty, Americans inconsistently sought to escape from democratic equality in the aristocratic hierarchies of lodges. The legitimate stage still flourished, as appreciative audiences responded to the lure of the footlights. Vaudeville, with its coarse jokes and graceful acrobats, continued to be immensely popular during the 1880s and 1890s, as were minstrel shows in the South, now performed by black singers and dancers rather than by blackfaced whites as in the North before the Civil War.

The circus—high-tented and multiringed—finally emerged full-blown. Phineas T. Barnum, the master showman who had early discovered that "the public likes to be humbugged," joined hands with James A. Bailey in 1881 to stage the "Greatest Show on Earth."*

Colorful "Wild West" shows, first performed in 1883, were even more distinctively American. Headed by the knightly, goateed, and free-drinking William F. ("Buffalo Bill") Cody, the troupe included war-whooping Indians, live buffalo, and deadeye marksmen. Among them was the girlish Annie Oak-

ley. Rifle in hand, she could at thirty paces perforate a tossed-up card half a dozen times before it fluttered to the ground (hence the term *Annie Oakley* for a punched ticket, later for a free pass).

Baseball, already widely played before the Civil War, was clearly emerging as the national pastime, if not a national mania. A league of professional players was formed in the 1870s, and in 1888 an all-star baseball team toured the world, using the pyramids as a backstop while in Egypt.

A gladiatorial trend toward spectator sports, rather than participative sports, was exemplified by football. This rugged game, with its dangerous flying wedge, had become popular well before 1889, when Yaleman Walter C. Camp chose his first "All American" team. The Yale-Princeton game of 1893 drew fifty thousand cheering fans, while foreigners jeered that the nation was getting sports "on the brain."

Even pugilism, with its long background of bare-knuckle brutality, gained a new and gloved respectability in 1892. Agile "Gentleman Jim" Corbett, a scientific boxer, wrestled the world championship from the aging and alcoholic John L. Sullivan, the fabulous "Boston Strong Boy."

Two crazes swept the country in the closing decades of the century. Croquet became all the rage, though condemned by moralists of the "naughty nineties" because it exposed feminine ankles and promoted flirtation. The low-framed "safety" bicycle came to replace the high-seated model. By 1893

---

*Now Ringling Bros. and Barnum & Bailey Circus.

a million bicycles were in use, and thousands of young women, jokesters remarked, were turning to this new "spinning wheel," one that offered freedom, not tedium.

Basketball was invented in 1891 by James Naismith, a YMCA instructor in Springfield, Massachusetts. Designed as an active indoor sport that could be played during the winter months, it spread rapidly and enjoyed enormous popularity in the next century.

The land of the skyscraper was plainly becoming more standardized, owing largely to the new industrialization. Although race and ethnicity assigned urban Americans to distinctive neighborhoods and workplaces, to an increasing degree they shared a common popular culture—playing, reading, shopping, and talking alike. As the century drew to a close, the explosion of cities paradoxically made Americans more diverse and more similar at the same time.

Chronology

1859 Charles Darwin publishes *On the Origin of Species*

1862 Morrill Act provides public land for higher education

1866 American Society for the Prevention of Cruelty to Animals (ASPCA) created

1869 Wyoming Territory grants women the right to vote

1871 *Woodhull and Claflin's Weekly* published

1873 Comstock Law passed

1874 Woman's Christian Temperance Union (WCTU) organized
Chautauqua education movement launched

1876 Johns Hopkins University graduate school established

1879 Henry George publishes *Progress and Poverty*
Dumbbell tenement introduced
Mary Baker Eddy establishes Christian Science
Salvation Army begins work in America

1881 Booker T. Washington becomes head of Tuskegee Institute
American Red Cross founded
Barnum and Bailey first join to stage the "Greatest Show on Earth"

1882 First immigration-restriction laws passed

1883 Brooklyn Bridge completed
Metropolitan Opera House built in New York

1884 Mark Twain publishes *The Adventures of Huckleberry Finn*

1885 Louis Sullivan builds the first skyscraper, in Chicago
Linotype invented

1886 Statue of Liberty erected in New York harbor

1887 American Protective Association (APA) formed
Hatch Act supplements Morrill Act

1888 Edward Bellamy publishes *Looking Backward*
American all-star baseball team tours the world

1889 Jane Addams founds Hull House in Chicago
Moody Bible Institute established in Chicago

1890 National American Woman Suffrage Association formed

1891 Basketball invented

1893 Lillian Wald opens Henry Street Settlement in New York
Anti-Saloon League formed
Columbian Exposition held in Chicago

1897 Library of Congress opens

1898 Charlotte Perkins Gilman publishes *Women and Economics*

1899 Kate Chopin publishes *The Awakening*

1900 Theodore Dreiser publishes *Sister Carrie*

1910 National Association for the Advancement of Colored People (NAACP) founded

For further reading, see page A18 of the Appendix. For web resources, go to **http://college.hmco.com.**

The Great West and the Agricultural Revolution

1865–1896

Up to our own day American history has been in a large degree the history of the colonization of the Great West. The existence of an area of free land, its continuous recession, and the advance of American settlement westward, explain American development.

FREDERICK JACKSON TURNER, 1893

When the Civil War crashed to a close, the frontier line was still wavering westward. A long fringe of settlement, bulging outward here and there, ran roughly north through central Texas and on to the Canadian border. Between this jagged line and the settled areas on the Pacific slope, there were virtually no white people. The few exceptions were the islands of Mormons in Utah, occasional trading posts and gold camps, and several scattered Spanish-Mexican settlements throughout the Southwest.

Sprawling in expanse, the Great West was a rough square that measured about a thousand miles on each side. Embracing mountains, plateaus, deserts, and plains, it was the habitat of the Indian, the buffalo, the wild horse, the prairie dog, and the coyote. Twenty-five years later—that is, by 1890—the entire domain had been carved into states and the four territories of Utah, Arizona, New Mexico, and "Indian Territory," or Oklahoma. Pioneers flung themselves greedily on this enormous prize, as if to ravish it. Probably never before in human experience had so huge an area been transformed so rapidly.

The Clash of Cultures on the Plains

Native Americans numbered about 360,000 in 1860, many of them scattered about the vast grasslands of the trans-Missouri West. But to their eternal misfortune, the Indians stood in the path of the advancing white pioneers. An inevitable clash loomed between an acquisitive, industrializing civilization and the Indians' highly evolved lifeways, adapted over centuries to the demanding environment of the sparsely watered western plains.

Migration and conflict—and sometimes dramatic cultural change—were no strangers in the arid West, even before the whites began to arrive. The Comanches had driven the Apaches off the central plains into the upper Rio Grande valley in the eighteenth century. Harried by the Mandans and Chippewas, the Cheyenne had abandoned their villages along the upper reaches of the Mississippi and Missouri Rivers in the century before the Civil War. The Sioux, displaced from the Great Lakes woodlands in the late eighteenth century, emerged onto the plains to prey upon the Crows, Kiowas, and Pawnees. Mounted on Spanish-introduced horses, peoples like the Cheyenne and the Sioux transformed themselves within just a few generations from foot-traveling, crop-growing villagers to wideranging nomadic traders and deadly efficient buffalo hunters—so deadly that they threatened to extinguish the vast bison herds that had lured them onto the plains in the first place.

When white soldiers and settlers edged onto the plains in the decades just before the Civil War, they accelerated a fateful cycle that exacerbated already fierce enmities among the Indians and ultimately undermined the foundations of Native American culture. White intruders unwittingly spread cholera,

As early as the Coronado expedition in 1541, Spanish explorers marveled at the Plains Indians' reliance on the buffalo:

"With the skins [the Indians] build their houses; with the skins they clothe and shoe themselves; from the skins they make ropes and also obtain wool. From the sinews they make thread, with which they sew their clothing and likewise their tents. From the bones they shape awls, and the dung they use for firewood, since there is no fuel in all that land. The bladders serve as jugs and drinking vessels. They sustain themselves on the flesh of the animals, eating it slightly roasted and sometimes uncooked. Taking it in their teeth, they pull with one hand; with the other they hold a large flint knife and cut off mouthfuls, swallowing it half chewed, like birds. They eat raw fat, without warming it."

typhoid, and smallpox among the native peoples of the plains, with devastating results. Equally harmful, whites put further pressure on the steadily shrinking bison population by hunting and by grazing their own livestock on the prairie grasses. As the once-mammoth buffalo herds dwindled, warfare

The Buffalo Hunt, by Frederic Remington, 1890 A New Yorker who first went west at the age of nineteen as a cowboy and ranch cook, Remington (1861–1909) became the foremost artist of the vanishing way of life of the old Far West. Once a common sight on the high plains, the kind of buffalo kill that Remington records here was a great rarity by the time he painted this scene in 1890. The once-vast herds of bison had long since been reduced to a pitiful few by the white man's rifles.

Pawnee Indians in Front of Their Lodge, c. 1868 The Pawnees of central Nebraska never made war on the United States, which they regarded as an ally in their own struggles against the marauding Sioux.

intensified among the plains tribes for ever-scarcer hunting grounds. "I am traveling all over this country, and am cutting the trees of my brothers," an Arikara Indian told a U.S. Army officer along the Platte River in 1835. "I am killing their buffalo before my friends arrive so that when they come up, they can find no buffalo."

The federal government tried to pacify the Plains Indians by signing treaties with the "chiefs" of various "tribes" at Fort Laramie in 1851 and at Fort Atkinson in 1853. The treaties marked the beginnings of the reservation system in the West. They established boundaries for the territory of each tribe and attempted to separate the Indians into two great "colonies" to the north and south of a corridor of intended white settlement.

But the white treaty makers misunderstood both Indian government and Indian society. "Tribes" and "chiefs" were often fictions of the white imagination, which could not grasp the fact that Native Americans, living in scattered bands, usually recognized no authority outside their immediate family, or perhaps a village elder. And the nomadic culture of the Plains Indians was utterly alien to the concept of living out one's life in the confinement of a defined territory.

In the 1860s the federal government intensified this policy and herded the Indians into still smaller confines, principally the "Great Sioux reservation" in Dakota Territory, and Indian Territory in present-day Oklahoma, into which dozens of southern Plains tribes were forced.

One disheartened Indian complained to the white Sioux Commission created by Congress,

"Tell your people that since the Great Father promised that we should never be removed we have been moved five times. . . . I think you had better put the Indians on wheels and you can run them about wherever you wish."

The Indians surrendered their ancestral lands only when they had received solemn promises from Washington that they would be left alone and provided with food, clothing, and other supplies. Regrettably, the federal Indian agents were often corrupt. They palmed off moth-eaten blankets, spoiled beef, and other defective provisions on the friendless Indians. One of these cheating officials, on an annual salary of $1,500, returned home after four years with an estimated "savings" of $50,000.

For more than a decade after the Civil War, fierce warfare between Indians and the U.S. Army raged in various parts of the West. Army troops, many of them recent immigrants who had, ironically, fled Europe to avoid military service, met formidable adversaries in the Plains Indians, whose superb horsemanship gave them baffling mobility. Fully one-fifth of all U.S. Army personnel on the

On the Southern Plains, by Frederic Remington, 1907

frontier were African-American—dubbed "Buffalo Soldiers" by the Indians, supposedly because of the resemblance of their hair to the bison's furry coat.

Receding Native Population

The Indian wars in the West were often savage clashes. Aggressive whites sometimes shot peaceful Indians on sight, just to make sure they would give no trouble. At Sand Creek, Colorado, in 1864, Colonel J. M. Chivington's militia massacred in cold blood some four hundred Indians who apparently thought they had been promised immunity. Women were shot praying for mercy, children had their brains dashed out, and braves were tortured, scalped, and unspeakably mutilated.

Cruelty begot cruelty. In 1866 a Sioux war party attempting to block construction of the Bozeman Trail to the Montana goldfields ambushed Captain William J. Fetterman's command of eighty-one soldiers and civilians in Wyoming's Bighorn Mountains. The Indians left not a single survivor and grotesquely mutilated the corpses. One trooper's face was spitted with 105 arrows. George Armstrong Custer, the buckskin-clad "boy general" of Civil War fame, now demoted to colonel and turned Indian fighter, wrote that Fetterman's annihilation "awakened a bitter feeling toward the savage perpetrators." The cycle of ferocious warfare intensified.

The Fetterman massacre led to one of the few—though short-lived—Indian triumphs in the plains wars. In another Treaty of Fort Laramie, signed in 1868, the government abandoned the Bozeman Trail. The sprawling "Great Sioux reservation" was guaranteed to the Sioux tribes. But in 1874 a new round of warfare with the Plains Indians began when Custer led a "scientific" expedition into the Black Hills of South Dakota (part of the Sioux reservation) and announced that he had discovered gold. Hordes of greedy gold-seekers swarmed into the Sioux lands. The aggrieved Sioux took to the warpath, inspired by the influential and wily Sitting Bull.

Colonel Custer's Seventh Cavalry, nearly half of them immigrants, set out to suppress the Indians and to return them to the reservation. Attacking what turned out to be a superior force of some 2,500 well-armed warriors camped along the Little Bighorn River in present-day Montana, the "White

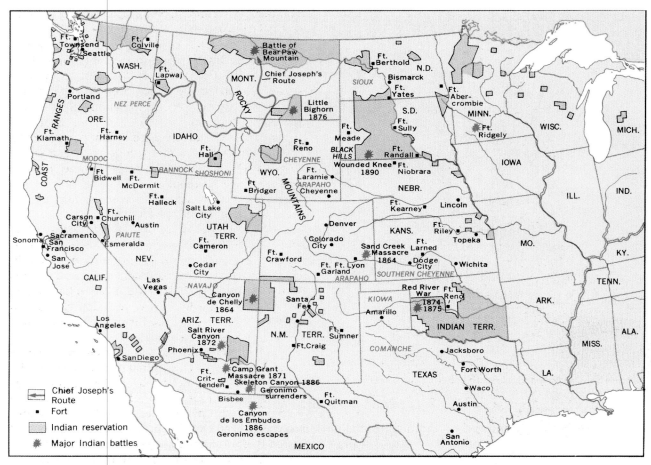

Indian Wars, 1860–1890   Surrendering in 1877, Chief Joseph of the Nez Percé declared, "Our chiefs are killed. . . . The old men are all dead. . . . The little children are freezing to death. . . . I want to have time to look for my children. . . . Hear me, my chiefs. My heart is sick and sad. From where the sun now stands I will fight no more forever."

A young lieutenant told Colonel Chivington that to attack the Indians would be a violation of pledges:

"His reply was, bringing his fist down close to my face, 'Damn any man who sympathizes with Indians.' I told him what pledges were given the Indians. He replied that he 'had come to kill Indians, and believed it to be honorable to kill Indians under any and all circumstances.'"

Chief with Yellow Hair" and his 264 officers and men were completely wiped out in 1876 when two supporting columns failed to come to their rescue.* But in a series of battles across the northern plains in the ensuing months, the U.S. Army relentlessly hunted down the Indians who had humiliated Custer.

One band of Nez Percé Indians in northeastern Oregon were goaded into daring flight in 1877, when U.S. authorities tried to herd them onto a

---

*When whites wiped out Indians, the engagement (in white history books) was usually a "battle"; when Indians wiped out whites, it was a "massacre." "Strategy" when practiced by Indians was "treachery."

Geronimo (c. 1823–1909) Also Known by His Apache Name, Goyahkla (One Who Yawns) In 1851 Mexican troops killed Geronimo's mother, wife, and three of his children, initiating Geronimo's lifelong hatred of Mexicans—though in later life, ironically, he repeatedly fled the intolerable confinement of reservations in the United States and sought refuge—and freedom—in Mexico. Persuaded at last to surrender to American authorities in 1886, he spent the remainder of his life on reservations in Florida, Alabama, and Oklahoma.

reservation. Chief Joseph finally surrendered his breakaway band of some seven hundred Indians after a tortuous, seventeen-hundred-mile, three-month trek across the Continental Divide toward Canada. There Joseph hoped to rendezvous with Sitting Bull, who had taken refuge north of the border after the Battle of Little Bighorn. Betrayed into believing they would be returned to their ancestral lands in Idaho, the Nez Percés instead were sent to a dusty reservation in Kansas, where 40 percent of them perished from disease. The survivors were eventually allowed to return to Idaho.

Fierce Apache tribes of Arizona and New Mexico were the most difficult to subdue. Led by Geronimo, whose eyes blazed hatred of the whites, they were pursued into Mexico by federal troops using the sun-flashing heliograph, a communication device that impressed the Indians as "big medicine." Scattered remnants of the warriors were finally persuaded to surrender after the Apache women had been exiled to Florida. The Apaches ultimately became successful farmers in Oklahoma.

This relentless fire-and-sword policy of the whites at last shattered the spirit of the Indians. The vanquished Native Americans were finally ghettoized on reservations where they could theoretically preserve their cultural autonomy but were in fact compelled to eke out a sullen existence as wards of the government. Their white masters had at last discovered that the Indians were much cheaper to feed than to fight. Even so, for many decades they were almost ignored to death.

The "taming" of the Indians was engineered by a number of factors. Of cardinal importance was the railroad, which shot an iron arrow through the heart of the West. Locomotives could bring out unlimited numbers of troops, farmers, cattlemen, sheepherders, and settlers. The Indians were also ravaged by the white people's diseases, to which they showed little resistance, and by their firewater, to which they showed almost no resistance. Above all, the virtual extermination of the buffalo doomed the Plains Indians' nomadic way of life.

Bellowing Herds of Bison

Tens of millions of buffalo—described by early Spaniards as "hunchback cows"—blackened the western prairies when the white Americans first arrived. These shaggy, lumbering animals were the staff of life for Native Americans (see "Makers of America: The Plains Indians," pp. 598–599). Their flesh provided food; their dried dung provided fuel ("buffalo chips"); their hides provided clothing, lariats, and harnesses.

When the Civil War closed, some 15 million of these meaty beasts were still grazing on the western plains. In 1868 a Kansas Pacific locomotive had to wait eight hours for a herd to amble across the tracks.

Much of the food supply of the railroad construction gangs came from leathery buffalo steaks. William "Buffalo Bill" Cody—sinewy, telescope-eyed, and a crack shot—killed over 4,000 animals in eighteen months while employed by the Kansas Pacific.

With the building of the railroad, the massacre of the herds began in deadly earnest. The creatures were slain for their hides, for their tongues or a few other choice cuts, or for sheer amusement. "Sportsmen" on lurching railroad trains would lean out the windows and blaze away at the animals to satisfy their lust for slaughter or excitement. Such wholesale butchery left fewer than a thousand buffalo alive by 1885, and the once-numerous beasts were in danger of complete extinction. The whole story is a shocking example of the greed and waste that accompanied the conquest of the continent.

The End of the Trail

By the 1880s the national conscience began to stir uneasily over the plight of the Indians. Helen Hunt Jackson, a Massachusetts writer of children's litera-ture, pricked the moral sense of Americans in 1881, when she published *A Century of Dishonor.* The book chronicled the sorry record of government ruthlessness and chicanery in dealing with the Indians. Her later novel *Ramona* (1884), a love story of injustice to the California Indians, sold some 600,000 copies and further inspired sympathy for the Indians.

Debate seesawed. Humanitarians wanted to treat the Indians kindly and persuade them thereby to "walk the white man's road." Yet hard-liners insisted on the current policy of forced containment and brutal punishment. Neither side showed much respect for Native American culture. Christian reformers, who often administered educational facilities on the reservations, sometimes withheld food to force the Indians to give up their tribal religion and assimilate to white society. In 1884 these zealous white souls joined with military men in successfully persuading the federal government to outlaw the sacred Sun Dance. When the "Ghost Dance" cult later spread to the Dakota Sioux, the army bloodily stamped it out in 1890 at the so-called Battle of Wounded Knee. In the fighting thus provoked, an estimated two hundred Indian men, women, and children were killed, as well as twenty-nine invading soldiers.

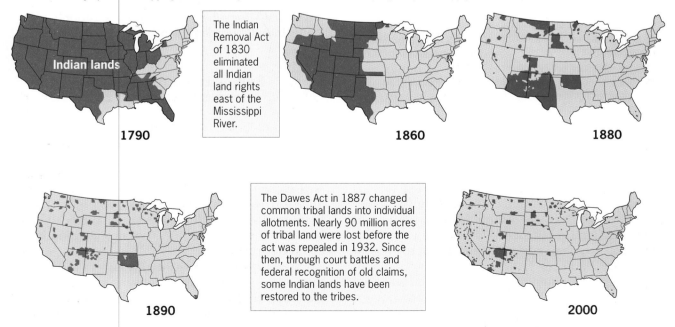

Vanishing Lands   Once masters of the continent, Native Americans have been squeezed into just 2 percent of U.S. territory. (Source: Copyright © 2000 by The New York Times Company. Reprinted by permission.)

The Indian Removal Act of 1830 eliminated all Indian land rights east of the Mississippi River.

1790   **1860**   **1880**

The Dawes Act in 1887 changed common tribal lands into individual allotments. Nearly 90 million acres of tribal land were lost before the act was repealed in 1932. Since then, through court battles and federal recognition of old claims, some Indian lands have been restored to the tribes.

1890   **2000**

Civil War veteran and long-time Indian fighter General Philip Sheridan (1831–1888) reflected on the wars against the Indians:

"We took away their country and their means of support, broke up their mode of living, their habits of life, introduced disease and decay among them, and it was for this and against this they made war. Could anyone expect less?"

Arapaho Chief Hail Wearing Ghost Dance Shirt, c. 1890
The Ghost Dance cult originated among the Paiute Indians in the 1870s and spread swiftly throughout the western tribes. It held out the promise of a revival of traditional Indian culture and revenge on the invading whites, but it was ruthlessly suppressed by the U.S. authorities. Ghost Dance shirts like this one were thought by their wearers to be impermeable to bullets.

The misbegotten offspring of the movement to reform Indian policy was the Dawes Severalty Act of 1887. Reflecting the forced-civilization views of the reformers, the act dissolved many tribes as legal entities, wiped out tribal ownership of land, and set up individual Indian family heads with 160 free acres. If the Indians behaved themselves like "good white settlers," they would get full title to their holdings, as well as citizenship, in twenty-five years. The probationary period was later extended, but full citizenship was granted to all Indians in 1924.

Reservation land not allotted to the Indians under the Dawes Act was to be sold to railroads and white settlers, with the proceeds used by the federal government to educate and "civilize" the native peoples. In 1879 the government had already funded the Carlisle Indian School in Pennsylvania, where Native American children, separated from their tribes, were taught English and inculcated with white values and customs. "Kill the Indian and save the man" was the school founder's motto. In the 1890s the government expanded its network of Indian boarding schools and sent "field matrons" to the reservations to teach Native American women the art of sewing and to preach the virtues of chastity and hygiene.

The Dawes Act struck directly at tribal organization and tried to make rugged individualists out of the Indians. This legislation ignored the inherent reliance of traditional Indian culture on tribally held land, literally pulling the land out from under them. By 1900 Indians had lost 50 percent of the 156 million acres they had held just two decades earlier. The forced-assimilation doctrine of the Dawes Act remained the cornerstone of the government's official Indian policy for nearly half a century, until the

The Indian spokesman Plenty Coups said in 1909,

"I see no longer the curling smoke rising from our lodge poles. I hear no longer the songs of the women as they prepare the meal. The antelope have gone; the buffalo wallows are empty. Only the wail of the coyote is heard. The white man's medicine is stronger than ours. . . . We are like birds with a broken wing."

The Plains Indians

The last of the native peoples of North America to bow before the military might of the whites, the Indians of the northern Great Plains long defended their lands and their ways of life against the American cavalry. After the end of the Indian wars, toward the close of the nineteenth century, the Plains tribes struggled on, jealously guarding their communities against white encroachment. Crowded onto reservations, subject to ever-changing federal Indian policies, assailed by corrupt settlers and Indian agents, the Plains Indians have nonetheless preserved much of their ancestral culture to this day.

Before Europeans first appeared in North America in the sixteenth century, the vast plain from northern Texas to Saskatchewan was home to some thirty different tribes. There was no typical Plains Indian; each tribe spoke a distinct language, practiced its own religion, and formed its own government. When members of different bands met on the prairies, communication depended on a special sign language.

Indians had first trod the arid plains to pursue sprawling herds of antelope, elk, and especially buffalo. But these early peoples of the plains were not exclusively hunters: the women were expert farmers, coaxing lush gardens of pumpkins, squash, corn, and beans from the dry but fertile soil. Still, the shaggy pelt and heavy flesh of the buffalo constituted the staff of life on the plains. Hunted by men, the great bison were butchered by women, who used every part of the beast. They fashioned horns and hooves into spoons, and intestines into containers. They stretched sinews into strong bowstrings and wove buffalo hair into ropes. Meat not immediately eaten was pounded into pemmican—thin strips of smoked or sun-dried buffalo flesh mixed with berries and stuffed into rawhide bags.

A Comanche Village, by George Catlin, 1834

(above) A Sioux Carving
Horses were essential to the culture of the Plains Indians, and they often carved likenesses of horses killed in battle. Note the red-stained holes depicting this horse's wounds.

(right) A Cheyenne Cradleboard for Carrying a Baby

Chan-Chä-Uiá-Teüin, Teton Sioux Woman, by Karl Bodmer, c. 1830s   Bodmer, a German artist, painted this woman's portrait during an expedition to the Great Plains. Her name means "Woman of the Crow Nation," which seems to suggest that she was taken captive from the Sioux's mortal enemies, the Crows.

The nomadic Plains Indians sought what shelter they could in small bands throughout the winter, gathering together in summer for religious ceremonies, socializing, and communal buffalo hunts. At first these seasonal migrations required arduous loading and carting. The Indians carried all their possessions or heaped them on wheelless carts called travois, which were dragged by dogs—their only beasts of burden.

Then in the sixteenth century, the mounted Spanish *conquistadores* ventured into the New World. Their steeds—some of them escaping to become mustangs, the wild horses of the American West, and others acquired by the Indians in trade—quickly spread over the plains. The horse revolutionized Indian societies, turning the Plains tribes into efficient hunting machines that promised to banish hunger from the prairies. But the plains pony also ignited a furious competition for grazing lands, for trade goods, and for ever more horses, so that wars of aggression and of revenge became increasingly bitter and frequent.

The European invasion soon eclipsed the short-lived era of the horse. After many battles the Plains Indians found themselves crammed together on tiny reservations, clinging with tired but determined fingers to their traditions. Although much of Plains Indian culture persists to this day, the Indians' free-ranging way of life has passed into memory. As Black Elk, an Oglala Sioux, put it, "Once we were happy in our own country and we were seldom hungry, for then the two-leggeds and the four-leggeds lived together like relatives, and there was plenty for them and for us. But then the Wasichus [white people] came, and they made little islands for us . . . and always these islands are becoming smaller, for around them surges the gnawing flood of Wasichus."

Indian Reorganization Act (the "Indian New Deal") of 1934 partially reversed the individualistic approach and belatedly tried to restore the tribal basis of Indian life (see p. 790).

Under these new federal policies, defective though they were, the Indian population started to mount slowly. The total number had been reduced by 1887 to about 243,000—the result of bullets, bottles, and bacteria—but the census of 2000 counted more than 1.5 million Native Americans, urban and rural.

Mining: From Dishpan to Ore Breaker

The conquest of the Indians and the coming of the railroad were life-giving boons to the mining frontier. The golden gravel of California continued to yield "pay dirt," and in 1858 an electrifying discovery convulsed Colorado. Avid "fifty-niners" or "Pike's Peakers" rushed west to rip at the ramparts of the Rockies. But there were more miners than minerals; and many gold-grubbers, with "Pike's Peak or Bust" inscribed on the canvas of their covered wagons, creaked wearily back with the added inscription, "Busted, by Gosh." Yet countless bearded fortune seekers stayed on, some to strip away the silver deposits, others to extract nonmetallic wealth from the earth in the form of golden grain.

"Fifty-niners" also poured feverishly into Nevada in 1859, after the fabulous Comstock Lode had been uncovered. A fantastic amount of gold and silver, worth more than $340 million, was mined by the "Kings of the Comstock" from 1860 to 1890. The scantily populated state of Nevada, "child of the Comstock Lode," was prematurely railroaded into the Union in 1864, partly to provide three electoral votes for President Lincoln.

Smaller "lucky strikes" drew frantic gold- and silver-seekers into Montana, Idaho, and other western states. Boomtowns, known as "Helldorados," sprouted from the desert sands like magic. Every third cabin was a saloon, where sweat-stained miners drank adulterated liquor ("rotgut") in the company of accommodating women. Lynch law and hempen vigilante justice, as in early California, preserved a crude semblance of order in the towns. And when the "diggings" petered out, the gold-seekers decamped, leaving eerily picturesque "ghost towns," such as Virginia City, Nevada, silhouetted in the desert. Begun with a boom, these towns ended with a whimper.

Dance-Hall Girl, Virginia City, Nevada, c. 1890
Women as well as men sought their fortunes in the frontier West—especially in wide-open mining towns like Virginia City.

Once the loose surface gold was gobbled up, ore-breaking machinery was imported to smash the gold-bearing quartz. This operation was so expensive that it could ordinarily be undertaken only by corporations pooling the wealth of stockholders. Gradually the age of big business came to the mining industry. Dusty, bewhiskered miners, dishpans in hand, were replaced by the impersonal corporations, with their costly machinery and trained engineers. The once-independent gold-washer became just another day laborer.

Yet the mining frontier had played a vital role in subduing the continent. Magnetlike, it attracted population and wealth, while advertising the wonders of the Wild West. Women as well as men found opportunity, running boardinghouses or working as prosti-

Cattle Trails

Dressed to Kill Cowboys came in all varieties and sizes in the wild and woolly frontier West—and in all kinds of garb as well.

tutes. They won a kind of equality on the rough frontier that earned them the vote in Wyoming (1869), Utah (1870), Colorado (1893), and Idaho (1896) long before their sisters in the East could cast a ballot.

The amassing of precious metals helped finance the Civil War, facilitated the building of railroads, and intensified the already bitter conflict between whites and Indians. The outpouring of silver and gold enabled the Treasury to resume specie payments in 1879 and injected the silver issue into American politics. "Silver Senators," representing the thinly peopled "acreage states" of the West, used their disproportionate influence to promote the interests of the silver miners. Finally, the mining frontier added to American folklore and literature, as the writings of Bret Harte and Mark Twain so colorfully attest.

Beef Bonanzas and the Long Drive

When the Civil War ended, the grassy plains of Texas supported several million tough, long-horned cattle. These scrawny beasts, whose horn spread sometimes reached eight feet, were killed primarily for their hides. There was no way of getting their meat profitably to market.

The problem of marketing was neatly solved when the transcontinental railroads thrust their iron fingers into the West. Cattle could now be shipped bodily to the stockyards, and under "beef barons" like the Swifts and Armours, the highly industrialized meatpacking business sprang into existence as a main pillar of the economy. Drawing upon the gigantic stockyards at Kansas City and Chicago, the meatpackers could ship their fresh products to the East Coast in the newly perfected refrigerator cars.

A spectacular feeder of the new slaughterhouses was the "Long Drive." Texas cowboys—black, white, and Mexican—drove herds numbering from one thousand to ten thousand head slowly over the unfenced and unpeopled plains until they reached a railroad terminal. The bawling beasts grazed en route on the free government grass. Favorite terminal points were flyspecked "cow towns" like Dodge City—"the Bibulous Babylon of the Frontier"—and Abilene (Kansas), Ogallala (Nebraska), and Cheyenne (Wyoming). At Abilene order was maintained by Marshal James B. ("Wild Bill") Hickok, a fabulous gunman who reputedly killed only in self-defense or in the line of duty and who was fatally shot in the back in 1876, while playing poker.

As long as lush grass was available, the Long Drive proved profitable—that is, to the luckier cattlemen who escaped Indians, stampedes, cattle fever, and other hazards. From 1866 to 1888, bellowing herds, totaling over 4 million steers, were driven northward from the beef bowl of Texas. The steer was king in a Cattle Kingdom richly carpeted with grass.

What the Lord giveth, the Lord also can taketh away. The railroad made the Long Drive, and the railroad unmade the Long Drive, primarily because the locomotives ran both ways. The same rails that bore the cattle from the open range to the kitchen range brought out the homesteader and the sheepherder. Both of these intruders, sometimes amid flying bullets, built barbed-wire fences that were too numerous to be cut down by the cowboys. Furthermore, the terrible winter of 1886–1887, with blinding blizzards reaching 68 degrees below zero, left thousands of dazed cattle starving and freezing. Overexpansion and overgrazing likewise took their toll, as the cowboys slowly gave way to plowboys.

The only escape for the stockmen was to make cattle-raising a big business and avoid the perils of overproduction. Breeders learned to fence their ranches, lay in winter feed, import blooded bulls, and produce fewer and meatier animals. They also learned to organize. The Wyoming Stock-Growers' Association, especially in the 1880s, virtually controlled the state and its legislature.

This was the heyday of the cowboy. The equipment of the cowhand—from "shooting irons" and ten-gallon hat to chaps and spurs—served a useful, not an ornamental, function. A "genuwine" gun-toting cowpuncher, riding where men were men and smelled like horses, could justifiably boast of his toughness.

These bowlegged Knights of the Saddle, with their colorful trappings and cattle-lulling songs, became part of American folklore. Many of them, perhaps five thousand, were blacks, who especially enjoyed the newfound freedom of the open range.

The Farmers' Frontier

Miners and cattlemen created the romantic legend of the West, but it was the sober sodbuster who wrote the final chapter of frontier history. A fresh

The Homesteader's Wife, by Harvey Dunn   Women as well as men toiled without shade or respite on the sun-scorched and wind-parched Great Plains.

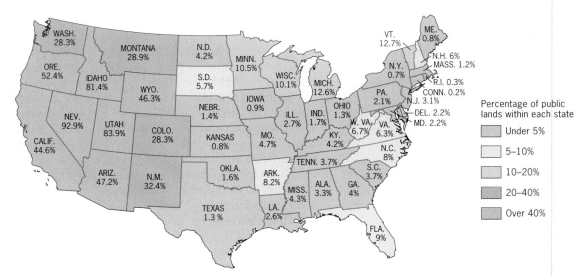

Myth and Reality in the West   American folklore pictures the western United States as a land of rugged individualists who tamed the wild region with grit and brawn. The reality is that the federal government is by far the West's largest landowner—and that federal projects, especially dam-building, have done more to shape the region than all the cowboys and farmers put together. (Source: Center of the American West.)

day dawned for western farmers with the Homestead Act of 1862. The new law allowed a settler to acquire as much as 160 acres of land (a quarter-section) by living on it for five years, improving it, and paying a nominal fee of about $30.

The Homestead Act marked a drastic departure from previous policy. Before the act, public land had been sold primarily for revenue; now it was to be given away to encourage a rapid filling of empty spaces and to provide a stimulus to the family farm—"the backbone of democracy." The new law was a godsend to a host of farmers who could not afford to buy large holdings. During the forty years after its passage, about half a million families took advantage of the Homestead Act to carve out new homes in the vast open stretches. Yet five times that many families *purchased* their land from the railroads, the land companies, or the states.

The Homestead Act often turned out to be a cruel hoax. The standard 160 acres, quite adequate in the well-watered Mississippi basin, frequently proved pitifully inadequate on the rain-scarce Great Plains. Thousands of homesteaders, perhaps two out of three, were forced to give up the one-sided

struggle against drought. Uncle Sam, it was said, bet 160 acres against ten dollars that the settlers could not live on their homesteads for five years. One of these unsuccessful gambles in Greer County, western Oklahoma, inspired a folk song:

> *Hurrah for Greer County! The land of the free,*
> *The land of the bedbug, grasshopper, and flea;*
> *I'll sing of its praises, I'll tell of its fame,*
> *While starving to death on my government*
>   *claim.*

Naked fraud was spawned by the Homestead Act and similar laws. Perhaps ten times more of the public domain wound up in the clutches of land-grabbing promoters than in the hands of bona fide farmers. Unscrupulous corporations would use "dummy" homesteaders—often their employees or aliens bribed with cash or a bottle of beer—to grab the best properties containing timber, minerals, and oil. Settlers would later swear that they had "improved" the property by erecting a "twelve by fourteen" dwelling, which turned out to measure twelve by fourteen *inches.*

In making the arduous journey across the western prairies, many women settlers discovered new confidence in their abilities. Early on in her trek, Mary Richardson Walker (1811–1897) confided in her diary that

". . . my circumstances are rather trying. So much danger attends me on every hand. A long journey before me, going I know not whither, without mother or sister to attend me, can I expect to survive it all?"

Only a month later, she recorded that

"in the afternoon we rode thirty-five miles without stopping. Pretty well tired out, all of us. Stood it pretty well myself."

The railways also played a major role in developing the agricultural West, largely through the profitable marketing of crops. Some railroad companies induced Americans and European immigrants to buy the cheap lands earlier granted by the government. The Northern Pacific Railroad at one time had nearly a thousand paid agents in Europe distributing roseate leaflets in various languages.

Shattering the myth of the Great American Desert opened the gateways to the agricultural West even wider. The windswept prairies were for the most part treeless, and the tough sod had been pounded solid by millions of buffalo hooves. Pioneer explorers and trappers had assumed that the soil must be sterile, simply because it was not heavily watered and did not support immense forests. But once the prairie sod was broken with heavy iron plows pulled by four yokes of oxen—the "plow that broke the plains"—the earth proved astonishingly fruitful. "Sodbusters" poured onto the prairies. Lacking trees for lumber and fuel, they built homes from the very sod they dug from the ground, and burned corncobs for warmth.

Lured by higher wheat prices resulting from crop failures elsewhere in the world, settlers in the 1870s rashly pushed still farther west, onto the poor, marginal lands beyond the 100th meridian. That imaginary line, running north to south from the Dakotas through west Texas, separated two climatological regions—a well-watered area to the east, and a semiarid area to the west. Bewhiskered and one-armed geologist John Wesley Powell, explorer of the Colorado River's Grand Canyon and director of the U.S. Geological Survey, warned in 1874 that beyond the 100th meridian so little rain fell that agriculture was impossible without massive irrigation.

Ignoring Powell's advice, farmers heedlessly chewed up the crusty earth in western Kansas, eastern Colorado, and Montana. They quickly went broke as a six-year drought in the 1880s further desiccated the already dusty region. Western Kansas lost half its population between 1888 and 1892. "There is no God west of Salina," one hapless homesteader declared.

In the wake of the devastating drought, the new technique of "dry farming" took root on the plains. Its methods of frequent shallow cultivation supposedly were adapted to the arid western environment, but over time "dry farming" created a finely pulverized surface soil that contributed to the notorious "Dust Bowl" several decades later (see p. 789).

Other adaptations to the western environment were more successful. Tough strains of wheat, resistant to cold and drought, were imported from Russia and blossomed into billowing yellow carpets. Wise farmers abandoned corn in favor of sorghum and other drought-resistant grains. Barbed wire, perfected by Joseph F. Glidden in 1874, solved the problem of how to build fences on the treeless prairies.

Eventually federally financed irrigation projects —on a colossal scale, beyond even what John Wesley Powell had dreamed—caused the Great American Desert to bloom. A century after Powell's predictions, arching dams had tamed the Missouri and Columbia Rivers and had so penned up and diverted the canyon-gnawing Colorado that its mouth in the Gulf of California was dry. More than 45 million acres were irrigated in seventeen western states. In the long run, the hydraulic engineers had more to do with shaping the modern West than all the trappers, miners, cavalrymen, and cowboys there ever were. As one engineer boasted, "We enjoy pushing rivers around."

The Far West Comes of Age

The Great West experienced a fantastic growth in population from the 1870s to the 1890s. A parade of new western states proudly joined the Union. Boomtown Colorado, offspring of the Pike's Peak

EXAMINING THE EVIDENCE

Robert Louis Stevenson's Transcontinental Journey, 1879 The celebrated Scottish writer Robert Louis Stevenson, author of such enduring classics as *Treasure Island, Kidnapped,* and *The Strange Case of Dr. Jekyll and Mr. Hyde,* journeyed from Scotland to California in 1879 to rendezvous with his American fiancée, Frances Osbourne. Between New York and San Francisco, Stevenson traveled on the transcontinental railroad line completed just ten years earlier, and he dutifully recorded his impressions of America, the West in particular, as he made his way toward California. Stevenson's account of his trip provides an unusually gifted writer's vivid portrait of the trans-Mississippi West at the close of the era of the Indian wars. Like all travelogues, Stevenson's colorful tale may reveal as much about the traveler as it does about the things he saw. Yet historians frequently make use of such documents to reconstruct the original appearance and texture of places that were once the exotic destinations of adventurous travelers, before they were transformed by the onrush of modernity. In the passages reproduced here, inspired by the view as Stevenson's train passed through Nebraska and Wyoming, what features of the landscape does the author find most remarkable? How does he portray the railroad?

THE PLAINS OF NEBRASKA

. . . We were at sea—there is no other adequate expression—on the plains of Nebraska. . . . It was a world almost without a feature; an empty sky, an empty earth; front and back, the line of railway stretched from horizon to horizon, like a cue across a billiard-board; on either hand, the green plain ran till it touched the skirts of heaven. . . . [G]razing beasts were seen upon the prairie at all degrees of distance and diminution; and now and again we might perceive a few dots beside the railroad which grew more and more distinct as we drew nearer till they turned into wooden cabins, and then dwindled and dwindled in our wake until they melted into their surroundings, and we were once more alone upon the billiard-board. The train toiled over this infinity like a snail; and being the one thing moving, it was wonderful what huge proportions it began to assume in our regard. . . .

[That] evening we left Laramie [Wyoming]. . . . And yet when day came, it was to shine upon the same broken and unsightly quarter of the world. Mile upon mile, and not a tree, a bird, or a river. Only down the long, sterile cañons, the train shot hooting and awoke the resting echo. That train was the one piece of life in all the deadly land; it was the one actor, the one spectacle fit to be observed in this paralysis of man and nature. And when I think how the railroad has been pushed through this unwatered wilderness and haunt of savage tribes, and now will bear an emigrant for some £12 from the Atlantic to the Golden Gates; how at each stage of the construction, roaring, impromptu cities, full of gold and lust and death, sprang up and then died away again, and are now but wayside stations in the desert; how in these uncouth places pig-tailed Chinese pirates worked side by side with border ruffians and broken men from Europe, talking together in a mixed dialect, mostly oaths, gambling, drinking, quarrelling and murdering like wolves; how the plumed hereditary lord of all America heard, in this last fastness, the scream of the 'bad medicine waggon' charioting his foes; and then when I go on to remember that all this epical turmoil was conducted by gentlemen in frock coats, and with a view to nothing more extraordinary than a fortune and a subsequent visit to Paris, it seems to me, I own, as if this railway were the one typical achievement of the age in which we live, as if it brought together into one plot all the ends of the world and all the degrees of social rank, and offered to some great writer the busiest, the most extended, and the most varied subject for an enduring literary work. . . .

Source: *Across the Plains,* by Robert Louis Stevenson (New York: Charles Scribner's Sons, 1897).

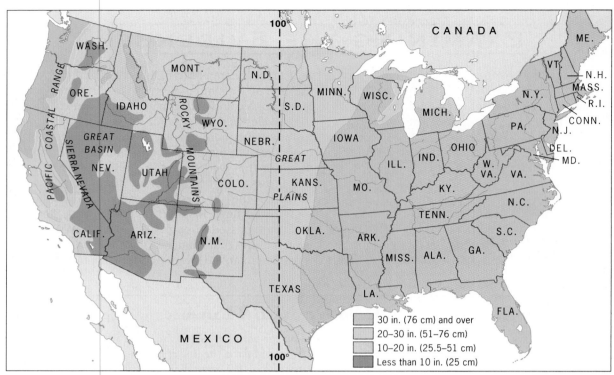

Average Annual Precipitation In the Northern Hemisphere, storms usually circle the globe in a west-to-east direction. Much of the life-nourishing water in these storms is dumped as rainfall on the western slopes of the cloud-high Pacific coastal ranges and the Rocky Mountains. This weather pattern creates deep, dry "rain shadows" in the Great Basin and in the plains area immediately east of the Rockies.

gold rush, was greeted in 1876 as "the Centennial State." In 1889–1890 a Republican Congress, eagerly seeking more Republican electoral and congressional votes, admitted in a wholesale lot six new states: North Dakota, South Dakota, Montana, Washington, Idaho, and Wyoming. The Mormon Church formally and belatedly banned polygamy in 1890, but not until 1896 was Utah deemed worthy of admission. Only Oklahoma, New Mexico, and Arizona remained to be lifted into statehood from contiguous territory on the mainland of North America.

In a last gaudy fling, the federal government made available to settlers vast stretches of fertile plains formerly occupied by the Indians in the district of Oklahoma ("the Beautiful Land"). Scores of overeager and well-armed "sooners," illegally jumping the gun, had entered Oklahoma Territory. They had to be evicted repeatedly by federal troops, who on occasion would shoot the intruders' horses. On April 22, 1889, all was in readiness for the legal

opening, and some 50,000 "boomers" were poised expectantly on the boundary line. At high noon the bugle shrilled, and a horde of "eighty-niners" poured in on lathered horses or careening vehicles. That night a lonely spot on the prairie had mushroomed into the tent city of Guthrie, with over 10,000 people. By the end of the year, Oklahoma boasted 60,000 inhabitants, and Congress made it a territory. In 1907 it became the "Sooner State."

The Fading Frontier

In 1890—a watershed date—the superintendent of the census announced that for the first time in America's experience, a frontier line was no longer discernible. All the unsettled areas were now broken into by isolated bodies of settlement. The "closing" of the frontier inspired one of the most influential essays ever written about American history—Frederick Jackson Turner's "The Significance of the Frontier in American History" in 1893.

As the nineteenth century neared its sunset, the westward-tramping American people were disturbed to find that their fabled free land was going or had gone. The secretary of war had prophesied in 1827 that five hundred years would be needed to fill the West. But as the nation finally recognized that its land was not inexhaustible, seeds were planted to preserve the vanishing resource. The government set aside land for national parks—first Yellowstone in 1872, followed by Yosemite and Sequoia in 1890.

But the frontier was more than a place; it was also a state of mind and a symbol of opportunity. Its passing ended a romantic phase of the nation's internal development and created new economic and psychological problems.

Traditionally footloose, Americans have been notorious for their mobility. The nation's farmers, unlike the peasants of Europe, have seldom remained rooted to their soil. The land, sold for a profit as settlement closed in, was often the settler's most profitable crop.

Much has been said about the frontier as a "safety valve." The theory is that when hard times came, the unemployed who cluttered the city pavements merely moved west, took up farming, and prospered.

In truth, relatively few city dwellers, at least in the populous eastern centers, migrated to the frontier during depressions. Most of them did not know how to farm; few of them could raise enough money to transport themselves west and then pay for livestock and expensive machinery.

But the safety-valve theory does have some validity. Free acreage did lure to the West a host of immigrant farmers who otherwise might have remained in the eastern cities to clog the job markets and to crowd the festering and already overpopulated slums. And the very *possibility* of westward migration may have induced urban employers to maintain wage rates high enough to discourage workers from leaving. But the real safety valve by the late nineteenth century was in western cities like Chicago, Denver, and San Francisco, where failed farmers, busted miners, and displaced easterners found ways to seek their fortunes. Indeed, after about 1880 the area from the Rocky Mountains to the Pacific Coast was the most urbanized region in America, measured by the percentage of people living in cities.

U.S. history cannot be properly understood unless it is viewed in light of the westward-moving experience. As Frederick Jackson Turner wrote, "American history has been in a large degree the history of the colonization of the Great West." The story of settling and taming the trans-Mississippi West in the late nineteenth century was but the last chapter in the saga of colonizing various American "wests" since Columbus's day—from the West Indies to the Chesapeake shore, from the valleys of the Hudson and Connecticut Rivers to the valleys of the Tennessee and Ohio Rivers.

Homesteads from the Public Lands (acreage legally transferred to private ownership) (See related map, p. 603.)

Harvesting in Washington State   Humans, horses, and machine join forces in this turn-of-the-century scene.

And yet the trans-Mississippi West formed a distinct chapter in that saga and retains even to this day much of its uniqueness. There the Native American peoples made their last and most desperate struggle against colonization, and there most Native Americans live today. There "Anglo" culture collided most directly with Hispanic culture—the historic rival of the Anglo-Americans for dominance in the New World—and the Southwest remains the most Hispanicized region in America. There America faced across the Pacific to Asia, and there most Asian-Americans dwell today. There the scale and severity of the environment posed their largest challenges to human ambitions, and there the environment, with its aridity and still-magical emptiness, continues to mold social and political life, and the American imagination, as in no other part of the nation. And in no other region has the federal government, with its vast landholdings, its subsidies to the railroads, and its massive irrigation projects, played so conspicuous a role in economic and social development.

The westward-moving pioneers and the country they confronted have assumed mythic proportions in the American mind. They have been immortalized by such writers as Bret Harte, Mark Twain, Helen Hunt Jackson, and Francis Parkman, and by such painters as George Catlin, Frederic Remington, and Albert Bierstadt. For better or worse, those pioneers planted the seeds of civilization in the immense western wilderness. The life we live, they dreamed of; the life they lived, we can only dream.

The Farm Becomes a Factory

The situation of American farmers, once jacks-and-jills-of-all-trades, was rapidly changing. They had raised their own food, fashioned their own clothing, and bartered for other necessities with neighbors. Now high prices persuaded farmers to concentrate on growing single "cash" crops, such as wheat or corn, and use their profits to buy foodstuffs at the general store and manufactured goods in town or by mail order. The Chicago firm of Aaron Montgomery Ward sent out its first catalogue—a single sheet—in 1872.

Large-scale farmers, especially in the immense grain-producing areas of the Mississippi Valley, were now both specialists as well as business-people. As cogs in the vast industrial machine, these farmers were intimately tied to banking, railroading, and manufacturing. They had to buy expensive machinery in order to plant and to harvest their crops. A powerful steam engine could drag behind it simultaneously the plow, seeder, and harrow. The speed of harvesting wheat was dramatically increased in the 1870s by the invention of the twine binder and then in the 1880s by the "combine"—the combined reaper-thresher, which was drawn by twenty to forty horses and which both reaped and bagged the grain. Widespread use of such costly equipment naturally called for first-class management. But the farmers, often unskilled as businesspeople, were inclined to blame the

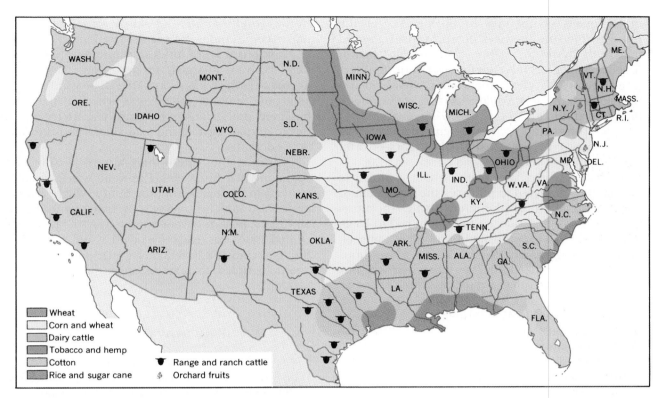

American Agriculture in 1900

banks and railroads or the volatility of the global marketplace rather than their own shortcomings, for their losses.

This amazing mechanization of agriculture in the postwar years was almost as striking as the mechanization of industry. In fact, agricultural modernization drove many marginal farmers off the land, thus swelling the ranks of the new industrial work force. As the rural population steadily decreased, those farmers who remained achieved miracles of production, making America the world's breadbasket and butcher shop. The farm was attaining the status of a factory—an outdoor grain factory. Bonanza wheat farms of the Minnesota–North Dakota area, for example, were enormous. By 1890 at least a half-dozen of them were larger than fifteen thousand acres, with communication by telephone from one part to another. These bonanza farms foreshadowed the gigantic agribusinesses of the next century.

Agriculture was a big business from its earliest days in California's phenomenally productive (and phenomenally irrigated) Central Valley. California farms, carved out of giant Spanish-Mexican land grants and the railroads' huge holdings, were from the outset more than three times larger than the national average. The reformer Henry George in 1871 described the Golden State as "not a country of farms but a country of plantations and estates." With the advent of the railroad refrigerator car in the 1880s, California fruit and vegetable crops, raised on sprawling tracts by ill-paid migrant Mexican and Chinese farmlands, sold at a handsome profit in the rich urban markets of the East.

Deflation Dooms the Debtor

Once the farmers became chained to a one-crop economy—wheat or corn—they were in the same leaky boat with the southern cotton growers. As long as prices stayed high, all went well. But when they skidded in the 1880s, bankruptcy fell like a blight on the farm belts.

The grain farmers were no longer the masters of their own destinies. They were engaged in one of the most fiercely competitive of businesses, for the price of their product was determined in a world market by the world output. If the wheat fields of Argentina, Russia, and other foreign countries flourished, the price of the farmers' grain would fall and American sodbusters would face ruin, as they did in the 1880s and 1890s.

Low prices and a deflated currency were the chief worries of the frustrated farmers—North, South, and West. If a family had borrowed $1,000 in 1855, when wheat was worth about a dollar a bushel, they expected to pay back the equivalent of one thousand bushels, plus interest, when the mortgage fell due. But if they let their debt run to 1890, when wheat had fallen to about fifty cents a bushel, they would have to pay back the price of two thousand bushels for the $1,000 they had borrowed, plus interest. This unexpected burden struck them as unjust, though their steely-eyed creditors often branded the complaining farmers as slippery and dishonest rascals.

The deflationary pinch on the debtor flowed partly from the static money supply. There were simply not enough dollars to go around, and as a result, prices were forced down. In 1870 the currency in circulation for each person was $19.42; in 1890 it was only $22.67. Yet during these twenty years, business and industrial activity, increasing manyfold, had intensified the scramble for available currency.

The forgotten farmers were caught on a treadmill. Despite unremitting toil, they operated year after year at a loss and lived off their fat as best they could. In a vicious circle, their farm machinery increased their output of grain, lowered the price, and drove them even deeper into debt. Mortgages engulfed homesteads at an alarming rate; by 1890 Nebraska alone reported more than 100,000 farms blanketed with mortgages. The repeated crash of the sheriff-auctioneer's hammer kept announcing

A contemporary farm protest song, "The Kansas Fool," ran,

The bankers followed us out west;
And did in mortgages invest;
They looked ahead and shrewdly planned,
And soon they'll have our Kansas land.

to the world that another sturdy American farmer had become landless in a landed nation.

Ruinous rates of interest, running from 8 to 40 percent, were charged on mortgages, largely by agents of eastern loan companies. The windburned sons and daughters of the sod, who felt that they deserved praise for developing the country, cried out in despair against the loan sharks and the Wall Street octopus.

Farm tenancy rather than farm ownership was spreading like stinkweed. The trend was especially marked in the sharecropping South, where cotton prices also sank dismayingly. By 1880 one-fourth of all American farms were operated by tenants. The United States was ready to feed the world, but under the new industrial feudalism, the farmers were about to sink into a status suggesting Old World serfdom.

Unhappy Farmers

Even Mother Nature ceased smiling, as her powerful forces conspired against agriculture. Mile-wide clouds of grasshoppers, leaving "nothing but the mortgage," periodically ravaged prairie farms. The terrible cotton-boll weevil was also wreaking havoc in the South by the early 1890s.

The good earth was going sour. Floods added to the waste of erosion, which had already washed the topsoil off millions of once-lush southern acres. Expensive fertilizers were urgently needed. A long succession of droughts seared the trans-Mississippi West, beginning in the summer of 1887. Whole towns were abandoned. "Going home to the wife's folks" and "In God we trusted, in Kansas we busted" were typical laments of many impoverished farmers, as they fled their weather-beaten shacks and sun-baked sod houses. One irate "poet" snarled,

> *Fifty miles to water,*
> *A hundred miles to wood,*
> *To hell with this damned country,*
> *I'm going home for good.*

To add to their miseries, the soil-tillers were gouged by their government—local, state, and national. Their land was overassessed, and they paid painful local taxes, whereas wealthy easterners could conceal their stocks and bonds in safe-deposit boxes. High protective tariffs in these years poured

Nebraska Homesteaders in Front of Their Sod House, 1887 These two brothers and their families had escaped to Canada from the slave South during the Civil War. Returning to the United States in the 1880s, they took advantage of the Homestead Act to stake out farms in Custer County, Nebraska.

profits into the pockets of manufacturers. Farmers, on the other hand, had no choice but to sell their low-priced products in a fiercely competitive, unprotected world market, while buying high-priced manufactured goods in a protected home market.

The farmers were also "farmed" by the corporations and processors. They were at the mercy of the harvester trust, the barbed-wire trust, and the fertilizer trust, all of which could control output and raise prices to extortionate levels. Middlemen took a juicy "cut" from the selling price of the goods that the farmers bought, while operators pushed storage rates to the ceiling at grain warehouses and elevators.

In addition, the railroad octopus had the grain growers in its grip. Freight rates could be so high that the farmers sometimes lost less if they burned their corn for fuel than if they shipped it. If they raised their voices in protest, the ruthless railroad operators might let their grain spoil in damp places or refuse to provide them with cars when needed.

Farmers still made up nearly one-half the population in 1890, but they were hopelessly disorganized. The manufacturers and the railroad barons knew how to combine to promote their interests, and so, increasingly, did industrial workers. But the farmers were by nature independent and individualistic—dead set against consolidation or regimentation. No really effective Carnegie or Gompers arose among them to preach the gospel of economic integration and concentration. They never did organize successfully to restrict production until forced to by the federal government nearly half a century later, in Franklin Roosevelt's New Deal days. What they did manage to organize was a monumental political uprising.

The Farmers Take Their Stand

Agrarian unrest had flared forth earlier, in the Greenback movement shortly after the Civil War. Prices sagged in 1868, and a host of farmers unsuccessfully sought relief from low prices and high indebtedness by demanding an inflation of the currency with paper money.

The National Grange of the Patrons of Husbandry—better known as the Grange—was organized in 1867. Its leading spirit was Oliver H. Kelley, a shrewd and energetic Minnesota farmer then working as a clerk in Washington. Kelley's first objective was to enhance the lives of isolated farmers through social, educational, and fraternal activities. Farm men and women, cursed with loneliness in widely separated farmhouses, found the Grange's picnics, concerts, and lectures a godsend. Kelley, a Mason, even found farmers receptive to his mumbo-jumbo of passwords and secret rituals, as well as his four-ply hierarchy, ranging (for men) from Laborer to Husbandman and (for women) from Maid to

The Farmers' Grievances
This poster from 1875 expresses one of the agrarian radicals' fundamental premises: that all other walks of life were dependent—or even parasitic—on the indispensable work of farmers. In his famous "Cross of Gold" speech in 1896 (see p. 617), Populist presidential candidate William Jennings Bryan put it this way: "Burn down your cities and leave our farms, and your cities will spring up again as if by magic; but destroy our farms and the grass will grow in the streets of every city in the country."

Matron. The Grange spread like an old-time prairie fire and by 1875 claimed 800,000 members, chiefly in the Midwest and South. Buzzing with gossip, these calicoed and calloused folk often met in red schoolhouses around potbellied stoves.

The Grangers gradually raised their goals from individual self-improvement to improvement of the farmers' collective plight. In a determined effort to escape the clutches of the trusts, they established cooperatively owned stores for consumers and cooperatively owned grain elevators and warehouses for producers. Their most ambitious experiment was an attempt to manufacture harvesting machinery, but this venture, partly as a result of mismanagement, ended in financial disaster.

Embattled Grangers also went into politics, enjoying their most gratifying success in the grain-growing regions of the upper Mississippi Valley, chiefly in Illinois, Wisconsin, Iowa, and Minnesota. There, through state legislation, they strove to regulate railway rates and the storage fees charged by railroads and by the operators of warehouses and grain elevators. Many of the state courts, notably in Illinois, were disposed to recognize the principle of public control of private business for the general welfare. A number of the so-called Granger Laws, however, were badly drawn, and they were bitterly fought through the high courts by the well-paid lawyers of the "interests." Following judicial reverses, most severely at the hands of the Supreme Court in the famous *Wabash* decision of 1886 (see p. 536), the Grangers' influence faded. But their organization has lived on as a vocal champion of farm interests, while brightening rural life with social activities.

Farmers' grievances likewise found a vent in the Greenback Labor party, which combined the inflationary appeal of the earlier Greenbackers with a program for improving the lot of labor. In 1878, the high-water mark of the movement, the Greenback Laborites polled over a million votes and elected fourteen members of Congress. In the presidential election of 1880, the Greenbackers ran General James B. Weaver, an old Granger who was a favorite of the Civil War veterans and who possessed a remarkable voice and bearing. He spoke to perhaps a half-million citizens in a hundred or so speeches but polled only 3 percent of the total popular vote.

Prelude to Populism

A striking manifestation of rural discontent came through the Farmers' Alliance, founded in Texas in the late 1870s (see p. 521). Farmers came together in the Alliance to socialize, but more importantly to break the strangling grip of the railroads and manufacturers through cooperative buying and selling. Local chapters spread throughout the South and the Great Plains during the 1880s, until by 1890 members numbered more than a million hard-bitten souls.

Unfortunately, the Alliance weakened itself by ignoring the plight of landless tenant farmers, sharecroppers, and farmworkers. Even more debilitating was the Alliance's exclusion of blacks, who counted for nearly half the agricultural population of the South. In the 1880s a separate Colored Farmers' National Alliance emerged to attract black farmers, and by 1890 membership numbered more than 250,000. The long history of racial division in the South, however, made it difficult for white and black farmers to work together in the same organization.

Out of the Farmers' Alliances a new political party emerged in the early 1890s—the People's party. Better known as the Populists, these frustrated farmers attacked Wall Street and the "money trust." They called for nationalizing the railroads, telephones, and telegraph; instituting a graduated income tax; and creating a new federal "subtreasury"—a scheme to provide farmers with loans for crops stored in government-owned warehouses, where they could be held until market prices rose. They also wanted the free and unlimited coinage of silver—yet another of the debtors' demands for inflation that echoed continuously throughout the Gilded Age.

Numerous fiery prophets leapt forward to trumpet the Populist cause. The free coinage of silver struck many Populists as a cure-all, especially after the circulation of an enormously popular pamphlet titled *Coin's Financial School* (1894). Written by William Hope Harvey, it was illustrated by clever woodcuts, one of which depicted the gold ogre beheading the beautiful silver maiden. In fiction parading as fact, the booklet showed how the "little professor"—"Coin" Harvey—overwhelmed the bankers and professors of economics with his brilliant arguments on behalf of free silver. Another notorious spellbinder was red-haired Ignatius Donnelly

Mary E. Lease (1853–1933) She was so eloquent as to be called the "Patrick Henry in petticoats."

of Minnesota, three times elected to Congress. The queen of the Populist "calamity howlers" was Mary Elizabeth ("Mary Yellin'") Lease, a tall, athletic woman known as the "Kansas Pythoness." She reportedly demanded that Kansans should raise "less corn and more hell." The big-city *New York Evening Post* snarled, "We don't want any more states until we can civilize Kansas." To many easterners, complaint, not corn, was rural America's staple crop.

Yet the Populists, despite their oddities, were not to be laughed away. They were leading a deadly earnest and impassioned campaign to relieve the farmers' many miseries. Smiles faded from Republican and Democratic faces alike as countless thousands of Populists began to sing "Good-bye, My Party, Good-bye." In 1892 the Populists had jolted the traditional parties by winning several congressional seats and polling more than 1 million votes for their presidential candidate, James B. Weaver. Racial divisions continued to hobble the Populists in the South, but in the West their ranks were swelling. Could the People's party now reach beyond its regional bases in agrarian America, join hands with urban workers, and mount a successful attack on the northeastern citadels of power?

Coxey's Army and the Pullman Strike

The panic of 1893 and the severe ensuing depression strengthened the Populists' argument that farmers and laborers alike were being victimized by an oppressive economic and political system. Ragged armies of the unemployed began marching to protest their plight. In the growing hordes of displaced industrial toilers, the Populists saw potential political allies.

The most famous marcher was "General" Jacob S. Coxey, a wealthy Ohio quarry owner. He set out for Washington in 1894 with a few score of supporters and a swarm of newspaper reporters. His platform included a demand that the government relieve unemployment by an inflationary public works program, supported by some $500 million in legal tender notes to be issued by the Treasury. Coxey himself rode in a carriage with his wife and infant son, appropriately named Legal Tender Coxey, while his tiny "army" tramped along behind, singing,

> We're coming, Grover Cleveland,
>   500,000 strong,
> We're marching on to Washington
>   to right the nation's wrong.

The "Commonweal Army" of Coxeyites finally straggled into the nation's capital, but the invasion took on the aspects of a comic opera when "General" Coxey and his "lieutenants" were arrested for walking on the grass.

Elsewhere, violent flare-ups accompanied labor protests, notably in Chicago. Most dramatic was the crippling Pullman strike of 1894. Eugene V. Debs, a charismatic labor leader, had helped organize the American Railway Union of about 150,000 members. The Pullman Palace Car Company, which maintained a model town near Chicago for its employees, was hit hard by the depression and cut wages by about one-third, while holding the line on rent for the company houses. The workers finally struck—in some places overturning Pullman cars—and paralyzed railway traffic from Chicago to the Pacific coast. The American Federation of Labor conspicuously declined to support the Pullman strikers, thus enhancing the AF of L's reputation for "respectability" even while weakening labor's cause by driving a large wedge into the workers' ranks.

Coxey's Army on the Outskirts of Washington, D.C., 1894
Jacob Sechler Coxey arrived at the nation's capital with 500 men, not the 100,000 he predicted, to make a "living petition" of the unemployed.

The Pullman Strike, 1894
Illinois National Guardsmen fire on Pullman Company strikers, July 7, 1894. Police clubs and U.S. Army rifles and bayonets finally broke the back of a strike that halted railroads throughout the country.

The turmoil in Chicago was serious but not yet completely out of hand. At least this was the judgment of Governor John Peter Altgeld of Illinois, a friend of the downtrodden, who had pardoned the Haymarket Square anarchists the year before (see p. 551). But U.S. Attorney General Richard Olney, an archconservative and an ex–railroad attorney, urged the dispatch of federal troops. His legal grounds were that the strikers were interfering with the transit of the U.S. mail. President Cleveland supported Olney with the ringing declaration, "If it takes the entire army and navy to deliver a postal card in Chicago, that card will be delivered."

To the delight of conservatives, federal troops, bayonets fixed, crushed the Pullman strike. Debs was sentenced to six months' imprisonment for contempt of court because he had defied a federal court injunction to cease striking. Ironically, the lean labor agitator spent much of his enforced leisure reading radical literature, which led to his later leadership of the socialist movement in America.

Embittered cries of "government by injunction" now burst from organized labor. This was the first time that such a legal weapon had been used conspicuously by Washington to break a strike, and it was all the more distasteful because defiant workers who were held in contempt could be imprisoned without a jury trial. Signs multiplied that employers were striving to smash labor unions by court action. Nonlabor elements of the country, including the Populists and other debtors, were likewise incensed. They saw in the brutal Pullman episode further proof of an unholy alliance between business and the courts.

After the Pullman strike collapsed, Eugene Debs (1855–1926) said,

"No strike has ever been lost."

In 1897 he declared,

"The issue is Socialism versus Capitalism. I am for Socialism because I am for humanity."

Golden McKinley and Silver Bryan

The smoldering grievances of the long-suffering farmers and the depression-plagued laborers gave ominous significance to the election of 1896. Conservatives of all stripes feared an impending

McKinley Campaign Headquarters, Chicago, 1896   Those few black Americans who could exercise their right to vote in the 1890s still remained faithful to "the party of Lincoln."

iron business and now coveted the role of president maker. "I love McKinley," he once said. As a whole-hearted Hamiltonian, Hanna believed that a prime function of government was to aid business. Honest, earnest, tough, and direct, he became the personification of big industry in politics. He was often caricatured in cartoons, quite unfairly, as a bloated bully in a loud checkered suit with a dollar sign in each square. He believed that in some measure prosperity "trickled down" to the laborer, whose dinner pail was full when business flourished. Critics assailed this idea as equivalent to feeding the horses in order to feed the sparrows.

The hardheaded Hanna, although something of a novice in politics, organized his preconvention campaign for McKinley with consummate skill and with a liberal outpouring of his own money. The convention steamroller, well lubricated with Hanna's dollars, nominated McKinley on the first ballot in St. Louis in June 1896. The Republican platform cleverly straddled the money question but leaned toward hard-money policies. It declared for

Crying for Protection, 1896
Uncle Sam is called on in this cartoon to nurse so-called infant industries—some of which had in fact long since grown into vigorous adulthood.

upheaval, while down-and-out husbandmen and discontented workers cast about desperately for political salvation. Increasingly, monetary policy—whether to maintain the gold standard or inflate the currency by monetizing silver—loomed as the issue on which the election would turn.

The leading candidate for the Republican presidential nomination in 1896 was former congressman William McKinley of Ohio, sponsor of the ill-starred tariff bill of 1890 (see p. 521). He had established a creditable Civil War record, having risen to the rank of major; he hailed from the electorally potent state of Ohio; and he could point to long years of honorable service in Congress, where he had made many friends with his kindly and conciliatory manner.

As a presidential candidate, McKinley was largely the creature of a fellow Ohioan, Marcus Alonzo Hanna, who had made his fortune in the

the gold standard, even though McKinley's voting record in Congress had been embarrassingly friendly to silver. The platform also condemned hard times and Democratic incapacity, while pouring praise on the protective tariff.

Dissension riddled the Democratic camp. Cleveland no longer led his party. The depression had driven the last nail into his political coffin. Dubbed "the Stuffed Prophet," he was undeniably the most unpopular man in the country. Labor-debtor groups remembered too vividly his intervention in the Pullman strike, the backstairs Morgan bond deal, and especially his stubborn hard-money policies. Ultraconservative in finance, Cleveland now looked more like a Republican than a Democrat on the money issue.

Rudderless, the Democratic convention met in Chicago in July 1896, with the silverites lusting for victory. Shouting insults at the absent Cleveland, the delegates refused, by a suicidal vote of 564 to 357, to endorse their own administration. They had the enthusiasm and the numbers; all they lacked was a leader.

A new Moses suddenly appeared in the person of William Jennings Bryan of Nebraska. Then only thirty-six years of age and known as "the Boy Orator of the Platte,"* he stepped confidently onto the platform before fifteen thousand people. His masterful presence was set off by a peninsular jaw and raven-black hair. He radiated honesty, sincerity, and energy.

The convention-hall setting was made to order for a magnificent oratorical effort. A hush fell over the delegates as Bryan stood before them. With an organlike voice that rolled into the outer corners of the huge hall, he delivered a fervent plea for silver. Rising to supreme heights of eloquence, he thundered, "We will answer their demands for a gold standard by saying to them: 'You shall not press down upon the brow of labor this crown of thorns, you shall not crucify mankind upon a cross of gold.'"

The Cross of Gold speech was a sensation. Swept off its feet in a tumultuous scene, the Democratic convention nominated Bryan the next day on the fifth ballot. The platform demanded inflation

through the unlimited coinage of silver at the ratio of 16 ounces of silver to 1 of gold, though the market ratio was about 32 to 1. This meant that the silver in a dollar would be worth about fifty cents.

Democratic "Gold Bugs," unable to swallow Bryan, bolted their party over the silver issue. A conservative senator from New York, when asked if he was a Democrat still, reportedly replied, "Yes, I am a Democrat still—very still." The Democratic minority, including Cleveland, charged that the Populist-silverites had stolen both the name and the clothes of their party. They nominated a lost-cause ticket of their own, and many of them, including Cleveland, not too secretly hoped for a McKinley victory.

The Populists now faced a dilemma, because the Democratic majority had appropriated their main plank—"16 to 1," that "heaven-born ratio." The bulk of the Populists, fearing a hard-money McKinley victory, endorsed both "fusion" with the Democrats and Bryan for president, sacrificing their identity in the mix. Singing "The Jolly Silver Dollar of the Dads," they became in effect the "Demo-Pop" party, though a handful of the original Populists refused to support Bryan and went down with their colors nailed to the mast.

Class Conflict: Plowholders Versus Bondholders

Mark Hanna smugly assumed that he could make the tariff the focus of the campaign. But Bryan, a dynamo of energy, forced the free-trade issue into the back seat when he took to the stump in behalf of free silver. Sweeping through 27 states and traveling 18,000 miles, he made nearly 600 speeches—36 in one day—and even invaded the East, "the enemy's country." Vachel Lindsay caught the spirit of his oratorical orgy:

> *Prairie avenger, mountain lion,*
> *Bryan, Bryan, Bryan, Bryan,*
> *Gigantic troubadour, speaking like a siege gun,*
> *Smashing Plymouth Rock with his boulders*
> *from the West.**

---

*One contemporary sneered that Bryan, like the Platte River in his home state of Nebraska, was "six inches deep and six miles wide at the mouth."

*Reprinted with the permission of Scribner, a Division of Simon & Schuster, Inc., from *Collected Poems* by Vachel Lindsay. Copyright © 1920 by Macmillan Publishing Company; copyright renewed 1948 by Elizabeth C. Lindsay.

William Jennings Bryan, Campaigning (Again) in 1908
The premier orator of his day, Bryan also became a perennial presidential candidate, running in 1896, 1900, and 1908. He lost every time.

Free silver became almost as much a religious as a financial issue. Hordes of fanatical free-silverites hailed Bryan as the messiah to lead them out of the wilderness of debt. They sang "We'll All Have Our Pockets Lined with Silver" and "No Crown of Thorns, No Cross of Gold."

Bryan created panic among eastern conservatives with his threat of converting their holdings overnight into fifty-cent dollars. The "Gold Bugs" responded with their own free and unlimited coinage of verbiage. They vented their alarm in abusive epithets, ringing from "fanatic" and "madman" to "traitor" and "murderer." "In God We Trust, with Bryan We Bust," the Republicans sneered, while one eastern clergyman cried, "That platform was made in Hell." Widespread fear of Bryan and the "silver lunacy" enabled "Dollar Mark" Hanna, now chairman of the Republican National Committee, to shine as a money-raiser. He "shook down" the trusts and plutocrats and piled up an enormous "slush fund" for a "campaign of education"—or of propaganda, depending on one's point of view. Reminding

the voters of Cleveland's "Democratic panic," Republicans appealed to the "belly vote" with their prize slogan, "McKinley and the Full Dinner Pail." The McKinleyites amassed the most formidable political campaign chest thus far in American history. At all levels—national, state, and local—it amounted to about $16 million, as contrasted with about $1 million for the poorer Democrats (roughly "16 to 1"). With some justification, the Bryanites accused Hanna of "buying" the election and of floating McKinley into the White House on a tidal wave of mud and money.

Bryan's cyclonic campaign began to lose steam as the weeks passed. Fear was probably Hanna's strongest ally, as it was Bryan's worst enemy. Republican businesspeople placed contracts with manufacturers, contingent on the election of McKinley. A few factory owners, with thinly veiled intimidation, paid off their workers and told them not to come to work on Wednesday morning if Bryan won. Reports also circulated that employers were threatening to pay their employees in fifty-cent pieces, instead of in dol-

The Sacrilegious Candidate A hostile cartoonist makes sport of Bryan's notorious Cross of Gold speech in 1896.

lars, if Bryan triumphed. Such were some of the "dirty tricks" of the "Stop Bryan, Save America" crusade.

Hanna's campaign methods paid off. On election day McKinley triumphed decisively. The vote was 271 to 176 in the Electoral College and 7,102,246 to 6,492,559 in the popular election. Driven by fear and excitement, an unprecedented outpouring of voters flocked to the polls. McKinley ran strongly in the populous East, where he carried every county of New England, and in the upper Mississippi Valley. Bryan's states, concentrated in the debt-burdened South and the trans-Mississippi West, boasted more acreage than McKinley's but less population.

The free-silver election of 1896 was perhaps the most significant political turning point since Lincoln's victories in 1860 and 1864. Despite Bryan's strength in the South and West, the results vividly demonstrated his lack of appeal to the unmortgaged farmer and especially to the eastern urban laborer. Many wage earners in the East voted for their jobs and full dinner pails, threatened as they were by free silver, free trade, and fireless factories. Living precariously on a fixed wage, the factory workers had no reason to favor inflation, which was the heart of the Bryanites' program.

The Bryan-McKinley battle heralded the advent of a new era in American politics. At first glance the election seemed to be the age-old story of the underprivileged many against the privileged few, of the indebted backcountry against the wealthier seaboard, of the country against the city, of the agrarians against the industrialists, of Main Street against Wall Street, of the nobodies against the somebodies. Yet when Bryan made his evangelical appeal to all those supposed foes of the existing social order, not enough of them banded together to form a political majority.

The outcome was instead a resounding victory for big business, the big cities, middle-class values, and financial conservatism. Bryan's defeat marked the last serious effort to win the White House with mostly agrarian votes. The future of presidential politics lay not on the farms, with their dwindling population, but in the mushrooming cities, with their growing hordes of freshly arriving immigrants.

The smashing Republican victory of 1896 also heralded a Republican grip on the White House for sixteen consecutive years—indeed, for all but eight of the next thirty-six years. McKinley's election thus imparted a new character to the American political system. The long reign of Republican political dominance that it ushered in was accompanied by diminishing voter participation in elections, the weakening of party organizations, and the fading away of issues like the money question and civil-

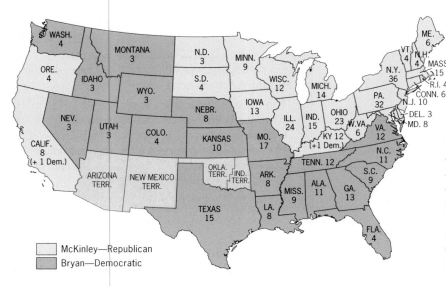

McKinley—Republican
Bryan—Democratic

Presidential Election of 1896 (with electoral vote by state) This election tolled the death knell of the Gilded Age political party system, with its razor-close elections, strong party loyalties, and high voter turnouts. For years after 1896, Republicans predominated, and citizens showed a declining interest in either joining parties or voting.

Campaign Gimcrack, 1896 This McKinley paper hat was distributed in a Boston Sunday newspaper.

service reform, which came to be replaced by concern for industrial regulation and the welfare of labor. Scholars have dubbed this new political era the period of the "fourth party system."*

---

*The first party system, marked by doubts about the very legitimacy of parties, embraced the Federalist-Republican clashes of the 1790s and early 1800s. The second party system took shape after 1828 with the emergence of mass-based politics in the Jacksonian era, and pitted Democrats against Whigs. The third party system, beginning in 1860, was characterized by the precarious equilibrium between Republicans and Democrats, as well as the remarkably high electoral participation rates that endured from the end of the Civil War to McKinley's election. The fourth party system is described above. The fifth party system emerged with Franklin Roosevelt's New Deal in the 1930s, initiating a long period of Democratic ascendancy. Each "system," with the conspicuous exception of the fifth, lasted about three and one-half decades—a cyclical regularity that has long intrigued political scientists and historians. Debate still rages about whether the country passed into a sixth party system with Richard Nixon's election in 1968.

Republican Stand-pattism Enthroned

An eminently "safe" McKinley took the inaugural oath in 1897. With his impeccable white vest, he seemed never to perspire, even in oppressively muggy Washington. Though a man of considerable ability, he was an ear-to-the-ground politician who seldom got far out of line with majority opinion. His cautious, conservative nature caused him to shy away from the flaming banner of reform. Business was given a free rein, and the trusts, which had trusted him in 1896, were allowed to develop more mighty muscles without serious restraints.

Almost as soon as McKinley took office, the tariff issue, which had played second fiddle to silver in the "Battle of '96," quickly forced itself to the fore. The current Wilson-Gorman law was not raising enough revenue to cover the annual Treasury deficits, and the Republican trusts thought that they had purchased the right to additional tariff protection by their lush contributions to Hanna's war chest. In due course the Dingley Tariff Bill was jammed through the House in 1897, under the pounding gavel of the rethroned "Czar" Reed. The proposed new rates were high, but not high enough to satisfy the paunchy lobbyists, who once again descended upon the Senate. Over 850 amendments were tacked onto the overburdened bill. The resulting piece of patchwork finally established the average rates at 46.5 percent, substantially higher than the Democratic Wilson-Gorman Act of 1894 and in some categories even higher than the McKinley Act of 1890. (See the chart in the Appendix.)

Prosperity, long lurking around the corner, began to return with a rush in 1897, the first year of McKinley's term. The depression of 1893 had run its course, and farm prices rose. Paint-thirsty midwestern barns blossomed in new colors, and the wheels of industry resumed their hum. Republican politicians, like crowing roosters believing they caused the sun to rise, claimed credit for attracting the sunlight of prosperity.

With the return of prosperity, the money issue that had overshadowed politics since the Civil War gradually faded away. The Gold Standard Act of 1900, passed over last-ditch silverite opposition, provided that the paper currency be redeemed freely in gold. Nature and science gradually provided an inflation that the "Gold Bug" East had fought so frantically to prevent. Electrifying discoveries of new gold deposits in Canada's fabled Klondike, as well as in Alaska, South Africa, and Australia, brought huge quantities of gold onto world markets, as did the perfecting of the cheap cyanide process for extracting gold from low-grade ore. Moderate inflation thus took care of the currency needs of an explosively expanding nation, as its circulatory system greatly improved. The tide of "silver heresy" rapidly receded, and the "Popocratic" fish were left gasping high and dry on a golden-sanded beach.

Chronology

c. 1700-1800	New Indian peoples move onto Great Plains
1858	Pike's Peak gold rush
1859	Nevada Comstock Lode discovered
1862	Homestead Act
1864	Sand Creek massacre Nevada admitted to the Union
1867	National Grange organized
1876	Battle of Little Bighorn Colorado admitted to the Union
1877	Nez Percé Indian War
1881	Helen Hunt Jackson publishes *A Century of Dishonor*
1884	Federal government outlaws Indian Sun Dance
1885-1890	Local chapters of Farmers' Alliance formed
1887	Dawes Severalty Act
1889	Oklahoma opened to settlement
1889-1890	North Dakota, South Dakota, Montana, Washington, Idaho, and Wyoming admitted to the Union
1890	Census Bureau declares frontier line ended Emergence of People's party (Populists) Battle of Wounded Knee
1892	Populist party candidate James B. Weaver polls more than 1 million votes in presidential election
1893	Frederick Jackson Turner publishes "The Significance of the Frontier in American History"
1894	"Coxey's Army" marches on Washington Pullman strike
1896	Utah admitted to the Union McKinley defeats Bryan for presidency
1897	Dingley Tariff Act
1900	Gold Standard Act
1907	Oklahoma admitted to the Union
1924	Indians granted U.S. citizenship
1934	Indian Reorganization Act

VARYING VIEWPOINTS

Was the West Really "Won"?

For more than half a century, the Turner thesis dominated historical writing about the West. In his famous essay of 1893, "The Significance of the Frontier in American History," historian Frederick Jackson Turner argued that the frontier experience molded both region and nation. Not only the West, Turner insisted, but the national character had been uniquely shaped by the westward movement. Pioneers had brought the raw West into the embrace of civilization. And the struggle to overcome the hazards of the western wilderness—including distance, deserts, drought, and Indians—had transformed *Europeans* into tough, inventive, and self-reliant *Americans.*

Turner's thesis raised a question that Americans found especially intriguing in 1893. Just three years earlier, the superintendent of the census declared that the frontier, defined as a zone with little or no settled population, had closed forever. What new forces, Turner now asked, would shape a distinctive American national character, now that the testing ground of the frontier had been plowed and tamed?

Turner's hypothesis that the American character was forged in the western wilderness is surely among the most provocative statements ever made about the formative influences on the nation's development. But as the frontier era recedes ever further into the past, scholars are less persuaded that Turner's thesis adequately explains the national character. American society is still conspicuously different from European and other cultures, even though Turner's frontier disappeared more than a century ago.

Modern scholars charge that Turner based his thesis on several questionable assumptions. Historian David J. Weber, for example, suggests that the line of the frontier did not define the quavering edge of "civilization" but marked the boundary between diverse cultures, each with its own claims to legitimacy and, indeed, to legitimate possession of the land. The frontier should therefore be understood not as the place where "civilization" triumphed over "savagery," but as the principal site of interaction between those cultures.

Several so-called New Western historians take this argument still further. Scholars such as Patricia Nelson Limerick, Richard White, and Donald Worster suggest that the cultural and ecological damage inflicted by advancing "civilization" must be reckoned with in any final accounting of what the pioneers accomplished. These same scholars insist that the West did not lose its regional identity after the frontier line was no longer recognizable in 1890. The West, they argue, is still a unique part of the national mosaic, a region whose history, culture, and identity remain every bit as distinctive as those of New England or the Old South.

But where Turner saw the frontier as the principal shaper of the region's character, the New Western historians emphasize the effects of ethnic and racial confrontation, topography, climate, and the roles of government and big business as the factors that have made the modern West. The New Western historians thus reject Turner's emphasis on the triumphal civilizing of the wilderness. As they see the matter, European and American settlers did not tame the West, but rather conquered it, by suppressing the Native American and Hispanic peoples who had preceded them into the region. But those conquests were less than complete, so the argument goes, and the West therefore remains, uniquely among American regions, an unsettled arena of commingling and competition among those groups. Moreover, in these accounts the West's distinctively challenging climate and geography yielded to human habitation not through the efforts of heroic individual pioneers, but only through massive corporate—and especially federal government—investments in transportation systems (like the transcontinental railroad) and irrigation projects (like the watering of California's Central Valley). Such developments still give western life its special character today.

For further reading, see page A19 of the Appendix. For web resources, go to **http://college.hmco.com**.

The Path of Empire

—⁂—

1890–1899

We assert that no nation can long endure half republic and half empire, and we warn the American people that imperialism abroad will lead quickly and inevitably to despotism at home.

DEMOCRATIC NATIONAL PLATFORM, 1900

In the years immediately following the Civil War, Americans remained astonishingly indifferent to the outside world. Enmeshed in struggles over Reconstruction policies and absorbed in efforts to heal the wounds of war, build an industrial economy, make their cities habitable, and settle the sprawling West, most citizens took little interest in international affairs. But the sunset decades of the nineteenth century witnessed a momentous shift in U.S. foreign policy. America's new diplomacy reflected the far-reaching changes that were reshaping agriculture, industry, and the social structure. American statesmen also responded to the intensifying scramble of several other nations for international advantage in the dawning "age of empire." By century's end America itself would become an imperial power, an astonishing departure from its venerable anticolonial traditions.

Imperialist Stirrings

Many developments fed the nation's ambition for overseas expansion. Both farmers and factory owners began to look beyond American shores as agricultural and industrial production boomed. Many Americans believed that the United States had to expand or explode. Their country was bursting with a new sense of power generated by the robust growth in population, wealth, and productive capacity—and it was trembling from the hammer blows of labor violence and agrarian unrest. Overseas markets might provide a safety valve to relieve those pressures.

Other forces also whetted the popular appetite for overseas involvement. The lurid "yellow press" of Joseph Pulitzer and William Randolph Hearst

BILL OF FARE

HAVANA MATANZAS
CUBA STEAK SANTIAGO

PORTO SAN JUAN
RICO BAYAMON
PIG ARECIBO
MATACHEZ
PONCE

PHILIPPINE SANDWICH
FLOATING ISLANDS
ISLANDS

WELL, I HARDLY KNOW WHICH TO TAKE FIRST!

The Imperial Menu
A pleased Uncle Sam gets ready to place his order with headwaiter William McKinley. Swallowing some of these possessions eventually produced political indigestion.

described foreign exploits as manly adventures, the kind of dashing derring-do that was the stuff of young boys' dreams. Pious missionaries, inspired by books like the Reverend Josiah Strong's *Our Country: Its Possible Future and Its Present Crisis,* looked overseas for new souls to harvest. Strong trumpeted the superiority of Anglo-Saxon civilization and summoned Americans to spread their religion and their values to the "backward" peoples. He cast his seed on fertile ground. At the same time, aggressive Americans like Theodore Roosevelt and Congressman Henry Cabot Lodge were interpreting Darwinism to mean that the earth belonged to the strong and the fit—that is, to Uncle Sam. This view was strengthened as latecomers to the colonial scramble scooped up leavings from the banquet table of earlier diners. Africa, previously unexplored and mysterious, was partitioned by the Europeans in the 1880s in a pell-mell rush of colonial conquest. In the 1890s Japan, Germany, and Russia all extorted concessions from the anemic Chinese Empire. If America was to survive in the competition of modern nation-states, perhaps it, too, would have to become an imperial power.

The development of a new steel navy also focused attention overseas. Captain Alfred Thayer Mahan's book of 1890, *The Influence of Sea Power*

upon History, 1660–1783, argued that control of the sea was the key to world dominance. Read by the English, Germans, and Japanese, as well as by his fellow Americans, Mahan helped stimulate the naval race among the great powers that gained momentum around the turn of the century. Red-blooded Americans joined in the demands for a mightier navy and for an American-built isthmian canal between the Atlantic and the Pacific.

America's new international interest manifested itself in several ways. As secretary of state, first in the Garfield administration and later in the Harrison administration, James G. Blaine pushed his "Big Sister" policy. It aimed to rally the Latin American nations behind Uncle Sam's leadership and to open Latin American markets to Yankee traders. Blaine's efforts bore modest fruit in 1889, when he presided over the first Pan-American Conference, held in Washington, D.C. Although the frock-coated delegates did little more than sketch a vague plan for economic cooperation through reciprocal tariff reduction, they succeeded in blazing the way for a long and increasingly important series of inter-American assemblages.

A number of diplomatic crises or near-wars also marked the path of American diplomacy in the late 1880s and early 1890s. The American and German navies nearly came to blows in 1889 over the far-away Samoan Islands in the South Pacific. The lynching of eleven Italians in New Orleans in 1891 brought America and Italy to the brink of war; the crisis was defused when the United States agreed to pay compensation. In the ugliest affair, American demands on Chile after the deaths of two American sailors in the port of Valparaiso in 1892 made hostilities between the two countries seem inevitable. The threat of attack by Chile's modern navy spread alarm on the Pacific Coast, until American power finally forced the Chileans to pay an indemnity. A simmering argument between the United States and Canada over seal hunting near the Pribilof Islands off the coast of Alaska was resolved by arbitration in 1893. The willingness of Americans to risk war over such distant and minor disputes demonstrated the aggressive new national mood.

Monroe's Doctrine and the Venezuelan Squall

America's anti-British feeling, which periodically came to a head, flared ominously in 1895–1896 over Venezuela. For more than a half-century, the jungle boundary between British Guiana and Venezuela had been in dispute. The Venezuelans, whose claims on the whole were extravagant, had repeatedly urged arbitration. But the prospect of a peaceful settlement faded when gold was discovered in the contested area.

President Cleveland, a champion of righteousness and no lover of Britain, at length decided upon a strong protest. His no less pugnacious secretary of state, Richard Olney, was authorized to present to London a smashing note, which Cleveland later dubbed a "twenty-inch gun" blast. Olney declared in effect that the British, by attempting to dominate Venezuela in this quarrel and acquire more territory, were flouting the Monroe Doctrine. London should therefore submit the dispute to arbitration. Not content to stop there, Olney haughtily informed the world's number one naval power that the United

The Venezuela–British Guiana Boundary Dispute

The World's Plunderers, 1885

States was now calling the tune in the Western Hemisphere.

British officials, unimpressed, took four months to prepare their reply. Preoccupied elsewhere, they were inclined to shrug off Olney's lengthy salvo as just another twist of the lion's tail designed to elicit cheers from Irish-American voters. When London's answer finally came, it flatly denied the relevance of the Monroe Doctrine, while no less emphatically spurning arbitration. In short, said John Bull, the affair was none of Uncle Sam's business.

President Cleveland—"mad clear through," as he put it—sent a bristling special message to Congress. He urged an appropriation for a commission of experts, who would run the line where it ought to go. Then, he implied, if the British would not accept this rightful boundary, the United States would fight for it.

The entire country, irrespective of political party, was swept off its feet in an outburst of hysteria. War seemed inevitable, even though Britain had thirty-two warships of the battleship class to only five flying Old Glory.

Fortunately, sober second thoughts prevailed on both sides of the Atlantic. The British, though vastly annoyed by their upstart cousins, had no real urge to fight. Canada was vulnerable to yet-to-be-raised American armies, and Britain's rich merchant marine was vulnerable to American commerce raiders. The European atmosphere was menacing, for Britain's traditional policy of "splendid isolation" was bringing insecure isolation. Russia and France were unfriendly, and Germany, under the saber-rattling Kaiser Wilhelm II, was about to challenge British naval supremacy.

The German kaiser, blunderingly and unwittingly, increased chances of a peaceful solution to the Venezuelan crisis. An unauthorized British raiding party of six hundred armed men was captured by the Dutch-descended Boers in South Africa, and Wilhelm forthwith cabled his congratulations to the victors. Overnight, British anger against America was largely deflected to Germany, and London consented to arbitrate the Venezuelan dispute. The final decision, ironically, awarded the British the bulk of what they had claimed from the beginning.

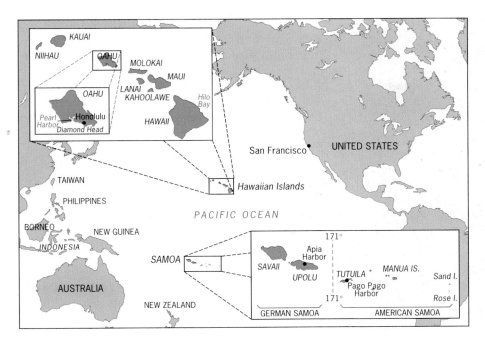

The Pacific
The enlargements show the Hawaiian Islands and the Samoas, both areas of American imperialistic activity in the late nineteenth century.

America had skated close to the thin ice of a terrible war, but the results on the whole were favorable. The prestige of the Monroe Doctrine was immensely enhanced. Europe was irked by Cleveland's claim to domination in this hemisphere, but he had made his claim stick. Many Latin American republics were pleased by the determination of the United States to protect them, and when Cleveland died in 1908, some of them lowered their flags to half-mast.

The chastened British, their eyes fully opened to the European peril, were now determined to cultivate Yankee friendship. The British inaugurated an era of "patting the eagle's head," which replaced a century or so of America's "twisting the lion's tail." Sometimes called the Great Rapprochement—or reconciliation—between the United States and Britain, the new Anglo-American cordiality became a cornerstone of both nations' foreign policies as the twentieth century opened.

Spurning the Hawaiian Pear

Enchanted Hawaii had early attracted the attention of Americans. In the morning years of the nineteenth century, the breeze-brushed islands were a way station and provisioning point for Yankee shippers, sailors, and whalers. In 1820 came the first New England missionaries, who preached the twin blessings of Protestant Christianity and protective calico. They came to do good—and did well; their children did even better. In some respects Honolulu took on the earmarks of a typical New England town.

Americans gradually came to regard the Hawaiian Islands as a virtual extension of their own coastline. The State Department, beginning in the 1840s, sternly warned other powers to keep their grasping hands off. America's grip was further tightened in 1875 by a commercial reciprocity agreement and in 1887 by a treaty with the native government guaranteeing priceless naval-base rights at spacious Pearl Harbor.

But trouble, both economic and political, was brewing in the insular paradise. Sugar cultivation, which had become immensely profitable, went somewhat sour in 1890 when the McKinley Tariff raised barriers against the Hawaiian product. White planters, mostly Americans, quickly concluded that the best way to overcome the tariff was to annex Hawaii to the United States. But that ambition was blocked by the strong-willed Queen Liliuokalani, who insisted that native Hawaiians should control the islands. Desperate whites, though only a tiny

Queen Liliuokalani (1838–1917)   She was the last reigning queen of Hawaii, whose defense of native Hawaiian self-rule led to a revolt by white settlers and to her dethronement. She wrote many songs, the most famous of which was "Aloha Oe," or Farewell to Thee, played countless times by Hawaiian bands for departing tourists.

minority, organized a successful revolt early in 1893. It was openly assisted by American troops, who landed under the unauthorized orders of the expansionist American minister in Honolulu. "The Hawaiian pear is now fully ripe," he wrote exultantly to his superiors in Washington, "and this is the golden hour for the United States to pluck it."

Hawaii, like Texas of earlier years, seemed ready for annexation—at least in the eyes of the ruling American whites. An appropriate treaty was rushed to Washington. But before it could be railroaded through the Senate, Republican president Harrison's term expired and Democratic president Cleveland came in. "Old Grover," who set great store by "national honesty," suspected that his powerful nation had gravely wronged the deposed Queen Liliuokalani.

Cleveland abruptly withdrew the treaty from the Senate early in 1893 and then sent a special investigator to Hawaii. The subsequent probe revealed the damning fact that a majority of the Hawaiian natives did not favor annexation at all. But the white revolutionists were firmly in the saddle, and Cleveland could not unhorse them without using armed force—a step American public opinion would not have tolerated. Although Queen Liliuokalani could not be reinstated, the sugarcoated move for annexation had to be abandoned temporarily—until 1898.

The question of annexing Hawaii touched off the first full-fledged imperialistic debate in American experience. Cleveland was savagely criticized for trying to stem the new Manifest Destiny, and a popular jingle ran,

> . . . *Liliuokalani,*
> *Give us your little brown hannie.*

But Cleveland's motives, in a day of international land-grabbing, were honorable both to himself and to his country. The Hawaiian pear continued to ripen for five more years.

Cubans Rise in Revolt

Cuba's masses, frightfully misgoverned, again rose against their Spanish oppressor in 1895. The roots of their revolt were partly economic, with partial origins in the United States. Sugar production—the backbone of the island's prosperity—was crippled when the American tariff of 1894 restored high duties on the toothsome product.

Driven to desperation, the insurgents now adopted a scorched-earth policy. They reasoned that if they did enough damage, Spain might be willing to move out. Or the United States might move in and help the Cubans win their independence. In pursuance of this destructive strategy, the *insurrectos* torched canefields and sugar mills; they even dynamited passenger trains.

American sympathies, ever on the side of patriots fighting for freedom, went out to the Cuban underdogs. Aside from pure sentiment, the United States had an investment stake of about $50 million in Cuba and an annual trade stake of about $100 million. Moreover, Spanish misrule in Cuba menaced the shipping routes of the West Indies and the Gulf of Mexico, and less directly the future isthmian canal.

Fuel was added to the Cuban conflagration in 1896 with the coming of the Spanish general

The Explosion of the *Maine*, February 15, 1898   Encouraged and amplified by the "yellow press," the outcry over the tragedy of the *Maine* helped drive the country into an impulsive war against Spain.

("Butcher") Weyler. He undertook to crush the rebellion by herding many civilians into barbed-wire reconcentration camps, where they could not give assistance to the armed *insurrectos*. Lacking proper sanitation, these enclosures turned into deadly pestholes; the victims died like dogs.

An outraged American public demanded action. Congress in 1896 overwhelmingly passed a resolution that called upon President Cleveland to recognize the belligerency of the revolted Cubans. But as the government of the insurgents consisted of hardly more than a few fugitive leaders, Cleveland—an antijingoist and anti-imperialist—refused to budge. He defiantly vowed that if Congress declared war, the commander in chief would not issue the necessary order to mobilize the army.

The Mystery of the *Maine* Explosion

Atrocities in Cuba were made to order for the sensational new "yellow journalism." William R. Hearst and Joseph Pulitzer, then engaged in a titanic duel for circulation, attempted to outdo each other with screeching headlines and hair-raising "scoops." Lesser competitors zestfully followed suit.

Where atrocity stories did not exist, they were invented. Hearst sent the gifted artist Frederic Remington to Cuba to draw sketches, and when the latter reported that conditions were not bad enough to warrant hostilities, Hearst is alleged to have replied, "You furnish the pictures and I'll furnish the war."

Among other outrages, Remington depicted Spanish customs officials brutally disrobing and searching an American woman. Most readers of Hearst's *Journal,* their indignation soaring, had no way of knowing that such tasks were performed by female attendants. "Butcher" Weyler was removed in 1897, yet conditions steadily worsened. There was some talk in Spain of granting the restive island a type of self-government, but such a surrender was so bitterly opposed by many Spaniards in Cuba that they engaged in furious riots. Early in 1898 Washington sent the battleship *Maine* to Cuba, ostensibly for a "friendly visit" but actually to protect and evacuate Americans if a dangerous flare-up should again occur.

This already explosive situation suddenly grew acute on February 9, 1898, when Hearst sensationally headlined a private letter written by the Spanish minister in Washington, Dupuy de Lôme. The indiscreet epistle, which had been stolen from the mails, described President McKinley as an ear-to-the-ground politician who lacked good faith. The resulting uproar was so violent that Dupuy de Lôme was forced to resign.

A tragic climax came a few days later, on February 15, 1898, when the *Maine* mysteriously blew up in Havana harbor, with a loss of 260 officers and men. Two investigations of the iron coffin were undertaken, one by U.S. naval officers, and the other by Spanish officials, whom the Americans would not trust near the wreck. The Spanish commission stated

Many Spaniards felt that accusations about their blowing up the Maine *reflected on Spanish honor. One Madrid newspaper spoke up:*

"The American jingoes . . . imagine us capable of the most foul villainies and cowardly actions. Scoundrels by nature, the American jingoes believe that all men are made like themselves. What do they know about noble and generous feelings? . . . We should not in any way heed the jingoes: they are not even worth our contempt, or the saliva with which we might honor them in spitting at their faces."

that the explosion had been internal and presumably accidental; the American commission reported that the blast had been caused by a submarine mine. Washington, not unmindful of popular indignation, spurned Spanish proposals of arbitration.

Various theories have been advanced as to how the *Maine* was blown up. The least convincing explanation of all is that the Spanish officials in Cuba were guilty, for they were under the American gun and Spain was far away. Not until 1976 did Admiral H. G. Rickover, under U.S. Navy auspices, give what appears to be the final answer. He presented overwhelming evidence that the initial explosion had resulted from spontaneous combustion in one of the coal bunkers adjacent to a powder magazine. Ironically, this is essentially what the Spanish commission had deduced in 1898.

But Americans in 1898, now war-mad, blindly accepted the least likely explanation. Lashed to fury by the yellow press, they leapt to the conclusion that the Spanish government had been guilty of intolerable treachery. The battle cry of the hour became,

> *Remember the* Maine!
> *To hell with Spain!*

Nothing would do but to hurl the "dirty" Spanish flag from the hemisphere.

McKinley Unleashes the Dogs of War

The national war fever burned higher, even though American diplomats had already gained Madrid's agreement to Washington's two basic demands: an end to the reconcentration camps and an armistice with Cuban rebels. The cautious McKinley did not want hostilities. The hesitant chief executive was condemned by jingoes as "Wobbly Willie" McKinley, while fight-hungry Theodore Roosevelt reportedly snarled that the "white-livered" occupant of the White House did not have "the backbone of a chocolate éclair." The president, whose shaken nerves required sleeping pills, was even being hanged in effigy. Many critics did not realize that backbone was needed to stay out of war, not to plunge into it.

McKinley's private desires clashed sharply with opinions now popular with the public. He did not want hostilities, for he had seen enough bloodshed as a major in the Civil War. Mark Hanna and Wall

"Cuba Libre," by Captain Fritz W. Guerin of St. Louis, 1898 This elaborately staged tableau depicts Confederate and Union officers reconciled three decades after the Civil War as they join hands to liberate innocent Cuba from her chains of bondage to Spain.

Street did not want war, for business might be unsettled. But the public, prodded by the yellow press and the appeals of Cuban exiles in the United States, clamored for a fight. The president, recognizing the inevitable, finally yielded and gave the people what they wanted.

But public pressures did not fully explain McKinley's course. He had no faith in Spain's promises regarding Cuba; Madrid had spoken them and broken them before. He was certain that a showdown would have to come sooner or later. He believed in the democratic principle that the people should rule, and he hesitated to deny Americans what they demanded—even if it was not good for them. He also perceived that if he stood out against war, the Democrats would make political capital out of his stubbornness. Bryan might sweep into the presidency two years later under a banner inscribed "Free Cuba and Free Silver." Gold-standard McKinley was a staunch party man, and to him it seemed better to break up the remnants of Spain's once-

glorious empire than to break up the Grand Old Party—especially since war seemed inevitable.

On April 11, 1898, McKinley sent his war message to Congress, urging armed intervention to free the oppressed Cubans. The legislators responded uproariously with what was essentially a declaration of war. In a burst of self-righteousness, they likewise adopted the hand-tying Teller Amendment. This proviso proclaimed to the world that when the United States had overthrown Spanish misrule, it would give the Cubans their freedom—a declaration that caused imperialistic Europeans to smile skeptically.

Dewey's May Day Victory at Manila

The American people plunged into the war lightheartedly, like schoolchildren off to a picnic. Bands blared incessantly "There'll Be a Hot Time in the Old

Town Tonight" and "Hail, Hail, the Gang's All Here," thus leading foreigners to believe that those were national anthems.

But such jubilation seemed premature to European observers. The regular army, which was commanded by corpulent Civil War oldsters, was unprepared for a war under tropical skies. It numbered only 2,100 officers and 28,000 men, as compared with some 200,000 Spanish troops in Cuba. The American navy, at least to transatlantic experts, seemed slightly less powerful than Spain's. European powers, moreover, were generally friendly to their Old World associate. The only conspicuous exception was the ally-seeking British, who now were ardently wooing their American cousins.

Yet in one important respect, Spain's apparent superiority was illusory. Its navy, though formidable on paper, was in wretched condition. It labored under the added handicap of having to operate thousands of miles from its home base. But the new American steel navy, now fifteen years old and ranking about fifth among the fleets of the world, was in fairly good trim, though the war was to lay bare serious defects.

The readiness of the navy owed much to two men: the easygoing navy secretary John D. Long and his bellicose assistant secretary Theodore Roosevelt. The secretary hardly dared leave his desk for fear that his overzealous underling would stir up a hornet's nest. On February 25, 1898, while Long was away for a weekend, Roosevelt had cabled Commodore George Dewey, commanding the American Asiatic Squadron at Hong Kong, to descend upon Spain's Philippines in the event of war. McKinley subsequently confirmed these instructions, even though an attack in the distant Far East seemed like a strange way to free nearby Cuba.

Dewey carried out his orders magnificently on May 1, 1898. Sailing boldly with his six warships at night into the fortified harbor of Manila, he trained his guns the next morning on the ten-ship Spanish fleet, one of whose craft was only a moored hulk without functioning engines. The entire collection of antiquated and overmatched vessels was quickly destroyed, with a loss of nearly four hundred Spaniards killed and wounded, and without the loss of a single life in Dewey's fleet. An American consul who was there wrote that all the American sailors needed was cough drops for throats made raw by cheers of victory.

Unexpected Imperialistic Plums

Taciturn George Dewey became a national hero overnight. He was promptly promoted to the rank of admiral, as the price of flags rose sharply. An amateur poet blossomed forth with this:

> Oh, dewy was the morning
> Upon the first of May,
> And Dewey was the Admiral,
> Down in Manila Bay.
> And dewy were the Spaniards' eyes,
> Them orbs of black and blue;
> And dew we feel discouraged?
> I dew not think we dew!

Yet Dewey was in a perilous position. He had destroyed the enemy fleet, but he could not storm the forts of Manila with his sailors. His nerves frayed, he was forced to wait in the steaming-hot bay while troop reinforcements were slowly assembled in America.

Dewey's Route in the Philippines, 1898

Emilio Aguinaldo (c. 1869–1964) and Followers, 1900 Aguinaldo had a colorfully checkered career. Exiled from the Philippines by the Spanish in 1897, he was brought back in 1898 to assist the American invasion. A year later he led the Filipino insurrection against the new American rulers. Captured in 1901, he declared his loyalty to the United States. During World War II, he collaborated with the Japanese when they occupied the Philippines. After a lifetime of political intrigue and armed struggle, Aguinaldo died peacefully in Manila in 1964 in his ninety-fifth year.

Foreign warships meanwhile had begun to gather in the harbor, ostensibly to safeguard their nationals in Manila. The Germans sent five vessels—a naval force more powerful than Dewey's—and their haughty admiral defied the American blockade regulations. After several disagreeable incidents, Dewey lost his temper and threatened the arrogant German with war "as soon as you like." Happily, the storm blew over. The British commander, by contrast, was conspicuously successful in carrying out London's new policy of friendliness. A false tale subsequently circulated that the British dramatically interposed their ships to prevent the Germans from blowing the Americans out of the water.

Long-awaited American troops, finally arriving in force, captured Manila on August 13, 1898. They collaborated with the Filipino insurgents, commanded by their well-educated, part-Chinese leader, Emilio Aguinaldo. Dewey, to his later regret, had brought this shrewd and magnetic revolutionary from exile in Asia, so that he might weaken Spanish resistance.

These thrilling events in the Philippines had meanwhile focused attention on Hawaii. An impression spread that America needed the archipelago as a coaling and provisioning way station, in order to send supplies and reinforcements to Dewey. The truth is that the United States could have used these island "Crossroads of the Pacific" without annexing them, so eager was the white-dominated Honolulu government to compromise its neutrality and risk the vengeance of Spain. But an appreciative American public would not leave Dewey in the lurch. A joint resolution of annexation was rushed through Congress and approved by McKinley on July 7, 1898.

The residents of Hawaii were granted U.S. citizenship with annexation and received full territorial status in 1900. These events in the idyllic islands, though seemingly sudden, were but the culmination of nearly a century of Americanization by sailors, whalers, traders, and missionaries.

The Confused Invasion of Cuba

Shortly after the outbreak of war, the Spanish government ordered a fleet of warships to Cuba. It was commanded by Admiral Cervera, who protested that his wretchedly prepared ships were flirting with suicide. Four armored cruisers finally set forth (one without its main battery of guns). They were accompanied by six torpedo boats, three of which had to be abandoned en route.

Panic seized the eastern seaboard of the United States. American vacationers abandoned their seashore cottages, while nervous investors moved their securities to inland depositories. Demands for protection poured in on Washington from nervous citizens, and the Navy Department was forced to dispatch some useless old Civil War ships to useless

Colonel Theodore Roosevelt with Some of the "Rough Riders" Roosevelt later described his first encounter with the Spanish enemy: "Soon we came to the brink of a deep valley. There was a good deal of cracking of rifles way off in front of us, but as they used smokeless powder we had no idea as to exactly where they were, or who they were shooting at. Then it dawned on us that we were the target. The bullets began to come overhead, making a sound like the ripping of a silk dress, with sometimes a kind of pop. . . . We advanced, firing at them, and drove them off."

places for morale purposes. Cervera finally found refuge in bottle-shaped Santiago harbor, Cuba, where he was blockaded by the much more powerful American fleet.

Sound strategy seemed to dictate that an American army be sent in from the rear to drive out Cervera. Leading the invading force was the grossly overweight General William R. Shafter, a leader so blubbery and gout-stricken that he had to be car-

---

With a mixture of modesty and immodesty, Colonel Theodore Roosevelt (1858–1919) wrote privately in 1903 of his "Rough Riders,"

"In my regiment nine-tenths of the men were better horsemen than I was, and probably two-thirds of them better shots than I was, while on the average they were certainly hardier and more enduring. Yet after I had had them a very short while they all knew, and I knew too, that nobody else could command them as I could."

---

ried about on a door. The ill-prepared Americans were unequipped for war in the tropics; they had been amply provided with heavy woolen underwear and uniforms designed for subzero operations against the Indians.

The "Rough Riders," a part of the invading army, now charged onto the stage of history. This colorful regiment of volunteers, short on discipline but long on dash, consisted largely of western cowboys and other hardy characters, with a sprinkling of ex–polo players and ex-convicts. Commanded by Colonel Leonard Wood, the group was organized principally by the glory-hungry Theodore Roosevelt, who had resigned from the Navy Department to serve as lieutenant colonel. Although totally without military experience, he used his strong political pull to secure his commission and to bypass physical standards. He was so nearsighted that as a safeguard he took along a dozen pairs of spectacles, cached in handy spots on his person or nearby.

About the middle of June, a bewildered American army of seventeen thousand men finally embarked at congested Tampa, Florida, amid scenes of indescribable confusion. The Rough Riders, fearing that they would be robbed of glory, rushed one of the transports and courageously held

The U.S. Cruiser *Olympia*, c. 1898 Naval vessels such as this played crucial roles in the battles of Santiago and Manila Bay.

their place for almost a week in the broiling tropical sun. About half of them finally got to Cuba without most of their horses, and the bowlegged regiment then came to be known as "Wood's Weary Walkers."

Shafter's landing near Santiago, Cuba, was made without serious opposition. Defending Spaniards, even more disorganized than the Americans, were unable to muster at this spot more than two thousand men. Brisk fighting broke out on July 1 at El Caney and San Juan Hill, up which Colonel Roosevelt and his horseless Rough Riders charged, with strong support from two crack black regiments. They suffered heavy casualties, but the colorful colonel, having the time of his life, shot a Spaniard with his revolver, and rejoiced to see his victim double up like a jackrabbit. He later wrote a book on his exploits, which the famed satirist, "Mr. Dooley" remarked, ought to have been entitled *Alone in Cubia* [sic].

Curtains for Spain in America

The American army, fast closing in on Santiago, spelled doom for the Spanish fleet. Admiral Cervera, again protesting against suicide, was flatly ordered to fight for the honor of the flag. The odds against him were heavy: the guns of the USS *Oregon* alone

threw more metal than his four armored cruisers combined. After a running chase, on July 3 the

The Cuban Campaign, 1898

foul-bottomed Spanish fleet was entirely destroyed, as the wooden decks caught fire and the blazing infernos were beached. About five hundred Spaniards were killed, as compared with one death for the Americans. "Don't cheer, men," admonished Captain Philip of the *Texas.* "The poor devils are dying." Shortly thereafter Santiago surrendered.

Hasty preparations were now made for a descent upon Puerto Rico before the war should end. The American army, commanded by the famed Indian-fighter General Nelson A. Miles, met little resistance, as most of the population greeted the invaders as liberating heroes. "Mr. Dooley" was led to refer to "Gin'ral Miles' Gran' Picnic an' Moonlight Excursion." By this time Spain had satisfied its honor, and on August 12, 1898, it signed an armistice.

If the Spaniards had held out a few months longer in Cuba, the American army might have melted away. The inroads of malaria, typhoid, dysentery, and yellow fever became so severe that hundreds were incapacitated—"an army of convalescents." Others suffered from odorous canned meat known as "embalmed beef." Fiery and insubordinate Colonel Roosevelt, who had no regular military career to jeopardize, was a ringleader in making "round-robin"* demands on Washington that the army be moved before it perished. About twenty-five thousand men, 80 percent of them ill, were transferred to chilly Long Island, where their light summer clothing finally arrived.

One of the war's worst scandals was the high death rate from sickness, especially typhoid fever. This disease was rampant in the unsanitary training camps in the United States. All told, nearly four hundred men lost their lives to bullets; over five thousand succumbed to bacteria and other causes.

McKinley Heeds Duty, Destiny, and Dollars

Late in 1898 the Spanish and American negotiators met in Paris, there to begin heated discussions. McKinley had sent five commissioners, including

Uncle Sam's White Elephant, 1898

three senators, who would have a final vote on their own handiwork. War-racked Cuba, as expected, was freed from its Spanish overlords. The Americans had little difficulty in securing the remote Pacific island of Guam, which they had captured early in the conflict from astonished Spaniards who, lacking a cable, had not known that a war was on. They also picked up Puerto Rico, the last remnant of what had been Spain's vast New World empire. In the decades to come, American investment in the island and Puerto Rican immigration to the United States would make this acquisition one of the weightier consequences of this somewhat carefree war (see "Makers of America: The Puerto Ricans," pp. 640–641).

Knottiest of all was the problem of the Philippines, a veritable apple of discord. These lush islands not only embraced an area larger than the British Isles but also contained a completely alien population of some 7 million souls. McKinley was confronted with a devil's dilemma. He did not feel that America could honorably give the islands back to Spanish misrule, especially after it had fought a

---

*A "round robin" is a document signed in circular form around the edges so that no one person can be identified (and punished) as the first signer.

President William McKinley (1843–1901) later described his decision to annex the Philippines:

"When next I realized that the Philippines had dropped into our laps, I confess I did not know what to do with them. . . . I went down on my knees and prayed Almighty God for light and guidance. . . . And one night late it came to me this way. . . . That there was nothing left for us to do but to take them all, and to educate the Filipinos, and uplift and civilize and Christianize them and by God's grace do the very best we could by them, as our fellow men, for whom Christ also died. And then I went to bed and went to sleep, and slept soundly."

war to free Cuba. And America would be turning its back upon its responsibilities in a cowardly fashion, he believed, if it simply pulled up anchor and sailed away.

McKinley viewed other alternatives open to him as trouble-fraught. The Filipinos, if left to govern themselves, might fall into anarchy. One of the major powers, possibly aggressive Germany, might then try to seize them, and the result might be a world war into which the United States would be sucked. Seemingly the least of the evils consistent with national honor and safety was to acquire all the Philippines and then perhaps give the Filipinos their freedom later.

President McKinley, ever sensitive to public opinion, kept a carefully attuned ear to the ground. The rumble that he heard seemed to call for the entire group of islands. Zealous Protestant missionaries were eager for new converts from Spanish Catholicism,* and the invalid Mrs. McKinley, to whom her husband was devoted, expressed deep concern about the welfare of the Filipinos. Wall

---

*The Philippines had been substantially Christianized by Catholics before the founding of Jamestown in 1607.

Street had generally opposed the war, but awakened by the booming of Dewey's guns, it was clamoring for profits in the Philippines. "If this be commercialism," cried Mark Hanna, then "for God's sake let us have commercialism."

A tormented McKinley, so he was later reported as saying, finally went down on his knees seeking divine guidance. An inner voice seemed to tell him to take all the Philippines and Christianize and civilize them. This solution apparently coincided with the demands of the American people as well as with the McKinley-Hanna outlook. The mixture of things spiritual and material in McKinley's reasoning was later slyly summarized by a historian: "God directs us—perhaps it will pay." Profits thus joined hands with piety.

Fresh disputes broke out with the Spanish negotiators in Paris, once McKinley had reached the thorny decision to keep the Philippines. Manila had been captured the day *after* the armistice was signed, and the islands could not properly be listed among the spoils of war. The deadlock was broken when the Americans at length agreed to pay Spain $20 million for the Philippine Islands—one of the best bargains the Spaniards ever drove and their last great haul from the New World. House Speaker "Czar" Reed sneered at America's having acquired millions of Malays, at three dollars a head, "in the bush." He resigned in protest against America's new imperial adventure.

America's Course (Curse?) of Empire

The signing of the pact of Paris touched off one of the most impassioned debates in American history. Except for glacial Alaska, coral-reefed Hawaii, and a handful of Pacific atolls acquired mostly for whaling stations, the Republic had hitherto acquired only contiguous territory on the continent. All previous acquisitions had been thinly peopled and capable of ultimate statehood. But in the Philippines, the nation had on its hands a distant tropical area, thickly populated by Asians of alien race, culture, tongue, religion, and government institutions.

The Anti-Imperialist League sprang into being to fight the McKinley administration's expansionist moves. The organization counted among its members some of the most prominent people in the

United States, including the presidents of Stanford and Harvard Universities, the philosopher William James, and the novelist Mark Twain. The anti-imperialist blanket even stretched over such strange bedfellows as the labor leader Samuel Gompers and steel titan Andrew Carnegie. "God-damn the United States for its vile conduct in the Philippine Isles!" burst out the usually mild-mannered Professor James. The Harvard philosopher could not believe that the United States could "puke up its ancient soul in five minutes without a wink of squeamishness."

Anti-imperialists had still other arrows in their quiver. The Filipinos panted for freedom, and to annex them would violate the "consent of the governed" philosophy in the Declaration of Independence. Despotism abroad might well beget despotism at home. Finally, annexation would propel the United States into the political and military cauldron of the Far East.

Yet the expansionists or imperialists could sing a seductive song. They appealed to patriotism and to the glory of annexation—"don't let any dastard dishonor the flag by hauling it down." Stressing the opportunities for exploiting the islands, they played up possible trade profits. Manila, in fact, might become another Hong Kong. The richer the natural resources of the islands appeared to be, the less capable of self-government the Filipinos seemed to be. Rudyard Kipling, the British poet laureate of imperialism, urged America down the slippery path:

Take up the White Man's burden—
Ye dare not stoop to less—
Nor call too loud on Freedom
To cloak your weariness.

Uncle Sam and People from His Colonies, c. 1900 The acquisition of Puerto Rico, the Philippines, Hawaii, and other Pacific Islands brought millions of people of color under the American flag. Whether they would eventually become citizens or remain colonial subjects was hotly debated in the United States. Many anti-imperialists opposed colonial expansion precisely because they regarded the exotic new peoples as "unassimilable."

In short, the wealthy Americans must help to uplift (and exploit) the underprivileged, underfed, and underclad of the world.

In the Senate the Spanish treaty ran into such heated opposition that it seemed doomed to defeat. But at this juncture the silverite Bryan unexpectedly sallied forth as its champion. As a Democratic volunteer colonel whom the Republicans had kept out of Cuba, he apparently had no reason to help the McKinley administration out of a hole. But free silver was dead as a political issue. Bryan's foes assumed that he was preparing to fasten the stigma of imperialism on the Republicans and then sweep into the presidency in 1900 under the flaming banner of anti-imperialism.

Bryan could support the treaty on plausible grounds. He argued that the war would not officially end until America had ratified the pact. It already had the islands on its hands, and the sooner it accepted the document, the sooner it could give the Filipinos their independence. After Bryan had used his personal influence with certain Democratic senators, the treaty was approved on February 6, 1899, with only one vote to spare. But the responsibility, as Bryan had foreseen, rested primarily with the Republicans.

Perplexities in Puerto Rico and Cuba

Many of Puerto Rico's 1 million inhabitants lived in poverty. The island's population grew faster than its economy. By the Foraker Act of 1900, Congress accorded the Puerto Ricans a limited degree of popular government and, in 1917, granted them U.S. citizenship. Although the American regime worked wonders in education, sanitation, transportation, and other tangible improvements, many of the inhabitants still aspired to independence. Great numbers of Puerto Ricans ultimately moved to New York City, where they added to the diversity of its immigrant culture.

A thorny legal problem was posed by the questions, Did the Constitution follow the flag? Did American laws, including tariff laws and the Bill of Rights, apply with full force to the newly acquired possessions? Beginning in 1901 with the *Insular Cases*, a badly divided Supreme Court decreed, in effect, that the flag did outrun the Constitution, and that the outdistanced document did not necessarily extend with full force to the new windfalls. The Filipinos and Puerto Ricans might be subject to American rule, but they did not enjoy all American rights.

Cuba, scorched and chaotic, presented another headache. An American military government, set up under the administrative genius of General Leonard Wood of Rough Rider fame, wrought miracles in government, finance, education, agriculture, and public health. Under his leadership a frontal attack was launched on yellow fever. Spectacular experiments were performed by Dr. Walter Reed and others upon American soldiers, who volunteered as human guinea pigs, and the stegomyia mosquito was proved to be the lethal carrier. A cleanup of breeding places for mosquitoes wiped out yellow fever in Havana, while removing the recurrent fear of epidemics in cities of the South and Atlantic seaboard.

The United States, honoring its self-denying Teller Amendment of 1898, withdrew from Cuba in 1902. Old World imperialists could scarcely believe their eyes. But the Washington government could not turn this rich and strategic island completely loose on the international sea; a grasping power like Germany might secure dangerous lodgment near America's soft underbelly. The Cubans were therefore forced to write into their own constitution of 1901 the so-called Platt Amendment.

The hated restriction severely hobbled the Cubans. They reluctantly bound themselves not to impair their independence by treaty or by contracting a debt beyond their resources. They further agreed that the United States might intervene with troops to restore order and to provide mutual protection. Finally, the Cubans promised to sell or lease needed coaling or naval stations, ultimately two and then only one (Guantanamo), to their powerful "benefactor." The United States still occupies its twenty-eight-thousand-acre beachhead under an agreement that can be revoked only by the consent of both parties.

New Horizons in Two Hemispheres

In essence, the Spanish-American War was a kind of colossal coming-out party. Despite a common misconception, the conflict did not cause the United States to become a world power. Dewey's thundering guns merely advertised the fact that the nation was already a world power.

The Puerto Ricans

At dawn on July 26, 1898, the U.S. warship *Gloucester* steamed into Puerto Rico's Guánica harbor, fired at the Spanish blockhouse, and landed some thirty-three hundred troops. Within days the Americans had taken possession of the militarily strategic Caribbean island a thousand miles southeast of Florida. In so doing they set in motion changes on the island that ultimately brought a new wave of immigrants to U.S. shores.

Puerto Rico had been a Spanish possession since Christopher Columbus claimed it for Castile in 1493. The Spaniards enslaved many of the island's forty thousand Taino Indians and set them to work on farms and in mines. Many Tainos died of exhaustion and disease, and in 1511 the Indians rebelled. The Spaniards crushed the uprising, killed thousands of Indians, and began importing African slaves—thus establishing the basis for Puerto Rico's multiracial society.

The first Puerto Rican immigrants to the United States arrived as political exiles in the nineteenth century. From their haven in America, they agitated for the island's independence from Spain. In 1897 Spain finally granted the island local autonomy; ironically, however, the Spanish-American War the following year placed it in American hands. Puerto Rican political émigrés in the United States returned home, but they were soon replaced by poor islanders looking for work.

Changing conditions in Puerto Rico after the U.S. takeover had driven these new immigrants north. Although slow to grant Puerto Ricans U.S. citizenship, the Americans quickly improved health and sanitation on the island, triggering a population surge in the early twentieth century. At the same time, growing monopoly control of Puerto Rico's sugar cane plantations undermined the island's subsistence economy, and a series of hurricanes devastated the coffee plantations that had employed large numbers of people. With almost no industry to provide wage labor, Puerto Rico's unemployment rate soared.

Thus when Congress finally granted Puerto Ricans U.S. citizenship in 1917, thereby eliminating immigration hurdles, many islanders hurried north to find jobs. Over the ensuing decades, Puerto Ricans went to work in Arizona cotton fields, New Jersey soup factories, and Utah mines. The majority, however, clustered in New York City and found work in the city's cigar factories, shipyards, and garment industry. Migration slowed somewhat after the 1920s as the Great Depression shrank the job market on the mainland and as World War II made travel hazardous.

The First Puerto Ricans The Spanish *conquistadores* treated the native Taino people in Puerto Rico with extreme cruelty, and the Indians were virtually extinct by the mid-1500s.

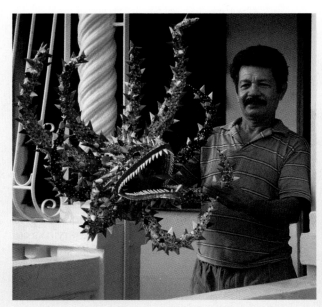

Preparing for *Carnaval* (Carnival) This mask-maker displays an elaborate *máscara de cartón* (papier-mâché mask) made for the annual Puerto Rican festival. Masked figures at *Carnaval* have been part of Puerto Rican culture for more than two centuries.

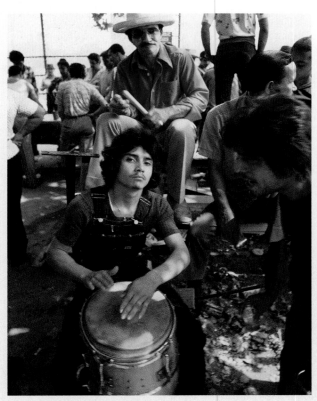

***Carnaval* in New York** Puerto Rican Americans making music in New York City.

When World War II ended in 1945, the sudden advent of cheap air travel sparked an immigration explosion. As late as the 1930s, the tab for a boat trip to the mainland exceeded the average Puerto Rican's yearly earnings. But with an airplane surplus after World War II, the six-hour flight from Puerto Rico to New York cost under fifty dollars. The Puerto Rican population on the mainland quadrupled between 1940 and 1950 and tripled again by 1960. In 1970, 1.5 million Puerto Ricans lived in the United States, one-third of the island's total population.

U.S. citizenship and affordable air travel made it easy for Puerto Ricans to return home. Thus to a far greater degree than most immigrant groups, Puerto Ricans kept one foot in the United States and the other on their native island. By some estimates, 2 million people a year journeyed to and from the island during the postwar period. Puerto Rico's gubernatorial candidates sometimes campaigned in New York for the thousands of voters who were expected to return to the island in time for the election.

This transience worked to keep Puerto Ricans' educational attainment and English proficiency far below the national average. At the same time, the immigrants encountered a deep-seated racism in America unlike anything on their multiracial island. Throughout the postwar years, Puerto Ricans remained one of the poorest groups in the United States, with a median family income below that of African-Americans and Mexican-Americans.

Still, Puerto Ricans have fared better economically in the United States than on the island, where, in 1970, 60 percent of all inhabitants lived below the poverty line. In recent years Puerto Ricans have attained more schooling, and many have attended college. Invigorated by the civil rights movement of the 1960s, Puerto Ricans also became more politically active, electing growing numbers of congressmen and state and city officials.

The New Jingoism An enthusiastic Uncle Sam cheers the U.S. Navy in the "splendid little war" of 1898. Many Americans, however, were less than enthused about America's new imperial adventure.

Three years after the Spanish-American War ended, a foreign diplomat in Washington remarked,

"I have seen two Americas, the America before the Spanish American War and the America since."

The war itself was short (113 days), spectacular, low in casualties, and uninterruptedly successful—despite the bungling. American prestige rose sharply, and the European powers grudgingly accorded the Republic more respect. In Germany Prince Bismarck reportedly growled that there was a special Providence that looked after drunkards, fools, and the United States of America. At times it seemed as though not only Providence but the Spaniards were fighting on the side of the Yankees. So great, in fact, was America's good fortune that rejoicing citizens found in the victories further support—misleading support—for their indifference to adequate preparedness.

An exhilarating new spirit thrilled America, buoyed along by the newly popular military marching-band music of John Philip Sousa. National pride was touched and cockiness was increased by what John Hay called a "splendid little war."* Enthusiasm over these triumphs made easier the rush down the thorny path of empire. America did not start the war with imperialistic motives, but after falling through the cellar door of imperialism in a drunken fit of idealism, it wound up with imperialistic and colonial fruits in its grasp. The much-criticized British imperialists were pleased, partly because of the newfound friendship, partly because misery loves company. But America's German rival was envious, and Latin American neighbors were deeply suspicious of Yankee greed.

By taking on the Philippine Islands, the United States became a full-fledged Far Eastern power. Hereafter these distant islands were to be a "heel of Achilles"—a kind of indefensible hostage given to Japan, as events proved in 1941. With singular short-sightedness, the Americans assumed dangerous commitments that they were later unwilling to defend by proper naval and military outlays.

But the lessons of unpreparedness were not altogether lost. Captain Mahan's big-navyism seemed vindicated, and pride in the exploits of the navy energized popular support for more and better battleships. A masterly organizer, Elihu Root, took over the reins at the War Department. He estab-

---

*Anti-imperialist William James called it "our squalid war with Spain."

lished a general staff and founded the War College in Washington. His genius later paid dividends when the United States found itself involved in the world war of 1914–1918.

One of the happiest results of the conflict was the further closing of the "bloody chasm" between North and South. Thousands of patriotic southern-ers had flocked to the Stars and Stripes, and the gray-bearded General Joseph ("Fighting Joe") Wheeler—a Confederate cavalry hero of about a thousand Civil War skirmishes and battles—was given a command in Cuba. He allegedly cried, in the heat of battle, "To hell with the Yankees! Dammit, I mean the Spaniards."

Chronology

1820	New England missionaries arrive in Hawaii
1889	Samoa crisis with Germany Pan-American Conference
1890	Mahan publishes *The Influence of Sea Power upon History*
1891	New Orleans crisis with Italy
1892	Valparaiso crisis with Chile
1893	Pribilof Islands dispute with Canada White planter revolt in Hawaii Cleveland refuses Hawaii annexation
1895	Cubans revolt against Spain
1895-1896	Venezuelan boundary crisis with Britain
1898	*Maine* explosion in Havana harbor Spanish-American War Teller Amendment Dewey's victory at Manila Bay Hawaii annexed
1899	Senate ratifies treaty acquiring the Philippines
1900	Hawaii receives full territorial status Foraker Act for Puerto Rico
1901	Supreme Court *Insular Cases* Platt Amendment
1902	U.S. troops leave Cuba
1917	Puerto Ricans granted U.S. citizenship

For further reading, see page A19 of the Appendix. For web resources, go to **http://college.hmco.com.**

PART FIVE

STRUGGLING FOR JUSTICE AT HOME AND ABROAD

---◆◆---

1899–1945

The new century brought astonishing changes to the United States. Victory in the Spanish-American War made it clear that the United States was now a world power. Industrialization ushered in giant corporations, sprawling factories, sweatshop labor, and the ubiquitous automobile. A huge wave of immigration was altering the face of the nation, especially the cities, where a majority of Americans lived by 1920. With bigger cities came bigger fears—of crime, vice, poverty, and disease.

Changes of such magnitude raised vexing questions. What role should the United States play in the world? How could the enormous power of industry be controlled? How would the millions of new immigrants make their way in America? What should the country do about poverty, disease, and the continuing plague of racial inequality? All these issues turned on a fundamental point: should government remain narrowly limited in its powers, or did the times require a more potent government that would actively shape society and secure American interests abroad?

The progressive movement represented the first attempt to answer those questions. Reform-minded men and women from all walks of life and from both major parties shared in the progressive crusade for greater government activism. Buoyed by this outlook, Presidents Theodore Roosevelt, William Howard Taft, and Woodrow Wilson enlarged the capacity of government to fight graft, "bust" business trusts, regulate corporations, and promote fair labor prac-

Stars and Stripes Roll for Women's Suffrage
Reformers fought on many fronts in the Progressive Era. These suffragists and their daughters aimed to convince parade watchers that nothing was more patriotic than giving the vote to American women.

tices, child welfare, conservation, and consumer protection. These progressive reformers, convinced that women would bring greater morality to politics, bolstered the decades-long struggle for female suffrage. Women finally secured the vote in 1920 with the ratification of the Nineteenth Amendment.

The progressive era presidents also challenged America's tradition of isolationism in foreign policy. They felt the country had a moral obligation to spread democracy and an economic opportunity to reap profits in foreign markets. Roosevelt and Taft launched diplomatic initiatives in the Caribbean, Central America, and East Asia. Wilson aspired to "make the world safe for democracy" by rallying support for American intervention in the First World War.

The progressive spirit waned, however, as the United States retreated during the 1920s into what President Harding called "normalcy." Isolationist sentiment revived with a vengeance. Blessed with a booming economy, Americans turned their gaze inward to baseball heroes, radio, jazz, movies, and the first mass-produced American automobile, the Model T Ford. Presidents Harding, Coolidge, and Hoover backed off from the economic regulatory zeal of their predecessors.

"Normalcy" also had a brutal side. Thousands of suspected radicals were jailed or deported in the Red Scare of 1919 and 1920. Anti-immigrant passions flared until immigration quotas in 1924 squeezed the flow of newcomers to a trickle. Race riots scorched several northern cities in the summer of 1919, a sign of how embittered race relations had become in the wake of the "Great Migration" of southern blacks to wartime jobs in northern industry. A reborn Ku Klux Klan staged a comeback, not just in the South but in the North and West as well.

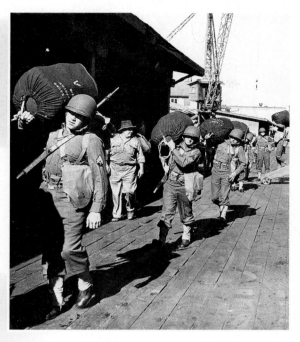

"Normalcy" itself soon proved short-lived, a casualty of the stock market crash of 1929 and the Great Depression that followed. As Americans watched banks fail, and businesses collapse, and millions of people lose their jobs, they asked with renewed urgency what role the government should play in rescuing the nation. President Franklin D. Roosevelt's answer was the "New Deal" —an ambitious array of relief programs, public works, and economic regulations that failed to cure the Depression but furnished an impressive legacy of social reforms.

Most Americans came to accept an expanded federal governmental role at home under FDR's leadership in the 1930s, but they still clung stubbornly to isolationism. The United States did little in the 1930s to check the rising military aggression of Japan and Germany. By the early 1940s, events forced Americans to reconsider. Once Hitler's Germany had seized control of most of Europe, Roosevelt, who had long opposed the isolationists, found ways to aid a beleaguered Britain. When Japan attacked the American naval base at Pearl Harbor in December 1941, isolationists at last fell silent. Roosevelt led a stunned but determined nation into the Second World War, and victory in 1945 positioned the United States to assume a commanding position in the postwar world order.

The Great Depression and the Second World War brought to a head a half-century of debate over the role of government and the place of the United States in the world. In the name of a struggle for justice, Roosevelt established a new era of government activism at home and internationalism abroad. The New Deal's legacy set the terms of debate in American political life for the rest of the century.

Bound for Guadalcanal, 1942
These troops were headed for one of the bloodiest battles of World War II, in the southwest Pacific's Solomon Islands. America threw some 15 million men and the full weight of its enormous economy into the struggle against German and Japanese aggression.

America on the World Stage

∽

1899–1909

I never take a step in foreign policy unless I am assured that I shall be able eventually to carry out my will by force.

THEODORE ROOSEVELT, 1905

Liberty-loving Filipinos assumed that they, like the Cubans, would be granted their freedom after the Spanish-American War. They were tragically deceived. The Senate refused to pass such a resolution granting Filipino independence. Bitterness toward the American troops mounted. It finally erupted into open insurrection on February 4, 1899, under Emilio Aguinaldo.

The war with the Filipinos, unlike the "splendid" little set-to with Spain, was sordid and prolonged. It involved more savage fighting, more soldiers killed, and far more scandal. Anti-imperialists redoubled their protests. In their view the United States, having plunged into war with Spain to free Cuba, was now fighting ten thousand miles away to rivet shackles on a people who asked for nothing but liberty—in the American tradition.

"Little Brown Brothers" in the Philippines

As the ill-equipped Filipino armies were defeated, they melted into the jungle to wage vicious guerrilla warfare. Many of the outgunned Filipinos used barbarous methods, and the infuriated American troops responded in kind. A brutal soldier song betrayed inner feelings:

Damn, damn, damn the Filipinos!
Cross-eyed kakiak ladrones [thieves]!
    Underneath the starry flag
    Civilize 'em with a Krag [rifle],
And return us to our own beloved homes.

Atrocity tales shocked and rocked the United States, for such methods did not reflect America's

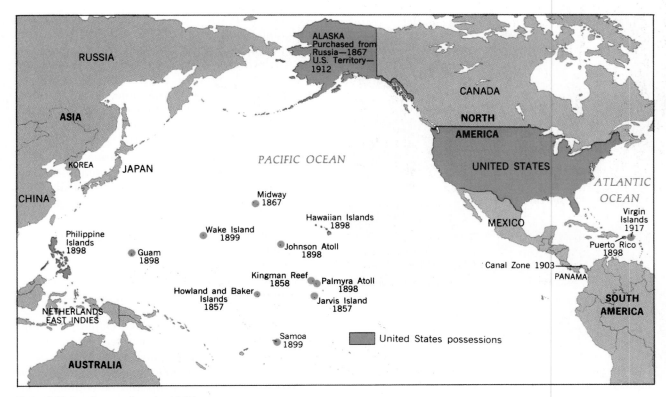

United States Possessions to 1917

better self. Uncle Sam's soldiers resorted to such extremes as the painful "water cure"—that is, forcing water down victims' throats until they yielded information or died. Reconcentration camps were even established that strongly suggested those of "Butcher" Weyler in Cuba. America, having begun the Spanish war with noble ideals, now dirtied its hands. One New York newspaper published a reply to Rudyard Kipling's famous poem:

We've taken up the white man's burden
Of ebony and brown;
Now will you kindly tell us, Rudyard,
How we may put it down?

The backbone of the Filipino insurrection was finally broken in 1901, when American soldiers cleverly infiltrated a guerrilla camp and captured Aguinaldo. But sporadic fighting dragged on for many dreary months.

The problem of a government for the conquered islanders worried President McKinley, who, in 1899, appointed the Philippine Commission to make appropriate recommendations. In its second year, this body was headed by future president William H. Taft, an able and amiable lawyer-judge from Ohio who weighed about 350 pounds. Forming a strong attachment to the Filipinos, he called them his "little brown brothers" and danced light-footedly with their tiny women. But among the American soldiers, sweatily combing the jungles, a different view of the insurgent prevailed:

He may be a brother of Big Bill Taft,
But he ain't no brother of mine.

McKinley's "benevolent assimilation" of the Philippines proceeded with painful slowness. Millions of American dollars were poured into the islands to improve roads, sanitation, and public health. Important economic ties, including trade in sugar, developed between the two peoples. American teachers—"pioneers of the blackboard"—set up an unusually good school system and helped

Captured Filipino Insurrectionists, c. 1899   For three years after its annexation of the Philippine Islands in 1898, the United States fought a savage war to suppress a Filipino rebellion against American rule. Some 600,000 Filipinos perished. There was bitter irony in this clash, as the Americans had claimed to be "liberating" the Filipinos from their oppressive Spanish masters; now the Yankee liberators appeared to be no less oppressive than the Spaniards they had ousted.

they began to tear away valuable leaseholds and economic spheres of influence from the Manchu government.

A growing group of Americans viewed the vivisection of China with alarm. Churches worried about their missionary strongholds; manufacturers and exporters feared that Chinese markets would be monopolized by Europeans. An alarmed American public, openly prodded by the press and slyly nudged by certain free-trade Britons, demanded that Washington do something. Secretary of State John Hay, a quiet but witty poet-novelist-diplomat with a flair for capturing the popular imagination, finally decided upon a dramatic move.

In the summer of 1899, Hay dispatched to all the great powers a communication soon known as the Open Door note. He urged them to announce that in their leaseholds or spheres of influence they would respect certain Chinese rights and the ideal of fair competition.

The phrase *Open Door* quickly caught the public fancy and gained wide acceptance. Hay's proposal caused much squirming in the leading capitals of the world. It was like asking all those who did not have thieving designs to stand up and be counted. Italy alone accepted the Open Door unconditionally; it was the only major power that had no leasehold or

make English a second language. But all this vast expenditure, which profited America little, was ill received. The Filipinos, who hated compulsory Americanization, preferred liberty. Like caged hawks, they beat against their gilded bars until they finally got their freedom, on the Fourth of July, 1946. In the meantime, thousands of Filipinos emigrated to the United States (see "Makers of America: The Filipinos," pp. 650–651).

Hinging the Open Door in China

Exciting events had meanwhile been brewing in faraway and enfeebled China. Following its defeat by Japan in 1894–1895, the imperialistic European powers, notably Russia and Germany, moved in. Like vultures descending upon a wounded whale,

The commercial interests of Britain and America were imperiled by the power grabs in China, and a close concert between the two powers would have helped both. Yet as Secretary of State John Hay (1838–1905) wrote privately in June 1900,

"Every Senator I see says, 'For God's sake, don't let it appear we have any understanding with England.' How can I make bricks without straw? That we should be compelled to refuse the assistance of the greatest power in the world [Britain], in carrying out our own policy, because all Irishmen are Democrats and some [American] Germans are fools—is enough to drive a man mad."

American Missionary Grace Roberts Teaching in China, 1903 A long history of American missionary involvement in China nurtured a sentimental affection for that country among Americans that persisted well into the twentieth century.

sphere of influence in China. Britain, Germany, France, and Japan all accepted, but subject to the condition that the others acquiesce unconditionally. Russia, with covetous designs on China's Manchuria, politely declined. But John Hay artfully interpreted the Russian refusal as an acceptance and proclaimed that the Open Door was in effect. Under such dubious midwifery was the infant born, and no one should have been surprised when the child proved to be sickly and relatively short-lived.

Open Door or not, patriotic Chinese did not care to be used as a doormat by the Europeans. In 1900 a superpatriotic group known as the "Boxers" broke loose with the cry, "Kill Foreign Devils." Over two hundred missionaries and other ill-fated whites were murdered, and a number of foreign diplomats were besieged in the capital, Beijing (Peking).

A multinational rescue force of some eighteen thousand soldiers, including twenty-five hundred Americans, arrived in the nick of time and quelled the rebellion. Such participation in a joint military operation, especially in Asia, was plainly contrary to the nation's time-honored principles of nonentanglement and noninvolvement.

The victorious allied invaders acted angrily and vindictively. They assessed prostrate China an excessive indemnity of $333 million, of which America's share was to be $24.5 million. When Washington discovered that this sum was much more than enough to pay damages and expenses, it remitted about $18 million. The Beijing government, appreciating this gesture of goodwill, set aside the money to educate a selected group of Chinese students in the United States. These bright young scholars later played a significant role in the westernization of Asia.

Secretary Hay now let fly another paper broadside, for he feared that the triumphant powers might use the Boxer outrages as a pretext for carving up China outright. His new circular note to the powers in 1900 announced that henceforth the Open Door would embrace the territorial integrity of China, in addition to its commercial integrity.

Defenseless China was spared partition during these troubled years. But its salvation was probably due not to Hay's fine phrases, but to the strength of the competing powers. None of them could trust the others not to seek their own advantage.

The Filipinos

At the beginning of the twentieth century, the United States, its imperial muscles just flexed in the war with Spain, found itself in possession of the Philippines. Uncertain of how to manage this empire, which seethed resentfully against its new masters, the United States promised to build democracy in the Philippines and to ready the islanders for home rule. Almost immediately after annexation, the American governor of the archipelago sent a corps of Filipino students to the United States, hoping to forge future leaders steeped in American ways who would someday govern an independent Philippines. Yet this small student group found little favor in their adopted country, although in their native land many went on to become respected citizens and leaders.

Most Filipino immigrants to the United States in these years, however, came not to study but to toil. With Chinese immigration banned, Hawaii and the Pacific Coast states turned to the Philippines for cheap agricultural labor. Beginning in 1906 the Hawaiian Sugar Planters Association aggressively recruited Filipino workers. Enlistments grew slowly at first, but by the 1920s thousands of young Filipino men had reached the Hawaiian Islands and been assigned to sugar plantations or pineapple fields.

Typically a young Filipino wishing to emigrate first made his way to Manila, where he signed a contract with the growers that promised three years' labor in return for transportation to Hawaii, wages, free housing and fuel, and return passage at the end of the contract. Not all of the emigrants returned; there remain in Hawaii today some former field workers still theoretically eligible for free transport back to their native land.

Those Filipinos venturing as far as the American mainland found work less arduous but also less certain than did their countrymen on Hawaiian plantations. Many mainlanders worked seasonally—in winter as domestic servants, busboys, or bellhops; in summer journeying to the fields to harvest lettuce, strawberries, sugar beets, and potatoes. Eventually Filipinos, along with Mexican immigrants, shared the dubious honor of making up California's agricultural work force.

A mobile society, Filipino-Americans also were overwhelmingly male; there was only one Filipino woman for every fourteen Filipino men in California in 1930. Thus the issue of intermarriage became acutely sensitive. California and many other states prohibited the marriage of Asians and Caucasians in demeaning laws that remained on the books until 1948. And if a Filipino so much as approached a

Filipino Laborers at Work on a Hawaiian Pineapple Plantation, 1930s

Caucasian woman, he could expect reprisals—sometimes violent. For example, white vigilante groups roamed the Yakima Valley in Washington and the San Joaquin and Salinas Valleys in California, intimidating and even attacking Filipinos whom they accused of improperly accosting white women. In 1930 one Filipino was murdered and others wounded after they invited some Caucasian women to a dance. Undeterred, the Filipinos challenged the restrictive state laws and the hooligans who found in them an excuse for mayhem. But Filipinos, who did not become eligible for American citizenship until 1946, long lacked political leverage.

After World War II, Filipino immigration accelerated. Between 1950 and 1970, the number of Filipinos in the United States nearly doubled, with women and men stepping aboard the new transpacific airliners in roughly equal numbers. Many of these recent arrivals sprang from sturdy middle-class stock and sought in America a better life for their children than the Philippines seemed able to offer. Today the war-torn and perpetually depressed archipelago sends more immigrants to American shores than does any other Asian nation.

Filipino Workers Arriving in Honolulu, 1940s Tags around their necks indicated the plantations to which they had been assigned.

A Filipino Day Parade, New York City

The Boxer Rebellion, 1900   Chinese nationalists, known as "Boxers," rose up against foreign domination of China in 1900. This map illustrates the Boxers' resentment against Russian, British, Japanese, and American incursions in China. Note the Russian bear and the American eagle.

Imperialism or Bryanism in 1900?

President McKinley's renomination by the Republicans in 1900 was a foregone conclusion. He had piloted the country through a victorious war; he had acquired rich, though burdensome, real estate; he had established the gold standard; and he had brought the promised prosperity of the full dinner pail. "We'll stand pat!" was the poker-playing counsel of Mark Hanna, since 1897 a senator from Ohio. McKinley was renominated at Philadelphia on a platform that smugly endorsed prosperity, the gold standard, and overseas expansion.

An irresistible vice-presidential boom had developed for "Teddy" Roosevelt (TR), the cowboy-hero of San Juan Hill. Capitalizing on his war-born popularity, he had been elected governor of New York, where the local political bosses had found him headstrong and difficult to manage. They therefore devised a scheme to kick the colorful colonel upstairs into the vice presidency.

This plot to railroad Roosevelt worked beautifully. Gesticulating wildly, he attended the nominating convention, where his western-style cowboy hat had made him stand out like a white crow. He had no desire to die of slow rot in the vice-presidential "burying ground," but he was eager to prove that he could get the nomination if he wanted it. He finally gave in to a chanting chorus of "We want Teddy!" He received a unanimous vote, except for his own. A frantic Hanna reportedly moaned that there would be only one heartbeat between that wild-eyed "madman"—"that damned cowboy"—and the presidency of the United States.

William Jennings Bryan was the odds-on choice of the Democrats, meeting at Kansas City. The free-silver issue was now as defunct as an abandoned mine, but Bryan, a slave to consistency, forced a silver plank down the throats of his protesting associates. Choking on its candidate's obstinacy, the Democratic platform proclaimed, as did Bryan, that the paramount issue was Republican overseas imperialism.

Campaign history partially repeated itself in 1900. McKinley, the soul of dignity, sat safely on his front porch, as before. Bryan, also as before, took to the stump in a cyclonic campaign, assailing both imperialism and Republican-fostered trusts.

The superenergetic, second-fiddle Roosevelt out-Bryaned Bryan. He toured the country with revolver-shooting cowboys, and his popularity cut heavily into Bryan's support in the Midwest. Flashing his magnificent teeth and pounding his fist fiercely into his palm, Roosevelt denounced all dastards who would haul down Old Glory.

Bryanites loudly trumpeted their "paramount" issue of imperialism. Lincoln, they charged, had abolished slavery for 3.5 million Africans; McKinley had reestablished it for 7 million Filipinos. Republicans responded by charging that "Bryanism," not imperialism, was the paramount issue. By this accusation they meant that Bryan would rock the boat of prosperity once he got into office with his free-silver lunacy and other dangerous ideas. The voters were much less concerned about imperialism than about "Four Years More of the Full Dinner Pail."

When the smoke cleared, McKinley had triumphed by a much wider margin than in 1896:

7,218,491 to 6,356,734 popular votes, and 292 to 155 electoral votes. But victory for the Republicans was not a mandate for or against imperialism. Many citizens who favored Bryan's anti-imperialism feared his free silver; many who favored McKinley's "sound money" hated his imperialism. One citizen wrote to former president Cleveland: "It is a choice between evils, and I am going to shut my eyes, hold my nose, vote, go home and disinfect myself." If there was any mandate at all it was for the two *P*s: prosperity and protection. Content with good times, the country anticipated four more years of a full dinner pail crammed with fried chicken. "Boss" Platt of New York gleefully looked forward to Inauguration Day, when he would see Roosevelt exit Albany and "take the veil" as vice president.

Bryan's Miscalculation   While the venerable Democratic party boss and former New York Senator David Hill looks on skeptically, Democratic presidential candidate William Jennings Bryan prepares to commit political suicide in 1900 by embracing the moribund silver issue as well as a highly unpopular position critical of overseas expansion. Bryan lost badly to William McKinley in 1900, but he survived to wage—and lose—one last presidential campaign in 1908.

IS SUICIDE A CRIME?

THOSE IN THE BACKGROUND: "It's sixteen to one he doesn't pull through alive this time."

TR: Brandisher of the Big Stick

Kindly William McKinley had scarcely served another six months when, in September 1901, he was murdered by a deranged anarchist. Roosevelt became president at age forty-two, the youngest thus far in American history. Knowing he had a reputation for impulsiveness and radicalism, he sought to reassure the country by proclaiming that he would carry out the policies of his predecessor. Cynics sneered that he would indeed carry them out— to the garbage heap.

What manner of man was Theodore Roosevelt, the red-blooded blue blood? Born into a wealthy and distinguished New York family, he had fiercely built up his spindly, asthmatic body by a stern and self-imposed routine of exercise. Graduating from Harvard with Phi Beta Kappa honors, he published at the age of twenty-four the first of some thirty volumes of muscular prose. Then came busy years,

---

The contest over American imperialism took place on the Senate floor as well as around the globe. In 1900 Senator Albert J. Beveridge (1862–1927), Republican from Indiana, returned from an investigative trip to the Philippines to defend its annexation:

"The Philippines are ours forever. . . . And just beyond the Philippines are China's illimitable markets. We will not retreat from either. We will not abandon our opportunity in the Orient. We will renounce our part in the mission of our race: trustee, under God, of the civilization of the world."

Two years later Senator George F. Hoar (1826–1904), Republican from Massachusetts, broke with his party to denounce American annexation of the Philippines and other territories:

"You cannot maintain despotism in Asia and a republic in America. If you try to deprive even a savage or a barbarian of his just rights you can never do it without becoming a savage or a barbarian yourself."

which involved duties as a ranch owner and bespectacled cowboy ("Four Eyes") in the Dakotas, followed by various political posts. When fully developed, he was a barrel-chested five feet ten inches, with prominent teeth, squinty eyes, droopy mustache, and piercing voice.

The Rough Rider's high-voltage energy was electrifying. Believing that it was better to wear out than to rust out, he would shake the hands of some six thousand people at one stretch or ride horseback many miles in a day as an example for portly cavalry officers. Not surprisingly, he gathered about him a group of athletic, tennis-playing cronies, who were popularly dubbed "the tennis cabinet."

Incurably boyish and bellicose, Roosevelt loved to fight—"an elegant row." He never ceased to preach the virile virtues and to denounce civilized softness, with its pacifists and other "flubdubs" and "mollycoddles." An ardent champion of military and naval preparedness, he adopted as his pet proverb, "Speak softly and carry a big stick, [and] you will go far." If statesmen had the big stick, they could work their will among foreign nations without shouting; if they lacked it, shouting would do no good. TR had both a big stick and a shrill voice.

Wherever Roosevelt went, there was a great stir. At a wedding he eclipsed the bride, at a funeral the corpse. Shockingly unconventional, he loved to break hoary precedents—the hoarier the better. He was a colossal egoist, and his self-confidence merged with self-righteousness. So sure was he of the correctness of his convictions that he impetuously branded people liars who disagreed with him. As a true cosmopolite, he loved people and mingled with those of all ranks, from Catholic cardinals to professional prizefighters, one of whom blinded a Rooseveltian eye in a White House bout.

An outspoken moralizer and reformer, Roosevelt preached virtue from the White House pulpit. Yet he was an opportunist who would cut a deal rather than butt his head against a stone wall. He was, in reality, much less radical than his blustery actions would indicate. A middle-of-the-roader, he stood just a little left of center and bared his mule-like molars at liberals and reactionaries alike.

Roosevelt rapidly developed into a master politician with an idolatrous personal following. After visiting him, a journalist wrote, "You go home and wring the personality out of your clothes." TR—as he was called—had an enormous popular

Theodore Roosevelt Roosevelt gives a speech with both voice and body language in North Carolina in 1902.

appeal, partly because the common people saw in him a fiery champion. A magnificent showman, he was always front-page copy; his cowboyism, his bear shooting, his outsize teeth, and his pince-nez glasses were ever the delight of cartoonists. Though a staunch party man, he detested many of the dirty-handed bosses. But he learned, as Cleveland never did, to hold his nose and work with them.

Above all, Roosevelt was a direct-actionist. He believed that the president should lead, and although he made mistakes, he kept things noisily moving—generally forward. Never a lawyer, he condemned the law and the courts as too slow. He had no real respect for the delicate checks and balances among the three branches of the government. Finding the Constitution too rigid, he would on occasion ignore it; finding Congress too rebellious, he tried a mixture of coercion and compromise on it. The president, he felt, may take any action in the general interest that is not specifically forbidden by the laws of the Constitution. As one poet noted,

The Constitution rides behind
And the Big Stick rides before,
(Which is the rule of precedent
In the reign of Theodore.)

Colombia Blocks the Canal

Foreign affairs absorbed much of Roosevelt's bullish energy. Having traveled extensively in Europe, he enjoyed a far more intimate knowledge of the outside world than most of his predecessors.

The Spanish-American War had emphasized the need for the long-talked-about canal across the Central American isthmus, through which only printer's ink had ever flowed. Americans had learned a sobering lesson when the battleship *Oregon*, stationed on the Pacific Coast at the outbreak of war in 1898, had to steam all the way around South America to join the fleet in Cuban waters. An isthmian canal would plainly augment the strength of the navy by increasing its mobility. Such a waterway would also make easier the defense of such recent acquisitions as Puerto Rico, Hawaii, and the Philippines, while facilitating the operations of the American merchant marine.

Initial obstacles in the path of the canal builders were legal rather than geographical. By the terms of the ancient Clayton-Bulwer Treaty, concluded with Britain in 1850, the United States could not secure exclusive control over such a route. But by 1901 America's British cousins were willing to yield ground. Confronted with an unfriendly Europe and bogged down in the South African Boer War, they consented to the Hay-Pauncefote Treaty in 1901. It not only gave the United States a free hand to build the canal but conceded the right to fortify it as well.

Legal barriers now removed, the next question was, Where should the canal be dug? Many American experts favored the Nicaraguan route, but agents of the old French Canal Company were eager to salvage something from their costly failure at S-shaped Panama. Represented by a young, energetic, and unscrupulous engineer, Philippe Bunau-Varilla, the New Panama Canal Company suddenly dropped the price of its holdings from $109 million to the fire-sale price of $40 million.

After much debate, Congress in June 1902 decided on the Panama route. The scene now shifted to Colombia, of which Panama was an unwilling part. A treaty highly favorable to the United States was negotiated between Washington and a Colombian government agent in Bogota. It granted to the United States a lease for a six-mile-wide zone in perpetuity in exchange for $10 million and an annual payment of $250,000. The Colombian senate rejected the treaty, putting a higher value on this precious isthmian strip. Evidence later unearthed indicates that had Washington been willing to pay an additional $15 million, the pact would have been approved.

Roosevelt was infuriated by his setback at the hands of what he called "those dagoes." Frantically eager to be elected president "in his own right" in 1904, he was anxious to "make the dirt fly" to impress the voters. "Damn the law," he reportedly cried in private, "I want the canal built!" He assailed "the blackmailers of Bogota" who, like armed highwaymen, were blocking the onward march of civilization. He failed to note that the U.S. Senate also rejects treaties.

Uncle Sam Creates Puppet Panama

Impatient Panamanians, who had rebelled numerous times, were ripe for another revolt. They had counted on a wave of prosperity to follow construction of the canal, and they feared that the United States would now turn to the Nicaraguan route. Scheming Bunau-Varilla was no less disturbed by the prospect of losing the company's $40 million. Working hand in glove with the Panama revolutionists, he raised a tiny "patriot" army consisting largely of members of the Panamanian fire department, plus five hundred "bought" Colombian troops—for a reported price of $100,000.

The Panama revolution occurred on November 3, 1903, with the incidental killing of a Chinese civilian and a donkey. Colombian troops were gathered to crush the uprising, but U.S. naval forces would not let them cross the isthmus. Roosevelt justified this highly questionable interference by a strained interpretation of the treaty of 1846 with Colombia. (This pact obligated Washington to maintain

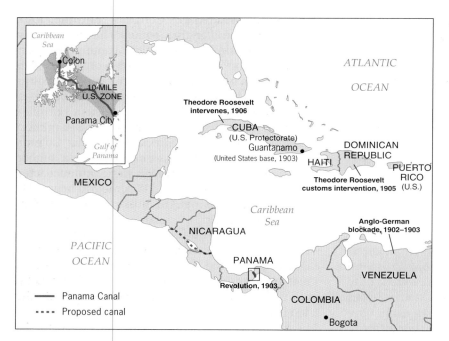

Big Stick in the Caribbean

In 1901 Roosevelt declared, "If a man continually blusters . . . a big stick will not save him from trouble; and neither will speaking softly avail, if back of the softness there does not lie strength, power. . . . If the boaster is not prepared to back up his words, his position becomes absolutely contemptible."

the "perfect neutrality" of the isthmus, obviously against outsiders.)

Roosevelt moved rapidly to make steamy Panama a virtual outpost of the United States. Three days after the uprising, he hastily extended the right hand of recognition. Fifteen days later, Bunau-Varilla, who was now the Panamanian minister despite his French citizenship, signed the Hay–Bunau-Varilla treaty in Washington. The price of the canal strip was left the same, but the zone was widened from six to ten miles. The French company gladly pocketed its $40 million from the U.S. Treasury.

Roosevelt, it seems clear, did not actively plot to tear Panama from the side of Colombia. But the conspirators knew of his angrily expressed views, and they counted on his using the big stick to hold Colombia at bay. Yet the Rough Rider became so indiscreetly involved in the Panama affair as to create the impression that he had been a secret party to the intrigue.

Unhappily, the United States suffered a black eye as a result of Roosevelt's "cowboy diplomacy." European imperialists, who were old hands at this sort of thing, could now raise their eyebrows in scorn at America's superior moral pretensions—and they did.

Roosevelt in Panama When he visited the Panama Canal construction site in 1906 to see "the dirt fly," Roosevelt was the first president to leave the United States for foreign soil.

Completing the Canal and Appeasing Colombia

The so-called rape of Panama marked an ugly downward lurch in U.S. relations with Latin America. Much fear had already been aroused by the recent seizure of Puerto Rico and by the Yankee stranglehold on Cuba. The fate of Colombia, when it dared defy the Colossus of the North, indicated that its weak fellow republics were not safe. The era of the bullying "Big Brother" policy was brazenly launched.

Roosevelt heatedly defended himself against all charges of evildoing. He claimed that he had received a "mandate from civilization" to start the canal and that Colombia had wronged the United States by not permitting itself to be benefited. To deal with these "blackmailers," he insisted, was like "nailing currant jelly to the wall."

But TR was not completely candid. He failed to point out that the Nicaragua route was about equally feasible and that it was available without a revolution. Yet this alternative would have involved some delay, and the presidential election of 1904 was fast approaching.

Active work was begun on "making the dirt fly" in 1904, but grave difficulties were encountered, ranging from labor troubles to landslides. The organization was finally perfected under an energetic but autocratic West Point engineer, Colonel George Washington Goethals. At the outset sanitation proved to be more important than excavation. Colonel William C. Gorgas, the quiet and determined exterminator of yellow fever in Havana, ultimately made the Canal Zone "as safe as a health resort."

Americans finally succeeded where the French had failed. In 1914 the colossal canal project was completed at an initial cost of about $400 million, just as World War I was breaking out. The whole enterprise, in the words of the English writer James Bryce, was "the greatest liberty Man has ever taken with Nature."

TR's Perversion of Monroe's Doctrine

Latin American debt defaults created the conditions for further Rooseveltian involvement in affairs south of the border. Nations such as Venezuela and the Dominican Republic were chronically in arrears in their payments to European creditors, particularly Britain and Germany. Seeking to force payment, German warships sank two Venezuelan gunboats and bombarded a town in early 1903.

This ironfisted intervention aroused Roosevelt. He feared that if the Germans or British got their foot in the door as bill collectors, they might remain in Latin America, in flagrant violation of the Monroe Doctrine. Roosevelt therefore devised a devious policy of "preventive intervention," better known as the Roosevelt Corollary to the Monroe Doctrine. He declared that in the event of future financial malfeasance by the Latin American nations, the United States itself would intervene, take over the customshouses, pay off the debts, and keep the troublesome powers on the other side of the Atlantic. In short, no outsiders could push around the Latin nations except Uncle Sam, Policeman of the Caribbean.

This new brandishing of the big stick in the Caribbean became effective in 1905, when the United States took over the management of tariff collections in the Dominican Republic, an arrangement formalized in a treaty with the Dominicans two years later. Dominican officials, who had raked in much juicy graft, were not happy with such interference, and they acquiesced only after some strenuous arm-twisting from Washington. But from a debt-collecting point of view, the customshouse intervention was a success.

Roosevelt's corollary, though tacked onto the Monroe Doctrine, bore only a strained relation to the original dictum of 1823. Monroe had in effect

---

Theodore Roosevelt (1858–1919) wrote to a correspondent in February 1904,

"I have been hoping and praying for three months that the Santo Domingans would behave so that I would not have to act in any way. I want to do nothing but what a policeman has to do. . . . As for annexing the island, I have about the same desire to annex it as a gorged boa-constrictor might have to swallow a porcupine wrong-end-to."

said to the European powers, "Thou shalt not intervene." TR changed this warning to mean, "We shall intervene to prevent you from intervening." The Roosevelt doctrine was actually so radical as to be a completely new policy, but it gained readier acceptance by being associated with the honored name of Monroe. Yet in its own right, the corollary had considerable merit as a preemptive stroke.

Roosevelt's rewriting of Monroe's doctrine had its dark side. It probably did more than any other single step to promote the "Bad Neighbor" policy begun in these years. As time wore on, the new corollary was used to justify wholesale interventions and repeated landings of the marines, all of which helped turn the Caribbean into a "Yankee lake." Latin Americans mistakenly cursed the unoffending Monroe, when they should have cursed the offending Roosevelt. To them it seemed as though the Monroe Doctrine, far from providing a shield, was a cloak behind which the United States sought to strangle them.

The shadow of the big stick likewise fell on Cuba in 1906. Revolutionary disorders brought an appeal from the Cuban president, and "necessity being the mother of invention," U.S. Marines were landed. These police forces were withdrawn temporarily in 1909, but in Latin American eyes the episode was but another example of the creeping power of the Colossus of the North.

Roosevelt on the World Stage

Booted and spurred, Roosevelt charged into international affairs far beyond Latin America. The outbreak of war between Russia and Japan in 1904 gave him a chance to perform as a global statesman. The Russian bear, having lumbered across Asia, was seeking to bathe its frostbitten paws in the ice-free ports of China's Manchuria, particularly Port Arthur. In Japanese eyes, Manchuria and Korea in tsarist hands were pistols pointed at Japan's strategic heart. Russian troops had invaded Manchuria during the Boxer outburst of 1900 and, despite solemn promises, were not withdrawing. The tsar was obviously stalling until his trans-Siberian railroad could be finished, as it would be in a few months. With the clock ticking against them, the Japanese suddenly began war in 1904 with a devastating surprise pounce on the Russian fleet at Port Arthur. They proceeded to administer a humiliating series of beatings to the inept Russians—the first serious military setback to a European power by a non-European force since the Turkish invasions of

Uncle Sam Gets Cocky, 1901 American policy toward Latin America grew more assertive, even aggressive, around the turn of the century, alarming both Latin Americans and Europeans. In this cartoon the European chickens complain to a giant Uncle Sam that "you're not the only rooster in South America," to which he replies, "I was aware of that when I cooped you up!" (with the Monroe Doctrine). The Latin American republics themselves, meanwhile, are dwarfed by the American rooster.

Theodore Roosevelt and His Big Stick in the Caribbean, 1904
Roosevelt's policies seemed to be turning the Caribbean into a Yankee pond.

the sixteenth century. But as the war dragged on, Japan began to run short of men and yen—a weakness it did not want to betray to the enemy. Tokyo officials therefore approached Roosevelt in the deepest secrecy and asked him to help sponsor peace negotiations.

Roosevelt agreed and shepherded the delegates of the two sides together at Portsmouth, New Hampshire, in 1905. The Japanese presented stern demands for a huge indemnity and the entire strategic island of Sakhalin, while the Russians stubbornly refused to admit the depths of their defeat. Blustering at both sides behind the scenes, Roosevelt forced through an accord in which the Japanese received no indemnity for the losses and only the southern half of Sakhalin.

For achieving this agreement, as well as for helping arrange an international conference at Algeciras, Spain, in 1906 to mediate North African disputes, Roosevelt received the Nobel Peace Prize in 1906. But the price of TR's diplomatic glory was high for U.S. foreign relations. Two historic friend-

ships withered on the windswept plains of Manchuria. American relations with Russia, once friendly, soured as the Russians implausibly accused Roosevelt of robbing them of military victory. Revelations about savage massacres of Russian Jews further poisoned American feeling against Russia. Japan, once America's protégé, felt robbed of its due compensation. Both newly powerful, Japan and America now became rivals in Asia, as fear and jealousy between them grew. To many Americans, the Japanese were getting too big for their kimonos.

Japanese Laborers in California

Adding to tensions between America and Japan was the issue of Japanese migration to America's Pacific Coast. The Japanese government prohibited emigration of its citizens until 1884, when it began allowing temporary laborers to work on sugar plantations in Hawaii. From there thousands of Japanese were recruited for work in California as farm laborers, railroad workers, and servants. Like the Chinese before them, Japanese immigrants did the nation's most arduous, dangerous work but were barred from becoming citizens. And like the Chinese, Japanese immigrants confronted racist hostility. Although Japanese residents never amounted to more than 3 percent of the state's population, white Californians ranted about a new "yellow peril" and feared being drowned in an Asian sea.

A showdown on the influx came in 1906 when San Francisco's school board, coping with the aftermath of a frightful earthquake and fire, ordered the segregation of Chinese, Japanese, and Korean students in a special school to free more space for whites. Instantly the incident boiled into an international crisis. The people of Japan, who were highly sensitive on questions of race, regarded this discrimination as an insult to them and their beloved children. On both sides of the Pacific, irresponsible war talk sizzled in the yellow press—the real "yellow peril." Roosevelt, who as a Rough Rider had relished shooting, was less happy over the prospect that California might stir up a war that all the other states would have to wage. He therefore invited the entire San Francisco Board of Education, headed by a bassoon-playing mayor under indictment for graft, to come to the White House.

Roosevelt at Portsmouth Conference   Roosevelt meets with the two Russian and two Japanese delegates in 1905. Roosevelt wrote that dealing with U.S. senators was a tough job but dealing with these peace envoys was even tougher. He had to be "polite and sympathetic and patient in explaining for the hundredth time something perfectly obvious . . . when I really want to give utterance to whoops of rage and jump up and knock their heads together."

Japanese Workers Building a Road in California, c. 1910

TR finally broke the deadlock, but not until he had brandished his big stick and bared his big teeth. The Californians were induced to repeal the offensive school order and to accept what came to be known as the "Gentlemen's Agreement." This secret understanding was worked out, during 1907–1908, by an exchange of diplomatic notes between Washington and Tokyo. The Japanese, for their part, agreed to stop the flow of laborers to the American mainland by withholding passports.

Roosevelt worried that his intercession between California and Japan might be interpreted in Tokyo as prompted by fear of the Japanese. Accordingly, he hit upon a dramatic scheme to impress the Japanese with the heft of his big stick. He daringly decided to send the entire battleship fleet on a highly visible voyage around the world.

Late in 1907 sixteen sparkling-white, smoke-belching battleships started from Virginia waters. Their commander pointedly declared that he was ready for "a feast, a frolic, or a fight." The Great White Fleet—saluted by cannonading champagne corks—received tumultuous welcomes in Latin America, Hawaii, New Zealand, and Australia.

As events turned out, an overwhelming reception in Japan was the high point of the trip. Tens of thousands of kimonoed schoolchildren had been trained to wave tiny American flags and sing "The Star-Spangled Banner"—reportedly in English. In the warm diplomatic atmosphere created by the visit of the fleet, the Root-Takahira agreement of 1908 was reached with Japan. The United States and Japan solemnly pledged themselves to respect each other's territorial possessions in the Pacific and to uphold the Open Door in China. The once fight-thirsty Roosevelt, who thus went out of his way to avoid a war with Japan, regarded the battleship cruise as his most important contribution to peace. The voyage of the white fleet also gave Uncle Sam a new recruiting slogan: "Join the Navy and See the World."

Chronology

1899 Aguinaldo launches rebellion against United States in the Philippine Islands
First American Open Door note

1900 Boxer Rebellion and U.S. expedition to China
Second Open Door note
McKinley defeats Bryan for presidency

1901 McKinley assassinated; Roosevelt assumes presidency
Filipino rebellion defeated
Hay-Pauncefote Treaty

1902 Colombian senate rejects canal treaty

1903 Panamanian revolution against Colombia
Hay–Bunau-Varilla treaty

1904 Roosevelt Corollary to the Monroe Doctrine

1904-1914 Construction of the Panama Canal

1905 United States takes over Dominican Republic customs
Roosevelt mediates Russo-Japanese peace treaty

1906 San Francisco Japanese education crisis
Roosevelt arranges Algeciras conference

1906-1909 U.S. Marines occupy Cuba

1907 Great White Fleet

1907-1908 "Gentlemen's Agreement" with Japan

1908 Root-Takahira agreement

VARYING VIEWPOINTS

Why Did America Become a World Power?

American imperialism has long been an embarrassing topic for students of American history, who remember the Republic's own revolutionary origins and anti-colonial tradition. Perhaps for that reason, many historians have tried to explain the dramatic overseas expansionism of the 1890s as some kind of aberration—a sudden, singular, and short-lived departure from time-honored American principles and practices. Various explanations have been offered to account for this spasmodic lapse. Scholars such as Julius Pratt pointed to the irresponsible behavior of the yellow press. Richard Hofstadter ascribed America's imperial fling to the "psychic crisis of the 1890s," a crisis brought on, he argued, by the strains of the decade's economic depression and the Populist upheaval. Howard K. Beale emphasized the contagious scramble for imperial possessions by the European powers, as well as Japan, in these years.

In Beale's argument, the United States—and Theodore Roosevelt in particular—succumbed to a kind of international peer pressure: if other countries were expanding their international roles and even establishing colonies around the globe, could the United States safely refrain from doing the same? In Beale's view, Theodore Roosevelt was no simple-minded imperial swashbuckler, but a coolly calculating diplomatic realist who perceived that if the United States did not hold its own against other powers, it would soon risk being pushed around, even in its own hemisphere, despite the Monroe Doctrine.

Perhaps the most controversial interpretation of American imperialism has come from a so-called New Left school of writers, inspired by William Appleman Williams (and before him by V. I. Lenin's 1916 book *Imperialism: The Highest Stage of Capitalism*). Historians such as Williams and Walter LaFeber argue that the explanation for political and military expansion abroad is to be found in economic expansion at home. Increasing industrial output, so the argument goes, required ever more raw materials and, especially, overseas markets. To meet those needs, the nation adopted a strategy of "informal empire," shunning formal territorial possessions (with the conspicuous exception of the Philippines), but seeking economic dominance over foreign markets, materials, and investment outlets. That "revisionist" interpretation, in turn, has been sharply criticized by scholars who point out that foreign trade accounted for only a tiny share of American output and that the diplomacy of this period was far too complex to be reduced to "economic need."

Most recently, historians have highlighted the importance of race and gender in the march toward empire. Roosevelt and other imperialists perceived their world in gendered terms. American society, many feared, was losing touch with the manly virtues. It had grown soft and "feminine" since the closing of the frontier. Imperialists also saw the nations of the world in a strict racial hierarchy, with "primitive" blacks and Indians at the bottom and "civilized" Anglo-Saxons at the top. In this worldview the conquest of "inferior" peoples seemed natural—a tropical tonic to restore the nation's masculine virility. Scholars who emphasize these explanations of imperialism are less likely to see the expansionism of the 1890s as an aberration in American history. Instead, they argue, these overseas adventures were part of a long tradition of race-fueled militarism, from the nation's earliest Indian wars to Cold War engagements in Korea and Vietnam.

For further reading, see page A20 of the Appendix. For web resources, go to **http://college.hmco.com.**

Progressivism and the Republican Roosevelt

1901–1912

*When I say I believe in a square deal I do not mean . . . to give
every man the best hand. If the cards do not come to any man,
or if they do come, and he has not got the power to play them,
that is his affair. All I mean is that there shall be no crookedness
in the dealing.*

THEODORE ROOSEVELT, 1905

Nearly 76 million Americans greeted the new century in 1900. Of them, almost one in seven was foreign-born. In the fourteen years of peace that remained before the Great War of 1914 engulfed the globe, 13 million more migrants would carry their bundles down the gangplanks to the land of promise.

Hardly had the twentieth century dawned on the ethnically and racially mixed American people than they were convulsed by a reform movement, the like of which the nation had not seen since the 1840s. The new crusaders, who called themselves "progressives," waged war on many evils, notably monopoly, corruption, inefficiency, and social injustice. The progressive army was large, diverse, and widely deployed, but it had a single battle cry: "Strengthen the State." The "real heart of the movement," explained one of the progressive reformers, was "to use government as an agency of human welfare."

Progressive Roots

The groundswell of the new reformist wave went far back—to the Greenback Labor party of the 1870s and the Populists of the 1890s, to the mounting unrest throughout the land as grasping industrialists concentrated more and more power in fewer and fewer hands. An outworn philosophy of hands-off individualism seemed increasingly out of place in the modern machine age. Social and economic problems were now too complex for the intentionally feeble Jeffersonian organs of government. Progressive theorists were insisting that society could no longer afford the luxury of a limitless "let-alone" (laissez-faire) policy. The people, through government, must substitute mastery for drift.

Well before 1900, perceptive politicians and writers had begun to pinpoint targets for the progressive attack. Bryan, Altgeld, and the Populists loudly branded the "bloated trusts" with the stigma of corruption and wrongdoing. In 1894 Henry Demarest Lloyd charged headlong into the Standard Oil Company with his book *Wealth Against Commonwealth.* Eccentric Thorstein Veblen assailed the new rich with his prickly pen in *The Theory of the Leisure Class* (1899), a savage attack on "predatory wealth" and "conspicuous consumption."

Other pen-wielding knights likewise entered the fray. The keen-eyed and keen-nosed Danish immigrant Jacob A. Riis, a reporter for the *New York Sun,* shocked middle-class Americans in 1890 with *How the Other Half Lives.* His account was a damning indictment of the dirt, disease, vice, and misery of the rat-gnawed human rookeries known as New York slums. The book deeply influenced a future New York City police commissioner, Theodore Roosevelt. Novelist Theodore Dreiser used his blunt prose to batter promoters and profiteers in *The Financier* (1912) and *The Titan* (1914).

Caustic critics of social injustice issued from several other corners. Socialists, many of whom were European immigrants inspired by the strong movement for state socialism in the Old World, began to register appreciable strength at the ballot

Saluting the Flag   Flooded with immigrant children, many of whom could scarcely speak English, schools like this one in New York in 1892 cultivated loyalty to the newcomers' adopted land by teaching courses in "civics" and encouraging patriotic rituals like the Pledge of Allegiance to the U.S. flag.

box. High-minded messengers of the social gospel promoted a brand of progressivism based in Christian teachings. They used religious doctrine to demand better housing and living conditions for the urban poor. Feminists in multiplying numbers added social justice to suffrage on their list of

Room in a Tenement Flat, 1910 Tenement life on the Lower East Side of New York City was exposed by the camera of Jacob Riis, who compiled a large photographic archive of turn-of-the-century urban life. Many families counted themselves lucky to share a single room, no matter how squalid.

needed reforms. With urban pioneers like Jane Addams in Chicago and Lillian Wald in New York blazing the way, women entered the fight to improve the lot of families living and working in the festering cities.

Raking Muck with the Muckrakers

Beginning about 1902 the exposing of evil became a flourishing industry among American publishers. A group of aggressive ten- and fifteen-cent popular magazines surged to the front, notably *McClure's, Cosmopolitan, Collier's,* and *Everybody's.* Waging fierce circulation wars, they dug deep for the dirt that the public loved to hate. Enterprising editors financed extensive research and encouraged pugnacious writing by their bright young reporters, whom President Roosevelt branded as "muckrakers" in 1906. Annoyed by their excess of zeal, he compared the mudslinging magazine dirt-diggers to the figure in Bunyan's *Pilgrim's Progress* who was so intent on raking manure that he could not see the celestial crown dangling overhead.

Despite presidential scolding, these muckrakers boomed circulation, and some of their most scandalous exposures were published as best-selling books. The reformer-writers ranged far, wide, and deep in their crusade to lay bare the muck of iniquity in American society. In 1902 a brilliant New York reporter, Lincoln Steffens, launched a series of articles in *McClure's* titled "The Shame of the Cities." He fearlessly unmasked the corrupt alliance between big business and municipal government. Steffens was followed in the same magazine by Ida M. Tarbell, a pioneering journalist who published a devastating but factual exposé of the Standard Oil Company. (Her father had been ruined by the oil interests.) Fearing legal reprisals, the muckraking magazines went to great pains and expense to check their material—paying as much as three thousand dollars to verify a single Tarbell article.

Plucky muckrakers fearlessly tilted their pen-lances at varied targets. They assailed the malpractices of life insurance companies and tariff lobbies. They roasted the beef trust, the "money trust," the railroad barons, and the corrupt amassing of American fortunes. Thomas W. Lawson, an erratic speculator who had himself made $50 million on the stock market, laid bare the practices of his accom-

Ida Tarbell (1857–1944) in Her Office
Tarbell was the most eminent woman in the muckraking movement and one of the most respected business historians of her generation. In 1904, she earned a national reputation for publishing a scathing history of the Standard Oil Company, the "Mother of Trusts." Two years later she joined Ray Stannard Baker, William Allen White, and other muckrakers in purchasing the *American* magazine, which became a journalistic podium in their campaign for honest government and an end to business abuses.

plices in "Frenzied Finance." This series of articles, appearing in 1905–1906, rocketed the circulation of *Everybody's.* Lawson, by fouling his own nest, made many enemies among his rich associates, and he died a poor man.

David G. Phillips shocked an already startled nation by his series in *Cosmopolitan* titled "The Treason of the Senate" (1906). He boldly charged that seventy-five of the ninety senators did not represent the people at all but the railroads and trusts. This withering indictment, buttressed by facts, impressed President Roosevelt. Phillips continued his attacks through novels and was fatally shot in 1911 by a deranged young man whose family he had allegedly maligned.

Some of the most effective fire of the muckrakers was directed at social evils. The ugly list included the immoral "white slave" traffic in women, the rickety slums, and the appalling number of industrial accidents. The sorry subjugation of America's 9 million blacks—of whom 90 percent still lived in the South and one-third were illiterate—was spotlighted in Ray Stannard Baker's *Following the Color Line* (1908). The abuses of child labor were brought luridly to light by John Spargo's *The Bitter Cry of the Children* (1906).

Vendors of potent patent medicines (often heavily spiked with alcohol) likewise came in for bitter criticism. These conscienceless vultures sold incredible quantities of adulterated or habit-forming drugs, while "doping" the press with lavish advertising. Muckraking attacks in *Collier's* were ably reinforced by Dr. Harvey W. Wiley, chief chemist of the Department of Agriculture, who with his famous "Poison Squad" performed experiments on himself.

Full of sound and fury, the muckrakers signified much about the nature of the progressive reform movement. They were long on lamentation and short on sweeping remedies. To right social wrongs, they counted on publicity and an aroused public conscience, not drastic political change. They sought not to overthrow capitalism but to cleanse it. The cure for the ills of American democracy, they earnestly believed, was more democracy.

Political Progressivism

Progressive reformers were mainly middle-class men and women who felt themselves squeezed from above and below. They sensed pressure from the new giant corporations, the restless immigrant hordes, and the aggressive labor unions. The progressives simultaneously sought two goals: to use state power to curb the trusts and to stem the socialist threat by generally improving the common person's conditions of life and labor. Progressives emerged in both major parties, in all regions, and at all levels of government. The truth is that progressivism was less a minority movement and more a majority mood.

One of the first objectives of progressives was to regain the power that had slipped from the hands of the people into those of the "interests." These ardent reformers pushed for direct primary elections so as to undercut power-hungry party bosses. They favored the "initiative" so that voters could directly propose legislation themselves, thus bypassing the boss-bought state legislatures. Progressives also agitated for the "referendum." This device would place laws on the ballot for final approval by the people, especially laws that had been railroaded through a compliant legislature by free-spending agents of big business. The "recall" would enable the voters to remove faithless elected officials, particularly those who had been bribed by bosses or lobbyists.

Suffragette Parade in Brooklyn, New York
The enormous political effort of American suffragists finally achieved victory with the
ratification of the Nineteenth Amendment in 1920.

Rooting out graft also became a prime goal of earnest progressives. A number of the state legislatures passed corrupt-practices acts, which limited the amount of money that candidates could spend for their election. Such legislation also restricted huge gifts from corporations, for which the donors would expect special favors. The secret Australian ballot was likewise being introduced more widely in the states to counteract boss rule. Bribery was less feasible when bribers could not tell if they were getting their money's worth from the bribed.

Direct election of U.S. senators became a favorite goal of progressives, especially after the muckrakers had exposed the scandalous intimacy between greedy corporations and Congress. By 1900 the Senate had so many rich men that it was often sneered at as the "Millionaires' Club." Too many of these prosperous solons, elected as they then were by trust-dominated legislatures, heeded the voice of their "masters" rather than the voice of the masses.

A constitutional amendment to bring about the popular election of senators had rough sledding in Congress, for the plutocratic members of the Senate were happy with existing methods. But a number of states established primary elections in which the voters expressed their preferences for the Senate. The local legislatures, when choosing senators, found it politically wise to heed the voice of the people. Partly as a result of such pressures, the Seventeenth Amendment to the Constitution, approved in 1913, established the direct election of U.S. senators. (See the Appendix.) But the expected improvement in caliber was slow in coming.

The suffrage campaign of the early twentieth century benefited from a new generation of women who considered themselves "feminists." At a mass meeting in New York in 1914, Marie Jenny Howe (1870–1934), a minister by training as well as a prominent early feminist, proclaimed,

"We intend simply to be ourselves, not just our little female selves, but our whole big human selves."

Woman suffrage, the goal of feminists for many decades, likewise received powerful new support from the progressives early in the 1900s. The political reformers believed that women's votes would elevate the political tone, and the foes of the saloon felt that they could count on the support of enfranchised females. The suffragists, with their cry of "Votes for Women" and "Equal Suffrage for Men and Women," protested bitterly against "Taxation Without Representation." Many of the states, especially the more liberal ones in the West, gradually extended the vote to women. But by 1910 nationwide female suffrage was still a decade away, and a suffragist could still be sneeringly defined as "one who has ceased to be a lady and has not yet become a gentleman."

Progressivism in the Cities and States

Progressives scored some of their most impressive gains in the cities. Frustrated by the inefficiency and corruption of machine-oiled city government, many localities followed the pioneering example of Galveston, Texas. In 1901 it had appointed expert-staffed commissions to manage urban affairs. Other communities adopted the city-manager system, also designed to take politics out of municipal administration. Some of these "reforms" obviously valued efficiency more highly than democracy, as control of civic affairs was further removed from the people's hands.

Urban reformers likewise attacked "slumlords," juvenile delinquency, and wide-open prostitution (vice-at-a-price), which flourished in red-light districts unchallenged by bribed police. Public-spirited city dwellers also moved to halt the corrupt sale of franchises for streetcars and other public utilities.

Progressivism naturally bubbled up to the state level, notably in Wisconsin, which became a yeasty laboratory of reform. The governor of the state, pompadoured Robert M. ("Fighting Bob") La Follette, was an undersized but overbearing crusader who emerged as the most militant of the progressive Republican leaders. After a desperate fight with entrenched monopoly, he reached the governor's chair in 1901. Routing the lumber and railroad "interests," he wrested considerable control from the crooked corporations and returned it to the people.

He also perfected a scheme for regulating public utilities, while laboring in close association with experts on the faculty of the state university at Madison.

Other states marched steadily toward the progressive camp, as they undertook to regulate railroads and trusts, chiefly through public utilities commissions. Oregon was not far behind Wisconsin, and California made giant bootstrides under the stocky Hiram W. Johnson. Elected Republican governor in 1910, this dynamic prosecutor of grafters helped break the dominant grip of the Southern Pacific Railroad on California politics and then, like La Follette, set up a political machine of his own. Heavily whiskered Charles Evans Hughes, the able and audacious reformist Republican governor of New York, had earlier gained national fame as an investigator of malpractices by gas and insurance companies and by the coal trust.

Progressive Women

Women proved themselves an indispensable part of the progressive army. A crucial focus for women's activism was the settlement house movement (see p. 565). At a time when women could neither vote nor hold political office, settlement houses offered a side door to public life. They exposed middle-class women to the problems plaguing America's cities, including poverty, political corruption, and intolerable working and living conditions. They also gave them the skills and confidence to attack those evils. The women's club movement provided an even broader civic entryway for many middle-class women. Literary clubs, where educated women met to improve themselves with poetry and prose, had existed for decades. But in the late nineteenth and early twentieth centuries, many of these clubs set aside Shakespeare and Henry James for social issues and current events. "Dante has been dead for several centuries," observed the president of the General Federation of Women's Clubs in 1904. "I think it is time that we dropped the study of his *Inferno* and turned our attention to our own."

Nineteenth-century notions of "separate spheres" dictated that a woman's place was in the home, so most female progressives defended their new activities as an extension—not a rejection—of the traditional roles of wife and mother. Thus they were often drawn to moral and "maternal" issues like keeping children out of smudgy mills and sweltering sweatshops, attacking the scourge of tuberculosis bred in airless tenements, winning pensions for mothers with dependent children, and ensuring that only safe food products found their way to the family table. Female activists agitated through organizations like the Women's Trade Union League and the National Consumers League, as well as through two new federal agencies, the Children's Bureau (1912) and the Women's Bureau (1920), both in the Department of Labor. These wedges into the federal bureaucracy, however small, gave female reformers a national stage for social investigation and advocacy.

Campaigns for factory reform and temperance particularly attracted women foot soldiers. Unsafe and unsanitary sweatshops—factories where workers toiled long hours for low wages—were a public scandal in many cities. Florence Kelley, a former resident of Jane Addams's Hull House, became the state of Illinois's first chief factory inspector and one of the nation's leading advocates for improved factory conditions. In 1899 Kelley took control of the newly founded National Consumers League, which mobilized female consumers to pressure for laws safeguarding women and children in the workplace. In the landmark case *Muller* v. *Oregon* (1908), crusading attorney Louis D. Brandeis persuaded the Supreme Court to accept the constitutionality of laws protecting women workers by presenting evidence of the harmful effects of factory labor on women's weaker bodies. Although this argument calling for special protection for women seemed discriminatory by later standards and closed many "male" jobs to women, progressives at the time hailed Brandeis's achievement as a triumph over existing legal doctrine, which afforded employers total control over the workplace. The American

Jane Addams and Fellow Pacifists, 1915   Addams co-founded the Women's Peace Party in 1915, its pacifist platform said to represent the views of the "mother half of humanity." Although the party initially attracted 25,000 members, America's entry into the war two years later eroded popular support, as pacifist internationalism became suspect as anti-American.

EXAMINING THE EVIDENCE

***Muller* v. *Oregon,* 1908** Court records provide notably fruitful sources for historians. They not only tell often-colorful stories about the lives of ordinary men and women caught up in the legal system; they also by their very nature testify to the norms and values that lawyers employ to make their cases and that judges invoke to explain their decisions. The case of *Muller* v. *Oregon* (see p. 670) is especially instructive on both counts. The official Supreme Court records tell how on September 4, 1905, Joe Haselbock, a supervisor in Curt Muller's Grand Laundry in Portland, Oregon, asked an employee, Mrs. E. Gotcher, to remain after hours to do an extra load of laundry. That request violated Oregon's law prohibiting women from working more than ten hours per day. Mrs. Gotcher later complained to the authorities, and Muller was fined $10. Muller refused to pay, and took his case all the way to the United States Supreme Court. In its landmark decision, the Court upheld the constitutionality of the Oregon statute, and Muller at last had to cough up his fine. On what grounds did the Court justify its ruling? What does Justice Brewer's argument on behalf of the Court's decision suggest about the cultural identity and social role of women in early-twentieth-century American society?

(208 U.S. 412)
CURT MULLER, Plff. in Err.,
v.
STATE OF OREGON.

. . . That woman's physical structure and the performance of material functions place her at a disadvantage in the struggle for subsistence is obvious. This is especially true when the burdens of motherhood are upon her. . . . and as healthy mothers are essential to vigorous offspring, the physical well-being of woman becomes an object of public interest and care in order to preserve the strength and vigor of the race.

Still again, history discloses the fact that woman has always been dependent upon man. He established his control at the outset by superior physical strength, and this control in various forms, with diminishing intensity, has continued to the present. . . . It is still true that in the struggle for subsistence she is not an equal competitor with her brother. . . . Differentiated by these matters from the other sex, she is properly placed in a class by herself, and legislation designed for her protection may be sustained, even when like legislation is not necessary for men, and could not be sustained. It is impossible to close one's eyes to the fact that she still looks to her brother and depends upon him. . . . The two sexes differ in structure of body, in the functions to be performed by each, in the amount of physical strength, in the capacity for long continued labor, particularly when done standing, the influence of vigorous health upon the future well-being of the race, the self-reliance which enables one to assert full rights, and in the capacity to maintain the struggle for subsistence. This difference justifies a difference in legislation, and upholds that which is designed to compensate for some of the burdens which rest upon her.

We have not referred in this discussion to the denial of the elective franchise in the state of Oregon, for while that may disclose a lack of political equality in all things with her brother, that is not of itself decisive. The reason runs deeper, and rests in the inherent difference between the two sexes, and in the different functions in life which they perform. . . .

welfare state that emerged from female activism focused more on protecting women and children than on granting benefits to everyone, as was the case in much of western Europe, with its stronger labor movements.

Crusaders for these humane measures did not always have smooth sailing. One dismaying setback came in 1905, when the Supreme Court, in *Lochner* v. *New York,* invalidated a New York law establishing a ten-hour day for bakers. Yet the reformist progressive wave finally washed up into the judiciary, and in 1917 the Court upheld a ten-hour law for factory workers.

Laws regulating factories were worthless if not enforced, a truth horribly demonstrated by a lethal fire in 1911 at the Triangle Shirtwaist Company in New York City. Locked doors and other flagrant violations of the fire code turned the factory into a death trap. One hundred forty-six workers, most of them young immigrant women, were incinerated or leapt from eighth- and ninth-story windows to their deaths. Lashed by the public outcry, including a massive strike by women in the needle trades, the New York legislature passed much stronger laws regulating the hours and conditions of sweatshop toil. Other legislatures followed, and by 1917 thirty states had put workers' compensation laws on the books, providing insurance to workers injured in industrial accidents. Gradually the concept of the employer's responsibility to society was replacing the old dog-eat-dog philosophy of unregulated free enterprise.

Corner saloons, with their shutter doors, naturally attracted the ire and fire of progressives. Alcohol was intimately connected with prostitution in red-light districts, with the drunken voter, with crooked city officials dominated by "booze" interests, and with the blowsy "boss" who counted poker chips by night and miscounted ballots by day (including the "cemetery vote"). By 1900 cities like New York and San Francisco had one saloon for about every two hundred people.

Antiliquor campaigners received powerful support from several militant organizations, notably the Woman's Christian Temperance Union (WCTU). Founder Frances E. Willard, who would fall to her knees in prayer on saloon floors, mobilized nearly 1 million women to "make the world homelike" and built the WCTU into the largest organization of women in the world. She found a vigorous ally in the Anti-Saloon League, which was aggressive, well organized, and well financed.

Out of Work and the Reason Why, 1899   This temperance propaganda from an 1899 magazine illustrates the role of women in the temperance movement. Alcohol abuse threatened the stability of the family, still predominantly the "woman's sphere" in the late nineteenth century.

Caught up in the crusade, some states and numerous counties passed "dry" laws, which controlled, restricted, or abolished alcohol. The big cities were generally "wet," for they had a large immigrant vote accustomed in the Old Country to the free flow of wine and beer. When World War I erupted in 1914, nearly one-half of the population lived in "dry" territory, and nearly three-fourths of the total area had outlawed saloons. Demon Rum was groggy and about to be floored—temporarily—by the Eighteenth Amendment in 1919.

TR's Square Deal for Labor

Theodore Roosevelt, although something of an imperialistic busybody abroad, was touched by the progressive wave at home. Like other reformers, he feared that the "public interest" was being sub-merged in the drifting seas of indifference. Every-body's interest was nobody's interest. Roosevelt decided to make it his. His sportsman's instincts spurred him into demanding a "Square Deal" for capital, labor, and the public at large. Broadly speaking, the president's program embraced three C's: control of the corporations, consumer protection, and conservation of natural resources.

The Square Deal for labor received its acid test in 1902, when a crippling strike broke out in the anthracite coal mines of Pennsylvania. Some 140,000 besooted workers, many of them illiterate immigrants, had long been frightfully exploited and accident-plagued. They demanded, among other improvements, a 20 percent increase in pay and a reduction of the working day from ten to nine hours.

Unsympathetic mine owners, confident that a chilled public would react against the miners, refused to arbitrate or even negotiate. One of their spokesmen, multimillionaire George F. Baer, reflected the high-and-mighty attitude of certain ungenerous employers. Workers, he wrote, would be cared for "not by the labor agitators, but by the Christian men to whom God in His infinite wisdom has given the control of the property interests of this country."

As coal supplies dwindled, factories and schools were forced to shut down, and even hospitals felt the icy grip of winter. Desperately seeking a solution, Roosevelt summoned representatives of the striking miners and the mine owners to the White House. He was profoundly annoyed by the "extraordinary stupidity and bad temper" of the "wooden-headed gentry" who operated the mines. As he later confessed, if it had not been for the dignity of his high office, he would have taken one of them "by the seat of the breeches" and "chucked him out of the window."

Roosevelt finally resorted to his trusty big stick when he threatened to seize the mines and operate them with federal troops. Faced with this first-time-ever threat to use federal bayonets against capital, rather than labor, the owners grudgingly consented to arbitration. A compromise decision ultimately gave the miners a 10 percent pay boost and a working day of nine hours. But their union was not officially recognized as a bargaining agent.

Keenly aware of the mounting antagonisms between capital and labor, Roosevelt urged Congress to create the new Department of Commerce and Labor. This goal was achieved in 1903. (Ten years later the agency was split in two.) An important arm of the newborn cabinet body was the Bureau of Corporations, which was authorized to probe businesses engaged in interstate commerce. The bureau was highly useful in helping to break the stranglehold of monopoly and in clearing the road for the era of "trust-busting."

TR Corrals the Corporations

The sprawling railroad octopus sorely needed restraint. The Interstate Commerce Commission, created in 1887 as a feeble sop to the public, had proved woefully inadequate. Railroad barons could simply appeal the commission's decisions on rates to the federal courts—a process that might take ten years.

Spurred by the former-cowboy president, Congress passed effective railroad legislation, beginning with the Elkins Act of 1903. This curb was aimed primarily at the rebate evil. Heavy fines could now be imposed both on the railroads that gave rebates and on the shippers that accepted them.

Still more effective was the Hepburn Act of 1906. Free passes, with their hint of bribery, were

---

Roosevelt was a charismatic figure who made a powerful impression on his contemporaries. The journalist William Allen White (1868–1944) later wrote of his first meeting with TR in 1897,

"He sounded in my heart the first trumpet call of the new time that was to be. . . . I had never known such a man as he, and never shall again. He overcame me. And in the hour or two we spent that day at lunch, and in a walk down F Street, he poured into my heart such visions, such ideals, such hopes, such a new attitude toward life and patriotism and the meaning of things, as I had never dreamed men had. . . . After that I was his man."

severely restricted. The once-infantile Interstate Commerce Commission was expanded, and its reach was extended to include express companies, sleeping-car companies, and pipelines. For the first time, the commission was given real molars when it was authorized, on complaint of shippers, to nullify existing rates and stipulate maximum rates.

Railroads also provided Roosevelt with an opportunity to brandish his antitrust bludgeon. *Trusts* had come to be a fighting word in the progressive era. Roosevelt believed that these industrial behemoths, with their efficient means of production, had arrived to stay. He concluded that there were "good" trusts, with public consciences, and "bad" trusts, which lusted greedily for power. He was determined to respond to the popular outcry against the trusts but was also determined not to throw out the baby with the bathwater by indiscriminately smashing all large businesses.

Roosevelt, as a trustbuster, first burst into the headlines in 1902 with an attack on the Northern Securities Company, a railroad holding company organized by financial titan J. P. Morgan and empire builder James J. Hill. These Napoleonic moguls of money sought to achieve a virtual monopoly of the railroads in the Northwest. Roosevelt was therefore challenging the most regal potentates of the industrial aristocracy.

The railway promoters appealed to the Supreme Court, which in 1904 upheld Roosevelt's antitrust suit and ordered the Northern Securities Company to be dissolved. The *Northern Securities* decision jolted Wall Street and angered big business but greatly enhanced Roosevelt's reputation as a trust smasher.

Roosevelt's big stick crashed down on other giant monopolies, as he initiated over forty legal proceedings against them. The Supreme Court in 1905 declared the beef trust illegal, and the heavy fist of justice fell upon monopolists controlling sugar, fertilizer, harvesters, and other key products.

Much mythology has inflated Roosevelt's reputation as a trustbuster. The Rough Rider understood the political popularity of monopoly-smashing, but he did not consider it sound economic policy. Combination and integration, he felt, were the hallmarks of the age, and to try to stem the tide of economic progress by political means he considered the rankest folly. Bigness was not necessarily badness, so why punish success? Roosevelt's real purpose in

Roosevelt Turns the Screws on the Trusts   This cartoon exaggerates Roosevelt's impact on the corporate giants. He wanted to bring the trusts under government control, but not necessarily wring them dry of their wealth.

assaulting the Goliaths of industry was symbolic: to prove conclusively that the government, not private business, ruled the country. He believed in regulating, not fragmenting, the big business combines. The threat of dissolution, he felt, might make the sultans of the smokestacks more amenable to federal regulation—as it did.

In truth, Roosevelt never swung his trust-crushing stick with maximum force. In many ways the huge industrial behemoths were healthier—though perhaps more "tame"—at the end of Roosevelt's reign than they had been before. His successor, William Howard Taft, actually "busted" more trusts than TR did. In one celebrated instance in 1907, Roosevelt even gave his personal blessing to J. P. Morgan's plan to have U.S. Steel absorb the Tennessee Coal and Iron Company, without fear of antitrust reprisals. When Taft then launched a suit against U.S. Steel in 1911, the political reaction from TR was explosive.

Caring for the Consumer

Roosevelt backed a noteworthy measure in 1906 that benefited both corporations and consumers. Big meatpackers were being shut out of certain European markets because some American meat—from the small packinghouses, claimed the giants—had been found to be tainted. Foreign governments were even threatening to ban all American meat imports by throwing out the good beef with the bad botulism.

At the same time, American consumers hungered for safer canned products. Their appetite for reform was whetted by Upton Sinclair's sensational novel *The Jungle,* published in 1906. Sinclair intended his revolting tract to focus attention on the plight of the workers in the big canning factories, but instead he appalled the public with his description of disgustingly unsanitary food products. (As he put it, he aimed for the nation's heart but hit its stomach.) The book described in noxious detail the filth, disease, and putrefaction in Chicago's damp, ill-ventilated slaughterhouses. Many readers, including Roosevelt, were so sickened that for a time they found meat unpalatable. The president was moved by the loathsome mess in Chicago to appoint a special investigating commission, whose cold-blooded report almost outdid Sinclair's novel. It related how piles of poisoned rats, rope ends, splinters, and other debris were scooped up and canned as potted ham. A cynical jingle of the time ran,

> *Mary had a little lamb,*
> *And when she saw it sicken,*
> *She shipped it off to Packingtown,*
> *And now it's labeled chicken.*

Backed by a nauseated public, Roosevelt induced Congress to pass the Meat Inspection Act of 1906. It decreed that the preparation of meat shipped over state lines would be subject to federal inspection from corral to can. Although the largest packers resisted certain features of the act, they accepted it as an opportunity to drive their smaller, fly-by-night competitors out of business. At the same time, they could receive the government's seal of approval on their exports. As a companion to the Meat Inspection Act, the Pure Food and Drug Act of 1906 was designed to prevent the adulteration and mislabeling of foods and pharmaceuticals.

Sausage Making, c. 1906
White-jacketed inspectors like those on the right made some progress in cleaning up the septic slaughterhouses after the passage of the Meat Inspection Act in 1906.

Earth Control

Wasteful Americans, assuming that their natural resources were inexhaustible, had looted and polluted their incomparable domain with unparalleled speed and greed. Western ranchers and timbermen were especially eager to accelerate the destructive process, for they panted to build up the country, and the environmental consequences be hanged. But even before the end of the nineteenth century, farvisioned leaders saw that such a squandering of the nation's birthright would have to be halted, or America would sink from resource richness to despoiled dearth.

A first feeble step toward conservation had been taken with the Desert Land Act of 1877, under which the federal government sold arid land cheaply on the condition that the purchaser irrigate the thirsty soil within three years. More successful was the Forest Reserve Act of 1891, authorizing the president to set aside public forests as national parks and other reserves. Under this statute some 46 million acres of magnificent trees were rescued from the lumberman's saw in the 1890s and preserved for posterity. The Carey Act of 1894 distributed federal land to the states on the condition that it be irrigated and settled.

A new day in the history of conservation dawned with Roosevelt. Huntsman, naturalist, rancher, lover of the great outdoors, he was appalled by the pillaging of timber and mineral resources. Other dedicated conservationists, notably Gifford Pinchot, head of the federal Division of Forestry, had broken important ground before him. But Roosevelt seized

High Point for Conservation Roosevelt and famed naturalist John Muir visit Glacier Point, on the rim of Yosemite Valley, California. In the distance is Yosemite Falls; a few feet behind Roosevelt is a sheer drop of 3,254 feet.

In his annual message to Congress (1907), Roosevelt declared prophetically,

"We are prone to speak of the resources of this country as inexhaustible; this is not so. The mineral wealth of the country, the coal, iron, oil, gas, and the like, does not reproduce itself, and therefore is certain to be exhausted ultimately; and wastefulness in dealing with it to-day means that our descendants will feel the exhaustion a generation or two before they otherwise would."

---

the banner of leadership and charged into the fray with all the weight of his prestige, his energy, his firsthand knowledge, and his slashing invective.

The thirst of the desert still unslaked, Congress responded to the whip of the Rough Rider by passing the landmark Newlands Act of 1902. Washington was authorized to collect money from the sale of public lands in the sun-baked western states and then use these funds for the development of irrigation projects. Settlers repaid the cost of reclamation from their now-productive soil, and the money was put into a revolving fund to finance more such enterprises. The giant Roosevelt Dam, constructed on Arizona's Salt River, was appropriately dedicated by Roosevelt in 1911. Thanks to this epochal legislation, dozens of dams were thrown across virtually every major western river in the ensuing decades.

Loggers in the State of Washington, 1912 It took the sweat and skill of many men to conquer a giant Douglas fir like this one. An ax-wielding "sniper" had rounded the edges of this log so that a team of oxen, driven by a "bullwhacker," could more easily drag it out of the woods along a "skid road." *Skid road* (sometimes corrupted as *skid row*) was also a name for the often-sleazy sections of logging towns, where loggers spent their time in the off-season.

Roosevelt pined to preserve the nation's shrinking forests. By 1900 only about a quarter of the once-vast virgin timberlands remained standing. Lumbermen had already logged off most of the first-growth timber from Maine to Michigan, and the sharp thud of their axes was beginning to split the silence in the great fir forests of the Pacific slope. Roosevelt proceeded to set aside in federal reserves some 125 million acres, or almost three times the acreage thus saved from the saw by his three predecessors. He similarly earmarked millions of acres of coal deposits, as well as water resources useful for irrigation and power. To set a shining example, in 1902 he banned Christmas trees from the White House.

Conservation, including reclamation, may have been Roosevelt's most enduring tangible achievement. He was buoyed in this effort by an upwelling national mood of concern about the disappearance of the frontier—believed to be the source of such national characteristics as individualism and democracy. An increasingly citified people worried that too much civilization might not be good for the national soul. City dwellers snapped up Jack London's *Call of the Wild* (1903) and other books about nature, and urban youngsters made the outdoor-oriented Boy Scouts of America the country's largest youth organization. The Sierra Club, founded in 1892, dedicated itself to preserving the wildness of the western landscape.

The preservationists lost a major battle in 1913 when the federal government allowed the city of San Francisco to build a dam for its municipal water supply in the spectacular, high-walled Hetch Hetchy Valley in Yosemite National Park. The Hetch Hetchy controversy laid bare a deep division among conservationists that persists to the present day. To the preservationists of the Sierra Club, including famed naturalist John Muir, Hetch Hetchy was a "temple"

Gifford Pinchot (1865–1946), a leading conservationist in the Roosevelt administration, wrote,

"The object of our forest policy is not to preserve the forests because they are refuges for the wild creatures of the wilderness, but the making of prosperous homes. Every other consideration comes as secondary. . . . The test of utility . . . implies that no lands will be permanently reserves which can serve the people better in any other way."

The Environmentalists

Humans have long been awed by nature, but they have also yearned to be its masters. Native American peoples did what they could to shape the natural environment to serve their purposes—burning forest and grasslands, for example, to improve hunting habitats—but they lacked the tools to make Mother Earth bow deeply to their will. The earliest European colonists saw North America as a "howling wilderness" and toiled mightily with ax and plow to tame it. By the mid-nineteenth century, Americans commanded powerful new technologies like the railroad and steam-powered drills and dredges, which promised unbridled dominion over the natural world. Only then did voices begin to be heard in defense of the wounded earth—the faint first stirrings of what would come to be called "environmentalism."

In a pattern that would often be repeated, nature's earliest defenders tended to be well-off townsfolk and city dwellers, like Henry David Thoreau and Ralph Waldo Emerson. The Americans most likely to appreciate the value of the pristine wilderness, it seemed, were those who had ceased to struggle against it. ("Cities, not log cabins, produce Sierra Clubbers," one historian noted.) For the loggers, miners, and farmers who continued to sweat their living out of nature's grudging embrace, concern for environmental niceties often seemed like the sanctimonious piety of a privileged elite.

By the dawn of the twentieth century, many genteel, urban Americans had come to romanticize their pioneer forebears. They reinvented hunting and fishing as sports for the well-to-do, not simply as ways to put food on the table. Preservationists like John Muir waxed lyrical about the mystic allure of unspoiled nature. Seizing the popular mood, Theodore Roosevelt deliberately constructed a public image of himself as a manly outdoorsman—raising cattle in the Dakotas, shooting lions in Africa, rafting down wild rivers in the Amazon basin—and as president he greatly expanded the system of national forests. But Roosevelt was also a pioneer of another sort—as a

prominent promoter of the progressive-era "conservation" movement, composed of a loose coalition of scientists, bureaucrats, and businesspeople dependent on America's endowment of natural resources. Progressive conservationists believed that nature must be neither uncritically reverenced nor wastefully exploited, but must instead be efficiently utilized. Thus the same TR who admired the wonders of Yosemite Valley in the company of John Muir also supported the professional forester Gifford Pinchot, who declared that "the object of our forest policy is not to preserve the forests because they are beautiful or because they are refuges for the wild creatures of the wilderness, but the making of prosperous homes. Use must be the test by which the forester tries himself."

Pinchot's "rational use" philosophy guided America's natural resource policy until the mid-twentieth century. It justified the systematic harvesting of millions of trees in the sprawling national forests whose boundaries Roosevelt had expanded, and the drowning of vast river valleys behind massive dams that Roosevelt's Reclamation Service helped to build. This attitude toward nature tri-

Gifford Pinchot Going Trout Fishing
The father of the modern Forest Service, Pinchot championed the concept of "rational use" as the guiding principle of the federal government's natural resource management policies.

umphed in the New Deal era of the 1930s, when the federal government initiated colossal projects that undertook nothing less than reengineering the face of the continent—including the Tennessee Valley Authority, the Soil Conservation Service, and the Shelterbelt tree-planting project on the Great Plains. The huge reach of these New Deal projects also introduced millions of Americans for the first time to the concept that nature had to be treated with respect, helping to stimulate the post–World War II grassroots environmental movement.

The rise of ecological science in the post–World War II era fundamentally changed the debate about the relation of nature to civilization. Ecologists charged that the apparent "rationality" of the earlier conservationists dangerously neglected the fateful intricacies of biological systems. They called attention to the stunningly complex webs of interrelationships that linked together seemingly unrelated organisms—and to the perils of tampering even slightly with the delicate biological fabrics that nature had taken millennia to weave. Rachel Carson helped to popularize the new outlook in her sensational 1962 exposé, *Silent Spring*, about the far-reaching effects of pesticides on birds, plants, and animals—including humans.

The advent of ecological studies coincided with a revival of preservationist sentiment, especially in the suburbs, where Americans increasingly dwelled. Hordes of affluent baby boomers took to America's trails, slopes, and waterways to hike, bike, ski, fish, boat, and otherwise recreate—often on public lands like Arizona's wondrous Grand Canyon National Park, or public waters like Utah's shimmering (and man-made) Lake Powell. Membership in environmental organizations such as the Sierra Club and the Audubon Society soared, as a generation infatuated with nature demanded a clean and green world. The first celebration of Earth Day, on April 22, 1970, marked the political maturation of modern-day environmentalism, which wedded scientific analysis with respect for nature's majesty. That same year saw the creation of the federal Environmental Protection Agency (EPA), soon followed by the Endangered Species Act and other legislation designed to regulate the relationship between humans and nature.

At the outset of the twenty-first century, developments like global warming served dramatic notice that planet earth was the biggest ecological system of them all—one that did not recognize national boundaries. Yet while Americans took pride in the efforts they had made to clean up their own turf, who were they, having long since consumed much of their own timberlands, to tell the Brazilians that they should not cut down the Amazon rain forest? Who were they, having tamed virtually all their own free-flowing waters, to tell the Chinese not to dam their rivers? For the peoples of the developing world, struggling to match America's standard of living, environmentalists often seemed like spoiled spoilers, preaching the same privileged pieties that had infuriated generations of working Americans.

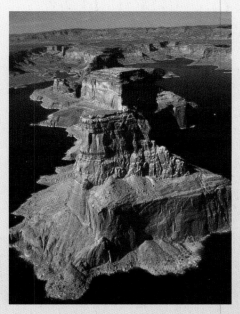

Lake Powell, Utah Named for the famed explorer John Wesley Powell and formed by one of the several dams on the Colorado River, Lake Powell has been a focus of intense controversy. It drowned the spectacularly beautiful Glen Canyon, but created recreational facilities for countless Americans.

Earth Day, 1999
Some 1,500 school children gathered on the shoreline near Los Angeles to participate in a beach clean-up project. The "O" represents planet earth; inside it are represented the North and South American continents.

of nature that should be held inviolable by the civilizing hand of humanity. But other conservationists, among them President Roosevelt's chief forester, Gifford Pinchot, believed that "wilderness was waste." Pinchot and Roosevelt wanted to *use* the nation's natural endowment intelligently. In their eyes they had to battle on two fronts: against greedy commercial interests who abused nature, as well as against romantic preservationists in thrall to simple "woodman-spare-that-tree" sentimentality.

Under Roosevelt, professional foresters and engineers developed a policy of "multiple-use resource management." They sought to combine recreation, sustained-yield logging, watershed pro-

tection, and summer stock grazing on the same expanse of federal land.

At first many westerners resisted the federal management of natural resources, but they soon learned how to take advantage of new agencies like the Forest Service and especially the Bureau of Reclamation. The largest ranches and timber companies in particular figured out how to work hand in glove with federal conservation programs devoted to the rational, large-scale, and long-term use of natural resources. The one-man-and-a-mule logger or the one-man-and-a-dog sheepherder had little clout in the new resources bureaucracy. Single-person enterprises were shouldered aside, in the

Sunrise, Yosemite Valley, by Albert Bierstadt, c. 1870
A German-born artist, Bierstadt romanticized the already awesome beauty of the American West.

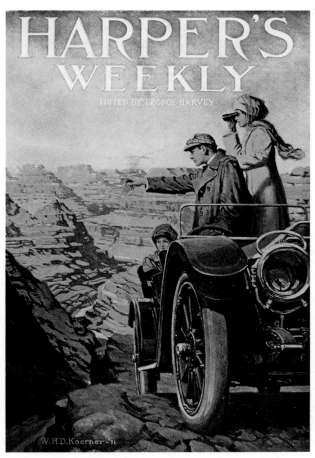

The Machine and Nature   These hardy sightseers at the Grand Canyon in 1911 ironically and probably unwittingly foreshadowed the mass tourism that arrived with the dawning automobile age. Soon millions of motorized Americans would regularly flee from the cities and suburbs to "get away from it all" in wilderness sites increasingly overrun by their fellow refugees from "civilization."

interest of efficiency, by the combined bulk of big business and big government.

The "Roosevelt Panic" of 1907

Roosevelt was handily elected president "in his own right" in 1904 and entered his new term buoyed by his enormous personal popularity—the cuddly "teddy bear" honored one of his bear-hunting exploits (when he saved the life of a cub), and chil-dren piped vigorously on whistles modeled on his famous teeth. Yet the conservative Republican bosses considered him as dangerous and unpredictable as a rattlesnake. They grew increasingly restive as Roosevelt in his second term called ever more loudly for regulating the corporations, taxing incomes, and protecting workers. Roosevelt, meanwhile, had partly defanged himself after his election in 1904 by announcing that under no circumstances would he be a candidate for a third term. This was a tactical blunder, for the power of the king wanes when the people know he will be dead in four years.

Roosevelt suffered a sharp setback in 1907, when a short but punishing panic descended on Wall Street. The financial flurry featured frightened "runs" on banks, suicides, and criminal indictments against speculators.

The financial world hastened to blame Roosevelt for the storm. It cried that this "quack" had unsettled industry with his boat-rocking tactics. Conservatives damned him as "Theodore the Meddler" and branded the current distress the "Roosevelt panic." The hot-tempered president angrily lashed back at his critics when he accused "certain malefactors of great wealth" of having deliberately engineered the monetary crisis to force the government to relax its assaults on trusts.

Fortunately, the panic of 1907 paved the way for long-overdue fiscal reforms. Precipitating a currency shortage, the flurry laid bare the need for a more elastic medium of exchange. In a crisis of this sort, the hard-pressed banks were unable to increase the volume of money in circulation, and those with ample reserves were reluctant to lend to their less fortunate competitors. Congress in 1908 responded by passing the Aldrich-Vreeland Act, which authorized national banks to issue emergency currency backed by various kinds of collateral. The path was thus smoothed for the momentous Federal Reserve Act of 1913 (see p. 692).

The Rough Rider Thunders Out

Still warmly popular in 1908, Roosevelt could easily have won a second presidential nomination and almost certainly the election. But he felt bound by his impulsive postelection promise after his victory in 1904.

Baby, Kiss Papa Good-bye Theodore Roosevelt leaves his baby, "My Policies," in the hands of his chosen successor, William Howard Taft. Friction between Taft and Roosevelt would soon erupt, however, prompting Roosevelt to return to politics and challenge Taft for the presidency.

The departing president thus naturally sought a successor who would carry out "my policies." The man of his choice was amiable, ample-girthed, and huge-framed William Howard Taft, secretary of war and a mild progressive. As an heir apparent, he had often been called upon in Roosevelt's absence to "sit on the lid"—all 350 pounds of him. At the Republican convention of 1908 in Chicago, Roosevelt used his control of the party machinery—the "steamroller"—to push through Taft's nomination on the first ballot. Three weeks later, in mile-high Denver, in the heart of silver country, the Democrats nominated twice-beaten William Jennings Bryan.

The dull campaign of 1908 featured the rotund Taft and the now-balding "Boy Orator" both trying to don the progressive Roosevelt mantle. The solid Judge Taft read cut-and-dried speeches, while Bryan griped that Roosevelt had stolen his policies from the Bryanite camp. A majority of voters chose stabil-ity with Roosevelt-endorsed Taft, who polled 321 electoral votes to 162 for Bryan. The victor's popular count was 7,675,320 to 6,412,294. The election's only surprise came from the Socialists, who amassed 420,793 votes for Eugene V. Debs, the hero of the Pullman strike of 1894 (see pp. 614–615).

Roosevelt, ever in the limelight, left soon after the election for a lion hunt in Africa. His numerous enemies clinked glasses while toasting "Health to the lions," and a few irreverently prayed that some big cat would "do its duty." But TR survived, still bursting with energy at the age of fifty-one in 1909.

Roosevelt was branded by his adversaries as a wild-eyed radical, but his reputation as an eater of errant industrialists now seems inflated. He fought many a sham battle, and the number of laws he inspired was certainly not in proportion to the amount of noise he emitted. He was often under attack from the reigning business lords, but the more enlightened of them knew that they had a friend in the White House. Roosevelt should be remembered first and foremost as the cowboy who started to tame the bucking bronco of adolescent capitalism, thus ensuring it a long adult life.

Taft Campaigning A powerful voice was a political necessity in the pre-electronic age.

> *Roosevelt, who preached the doctrine of the "strenuous life," practiced it until almost the end. In 1913 he sent a political message on a still-preserved phonograph recording to the Boys' Progressive League:*
>
> "Don't flinch, don't foul, and hit the line hard."

TR's enthusiasm and perpetual youthfulness, like an overgrown Boy Scout's, appealed to the young of all ages. "You must always remember," a British diplomat cautioned his colleagues, "that the president is about six." He served as a political lightning rod to protect capitalists against popular indignation—and against socialism, which Roosevelt regarded as "ominous." He strenuously sought the middle road between unbridled individualism and paternalistic collectivism. His conservation crusade, which tried to mediate between the romantic wilderness-preservationists and the rapacious resource-predators, was probably his most typical and his most lasting achievement.

Several other contributions of Roosevelt lasted beyond his presidency. First, he greatly enlarged the power and prestige of the presidential office—and masterfully developed the technique of using the big stick of publicity as a political bludgeon. Second, he helped shape the progressive movement and beyond it the liberal reform campaigns later in the century. His Square Deal, in a sense, was the grandfather of the New Deal later launched by his fifth cousin, Franklin D. Roosevelt. Finally, to a greater degree than any of his predecessors, TR opened the eyes of Americans to the fact that they shared the world with other nations. As a great power, they had fallen heir to responsibilities—and had been seized by ambitions—from which there was no escaping.

Taft: A Round Peg in a Square Hole

William Howard Taft, with his ruddy complexion and upturned mustache, at first inspired widespread confidence. "Everybody loves a fat man," the saying goes, and the jovial Taft, with "mirthquakes" of laughter bubbling up from his abundant abdomen, was personally popular. He had graduated second in his class at Yale and had established an enviable reputation as a lawyer and judge, though he was widely regarded as hostile to labor unions. He had been a trusted administrator under Roosevelt—in the Philippines, at home, and in Cuba, where he had served capably as a troubleshooter.

But "good old Will" suffered from lethal political handicaps. Roosevelt had led the conflicting elements of the Republican party by the sheer force of his personality. Taft, in contrast, had none of the arts of a dashing political leader and none of Roosevelt's zest for the fray. Recoiling from the clamor of controversy, he generally adopted an attitude of passivity toward Congress. He was a poor judge of public opinion, and his candor made him a chronic victim of "foot-in-mouth" disease.

"Peaceful Bill" was no doubt a mild progressive, but at heart he was more wedded to the status quo than to change. Significantly, his cabinet did not contain a single representative of the party's "insurgent" wing, which was on fire for reform of current abuses, especially the tariff.

The Dollar Goes Abroad as a Diplomat

Though ordinarily lethargic, Taft bestirred himself to use the lever of American investments to boost American political interests abroad, an approach to foreign policy that his critics denounced as "dollar diplomacy." Washington warmly encouraged Wall Street bankers to sluice their surplus dollars into foreign areas of strategic concern to the United States, especially in the Far East and in the regions critical to the security of the Panama Canal. By preempting investors from rival powers, such as Germany, New York bankers would thus strengthen American defenses and foreign policies, while bringing further prosperity to their homeland—and to themselves. The almighty dollar thereby supplanted the big stick.

China's Manchuria was the object of Taft's most spectacular effort to inject the reluctant dollar into the Far Eastern theater. Newly ambitious Japan and imperialistic Russia, recent foes, controlled the railroads of this strategic province. President Taft saw in the Manchurian railway monopoly a possible strangulation of Chinese economic interests and a consequent slamming of the Open Door in the faces of U.S. merchants. In 1909 Secretary of State

Ex-President Theodore Roosevelt Watches President Taft Struggle with the Demands of Government, 1910

Philander C. Knox blunderingly proposed that a group of American and foreign bankers buy the Manchurian railroads and then turn them over to China under a self-liquidating arrangement. Both Japan and Russia, unwilling to be jockeyed out of their dominant position, bluntly rejected Knox's overtures. Taft was showered with ridicule.

Another dangerous new trouble spot was the revolution-riddled Caribbean—now virtually a Yankee lake. Hoping to head off trouble, Washington urged Wall Street bankers to pump dollars into the financial vacuums in Honduras and Haiti to keep out foreign funds. The United States, under the Monroe Doctrine, would not permit foreign nations to intervene, and consequently felt obligated to put its money where its mouth was to prevent economic and political instability.

Again necessity was the mother of armed Caribbean intervention. Sporadic disorders in palm-fronded Cuba, Honduras, and the Dominican Republic brought American forces to these countries to restore order and protect American investment. A revolutionary upheaval in Nicaragua, regarded as perilously close to the nearly completed Panama Canal, resulted in the landing of twenty-five hundred marines in 1912. The marines remained in Nicaragua for thirteen years. (See the map on p. 695.)

Taft the Trustbuster

Taft managed to gain some fame as a smasher of monopolies. The ironic truth is that the colorless Taft brought 90 suits against the trusts during his 4 years in office, as compared with some 44 for Roosevelt in $7\frac{1}{2}$ years.

By fateful happenstance the most sensational judicial actions during the Taft regime came in 1911. In that year the Supreme Court ordered the dissolution of the mighty Standard Oil Company, which was judged to be a combination in restraint of trade in violation of the Sherman Anti-Trust Act of 1890. At the same time, the Court handed down its famous "rule of reason." This doctrine held that only those combinations that "unreasonably" restrained trade were illegal. This fine-print proviso ripped a huge hole in the government's antitrust net.

Even more explosively, in 1911 Taft decided to press an antitrust suit against the U.S. Steel Corporation. This initiative infuriated Roosevelt, who had personally been involved in one of the mergers that prompted the suit. Once Roosevelt's protégé, President Taft was increasingly taking on the role of his antagonist. The stage was being set for a bruising confrontation.

Taft Splits the Republican Party

Lowering the barriers of the formidable protective tariff—the "Mother of Trusts"—was high on the agenda of the progressive members of the Republican party, and they at first thought they had a friend and ally in Taft. True to his campaign promises to reduce tariffs, Taft called Congress into special session in March 1909. The House proceeded to pass a moderately reductive bill, but senatorial reactionaries, led by Senator Nelson W. Aldrich of Rhode Island, tacked on hundreds of upward tariff revisions. Only items such as hides, sea moss, and canary-bird seed were left on the duty-free list.

After much handwringing, Taft signed the Payne-Aldrich Bill, thus betraying his campaign promises and outraging the progressive wing of his party, heavily drawn from the Midwest. Taft rubbed salt in the wound by proclaiming it "the best bill that the Republican party ever passed."

Taft revealed a further knack for shooting himself in the foot in his handling of conservation. The portly president was a dedicated conservationist, and his contributions actually equaled or surpassed those of Roosevelt. He established the Bureau of Mines to control mineral resources, rescued millions of acres of western coal lands from exploitation, and protected water-power sites from private development. But those praiseworthy accomplishments were largely erased in the public mind by the noisy Ballinger-Pinchot quarrel that erupted in 1910.

When Secretary of the Interior Richard Ballinger opened public lands in Wyoming, Montana, and Alaska to corporate development, he was sharply criticized by Gifford Pinchot, chief of the Agriculture Department's Division of Forestry and a stalwart Rooseveltian. When Taft dismissed Pinchot on the narrow grounds of insubordination, a storm of protest arose from conservationists and from Roosevelt's friends, who were legion. The whole unsavory episode further widened the growing rift between the president and the former president, one-time bosom political partners.

The reformist wing of the Republican party was now up in arms, while Taft was being pushed increasingly into the embrace of the stand-pat Old Guard. By the spring of 1910, the Grand Old Party was split wide open, owing largely to the clumsiness of Taft. A suspicious Roosevelt returned triumphantly to New York in June 1910 and shortly thereafter stirred up a tempest. Unable to keep silent, he took to the stump at Osawatomie, Kansas, and shocked the Old Guard with a flaming speech. The doctrine that he proclaimed—popularly known as the "New Nationalism"—urged the national government to increase its power to remedy economic and social abuses.

Weakened by these internal divisions, the Republicans lost badly in the congressional elections of 1910. In a victory of landslide proportions, the Democrats emerged with 228 seats, leaving the once-dominant Republicans with only 161. In a further symptom of the reforming temper of the times, a Socialist representative, Austrian-born Victor L. Berger, was elected from Milwaukee.* The Republicans, by virtue of holdovers, retained the Senate, 51 to 41, but the insurgents in their midst were numerous enough to make that hold precarious.

The Taft-Roosevelt Rupture

The sputtering uprising in Republican ranks had now blossomed into a full-fledged revolt. Early in 1911 the National Progressive Republican League was formed, with the fiery, white-maned Senator La Follette of Wisconsin its leading candidate for the Republican presidential nomination. The assumption was that Roosevelt, an anti–third termer, would not permit himself to be "drafted."

But the restless Rough Rider began to change his views about third terms as he saw Taft, hand in glove with the hated Old Guard, discard "my policies." In February 1912 Roosevelt formally wrote to seven state governors that he was willing to accept the Republican nomination. His reasoning was that the third-term tradition applied to three *consecutive elective* terms. Exuberantly he cried, "My hat is in the ring!" and "The fight is on and I am stripped to the buff!"

Roosevelt forthwith seized the Progressive banner, while La Follette, who had served as a convenient pathbreaker, was protestingly elbowed aside. Girded for battle, the Rough Rider came clattering into the presidential primaries then being held in many states. He shouted through half-clenched teeth that the president had fallen under the thumb of the reactionary bosses and that,

---

*He was eventually denied his seat in 1919, during a wave of antired hysteria.

Roosevelt the Take-Back Giver

although Taft "means well, he means well feebly." The once-genial Taft, now in a fighting mood, retorted by branding Roosevelt supporters "emotionalists and neurotics."

A Taft-Roosevelt explosion was near in June 1912, when the Republican convention met in Chicago. The Rooseveltites, who were about 100 delegates short of winning the nomination, challenged the right of some 250 Taft delegates to be seated.

Most of these contests were arbitrarily settled in favor of Taft, whose supporters held the throttle of the convention steamroller. The Roosevelt adherents, crying "fraud" and "naked theft," in the end refused to vote, and Taft triumphed.

Roosevelt, the supposedly good sportsman, refused to quit the game. Having tasted for the first time the bitter cup of defeat, he was now on fire to lead a third-party crusade.

Chronology

1901 Commission system established in Galveston, Texas
Progressive Robert La Follette elected governor of Wisconsin

1902 Lincoln Steffens and Ida Tarbell publish muckraking exposés
Anthracite coal strike
Newlands Act

1903 Department of Commerce and Labor established
Elkins Act

1904 *Northern Securities* case
Roosevelt defeats Alton B. Parker for presidency

1905 *Lochner* v. *New York*

1906 Hepburn Act
Upton Sinclair publishes *The Jungle*
Meat Inspection Act

1906 Pure Food and Drug Act

1907 "Roosevelt panic"

1908 *Muller* v. *Oregon*
Taft defeats Bryan for presidency
Aldrich-Vreeland Act

1909 Payne-Aldrich Tariff

1910 Ballinger-Pinchot affair

1911 Triangle Shirtwaist Company fire
Standard Oil antitrust case
U.S. Steel Corporation antitrust suit

1912 Taft wins Republican nomination over Roosevelt

1913 Seventeenth Amendment passed (direct election of U.S. senators)
Federal Reserve Act

For further reading, see page A20 of the Appendix. For web resources, go to **http://college.hmco.com**.

Wilsonian Progressivism at Home and Abroad

—◈—

1912–1916

American enterprise is not free; the man with only a little capital is finding it harder and harder to get into the field, more and more impossible to compete with the big fellow. Why? Because the laws of this country do not prevent the strong from crushing the weak.

WOODROW WILSON, THE NEW FREEDOM, 1913

Office-hungry Democrats—the "outs" since 1897—were jubilant over the disruptive Republican brawl at the convention in Chicago. If they could come up with an outstanding reformist leader, they had an excellent chance to win the White House. Such a leader appeared in Dr. Woodrow Wilson, once a mild conservative but now a militant progressive. Beginning professional life as a brilliant academic lecturer on government, he had risen in 1902 to the presidency of Princeton University, where he had achieved some sweeping educational reforms.

Wilson entered politics in 1910 when New Jersey bosses, needing a respectable "front" candidate for the governorship, offered him the nomination. They expected to lead the academic novice by the nose, but to their surprise, Wilson waged a passionate reform campaign in which he assailed the "predatory" trusts and promised to return state government to the people. Riding the crest of the progressive wave, the "Schoolmaster in Politics" was swept into office.

Once in the governor's chair, Wilson drove through the legislature a sheaf of forward-looking measures that made reactionary New Jersey one of the more liberal states. Filled with righteous indignation, Wilson revealed irresistible reforming zeal, burning eloquence, superb powers of leadership, and a refreshing habit of appealing over the heads of the scheming bosses to the sovereign people. Now a figure of national eminence, Wilson was being widely mentioned for the presidency.

GOP Divided by Bull Moose Equals Democratic Victory, 1912

The "Bull Moose" Campaign of 1912

When the Democrats met at Baltimore in 1912, Wilson was nominated on the forty-sixth ballot, aided by William Jennings Bryan's switch to his side. The Democrats gave Wilson a strong progressive platform to run on; dubbed the "New Freedom" program, it included calls for stronger antitrust legislation, banking reform, and tariff reductions.

Surging events had meanwhile been thrusting Roosevelt to the fore as a candidate for the presidency on a third-party Progressive Republican ticket. The fighting ex-cowboy, angered by his recent rebuff, was eager to lead the charge. A pro-Roosevelt Progressive convention, with about two thousand delegates from forty states, assembled in Chicago during August 1912. Dramatically symbolizing the rising political status of women, as well as Progressive support for the cause of social justice, settlement-house pioneer Jane Addams placed Roosevelt's name in nomination for the presidency. Roosevelt was applauded tumultuously as he cried in a vehement speech, "We stand at Armageddon, and we battle for the Lord!" The hosanna spirit of a religious revival meeting suffused the convention, as the hoarse delegates sang "Onward Christian Soldiers" and "Battle Hymn of the Republic." William Allen White, the caustic Kansas journalist, later wrote, "Roosevelt bit me and I went mad."

Fired-up Progressives entered the campaign with righteousness and enthusiasm. Roosevelt boasted that he felt "as strong as a bull moose," and the bull moose took its place with the donkey and the elephant in the American political zoo. As one poet whimsically put it,

I want to be a Bull Moose,
And with the Bull Moose stand
With antlers on my forehead
And a Big Stick in my hand.

Roosevelt and Taft were bound to slit each other's political throats; by dividing the Republican vote, they virtually guaranteed a Democratic victory. The two antagonists tore into each other as only former friends can. "Death alone can take me out now," cried the once-jovial Taft, as he branded Roosevelt a "dangerous egotist" and a "demagogue." Roosevelt, fighting mad, assailed Taft as a "fathead" with the brain of a "guinea pig."

Beyond the clashing personalities, the overshadowing question of the 1912 campaign was which of two varieties of progressivism would prevail—Roosevelt's New Nationalism or Wilson's New Freedom. Both men favored a more active government role in economic and social affairs, but they disagreed sharply over specific strategies. Roosevelt preached the theories spun out by the progressive thinker Herbert Croly in his book *The Promise of American Life* (1910). Croly and TR both favored continued consolidation of trusts and labor unions, paralleled by the growth of powerful regulatory agencies in Washington. Roosevelt and his "bull moosers" also campaigned for woman suffrage and a broad program of social welfare, including minimum-wage laws and "socialistic" social insurance. Clearly, the bull moose Progressives looked forward to the kind of activist welfare state that Franklin Roosevelt's New Deal would one day make a reality.

Wilson's New Freedom, by contrast, favored small enterprise, entrepreneurship, and the free functioning of unregulated and unmonopolized markets. The Democrats shunned social-welfare proposals and pinned their economic faith on competition—on the "man on the make," as Wilson put it. The keynote of Wilson's campaign was not regulation but fragmentation of the big industrial combines, chiefly by means of vigorous enforcement of the antitrust laws. The election of 1912 thus offered the voters a choice not merely of policies but of political and economic philosophies—a rarity in U.S. history.

The heat of the campaign cooled a bit when, in Milwaukee, Roosevelt was shot in the chest by a fanatic. The Rough Rider suspended active campaigning for more than two weeks after delivering, with bull moose gameness and a bloody shirt, his scheduled speech.

Woodrow Wilson: A Minority President

Former professor Wilson won handily, with 435 electoral votes and 6,296,547 popular votes. The "third-party" candidate, Roosevelt, finished second, receiving 88 electoral votes and 4,118,571 popular votes. Taft won only 8 electoral votes and 3,486,720 popular votes (see the map on p. 690).

The election figures are fascinating. Wilson, with only 41 percent of the popular vote, was clearly a minority president, though his party won a majority in Congress. His popular total was actually smaller than Bryan had amassed in any of his three defeats, despite the increase in population. Taft and Roosevelt together polled over 1.25 million more votes than the Democrats. Progressivism rather than Wilson was the runaway winner. Although the Democratic total obviously included many conservatives in the solid South, the combined progressive vote for Wilson and Roosevelt exceeded the tally of the more conservative Taft. To the progressive tally must be added some support for the Socialist candidate, persistent Eugene V. Debs, who rolled up 900,672 votes, or more than twice as many as he had netted four years earlier. Starry-eyed Socialists dreamed of being in the White House within eight years.

Roosevelt's lone-wolf course was tragic both for himself and for his former Republican associates. Perhaps, to rephrase William Allen White, he had bitten himself and gone mad. The Progressive party, which was primarily a one-man show, had no future because it had elected few candidates to state and local offices; the Socialists, in contrast, elected more than a thousand. Without patronage plums to hand out to the faithful workers, death by slow starvation was inevitable for the upstart party. Yet the Progressives made a tremendous showing for a hastily organized third party and helped spur the enactment of many of their pet reforms by the Wilsonian Democrats.

As for the Republicans, they were thrust into unaccustomed minority status in Congress for the next six years and were frozen out of the White House for eight years. Taft himself had a fruitful old age. He taught law for eight pleasant years at Yale University and in 1921 became chief justice of the Supreme Court—a job for which he was far more happily suited than the presidency.

Wilson: The Idealist in Politics

(Thomas) Woodrow Wilson, the second Democratic president since 1861, looked like the ascetic intellectual he was, with his clean-cut features, pinched-on eyeglasses, and trim figure. Born in Virginia

The Presidential Vote, 1912

Candidate	Party	Electoral Vote	Popular Vote	Approximate Percentage
Woodrow Wilson	Democratic	435	6,296,547	41%
Theodore Roosevelt	Progressive	88	4,118,571	27
William H. Taft	Republican	8	3,486,720	23
Eugene V. Debs	Socialist	—	900,672	6
E. W. Chafin	Prohibition	—	206,275	1
A. E. Reimer	Socialist-Labor	—	28,750	0.2

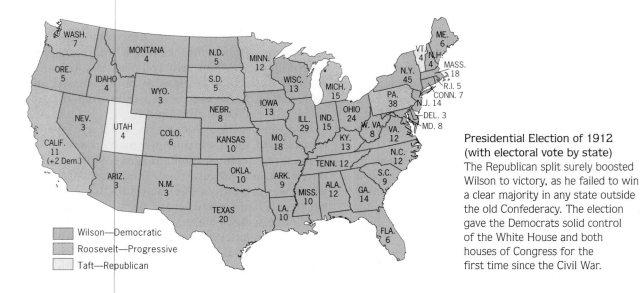

Presidential Election of 1912 (with electoral vote by state) The Republican split surely boosted Wilson to victory, as he failed to win a clear majority in any state outside the old Confederacy. The election gave the Democrats solid control of the White House and both houses of Congress for the first time since the Civil War.

shortly before the Civil War and reared in Georgia and the Carolinas, the professor-politician was the first man from one of the seceded southern states to reach the White House since Zachary Taylor, sixty-four years earlier.

The impact of Dixieland on young "Tommy" Wilson was profound. He sympathized with the Confederacy's gallant attempt to win its independence, a sentiment that partly inspired his ideal of self-determination for people of other countries. Steeped in the traditions of Jeffersonian democracy, he shared Jefferson's faith in the masses—if they were properly informed.

Son of a Presbyterian minister, Wilson was reared in an atmosphere of fervent piety. He later used the presidential pulpit to preach his inspirational political sermons. A moving orator, Wilson could rise on the wings of spiritual power to soaring eloquence. Skillfully using a persuasive voice, he relied not on arm-waving but on sincerity and moral appeal. As a lifelong student of finely chiseled words, he turned out to be a "phraseocrat" who coined many noble epigrams. Someone has remarked that he was born halfway between the Bible and the dictionary and never strayed far from either.

A profound student of government, Wilson believed that the chief executive should play a dynamic role. He was convinced that Congress could not function properly unless the president,

like a kind of prime minister, got out in front and provided leadership. He enjoyed dramatic success, both as governor and as president, in appealing over the heads of legislators to the sovereign people.

Splendid though Wilson's intellectual equipment was, he suffered from serious defects of personality. Though jovial and witty in private, he could be cold and standoffish in public. Incapable of unbending and acting the showman, like "Teddy" Roosevelt, he lacked the common touch. He loved humanity in the mass rather than the individual in person. His academic background caused him to feel most at home with scholars, although he had to work with politicians. An austere and somewhat arrogant intellectual, he looked down his nose through pince-nez glasses upon lesser minds, including journalists. He was especially intolerant of stupid senators, whose "bungalow" minds made him "sick."

Wilson's burning idealism—especially his desire to reform ever-present wickedness—drove him forward faster than lesser spirits were willing to go. His sense of moral righteousness was such that he often found compromise difficult; black was black, wrong was wrong, and one should never compromise with wrong. President Wilson's Scottish Presbyterian ancestors had passed on to him an inflexible stubbornness. When convinced that he was right, the principled Wilson would break before he would bend, unlike the pragmatic Roosevelt.

Woodrow Wilson (1856–1924) at Princeton Commencement with Andrew Carnegie, 1906   Before his election to the presidency of the United States in 1912, Wilson (left) served as president of Princeton University (1902–1910) and governor of New Jersey (1910–1912). In all three offices he undertook substantial reforms. Fighting desperately later for the League of Nations, at the cost of his health, Wilson said, "I would rather fail in a cause that I know some day will triumph than to win in a cause that I know some day will fail."

Wilson Tackles the Tariff

Few presidents have arrived at the White House with a clearer program than Wilson's or one destined to be so completely achieved. The new president called for an all-out assault on what he called "the triple wall of privilege": the tariff, the banks, and the trusts.

He tackled the tariff first, summoning Congress into special session in early 1913. In a precedent-shattering move, he did not send his presidential message over to the Capitol to be read loudly by a bored clerk, as had been the custom since Jefferson's day. Instead he appeared in person before a joint session of Congress and presented his appeal with stunning eloquence and effectiveness.

Moved by Wilson's aggressive leadership, the House swiftly passed the Underwood Tariff Bill, which provided for a substantial reduction of rates. When a swarm of lobbyists descended on the Senate seeking to disembowel the bill, Wilson promptly issued a combative message to the people, urging them to hold their elected representatives in line. The tactic worked. The force of public opinion, aroused by the president's oratory, secured late in 1913 final approval of the bill Wilson wanted.

The new Underwood Tariff substantially reduced import fees. It also was a landmark in tax legislation. Under authority granted by the recently ratified Sixteenth Amendment, Congress enacted a graduated income tax, beginning with a modest levy on incomes over $3,000 (then considerably higher than the average family's income). By 1917 revenue from the income tax shot ahead of receipts from the tariff. This gap has since been vastly widened.

Wilson Battles the Bankers

A second bastion of the "triple wall of privilege" was the antiquated and inadequate banking and currency system, long since outgrown by the Republic's lusty economic expansion. The country's financial structure, still creaking along under the Civil War National Banking Act, revealed glaring defects. Its most serious shortcoming, as exposed by the panic of 1907, was the inelasticity of the currency. Banking reserves were heavily concentrated in New York and a handful of other large cities and could not be mobilized in times of financial stress into areas that were badly pinched.

In 1908 Congress had authorized an investigation headed by a mossback banker, Republican senator Aldrich. Three years later Aldrich's special commission recommended a gigantic bank with numerous branches—in effect, a third Bank of the United States.

For their part, Democratic banking reformers heeded the findings of a House committee chaired by Congressman Arsene Pujo, which traced the tentacles of the "money monster" into the hidden vaults of American banking and business. President Wilson's confidant, progressive-minded Massachusetts attorney Louis D. Brandeis, further fanned the flames of reform with his incendiary though scholarly book *Other People's Money and How the Bankers Use It* (1914).

In June 1913, in a second dramatic personal appearance before both houses of Congress, the president delivered a stirring plea for sweeping reform of the banking system. He ringingly endorsed Democratic proposals for a decentralized bank in government hands, as opposed to Republican demands for a huge private bank with fifteen branches.

Again appealing to the sovereign people, Wilson scored another triumph. In 1913 he signed the epochal Federal Reserve Act, the most important piece of economic legislation between the Civil War and the New Deal. The new Federal Reserve Board, appointed by the president, oversaw a nationwide system of twelve regional reserve districts, each with its own central bank. Although these regional banks were actually bankers' banks, owned by member financial institutions, the final authority of the Federal Reserve Board guaranteed a substantial measure of public control. The board was also empowered to issue paper money—"Federal Reserve Notes"—backed by commercial paper, such as promissory notes of businesspeople. Thus the amount of money in circulation could be swiftly increased as needed for the legitimate requirements of business.

The Federal Reserve Act was a red-letter achievement. It carried the nation with flying banners through the financial crises of the First World War of 1914–1918. Without it, the Republic's progress toward the modern economic age would have been seriously retarded.

The President Tames the Trusts

Without pausing for breath, Wilson pushed toward the last remaining rampart in the "triple wall of privilege"—the trusts. Early in 1914 he again went before Congress in a personal appearance that still carried drama.

Nine months and thousands of words later, Congress responded with the Federal Trade Commission Act of 1914. The new law empowered a presidentially appointed commission to turn a searchlight on industries engaged in interstate commerce, such as the meatpackers. The commissioners were expected to crush monopoly at the source by rooting out unfair trade practices, including unlawful competition, false advertising, mislabeling, adulteration, and bribery.

The knot of monopoly was further cut by the Clayton Anti-Trust Act of 1914. It lengthened the shopworn Sherman Act's list of business practices that were deemed objectionable, including price discrimination and interlocking directorates (whereby the same individuals served as directors of supposedly competing firms).

The Clayton Act also conferred long-overdue benefits on labor. Conservative courts had unexpectedly been ruling that trade unions fell under the antimonopoly restraints of the Sherman Act. A classic case involved striking hatmakers in Danbury, Connecticut, who were assessed triple damages of more than $250,000, which resulted in the loss of their savings and homes. The Clayton Act therefore sought to exempt labor and agricultural organizations from antitrust prosecution, while explicitly legalizing strikes and peaceful picketing.

Union leader Samuel Gompers hailed the act as the Magna Carta of labor because it legally lifted human labor out of the category of "a commodity or article of commerce." But the rejoicing was premature, as conservative judges in later years continued to clip the wings of the union movement.

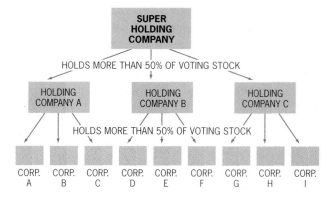

Organization of Holding Companies   Keep in mind that the voting stock of a corporation is often only a fraction of the total stock.

Reading the Death Warrant   This cartoon appeared in a New York newspaper soon after Woodrow Wilson called for dramatic reform of the banking system before both houses of Congress. With the "money trust" of bankers and businessmen cowed, Wilson was able to win popular and congressional support for the Federal Reserve Act of 1913.

Wilsonian Progressivism at High Tide

Energetically scaling the "triple wall of privilege," Woodrow Wilson had treated the nation to a dazzling demonstration of vigorous presidential leadership. He proved nearly irresistible in his first eighteen months in office. For once, a political creed was matched by deed, as the progressive reformers racked up victory after victory.

Standing at the peak of his powers at the head of the progressive forces, Wilson pressed ahead with further reforms. The Federal Farm Loan Act of 1916 made credit available to farmers at low rates of interest—as long demanded by the Populists. The Warehouse Act of 1916 authorized loans on the security of staple crops—another Populist idea. Other laws benefited rural America by providing for highway construction and the establishment of agricultural extension work in the state colleges.

Sweaty laborers also made gains as the progressive wave foamed forward. Sailors, treated brutally from cat-o'-nine-tails days onward, were given relief by the La Follette Seamen's Act of 1915. It required decent treatment and a living wage on American merchant ships. One unhappy result of this well-intentioned law was the crippling of America's merchant marine, as freight rates spiraled upward with the crew's wages.

Wilson further helped the workers with the Workingmen's Compensation Act of 1916, granting assistance to federal civil-service employees during periods of disability. In the same year, the president approved an act restricting child labor on products flowing into interstate commerce, though the standpat Supreme Court soon invalidated the law. Railroad workers, numbering about 1.7 million, were not sidetracked. The Adamson Act of 1916 established an eight-hour day for all employees on trains in interstate commerce, with extra pay for overtime.

Wilson earned the enmity of businesspeople and bigots but endeared himself to progressives when in 1916 he nominated for the Supreme Court the prominent reformer Louis D. Brandeis—the first Jew to be called to the high bench. Yet even Wilson's progressivism had its limits, and it clearly stopped short of better treatment for blacks. The southern-bred Wilson actually presided over accelerated segregation in the federal bureaucracy. When a delegation of black leaders personally protested to him, the schoolmasterish president virtually froze them out of his office.

Despite these limitations, Wilson knew that to be reelected in 1916, he needed to identify himself clearly as the candidate of progressivism. He appeased businesspeople by making conservative appointments to the Federal Reserve Board and the Federal Trade Commission, but he devoted most of his energies to cultivating progressive support. Wilson's election in 1912 had been something of a fluke, owing largely to the Taft-Roosevelt split in the Republican ranks. To remain in the White House, the president would have to woo the bull moose voters into the Democratic fold.

New Directions in Foreign Policy

In one important area, Wilson chose not to answer the trumpet call of the bull moosers. In contrast to Roosevelt and even Taft, Wilson recoiled from an aggressive foreign policy. Hating imperialism, he was repelled by TR's big stickism. Suspicious of Wall Street, he detested the so-called dollar diplomacy of Taft.

In office only a week, Wilson declared war on dollar diplomacy. He proclaimed that the government would no longer offer special support to American investors in Latin America and China. Shivering from this Wilsonian bucket of cold water, American bankers pulled out of the Taft-engineered six-nation loan to China the next day.

In a similarly self-denying vein, Wilson persuaded Congress in early 1914 to repeal the Panama Canal Tolls Act of 1912, which had exempted American coastwise shipping from tolls and thereby provoked sharp protests from injured Britain. The president further chimed in with the anti-imperial song of Bryan and other Democrats when he signed the Jones Act in 1916. It granted to the Philippines the boon of territorial status and promised independence as soon as a "stable government" could be established. That glad day came thirty years later, on July 4, 1946.

Wilson also partially defused a menacing crisis with Japan in 1913. The California legislature, still seeking to rid the Golden State of Japanese settlers, prohibited them from owning land. Tokyo, understandably irritated, lodged vigorous protests. At Fortress Corregidor, in the Philippines, American gunners were put on around-the-clock alert. But when Wilson dispatched Secretary of State William Jennings Bryan to plead with the California legislature to soften its stand, tensions eased somewhat.

Political turmoil in Haiti soon forced Wilson to eat some of his anti-imperialist words. The climax of the disorders came in 1914–1915, when an outraged populace literally tore to pieces the brutal Haitian president. In 1915 Wilson reluctantly dispatched marines to protect American lives and property. In 1916 he stole a page from Roosevelt's corollary to the Monroe Doctrine and concluded a treaty with Haiti providing for U.S. supervision of finances and the police. In the same year, he sent the leather-necked marines to quell riots in the Dominican Republic, and that debt-cursed land came under the shadow of the American eagle's wings for the next eight years. In 1917 Wilson purchased from Denmark the Virgin Islands, in the West Indies, tightening the grip of Uncle Sam in these shark-infested waters. Increasingly, the Caribbean Sea, with its vital approaches to the now navigable Panama Canal, was taking on the earmarks of a Yankee preserve.

Moralistic Diplomacy in Mexico

Rifle bullets whining across the southern border served as a constant reminder that all was not quiet in Mexico. For decades Mexico had been sorely

U.S. Marines in Haiti, 1919
The United States sent the marines to Haiti in 1915 to protect American economic interests. They remained for nineteen years.

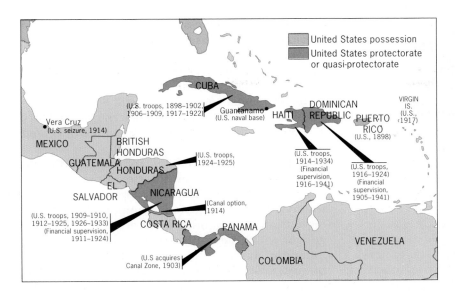

United States possession

United States protectorate or quasi-protectorate

The United States in the Caribbean
This map explains why many Latin Americans accused the United States of turning the Caribbean Sea into a Yankee lake. It also suggests that Uncle Sam was much less "isolationist" in his own backyard than he was in faraway Europe or Asia.

exploited by foreign investors in oil, railroads, and mines. By 1913 American capitalists had sunk about a billion dollars into the underdeveloped but generously endowed country.

But if Mexico was rich, the Mexicans were poor. Fed up with their miserable lot, they at last revolted. Their revolution took an ugly turn in 1913, when a conscienceless clique murdered the popular new revolutionary president and installed General Victoriano Huerta, an Indian, in the president's chair. All this chaos accelerated a massive migration of Mexicans to the United States. More than a million Spanish-speaking newcomers tramped across the southern border in the first three decades of the twentieth century. Settling mostly in Texas, New Mexico, Arizona, and California, they swung picks building highways and railroads or followed the fruit harvests as pickers. Though often segregated in Spanish-speaking enclaves, they helped to create a unique borderland culture that blended Mexican and American folkways.

The revolutionary bloodshed also menaced American lives and property in Mexico. Cries for intervention burst from the lips of American jingoes. Prominent among those chanting for war was the influential chain-newspaper publisher William Randolph Hearst, whose views presumably were colored by his ownership of a Mexican ranch larger than Rhode Island. Yet President Wilson stood firm against demands to step in. It was "perilous," he

declared, to determine foreign policy "in the terms of material interest."

But though he refused to intervene, Wilson also refused to recognize officially the murderous government of "that brute" Huerta, even though most foreign powers acknowledged Huerta's bloody-handed regime. "I am going to teach the South American republics to elect good men," the former professor declared. He put his munitions where his mouth was in 1914, when he allowed American arms to flow to Huerta's principal rivals, white-bearded

A Republican congressman voiced complaints against Wilson's Mexican policy in 1916:

"It is characterized by weakness, uncertainty, vacillation, and uncontrollable desire to intermeddle in Mexican affairs. He has not had the courage to go into Mexico nor the courage to stay out. . . . I would either go into Mexico and pacify the country or I would keep my hands entirely out of Mexico. If we are too proud to fight, we should be too proud to quarrel. I would not choose between murderers."

Thorny Problems in Mexico President Huerta clung to power for more than a year in 1913–1914, despite Woodrow Wilson's strong disapproval of his regime.

Venustiano Carranza and the firebrand Francisco ("Pancho") Villa.

The Mexican volcano erupted at the Atlantic seaport of Tampico in April 1914, when a small party of American sailors was arrested. The Mexicans promptly released the captives and apologized, but they refused the affronted American admiral's demand for a salute of twenty-one guns. Wilson, heavy-hearted but stubbornly determined to eliminate Huerta, asked Congress for authority to use force against Mexico. Before Congress could act, Wilson ordered the navy to seize the Mexican port of Vera Cruz. Huerta as well as Carranza hotly protested against this high-handed Yankee maneuver.

Just as a full-dress shooting conflict seemed inevitable, Wilson was rescued by an offer of mediation from the ABC Powers—Argentina, Brazil, and Chile. Huerta collapsed in July 1914 under pressure from within and without. He was succeeded by his archrival, Venustiano Carranza, still fiercely resentful of Wilson's military meddling. The whole sorry episode did not augur well for the future of United States–Mexican relations.

"Pancho" Villa, a combination of bandit and Robin Hood, had meanwhile stolen the spotlight. He emerged as the chief rival to President Carranza, whom Wilson now reluctantly supported. Challenging Carranza's authority while also punishing the gringos, Villa's men ruthlessly hauled sixteen young American mining engineers off a train traveling through northern Mexico in January 1916 and killed them. A month later Villa and his followers, hoping to provoke a war between Wilson and Carranza, blazed across the border into Columbus, New Mexico, and murdered another nineteen Americans.

General John J. ("Black Jack"[*]) Pershing, a grim-faced and ramrod-erect veteran of the Cuban and Philippine campaigns, was ordered to break up the bandit band. His hastily organized force of several thousand mounted troops penetrated deep into rugged Mexico with surprising speed. They clashed with Carranza's forces and mauled the Villistas but missed capturing Villa himself. As the threat of war with Germany loomed larger, the invading army was withdrawn in January 1917.

Thunder Across the Sea

Europe's powder magazine, long smoldering, blew up in the summer of 1914, when the flaming pistol of a Serb patriot killed the heir to the throne of Austria-Hungary in Sarajevo. An outraged Vienna government, backed by Germany, forthwith presented a stern ultimatum to neighboring Serbia.

An explosive chain reaction followed. Tiny Serbia, backed by its powerful Slav neighbor Russia, refused to bend the knee sufficiently. The Russian tsar began to mobilize his ponderous war machine, menacing Germany on the east, even as his ally,

---

[*]So called from his earlier service as an officer with the crack black Tenth Cavalry.

"Pancho" Villa with His Ragtag Army in Mexico, c. 1916
His daring, impetuosity, and horsemanship made Villa a hero to the masses of northern Mexico. Yet he proved to be a violent and ineffective crusader against social abuses, and he was assassinated in 1923.

France, confronted Germany on the west. In alarm, the Germans struck suddenly at France through unoffending Belgium; their objective was to knock their ancient enemy out of action so that they would have two free hands to repel Russia. Great Britain, its coastline jeopardized by the assault on Belgium, was sucked into the conflagration on the side of France.

Almost overnight most of Europe was locked in a fight to the death. On one side were arrayed the Central Powers: Germany and Austria-Hungary, and later Turkey and Bulgaria. On the other side were the Allies: principally France, Britain, and Russia, and later Japan and Italy.

Americans thanked God for the ocean moats and self-righteously congratulated themselves on having had ancestors wise enough to have abandoned the hell pits of Europe. America felt strong, snug, smug, and secure—but not for long.

A Precarious Neutrality

President Wilson's grief at the outbreak of war was compounded by the recent death of his wife. He sorrowfully issued the routine neutrality proclamation and called on Americans to be neutral in thought as well as deed. But such scrupulous evenhandedness proved difficult.

Both sides wooed the United States, the great neutral in the West. The British enjoyed the boon of close cultural, linguistic, and economic ties with America and had the added advantage of controlling most of the transatlantic cables. Their censors sheared away war stories harmful to the Allies and drenched the United States with tales of German bestiality.

The Germans and the Austro-Hungarians counted on the natural sympathies of their transplanted countrymen in America. Including persons with at least one foreign-born parent, people with blood ties to the Central Powers numbered some 11 million in 1914. Some of these recent immigrants expressed noisy sympathy for the fatherland, but most were simply grateful to be so distant from the fray.

Most Americans were anti-German from the outset. With his villainous upturned mustache, Kaiser Wilhelm II seemed the embodiment of arrogant autocracy, an impression strengthened by Germany's ruthless strike at neutral Belgium. German and Austrian agents further tarnished the image of the Central Powers in American eyes when they resorted to violence in American factories and ports. When a German operative in 1915 absent-mindedly left his briefcase on a New York elevated car, its documents detailing plans for industrial sabotage were quickly discovered and publicized. American opinion, already ill disposed, was further

PUNCH, OR THE LONDON CHARIVARI.—October 21, 1914.

UNCONQUERABLE.

THE KAISER. "SO, YOU SEE—YOU'VE LOST EVERYTHING."
THE KING OF THE BELGIANS. "NOT MY SOUL."

American Contempt for the Kaiser Resentment against German submarine attacks inflamed anti-German opinion in America. Here the German Kaiser is cast as a war monger, paving the road to the Battle of Verdun in France, where nearly 700,000 German and French soldiers cruelly lost their lives.

inflamed against the kaiser and Germany. Yet the great majority of Americans earnestly hoped to stay out of the horrible war.

America Earns Blood Money

When Europe burst into flames in 1914, the United States was bogged down in a worrisome business recession. But as fate would have it, British and French war orders soon pulled American industry out of the morass of hard times and onto a peak of war-born prosperity. Part of this boom was financed by American bankers, notably the Wall Street firm of J.P. Morgan and Company, which eventually advanced to the Allies the enormous sum of $2.3 billion during the period of American neutrality. The Central Powers protested bitterly against the immense trade between America and the Allies, but this traffic did not in fact violate the international neutrality laws. Germany was technically free to

Principal Foreign Elements in the United States (census of 1910; total U.S. population: 91,972,266)

Country of Origin		Foreign-Born	Natives with Two Foreign-Born Parents	Natives with One Foreign-Born Parent	Total
Central Powers	Germany	2,501,181	3,911,847	1,869,590	8,282,618
	Austria-Hungary	1,670,524	900,129	131,133	2,701,786
Allied Powers	Great Britain	1,219,968	852,610	1,158,474	3,231,052
	(Ireland)*	1,352,155	2,141,577	1,010,628	4,504,360
	Russia	1,732,421	949,316	70,938	2,752,675
	Italy	1,343,070	695,187	60,103	2,098,360
TOTAL (for all foreign countries, including those not listed)		13,345,545	12,916,311	5,981,526	32,243,282
Percentage of total U.S. population		14.5	14.0	6.5	35.0

*Ireland was not yet independent.

trade with the United States. It was prevented from doing so not by American policy but by geography and the British navy. Trade between Germany and America had to move across the Atlantic; but the British controlled the sea-lanes, and they threw a noose-tight blockade of mines and ships across the North Sea, gateway to German ports. Over the unavailing protests of American shippers, farmers, and manufacturers, the British began forcing American vessels off the high seas and into their ports. This harassment of American shipping proved highly effective, as trade between Germany and the United States virtually ceased.

Hard-pressed Germany did not tamely consent to being starved out. In retaliation for the British blockade, in February 1915 Berlin announced a submarine war area around the British Isles. The submarine was a weapon so new that existing international law could not be made to fit it. The old rule that a warship must stop and board a merchantman could hardly apply to submarines, which could easily be rammed or sunk if they surfaced.

The cigar-shaped marauders posed a dire threat to the United States—so long as Wilson insisted on maintaining America's neutral rights. Berlin officials declared that they would try not to sink *neutral* shipping, but they warned that mistakes would probably occur. Wilson now determined on a policy of calculated risk. He would continue to claim profitable neutral trading rights, while hoping that no high-seas incident would force his hand to grasp the sword of war. Setting his peninsular jaw, he emphatically warned Germany that it would be held to "strict accountability" for any attacks on American vessels or citizens.

The German submarines (known as U-boats, from the German *Unterseeboot,* or "undersea boat")

The Fatherland, *the chief German-American propaganda newspaper in the United States, cried,*

"We [Americans] prattle about humanity while we manufacture poisoned shrapnel and picric acid for profit. Ten thousand German widows, ten thousand orphans, ten thousand graves bear the legend 'Made in America.'"

meanwhile began their deadly work. In the first months of 1915, they sank about ninety ships in the war zone. Then the submarine issue became acute when the British passenger liner *Lusitania* was torpedoed and sank off the coast of Ireland on May 7, 1915, with the loss of 1,198 lives, including 128 Americans.

The *Lusitania* was carrying forty-two hundred cases of small-arms ammunition, a fact the Germans used to justify the sinking. But Americans were swept by a wave of shock and anger at this act of "mass murder" and "piracy." The eastern United States, closer to the war, seethed with talk of fighting, but the rest of the country showed a strong distaste for hostilities. The peace-loving Wilson had no stomach for leading a disunited nation into war. He well remembered the mistake in 1812 of his fellow Princetonian, James Madison. Instead, by a series of increasingly strong notes, Wilson attempted to bring the German warlords sharply to book. Even this measured approach was too much for Secretary of State Bryan, who resigned rather than sign a protestation that might spell shooting. But Wilson resolutely stood his ground. "There is such a thing,"

U.S. Exports to Belligerents, 1914–1916

Belligerent	1914	1915	1916	1916 Figure as a Percentage of 1914 Figure
Britain	$594,271,863	$911,794,954	$1,526,685,102	257%
France	159,818,924	369,397,170	628,851,988	393
Italy*	74,235,012	184,819,688	269,246,105	363
Germany	344,794,276	28,863,354	288,899	0.08

*Italy joined the Allies in April 1915.

British Military Area (declared November 3, 1914) and German Submarine War Zone (declared February 4, 1915)

A German U-boat   This deadly new weapon rendered useless existing rules of naval warfare, eventually forcing the United States to declare war against Germany in 1917.

he declared, "as a man being too proud to fight." This kind of talk incensed the war-thirsty Theodore Roosevelt. The Rough Rider assailed the spineless simperers who heeded the "weasel words" of the pacifistic professor in the White House.

Yet Wilson, sticking to his verbal guns, made some diplomatic progress. After another British liner, the *Arabic*, was sunk in August 1915, with the loss of two American lives, Berlin reluctantly agreed not to sink unarmed and unresisting passenger ships *without warning*.

This pledge appeared to be violated in March 1916, when the Germans torpedoed a French passenger steamer, the *Sussex*. The infuriated Wilson informed the Germans that unless they renounced the inhuman practice of sinking merchant ships without warning, he would break diplomatic relations—an almost certain prelude to war.

Germany reluctantly knuckled under to President Wilson's *Sussex* ultimatum, agreeing not to sink passenger ships and merchant vessels without giving warning. But the Germans attached a long string to their *Sussex* pledge: the United States would have to persuade the Allies to modify what Berlin regarded as their illegal blockade. This, obviously, was something that Washington could not do. Wil-

son promptly accepted the German pledge, without accepting the "string." He thus won a temporary but precarious diplomatic victory—precarious because Germany could pull the string whenever it chose, and the president might suddenly find himself tugged over the cliff of war.

Wilson Wins Reelection in 1916

Against this ominous backdrop, the presidential campaign of 1916 gathered speed. Both the bull moose Progressives and the Republicans met in Chicago. The Progressives uproariously renominated Theodore Roosevelt, but the Rough Rider,

Advertisement from the *New York Herald,* May 1, 1915
Six days later the *Lusitania* was sunk. Note the German warning.

who loathed Wilson and all his works, had no stom-ach for splitting the Republicans again and ensuring the reelection of his hated rival. In refusing to run, he sounded the death knell of the Progressive party.

Roosevelt's Republican admirers also clamored for "Teddy," but the Old Guard detested the rene-gade who had ruptured the party in 1912. Instead they drafted Supreme Court justice Charles Evans Hughes, a cold intellectual who had achieved a solid liberal record when he was governor of New York. The Republican platform condemned the Demo-cratic tariff, assaults on the trusts, and Wilson's wishy-washiness in dealing with Mexico and Germany.

The thick-whiskered Hughes ("an animated feather duster") left the bench for the campaign stump, where he was not at home. In anti-German areas of the country, he assailed Wilson for not standing up to the kaiser, whereas in isolationist areas he took a softer line. This fence-straddling operation led to the jeer, "Charles Evasive Hughes."

Hughes was further plagued by Roosevelt, who was delivering a series of skin-'em-alive speeches against "that damned Presbyterian hypocrite Wil-son." Frothing for war, TR privately scoffed at Hughes as a "whiskered Wilson"; the only difference between the two, he said, was "a shave."

Wilson, nominated by acclamation at the Dem-ocratic convention in St. Louis, ignored Hughes on the theory that one should not try to murder a man

---

During the 1916 campaign, J. A. O'Leary, the head of a pro-German and pro-Irish organ-ization, sent a scorching telegram to Wilson condemning him for having been pro-British in approving war loans and ammunition traffic. Wilson shot back an answer:

"Your telegram received. I would feel deeply
mortified to have you or anybody like you
vote for me. Since you have access to many
disloyal Americans and I have not, I will ask
you to convey this message to them."

President Wilson's devastating and somewhat insulting response probably won him more votes than it lost.

Theodore Roosevelt, War Hawk
The former president clamored for American intervention in the European war, but the country preferred peace in 1916. Ironically, Roosevelt's archrival, Woodrow Wilson, would take the country into the war just months after the 1916 election.

who is committing suicide. His campaign was built on the slogan, "He Kept Us Out of War."

Democratic orators warned that by electing Charles Evans Hughes, the nation would be electing a fight—with a certain frustrated Rough Rider leading the charge. A Democratic advertisement appealing to the American workingpeople read,

> *You are Working;*
> *—Not Fighting!*
> *Alive and Happy;*
> *—Not Cannon Fodder!*
> *Wilson and Peace with Honor?*
> *or*
> *Hughes with Roosevelt and War?*

On election day Hughes swept the East and looked like a surefire winner. Wilson went to bed that night prepared to accept defeat, while the New York newspapers displayed huge portraits of "The President-Elect—Charles Evans Hughes."

But the rest of the country turned the tide. Midwesterners and westerners, attracted by Wilson's progressive reforms and antiwar policies, flocked to the polls for the president. The final result, in doubt for several days, hinged on California, which Wilson carried by some 3,800 votes out of about a million cast.

Wilson barely squeaked through, with a final vote of 277 to 254 in the Electoral College, and 9,127,695 to 8,533,507 in the popular column. The pro-labor Wilson received strong support from the working class and from renegade bull moosers, whom Republicans failed to lure back into their camp. Wilson had not specifically promised to keep the country out of war, but probably enough voters relied on such implicit assurances to ensure his victory. Their hopeful expectations were soon rudely shattered.

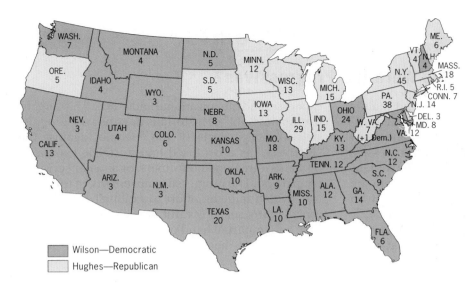

Presidential Election of 1916 (with electoral vote by state)
Wilson was so worried about being a lame duck president in a time of great international tensions that he drew up a plan whereby Hughes, if victorious, would be appointed secretary of state, Wilson and the vice president would resign, and Hughes would thus succeed immediately to the presidency.

Chronology

1912 Wilson defeats Taft and Roosevelt for presidency

1913 Underwood Tariff Act
Sixteenth Amendment (income tax) passed
Federal Reserve Act
Huerta takes power in Mexico
Seventeenth Amendment (direct election of senators) passed

1914 Clayton Anti-Trust Act
Federal Trade Commission established
U.S. occupation of Vera Cruz, Mexico
World War I begins in Europe

1915 La Follette Seamen's Act
Lusitania torpedoed and sunk by German U-boat

1915 U.S. Marines sent to Haiti

1916 *Sussex* ultimatum and pledge
Workingmen's Compensation Act
Federal Farm Loan Act
Warehouse Act
Adamson Act
Pancho Villa raids New Mexico
Brandeis appointed to Supreme Court
Jones Act
U.S. Marines sent to Dominican Republic
Wilson defeats Hughes for presidency

1917 United States buys Virgin Islands from Denmark

VARYING VIEWPOINTS

Who Were the Progressives?

Debate about progressivism has revolved mainly around a question that is simple to ask but devilishly difficult to answer: who were the progressives? It was once taken for granted that progressive reformers were simply the heirs of the Jeffersonian-Jacksonian-Populist reform crusades; they were the oppressed and downtrodden common folk who finally erupted in wrath and demanded their due.

But in his influential *Age of Reform* (1955), Richard Hofstadter astutely challenged that view. Progressive leaders, he argued, were not drawn from the ranks of society's poor and marginalized. Rather, they were middle-class people threatened from above by the emerging power of new corporate elites and from below by a restless working class. It was not economic deprivation, but "status anxiety," Hofstadter insisted, that prompted these people to become reformers. Their psychological motivation, Hofstadter concluded, rendered many of their reform efforts quirky and ineffectual.

By contrast, "New Left" historians, notably Gabriel Kolko, argue that progressivism was dominated by established business leaders who successfully directed "reform" to their own conservative ends. In this view government regulation (as embodied in new agencies like the Federal Reserve Board and the Federal Tariff Commission, and in legislation like the Meat Inspection Act) simply accomplished what two generations of private efforts had failed to accomplish: dampening cutthroat competition, stabilizing markets, and making America safe for monopoly capitalism.

Still other scholars, notably Robert H. Wiebe and Samuel P. Hays, argue that the progressives were neither the psychologically or economically disadvantaged nor the old capitalist elite, but were, rather, members of a rapidly emerging, self-confident social class possessed of the new techniques of scientific management, technological expertise, and organizational know-how. This "organizational school" of historians does not see progressivism as a struggle of the "people" against the "interests," as a confused and nostalgic campaign by status-threatened reformers, or as a conservative coup d'état. The progressive movement, in this view, was by and large an effort to rationalize and modernize many social institutions, by introducing the wise and impartial hand of government regulation.

This view has much to recommend it. Yet despite its widespread acceptance among historians, it is an explanation that cannot adequately account for the titanic political struggles of the progressive era over the very reforms that the "organizational school" regards as simple adjustments to modernity. The organizational approach also brushes over the deep philosophical differences that divided progressives themselves—such as the ideological chasm that separated Roosevelt's New Nationalism from Wilson's New Freedom. Nor can the organizational approach sufficiently explain why, as demonstrated by Otis Graham in *An Encore for Reform,* so many progressives—perhaps a majority—who survived into the New Deal era criticized that agenda for being too bureaucratic and for laying too heavy a regulatory hand on American society.

Recently scholars such as Robyn Muncy, Linda Gordon, and Theda Skocpol have stressed the role of women in advocating progressive reforms. Building the American welfare state in the early twentieth century, they argue, was fundamentally a gendered activity inspired by a "female dominion" of social workers and "social feminists." Moreover, in contrast to many European countries where labor movements sought a welfare state to benefit the working class, American female reformers promoted welfare programs specifically to protect women and children.

For further reading, see page A21 of the Appendix. For web resources, go to **http://college.hmco.com.**

The War to End War

1917–1918

The world must be made safe for democracy. Its peace must be planted upon the tested foundations of political liberty. We have no selfish ends to serve. We desire no conquest, no dominion. We seek no indemnities for ourselves, no material compensation for the sacrifices we shall freely make.

WOODROW WILSON, WAR MESSAGE, APRIL 2, 1917

Destiny dealt cruelly with Woodrow Wilson. The lover of peace, as fate would have it, was forced to lead a hesitant and peace-loving nation into war. As the last days of 1916 slipped through the hourglass, the president made one final, futile attempt to mediate between the embattled belligerents. On January 22, 1917, he delivered one of his most moving addresses, restating America's commitment to neutral rights and declaring that only a negotiated "peace without victory" would prove durable.

German's warlords responded with a blow of the mailed fist. On January 31, 1917, they announced to an astonished world their decision to wage *unrestricted* submarine warfare, sinking *all* ships, including America's, in the war zone.

Why this rash act? War with America was the last thing Germany wanted. But after three ghastly years in the trenches, Germany's leaders decided the distinction between combatants and noncombatants was a luxury they could no longer afford. Thus they jerked on the string they had attached to their *Sussex* pledge in 1916, desperately hoping to bring England to its knees before the United States entered the war. Wilson, his bluff called, broke diplomatic relations with Germany but refused to move closer to war unless the Germans undertook "overt" acts against American lives.

War by Act of Germany

To defend American interests short of war, the president asked Congress for authority to arm American merchant ships. When a band of midwestern senators launched a filibuster to block the measure,

"All the News That's Fit to Print."

The New York Times.

THE WEATHER
Fair, colder today; tomorrow warmer, probably rain; wind northwest.

VOL. , LXVI...NO. 21,619.   NEW YORK, TUESDAY, APRIL 3, 1917.—TWENTY-FOUR PAGES.   ONE CENT In New York City. | TWO CENTS New England and Middle States. | THREE CENTS Elsewhere.

PRESIDENT CALLS FOR WAR DECLARATION, STRONGER NAVY, NEW ARMY OF 500,000 MEN, FULL CO-OPERATION WITH GERMANY'S FOES

War! Attacks by German submarines finally forced Wilson's hand, and he asked Congress for a declaration of war on April 2, 1917. Four days later, after considerable debate and with fifty-six dissenting votes, Congress obliged the president.

Wilson denounced them as a "little group of willful men" who were rendering a great nation "helpless and contemptible." But their obstruction was a powerful reminder of the continuing strength of American isolationism.

Meanwhile, the sensational Zimmermann note was intercepted and published on March 1, 1917, infuriating Americans, especially westerners. German foreign secretary Arthur Zimmermann had secretly proposed a German-Mexican alliance, tempting anti-Yankee Mexico with veiled promises of recovering Texas, New Mexico, and Arizona.

On the heels of this provocation came the long-dreaded "overt" acts in the Atlantic, where German U-boats sank four unarmed American merchant vessels in the first two weeks of March. As one Philadelphia newspaper observed, "the difference between war and what we have now is that now we aren't fighting back." Simultaneously came the rousing news that a revolution in Russia had toppled the cruel regime of the tsars. America could now fight foursquare for democracy on the side of the Allies, without the black sheep of Russian despotism in the Allied fold.

Subdued and solemn, Wilson at last stood before a hushed joint session of Congress on the evening of April 2, 1917, and asked for a declaration of war. He had lost his gamble that America could pursue the profits of neutral trade without being sucked into the ghastly maelstrom. A myth developed in later years that America was dragged unwittingly into war by munitions makers and Wall Street bankers, desperate to protect their profits and loans. Yet the weapons merchants and financiers were already thriving, unhampered by wartime government restrictions and heavy taxation. Their slo-

gan might well have been "Neutrality Forever." The simple truth is that British harassment of American commerce had been galling but endurable; Germany had resorted to the mass killing of civilians. The difference was like that between a gang of thieves and a gang of murderers. President Wilson had drawn a clear, if risky, line against the depredations of the submarine. The German high command, in a last desperate throw of the dice, chose to cross it. In a figurative sense, America's war declaration of April 6, 1917, bore the unambiguous trademark "Made in Germany."

Wilsonian Idealism Enthroned

"It is a fearful thing to lead this great peaceful people into war," Wilson said in his war message. It was fearful indeed, not least of all because of the formidable challenge it posed to Wilson's leadership skills. Ironically, it fell to the scholarly Wilson, deeply respectful of American traditions, to shatter one of the most sacred of those traditions by entangling America in a distant European war.

How could the president arouse the American people to shoulder this unprecedented burden? For more than a century, they had prided themselves on their isolationism from the periodic outbursts of militarized violence that afflicted the Old World. Since 1914 their pride had been reinforced by the bountiful profits gained through neutrality. German U-boats had now roughly shoved a wavering America into the abyss, but ominously, no fewer than six senators and fifty representatives (including the first congresswoman, Jeannette Rankin of Montana) had voted against the war resolution. Wilson could whip up no enthusiasm, especially in the landlocked Midwest, by fighting to make the world safe from the submarine.

To galvanize the country, Wilson would have to proclaim more glorified aims. Radiating the spiritual fervor of his Presbyterian ancestors, he declared the twin goals of "a war to end war" and a crusade "to make the world safe for democracy." Brandishing the sword of righteousness, Wilson virtually hypnotized the nation with his lofty ideals. He contrasted the selfish war aims of the other belligerents, Allied and enemy alike, with America's shining altruism. America, he preached, did not fight for the sake of riches or territorial conquest. The Republic sought only to shape an international order in which democracy could flourish without fear of power-crazed autocrats and militarists.

In Wilsonian idealism the personality of the president and the necessities of history were perfectly matched. The high-minded Wilson genuinely believed in the principles he so eloquently intoned. And probably no other appeal could have successfully converted the American people from their historic hostility to involvement in European squabbles. Americans, it seemed, could be either isolationists or crusaders, but nothing in between.

Wilson's appeal worked—perhaps too well. Holding aloft the torch of idealism, the president fired up the public mind to a fever pitch. "Force, force to the utmost, force without stint or limit," he cried, while the country responded less elegantly with "Hang the kaiser." Lost on the gale was Wilson's earlier plea for "peace without victory."

Wilson's Fourteen Potent Points

Wilson quickly came to be recognized as the moral leader of the Allied cause. He scaled a summit of inspiring oratory on January 8, 1918, when he delivered his famed Fourteen Points Address to an enthusiastic Congress. Although one of his primary purposes was to keep reeling Russia in the war, Wilson's vision inspired all the drooping Allies to make mightier efforts and demoralized the enemy governments by holding out alluring promises to their dissatisfied minorities.

The first five of the Fourteen Points were broad in scope. (1) A proposal to abolish secret treaties pleased liberals of all countries. (2) Freedom of the seas appealed to the Germans, as well as to Americans who distrusted British sea power. (3) A removal of economic barriers among nations was comforting to Germany, which feared postwar vengeance. (4) Reduction of armament burdens was gratifying to taxpayers everywhere. (5) An adjustment of colonial claims in the interests of both native peoples and the colonizers was reassuring to the anti-imperialists.

Other points among the fourteen proved to be no less seductive. They held out the hope of independence ("self-determination") to oppressed minority groups, such as the Poles, millions of whom lay under the heel of Germany and Austria-Hungary. The capstone point, number fourteen, foreshadowed the League of Nations—an international organization that Wilson dreamed would provide a system of collective security. Wilson earnestly prayed that this new scheme would effectively guarantee the political independence and territorial integrity of all countries, whether large or small.

Yet Wilson's appealing points, though raising hopes the world over, were not everywhere applauded. Certain leaders of the Allied nations, with an eye to territorial booty, were less than enthusiastic. Hard-nosed Republicans at home grumbled, and some of them openly mocked the "fourteen commandments" of "God Almighty Wilson."

Creel Manipulates Minds

Mobilizing people's minds for war, both in America and abroad, was an urgent task facing the Washington authorities. For this purpose the Committee on Public Information was created. It was headed by a youngish journalist, George Creel, who, though outspoken and tactless, was gifted with zeal and imagination. His job was to sell America on the war and sell the world on Wilsonian war aims.

The Creel organization, employing some 150,000 workers at home and overseas, proved that words were indeed weapons. It sent out an army of 75,000 "four-minute men"—often longer-winded than that—who delivered countless speeches containing much "patriotic pep."

Creel's propaganda took varied forms. Posters were splashed on billboards in the "Battle of the Fences," as artists "rallied to the colors." Millions of

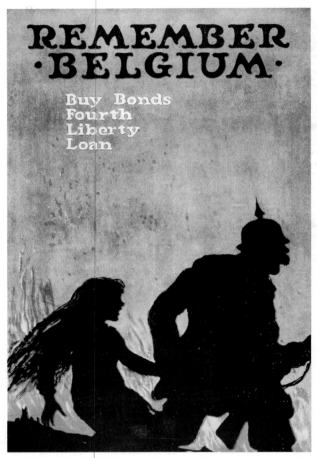

REMEMBER
·BELGIUM·

Buy Bonds
Fourth
Liberty
Loan

Anti-German Propaganda The government relied extensively on emotional appeals and hate propaganda to rally support for the First World War, which most Americans regarded as a distant "European" affair. This poster evokes the brutal German violation of Belgian neutrality in August 1914.

leaflets and pamphlets, which contained the most pungent Wilsonisms, were showered like confetti upon the world. Propaganda booklets with red-white-and-blue covers were printed by the millions.

Hang-the-kaiser movies, carrying such titles as *The Kaiser, the Beast of Berlin* and *To Hell with the Kaiser*, revealed the helmeted "Hun" at his bloodiest. Arm-waving conductors by the thousands led huge audiences in songs that poured scorn on the enemy and glorified the "boys" in uniform.

The entire nation, catching the frenzied spirit of a religious revival, burst into song. This was undoubtedly America's singingest war. Most memorable was George M. Cohan's spine-tingling "Over There":

*Over there, over there
Send the word, send the word over there,
That the Yanks are coming, the Yanks are coming
The drums rum-tumming ev'rywhere.*

Creel typified American war mobilization, which relied more on aroused passion and voluntary compliance than on formal laws. But he oversold the ideals of Wilson and led the world to expect too much. When the president proved to be a mortal and not a god, the resulting disillusionment both at home and abroad was disastrous.

Enforcing Loyalty and Stifling Dissent

German-Americans numbered over 8 million, counting those with at least one parent foreign-born, out of a total population of 100 million. On the whole they proved to be dependably loyal to the United States. Yet rumormongers were quick to spread tales of spying and sabotage; even trifling epidemics of diarrhea were blamed on German agents. A few German-Americans were tarred, feathered, and beaten; in one extreme case a German Socialist in Illinois was lynched by a drunken mob.

As emotion mounted, hysterical hatred of Germans and things Germanic swept the nation. Orchestras found it unsafe to present German-composed music, like that of Wagner or Beethoven. German books were removed from library shelves, and German classes were canceled in high schools and colleges. Sauerkraut became "liberty cabbage," hamburger "liberty steak." Even beer became suspect, as patriotic Americans fretted over the loyalty of breweries with names like Schlitz and Pabst.

Both the Espionage Act of 1917 and the Sedition Act of 1918 reflected current fears about Germans and antiwar Americans. Especially visible among the 1,900 prosecutions undertaken under these laws were antiwar Socialists and members of the radical Industrial Workers of the World (IWW). Kingpin Socialist Eugene V. Debs was convicted under the Espionage Act in 1918 and sentenced to ten years in a federal penitentiary. IWW leader William D. ("Big Bill") Haywood and ninety-nine associates were similarly convicted. Virtually any criticism of the government could be censored and punished. Some critics claimed the new laws were bending, if not breaking, the First Amendment. But in *Schenck* v. *United States* (1919), the Supreme Court affirmed

Socialist Leader Eugene V. Debs Addresses an Antiwar Rally in Columbus, Ohio, 1918 For his remarks in this speech, Debs was convicted under the Espionage Act of 1917 and sent to federal prison. He ran as a presidential candidate in 1920 while still incarcerated in his cell and received nearly a million votes.

their legality, arguing that freedom of speech could be revoked when such speech posed a "clear and present danger" to the nation.

These prosecutions form an ugly chapter in the history of American civil liberty. With the dawn of peace, presidential pardons were rather freely granted, including President Harding's to Eugene Debs in 1921. Yet a few victims lingered behind bars into the 1930s.

The Nation's Factories Go to War

Victory was no foregone conclusion, especially since the Republic, despite ample warning, was caught flat-footedly unready for its leap into global war. The pacifistic Wilson had only belatedly backed some mild preparedness measures beginning in 1915, including the creation of a civilian Council of National Defense to study problems of economic mobilization. He had also launched a shipbuilding program (as much to capture the belligerents' war-disrupted foreign trade as to anticipate America's possible entry into the war) and endorsed a modest beefing-up of the army, which with 100,000 regulars then ranked about fifteenth among the armies of the world, in the same category with Persia's. It would take a herculean effort to marshal America's daunting but disorganized resources and throw them into the field quickly enough to bolster the Allied war effort.

Towering obstacles confronted economic mobilizers. Sheer ignorance was among the biggest roadblocks. No one knew precisely how much steel or explosive powder the country was capable of producing. Old ideas also proved to be liabilities, as traditional fears of big government hamstrung efforts to orchestrate the economy from Washington. States' rights Democrats and businesspeople alike balked at federal economic controls, even though the embattled nation could ill afford the freewheeling, hit-or-miss chaos of the peacetime economy.

Late in the war, and after some bruising political battles, Wilson succeeded in imposing some order on this economic confusion. In March 1918 he appointed lone-eagle stock speculator Bernard Baruch to head the War Industries Board. But the War Industries Board never had more than feeble formal powers, and it was disbanded within days after the armistice. Even in a globe-girdling crisis, the American preference for laissez-faire and for a weak central government proved amazingly strong.

Workers in Wartime

Spurred by the slogan, "Labor Will Win the War," American workers sweated their way to victory. In part they were driven by the War Department's "work or fight" rule of 1918, which threatened any unemployed male with being immediately drafted—

a powerful discouragement to go on strike. But for the most part, government tried to treat labor fairly. The National War Labor Board, chaired by former president Taft, exerted itself to head off labor disputes that might hamper the war effort. While pressing employers to grant concessions to labor, including high wages and the eight-hour day, the board stopped short of supporting labor's most important demand: a government guarantee of the right to organize into unions.

Fortunately for the Allied cause, Samuel Gompers and his American Federation of Labor (AF of L) loyally supported the war, though some smaller and more radical labor organizations, including the Industrial Workers of the World, did not. The IWW, known as the "Wobblies" and sometimes derided as the "I Won't Works," engineered some of the most damaging industrial sabotage, and not without rea-

Suppressing the Steel Strike: Pittsburgh, 1919 The big steel producers ferociously resisted the unionization of their industry. In Pittsburgh compliant local officials bent to the steel makers' will and issued an order banning all outdoor meetings of strikers. These mounted police enforced the order with flailing billy clubs. The steelworkers' strike eventually failed, leaving the steel industry un-unionized until the New Deal championed labor's cause in the Depression decade of the 1930s.

A Universal Draft, 1917 The prewar song "I Didn't Raise My Boy to Be a Soldier" was changed to "I Didn't Raise My Boy to Be a Slacker," which in turn inspired the cruel parody "I Didn't Raise My Dog to Be a Sausage."

son. As transient laborers in such industries as fruit and lumber, the Wobblies were victims of some of the shabbiest working conditions in the country. When they protested, many were viciously beaten, arrested, or run out of town.

Mainstream labor's loyalty was rewarded. At war's end, the AF of L had more than doubled its membership, to over 3 million, and in the most heavily unionized sectors—coal mining, manufacturing, and transportation—real wages (after adjusting for inflation) had risen more than 20 percent over prewar levels. A new day seemed to be dawning for the long-struggling union movement.

Yet labor harbored grievances. Recognition of the right to organize still eluded labor's grasp. War-time inflation threatened to eclipse wage gains (prices more than doubled between 1914 and 1920). Not even the call of patriotism and Wilsonian idealism could defuse all labor disputes. Some six thousand strikes, several stained by blood, broke

Race Riot, Chicago, 1919 The policeman apparently arrived too late to spare this victim from being pelted by stones from an angry mob.

out in the war years. In 1919 the greatest strike in American history rocked the steel industry. More than a quarter of a million steelworkers walked off their jobs in a bid to force their employers to recognize their right to organize and bargain collectively. The steel companies resisted mercilessly. They refused to negotiate with union representatives and brought in thirty thousand African-American strikebreakers to keep the mills running. After bitter confrontations that left more than a dozen workers dead, the steel strike collapsed, a grievous setback that crippled the union movement for more than a decade.

The black workers who entered the steel mills in 1919 were but a fraction of the tens of thousands of southern blacks drawn to the North in wartime by the magnet of war-industry employment. These migrants made up the small-scale beginnings of a great northward African-American trek that would eventually grow to massive proportions. Their sudden appearance in previously all-white areas sometimes sparked interracial violence. An explosive riot in East St. Louis, Missouri, in July 1917 left

nine whites and at least forty blacks dead. An equally gruesome race riot ripped through Chicago. The wartime Windy City was taut with racial tension as a growing black population expanded into white working-class neighborhoods and as African-Americans found jobs as strikebreakers in meat-packing plants. Triggered by an incident at a bathing beach in July 1919, a reign of terror descended on the city for nearly two weeks. Black and white gangs roamed Chicago's streets, eventually killing fifteen whites and twenty-three blacks.

Suffering Until Suffrage

Women also heeded the call of patriotism and opportunity. Thousands of female workers flooded into factories and fields, taking up jobs vacated by men who left the assembly line for the frontline. But the war split the women's movement deeply. Many progressive-era feminists were pacifists, inclined to oppose the participation both of America in the war and women in the war effort. This group found a voice in the National Woman's party, led by Quaker activist Alice Paul, which demonstrated against "Kaiser Wilson" with marches and hunger strikes.

In an open address to Congress in 1917, suffragist Carrie Chapman Catt (1859–1947) capitalized on the idealism of the day and invoked the founding principles of American democracy in arguing the case for women's right to vote:

"How can our nation escape the logic it has never failed to follow, when its last unenfranchised class calls for the vote? Behold our Uncle Sam floating the banner with one hand, 'Taxation without representation is tyranny,' and with the other seizing the billions of dollars paid in taxes by women to whom he refuses 'representation.' . . . Is there a single man who can justify such inequality of treatment, such outrageous discrimination? Not one. . . ."

But the larger part of the suffrage movement, represented by the National American Woman Suffrage Association, supported Wilson's war. Leaders echoed Wilson's justification for fighting by arguing that women must take part in the war effort to earn a role in shaping the peace. The fight for democracy abroad was women's best hope for winning true democracy at home.

War mobilization gave new momentum to the suffrage fight. Impressed by women's war work, President Wilson endorsed woman suffrage as "a vitally necessary war measure." In 1917 New York voted for suffrage at the state level; Michigan, Oklahoma, and South Dakota followed. Eventually the groundswell could no longer be contained. In 1920, eighty years after the first calls for suffrage at Seneca Falls, the Nineteenth Amendment was ratified, giving all American women the right to vote. (See the Appendix.)

Despite political victory, women's wartime economic gains proved fleeting. Although a permanent Women's Bureau did emerge after the war in the Department of Labor to protect women in the workplace, most women workers soon gave up their war jobs. Meanwhile, Congress affirmed its support for women in their traditional role as mothers when it passed the Sheppard-Towner Maternity Act of 1921, providing federally financed instruction in maternal and infant health care.

Feminists continued to flex their political muscle in the postwar decade, especially in campaigns

Women Working on the Railroad, 1918   The First World War created many new job opportunities for women, as illustrated by this 1918 photograph of the Union Pacific yards in Cheyenne, Wyoming. But the war ended too quickly for many women to secure a permanent foothold in occupations traditionally dominated by men.

Suffragists Picket the White House, 1917   Militant feminists sometimes handcuffed themselves to the White House fence to dramatize their appeal to the president.

for laws to protect women in the workplace and prohibit child labor. Complete success often eluded them in those crusades, but the developments of the World War I era nevertheless foreshadowed a future when women's wage-labor and political power would reshape the American way of life.

Forging a War Economy

Mobilization relied more on the heated emotions of patriotism than on the cool majesty of the laws. The largely voluntary and somewhat haphazard character of economic war organization testified unequivocally to ocean-insulated America's safe distance from the fighting—as well as to the still-modest scale of government powers in the progressive-era Republic.

As the larder of democracy, America had to feed itself and its allies. By a happy inspiration, the man chosen to head the Food Administration was the Quaker-humanitarian Herbert C. Hoover. He was already considered a hero because he had successfully led a massive charitable drive to feed the starving people of war-racked Belgium.

In common with other American war administrators, Hoover preferred to rely on voluntary compliance rather than on compulsory edicts. He deliberately rejected issuing ration cards, a practice used in Europe. Instead he waged a whirlwind propaganda campaign through posters, billboards, newspapers, pulpits, and movies. To save food for export, Hoover proclaimed wheatless Wednesdays and meatless Tuesdays—all on a voluntary basis. Even children, when eating apples, were urged to be "patriotic to the core."

The country soon broke out in a rash of vegetable "victory gardens," as perspiring patriots hoed their way to victory in backyards and vacant lots. Congress severely restricted the use of foodstuffs for manufacturing alcoholic beverages, and the war-spawned spirit of self-denial helped accelerate the wave of prohibition that was sweeping the country. Many leading brewers were German-descended, and this taint made the drive against alcohol all the more popular. The reformers' dream of a saloonless nation was finally achieved—temporarily—in 1919 with the passage of the Eighteenth Amendment, prohibiting all alcoholic drinks.

Thanks to the fervent patriotic wartime spirit, Hoover's voluntary approach worked. Farm produc-

Food for Thought Wartime agencies flooded the country with posters like this in 1917–1918, exhorting women on the homefront to "grow their own" and thus ease the pressure on food supplies.

tion increased by one-fourth, and food exports to the Allies tripled in volume. Hoover's methods were widely imitated in other war agencies. The Fuel Administration exhorted Americans to save fuel with "heatless Mondays," "lightless nights," and "gasless Sundays." The Treasury Department sponsored huge parades and invoked slogans like "Halt the Hun" to promote four great Liberty Loan drives, followed by a Victory Loan campaign in 1919. Together these efforts netted the then-fantastic sum of about $21 billion, or two-thirds of the current cost of the war to the United States. The remainder was raised by increased taxes, which, unlike the loan subscriptions, were obligatory. (The ultimate bill,

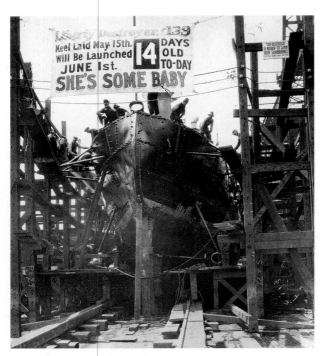

Miracles in Shipbuilding

including interest and veterans' benefits, mounted to some $112 billion.)

Pressures of various kinds, patriotic and otherwise, were used to sell bonds. The unfortunate German-American who could not display a Liberty Bond button might find his or her house bedaubed with yellow paint. A number of reluctant investors in war bonds were roughly handled. In at least one instance, a man signed for a bond with a rope around his neck.

Despite the Wilson administration's preference for voluntary means of mobilizing the economy, the government on occasion reluctantly exercised its sovereign formal power, notably when it took over the nation's railroads following indescribable traffic snarls in late 1917. Washington also hustled to get its hands on ships. It seized enemy merchant vessels trapped in America's harbors and orchestrated a gigantic drive to construct new tonnage. A few concrete vessels were launched, including one appropriately named *Faith*. A wooden-ship program was undertaken, though after months of war, birds were still nesting in the trees from which the vessels were to be hammered.

Making Plowboys into Doughboys

Most citizens, at the outset, did not dream of sending a mighty force to France. As far as fighting went, America would use its navy to uphold freedom of the seas. It would continue to ship war materials to the Allies and supply them with loans, which finally totaled nearly $10 billion. But in April and May of 1917, the European associates laid their cards on the table. They confessed that they were scraping the bottom not only of their money chests but, more ominously, of their manpower barrels. A huge American army would have to be raised, trained, and transported, or the whole western front would collapse.

Conscription was the only answer to the need for raising an immense army with all possible speed. Wilson disliked a draft, as did many other Americans with Civil War memories, but he eventually accepted and eloquently supported conscription as a disagreeable and temporary necessity.

The proposed draft bill immediately ran into a barrage of criticism in Congress. A congressman from Missouri, deploring compulsion, cried out in protest that there was "precious little difference between a conscript and a convict." Prophets of doom predicted that on draft-registration day, the streets would run red with blood. At length Congress—six weeks after declaring war—grudgingly got around to passing conscription.

Putting aside grizzly tales of the agonies of trench warfare, many young American men saw an opportunity for adventure and seized it. Author John Dos Passos (1896–1970) recollected how he felt going off to war in 1917:

"We had spent our boyhood in the afterglow of the peaceful nineteenth century. . . . What was war like? We wanted to see with our own eyes. We flocked into the volunteer services. I respected the conscientious objectors, and occasionally felt I should take that course myself, but hell, I wanted to see the show."

The draft act required the registration of all males between the ages of eighteen and forty-five. No "draft dodger" could purchase his exemption or hire a substitute, as in the days of the Civil War, though the law exempted men in key industries, such as shipbuilding.

The draft machinery, on the whole, worked effectively. Registration day proved to be a day of patriotic pilgrimages to flag-draped registration centers, and the sign-up saw no shedding of blood, as some had gloomily predicted. Despite precautions, some 337,000 "slackers" escaped the draft, and about 4,000 conscientious objectors were excused.

Within a few frantic months, the army grew to over 4 million men. For the first time, women were admitted to the armed forces; some 11,000 to the navy and 269 to the marines. African-Americans also served in the armed forces, though in strictly segregated units and usually under white officers. Reflecting racial attitudes of the time, military authorities hesitated to train black men for combat, and the majority of black soldiers were assigned to "construction battalions" or put to work unloading ships.

Recruits were supposed to receive six months of training in America and two more months overseas. But so great was the urgency that many doughboys were swept swiftly into battle scarcely knowing how to handle a rifle, much less a bayonet.

Fighting in France—Belatedly

Russia's collapse underscored the need for haste. The communistic Bolsheviks, after seizing power late in 1917, ultimately withdrew their beaten country from the "capitalistic" war early in 1918. This sudden defection released hundreds of thousands of battle-tested Germans from the eastern front facing Russia for the western front in France, where, for the first time in the war, they were developing a dangerous superiority in manpower.

Berlin's calculations as to American tardiness were surprisingly accurate. Germany had counted on knocking out Britain six months after the declaration of unlimited submarine warfare, long before America could get into the struggle. No really effective American fighting force reached France until about a year

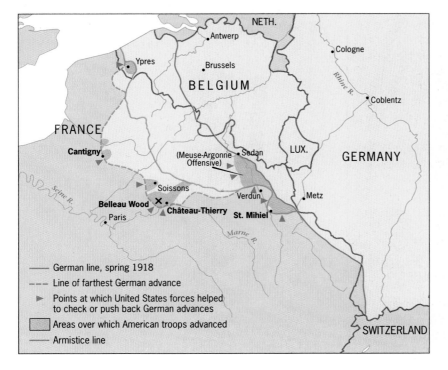

German line, spring 1918
Line of farthest German advance
Points at which United States forces helped to check or push back German advances
Areas over which American troops advanced
Armistice line

Major U.S. Operations in France, 1918 One doughboy recorded in his diary his baptism of fire at St. Mihiel: "Hiked through dark woods. No lights allowed, guided by holding on the pack of the man ahead. Stumbled through underbrush for about half mile into an open field where we waited in soaking rain until about 10:00 P.M. We then started on our hike to the St. Mihiel front, arriving on the crest of a hill at 1:00 A.M. I saw a sight which I shall never forget. It was the zero hour and in one instant the entire front as far as the eye could reach in either direction was a sheet of flame, while the heavy artillery made the earth quake."

after Congress declared war. Berlin had also reckoned on the inability of the Americans to transport their army, assuming that they were able to raise one. Here again the German predictions were not far from the mark, as shipping shortages plagued the Allies.

Nevertheless, France gradually began to bustle with American doughboys. The first trainees to reach the front were used as replacements in the Allied armies and were generally deployed in quiet sectors with the British and French. The newcomers soon made friends with the French girls—or tried to—and one of the most sung-about women in history was the fabled "Mademoiselle from Armentières." One of the printable stanzas ran

> *She was true to me, she was true to you,*
> *She was true to the whole damned army, too.*

American operations were not confined solely to France; small detachments fought in Belgium, Italy, and notably Russia. The United States, hoping to keep stores of munitions from falling into German hands when Bolshevik Russia quit fighting, contributed some 5,000 troops to an Allied invasion of northern Russia at Archangel. Wilson likewise sent nearly 10,000 troops to Siberia as part of an Allied expedition, which included more than 70,000

Japanese. Major American purposes were to prevent Japan from getting a stranglehold on Siberia, to rescue some 45,000 marooned Czechoslovak troops, and to snatch military supplies from Bolshevik control. Sharp fighting at Archangel and in Siberia involved casualties on both sides, including several hundred Americans. The Bolsheviks long resented these "capitalistic" interventions, which they regarded as high-handed efforts to suffocate their infant communist revolution in its cradle.

America Helps Hammer the "Hun"

The dreaded German drive on the western front exploded in the spring of 1918. Spearheaded by about half a million troops, the enemy rolled forward with terrifying momentum. So dire was the peril that the Allied nations for the first time united under a supreme commander, the quiet French marshal Foch, whose axiom was, "To make war is to attack." Until then the Allies had been fighting imperfectly coordinated actions.

At last the ill-trained "Yanks" were coming—and not a moment too soon. Late in May 1918, the Ger-

Over There   American troops man a trench gun in a bomb-blasted forest.

Gassed, by John Singer Sargent   The noted artist captures the horror of trench warfare in World War I. The enemy was often distant and unseen, and death came impersonally from gas or artillery fire. American troops, entering the line only in the war's final days, were only briefly exposed to this kind of brutal fighting.

man juggernaut, smashing to within forty miles of Paris, threatened to knock out France. Newly arrived American troops, numbering fewer than thirty thousand, were thrown into the breach at Château-Thierry, right in the teeth of the German advance. This was a historic moment—the first significant engagement of American troops in a European war. Battle-fatigued French soldiers watched incredulously as the roads filled with endless truckloads of American doughboys, singing New World songs at the top of their voices, a seemingly inexhaustible flood of fresh and gleaming youth. With their arrival it was clear that a new American giant had arisen in the West to replace the dying Russian titan in the East.

Approximate Comparative Losses in World War I

MEN KILLED IN BATTLE	
1,700,000	Russia
1,600,000	Germany
1,385,000	France
900,000	British Empire
800,000	Austria
462,000	Italy
53,000	United States

American weight in the scales was now being felt. By July 1918 the awesome German drive had spent its force, and keyed-up American men participated in a Foch counteroffensive in the Second Battle of the Marne. This engagement marked the beginning of a German withdrawal that was never effectively reversed. In September 1918 nine American divisions (about 243,000 men) joined four French divisions to push the Germans from the St. Mihiel salient, a German dagger in France's flank.

The Americans, dissatisfied with merely bolstering the British and French, had meanwhile been demanding a separate army. General John J. ("Black Jack") Pershing was finally assigned a front of eighty-five miles, stretching northwestward from the Swiss border to meet the French lines.

As part of the last mighty Allied assault, involving several million men, Pershing's army undertook the Meuse-Argonne offensive, from September 26 to November 11, 1918. One objective was to cut the German railroad lines feeding the western front. This battle, the most gargantuan thus far in American history, lasted forty-seven days and engaged 1.2 million American troops. With especially heavy fighting in the rugged Argonne Forest, the killed and wounded mounted to 120,000, or 10 percent of the Americans involved. The slow progress and severe losses from machine guns resulted in part from inadequate training, in part from dashing open-field tactics, with the bayonet liberally employed.

Tennessee-bred Alvin C. York, a member of an anti-war religious sect, became a hero when he single-handedly killed 20 Germans and captured 132 more.

Victory was in sight—and fortunately so. The slowly advancing American armies in France were eating up their supplies so rapidly that they were in grave danger of running short. But the battered Germans were ready to stagger out of the trenches and cry "Kamerad" ("Comrade"). Their allies were deserting them, the British blockade was causing critical food shortages, and the sledgehammer blows of the Allies rained down relentlessly. Propaganda leaflets, containing seductive Wilsonian promises, rained upon their crumbling lines from balloons, shells, and rockets.

The Fourteen Points Disarm Germany

Berlin was now ready to hoist the white flag. Warned of imminent defeat by the generals, it turned to the presumably softhearted Wilson in October 1918, seeking a peace based on the Fourteen Points. In stern responses the president made it clear that the kaiser must be thrown overboard before an armistice could be negotiated. War-weary Germans, whom Wilson had been trying to turn against their "military masters," took the hint. The kaiser was forced to flee to Holland, where he lived out his remaining twenty-three years, "unwept, unhonored, and unhung."

The exhausted Germans were through. They laid down their arms at eleven o'clock on the eleventh day of the eleventh month of 1918, and an eerie, numbing silence fell over the western front. War-taut America burst into a delirium of around-the-clock rejoicing, as streets were jammed with laughing, whooping, milling, dancing masses. The war to end wars had ended.

The United States' main contributions to the ultimate victory had been foodstuffs, munitions, credits, oil for this first mechanized war, and manpower—but not battlefield victories. The Yanks fought only two major battles, at St. Mihiel and the Meuse-Argonne, both in the last two months of the four-year war, and they were still grinding away in the Meuse-Argonne, well short of their objectives, when the war ended. It was the *prospect* of endless U.S. troop reserves, rather than America's actual military performance, that eventually demoralized the Germans.

Ironically enough, General Pershing in some ways depended more on the Allies than they depended on him. His army purchased more of its supplies in Europe than it shipped from the United States. Fewer than five hundred of Pershing's artillery pieces were of American manufacture. Virtually all his aircraft were provided by the British and French. Britain and France transported a majority of the doughboys to Europe. The United States, in short, was no arsenal of democracy in this war; that role awaited it in the next global conflict, two decades later.

Wilson Steps Down from Olympus

Woodrow Wilson had helped to win the war. What part would he now play in shaping the peace? Expectations ran extravagantly high. As the fighting in Europe crashed to a close, the American president towered at the peak of his popularity and power. In lonely huts in the mountains of Italy, candles burned before poster-portraits of the revered American prophet. In Poland starry-eyed university students would meet on the streets, clasp hands, and utter only one word: "Wilson." No other man

German "Repentance," 1918 A prophetic reflection of the view that the failure to smash Germany completely would lead to another world war.

Heroes' Welcome, 1917
The people of Harlem gathered to welcome home the black regiment known as the "Hell-fighters of Harlem." Black troops were confined to segregated units in World War I, and segregation followed some of them even into death. When Congress appropriated money in 1930 to send "Gold Star Mothers" to visit the graves of their slain soldier-sons in France, it provided for separate ships, hotels, and trains for African-American women. Several black mothers, preferring "to remain at home and retain our honor and self-respect," reluctantly refused to make the trip.

had ever occupied so dizzy a pinnacle as moral leader of the world. Wilson also had behind him the prestige of victory and the economic resources of the mightiest nation on earth. But at this fateful moment, his sureness of touch deserted him, and he began to make a series of tragic fumbles.

Under the slogan "Politics Is Adjourned," partisan political strife had been kept below the surface during the war crisis. Hoping to strengthen his hand at the Paris peace table, Wilson broke the truce by personally appealing for a Democratic victory in the

Theodore Roosevelt (1858–1919) favored the Germans' unconditional surrender. Referring to Wilson's practice of drafting diplomatic notes on his own typewriter, Roosevelt telegraphed several senators (October 24, 1918),

"Let us dictate peace by the hammering guns and not chat about peace to the accompaniment of clicking typewriters. The language of the fourteen points and the subsequent statements explaining or qualifying them are thoroughly mischievous."

congressional elections of November 1918. But the maneuver backfired when voters instead returned a narrow Republican majority to Congress. Having staked his reputation on the outcome, Wilson went to Paris as a diminished leader. Unlike all the parliamentary statesmen at the table, he did not command a legislative majority at home.

Wilson's decision to go in person to Paris to help make the peace infuriated Republicans. At that time no president had traveled to Europe, and Wilson's journey looked to his critics like flamboyant grandstanding. He further ruffled Republican feathers when he snubbed the Senate in assembling his peace delegation and neglected to include a single Republican senator in his official party. The logical choice was the new chairman of the Senate Committee on Foreign Relations, slender and aristocratically bewhiskered Henry Cabot Lodge of Massachusetts, a Harvard Ph.D. But including Lodge would have been problematic for the president. The senator's mind, quipped one critic, was like the soil of his native New England: "naturally barren but highly cultivated." Wilson loathed him, and the feeling was hotly reciprocated. An accomplished author, Lodge had been known as the "scholar in politics" until Wilson came on the scene. The two men were at daggers drawn, personally and politically.

An Idealist Battles the Imperialists in Paris

Woodrow Wilson, the great prophet arisen in the West, received tumultuous welcomes from the masses of France, England, and Italy late in 1918 and early in 1919. They saw in his idealism the promise of a better world. But the statesmen of France and Italy were careful to keep the new messiah at arm's length from worshipful crowds. He might so arouse the people as to prompt them to overthrow their leaders and upset finespun imperialistic plans.

The Paris Conference of great and small nations fell into the hands of an inner clique, known as the Big Four. Wilson, representing the richest and freshest great power, more or less occupied the driver's seat. He was joined by genial Premier Vittorio Orlando of Italy and brilliant Prime Minister David Lloyd George of Britain. Perhaps the most realistic of the quartet was cynical, hard-bitten Premier Georges Clemenceau of France, the seventy-eight-year-old "organizer of victory" known as "the Tiger."

Speed was urgent when the conference opened on January 18, 1919. Europe seemed to be slipping into anarchy; the red tide of communism was licking westward from Bolshevist Russia.

> *Grave concern was expressed by General Tasker H. Bliss (1853–1930), one of the five American peace commissioners (December 18, 1918):*
>
> "I am disquieted to see how hazy and vague our ideas are. We are going to be up against the wiliest politicians in Europe. There will be nothing hazy or vague about their ideas."

Wilson's ultimate goal was a world parliament to be known as the League of Nations, but he first bent his energies to preventing any vengeful parceling out of the former colonies and protectorates of the vanquished powers. He forced through a compromise between naked imperialism and Wilsonian idealism. The victors would not take possession of the conquered territory outright, but would receive it as trustees of the League of Nations. Strategic Syria, for example, was awarded to France, and oil-rich Iraq went to Britain. But in practice this half-loaf solution was little more than the old prewar colonialism, thinly disguised.

Wilson in Dover, England, 1919   Hailed by many Europeans in early 1919 as the savior of the Western world, Wilson was a fallen idol only a few months later, when Americans repudiated the peace treaty he had help to craft.

Meanwhile, Wilson had been serving as midwife for the League of Nations, which he envisioned as containing an assembly with seats for all nations and a council to be controlled by the great powers. He gained a signal victory over the skeptical Old World diplomats in February 1919, when they agreed to make the League Covenant, Wilson's brainchild, an integral part of the final peace treaty. At one point he spoke with such ardor for his plan that even the hard-boiled newspaper reporters forgot to take notes.

Hammering Out the Treaty

Domestic duties now required Wilson to make a quick trip to America, where ugly storms were brewing in the Senate. Certain Republican senators, Lodge in the lead, were sharpening their knives for Wilson. To them the League was either a useless "sewing circle" or an overpotent "super-state." Their hard core was composed of a dozen or so militant isolationists, led by senators William Borah of Idaho and Hiram Johnson of California, who were known as "irreconcilables" or "the Battalion of Death."

Thirty-nine Republican senators or senators-elect—enough to defeat the treaty—proclaimed that the Senate would not approve the League of Nations in its existing imperfect form. These difficulties delighted Wilson's Allied adversaries in Paris. They were now in a stronger bargaining position because Wilson would have to beg them for changes in the covenant that would safeguard the Monroe Doctrine and other American interests dear to the senators.

As soon as Wilson was back in Paris, hard-headed Premier Clemenceau pressed French demands for the German-inhabited Rhineland and the Saar Valley, a rich coal area. Faced with fierce Wilsonian opposition to this violation of self-determination, France settled for a compromise whereby the Saar basin would remain under the League of Nations for fifteen years, and then a popular vote would determine its fate.* In exchange for dropping its demands for the Rhineland, France got the Security Treaty, in which both Britain and America pledged to come to its aid in the event of another German invasion. The French later felt betrayed

Pilgrim Landing in America, 1919

when this pact was quickly pigeonholed by the U.S. Senate, which shied away from all entangling alliances.

Wilson's next battle was with Italy over Fiume, a valuable seaport inhabited by both Italians and Yugoslavs. When Italy demanded Fiume, Wilson insisted that the seaport go to Yugoslavia and appealed over the heads of Italy's leaders to the country's masses. The maneuver fell flat. The Italian delegates went home in a huff, while the Italian masses turned savagely against Wilson.

Another crucial struggle was with Japan over China's Shandong (Shantung) Peninsula and the German islands in the Pacific, which the Japanese had seized during the war. Japan was conceded the strategic Pacific islands under a League of Nations mandate,* but Wilson staunchly opposed Japanese control of Shandong as a violation of self-determination for its 30 million Chinese residents. But when the

---

*The Saar population voted overwhelmingly to rejoin Germany in 1935.

*In due time the Japanese illegally fortified these islands—the Marshalls, Marianas, and Carolines—and used them as bases against the United States in World War II.

Japanese threatened to walk out, Wilson reluctantly accepted a compromise whereby Japan kept Germany's economic holdings in Shandong and pledged to return the peninsula to China at a later date. The Chinese were outraged by this imperialistic solution, while Clemenceau jeered that Wilson "talked like Jesus Christ and acted like Lloyd George."

The Peace Treaty That Bred a New War

A completed Treaty of Versailles, after more weeks of wrangling, was handed to the Germans in June 1919—almost literally on the point of a bayonet. Germany had capitulated on the strength of assurances that it would be granted a peace based on the Fourteen Points. A careful analysis of the treaty shows that only about four of the twenty-three original Wilsonian points and subsequent principles were fully honored. Loud and bitter cries of betrayal burst from German throats—charges that Adolf Hitler would soon reiterate during his meteoric rise to power.

Wilson, of course, was guilty of no conscious betrayal. But the Allied powers were torn by conflicting aims, many of them sanctioned by secret treaties. There had to be compromise at Paris, or there would be no agreement. Faced with hard realities, Wilson was forced to compromise away some of his less cherished Fourteen Points in order to salvage the more precious League of Nations. He was much like the mother who had to throw her sickly younger children to the pursuing wolves to save her sturdy firstborn.

A troubled Wilson was not happy with the results. Greeted a few months earlier with frenzied acclaim in Europe, he was now a fallen idol, condemned alike by disillusioned liberals and frustrated imperialists. He was keenly aware of some of the injustices that had been forced into the treaty. But he was hoping that the League of Nations—a potent League with America as a leader—would iron out the inequities.

Yet the loudly condemned treaty had much to commend it. Not least among its merits was its liberation of millions of minority peoples, such as the Poles, from the yoke of an alien dynasty. Disappointing though Wilson's handiwork was, he saved the pact from being an old-time peace of grasping imperialism. His critics to the contrary, the settlement was almost certainly a fairer one because he had gone to Paris.

The Domestic Parade of Prejudice

Returning for the second and final time to America, Wilson sailed straight into a political typhoon. Isolationists raised a whirlwind of protest against the treaty, especially against Wilson's commitment to usher the United States into his newfangled League of Nations. Invoking the revered advice of Washington and Jefferson, they wanted no part of any "entangling alliance."

Nor were the isolationists Wilson's only problem. Critics showered the Treaty of Versailles with abuse from all sides.

Rabid Hun-haters, regarding the pact as not harsh enough, voiced their discontent. Principled liberals, like the editors of the New York *Nation*, thought it too harsh—and a gross betrayal to boot. German-Americans, Italian-Americans, and other "hyphenated" Americans were aroused because the peace settlement was not sufficiently favorable to their native lands.

Irish-Americans, traditional twisters of the British lion's tail, also denounced the League. They felt that with the additional votes of the five overseas British dominions, it gave Britain undue influence, and they feared that it could be used to force the United States to crush any rising for Irish independence. Crowds of Irish-American zealots hissed and booed Wilson's name.

Wilson's Tour and Collapse (1919)

Despite mounting discontent, the president had reason to feel optimistic. When he brought home the treaty, with the "Wilson League" firmly riveted in as Part I, a strong majority of the people still seemed favorable. At this time—early July 1919—Senator Lodge had no real hope of defeating the Treaty of Versailles. His strategy was merely to amend it in such a way as to "Americanize," "Republicanize," or "senatorialize" it. The Republicans could then claim political credit for the changes.

Lodge effectively used delay to muddle and divide public opinion. He read the entire 264-page treaty aloud in the Senate Foreign Relations Committee and held protracted hearings in which people of various nationalities aired their grievances.

Wilson fretted increasingly as the hot summer of 1919 wore on. The bulky pact was bogged down

Going to Talk to
the Boss, 1919

in the Senate, while the nation was drifting into confusion and apathy. He therefore decided to go to the country in a spectacular speechmaking tour. He would appeal over the heads of the Senate to the sovereign people—as he often had in the past.

The strenuous barnstorming campaign was undertaken in the face of protests by physicians and friends. Wilson had never been robust; he had entered the White House nearly seven years before with a stomach pump and with headache pills for his neuritis. His frail body had begun to sag under the strain of partisan strife, a global war, and a stressful peace conference. But he declared that he was willing to die, like the soldiers he had sent into battle, for the sake of the new world order.

The presidential tour, begun in September 1919, got off to a rather lame start. The Midwest received Wilson lukewarmly, partly because of strong German-American influence. Trailing after him like bloodhounds came two "irreconcilable" senators, Borah and Johnson, who spoke in the same cities a few days later. Hat-tossing crowds answered their attacks on Wilson, crying, "Impeach him, impeach him!"

But the reception was different in the Rocky Mountain region and on the Pacific Coast. These areas, which had elected Wilson in 1916, welcomed him with heartwarming outbursts. The high point—and the breaking point—of the return trip was at Pueblo, Colorado, September 25, 1919. Wilson, with tears coursing down his cheeks, pleaded for the League of Nations as the only real hope of preventing future wars. That night he collapsed from physical and nervous exhaustion.

Wilson was whisked back in the "funeral train" to Washington, where several days later a stroke paralyzed one side of his body. During the next few weeks, he lay in a darkened room in the White House, as much a victim of the war as the unknown soldier buried at Arlington. For more than seven months, he did not meet his cabinet.

Defeat Through Deadlock

Senator Lodge, coldly calculating, was now at the helm. After failing to amend the treaty outright, he finally came up with fourteen formal reservations to it—a sardonic slap at Wilson's Fourteen Points. These safeguards reserved the rights of the United States under the Monroe Doctrine and the Constitution and otherwise sought to protect American sovereignty. Senator Lodge and other critics were especially alarmed by Article X of the League because it *morally* bound the United States to aid any member victimized by external aggression. A jealous Congress wanted to reserve for itself the constitutional war-declaring power.

Wilson, hating Lodge, saw red at the mere suggestion of the Lodge reservations. He was quite willing to accept somewhat similar reservations sponsored by his faithful Democratic followers, but he insisted that the Lodge reservations "emasculated" the entire pact.

Although too feeble to lead, Wilson was still strong enough to obstruct. When the day finally came for the voting in the Senate, he sent word to all true Democrats to vote *against* the treaty with the odious Lodge reservations attached. Wilson hoped that when these were cleared away, the path would be open for ratification without reservations or with only some mild Democratic ones.

Loyal Democrats in the Senate, on November 19, 1919, blindly did Wilson's bidding. Combining with the "irreconcilables," mostly Republicans, they rejected the treaty with the Lodge reservations appended, 55 to 39.

The nation was too deeply shocked to accept the verdict as final. About four-fifths of the senators professed to favor the treaty, with or without reservations, yet a simple majority could not agree on a single proposition. So strong was public indignation that the Senate was forced to act a second time. In March 1920 the treaty was brought up again, with the Lodge reservations tacked on.

There was only one possible path to success. Unless the Senate approved the pact with the reservations, the entire document would be rejected. But the sickly Wilson, still sheltered behind drawn curtains and blind to disagreeable realities, again sent word to all loyal Democrats to vote down the treaty with the obnoxious reservations. He thus signed the death warrant of the treaty as far as America was concerned. On March 19, 1920, the treaty netted a simple majority but failed to get the necessary two-thirds majority by a count of 49 yeas to 35 nays.

Who defeated the treaty? The Lodge-Wilson personal feud, traditionalism, isolationism, disillusionment, and partisanship all contributed to the confused picture. But Wilson himself must bear a substantial share of the responsibility. He asked for all or nothing—and got nothing. One Democratic senator angrily charged that the president had strangled his own brainchild with his own palsied hands rather than let the Senate straighten its crooked limbs.

The "Solemn Referendum" of 1920

Wilson had his own pet solution for the deadlock, and this partly explains why he refused to compromise on Lodge's terms. He proposed to settle the treaty issue in the forthcoming presidential campaign of 1920 by appealing to the people for a "solemn referendum." This was sheer folly, for a true mandate on the League in the noisy arena of politics was clearly an impossibility.

Jubilant Republicans gathered in Chicago in June 1920 with wayward bull moosers back in the corral (after Theodore Roosevelt's death in 1919) and the senatorial Old Guard back in the saddle. The convention devised a masterfully ambiguous platform that could appeal to both pro-League and anti-League sentiment in the party. The nominee would run on a teeter-totter rather than a platform.

As the leading presidential contestants jousted with one another, the political weathervane began to veer toward genial Senator Warren G. Harding of Ohio. A group of Senate bosses, meeting rather casually in the historic "smoke-filled" Room 404 of the Hotel Blackstone, informally decided on the affable and malleable Ohioan. Their fair-haired boy was a prosperous, backslapping, small-town newspaper editor of the "folksy" type, quite the opposite of Wilson, who had earlier noted the senator's "disturbingly dull" mind. For vice president the party nominated frugal, grim-faced Governor Calvin ("Silent Cal") Coolidge of Massachusetts, who had attracted conservative support by breaking a police strike in Boston.

Meeting in San Francisco, Democrats nominated earnest Governor James M. Cox of Ohio, who strongly supported the League. His running mate was Assistant Navy Secretary Franklin D. Roosevelt, a young, handsome, vibrant New Yorker.

Democratic attempts to make the campaign a referendum on the League were thwarted by Senator Harding, who issued muddled and contradictory statements on the issue from his front porch. Pro-League and anti-League Republicans both claimed that Harding's election would advance their cause, while the candidate suggested that if elected he would work for a vague Association of Nations—*a* league but not *the* League.

With newly enfranchised women swelling the vote totals, Harding was swept into power with a prodigious plurality of over 7 million votes—16,143,407 to 9,130,328 for Cox. The electoral count was 404 to 127. Eugene V. Debs, federal prisoner number 9653 at the Atlanta Penitentiary, rolled up the largest vote ever for the left-wing Socialist party—919,799.

Public desire for a change found vent in a resounding repudiation of "high-and-mighty" Wilsonism. People were tired of professional highbrowism, star-reaching idealism, bothersome do-goodism, moral overstrain, and constant self-sacrifice. Eager to lapse back into "normalcy," they were willing to accept a second-rate president—and they got a third-rate one.

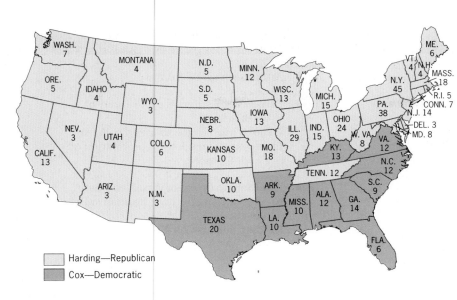

Presidential Election of 1920 (with electoral vote by state) Cox rashly claimed that "traitors" would vote Republican. But Harding and Coolidge ran successfully as small-town boys who had made good. Harding celebrated his fifty-fifth birthday on election day, and the voters presented him with the largest victory margin to date in a U.S. presidential election.

Although the election could not be considered a true referendum, Republican isolationists successfully turned Harding's victory into a death sentence for the League. Politicians increasingly shunned the League as they would a leper. When the legendary Wilson died in 1924, admirers knelt in the snow outside his Washington home. His "great vision" of a league for peace had perished long before.

The Betrayal of Great Expectations

America's spurning of the League was tragically shortsighted. The Republic had helped to win a costly war, but it foolishly kicked the fruits of victory under the table. Whether a strong international organization would have averted World War II in 1939 will always be a matter of dispute. But there can be no doubt that the orphaned League of Nations was undercut at the start by the refusal of the mightiest power on the globe to join it. The Allies themselves were largely to blame for the new world conflagration that flared up in 1939, but they found a convenient justification for their own shortcomings by pointing an accusing finger at Uncle Sam.

The ultimate collapse of the Treaty of Versailles must be laid, at least in some degree, at America's doorstep. This complicated pact, tied in with the four other peace treaties through the League Covenant, was a top-heavy structure designed to rest on a four-legged table. The fourth leg, the United States, was never put into place. This rickety structure teetered for over a decade and then crashed in ruins—a debacle that played into the hands of the German demagogue Adolf Hitler.

No less ominous events were set in motion when the Senate spurned the Security Treaty with France. The French, fearing that a new generation of Germans would follow in their fathers' goose steps, undertook to build up a powerful military force. Predictably resenting the presence of strong French armies, Germany began to rearm illegally. The seething cauldron of uncertainty and suspicion brewed an intoxicant that helped inflame the fanatical following of Hitler.

The United States, as the tragic sequel proved, hurt its own cause when it buried its head in the sand. Granted that the conduct of its Allies had been disillusioning, it had its own ends to serve by carrying through the Wilsonian program. It would have been well advised if it had forthrightly assumed its war-born responsibilities and had resolutely embraced the role of global leader proffered by the hand of destiny. In the interests of its own security, if for no other reason, the United States should have used its enormous strength to shape world-shaking events. Instead it permitted itself blithely to drift toward the abyss of a second and even more bloody international disaster.

Chronology

1915	Council of National Defense established	**1918**	Armistice ends World War I
1917	Germany resumes unrestricted submarine warfare Zimmermann note United States enters World War I Espionage Act of 1917	**1919**	Paris Peace Conference and Treaty of Versailles Wilson's pro-League tour and collapse Eighteenth Amendment (prohibition of alcohol) passed
1918	Wilson proposes the Fourteen Points Sedition Act of 1918 Battle of Château-Thierry Second Battle of the Marne Meuse-Argonne offensive	**1920**	Final Senate defeat of Versailles Treaty Nineteenth Amendment (woman suffrage) passed Harding defeats Cox for presidency

VARYING VIEWPOINTS

Woodrow Wilson: Realist or Idealist?

As the first president to take the United States into a foreign war, Woodrow Wilson was obliged to make a systematic case to the American people to justify his unprecedented European intervention. His ideas have largely defined the character of American foreign policy ever since—for better or worse.

"Wilsonianism" comprises three closely related principles: (1) the era of American isolation from world affairs has irretrievably ended; (2) the United States must infuse its own founding political and economic ideas—including democracy, the rule of law, free trade, and national self-determination (or anti-colonialism)—into the international order; and (3) American influence can eventually steer the world away from rivalry and warfare toward a cooperative and peaceful international system, maintained by the League of Nations or, later, the United Nations.

Whether that Wilsonian vision constitutes hard-nosed realism or starry-eyed idealism has excited scholarly debate for nearly a century. "Realists," such as George F. Kennan and Henry Kissinger, insist Wilson was anything but. They criticize the president as a naive, impractical dreamer who failed to understand that the international order is, and always will be, an anarchic, unruly arena, outside the rule of law, where only military force can effectively protect the nation's security. In a sharp critique in his 1950 study, *American Diplomacy*, Kennan condemned Wilson's vision as "moralism-legalism." In this view Wilson dangerously threatened to sacrifice American self-interests on the altar of his admirable but ultimately unworkable ideas.

Wilson's defenders, including conspicuously his principal biographer, Arthur S. Link, argue that Wilson's idealism was in fact a kind of higher realism, recognizing as it did that armed conflict on the scale of World War I could never again be tolerated and that some framework of peaceful international relations simply had to be found. The development of nuclear weapons in a later generation gave this argument still more force. This "liberal" defense of Wilsonianism derives from the centuries-old liberal faith that, given sufficient intelligence and willpower, the world can be made into a better place. Realists reject this notion of moral and political progress as hopelessly innocent, especially as applied to international affairs.

Some leftist scholars, such as William Appleman Williams, have argued that Wilson was in fact a realist of another kind: a subtle and wily imperialist whose stirring rhetoric cloaked a grasping ambition to make the United States the world's dominant economic power. Sometimes called "the imperialism of free trade," this strategy allegedly sought to decolonialize the world and open up international commerce not for the good of peoples elsewhere, but to create a system in which American economic might would irresistibly prevail. This criticism itself rests on a naive assumption that international relations are a "zero-sum game," in which one nation's gain must necessarily be another nation's loss. In a Wilsonian world, Wilson's defenders claim, *all* parties would be better off; altruism and self-interest are not mutually exclusive.

Still other scholars, especially John Milton Cooper, Jr., emphasize the absence of economic factors in shaping Wilson's diplomacy. Isolationism, so this argument goes, held such sway over American thinking precisely because the United States had such a puny financial stake abroad—no hard American economic interests were mortally threatened in 1917, nor for a long time thereafter. In these circumstances Wilson—and the Wilsonians who came after him, such as Franklin D. Roosevelt—had no choice but to appeal to abstract ideals and high principles. The "idealistic" Wilsonian strain in American diplomacy, in this view, may be an unavoidable heritage of America's historically isolated situation. If so, it was Wilson's genius to make practical use of those ideas in his bid for popular support of his diplomacy.

For further reading, see page A21 of the Appendix. For web resources, go to **http://college.hmco.com.**

32

American Life in the "Roaring Twenties"

1919–1929

*America's present need is not heroics but healing;
not nostrums but normalcy; not revolution but
restoration; . . . not surgery but serenity.*

WARREN G. HARDING, 1920

Bloodied by the war and disillusioned by the peace, Americans turned inward in the 1920s. Shunning diplomatic commitments to foreign countries, they also denounced "radical" foreign ideas, condemned "un-American" lifestyles, and clanged shut the immigration gates against foreign peoples. They partly sealed off the domestic economy from the rest of the world and plunged head-long into a dizzying decade of homegrown prosperity.

The boom of the golden twenties showered genuine benefits on Americans, as incomes and living standards rose for many. But there seemed to be something incredible about it all, even as people sang,

*My sister she works in the laundry,
My father sells bootlegger gin,
My mother she takes in the washing,
My God! how the money rolls in!*

New technologies, new consumer products, and new forms of leisure and entertainment made the twenties roar. Yet just beneath the surface lurked widespread anxieties about the future and fears that America was losing sight of its traditional ways.

Seeing Red

Hysterical fears of red Russia continued to color American thinking for several years after the Bolshevik revolution of 1917, which spawned a tiny Communist party in America. Tensions were heightened by an epidemic of strikes that convulsed the Republic at war's end, many of them the result of high prices and frustrated union-organizing drives. Upstanding Americans jumped to the conclusion that labor troubles were fomented by bomb-and-

Radicals on the Run, 1919   In the aftermath of the war, the American Legion, superpatriotic voice of veterans, joined the anti-Bolshevik chorus zealously attacking political leftists in the United States as "enemy reds."

whisker Bolsheviks. A general strike in Seattle in 1919, though modest in its demands and orderly in its methods, prompted a call from the mayor for federal troops to head off "the anarchy of Russia." Fire-and-brimstone evangelist Billy Sunday struck a responsive chord when he described a Bolshevik as "a guy with a face like a porcupine and a breath that would scare a pole cat. . . . If I had my way, I'd fill the jails so full of them that their feet would stick out the window."

The big "red scare" of 1919–1920 resulted in a nationwide crusade against left-wingers whose Americanism was suspect. Attorney General A. Mitchell Palmer, who "saw red" too easily, earned the title of the "Fighting Quaker" by his excess of zeal in rounding up suspects. They ultimately totaled about six thousand. This drive to root out radicals was redoubled in June 1919, when a bomb shattered both the nerves and the Washington home of Palmer. The "Fighting Quaker" was thereupon dubbed the "Quaking Fighter."

Other events highlighted the red scare. Late in December 1919, a shipload of 249 alleged alien radicals was deported on the *Buford* ("Soviet Ark") to the "workers' paradise" of Russia. One zealot cried, "My motto for the Reds is S.O.S.—ship or shoot." Hysteria was temporarily revived in September 1920, when a still-unexplained bomb blast on Wall Street killed thirty-eight people and wounded several hundred others.

Various states joined the pack in the outcry against radicals. In 1919–1920 a number of legislatures, reflecting the anxiety of "solid" citizens, passed criminal syndicalism laws. These antired statutes, some of which were born of the war, made unlawful the mere *advocacy* of violence to secure social change. Critics protested that mere words were not criminal deeds, that there was a great gulf between throwing fits and throwing bombs, and that "free screech" was for the nasty as well as the nice. Violence was done to traditional American concepts of free speech as IWW members and other radicals were vigorously prosecuted. The hysteria went so far that in 1920 five members of the New York legislature, all lawfully elected, were denied their seats simply because they were Socialists.

The red scare was a godsend to conservative businesspeople, who used it to break the backs of the fledgling unions. Labor's call for the "closed," or all-union, shop was denounced as "Sovietism in disguise." Employers, in turn, hailed their own antiunion campaign for the "open" shop as "the American plan."

Antiredism and antiforeignism were reflected in a notorious case regarded by liberals as a "judicial lynching." Nicola Sacco, a shoe-factory worker, and Bartolomeo Vanzetti, a fish peddler, were convicted in 1921 of the murder of a Massachusetts paymaster and his guard. The jury and judge were prejudiced

An author-soldier (Guy Empey) applauded the "deportation delirium" when he wrote,

"I believe we should place them [the reds] all on a ship of stone, with sails of lead, and that their first stopping place should be hell."

in some degree against the defendants because they were Italians, atheists, anarchists, and draft dodgers.

Liberals and radicals the world over rallied to the defense of the two aliens doomed to die. The case dragged on for six years until 1927, when the condemned men were electrocuted. Communists and other radicals were thus presented with two martyrs in the "class struggle," while many American liberals hung their heads. The evidence against the accused, though damaging, betrayed serious weaknesses. If the trial had been held in an atmosphere less charged with antiredism, the outcome might well have been only a prison term.

Hooded Hoodlums of the KKK

A new Ku Klux Klan, spawned by the postwar reaction, mushroomed fearsomely in the early 1920s. Despite the familiar sheets and hoods, it more closely resembled the antiforeign "nativist" movements of the 1850s than the antiblack nightriders of the 1860s. It was antiforeign, anti-Catholic, antiblack, anti-Jewish, antipacifist, anti-

KKK Parade of Forty Thousand Men in Washington, 1925

Communist, anti-internationalist, antievolutionist, antibootlegger, antigambling, antiadultery, and anti–birth control. It was also pro–Anglo-Saxon, pro–"native" American, and pro-Protestant. In short, the besheeted Klan betokened an extremist, ultraconservative uprising against many of the forces of diversity and modernity that were transforming American culture.

As reconstituted, the Klan spread with astonishing rapidity, especially in the Midwest and the "Bible Belt" South. At its peak in the mid-1920s, it claimed about 5 million dues-paying members and wielded potent political influence. It capitalized on the typically American love of on-the-edge adventure and in-group camaraderie, to say nothing of the adolescent ardor for secret ritual. "Knights of the Invisible Empire" included among their officials Imperial Wizards, Grand Goblins, King Kleagles, and other horrendous "kreatures." The most impressive displays were "konclaves" and huge flag-waving parades. The chief warning was the blazing cross. The principal weapon was the bloodied lash, supplemented by tar and feathers. Rallying songs were "The Fiery Cross on High," "One Hundred Percent American," and "The Ku Klux Klan and the Pope" (against kissing the Pope's toe). One brutal slogan was "Kill the Kikes, Koons, and Katholics."

This reign of hooded horror, so repulsive to the best American ideals, collapsed rather suddenly in the late 1920s. Decent people at last recoiled from the orgy of ribboned flesh and terrorism, while scandalous embezzling by Klan officials launched a congressional investigation. The bubble was punctured when the movement was exposed as a vicious racket based on a $10 initiation fee, $4 of which was kicked back to local organizers as an incentive to recruit. The KKK was an alarming manifestation of the intolerance and prejudice plaguing people anxious about the dizzying pace of social change in the 1920s. America needed no such cowardly apostles, whose white sheets concealed dark purposes.

Stemming the Foreign Flood

Isolationist America of the 1920s, ingrown and provincial, had little use for the immigrants who began to flood into the country again as peace settled soothingly on the war-torn world. Some 800,000 stepped ashore in 1920–1921, about two-

A recognized expert on American immigration, Henry P. Fairchild (1880–1956), wrote in 1926,

"The typical immigrant of the present does not really live in America at all, but, from the point of view of nationality, in Italy, Poland, Czecho-Slovakia, or some other foreign country."

thirds of them from southern and eastern Europe. The "one-hundred-percent Americans," recoiling at the sight of this resumed "New Immigration," once again cried that the famed poem at the base of the Statue of Liberty was all too literally true: they claimed that a sickly Europe was indeed vomiting on America "the wretched refuse of its teeming shore."

Congress temporarily plugged the breach with the Emergency Quota Act of 1921. Newcomers from Europe were restricted in any given year to a definite quota, which was set at 3 percent of the people of their nationality who had been living in the United States in 1910. This national-origins system was relatively favorable to the immigrants from southern and eastern Europe, for by 1910 immense numbers of them had already arrived.

This stopgap legislation of 1921 was replaced by the Immigration Act of 1924. Quotas for foreigners were cut from 3 percent to 2 percent. The national-origins base was shifted from the census of 1910 to that of 1890, when comparatively few southern Europeans had arrived.* Great Britain and Northern Ireland, for example, could send 65,721 a year as against 5,802 for Italy. Southern Europeans bitterly denounced the device as unfair and discriminatory—a triumph for the "nativist" belief that blue-eyed and fair-haired northern Europeans were of better blood. The purpose was clearly to freeze America's existing racial composition, which was largely northern European. A flagrantly discrimi-

The Only Way to Handle It

natory section of the Immigration Act of 1924 slammed the door absolutely against Japanese immigrants. Mass "Hate America" rallies erupted in Japan, and one Japanese superpatriot expressed his outrage by committing suicide near the American embassy in Tokyo. Exempt from the quota system were Canadians and Latin Americans, whose proximity made them easy to attract for jobs when times were good and just as easy to send back home when they were not.

The quota system effected a pivotal departure in American policy. It claimed that the nation was filling up and that a "No Vacancy" sign was needed. Immigration henceforth dwindled to a mere trickle. By 1931, probably for the first time in American experience, more foreigners left than arrived. Quotas thus caused America to sacrifice something of its tradition of freedom and opportunity, as well as its future ethnic diversity.

The Immigration Act of 1924 marked the end of an era—a period of virtually unrestricted immigration that in the preceding century had brought some 35 million newcomers to the United States, mostly from Europe. The immigrant tide was now cut off, but it left on American shores by the 1920s a

---

*Five years later the Act of 1929, using 1920 as the quota base, virtually cut immigration in half by limiting the total to 152,574 a year. In 1965 Congress abolished the national-origins quota system.

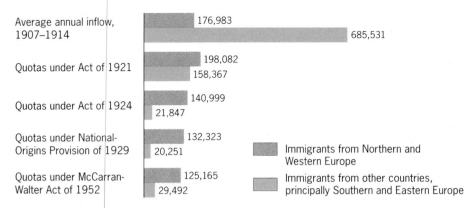

Average annual inflow, 1907–1914	176,983 — 685,531
Quotas under Act of 1921	198,082 — 158,367
Quotas under Act of 1924	140,999 — 21,847
Quotas under National-Origins Provision of 1929	132,323 — 20,251
Quotas under McCarran-Walter Act of 1952	125,165 — 29,492

Immigrants from Northern and Western Europe

Immigrants from other countries, principally Southern and Eastern Europe

Annual Immigration and the Quota Laws   The national-origins quota system was abolished in 1965. Legislation in that year capped the level of immigration at 170,000 per year but made exceptions for children, spouses, and parents of persons already arrived. It also restricted immigration from any single country to 20,000 people per year. The immigration laws were again significantly revised in 1986 (see p. 930 and p. 1023).

patchwork of ethnic communities separated from each other and from the larger society by language, religion, and customs. Many of the most recent arrivals, including the Italians, Jews, and Poles, lived in isolated enclaves with their own houses of worship, newspapers, and theaters (see Makers of America: The Poles, pp. 734–735). Efforts to organize labor unions repeatedly foundered on the rocks of ethnic differences. Immigrant workers on the same shop floor might share a common interest in wages and working conditions, but they often had no common language with which to forge common cause; indeed cynical employers often played upon ethnic rivalries to keep their workers divided and powerless. Ethnic variety thus undermined class and political solidarity. It was an old American story, but one that some reformers hoped would not go on forever.

The Prohibition "Experiment"

One of the last peculiar spasms of the progressive reform movement was prohibition, loudly supported by crusading churches and by many women. The arid new order was authorized in 1919 by the Eighteenth Amendment (see the Appendix), as implemented by the Volstead Act passed by Congress later that year. Together these laws made the world "safe for hypocrisy."

The legal abolition of alcohol was especially popular in the South and West. Southern whites were eager to keep stimulants out of the hands of blacks, lest they burst out of "their place." In the West prohibition represented an attack on all the vices associated with the ubiquitous western saloon: public drunkenness, prostitution, corruption, and crime. But despite the overwhelming ratification of the "dry" amendment, strong opposition persisted in the larger eastern cities. For many "wet" foreign-born people, Old World styles of sociability were built around drinking in beer gardens and cor-

Automaker Henry Ford (1863–1947), an ardent prohibitionist, posted this notice in his Detroit factory in 1922:

"From now on it will cost a man his job . . . to have the odor of beer, wine or liquor on his breath, or to have any of these intoxicants on his person or in his home. The Eighteenth Amendment is a part of the fundamental laws of this country. It was meant to be enforced. Politics has interfered with the enforcement of this law, but so far as our organization is concerned, it is going to be enforced to the letter."

ner taverns. Yet most Americans now assumed that prohibition had come to stay. Everywhere carousers indulged in last wild flings, as the nation prepared to enter upon a permanent "alcoholiday."

But prohibitionists were naive in the extreme. They overlooked the tenacious American tradition of strong drink and of weak control by the central government, especially over private lives. They forgot that the federal authorities had never satisfactorily enforced a law where the majority of the people—or a strong minority—were hostile to it. They ignored the fact that one cannot make a crime overnight out of something that millions of people have never regarded as a crime. Lawmakers could not legislate away a thirst.

Peculiar conditions hampered the enforcement of prohibition. Profound disillusionment over the aftermath of the war raised serious questions as to the wisdom of further self-denial. Slaking thirst became a cherished personal liberty, and many ardent wets believed that the way to bring about repeal was to violate the law on a large enough scale. Hypocritical, hip-flasked legislators spoke or voted dry while privately drinking wet. ("Let us strike a blow for liberty" was an ironic toast.) Frustrated soldiers, returning from France, complained that prohibition had been "put over" on them while they were "over there." Grimy workers bemoaned

the loss of their cheap beer, while pointing out that the idle rich could buy all the illicit alcohol they wanted. Flaming youth of the jazz age thought it "smart" to swill bootleg liquor—"liquid tonsillectomies." Millions of older citizens likewise found forbidden fruit fascinating, as they engaged in "bar hunts."

Prohibition might have started off on a better foot if there had been a larger army of enforcement officials. But the state and federal agencies were understaffed, and their snoopers, susceptible to bribery, were underpaid. The public was increasingly distressed as scores of people, including innocent bystanders, were killed by quick-triggered dry agents.

Prohibition simply did not prohibit. The old-time "men only" corner saloons were replaced by thousands of "speakeasies," each with its tiny grilled window through which the thirsty spoke softly before the barred door was opened. Hard liquor, especially the cocktail, was drunk in staggering volume by both men and women. Largely because of

Texas Guinan, Queen of the Nightclubs, in One of the "Speakeasies" That She Operated in New York City During Prohibition

Federal Agents Destroy Booze in Brooklyn

The Poles

The Poles were among the largest immigrant groups to respond to industrializing America's call for badly needed labor after the Civil War. Between 1870 and World War I, some 2 million Polish-speaking peasants boarded steamships bound for the United States. By the 1920s, when antiforeign feeling led to restrictive legislation that choked the immigrant stream to a trickle, Polish immigrants and their American-born children began to develop new identities as Polish-Americans.

The first Poles to arrive in the New World had landed in Jamestown in 1608 and helped to develop that colony's timber industry. Over the ensuing two and a half centuries, scattered religious dissenters and revolutionary nationalists also made their way from Poland to America. During the Revolution about one hundred Poles, including two officers recruited by Benjamin Franklin, served in the Continental Army.

But the Polish hopefuls who poured into the United States in the late nineteenth century came primarily to stave off starvation and to earn money to buy land. Known in their homeland as *za chlebem* ("for bread") emigrants, they belonged to the mass of central and eastern European peasants who had been forced off their farms by growing competition from the large-scale, mechanized agriculture of western Europe and the United States. An exceptionally high birthrate among the Catholic Poles compounded this economic pressure, creating an army of the land-poor and landless, who left their homes seasonally or permanently in search of work. In 1891 farmworkers and unskilled laborers in the United States earned about $1 a day, more than eight times as much as agricultural workers in the Polish province of Galicia. Such a magnet was irresistible.

These Polish-speaking newcomers emigrated not from a unified nation, but from a weakened country that had been partitioned in the eighteenth century by three great European powers: Prussia (later Germany), Austria-Hungary, and Russia. The Prussian Poles, driven from their homeland in part by the anti-Catholic policies that the German imperial government pursued in the 1870s, arrived in America first. Fleeing religious persecution as well as economic turmoil, many of these early immigrants came to the United States intending to stay. By contrast, most of those who came later from Austrian and Russian Poland simply hoped to earn enough American dollars to return home and buy land.

Some of the Polish peasants learned of America from propaganda spread throughout Europe by agents for U.S. railroad and steamship lines. But many more were lured by glowing letters from friends and relatives already living in the United States. The first wave of Polish immigrants had established a thriving network of self-help and fraternal associations organized around Polish Catholic parishes. Often Polish-American entrepreneurs helped their European compatriots make travel arrangements or find jobs in the United States. One of the most successful of these, the energetic Chicago grocer Anton Schermann, is credited with "bringing over" 100,000 Poles and causing the Windy City to earn the nickname the "American Warsaw."

Most of the Poles arriving in the United States in the late nineteenth century headed for booming industrial cities such as Buffalo, Pittsburgh, Detroit, Milwaukee, and Chicago. In 1907 four-fifths of the men toiled as unskilled laborers in coal mines, meatpacking factories, textile and steel mills, oil refineries, and garment-making shops. Although married women usually stayed home and contributed to the family's earnings by taking in laundry and boarders, children and single girls often joined their fathers and brothers on the job.

By putting the whole family to work, America's Polish immigrants saved tidy sums. By 1901 about one-third of all Poles in the United States owned real estate, and they sent so much money to relatives in Austria and Russia that American and European authorities fretted about the consequences: in 1907 a nativist U.S. immigration commission groused that the huge outflow of funds to eastern Europe was weakening the U.S. economy.

When an independent Poland was created after World War I, few Poles chose to return to their Old World homeland. Instead, like other immigrant groups in the 1920s, they redoubled their efforts to integrate into American society. Polish institutions like churches and fraternal organizations, which had served to perpetuate a distinctive Polish culture in the New World, now facilitated the transformation of Poles into Polish-Americans. When Poland was absorbed into the communist bloc after World War II, Polish-Americans clung still more tightly to their American identity, pushing for landmarks like Chicago's Pulaski Road to memorialize their culture in the New World.

Polish Coal Miners, c. 1905   It was common practice in American mines to segregate mining crews by ethnicity and race.

Solidarity Still, 1984   Even after generations of removal from their mother country, many Polish-Americans took a keen interest in the fate of their ancestral land, as shown by this pro-Solidarity banner at a Polish festival in Chicago.

the difficulties of transporting and concealing bottles, beverages of high alcoholic content were popular. Foreign rumrunners, often from the West Indies, had their inning, and countless cases of liquor leaked down from Canada. The zeal of American prohibition agents on occasion strained diplomatic relations with Uncle Sam's northern neighbor.

"Home brew" and "bathtub gin" became popular, as law-evading adults engaged in "alky cooking" with toy stills. The worst of the homemade "rotgut" produced blindness, even death. The affable bootlegger worked in silent partnership with the friendly undertaker.

Yet the "noble experiment" was not entirely a failure. Bank savings increased, and absenteeism in industry decreased, presumably because of the newly sober ways of formerly soused barflies. On the whole, probably less alcohol was consumed than in the days before prohibition, though strong drink continued to be available. As the legendary tippler remarked, prohibition was "a darn sight better than no liquor at all."

The Golden Age of Gangsterism

Prohibition spawned shocking crimes. The lush profits of illegal alcohol led to bribery of the police, many of whom were induced to see and smell no evil. Violent wars broke out in the big cities between rival gangs—often rooted in immigrant neighborhoods—who sought to corner the rich market in booze. Rival triggermen used their sawed-off shotguns and chattering "typewriters" (machine guns) to "erase" bootlegging competitors who were trying to "muscle in" on their "racket." In the gang wars of the 1920s in Chicago, about five hundred mobsters were murdered. Arrests were few and convictions were even fewer, as the button-lipped gangsters covered for one another with the underworld's code of silence.

Chicago was by far the most spectacular example of lawlessness. In 1925 "Scarface" Al Capone, a grasping and murderous booze distributor, began six years of gang warfare that netted him millions of blood-spattered dollars. He zoomed through the streets in an armor-plated car with bulletproof windows. A Brooklyn newspaper quipped,

Gangster Al Capone Fishing in Florida Capone may have looked like any Chicago businessman on vacation, but his business was bigger and nastier than most, as he often eliminated his competition by murder. He was reported as saying "Everybody calls me a racketeer. I call myself a businessman. When I sell liquor, it's bootlegging. When my patrons serve it on a silver tray on Lake Shore Drive, it's hospitality." He was finally jailed in 1932 for falsifying his income tax returns.

And the pistols' red glare,
Bombs bursting in air
Give proof through the night
That Chicago's still there.

Capone, though branded "Public Enemy Number One," could not be convicted of the cold-blooded massacre, on St. Valentine's Day in 1929, of seven disarmed members of a rival gang. But after serving most of an eleven-year sentence in a federal penitentiary for income-tax evasion, he was released as a syphilitic wreck.

Gangsters rapidly moved into other profitable and illicit activities: prostitution, gambling, and narcotics. Honest merchants were forced to pay "protection money" to the organized thugs; otherwise their windows would be smashed, their trucks overturned, or their employees or themselves beaten up. Racketeers even invaded the ranks of local labor unions as organizers and promoters. Organized crime had come to be one of the nation's most gigantic businesses. By 1930 the annual "take" of the underworld was estimated to be from $12 billion to $18 billion—several times the income of the Washington government.

Criminal callousness sank to new depths in 1932 with the kidnapping for ransom, and eventual murder, of the infant son of aviator-hero Charles A. Lindbergh. The entire nation was inexpressibly shocked and saddened, causing Congress in 1932 to pass the so-called Lindbergh Law, making interstate abduction in certain circumstances a death-penalty offense.

Monkey Business in Tennessee

Education in the 1920s continued to make giant bootstrides. More and more states were requiring young people to remain in school until age sixteen or eighteen, or until graduation from high school. The proportion of seventeen-year-olds who finished high school almost doubled in the 1920s, to more than one in four.

The most revolutionary contribution to educational theory during these yeasty years was made by mild-mannered Professor John Dewey, who served on the faculty of Columbia University from 1904 to 1930. By common consent one of America's few front-rank philosophers, he set forth the principles of "learning by doing" that formed the foundation of so-called progressive education, with its greater "permissiveness." He believed that the workbench was as essential as the blackboard, and that "education for life" should be a primary goal of the teacher.

Science also scored wondrous advances in these years. A massive public-health program, launched by the Rockefeller Foundation in the South in 1909, had virtually wiped out the ancient affliction of hookworm by the 1920s. Better nutrition and health care helped to increase the life expectancy of a newborn infant from fifty years in 1901 to fifty-nine years in 1929.

Yet both science and progressive education in the 1920s were subjected to unfriendly fire from the Fundamentalists. These old-time religionists charged that the teaching of Darwinian evolution

Hiram Wesley Evans (1881–1966), imperial wizard of the Ku Klux Klan, in 1926 poignantly described the cultural grievances that fueled the Klan and lay behind much of the Fundamentalist revolt against "Modernism":

"Nordic Americans for the last generation have found themselves increasingly uncomfortable and finally deeply distressed. . . . One by one all our traditional moral standards went by the boards, or were so disregarded that they ceased to be binding. The sacredness of our Sabbath, of our homes, of chastity, and finally even of our right to teach our own children in our own schools fundamental facts and truths were torn away from us. Those who maintained the old standards did so only in the face of constant ridicule. . . . We found our great cities and the control of much of our industry and commerce taken over by strangers. . . . We are a movement of the plain people, very weak in the matter of culture, intellectual support, and trained leadership. . . . This is undoubtedly a weakness. It lays us open to the charge of being 'hicks' and 'rubes' and 'drivers of second-hand Fords.'"

was destroying faith in God and the Bible, while contributing to the moral breakdown of youth in the jazz age. Numerous attempts were made to secure laws prohibiting the teaching of evolution, "the bestial hypothesis," in the public schools, and three southern states adopted such shackling measures. The trio of states included Tennessee, in the heart of

The bombastic Fundamentalist evangelist W. A. (Billy) Sunday (1862–1935) declared in 1925,

"If a minister believes and teaches evolution, he is a stinking skunk, a hypocrite, and a liar."

The Fundamentalist Outcry, 1925   Radicalism and science are both condemned as blasphemers.

the so-called Bible Belt South, where the spirit of evangelical religion was still robust.

The stage was set for the memorable "Monkey Trial" at the hamlet of Dayton, eastern Tennessee, in 1925. A likable high-school biology teacher, John T. Scopes, was indicted for teaching evolution. Batteries of newspaper reporters, armed with notebooks and cameras, descended upon the quiet town to witness the spectacle. Scopes was defended by nationally known attorneys, while former presidential candidate William Jennings Bryan, an ardent Presbyterian Fundamentalist, joined the prosecution. Taking the stand as an expert on the Bible, Bryan was made to appear foolish by the famed criminal lawyer Clarence Darrow. Five days after the trial was over, Bryan died of a stroke, no doubt brought on by the wilting heat and witness-stand strain.

This historic clash between theology and biology proved inconclusive. Scopes, the forgotten man of the drama, was found guilty and fined $100. But the supreme court of Tennessee, while upholding

the law, set aside the fine on a technicality.* The Fundamentalists at best won only a hollow victory, for the absurdities of the trial cast ridicule on their cause. Yet even though increasing numbers of Christians were coming to reconcile the revelations of religion with the findings of modern science, Fundamentalism, with its emphasis on literal reading of the Bible, remained a vibrant force in American spiritual life. It was especially strong in the Baptist Church and in the rapidly growing Churches of Christ, organized in 1906.

The Mass-Consumption Economy

Prosperity—real, sustained, and widely shared—put much of the "roar" into the twenties. The economy kicked off its war harness in 1919, faltered a few steps in the recession of 1920–1921, and then sprinted forward for nearly seven years. Both the recent war and Treasury Secretary Andrew Mellon's tax policies favored the rapid expansion of capital investment. Ingenious machines, powered by relatively cheap energy from newly tapped oil fields, dramatically increased the productivity of the laborer. Assembly-line production reached such perfection in Henry Ford's famed Rouge River plant near Detroit that a finished automobile emerged every ten seconds.

Great new industries suddenly sprouted forth. Supplying electrical power for the humming new machines became a giant business in the 1920s. Above all, the automobile, once the horseless chariot of the rich, now became the carriage of the common citizen. By 1930 Americans owned almost 30 million cars.

The nation's deepening "love affair" with the automobile headlined a momentous shift in the character of the economy. American manufacturers seemed to have mastered the problems of production; their worries now focused on consumption. Could they find the mass markets for the goods they had contrived to spew forth in such profusion?

Responding to this need, a new arm of American commerce came into being: advertising. By persuasion and ploy, seduction and sexual suggestion, advertisers sought to make Americans chronically

---

*The Tennessee law was not formally repealed until 1967.

discontented with their paltry possessions and want more, more, more. A founder of this new "profession" was Bruce Barton, prominent New York partner in a Madison Avenue firm. In 1925 Barton published a best-seller, *The Man Nobody Knows*, setting forth the provocative thesis that Jesus Christ was the greatest adman of all time. "Every advertising man ought to study the parables of Jesus," Barton preached. "They are marvelously condensed, as all good advertising should be." Barton even had a good word to say for Christ's executive ability: "He picked up twelve men from the bottom ranks of business and forged them into an organization that conquered the world."

Sports became big business in the consumer economy of the 1920s. Ballyhooed by the "image makers," home-run heroes like George H. ("Babe") Ruth were far better known than most statesmen. The fans bought tickets in such numbers that Babe's hometown park, Yankee Stadium, became known as "the house that Ruth built." In 1921 the slugging heavyweight champion, Jack Dempsey, knocked out the dapper French light heavyweight, Georges Carpentier. The Jersey City crowd in attendance had paid more than a million dollars—the first in a series of million-dollar "gates" in the golden 1920s.

Buying on credit was another innovative feature of the postwar economy. "Possess today and pay tomorrow" was the message directed at buyers. Once-frugal descendants of Puritans went ever deeper into debt to own all kinds of newfangled marvels—refrigerators, vacuum cleaners, and especially cars and radios—now. Prosperity thus accumulated an overhanging cloud of debt, and the economy became increasingly vulnerable to disruptions of the credit structure.

Putting America on Rubber Tires

A new industrial revolution slipped into high gear in America in the 1920s. Thrusting out steel tentacles, it changed the daily life of the people in unprecedented ways. Machinery was the new messiah—and the automobile was its principal prophet.

Of all the inventions of the era, the automobile cut the deepest mark. It heralded an amazing new industrial system based on assembly-line methods and mass-production techniques.

Americans adapted rather than invented the gasoline engine; Europeans can claim the original honor. By the 1890s a few daring American inventors and promoters, including Henry Ford and Ransom E. Olds (Oldsmobile), were developing the infant automotive industry. By 1910 sixty-nine car companies rolled out a total annual production of 181,000 units. The early contraptions were neither speedy nor reliable. Many a stalled motorist, profanely cranking a balky automobile, had to endure the jeer "Get a horse" from the occupants of a passing dobbin-drawn carriage.

An enormous industry sprang into being, as Detroit became the motorcar capital of America. The mechanized colossus owed much to the stopwatch efficiency techniques of Frederick W. Taylor, a prominent inventor, engineer, and tennis player, who sought to eliminate wasted motion. His epitaph reads "Father of Scientific Management."

Best known of the new crop of industrial wizards was Henry Ford, who more than any other individual

Babe Ruth: The "Sultan of Swat"

Henry Ford in His First Car, Built in 1896 He has been called the "Father of the Traffic Jam."

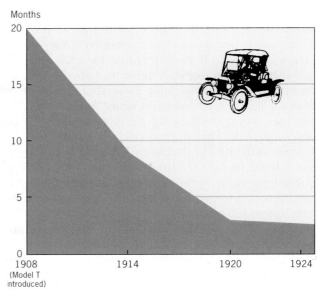

The Cost of a Model T Ford, 1908–1924
Henry Ford's mass-production techniques cut the costs of production dramatically and put the automobile within reach of the workingperson's purse. (Cost is shown in months of labor for an employee at the average national wage.)

put America on rubber tires. His high and hideous Model T ("Tin Lizzie") was cheap, rugged, and reasonably reliable, though rough and clattering. The parts of Ford's "flivver" were highly standardized, but the behavior of this rattling good car was so eccentric that it became the butt of numberless jokes.

Lean and silent Henry Ford, who was said to have wheels in his head, erected an immense personal empire on the cornerstone of his mechanical genius, though his associates provided much of the organizational talent. Ill educated, this multimillion-aire mechanic was socially and culturally narrow; "History is bunk," he once testified. But he dedicated himself with one-track devotion to the gospel of standardization. After two early failures, he grasped and applied fully the techniques of assembly-line production—"Fordism." He is supposed to have remarked that the purchaser could have his automo-

bile any color he desired—just as long as it was black. So economical were his methods that in the mid-1920s he was selling the Ford roadster for $260—well within the purse of a thrifty worker.

The flood of Fords was phenomenal. In 1914 the "Automobile Wizard" turned out his 500,000th Model T. By 1930 his total had risen to 20 million, or, on a bumper-to-bumper basis, more than enough to encircle the globe. A national newspaper and magazine poll conducted in 1923 revealed Ford to be the people's choice for the presidential nomination in 1924.

By 1929, when the great bull market collapsed, 26 million motor vehicles were registered in the United States. This figure, averaging 1 for every 4.9 Americans, represented far more automobiles than existed in all the rest of the world.

The Advent of the Gasoline Age

The impact of the self-propelled carriage on various aspects of American life was tremendous. A gigantic new industry emerged, dependent on steel but dis-

Gas Station, 1923 Gas stations like this one began to appear about 1913. Before that the nation's handful of automobile owners bought fuel from their local oil companies and stored it in tanks in their own yards.

placing steel from its kingpin role. Employing directly or indirectly about 6 million people by 1930, it was a major wellspring of the nation's prosperity. Thousands of new jobs, moreover, were created by supporting industries. The lengthening list would include rubber, glass, and fabrics, to say nothing of highway construction and thousands of service stations and garages. America's standard of living, responding to this infectious vitality, rose to an enviable level.

New industries boomed lustily; older ones grew sickly. The petroleum business experienced an

A lifelong resident of Muncie, Indiana, disguised as "Middletown" in Robert and Helen Lynd's exhaustive investigation of American life in a typical medium-size community during the 1920s, pooh-poohed their scientific sociological methods:

"Why on earth do you need to study what's changing this country? I can tell you what's happening in just four letters: A-U-T-O!"

explosive development. Hundreds of oil derricks shot up in California, Texas, and Oklahoma, as these states expanded wondrously and the wilderness frontier became an industrial frontier. The once-feared railroad octopus, on the other hand, was hard hit by the competition of passenger cars, buses, and trucks. An age-old story was repeated: one industry's gains were another industry's pains.

Other effects were widely felt. Speedy marketing of perishable foodstuffs, such as fresh fruits, was accelerated. A new prosperity enriched outlying farms, as city dwellers were provided with produce at attractive prices. Countless new roads ribboned out to meet the demand of the American motorist for smoother and faster highways, often paid for by taxes on gasoline. The era of mud ended as the nation made haste to construct the finest network of hard-surfaced roadways in the world. Lured by sophisicated advertising, and encouraged by tempting installment-plan buying, countless Americans with shallow purses acquired the habit of riding as they paid.

Zooming motorcars were agents of social change. At first a luxury, they rapidly became a necessity. Essentially devices for needed transportation, they soon developed into a badge of freedom and equality—a necessary prop for self-respect. To some, ostentation seemed more important than

The Ford Model A: New Wheels for the Masses   In 1927 Ford Motor Company ceased making its classic Model T, the first of its mass-produced automobiles. After shutting down its entire production line for several months in order to retool, Ford eventually unveiled its new product, the Model A, in 1928.

transportation. Leisure hours could now be spent more pleasurably, as tens of thousands of cooped-up souls responded to the call of the open road on joyriding vacations. Women were further freed from clinging-vine dependence on men. Isolation among the sections was broken down, and the less attractive states lost population at an alarming rate. By the late 1920s, Americans owned more automobiles than bathtubs. "I can't go to town in a bathtub," one homemaker explained.

Other social by-products of the automobile were visible. Autobuses made possible the consolidation of schools and to some extent of churches. The sprawling suburbs spread out still farther from the urban core, as America became a nation of commuters.

The demon machine, on the other hand, exacted a terrible toll by catering to the American mania for speed. Citizens were becoming statistics. Not counting the hundreds of thousands of injured and crippled, the one millionth American had died in a motor vehicle accident by 1951—more than all those killed on all the battlefields of all the nation's wars to that date. "The public be rammed" seemed to be the motto of the new age.

Virtuous home life partially broke down as joyriders of all ages forsook the parlor for the highway. The morals of flaming youth sagged correspondingly—at least in the judgment of their elders. What might young people get up to in the privacy of a closed-top Model T? An Indiana juvenile court judge voiced parents' worst fears when he condemned the automobile as "a house of prostitution on wheels." Even the celebrated crime waves of the 1920s and 1930s were aided and abetted by the motorcar, for gangsters could now make quick getaways.

Yet no sane American would plead for a return of the old horse and buggy, complete with fly-breeding manure. The automobile contributed notably to improved air and environmental quality, despite its later notoriety as a polluter. Life might be cut short on the highways, and smog might poison the air, but the automobile brought more convenience, pleasure, and excitement into more people's lives than almost any other single invention.

Humans Develop Wings

Gasoline engines also provided the power that enabled humans to fulfill the age-old dream of sprouting wings. After near-successful experiments by others with heavier-than-air craft, the Wright brothers, Orville and Wilbur, performed "the miracle at Kitty Hawk," North Carolina. On a historic day—December 17, 1903—Orville Wright took aloft a feebly engined plane that stayed airborne for 12 seconds and 120 feet. Thus the air age was launched by two obscure bicycle repairmen.

As aviation gradually got off the ground, the world slowly shrank. The public was made increas-

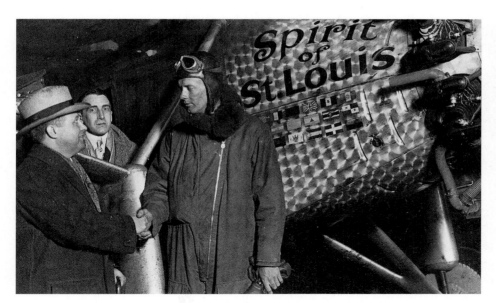

"Lucky Lindy" Charles A. Lindbergh (1902–1974), the first person to fly solo across the Atlantic, became a roving ambassador of goodwill for the United States after his historic 1927 flight, as the flags on his airplane attest. On a trip to Latin America in 1928, he met his future wife, Anne Morrow, daughter of the U.S. ambassador to Mexico.

ingly air-minded by unsung heroes—often martyrs—who appeared as stunt fliers at fairs and other public gatherings. Airplanes—"flying coffins"—were used with marked success for various purposes during the Great War of 1914–1918. Shortly thereafter private companies began to operate passenger lines with airmail contracts, which were in effect a subsidy from Washington. The first transcontinental airmail route was established from New York to San Francisco in 1920.

In 1927 modest and skillful Charles A. Lindbergh, the so-called Flyin' Fool, electrified the world by the first solo west-to-east conquest of the Atlantic. Seeking a prize of $25,000, the lanky stunt flier courageously piloted his single-engine plane, the *Spirit of St. Louis,* from New York to Paris in a grueling thirty-three hours and thirty-nine minutes.

Lindbergh's exploit swept Americans off their feet. Fed up with the cynicism and debunking of the jazz age, they found in this wholesome and handsome youth a genuine hero. They clasped the soaring "Lone Eagle" to their hearts much more warmly than the bashful young man desired. "Lucky Lindy" received an uproarious welcome in the "hero canyon" of lower Broadway, as eighteen hundred tons of ticker tape and other improvised confetti showered upon him. Lindbergh's achievement—it was more than a "stunt"—did much to dramatize and popularize flying, while giving a strong boost to the infant aviation industry.

The impact of the airship was tremendous. It provided the restless American spirit with yet another dimension. At the same time, it gave birth to a giant new industry. Unfortunately, the accident rate in the pioneer stages of aviation was high, though hardly more so than on the early railroads. But by the 1930s and 1940s, travel by air on regularly scheduled airlines was significantly safer than on many overcrowded highways.

Humanity's new wings also increased the tempo of an already breathless civilization. The floundering railroad received another setback through the loss of passengers and mail. A lethal new weapon was given to the gods of war, and with the coming of city-busting aerial bombs, people could well debate whether the conquest of the air was a blessing or a curse. The Atlantic Ocean was shriveling to about the size of the Aegean Sea in the days of Socrates, while isolation behind ocean moats was becoming a bygone dream.

The Radio Revolution

The speed of the airplane was far eclipsed by the speed of radio waves. Guglielmo Marconi, an Italian, invented wireless telegraphy in the 1890s, and his brainchild was used for long-range communication during World War I.

Family "Listening In" to the Radio, 1922   The Lacambanne family of San Francisco gathered in their parlor to listen to a concert broadcast over the radio. In the early years when only a handful of households could afford a radio, listening brought family and neighbors together to share a common experience.

Next came the voice-carrying radio, a triumph of many minds. A red-letter day was posted in November 1920, when the Pittsburgh radio station KDKA broadcast the news of the Harding landslide. Later miracles were achieved in transatlantic wireless phonographs, radiotelephones, and television. The earliest radio programs reached only local audiences. But by the late 1920s, technological improvements made long-distance broadcasting possible, and national commercial networks drowned out much local programming. Meanwhile, advertising "commercials" made radio another vehicle for American free enterprise, as contrasted with the government-owned systems of Europe.

Radio came in with a bang in the winter of 1921–1922. A San Francisco newspaper reported a discovery that countless citizens were making:

"There is radio music in the air, every night, everywhere. Anybody can hear it at home on a receiving set, which any boy can put up in an hour."

While other marvels of the era—like the automobile—were luring Americans away from home, the radio was drawing them back. For much of the decade, family and neighbors gathered around a household's sole radio as they once had around the toasty hearth. Radio knitted the nation together. Various regions heard voices with standardized accents, and countless millions "tuned in" to perennial comedy favorites like "Amos 'n' Andy." Programs sponsored by manufacturers and distributors of brand-name products, like the "A&P Gypsies" and the "Eveready Hour," helped to make radio-touted labels household words and purchases.

Educationally and culturally, the radio made a significant contribution. Sports were further stimulated. Politicians had to adjust their speaking techniques to the new medium, and millions rather than thousands of voters heard their promises and pleas. A host of listeners swallowed the gospel of their favorite newscaster or were even ringside participants in world-shaking events. Finally, the music of famous artists and symphony orchestras was beamed into countless homes.

Hollywood's Filmland Fantasies

The flickering movie was the fruit of numerous geniuses, including Thomas A. Edison. As early as the 1890s, this novel contraption, though still in crude form, had attained some popularity in the naughty peep-show penny arcades. The real birth of the movie came in 1903, when the first story sequence reached the screen. This breathless melodrama, *The Great Train Robbery,* was featured in the five-cent theaters, popularly called "nickelodeons." Spectacular among the first full-length classics was D. W. Griffith's *The Birth of a Nation* (1915), which glorified the Ku Klux Klan of Reconstruction days and defamed both blacks and Northern carpetbaggers. White southerners would fire guns at the screen during the attempted "rape" scene.

A fascinating industry was thus launched. Hollywood, in southern California, quickly became the movie capital of the world, for it enjoyed a maximum of sunshine and other advantages. Early producers featured nudity and heavy-lidded female vampires ("vamps"), and an outraged public forced the screen magnates to set up their own rigorous

> *In the face of protests against sex in the movies, the industry appointed a "movie czar," Will H. Hays (1879–1954), who issued the famous "Hays Code" in 1934. As he stated in a speech,*
>
> "This industry must have toward that sacred thing, the mind of a child, toward that clean virgin thing, that unmarked slate, the same responsibility, the same care about the impressions made upon it, that the best clergyman or the most inspired teacher of youth would have."

code of censorship. The motion picture really arrived during the World War of 1914–1918, when it was used as an engine of anti-German propaganda. Specially prepared "hang the kaiser" films aided powerfully in selling war bonds and in boosting morale.

A new era began in 1927 with the success of the first "talkie"—*The Jazz Singer,* starring the white performer Al Jolson in blackface. The age of the "silents" was ushered out as theaters everywhere were "wired for sound." At about the same time, reasonably satisfactory color films were being produced.

Movies eclipsed all other new forms of amusement in the phenomenal growth of their popularity. Movie "stars" of the first pulchritude commanded much larger salaries than the president of the United States, in some cases as much as $100,000 for a single picture. Many actors and actresses were far more widely known than the nation's political leaders.

Critics bemoaned the vulgarization of popular tastes wrought by the new technologies of radio and motion pictures. But the effects of the new mass media were not all negative. The parochialism of insular ethnic communities eroded as the immigrants' children, especially, forsook the neighborhood vaudeville theater for the downtown movie palace or turned away from Grandma's Yiddish storytelling to tune in "Amos 'n' Andy." Much of the rich diversity of the immigrants' Old Country cul-

tures was lost, but the standardization of tastes and of language hastened entry into the American mainstream—and set the stage for the emergence of a working-class political coalition that, for a time, would overcome the divisive ethnic differences of the past.

The Dynamic Decade

Far-reaching changes in lifestyles and values paralleled the dramatic upsurge of the economy. The census of 1920 revealed that for the first time most Americans no longer lived in the countryside but in urban areas. Women continued to find opportunities for employment in the cities, though they tended to cluster in a few low-paying jobs (such as retail clerking and office typing) that became classified as "women's work." An organized birth-control movement, led by fiery feminist Margaret Sanger, openly championed the use of contraceptives. Alice Paul's National Woman's party began in 1923 to campaign for an Equal Rights Amendment to the Constitution. (The campaign was still stalled short of success seven decades later.) To some defenders of traditional ways, it seemed that the world had suddenly gone mad.

Even the churches were affected. The Fundamentalist champions of the old-time religion lost ground to the Modernists, who liked to think that God was a "good guy" and the universe a pretty chummy place.

Some churches tried to fight the Devil with worldly weapons. Competing with joyriding automobiles and golf links, they turned to quality entertainment of their own, including wholesome moving pictures for young people. One uptown house of the Lord in New York advertised on a billboard, "Come to Church: Christian Worship Increases Your Efficiency."

Even before the war, one observer thought the chimes had "struck sex o'clock in America," and the 1920s witnessed what many old-timers regarded as a veritable erotic eruption. Advertisers exploited sexual allure to sell everything from soap to car tires. Once-modest maidens now proclaimed their new freedom as "flappers" in bobbed tresses and dresses. Young women appeared with hemlines elevated, stockings rolled, breasts taped flat, cheeks rouged,

The Flapper New dance styles, like the "Charleston," flamboyantly displayed the new social freedom of the "flapper," whose dress and antics frequently flummoxed the guardians of respectability.

and lips a "crimson gash" that held a dangling cigarette. Thus did the "flapper" symbolize a yearned-for and devil-may-care independence (some said wild abandon) in some American women. Still more

The Guardian of Morality Women's new one-piece bathing suits were a sensation in the 1920s. Here a check is carefully made to ensure that not too much leg is showing.

adventuresome females shocked their elders when they sported the new one-piece bathing suits.

Justification for this new sexual frankness could be found in the recently translated writings of Dr. Sigmund Freud. This Viennese physician appeared to argue that sexual repression was responsible for a variety of nervous and emotional ills. Thus not pleasure alone, but health, demanded sexual gratification and liberation.

Many taboos flew out the window as sex-conscious Americans let themselves go. As unknowing Freudians, teenagers pioneered the sexual frontiers. Glued together in rhythmic embrace, they danced to jazz music squeaking from phonographs. In an earlier day a kiss had been the equivalent of a proposal of marriage. But in the new era, exploratory young folk sat in darkened movie houses or took to the highways and byways in automobiles. There the youthful "neckers" and "petters" poached upon the forbidden territory of each other's bodies.

If the flapper was the goddess of the "era of wonderful nonsense," jazz was its sacred music. With its virtuoso wanderings and tricky syncopation, jazz moved up from New Orleans along with the migrating blacks during World War I. Tunes like W. C. Handy's "St. Louis Blues" became instant classics, as the wailing saxophone became the trumpet of the new era. Blacks such as Handy, "Jelly Roll" Morton, and Joseph ("Joe") King Oliver gave

EXAMINING THE EVIDENCE

The Jazz Singer, 1927   *The Jazz Singer* was the first feature-length "talkie," a motion picture in which the characters actually speak, and its arrival spelled the end for "silent" films, where the audience read subtitles with live or recorded music as background. Although moviegoers flocked to *The Jazz Singer* to hear recorded sound, when they got there they found a movie concerned with themes of great interest to the urban, first- or second-generation immigrant audiences who were Hollywood's major patrons. *The Jazz Singer* told the story of a poor, assimilating Jewish immigrant torn between following his father's wish that he train as an Orthodox cantor and his own ambition to make a success for himself as a jazz singer, performing in the popular blackface style. The movie's star, Al Jolson, was himself an immigrant Jew who had made his name as a blackface performer. White actors had gradually taken over the southern black minstrel show during the nineteenth century. By the early twentieth century, Jewish entertainers had entirely monopolized these roles. Jolson, like other Jewish blackface performers, used his ability to impersonate a black person to force his acceptance into mainstream white American society. This use of blackface seems ironic since black Americans in the 1920s were struggling with their own real-life battles against Jim Crow–era segregation, a blatant form of exclusion from American society. Besides the novelty of being a "talkie," what may have made *The Jazz Singer* a box office hit in 1927? How might different types of viewers in the audience have responded to the story? What does the popularity of blackface reveal about racial attitudes at the time?

King Oliver's Creole Jazz Band, Early 1920s   Joseph ("Joe") King Oliver arrived in Chicago from New Orleans in 1918. His band became the first important black jazz ensemble and made Chicago's Royal Garden Café a magnet for jazz lovers. Left to right: Honoré Dutrey, trombone; Baby Dodds, drums; King Oliver, cornet; Lil Hardin, piano; Bill Johnson, banjo; and Johnny Dodds, clarinet. Kneeling in the foreground is the young Louis Armstrong.

birth to jazz, but the entertainment industry soon spawned all-white bands—notably Paul Whiteman's. Caucasian impresarios cornered the profits, though not the creative soul, of America's most native music.

A new racial pride also blossomed in the northern black communities that burgeoned during and after the war. Harlem in New York City, counting some 100,000 African-American residents in the 1920s, was one of the largest black communities in the world. Harlem sustained a vibrant, creative culture that nourished poets like Langston Hughes, whose first volume of verses, *The Weary Blues*, appeared in 1926. Harlem in the 1920s also spawned a charismatic political leader, Marcus Garvey. The Jamaican-born Garvey founded the United Negro Improvement Association (UNIA) to promote the resettlement of American blacks in their own "African homeland." Within the United States, the UNIA sponsored stores and other businesses, like the Black Star Line Steamship Company, to keep blacks' dollars in black pockets. Most of Garvey's enterprises failed financially, and Garvey himself was convicted in 1927 for alleged mail fraud and deported by a nervous U.S. government. But the race pride that Garvey inspired among the 4 million blacks who counted themselves UNIA followers at the movement's height helped these newcomers to northern cities gain self-confidence and self-reliance. And his example proved important to the later founding of the Nation of Islam (Black Muslim) movement.

Langston Hughes (1902–1967)   Raised in the Midwest, Hughes arrived in New York City in 1921 to attend Columbia University. He spent most of his life in Harlem, making it so much the center of his prolific and versatile literary career that he was often introduced as "the Poet Laureate of Harlem."

Cultural Liberation

Likewise in literature, an older era seemed to have ground to a halt with the recent war. By the dawn of the 1920s, most of the custodians of an aging genteel culture had died—Henry James in 1916, Henry Adams in 1918, and William Dean Howells (the "Dean of American literature") in 1920. A few novelists who had been popular in the previous decades continued to thrive, notably the well-to-do, cosmopolitan New Yorker Edith Wharton and the Virginia-born Willa Cather, esteemed for her stark but sympathetic portrayals of pioneering on the prairies.

But in the decade after the war, a new generation of writers burst upon the scene. Many of them hailed from ethnic and regional backgrounds different from that of the Protestant New Englanders who traditionally had dominated American cultural life.

In A Farewell to Arms *(1929), Ernest Hemingway's (1899–1961) hero, Frederic Henry, confesses,*

"I was always embarrassed by the words sacred, glorious, and sacrifice and the expression in vain. . . . There were many words that you could not stand to hear and finally only the names of places had dignity. Certain numbers were the same way and certain dates and these with the names of the places were all you could say and have them mean anything. Abstract words such as glory, honor, courage, or hallow were obscene beside the concrete names of villages, the numbers of roads, the names of rivers, the numbers of regiments, and the dates."

F. Scott Fitzgerald and His Wife, Zelda   They are shown here in the happy, early days of their stormy marriage.

The newcomers exhibited the energy of youth, the ambition of excluded outsiders, and in many cases the smoldering resentment of ideals betrayed. They bestowed on American literature a new vitality, imaginativeness, and artistic quality.

A patron saint of many young authors was H. L. Mencken, the "Bad Boy of Baltimore." Little escaped his acidic wit. In the pages of his green-covered monthly *American Mercury,* he wielded a slashing rapier as much as a pen. He assailed marriage, patriotism, democracy, prohibition, Rotarians, and the middle-class American "booboisie." The South he contemptuously dismissed as "the Sahara of the Bozart" (a bastardization of *beaux arts,* French for the "fine arts"), and he scathingly attacked do-gooders as "Puritans." Puritanism, he jibed, was "the haunting fear that someone, somewhere, might be happy."

The war had jolted many young writers out of their complacency about traditional values and literary standards. With their pens they probed for new codes of morals and understanding, as well as fresh forms of expression. F. Scott Fitzgerald, a handsome Minnesota-born Princetonian then only twenty-four years old, became an overnight celebrity when he published *This Side of Paradise* in 1920. The book became a kind of Bible for the young. It was eagerly devoured by aspiring flappers and their ardent wooers, many of whom affected an air of bewildered abandon toward life. Catching the spirit of the hour (often about 4 A.M.), Fitzgerald found "all gods dead, all wars fought, all faiths in man shaken." He followed this melancholy success with *The Great Gatsby* (1925), a brilliant evocation of the glamour and cruelty of an achievement-oriented society. Theodore Dreiser's masterpiece of 1925 explored much the same theme: *An American Tragedy* dealt with the murder of a pregnant working girl by her socially ambitious young lover.

Ernest Hemingway, who had seen action on the Italian front in 1917, was among the writers most affected by the war. He responded to pernicious propaganda and the overblown appeal to patriotism by devising his own lean, word-sparing but word-perfect style. In *The Sun Also Rises* (1926), he told of disillusioned, spiritually numb American expatriates in Europe. In *A Farewell to Arms* (1929), he crafted one of the finest novels in any language about the war experience. A troubled soul, he finally blew out his brains with a shotgun blast in 1961.

Other writers turned to a caustic probing of American small-town life. Sherwood Anderson dissected various fictional personalities in *Winesburg, Ohio* (1919), finding them all in some way warped by their cramped psychological surroundings. Sinclair Lewis, a hotheaded, heavy-drinking journalist from Sauk Centre, Minnesota, sprang into prominence in 1920 with *Main Street,* the story of one woman's unsuccessful war against provincialism. In *Babbitt* (1922) he affectionately pilloried George F. Babbitt, a prosperous, vulgar, middle-class real estate broker who slavishly conforms to the respectable materialism of his group. The word *Babbittry* was quickly coined to describe his all-too-familiar lifestyle.

William Faulkner, a dark-eyed, pensive Mississippian, penned a bitter war novel, *Soldier's Pay,* in 1926. He then turned his attention to a fictional chronicle of an imaginary, history-rich Deep South county. In powerful books like *The Sound and the Fury* (1929) and *As I Lay Dying* (1930), Faulkner peeled back layers of time and consciousness from the constricted souls of his ingrown southern characters.

Nowhere was innovation in the 1920s more obvious than in poetry. Ezra Pound, a brilliantly erratic Idahoan who deserted America for Europe, rejected what he called "an old bitch civilization, gone in the teeth" and proclaimed his doctrine: "Make It New." Pound strongly influenced the Missouri-born and Harvard-educated T. S. Eliot, who

Langston Hughes (1902–1967) celebrated Harlem's role in energizing a generation of artists and writers in his poem "Esthete in Harlem" (1930):

"Strange,
That in this nigger place
I should meet life face to face;
When, for years, I had been seeking
Life in places gentler-speaking,
Until I came to this vile street
And found Life stepping on my feet!"*

took up residence in England. In "The Waste Land" (1922), Eliot produced one of the most impenetrable but influential poems of the century. Robert Frost, a San Francisco–born poet, wrote hauntingly about his adopted New England. The most daringly innovative of all was e.e. cummings, who relied on unorthodox diction and peculiar typesetting to produce startling poetical effects.

On the stage, Eugene O'Neill, a New York dramatist and Princeton dropout of globe-trotting background, laid bare Freudian notions of sex in plays like *Strange Interlude* (1928). A prodigious playwright, he authored more than a dozen productions in the 1920s and won the Nobel Prize in 1936.

O'Neill arose from New York's Greenwich Village, which before and after the war was a seething cauldron of writers, painters, musicians, actors, and other would-be artists. After the war a black cultural renaissance also took root uptown in Harlem, led by such gifted writers as Claude McKay, Langston Hughes, and Zora Neale Hurston, and by jazz artists like Louis Armstrong and Eubie Blake. In an outpouring of creative expression called the Harlem Renaissance, they proudly exulted in their black culture and argued for a "New Negro" who was a full citizen and a social equal to whites.

Architecture also married itself to the new materialism and functionalism. Long-range city planning was being intelligently projected, and

*From *Collected Poems* by Langston Hughes. Copyright © 1994 by the Estate of Langston Hughes. Reprinted by permission of Alfred A. Knopf, Inc.

architects like Frank Lloyd Wright were advancing the theory that buildings should grow from their sites and not slavishly imitate Greek and Roman importations. The machine age outdid itself in New York City when it thrust upward the cloud-brushing Empire State Building, 102 stories high. Dedicated in 1931, the "Empty State Building" towered partially vacant during the depressed 1930s.

Wall Street's Big Bull Market

Signals abounded that the economic joyride might end in a crash; even in the best years of the 1920s, several hundred banks failed annually. This something-for-nothing craze was well illustrated by real estate speculation, especially the fantastic Florida boom that culminated in 1925. Numerous underwater lots were sold to eager purchasers for preposterous sums. The whole wildcat scheme collapsed when the peninsula was devastated by a West Indian hurricane, which belied advertisements of a "soothing tropical wind."

The stock exchange provided even greater sensations. Speculation ran wild, and an orgy of boom-or-bust trading pushed the market up to dizzy peaks. "Never sell America short" and "Be a bull on America" were favorite catchwords, as Wall Street bulls gored one another and fleeced greedy lambs. The stock market became a veritable gambling den.

As the 1920s lurched forward, everybody seemed to be buying stocks "on margin"—that is, with a small down payment. Barbers, stenographers, and elevator operators cashed in on "hot tips" picked up while on duty. One valet was reported to have parlayed his wages into a quarter of a million dollars. "The cash register crashed the social register," as rags-to-riches Americans reverently worshiped at the altar of the ticker-tape machine. So powerful was the intoxicant of quick profits that few heeded the voices raised in certain quarters to warn that this kind of tinsel prosperity could not last forever.

Little was done by Washington to curb money-mad speculators. In the wartime days of Wilson, the national debt had rocketed from the 1914 figure of $1,188,235,400 to the 1921 peak of $23,976,250,608. Conservative principles of money management pointed to a diversion of surplus funds to reduce this financial burden.

Calvin Coolidge Presides over the "Jazz Age"
His hands-off policies were sweet music to big business.

A businesslike move toward economic sanity was made in 1921, when a Republican Congress created the Bureau of the Budget. The bureau's director was to assist the president in preparing careful estimates of receipts and expenditures for submission to Congress as the annual budget. This new reform, long overdue, was designed in part to prevent haphazardly extravagant appropriations.

The burdensome taxes inherited from the war were especially distasteful to Secretary of the Treasury Mellon, as well as to his fellow millionaires. Their theory was that such high levies forced the rich to invest in tax-exempt securities rather than in the factories that provided prosperous payrolls. The Mellonites also argued, with considerable persuasiveness, that high taxes not only discouraged business but, in so doing, also brought a smaller net return to the Treasury than moderate taxes.

Seeking to succor the "poor" rich people, Mellon helped engineer a series of tax reductions from 1921 to 1926. Congress followed his lead by repealing the excess-profits tax, abolishing the gift tax, and reducing excise taxes, the surtax, the income tax, and estate taxes. In 1921 a wealthy person with an income of $1 million had paid $663,000 in income taxes; in 1926 the same person paid about $200,000. Secretary Mellon's spare-the-rich policies thus shifted much of the tax burden from the wealthy to the middle-income groups.

Mellon, lionized by conservatives as the "greatest secretary of the Treasury since Hamilton," remains a controversial figure. True, he reduced the national debt by $10 billion—from about $26 billion to $16 billion. But foes of the emaciated multimillionaire charged that he should have bitten an even larger chunk out of the debt, especially while the country was pulsating with prosperity. He was also accused of indirectly encouraging the bull market. If he had absorbed more of the national income in taxes, there would have been less money left for frenzied speculation. His refusal to do so typified the single-mindedly probusiness regime that dominated the political scene throughout the postwar decade.

Chronology

1903	Wright brothers fly the first airplane First story-sequence motion picture
1919	Eighteenth Amendment (prohibition) ratified Volstead Act Seattle general strike Anderson publishes *Winesburg, Ohio*
1919-1920	"Red scare"
1920	Radio broadcasting begins Fitzgerald publishes *This Side of Paradise* Lewis publishes *Main Street*
1921	Sacco-Vanzetti trial Emergency Quota Act of 1921 Bureau of the Budget created
1922	Lewis publishes *Babbitt* Eliot publishes "The Waste Land"
1923	Equal Rights Amendment (ERA) proposed
1924	Immigration Act of 1924
1925	Scopes trial Florida real estate boom Fitzgerald publishes *The Great Gatsby* Dreiser publishes *An American Tragedy*
1926	Hughes publishes *The Weary Blues* Hemingway publishes *The Sun Also Rises*
1927	Lindbergh flies the Atlantic solo First talking motion pictures Sacco and Vanzetti executed
1929	Faulkner publishes *The Sound and the Fury* Hemingway publishes *A Farewell to Arms*

For further reading, see page A22 of the Appendix. For web resources, go to **http://college.hmco.com**.

33

The Politics of Boom and Bust

⎯ ❦ ⎯

1920–1932

We in America today are nearer to the final triumph over poverty than ever before in the history of any land. We have not yet reached the goal—but . . . we shall soon, with the help of God, be in sight of the day when poverty will be banished from this nation.

HERBERT HOOVER, 1928

Three Republican presidents—Warren G. Harding, Calvin Coolidge, and Herbert Hoover—steered the nation on the roller-coaster ride of the 1920s, a thrilling ascent from the depths of post–World War I recession to breathtaking heights of prosperity, followed by a terrifying crash into the Great Depression. In a retreat from progressive reform, Republicans sought to serve the public good less by direct government action and more through cooperation with big business. Some corrupt officials served themselves as well, exploiting public resources for personal profit. Meanwhile, the United States retreated from its brief internationalist fling during World War I and resumed with a vengeance its traditional foreign policy of military unpreparedness and political isolationism.

The Republican "Old Guard" Returns

Warren G. Harding, inaugurated in 1921, *looked* presidential. With erect figure, broad shoulders, high forehead, bushy eyebrows, and graying hair, he was one of the best-liked men of his generation. An easygoing, warm-handed backslapper, he exuded graciousness and love of people. So kindly was his nature that he would brush off ants rather than crush them.

Yet the charming, smiling exterior concealed a weak, inept interior. With a mediocre mind, Harding quickly found himself beyond his depth in the presidency. "God! What a job!" was his anguished cry on one occasion.

The Harding Scandals
This 1924 cartoon satirizing the misdemeanors of the Harding administration shows the sale of the Capitol, the White House, and even the Washington Monument.

Harding, like Grant, was unable to detect moral halitosis in his evil associates, and he was soon surrounded by his poker-playing, shirt-sleeved cronies of the "Ohio Gang." "A good guy," Harding was "one of the boys." He hated to hurt people's feelings, especially those of his friends, by saying no, and designing political leeches capitalized on this weakness. The difference between George Washington and Warren Harding, ran a current quip, was that while Washington could not tell a lie, Harding could not tell a liar. He "was not a bad man," said one Washington observer. "He was just a slob."

Candidate Harding, who admitted his scanty mental furnishings, had promised to gather about him the "best minds" of the party. Charles Evans Hughes—masterful, imperious, incisive, brilliant—brought to the position of secretary of state a dominating if somewhat conservative leadership. The new secretary of the Treasury was a lean and elderly Pittsburgh aluminum king, Andrew W. Mellon, multimillionaire collector of the paintings that are now displayed in Washington as his gift to the nation. Chubby-faced Herbert Hoover, famed feeder of the Belgians and wartime food administrator, became secretary of commerce. An energetic businessman and engineer, he raised his second-rate cabinet post to first-rate importance, especially in drumming up foreign trade for U.S. manufacturers.

But the "best minds" of the cabinet were largely offset by two of the worst. Senator Albert B. Fall of New Mexico, a scheming anticonservationist, was appointed secretary of the interior. As guardian of the nation's natural resources, he resembled the wolf hired to protect the sheep. Harry M. Daugherty, a small-town lawyer but a big-time crook in the "Ohio Gang," was supposed to prosecute wrongdoers as attorney general.

GOP Reaction at the Throttle

Well intentioned but weak-willed, Harding was a perfect "front" for enterprising industrialists. A McKinley-style old order settled back into place with a heavy thud at war's end, crushing the reform seedlings that had sprouted in the progressive era. A nest-feathering crowd moved into Washington and proceeded to hoodwink Harding, whom many regarded as an "amiable boob."

This new Old Guard hoped to improve on the old business doctrine of laissez-faire. Their plea was not simply for government to keep hands off business, but for government to help guide business along the path to profits. They subtly and effectively achieved their ends by putting the courts and the administrative bureaus into the safekeeping of fellow stand-patters for the duration of the decade.

The Supreme Court was a striking example of this trend. Harding lived less than three years as president, but he appointed four of the nine justices. Several of his choices were or became deep-dyed reactionaries, and they buttressed the dike against popular currents for nearly two decades. Harding's fortunate choice for chief justice was ex-president Taft, who not only performed his duties ably but surprisingly was more liberal than some of his cautious associates.

In the first years of the 1920s, the Supreme Court axed progressive legislation. It killed a federal child-labor law, stripped away many of labor's hard-won gains, and rigidly restricted government intervention in the economy. In the landmark case of *Adkins* v. *Children's Hospital* (1923), the Court reversed its own reasoning in *Muller* v. *Oregon* (see p. 670–672), which had declared women to be deserving of special protection in the workplace, and invalidated a minimum-wage law for women. Its strained ruling was that because women now had the vote (Nineteenth Amendment), they were the legal equals of men and could no longer be protected by special legislation. The contradictory premises of the *Muller* and *Adkins* cases framed a debate over gender differences that would continue for the rest of the century: were women sufficiently different from men that they merited special legal and social treatment, or were they effectively equal in the eyes of the law and therefore undeserving of special protections and preferences? (An analogous debate over *racial* differences haunted affirmative-action policies later in the century.)

Corporations, under Harding, could once more relax and expand. Antitrust laws were often ignored, circumvented, or feebly enforced by friendly prosecutors in the attorney general's office. The Interstate Commerce Commission, to single out one agency, came to be dominated by men who were personally sympathetic to the managers of the railroads. Harding reactionaries might well have boasted, "We care not what laws the Democrats pass as long as we are permitted to administer them."

Big industrialists, striving to reduce the rigors of competition, now had a free hand to set up trade associations. Cement manufacturers, for example,

Justice Oliver Wendell Holmes (1841–1935), wryly dissenting in the Adkins *case, said,*

"It would need more than the Nineteenth Amendment to convince me that there are no differences between men and women, or that legislation cannot take those differences into account."

would use these agencies to agree upon standardization of product, publicity campaigns, and a united front in dealing with the railroads and labor. Although many of these associations ran counter to the spirit of existing antitrust legislation, their formation was encouraged by Secretary Hoover. His sense of engineering efficiency led him to condemn the waste resulting from cutthroat competition, and his commitment to voluntary cooperation led him to urge businesses to regulate themselves rather than be regulated by big government.

The Aftermath of War

Wartime government controls on the economy were swiftly dismantled. The War Industries Board disappeared with almost indecent haste. With its passing, progressive hopes for more government regulation of big business evaporated.

Washington likewise returned the railroads to private management in 1920. Reformers had hoped that wartime government operation of the lines might lead to their permanent nationalization. Instead Congress passed the Esch-Cummins Transportation Act of 1920, which encouraged private consolidation of the railroads and pledged the Interstate Commerce Commission to guarantee their profitability. The new philosophy was not to save the country from the railroads, as in the days of the Populists, but to save the railroads for the country.

The federal government also tried to pull up anchor and get out of the shipping business. The Merchant Marine Act of 1920 authorized the Shipping Board, which controlled about fifteen hundred vessels, to dispose of much of the hastily built wartime fleet at bargain-basement prices. The board operated the remaining vessels without conspicuous success. Under the La Follette Seaman's Act of 1915, American shipping could not thrive in competition with foreigners, who all too often provided their crews with wretched food and starvation wages.

Labor, suddenly deprived of its wartime crutch of friendly government support, limped along badly in the postwar decade. A bloody strike in the steel industry was ruthlessly broken in 1919, partly by exploiting ethnic and racial divisions among the steelworkers and partly by branding the strikers as dangerous "reds." The Railway Labor Board, a successor body to the wartime labor boards, ordered a wage cut of 12 percent in 1922, provoking a two-month strike. It ended when Attorney General Daugherty, who fully shared Harding's big-business bias, clamped on the strikers one of the most sweeping injunctions in American history. Unions wilted in this hostile political environment, and membership shriveled by nearly 30 percent between 1920 and 1930.

Needy veterans were among the few nonbusiness groups to reap lasting gains from the war. Congress in 1921 generously created the Veterans Bureau, authorized to operate hospitals and provide vocational rehabilitation for the disabled.

Veterans quickly organized into pressure groups. The American Legion had been founded in Paris in 1919 by Colonel Theodore Roosevelt, Jr. Legionnaires met periodically to renew old hardships and let off steam in good-natured horseplay. The legion soon became distinguished for its militant patriotism, rock-ribbed conservatism, and zealous antiradicalism.

The legion also became notorious for its aggressive lobbying for veterans' benefits. The chief grievance of the former "doughboys" was monetary—they wanted their "dough." The former servicemen demanded "adjusted compensation" to make up for the wages they had "lost" when they turned in their factory overalls for military uniforms during the Great War.

Critics denounced this demand as a holdup "bonus," but the millions of veterans deployed heavy political artillery. They browbeat Congress into passing a bonus bill in 1922, which Harding promptly vetoed. Re-forming their lines, the repulsed veterans gathered for a final attack. In 1924 Congress again hoisted the white flag and passed the Adjusted Compensation Act. It gave every former soldier a paid-up insurance policy due in twenty years—adding about $3.5 billion to the total cost of the war. Penny-pinching Calvin Coolidge sternly vetoed the measure, but Congress overrode him, leaving the veterans with their loot.

America Seeks Benefits Without Burdens

Making peace with the fallen foe was the most pressing problem left on Harding's doorstep. The United States, having rejected the Treaty of Ver-

"I sympathize deeply with you, Madam, but I cannot associate with you." 1923   President Harding's Secretary of State Charles Evans Hughes broke the news to a desperate, war-tattered Europe that America was going, and staying, home.

sailles, was still technically at war with Germany, Austria, and Hungary nearly three years after the armistice. Peace was finally achieved by lone-wolf tactics. In July 1921 Congress passed a simple joint resolution that declared the war officially ended.

Isolation was enthroned in Washington. The Harding administration, with the Senate "irreconcilables" holding a hatchet over its head, continued to regard the League of Nations as a thing unclean. Harding at first refused even to support the League's world health program. But the new world body was much too important to be completely ignored. "Unofficial observers" were sent to its seat in Geneva, Switzerland, to hang around like detectives shadowing a suspected criminal.

Harding could not completely turn his back on the outside world, especially the Middle East, where a sharp rivalry developed between America and Britain for oil-drilling concessions. Remembering that the Allies had floated to victory on a flood of oil, experts recognized that liquid "black gold" would be as necessary as blood in the battles of tomorrow. Secretary Hughes eventually secured for American

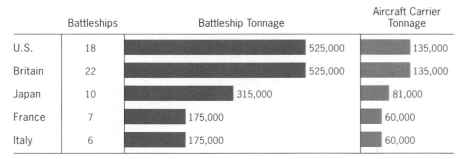

	Battleships	Battleship Tonnage	Aircraft Carrier Tonnage
U.S.	18	525,000	135,000
Britain	22	525,000	135,000
Japan	10	315,000	81,000
France	7	175,000	60,000
Italy	6	175,000	60,000

Limits Imposed by Washington Conference, 1921–1922 The pledge of the British and Americans to refrain from fortifying their Far Eastern possessions, while Japan was allowed to fortify its possessions, was the key to the naval limitation treaty. The United States and Great Britain thus won a temporary victory but later paid a horrendous price when they had to dislodge the well-entrenched Japanese from the Pacific in World War II.

oil companies the right to share in the exploitation of the sandy region's oil riches.

Disarmament was one international issue on which Harding, after much indecision, finally seized the initiative. He was prodded by businesspeople unwilling to dig deeper into their pockets for money to finance the ambitious naval building program started during the war. A deadly contest was shaping up with Britain and Japan, which watched with alarm as the oceans filled with American vessels. Britain still commanded the world's largest navy, but the clatter of American riveters proclaimed that the United States would soon overtake it.

Public agitation in America, fed by these worries, brought about the headline-making Washington "Disarmament" Conference in 1921–1922. Invitations went to all the major naval powers—except Bolshevik Russia, whose government the United States refused officially to recognize. The double agenda included naval disarmament and the situation in the Far East.

At the outset Secretary Hughes startled the delegates, who were expecting the usual diplomatic fence-straddling, with a comprehensive, concrete plan for declaring a ten-year "holiday" on construction of battleships and even for scrapping some of the huge dreadnoughts already built. He proposed that the scaled-down navies of America and Britain should enjoy parity in battleships and aircraft carriers, with Japan on the small end of a 5:5:3 ratio. This arrangement sounded to the sensitive Japanese ambassador like "Rolls-Royce, Rolls-Royce, Ford."

Complex bargaining followed in the wake of Hughes's proposals. The Five-Power Naval Treaty of 1922 embodied Hughes's ideas on ship ratios, but only after face-saving compensation was offered to the insecure Japanese. The British and Americans both conceded that they would refrain from fortifying their Far Eastern possessions, including the Philippines. The Japanese were not subjected to such restraints in their possessions. In addition, a Four-Power Treaty replaced the twenty-year-old Anglo-Japanese alliance. The new pact bound Britain, Japan, France, and the United States to preserve the status quo in the Pacific—another concession to the jumpy Japanese. Finally, the Washington Conference gave chaotic China—"the Sick Man of the Far East"—a shot in the arm with the Nine-Power Treaty of 1922, whose signatories agreed to nail wide open the Open Door in China.

When the final gavel banged, the Hardingites boasted with much fanfare—and some justification—of their globe-shaking achievement in disarmament. But their satisfaction was somewhat illusory. No restrictions had been placed on small warships, and the other powers churned ahead with the construction of cruisers, destroyers, and

As for the burdens of armament, the New York Independent, *a prominent magazine, noted in January 1921,*

"[The country is] more afraid of the tax collector than of any more distant foe."

submarines, while penny-pinching Uncle Sam lagged dangerously behind. Congress also pointedly declared that it was making no commitment to the use of armed force or any kind of joint action when it ratified the Four-Power Treaty. These reservations, in effect, rendered the treaty a dead letter. Ominously, the American people seemed content to rely for their security on words and wishful thinking rather than on weapons and hardheaded realism.

A similar sentimentalism welled up later in the decade, when Americans clamored for the "outlawry of war." The conviction spread that if quarreling nations would only take the pledge to foreswear war as an instrument of national policy, swords could be beaten into plowshares. Calvin Coolidge's secretary of state, Frank B. Kellogg, who later won the Nobel Peace Prize for his role, was lukewarm about the idea. But after petitions bearing more than 2 million signatures cascaded into Washington, he signed with the French foreign minister in 1928 the famed Kellogg-Briand Pact. Officially known as the Pact of Paris, it was ultimately ratified by sixty-two nations.

This new parchment peace was delusory in the extreme. Defensive wars were still permitted, and what scheming aggressor could not cook up an excuse of self-defense? Lacking both muscles and teeth, the pact was a diplomatic derelict—and virtually useless in a showdown. Yet it accurately—and dangerously—reflected the American mind in the 1920s, which was all too willing to be lulled into a false sense of security. This mood took even deeper hold in the ostrichlike neutralism of the 1930s.

Hiking the Tariff Higher

A comparable lack of realism afflicted foreign economic policy in the 1920s. Businesspeople, short-sightedly obsessed with the dazzling prospects in the prosperous home market, sought to keep that market to themselves by flinging up insurmountable tariff walls around the United States. They were spurred into action by their fear of a flood of cheap goods from recovering Europe, especially during the brief but sharp recession of 1920–1921.

In 1922 Congress passed the comprehensive Fordney-McCumber Tariff Law. Glib lobbyists once more descended upon Washington and helped boost schedules from the average of 27 percent under Wilson's Underwood Tariff of 1913 to an average of 38.5 percent, which was almost as high as Taft's Payne-Aldrich Tariff of 1909. (See the Appendix.) Duties on farm produce were increased, and the principle was proclaimed that the general rates were designed to equalize the cost of American and foreign production. A promising degree of flexibility was introduced for the first time, when the president was authorized, with the advice of the fact-finding Tariff Commission, to reduce or increase duties by as much as 50 percent.

Presidents Harding and Coolidge, true to their big-industry sympathies, were far more friendly to tariff increases than to reductions. In six years they authorized thirty-two upward changes, including on their list vital commodities like dairy products, chemicals, and pig iron. During the same period, the White House ordered only five reductions. These included mill feed and such trifling items as bobwhite quail, paintbrush handles, phenol, and cresylic acid.

The high-tariff course thus charted by the Republican regimes set off an ominous chain reaction. European producers felt the squeeze, for the American tariff walls prolonged their postwar chaos. An impoverished Europe needed to sell its manufactured goods to the United States, particularly if it hoped to achieve economic recovery and to pay its huge war debt to Washington. America needed to give foreign nations a chance to make a profit from it so that they could buy its manufactured articles and repay debts. International trade, Americans were slow to learn, is a two-way street. In general, they could not sell to others in quantity unless they bought from them in quantity—or lent them more U.S. dollars.

Erecting tariff walls was a game that two could play. The American example spurred European nations, throughout the feverish 1920s, to pile up higher barriers themselves. These artificial obstacles were doubly bad: they hurt not only American-made goods but the products of European countries as well. The whole vicious circle further deepened the international economic distress, providing one more rung on the ladder by which Adolf Hitler scrambled to power.

The Stench of Scandal

The loose morality and get-rich-quickism of the Harding era manifested themselves spectacularly in a series of scandals.

Early in 1923 Colonel Charles R. Forbes, one-time deserter from the army, was caught with his hand in the till and resigned as head of the Veterans Bureau. An appointee of the gullible Harding, he and his accomplices looted the government to the tune of about $200 million, chiefly in connection with the building of veterans' hospitals. He was sentenced to two years in a federal penitentiary.

Most shocking of all was the Teapot Dome scandal, an affair that involved priceless naval oil reserves at Teapot Dome (Wyoming) and Elk Hills (California). In 1921 the slippery secretary of the interior, Albert B. Fall, induced his careless colleague, the secretary of the navy, to transfer these valuable properties to the Interior Department. Harding indiscreetly signed the secret order. Fall then quietly leased the lands to oilmen Harry F. Sinclair and Edward L. Doheny, but not until he had received a bribe ("loan") of $100,000 from Doheny and about three times that amount in all from Sinclair.

Teapot Dome, no tempest in a teapot, finally came to a whistling boil. Details of the crooked transaction gradually began to leak out in March 1923, two years after Harding took office. Fall, Sinclair, and Doheny were indicted the next year, but the case dragged through the courts until 1929. Finally Fall was found guilty of taking a bribe and was sentenced to one year in jail. By a curious quirk of justice, the two bribe givers were acquitted while the bribe taker was convicted, although Sinclair served several months in jail for having "shadowed" jurors and for refusing to testify before a Senate committee.

The oily smudge from Teapot Dome polluted the prestige of the Washington government. Right-thinking citizens wondered what was going on when public officials could sell out the nation's vital resources, especially those reserved for the U.S. Navy. The acquittal of Sinclair and Doheny undermined faith in the courts, while giving further currency to the cynical sayings, "You can't put a million dollars in jail" and "In America everyone is assumed guilty until proven rich."

Still more scandals erupted. Persistent reports as to the underhanded doings of Attorney General Daugherty prompted a Senate investigation in 1924 of the illegal sale of pardons and liquor permits. Forced to resign, the accused official was tried in 1927 but was released after a jury twice failed to agree. During the trial Daugherty hid behind the trousers of the now-dead Harding by implying that persistent probing might uncover crookedness in the White House.

Harding was mercifully spared the full revelation of these iniquities, though his worst suspicions were aroused. While news of the scandals was beginning to break, he embarked upon a speech-making tour across the country all the way to Alaska. On the return trip, he died in San Francisco, on August 2, 1923, of pneumonia and thrombosis. His death may have been hastened by a broken heart resulting from the disloyalty of designing friends. Mourning millions, not yet fully aware of the graft in Washington, expressed genuine sorrow.

The brutal fact is that Harding was not a strong enough man for the presidency—as he himself privately admitted. Such was his weakness that he tolerated people and conditions that subjected the Republic to its worst disgrace since the days of President Grant.

Washington Officials Trying to Outpace the Teapot Dome Scandal, c. 1922

"Silent Cal" Coolidge

News of Harding's death was sped to Vice President Coolidge, then visiting at his father's New England farmhouse. By the light of two kerosene lamps, the elder Coolidge, a justice of the peace, used the old family Bible to administer the presidential oath to his son.

Farm-Bred Calvin Coolidge Revisits Vermont

This homespun setting was symbolic of Coolidge. Quite unlike Harding, the stern-faced Vermonter, with his thin nose and tightly set lips, embodied the New England virtues of honesty, morality, industry, and frugality. As a youth, his father reported, he seemed to get more sap out of a

Cash Register Chorus   Business croons its appreciation of "Coolidge prosperity."

maple tree than did any of the other boys. Practicing a rigid economy in both money and words, "Silent Cal" came to be known in Washington conversational circles for his brilliant flashes of silence. His dour, serious visage prompted the acid observation that he had been "weaned on a pickle."

Coolidge seemed to be a crystallization of the commonplace. Painfully shy, he was blessed with only mediocre powers of leadership. He would occasionally display a dry wit in private, but his speeches, delivered in a nasal New England twang, were invariably boring. A staunch apostle of the status quo, he was no knight in armor riding forth to tilt at wrongs. His only horse, in fact, was an electric-powered steed on which he took his exercise. True to Republican philosophy, he became the "high priest of the great god Business." He believed that "the man who builds a factory builds a temple" and that "the man who works there worships there."

The hands-off temperament of "Cautious Cal" Coolidge suited the times perfectly. His thrifty nature caused him to sympathize fully with Secretary of the Treasury Mellon's efforts to reduce both taxes and debts. No foe of industrial bigness, he let business have its head. "Coolidge luck" held during his five and a half prosperity-blessed years.

Ever a profile in caution, Coolidge slowly gave the Harding regime a badly needed moral fumigation. Teapot Dome had scalded the Republican party badly, but so transparently honest was the vinegary Vermonter that the scandalous oil did not rub off on him. The public, though at first shocked by the scandal, quickly simmered down, and an alarming tendency developed in certain quarters to excuse some of the wrongdoers on the grounds that "they had gotten away with it." Some critics even condemned the government prosecutors for continuing to rock the boat. America's moral sensibility was evidently being dulled by prosperity.

Frustrated Farmers

Sun-bronzed farmers were caught squarely in a boom-or-bust cycle in the postwar decade. While the fighting had raged, they had raked in money hand over gnarled fist; by the spring of 1920, the price of wheat had shot up to an incredible $3 a bushel. But peace brought an end to government-guaranteed high prices and to massive purchases by

Have you placed a Sentimental Value on your Horses out of proportion to the work they are able to perform?

BAILOR MOTOR CULTIVATORS

Mechanizing Agriculture
Just as the automobile replaced the horse on city streets, so did the gas-engine tractor replace horses and mules on the nation's farms in the 1920s. American farmers owned ten times more tractors in 1930 than they had in 1920. The smoke-belching tractors bolstered productivity but also increased the farmers' debt burden, as the Great Depression made tragically clear.

other nations, as foreign production reentered the stream of world commerce.

Machines also threatened to plow the farmers under an avalanche of their own overabundant crops. The gasoline-engine tractor was working a revolution on American farms. This steel mule was to cultivation and sowing what the McCormick reaper was to harvesting. Blue-denimed farmers no longer had to plod after the horse-drawn plow with high-footed gait. They could sit erect on their chugging mechanized chariots and turn under and harrow many acres in a single day. They could grow bigger crops on larger areas, using fewer horses and hired hands. The wartime boom had encouraged them to bring vast new tracts under cultivation, especially in the "wheat belt" of the upper Midwest. But such improved efficiency and expanded agricultural acreage helped to pile up more price-dampening surpluses. A withering depression swept through agricultural districts in the 1920s, when one farm in four was sold for debt or taxes. As a plaintive song of the period ran,

> *No use talkin', any man's beat,*
> *With 'leven-cent cotton and forty-cent meat.*

Schemes abounded for bringing relief to the hard-pressed farmers. A bipartisan "farm bloc" from the agricultural states coalesced in Congress in 1921 and succeeded in driving through some helpful laws. Noteworthy was the Capper-Volstead Act, which exempted farmers' marketing cooperatives from antitrust prosecution. The farm bloc's favorite proposal was the McNary-Haugen Bill, pushed energetically from 1924 to 1928. It sought to keep agricultural prices high by authorizing the government to buy up surpluses and sell them abroad. Government losses were to be made up by a special tax on the farmers. Congress twice passed the bill, but frugal Coolidge twice vetoed it. Farm prices stayed down, and farmers' political temperatures stayed high, reaching fever pitch in the election of 1924.

A Three-Way Race for the White House in 1924

Self-satisfied Republicans, chanting "Keep Cool and Keep Coolidge," nominated "Silent Cal" for the presidency at their convention in Cleveland in the simmering summer of 1924. Squabbling Democrats had more difficulty choosing a candidate when they met in New York's sweltering Madison Square Garden. Reflecting many of the cultural tensions of the decade, the party was hopelessly split between "wets" and "drys," urbanites and farmers, Fundamentalists and Modernists, northern liberals and southern stand-patters, immigrants and old-stock Americans. In one symptomatic spasm of discord, the conventioneers failed by just one vote to pass a resolution condemning the Ku Klux Klan.

Deadlocked for an unprecedented 102 ballots, the convention at last turned wearily, sweatily, and unenthusiastically to John W. Davis. A wealthy corporation lawyer connected with the Wall Street banking house of J. P. Morgan and Company, the polished nominee was no less conservative than cautious Calvin Coolidge.

The field was now wide open for a liberal candidate. The white-pompadoured Senator ("Fighting Bob") La Follette from Wisconsin, perennial aspirant to the presidency and now sixty-nine years of age, sprang forward to lead a new Progressive grouping. He gained the endorsement of the American Federation of Labor and enjoyed the support of the shrinking Socialist party, but his major constituency was made up of the price-pinched farmers. La Follette's new Progressive party, fielding only a presidential ticket, with no candidates for local office, was a head without a body. It proved to be only a shadow of the robust Progressive coalition of prewar days. Its platform called for government ownership of railroads and relief for farmers, lashed out at monopoly and antilabor injunctions, and urged a constitutional amendment to limit the Supreme Court's power to invalidate laws passed by Congress.

La Follette turned in a respectable showing, polling nearly 5 million votes. But "Cautious Cal" and the oil-smeared Republicans slipped easily back into office, overwhelming Davis, 15,718,211 to 8,385,283. The electoral count stood at 382 for Coolidge, 136 for Davis, and 13 for La Follette, all from his home state of Wisconsin (see the map below). As the so-called conscience of the calloused 1920s, La Follette injected a badly needed liberal tonic into a decade drugged on prosperity. But times were too good for too many for his reforming message to carry the day.

Foreign-Policy Flounderings

Isolation continued to reign in the Coolidge era. Despite presidential proddings, the Senate proved unwilling to allow America to adhere to the World Court—the judicial arm of the still-suspect League of Nations. Coolidge only halfheartedly—and unsuccessfully—pursued further naval disarmament after the loudly trumpeted agreements worked out at the Washington Conference in 1922.

A glaring exception to the United States' inward-looking indifference to the outside world was the armed interventionism in the Caribbean and Central America. American troops were withdrawn (after an eight-year stay) from the Dominican Republic in 1924, but they remained in Haiti

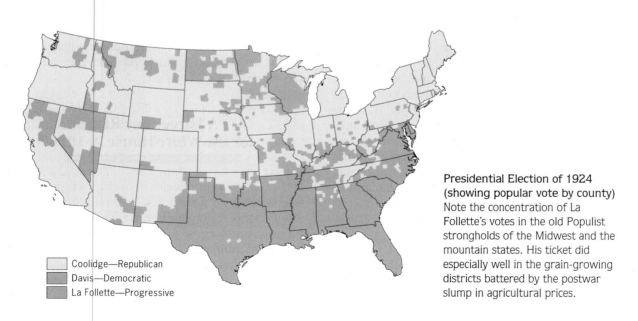

Presidential Election of 1924 (showing popular vote by county) Note the concentration of La Follette's votes in the old Populist strongholds of the Midwest and the mountain states. His ticket did especially well in the grain-growing districts battered by the postwar slump in agricultural prices.

Coolidge—Republican
Davis—Democratic
La Follette—Progressive

Harmony in Europe, 1932

refloat the war-shelled world economy. Americans, bewitched by lucrative investment opportunities in their domestic economy, did not lend nearly so large a fraction of their national income overseas as had the British in the prewar period.

The key knot in the debt tangle was the $10 billion that the U.S. Treasury had loaned to the Allies during and immediately after the war. Uncle Sam held their IOUs—and he wanted to be paid. The Allies, in turn, protested that the demand for repayment was grossly unfair. The French and the British pointed out, with much justice, that they had held up a wall of flesh and bone against the common foe until America the Unready had finally entered the fray. America, they argued, should write off its loans as war costs, just as the Allies had been tragically forced to write off the lives of millions of young men. The debtors also complained that the real effect of their borrowed dollars had been to fuel the boom in the already roaring wartime economy in America, where nearly all their purchases had been made. And the final straw, protested the Europeans, was that America's postwar tariff walls made it almost impossible for them to sell the goods to earn the dollars to pay their debts.

Unraveling the Debt Knot

America's tightfisted insistence on getting its money back helped to harden the hearts of the Allies against conquered Germany. The French and the British demanded that the Germans make enormous reparations payments, totaling some $32 billion, as compensation for war-inflicted damages. The Allies hoped to settle their debts to the United States with the money received from Germany. The French, seeking to extort lagging reparations payments, sent troops into Germany's industrialized Ruhr Valley in 1923. Berlin responded by permitting its currency to inflate astronomically. At one point in October 1923, a loaf of bread cost 480 million marks, or about $120 million in preinflation money. German society teetered on the brink of mad anarchy, and the whole international house of financial cards threatened to flutter down in colossal chaos.

Sensible statesmen now urged that war debts and reparations alike be drastically scaled down or even canceled outright. But to Americans such proposals smacked of "welshing" on a debt. "We went

from 1914 to 1934. President Coolidge in 1925 briefly removed American bayonets from troubled Nicaragua, where they had glinted intermittently since 1909, but in 1926 he sent them back, five thousand strong, and they stayed until 1933. American oil companies clamored for a military expedition to Mexico in 1926 when the Mexican government began to assert its sovereignty over oil resources. Coolidge kept cool and defused the Mexican crisis with some skillful diplomatic negotiating. But his mailed-fist tactics elsewhere bred sore resentments south of the Rio Grande, where angry critics loudly assailed "*yanqui* imperialism."

Overshadowing all other foreign-policy problems in the 1920s was the knotty issue of international debts, a complicated tangle of private loans, Allied war debts, and German reparations payments. Almost overnight, World War I had reversed the international financial position of the United States. In 1914 America had been a debtor nation in the sum of about $4 billion; by 1922 it had become a creditor nation in the sum of about $16 billion. The almighty dollar rivaled the pound sterling as the financial giant of the world. American investors loaned some $10 billion to foreigners in the 1920s, though even this huge river of money could not fully across, but they won't come across," cried a prominent politician. Scroogelike, Calvin Coolidge turned aside suggestions of debt cancellation with a typically terse question: "They hired the money, didn't they?" The Washington administration proved especially unrealistic in its dogged insistence that there was no connection whatever between debts and reparations.

Reality finally dawned in the Dawes Plan of 1924. Negotiated largely by Charles Dawes, about to be nominated as Coolidge's running mate, it rescheduled German reparations payments and opened the way for further American private loans to Germany. The whole financial cycle now became still more complicated, as U.S. bankers loaned money to Germany, Germany paid reparations to France and Britain, and the former Allies paid war debts to the United States. Clearly the source of this monetary merry-go-round was the flowing well of American credit. When that well dried up after the great crash in 1929, the jungle of international finance quickly turned into a desert. President Herbert Hoover declared a one-year debt moratorium in 1931, and before long all the debtors had defaulted—except "honest little Finland," which struggled along making payments until the last of its debt was discharged in 1976.

The United States never did get its money, but it harvested a bumper crop of ill will. Irate French crowds on occasion attacked American tourists, and throughout Europe Uncle Sam was caricatured as Uncle Shylock, greedily whetting his knife for the last pound of Allied flesh. The bad taste left in American mouths by the whole sorry episode contributed powerfully to the storm-cellar neutrality legislation passed by Congress in the 1930s.

The Triumph of Herbert Hoover, 1928

Poker-faced Calvin Coolidge, the tight-lipped "Sphinx of the Potomac," bowed out of the 1928 presidential race when he announced, "I do not choose to run." His logical successor was super-Secretary (of Commerce) Herbert Hoover, unpopular with the political bosses but the much-admired darling of the masses, who asked, "Hoo but Hoover?" He was nominated on a platform that clucked contentedly over both prosperity and prohibition.

Still-squabbling Democrats nominated Alfred E. Smith, four-time governor of New York and one of the most colorful personalities in American politics. He was a wisecracking, glad-handing liberal who suffered from several fatal political handicaps. "Al(cohol)" Smith was soakingly and drippingly "wet" at a time when the country was still devoted to the "noble experiment" of prohibition. To a nation that had only recently moved to the city, native New Yorker Smith seemed too abrasively urban. He was a Roman Catholic in an overwhelmingly Protestant—and unfortunately prejudiced—land. Many dry, rural, and Fundamentalist Dem-

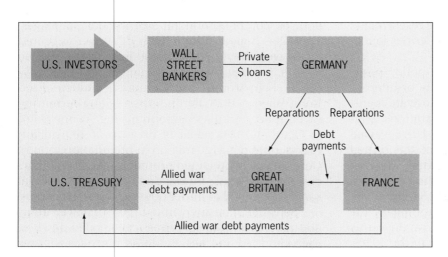

Aspects of the Financial Merry-go-round, 1921–1933 Great Britain, with a debt of over $4 billion owed to the U.S. Treasury, had a huge stake in proposals for inter-Allied debt cancellation, but France's stake was even larger. Less prosperous than Britain in the 1920s and more battered by the war, which had been fought on its soil, France owed nearly $3.5 billion to the United States and additional billions to Britain.

ocrats gagged on his candidacy, and they saddled the wet Smith with a dry running mate and a dry platform. Jauntily sporting a brown derby and a big cigar, Smith, "the Happy Warrior," tried to carry alcohol on one shoulder and water on the other. But his effort was doomed from the start.

Radio figured prominently in this campaign for the first time, and it helped Hoover more than Smith. The New Yorker had more personal sparkle, but he could not project it through the radio (which in his Lower East Side twang he pronounced "radd-dee-o," grating on the ears of many listeners). Iowa-born Hoover, with his double-breasted dignity, came out of the microphone better than he went in. Decrying un-American "socialism" and preaching "rugged individualism," he sounded both grass-rootish and statesmanlike.

Chubby-faced, ruddy-complexioned Herbert Hoover, with his painfully high starched collar, was a living example of the American success story and an intriguing mixture of two centuries. As a poor orphan boy who had worked his way through Stanford University, he had absorbed the nineteenth-century copybook maxims of industry, thrift, and self-reliance. As a fabulously successful mining engineer and a brilliant businessman, he had honed to a high degree the efficiency doctrines of the progressive era.

A small-town boy from Iowa and Oregon, he had traveled and worked abroad extensively. Long years of self-imposed exile had deepened his determination, abundantly supported by national tradition, to avoid foreign entanglements. His experiences abroad had further strengthened his faith in American individualism, free enterprise, and small government.

With his unshaken dignity and Quaker restraint, Hoover was a far cry from the typical backslapping politician. Though a citizen of the world and laden with international honors, he was quite shy, stand-offish, and stiff. Personally colorless in public, he had been accustomed during much of his life to giving orders to subordinates and not to soliciting votes. Never before elected to public office, he was thin-skinned in the face of criticism, and he did not adapt readily to the necessary give-and-take of political accommodation. His real power lay in his integrity, his humanitarianism, his passion for assembling the facts, his efficiency, his talents for administration, and his ability to inspire loyalty in close associates. They called him "the Chief."

Herbert Hoover on the Road   "Whistle-stop" campaigns, with candidates speaking from the rear platforms of trains, were a standard feature of American politics before the advent of television. Herbert Hoover here greets a crowd in Newark, New Jersey, during the 1928 campaign.

As befitted America's newly mechanized civilization, Hoover was the ideal businessperson's candidate. A self-made millionaire, he recoiled from anything suggesting socialism, paternalism, or "planned economy." Yet as secretary of commerce, he had exhibited some progressive instincts. He endorsed labor unions and supported federal regulation of the new radio broadcasting industry. He even flirted for a time with the idea of government-owned radio, similar to the British Broadcasting Corporation (BBC).

As bands blared Smith's theme song, "The Sidewalks of New York," the campaign sank into the sewers beneath the sidewalks. Despite the best efforts of Hoover and Smith, below-the-belt tactics were employed to a disgusting degree by lower-level campaigners. Religious bigotry raised its hideous head

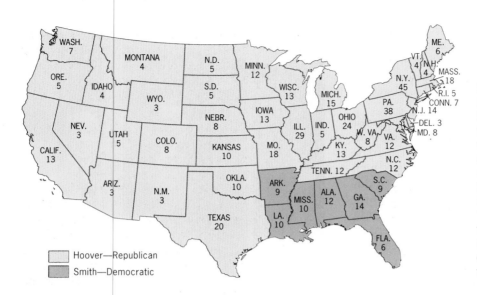

Presidential Election of 1928 (with electoral vote by state) Smith, despite his defeat, managed to poll almost as many votes as the victorious Coolidge had in 1924. By attracting to the party an immense urban or "sidewalk" vote, the breezy New Yorker foreshadowed Roosevelt's New Deal victory in 1932, when the Democrats patched together the solid South and the urban North. A cruel joke had Smith cabling the Pope a single word after the election: "Unpack."

over Smith's Catholicism. An irresponsible whispering campaign claimed that "A Vote for Al Smith Is a Vote for the Pope" and that the White House, under Smith, would become a branch of the Vatican—complete with "Rum, Romanism, and Ruin." Hoover's attempts to quash such rumors were in vain.

The proverbially solid South—"100 percent American" and a stronghold of Protestant Ku Klux Klanism—shied away from "city slicker" Al Smith. It might have accepted a Catholic, or a wet, or the descendant of Irish grandparents, or an urbanite. But a concoction of Catholicism, wettism, foreignism, and liberalism brewed on the sidewalks of New York was too bitter a dose for southern stomachs. Smith's theme song was a constant and rasping reminder that his upbringing had not been convincingly American.

Hoover triumphed in a landslide. He bagged 21,391,993 popular votes to 15,016,169 for his embittered opponent, while rolling up an electoral count of 444 to 87. A huge Republican majority was returned to the House of Representatives. Tens of thousands of dry southern Democrats—"Hoover-crats"—rebelled against Al Smith, and Hoover proved to be the first Republican candidate in fifty-two years, except for Harding's Tennessee victory in 1920, to carry a state that had seceded. He swept five states of the former Confederacy, as well as all the Border States.

President Hoover's First Moves

Prosperity in the late 1920s smiled broadly as the Hoover years began. Soaring stocks on the bull market continued to defy the laws of financial gravitation. But two immense groups of citizens were not getting their share of the riches flowing from the national cornucopia: the unorganized wage earners and especially the disorganized farmers.

Hoover's administration, in line with its philosophy of promoting self-help, responded to the outcry of the wounded farmers with legislative aspirin. The Agricultural Marketing Act, passed by Congress in June 1929, was designed to help the farmers help themselves, largely through producers' cooperatives. It set up the Federal Farm Board, with a revolving fund of half a billion dollars at its disposal. Money was lent generously to farm organizations seeking to buy, sell, and store agricultural surpluses.

In 1930 the Farm Board itself created both the Grain Stabilization Corporation and the Cotton Stabilization Corporation. The prime goal was to bolster sagging prices by buying up surpluses. But the two agencies were soon suffocated by an avalanche of farm produce, as wheat dropped to fifty-seven cents a bushel and cotton to five cents a pound.

Farmers had meanwhile clutched at the tariff as a possible straw to help keep their heads above the waters of financial ruin. During the recent presidential campaign, Hoover, an amateur in politics, had been stampeded into a politically unwise pledge. He had promised to call Congress into special session to consider agricultural relief and, specifically, to bring about "limited" changes in the tariff. These hope-giving assurances no doubt won many votes for Hoover in the midwestern farm belt.

The Hawley-Smoot Tariff of 1930 followed the well-worn pattern of Washington horse trading. It started out in the House as a fairly reasonable protective measure, designed to assist the farmers. But by the time the high-pressure lobbyists had pushed it through the Senate, it had acquired about a thousand amendments. It thus turned out to be the highest protective tariff in the nation's peacetime history. The average duty on nonfree goods was raised from 38.5 percent, as established by the Fordney-McCumber Act of 1922, to nearly 60 percent.

To angered foreigners, the Hawley-Smoot Tariff was a blow below the trade belt. It seemed like a declaration of economic warfare on the entire outside world. It reversed a promising worldwide trend toward reasonable tariffs and widened the yawning trade gaps. It plunged both America and other nations deeper into the terrible depression that had already begun. It increased international financial chaos and forced the United States further into the bog of economic isolationism. And economic isolationism, both at home and abroad, was playing directly into the hands of a hate-filled German demagogue, Adolf Hitler.

The Great Crash Ends the Golden Twenties

When Herbert Hoover confidently took the presidential oath on March 4, 1929, there were few black clouds on the economic horizon. The "long boom" seemed endless, with the painful exception of the debt-blanketed farm belt. America's productive colossus—stimulated by the automobile, radio, movie, and other new industries—was roaring along at a dizzy speed that suggested a permanent plateau of prosperity. Few people sensed that it might smother its own fires by pouring out too much.

The speculative bubble was actually near the bursting point. Prices on the stock exchange continued to spiral upward and create a fool's paradise of paper profits, despite Hoover's early but fruitless efforts to curb speculation through the Federal Reserve Board. A few prophets of disaster were bold enough to sound warnings but were drowned out by the mad chatter of the ticker-tape machine.

The Great Crash of 1929 The stock-market collapse caused fear to run like wildfire through the financial world. These anxious depositors lined up outside a New York bank, clamoring to withdraw their deposits before the bank failed. Ironically, "runs" on banks like this actually sped the downward economic spiral.

Index of Common Stock Prices
(1926 = 100)

A catastrophic crash came in October 1929. It was partially triggered by the British, who raised their interest rates in an effort to bring back capital lured abroad by American investments. Foreign investors and wary domestic speculators began to dump their "insecurities," and an orgy of selling followed. Tension built up to the panicky "Black Tuesday" of October 29, 1929, when 16,410,030 shares of stocks were sold in a save-who-may scramble. Wall Street became a wailing wall as gloom and doom replaced boom, and suicides increased alarmingly. A "sick joke" of the time had hotel room clerks ask registrants, "For sleeping or jumping?"

Losses, even in blue-chip securities, were unbelievable. By the end of 1929—two months after the initial crash—stockholders had lost $40 billion in paper values, or more than the total cost of World War I to the United States.

The stock-market collapse heralded a business depression, at home and abroad, that was the most prolonged and prostrating in American or world experience. No other industrialized nation suffered so severe a setback. By the end of 1930, more than 4 million workers in the United States were jobless; two years later the figure had about tripled. Hungry and despairing workers pounded pavements in search of nonexistent jobs ("We're firing, not hiring"). Where employees were not discharged, wages and salaries were often slashed. A current jingle ran,

> *Mellon pulled the whistle,*
> *Hoover rang the bell*
> *Wall Street gave the signal*
> *And the country went to hell.*

The misery and gloom were incalculable, as forests of dead chimneys stood stark against the sky. Over five thousand banks collapsed in the first three years of the depression, carrying down with them the life savings of tens of thousands of ordinary citizens. Countless thousands of honest, hard-working people lost their homes and farms to the forecloser's hammer. Bread lines formed, soup kitchens dispensed food, and apple sellers stood shivering on street corners trying to peddle their wares for five cents. Families felt the stress, as jobless fathers nursed their guilt and shame at not being able to provide for their households. Breadless breadwin-

---

The Depression spectacle of want in the shadow of surplus moved an observer to write in Current History *(1932),*

"We still pray to be given each day our daily bread. Yet there is too much bread, too much wheat and corn, meat and oil and almost every commodity required by man for his subsistence and material happiness. We are not able to purchase the abundance that modern methods of agriculture, mining and manufacture make available in such bountiful quantities. Why is mankind being asked to go hungry and cold and poverty stricken in the midst of plenty?"

The Unemployed, by John Langley Howard, 1937 In this painting Howard soberly evokes the dispirited state of millions of unemployed Americans during the depression.

ners often blamed themselves for their plight, despite abundant evidence that the economic system, not individual initiative, had broken down. Mothers meanwhile nursed fewer babies, as hard times reached even into the nation's bedrooms, precipitating a decade-long dearth of births. As cash registers gathered cobwebs, the song "My God, How the Money Rolls In" was replaced with "Brother, Can You Spare a Dime?"

Hooked on the Horn of Plenty

What caused the Great Depression? One basic explanation was overproduction by both farm and factory. Ironically, the depression of the 1930s was one of abundance, not want. It was the "great glut" or the "plague of plenty."

The nation's ability to produce goods had clearly outrun its capacity to consume or pay for them. Too much money was going into the hands of a few wealthy people, who in turn invested it in factories and other agencies of production. Not enough was going into salaries and wages, where revitalizing purchasing power could be more quickly felt.

Other maladies were at work. Overexpansion of credit through installment-plan buying overstimulated production. Paying on so-called easy terms caused many consumers to dive in beyond their depth. Normal technological unemployment, resulting from new laborsaving machines, also added its burden to the abnormal unemployment of the "threadbare thirties."

This already bleak picture was further darkened by economic anemia abroad. Britain and the Continent had never fully recovered from the upheaval of World War I. Depression in America was given a further downward push by a chain-reaction financial collapse in Europe, following the failure in 1931 of a prominent Vienna banking house. A drying up of international trade, moreover, had been hastened by the shortsighted Hawley-Smoot Tariff of 1930. European uncertainties over reparations, war debts, and defaults on loans owed to America caused tensions that reacted unfavorably on the United States.

"Hooverville" in Seattle, 1934 In the early years of the depression, desperate, homeless people constructed shacks out of scavenged materials. These shanty-towns sprang up in cities across the country.

Many of these conditions had been created or worsened by Uncle Sam's own narrow-visioned policies, but it was now too late to unscramble the omelet.

As if man-made disasters were not enough, a terrible drought scorched the Mississippi Valley in 1930. Thousands of farms were sold at auction for taxes, though in some cases kind neighbors would intimidate prospective buyers, bid one cent, and return the property to its original owner. Farm tenancy or rental—a species of peonage—was spreading at an alarming rate among both whites and blacks.

By 1930 the depression had become a national calamity. Through no fault of their own, a host of industrious citizens had lost everything. They wanted to work—but there was no work. The insidious effect of all this dazed despair on the nation's spirit was incalculable and long-lasting. America's "uniqueness" no longer seemed so unique or its Manifest Destiny so manifest. Hitherto the people had grappled with storms, trees, stones, and other physical obstacles. But the depression was a baffling wraith they could not grasp. Initiative and self-respect were stifled, as panhandlers begged for food or "charity soup." In extreme cases "ragged individualists" slept under "Hoover blankets" (old newspapers), fought over the contents of garbage cans, or cooked their findings in old oil drums in tin-and-paper shantytowns cynically named "Hoovervilles."

The very foundations of America's social and political structure trembled.

Rugged Times for Rugged Individualists

Hoover's exalted reputation as a wonder-worker and efficiency engineer crashed about as dismally as the stock market. He doubtless would have shone in the

> *Herbert Hoover (1874–1964) spoke approvingly in a campaign speech in 1928 of "the American system of Rugged Individualism." In 1930 he referred to Cleveland's 1887 veto of a bill to appropriate seed grain for the drought-stricken farmers of Texas:*
>
> "I do not believe that the power and duty of the General Government ought to be extended to the relief of individual suffering. . . . The lesson should be constantly enforced that though the people support the Government the Government should not support the people."

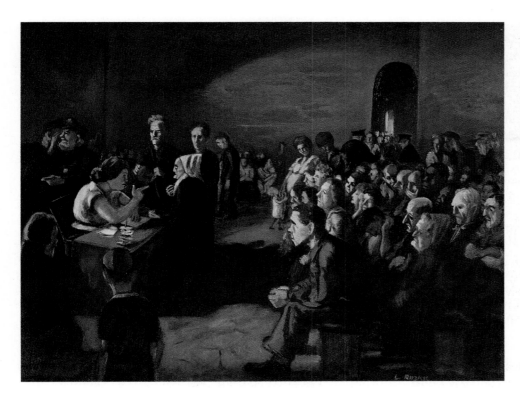

Home Relief Station, by Louis Ribak, 1935–1936
Destitute and despairing, millions of hard-working Americans like these had to endure the degradation and humiliation of going on relief as the pall of depression descended over the land.

prosperity-drenched Coolidge years, when he had foreseen the abolition of poverty and poor-houses. But damming the Great Depression proved to be a task beyond his engineering talents.

The perplexed president was impaled on the horns of a cruel dilemma. As a deservedly famed humanitarian, he was profoundly distressed by the widespread misery about him. Yet as a "rugged individualist," deeply rooted in an earlier era of free enterprise, he shrank from the heresy of government handouts. Convinced that industry, thrift, and self-reliance were the virtues that had made America great, President Hoover feared that a government doling out doles would weaken, perhaps destroy, the national fiber.

As the depression nightmare steadily worsened, relief by local government agencies broke down. Hoover was finally forced to turn reluctantly from his doctrine of log-cabin individualism and accept the proposition that the welfare of the people in a nationwide catastrophe is a direct concern of the national government.

The president at last worked out a compromise between the old hands-off philosophy and the "soul-destroying" direct dole then being used in England. He would assist the hard-pressed railroads, banks, and rural credit corporations, in the hope that if financial health were restored at the top of the economic pyramid, unemployment would be relieved at the bottom on a trickle-down basis.

Wall Streeter Martin Devries, observing President Herbert Hoover's struggle to keep his footing as the tidal wave of the Great Depression washed over him, decided he was a good man stuck in the wrong place, at the wrong time:

"Hoover happened to be in a bad spot. The Depression came on, and there he was. If Jesus Christ had been there, he'd have had the same problem. It's too bad for poor old Herbie that he happened to be there. This was a world-wide Depression. It wasn't Hoover's fault. In 1932, . . . a monkey could have been elected against him, no question about it."

Partisan critics sneered at the "Great Humanitarian"—he who had fed the faraway Belgians but would not use federal funds to feed needy Americans. Hostile commentators remarked that he was willing to lend government money to the big bankers, who allegedly had plunged the country into the mess. He would likewise lend money to agricultural organizations to feed pigs—but not people. Pigs, the cynics of the time noted, had no character to undermine.

Much of this criticism was unfair. Although continued suffering seemed to mock the effectiveness of Hoover's measures, his efforts probably prevented a more serious collapse than did occur. And his expenditures for relief, revolutionary for that day, paved the path for the enormous federal outlays of his New Deal successor, Franklin Roosevelt. Hoover proved that the old bootstrap-pulling techniques would no longer work in a crisis of this magnitude, especially when people lacked boots.

Herbert Hoover: Pioneer for the New Deal

President Hoover, in line with his "trickle-down" philosophy, at last recommended that Congress vote immense sums for useful public works. Though at heart an antispender, he secured from Congress appropriations totaling $2.25 billion for such projects.

Most imposing of the public enterprises was the gigantic Hoover Dam on the Colorado River. Voted by Congress in the days of Coolidge, it was begun in 1930 under Hoover and completed in 1936 under Roosevelt. It succeeded in creating a huge man-made lake for purposes of irrigation, flood control, and electric power.

But Hoover sternly fought all schemes that he regarded as "socialistic." Conspicuous among them was the Muscle Shoals Bill, designed to dam the Tennessee River and ultimately embraced by Franklin Roosevelt's Tennessee Valley Authority. Hoover emphatically vetoed this measure, primarily because he opposed the government's selling electricity in competition with its own citizens in private companies.

Early in 1932 Congress, responding to Hoover's belated appeal, established the Reconstruction Finance Corporation (RFC). With an initial working capital of half a billion dollars, this agency became a government lending bank. It was designed to provide indirect relief by assisting insurance companies, banks, agricultural organizations, railroads, and even hard-pressed state and local governments. But to preserve individualism and character, there would be no loans to individuals from this "billion-dollar soup kitchen."

"Pump-priming" loans by the RFC were no doubt of widespread benefit, though the organization was established many months too late for maximum usefulness. Projects that it supported were largely self-liquidating, and the government as a banker actually profited to the tune of many millions of dollars. Giant corporations so obviously benefited from this assistance that the RFC was dubbed—rather unfairly—"the millionaires' dole." The irony is that the thrifty and individualistic Hoover had sponsored the project, though with initial reluctance. It actually had a strong New Dealish flavor.

Hoover's administration also provided some indirect benefits for labor. After stormy debate, Congress passed the Norris–La Guardia Anti-Injunction Act in 1932, and Hoover signed it. The measure outlawed "yellow-dog" (antiunion) contracts and forbade the federal courts to issue injunctions to restrain strikes, boycotts, and peaceful picketing.

The truth is that Herbert Hoover, despite criticism of his "heartlessness," did inaugurate a significant new policy. In previous panics the masses had been forced to "sweat it out." Slow though Hoover was to abandon this nineteenth-century bias, by the end of his term he had started down the road toward government assistance for needy citizens— a road that Franklin Roosevelt would travel much farther.

Hoover's woes were increased by a hostile Congress. At critical times during his first two years, the Republican majority proved highly uncooperative. Friction worsened during his last two years. A depression-cursed electorate, rebelling in the congressional elections of 1930, so reduced the Republican majority that Democrats controlled the new House and almost controlled the Senate. Insurgent Republicans could—and did—combine with opposition Democrats to harass Hoover. Some of the president's troubles were deliberately manufactured by Congress, who, in his words, "played politics with human misery."

EXAMINING THE EVIDENCE

Lampooning Hoover, 1932 The pages of *The American Pageant* are filled with political cartoons for the pungent commentary they provide on historical events. With one image rather than many words, a cartoonist can convey a point of view much the way editorial writers do. This cartoon appeared in the *Washington Daily News* on July 25, 1932, three and one-half months before Republican President Hoover lost the presidential election to his Democratic challenger Franklin D. Roosevelt. The cartoonist foretells Hoover's defeat in November and departure from the White House the following March (not January, as at present), and expresses his support for the Home Loan Bank Bill. With this proposal, Hoover sought to come to the aid of home mortgage lenders in order to forestall them from foreclosing on homeowners. The cartoonist jokes that Hoover supported this bill because he identified with home owners about to lose their homes, but he also cleverly insinuates that Hoover's banking reform was motivated by electoral opportunism. Surely Hoover sought to win public support in return for his new banking program as he battled for reelection, but the Home Loan Bank Bill also reflected Hoover's growing recognition that the federal government had to take direct action to remedy flaws that had precipitated the crisis of the Great Depression. As Hoover later recorded in his memoirs, "All this seems dull economics, but the poignant American drama revolving around the loss of the old homestead had a million repetitions straight from life, not because of the designing villain but because of a fault in our financial system." How does the cartoonist use caricature to make his point? What accounts for the political cartoon's special power? Are there limitations to this genre? Find another cartoon in the book and subject it to similar analysis.

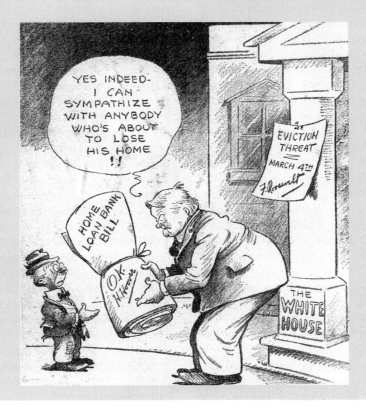

Routing the Bonus Army in Washington

Many veterans of World War I were numbered among the hard-hit victims of the depression. Industry had secured a "bonus"—though a dubious one—in the Hawley-Smoot Tariff. So the thoughts of the former soldiers naturally turned to what the government owed them for their services in 1917–1918, when they had "saved" democracy. A drive developed for the premature payment of the deferred bonus voted by Congress in 1924 and payable in 1945.

Thousands of impoverished veterans, both of war and of unemployment, were now prepared to move on to Washington, there to demand of Congress the immediate payment of their *entire* bonus. The "Bonus Expeditionary Force" (BEF), which mustered about twenty thousand souls, converged on the capital in the summer of 1932. These supplicants promptly set up unsanitary public camps and erected shacks on vacant lots—a gigantic "Hooverville." They thus created a menace to the public health, while attempting to intimidate Congress by their presence in force. After the pending bonus bill had failed in Congress by a narrow margin, Hoover arranged to pay the return fare of about six thousand bonus marchers. The rest refused to decamp, though ordered to do so.

Following riots that cost two lives, Hoover responded to the demands of the Washington authorities by ordering the army to evacuate the unwanted guests. Although Hoover charged that the "Bonus Army" was led by riffraff and reds, in fact only a sprinkling of them were former convicts and communist agitators. The eviction was carried out by General Douglas MacArthur with bayonets and tear gas, and with far more severity than Hoover had planned. A few of the former soldiers were injured as the torch was put to their pathetic shanties in the inglorious "Battle of Anacostia Flats." An eleven-month-old "bonus baby" allegedly died from exposure to tear gas.

This brutal episode brought down additional abuse on the once-popular Hoover, who by now was the most loudly booed man in the country. The Democrats, not content with Hoover's vulnerable record, employed professional "smear" artists to drive him from office. Cynics sneered that the "Great Engineer" had in a few months "ditched, drained, and damned the country." The existing panic was unfairly branded "the Hoover depression." In truth, Hoover had been oversold as a wizard, and the public grumbled when his magician's wand failed to produce rabbits. The time was ripening for the Democratic party—and Franklin D. Roosevelt—to cash in on Hoover's calamities.

Japanese Militarists Attack China

The Great Depression, which brewed enough distress at home, added immensely to difficulties abroad. Militaristic Japan stole the Far Eastern spotlight. In September 1931 the Japanese imperialists, noting that the Western world was badly mired in a depression, lunged into Manchuria. Alleging provocation, they rapidly overran the coveted Chinese province and proceeded to bolt shut the Open Door in the conquered area.

Peaceful peoples were stunned by this act of naked aggression, which was a flagrant violation of the League of Nations covenant, as well as of various other international agreements solemnly signed by Tokyo. Numerous indignant Americans, though by no means a majority, urged strong measures ranging from boycotts to blockades. Possibly a tight blockade by the League, backed by the United States, would have brought Japan sharply to book.

But the League was handicapped in taking two-fisted action by the nonmembership of the United States. Washington flatly rebuffed initial attempts in 1931 to secure American cooperation in applying economic pressure on Japan. Washington and Secretary of State Henry L. Stimson in the end decided to fire only paper bullets at the Japanese aggressors. The so-called Stimson doctrine, proclaimed in 1932, declared that the United States would not recognize any territorial acquisitions achieved by force. Righteous indignation—or a preach-and-run policy—would substitute for solid initiatives.

This verbal slap on the wrist from America did not deter the march of the Japanese militarists. Smarting under a Chinese boycott, they bombed Shanghai in 1932, with shocking losses to civilians. Outraged Americans launched informal boycotts of Japanese goods, chiefly dime-store knickknacks. But there was no real sentiment for armed intervention among a depression-ridden people, who remained strongly isolationist during the 1930s.

In a broad sense, collective security died and World War II was born in 1931 on the windswept

Japanese Aggression in Manchuria This American cartoon lambasts Japan for disregarding international treaty agreements when it seized Manchuria in 1931. The next year, the Japanese would set up the puppet state of Manchukuo.

plains of Manchuria. The League members had the economic and naval power to halt Japan but lacked the courage to act. One reason—though not the only one—was that they could not count on America's support. Even so, the Republic came closer to stepping into the chill waters of internationalism than American prophets would have dared to predict in the early 1920s.

Hoover later wrote of his differences with Secretary of State Stimson over economic boycotts,

"I was soon to realize that my able Secretary was at times more of a warrior than a diplomat. To him the phrase 'economic sanctions' was the magic wand of force by which all peace could be summoned from the vasty deep. . . . Ever since Versailles I had held that 'economic sanctions' meant war when applied to any large nation."

Hoover Pioneers the Good Neighbor Policy

Hoover's arrival in the White House brought a more hopeful turn to relations with America's southern neighbors. The new president was deeply interested in the often troubled nations below the Rio Grande. Shortly after his election in 1928, he had undertaken a goodwill tour of Latin America—on a U.S. battleship.

World depression softened an age-old aggressive attitude in the United States toward weak Latin neighbors. Following the stock-market collapse of 1929, Americans had less money to invest abroad. As millions of dollars' worth of investments in Latin America went sour, many Yankees felt as though they were more preyed upon than preying. So-called economic imperialism became much less popular in the United States than it had been in the golden twenties.

As an advocate of international goodwill, Hoover strove to abandon the interventionist twist given to the Monroe Doctrine by Theodore Roosevelt. In 1932 he negotiated a new treaty with the French-speaking republic of Haiti, and this pact, later supplanted by an executive agreement, provided for the complete withdrawal of American platoons by 1934. Further pleasing omens came early in 1933, when the last marine "leathernecks" sailed away from Nicaragua after an almost continuous stay of some twenty years.

Herbert Hoover, the engineer in politics, thus happily engineered the foundation stones of the "Good Neighbor" policy. Upon them rose an imposing edifice in the days of his successor, Franklin Roosevelt.

Chronology

1919	American Legion founded
	Chicago race riot
1920	Esch-Cummins Transportation Act
	Merchant Marine Act
1921	Veterans Bureau created
	Capper-Volstead Act
1922	Five-Power Naval Treaty
	Four-Power and Nine-Power Treaties on the Far East
	Fordney-McCumber Tariff Law
1923	*Adkins* v. *Children's Hospital*
	Teapot Dome scandal
	Harding dies; Coolidge assumes presidency
1924	Adjusted Compensation Act for veterans
	Dawes Plan for international finance
	U.S. troops leave the Dominican Republic
	Coolidge wins three-way presidential election
1926	U.S. troops occupy Nicaragua
1928	Kellogg-Briand Pact
	Hoover defeats Smith for presidency
	Hoover takes goodwill tour of Latin America
1929	Agricultural Marketing Act sets up Federal Farm Board
	Stock-market crash
1930	Hawley-Smoot Tariff
1931	Japanese invade Manchuria
1932	Reconstruction Finance Corporation (RFC) established
	Norris–La Guardia Anti-Injunction Act
	"Bonus Army" dispersed from Washington, D.C.

For further reading, see page A23 of the Appendix. For web resources, go to **http://college.hmco.com**.

The Great Depression and the New Deal

—◆—

1933–1939

The country needs and . . . demands bold, persistent experimentation. It is common sense to take a method and try it. If it fails, admit it frankly and try another. But above all, try something.

FRANKLIN D. ROOSEVELT, CAMPAIGN SPEECH, 1932

Voters were in an ugly mood as the presidential campaign of 1932 neared. Countless factory chimneys remained ominously cold, while more than 11 million unemployed workers and their families sank ever deeper into the pit of poverty. Herbert Hoover may have won the 1928 election by promising "a chicken in every pot," but three years later that chicken seemed to have laid a discharge slip in every pay envelope.

Hoover, sick at heart, was renominated by the Republican convention in Chicago without great enthusiasm. The platform indulged in extravagant praise of Republican antidepression policies, while halfheartedly promising to repeal national prohibition and return control of liquor to the states.

The rising star of the Democratic firmament was Governor Franklin Delano Roosevelt of New York, a fifth cousin of Theodore Roosevelt. Like the Rough Rider, he had been born to a wealthy New York family, had graduated from Harvard, had been elected as a kid-gloved politician to the New York legislature, had served as governor of the Empire State, had been nominated for the vice presidency (though not elected), and had served capably as assistant secretary of the navy. Although both men were master politicians, adept with the colorful phrase, FDR was suave and conciliatory, whereas TR was pugnacious and confrontational.

FDR: Politician in a Wheelchair

Infantile paralysis, while putting steel braces on Franklin Roosevelt's legs, put additional steel into his soul. Until 1921, when the dread disease struck,

Eleanor Roosevelt (1884–1962) She was America's most active First Lady and commanded enormous popularity and influence during FDR's presidency. Here she emerges, miner's cap in hand, from an Ohio coal mine.

young Roosevelt—tall (six feet two inches), athletic, and handsome—impressed observers as charming and witty yet at times a superficial and arrogant "lightweight." But suffering humbled him to the level of common clay. In courageously fighting his way back from complete helplessness to a hobbling mobility, he schooled himself in patience, tolerance, compassion, and strength of will. He once remarked that after trying for two years to wiggle one big toe, all else seemed easy.

Another of Roosevelt's great personal and political assets was his wife, Eleanor. The niece of Theodore Roosevelt, she was Franklin Roosevelt's distant cousin as well as his spouse. Tall, ungainly, and toothy, she overcame the misery of an unhappy

childhood and emerged as a champion of the dispossessed—and, ultimately, as the "conscience of the New Deal." FDR's political career was as much hers as it was his own. She traveled countless miles with him or on his behalf in all his campaigns, beginning with his run for the New York legislature before World War I, later considering herself "his legs." She was to become the most active First Lady in history. Through her lobbying of her husband, her speeches, and her syndicated newspaper column, she powerfully influenced the policies of the national government. Always she battled for the impoverished and the oppressed. At one meeting in Birmingham, Alabama, she confounded local authorities and flouted the segregation statutes by deliberately straddling the aisle separating the black and white seating sections. Sadly, her personal relationship with her husband was often rocky, due to his occasional infidelity. Condemned by conservatives and loved by liberals, she was one of the most controversial—and consequential—public figures of the twentieth century.

Franklin Roosevelt's political appeal was amazing. His commanding presence and his golden speaking voice, despite a sophisticated accent, combined to make him the premier American orator of his generation. He could turn on charm in private conversations as one would turn on a faucet. As a popular depression governor of New York, he had sponsored heavy state spending to relieve human suffering. Though favoring frugality, he believed that money, rather than humanity, was expendable. He revealed a deep concern for the plight of the "forgotten man"—a phrase he used in a 1932 speech—although he was assailed by the rich as a "traitor to his class."

Exuberant Democrats met in Chicago in June 1932 and speedily nominated Roosevelt. Fellow New Yorker Al Smith felt entitled to a second chance, and a beautiful friendship wilted when he was elbowed aside for Franklin Roosevelt. The Democratic platform came out more forthrightly than the Republican for repeal of prohibition, assailed the so-called Hoover depression, and promised not only a balanced budget but sweeping social and economic reforms. Roosevelt flew daringly through stormy weather to Chicago, where he smashed precedent by accepting the nomination in person. He electrified the delegates and the public with these words: "I pledge you, I pledge myself to a new deal for the American people."

Presidential Hopefuls of 1932

In the campaign that followed, Roosevelt seized the offensive with a slashing attack on the Republican Old Dealers. He was especially eager to prove that he was not an invalid ("Roosevelt Is Robust") and to display his magnificent torso and radiant personality to as many voters as possible.

Roosevelt consistently preached a New Deal for the "forgotten man," but he was annoyingly vague and somewhat contradictory. Many of his speeches were "ghostwritten" by the "Brains Trust" (popularly the "Brain Trust"), a small group of reform-minded intellectuals. They were predominantly youngish college professors, who, as a kind of kitchen cabinet, later authored much of the New Deal legislation. Roosevelt rashly promised a balanced budget and berated heavy Hooverian deficits, amid cries of "Throw the Spenders Out!" and "Out of the Red with Roosevelt." All of this was to make ironic reading in later months.

The high spirits of the Democrats found expression in the catchy air "Happy Days Are Here Again." This theme song fit FDR's indestructible smile, his jauntily angled cigarette holder, his breezy optimism, and his promises to do something, even at the risk of bold experimentation.

Grim-faced Herbert Hoover remained in the White House, conscientiously battling the depression through short lunches and long hours. Out on the firing line, his supporters halfheartedly assured half-listening voters, "The Worst Is Past," "It Might Have Been Worse," and "Prosperity Is Just Around the Corner." Hoover never ceased to insist that the uncertainty and fear produced by Roosevelt's impending victory plunged the nation deeper into the depression.

With the campaign going badly for the Republicans, a weary and despondent Hoover was persuaded to take to the stump. He stoutly reaffirmed his faith in American free enterprise and individual initiative, and gloomily predicted that if the Hawley-Smoot Tariff were repealed, the grass would grow "in the streets of a hundred cities." Such down-at-the-mouthism contrasted sharply with Roosevelt's tooth-flashing optimism and sparkling promises.

Hoover's Humiliation in 1932

Hoover had been swept into office on the rising tide of prosperity; he was swept out of office by the receding tide of depression. The flood of votes totaled 22,809,638 for Roosevelt and 15,758,901 for Hoover; the electoral count stood at 472 to 59. In all, the loser carried only six rock-ribbed Republican states.

One striking feature of the election was the beginning of a distinct shift of blacks, traditionally grateful to the Republican party of Lincoln, over to the Roosevelt camp. As the "last hired and first fired," black Americans had been among the worst sufferers from the depression. Beginning with the election of 1932, they became, notably in the great urban centers of the North, a vital element in the Democratic party.

Hard times unquestionably ruined the Republicans, for the electoral upheaval in 1932 was as much anti-Hoover as it was pro-Roosevelt. Democrats had only to harness the national grudge and let it pull them to victory. An overwhelming majority appear to have voiced a demand for change: *a* new deal rather than *the* New Deal, for the latter was only a gleam in the eyes of its sponsors. Any upstanding Democratic candidate probably could have won.

The preinauguration lame duck period now ground slowly to an end. Hoover, though defeated and repudiated, continued to be president for four long months, until March 4, 1933. But he was helpless to embark upon any long-range policies without the cooperation of Roosevelt—and the victorious president-elect proved rather uncooperative. Hoover at length succeeded in arranging two meetings with him to discuss the war-debt muddle. But Roosevelt, who airily remarked to the press, "It's not my baby," fought shy of assuming responsibility without authority. As Hoover privately confessed, he was trying to bind his successor to an anti-inflationary policy that would have made impossible many of the later New Deal experiments. But in politics the winner, not the loser, calls the tune.

With Washington deadlocked, the vast and vaunted American economic machine clanked to a virtual halt. One worker in four tramped the streets, feet weary and hands idle. Banks were locking their doors all over the nation, as people nervously stuffed paper money under their mattresses. Hooverites, then and later, accused Roosevelt of deliberately permitting the depression to worsen, so that he could emerge the more spectacularly as a savior.

FDR and the Three *R*'s: Relief, Recovery, Reform

Great crises often call forth gifted leaders, and the hand of destiny tapped Roosevelt on the shoulder. On a dreary Inauguration Day, March 4, 1933, his vibrant voice, broadcast nationally from a bulletproof stand, provided the American people with inspirational new hope. He denounced the "money changers" who had brought on the calamity and declared that the government must wage war on the Great Depression as it would wage war on an armed foe. His clarion note was, "Let me assert my firm belief that the only thing we have to fear is fear itself."

Roosevelt moved decisively. Now that he had full responsibility, he boldly declared a nationwide banking holiday, March 6–10, as a prelude to opening the banks on a sounder basis. He then summoned the overwhelmingly Democratic Congress into special session to cope with the national emergency. For the so-called Hundred Days (March 9–June 16, 1933), members hastily cranked out an unprecedented basketful of remedial legislation. Some of it derived from earlier progressivism, but these new measures mostly sought to deal with a desperate emergency.

Roosevelt's New Deal programs aimed at three *R*'s—relief, recovery, and reform. Short-range goals were relief and immediate recovery, especially in the first two years. Long-range goals were permanent recovery and reform of current abuses, particularly those that had produced the boom-or-bust catastrophe. The three-*R* objectives often overlapped and got in one another's way. But amid all the topsy-turvy haste, the gigantic New Deal program lurched forward.

The Inauguration of Franklin D. Roosevelt, March 4, 1933, by Covarrubias This highly stylized painting triumphantly celebrates FDR's inaugural.

Firmly ensconced in the driver's seat, President Roosevelt cracked the whip. A green Congress so fully shared the panicky feeling of the country that it was ready to rubber-stamp bills drafted by White House advisers—measures that Roosevelt called "must legislation." More than that, Congress gave the president extraordinary blank-check powers: some of the laws it passed expressly delegated

Principal New Deal Acts During Hundred Days Congress, 1933*
(items in parentheses indicate secondary purposes)

Recovery	Relief	Reform
FDR closes banks, March 6, 1933		
Emergency Banking Relief Act, March 9, 1933		
(Beer Act)	(Beer Act)	Beer and Wine Revenue Act, March 22, 1933
(CCC)	Unemployment Relief Act, March 31, 1933, creates Civilian Conservation Corps (CCC)	
FDR orders gold surrender, April 5, 1933		
FDR abandons gold standard, April 19, 1933		
(FERA)	Federal Emergency Relief Act, May 12, 1933, creates Federal Emergency Relief Administration (FERA)	
(AAA)	Agricultural Adjustment Act (AAA), May 12, 1933	
(TVA)	(TVA)	Tennessee Valley Authority Act (TVA), May 18, 1933 Federal Securities Act, May 27, 1933
Gold-payment clause repealed, June 5, 1933		
(HOLC)	Home Owners' Refinancing Act, June 13, 1933, creates Home Owners' Loan Corporation (HOLC)	
National Industrial Recovery Act, June 16, 1933, creates National Recovery Administration (NRA), Public Works Administration (PWA)	(NRA, PWA)	(NRA)
(Glass-Steagall Act)	(Glass-Steagall Act)	Glass-Steagall Banking Reform Act, June 16, 1933, creates Federal Deposit Insurance Corporation

*For later New Deal measures, see p. 784.

The Champ: FDR Chatting with Reporters   Roosevelt mastered the press as few presidents before or since have been able to do.

legislative authority to the chief executive. One senator complained that if FDR asked Congress "to commit suicide tomorrow, they'd do it."

Roosevelt was delighted to exert executive leadership, and Congress responded to it, although he did not always know precisely where he was going. He was inclined to do things by intuition—off the cuff. He was like the quarterback, as he put it, whose next play depends on the outcome of the previous play. So desperate was the mood of an action-starved public that *any* movement, even in the wrong direction, seemed better than no movement at all.

The frantic Hundred Days Congress passed many essentials of the New Deal "three *R*'s," though important long-range measures were added in later sessions. These reforms owed much to the legacy of the pre–World War I progressive movement. Many of them were long overdue, sidetracked by the war in Europe and the Old Guard reaction of the 1920s. The New Dealers, sooner or later, embraced such progressive ideas as unemployment insurance, old-age insurance, minimum-wage regulations, conservation and development of natural resources, and

restrictions on child labor. A few such reforms had already made limited gains in some of the states. Many of these forward-looking measures had been adopted a generation or so earlier by the more advanced countries of western Europe. In the area of social welfare, the United States, in the eyes of many Europeans, remained a "backward nation."

Roosevelt Tackles Money and Banking

Banking chaos cried aloud for immediate action. Congress pulled itself together and in an incredible eight hours had the Emergency Banking Relief Act of 1933 ready for Roosevelt's busy pen. The new law invested the president with power to regulate banking transactions and foreign exchange and to reopen solvent banks.

Bank Failures Before and After the Glass-Steagall Banking Reform Act of 1933

Roosevelt, the master showman, next turned to the radio to deliver the first of his thirty famous "fireside chats." As some 35 million people hung on his soothing words, he gave assurances that it was now safer to keep money in a reopened bank than "under the mattress." Confidence returned with a gush, and the banks began to unlock their doors.

The Emergency, or Hundred Days, Congress buttressed public reliance on the banking system by enacting the memorable Glass-Steagall Banking Reform Act. This measure provided for the Federal Deposit Insurance Corporation, which insured individual deposits up to $5,000 (later raised). Thus ended the disgraceful epidemic of bank failures, which dated back to the "wildcat" days of Andrew Jackson.*

Roosevelt moved swiftly elsewhere on the financial front, seeking to protect the melting gold reserve and to prevent panicky hoarding. He ordered all private holdings of gold to be surrendered to the Treasury in exchange for paper currency and then took the nation off the gold standard. The Emergency Congress responded to his recommendation by canceling the gold-payment clause in all contracts and authorizing repayment in paper money. A "managed currency" was well on its way.

The goal of Roosevelt's "managed currency" was inflation, which he believed would relieve debtors' burdens and stimulate new production. Roosevelt's principal instrument for achieving inflation was gold buying. He instructed the Treasury to purchase gold at increasing prices, ratcheting the dollar price of gold up from $21 an ounce in 1933 to $35 an ounce in early 1934, a price that held for nearly four decades. This policy did increase the amount of dollars in circulation, as holders of gold cashed it in at the elevated prices. But this inflationary result also provoked the wrath of "sound-money" critics, who gagged on the "baloney dollar." The gold-buying scheme came to an end in February 1934, when FDR returned the nation to a limited gold standard for purposes of international trade only. Thereafter (until 1971—see p. 954), the United States pledged itself to pay foreign bills, if requested, in gold at the rate of one ounce of gold for every $35 due. But domestic circulation of gold continued to be prohibited, and gold coins became collectors' items.

---

*When FDR was inaugurated in 1933, not a single Canadian bank had failed.

A CCC Camp in Idaho, 1930s   These Mexican-Americans from Los Angeles joined some 3 million of their countrymen at such camps in the 1930s. The CCC was among the most popular of all the New Deal programs. While undertaking valuable conservation projects, it provided employment, job training, and a healthy respite in the great outdoors from the conditions of urban life.

Creating Jobs for the Jobless

Overwhelming unemployment, even more than banking, clamored for prompt remedial action. One out of every four workers was jobless when FDR took his inaugural oath—the highest level of unemployment in the nation's history, before or since. Roosevelt had no hesitancy about using federal money to assist the unemployed and at the same time to "prime the pump" of industrial recovery. (A farmer has to pour a little water into a dry pump—that is, "prime it"—to start the flow.)

The Hundred Days Congress responded to Roosevelt's spurs when it created the Civilian Conservation Corps (CCC), which proved to be perhaps the most popular of all the New Deal "alphabetical agencies." This law provided employment in fresh-air government camps for about 3 million uniformed young men, many of whom might otherwise

Later Major New Deal Measures, 1933–1939 (items in parentheses indicate secondary purposes)

Recovery	Relief	Reform
(CWA)	FDR establishes Civil Works Administration (CWA), November 9, 1933	
Gold Reserve Act, January 30, 1934, authorizes FDR's devaluation, January 31, 1934		
		Securities and Exchange Commission (SEC) authorized by Congress, June 6, 1934
(Reciprocal Trade Agreements)	(Reciprocal Trade Agreements)	Reciprocal Trade Agreements Act, June 12, 1934 (see pp. 808–809)
		Indian Reorganization Act, June 18, 1934
(FHA)	National Housing Act, June 28, 1934, authorizes Federal Housing Administration (FHA)	(FHA)
(Frazier-Lemke Act)	Frazier-Lemke Farm Bankruptcy Act, June 28, 1934	
(Resettlement Administration)	FDR creates Resettlement Administration, April 30, 1935	
(WPA)	FDR creates Works Progress Administration (WPA), May 6, 1935, under act of April 8, 1935	
(Wagner Act)	(Wagner Act)	(Wagner) National Labor Relations Act, July 5, 1935
		Social Security Act, August 14, 1935
		Public Utility Holding Company Act, August 26, 1935
(Soil Conservation Act)	Soil Conservation and Domestic Allotment Act, February 29, 1936	
(USHA)	(USHA)	United States Housing Authority (USHA) established by Congress, September 1, 1937
(Second AAA)	Second Agricultural Adjustment Act, February 16, 1938	
(Fair Labor Standards)	(Fair Labor Standards)	Fair Labor Standards Act (Wages and Hours Bill), June 25, 1938
		Reorganization Act, April 3, 1939
		Hatch Act, August 2, 1939

have been driven by desperation into criminal habits. Their work was useful—including reforestation, fire fighting (forty-seven lost their lives), flood control, and swamp drainage. The recruits were required to help their parents by sending home most of their pay. Both human resources and natural resources were thus conserved, though there were minor complaints of "militarizing" the nation's youth. Critics charged that CCC "soldiers" would later claim pensions for exposure to poison ivy.

The first major effort of the new Congress to grapple with the millions of adult unemployed was the Federal Emergency Relief Act. Its chief aim was immediate relief rather than long-range recovery. The resulting Federal Emergency Relief Administration (FERA) was handed over to zealous Harry L. Hopkins, a painfully thin, shabbily dressed, chain-smoking New York social worker who had earlier won Roosevelt's friendship and who became one of his most influential advisers. Hopkins's agency in all granted about $3 billion to the states for direct dole payments or preferably for wages on work projects.*

Immediate relief was also given two large and hard-pressed special groups by the Hundred Days Congress. One section of the Agricultural Adjustment Act (AAA) made available many millions of dollars to help farmers meet their mortgages. Another law created the Home Owners' Loan Corporation (HOLC). Designed to refinance mortgages on nonfarm homes, it ultimately assisted about a million badly pinched households. The agency not only bailed out mortgage-holding banks, it also bolted the political loyalties of relieved middle-class homeowners securely to the Democratic party.

Harassed by the continuing plague of unemployment, FDR himself established the Civil Works Administration (CWA) late in 1933. As a branch of the FERA, it also fell under the direction of Hopkins. Designed to provide purely temporary jobs during the cruel winter emergency, it served a useful purpose. Tens of thousands of jobless were employed at leaf raking and other make-work tasks, which were dubbed "boondoggling." As this kind of labor put a premium on shovel-leaning slow motion, the scheme was widely criticized. "The only thing we have to fear," scoffers remarked, "is work itself."

---

*A boast attributed to Hopkins in 1938 was, "We will spend and spend, tax and tax, and elect and elect."

Huey Long (1893–1935) Long pursued progressive policies as governor of Louisiana, even while he ruled the state with a dictatorial hand. A flamboyant and unpredictable populist, he set the orthodox political establishment on its ear, especially after he became a U.S. senator in 1930. Long's admirers called him the "Kingfish"; Franklin Roosevelt called him "one of the two most dangerous men in the country." (The other, said Roosevelt, was General Douglas MacArthur.)

A Day for Every Demagogue

Direct relief from Washington to needy families helped pull the nation through the ghastly winter of 1933–1934. But the disheartening persistence of unemployment and suffering demonstrated that emergency relief measures had to be not only continued but supplemented. One danger signal was the appearance of various demagogues, notably a magnetic "microphone messiah," Father Charles Coughlin, a Catholic priest in Michigan who began broadcasting in 1930 and whose slogan was "Social Justice." His anti–New Deal harangues to some 40 million radio fans finally became so anti-Semitic, fascistic, and demagogic that he was silenced in 1942 by his ecclesiastical superiors.

Also notorious among the new brood of agitators were those who capitalized on popular discontent to make pie-in-the-sky promises. Most conspicuous of these individuals was Senator Huey P. ("Kingfish") Long of Louisiana, who was said to have more brass than a government mule. He used his abundant rabble-rousing talents to publicize his "Share Our Wealth" program, which promised to

In 1935 Father Charles Coughlin (1891–1979) single-handedly defeated President Roosevelt's effort to win Senate ratification of a treaty providing for American membership in the World Court, a judicial body of limited authority established by the League of Nations. What FDR saw as a symbolic embrace of international responsibility Coughlin convinced his radio listeners was a conspiracy of international monied interests against American sovereignty:

"Our thanks are due to Almighty God in that America retains her sovereignty. Congratulations to the aroused people of the United States who, by more than 200,000 telegrams containing at least 1,000,000 names, demanded that the principles established by Washington and Jefferson shall keep us clear from foreign entanglements and European hatreds."

tenant, former clergyman Gerald L. K. Smith, "the gutsiest, goriest, loudest and lustiest, the deadliest and damndest orator ever heard on this or any other earth, the champion boob-bumper of all time." Fear of Long's becoming a fascist dictator ended when he was shot by an assassin in the Louisiana state capitol in 1935.

Another Pied Piper was gaunt Dr. Francis E. Townsend of California, a retired physician whose savings had recently been wiped out. He attracted the trusting support of perhaps 5 million "senior citizens" with his fantastic plan that nonetheless spoke to earthly need. Each oldster sixty years of age or over was to receive $200 a month, provided that the money be spent within the month. One estimate had the scheme costing one-half of the national income.

Partly to quiet the groundswell of unrest produced by such crackbrained proposals, Congress authorized the Works Progress Administration (WPA) in 1935. The objective was employment on useful projects. Launched under the supervision of the ailing but energetic Hopkins, this remarkable agency ultimately spent about $11 billion on thousands of public buildings, bridges, and hard-surfaced roads. Not every WPA project strengthened the infrastructure: for instance, one controlled crickets in Wyoming, while another built a monkey pen in Oklahoma City. Predictably, missions like these caused critics to sneer that WPA meant "We Provide Alms." But the fact is that over a period of

make "Every Man a King." Every family was to receive $5,000, supposedly at the expense of the prosperous. H. L. Mencken called Long's chief lieu-

Mary McLeod Bethune (1875–1955)
The daughter of ex-slaves and founder of a college in Florida, Bethune became the highest ranking African-American in the Roosevelt administration when she was appointed director of the Office of Minority Affairs in the National Youth Administration (NYA). From this base, she organized the "Black Cabinet" to make sure blacks benefited from the New Deal programs along with whites. Here she is meeting with First Lady Eleanor Roosevelt and Aubrey Williams, executive director of the NYA.

eight years, nearly 9 million people were given jobs, not handouts.

Agencies of the WPA also found part-time occupations for needy high school and college students and for such unemployed white-collar workers as actors, musicians, and writers. John Steinbeck, future Nobel Prize novelist, counted dogs in his California county. Cynical taxpayers condemned lessons in tap dancing, as well as the painting of murals on post office walls. But much precious talent was nourished, self-respect was preserved, and more than a million pieces of art were created, many of them publicly displayed.

A Helping Hand for Industry and Labor

A daring attempt to stimulate a nationwide comeback was initiated when the Emergency Congress authorized the National Recovery Administration (NRA). This ingenious scheme was by far the most complex and far-reaching effort by the New Dealers to combine immediate relief with long-range recovery and reform. Triple-barreled, it was designed to assist industry, labor, and the unemployed.

Individual industries—over two hundred in all—were to work out codes of "fair competition," under which hours of labor would be reduced so that employment could be spread over more people. A ceiling was placed on the maximum hours of labor; a floor was placed under wages to establish minimum levels.

Labor, under the NRA, was granted additional benefits. Workers were formally guaranteed the right to organize and bargain collectively through representatives *of their own choosing*—not through handpicked agents of the company's choosing. The hated "yellow-dog," or antiunion, contract was expressly forbidden, and certain safeguarding restrictions were placed on the use of child labor.

Industrial recovery through the NRA "fair competition" codes would at best be painful, for these called for self-denial by both management and labor. Patriotism was aroused by mass meetings and monster parades, which included 200,000 marchers on New York City's Fifth Avenue. A handsome blue eagle was designed as the symbol of the NRA, and merchants subscribing to a code displayed it in their windows with the slogan "We Do Our Part." A newly formed professional football team was christened the Philadelphia Eagles. Such was the enthusiasm for the NRA that for a brief period, there was a marked upswing in business activity, although Roosevelt had warned, "We cannot ballyhoo our way to prosperity."

But the high-flying eagle gradually fluttered to earth. Too much self-sacrifice was expected of labor, industry, and the public for such a scheme to work. Critics began to brand NRA "National Run Around" and "Nuts Running America," symbolized by what Henry Ford called "that damn Roosevelt buzzard." A new "age of chiselry" dawned as certain unscrupulous businesspeople ("chiselers") publicly displayed the blue bird on their windows but secretly violated the codes. Complete collapse was imminent when, in 1935, the Supreme Court shot down the dying eagle in the famed *Schechter* "sick chicken" decision. The learned justices unanimously held that Congress could not "delegate legislative powers" to the executive. They further declared that congressional control of interstate commerce could not properly apply to a local fowl business, like that of the Schechter brothers in Brooklyn, New York.

Frances Perkins (1882–1965) The first woman cabinet member, she served as secretary of labor under Roosevelt. She was subjected to much undeserved criticism from male businessmen, laborites, and politicians. They sneered that FDR kept her in labor for many years.

Roosevelt was incensed by this "horse and buggy" interpretation of the Constitution, but actually the Court helped him out of a bad jam.

The same act of Congress that hatched the NRA eagle also authorized the Public Works Administration (PWA), likewise intended both for industrial recovery and for unemployment relief. The agency was headed by the secretary of the interior, acid-tongued Harold L. Ickes, a free-swinging former bull mooser. Long-range recovery was the primary purpose of the new agency, and in time over $4 billion was spent on some thirty-four thousand projects, which included public buildings, highways, and parkways. One spectacular achievement was the Grand Coulee Dam on the Columbia River—the largest structure erected by humans since the Great Wall of China. In the depths of the depression, the grand dam seemed the height of folly. It made possible the irrigation of millions of acres of new farmland—at a time when the government was desperately trying to reduce farm surpluses. It created more electrical power than the entire TVA—in a region with little industry and virtually no market for additional power. But with the outbreak of World War II and then postwar prosperity, the dam would come to seem a stroke of genius, transforming the entire region with abundant water and power.

Special stimulants aided the recovery of one segment of business—the liquor industry. The imminent repeal of the prohibition amendment afforded an opportunity to raise needed federal revenue and at the same time to provide a measure of employment. Prodded by Roosevelt, the Hundred Days Congress, in one of its earliest acts, legalized light wine and beer with an alcoholic content (presumably nonintoxicating) not exceeding 3.2 percent by weight, and levied a tax of $5 on every barrel so manufactured. Disgruntled drys, unwilling to acknowledge the breakdown of law and order begotten by bootlegging, damned Roosevelt as "a 3.2 percent American." Prohibition was officially repealed by the Twenty-first Amendment late in 1933 (see Appendix), and the saloon doors swung open.

Paying Farmers Not to Farm

Ever since the war-boom days of 1918, farmers had suffered from low prices and overproduction, especially in grain. During the depression, conditions

Per thousand farms

Farm Foreclosures and Defaults, 1929–1945

became desperate as innumerable mortgages were foreclosed, as corn was burned for fuel, and as embattled farmers tried to prevent shipment of crops to glutted markets. In Iowa several volatile counties were placed under martial law.

A radical new approach to farm recovery was embraced when the Emergency Congress established the Agricultural Adjustment Administration (AAA). Through "artificial scarcity" this agency was to establish "parity prices" for basic commodities. "Parity" was the price set for a product that gave it the same real value, in purchasing power, that it had enjoyed during the period from 1909 to 1914. The AAA would eliminate price-depressing surpluses by paying growers to reduce their crop acreage. The millions of dollars needed for these payments were to be raised by taxing processors of farm products, such as flour millers, who in turn would shift the burden to consumers.

Novelist John Steinbeck (1902–1968) related in his novel The Grapes of Wrath *(1939) that when the "Okies" and "Arkies" reached California, they found the big growers unwilling to pay more than twenty-five cents an hour for work in the fields. One owner mutters,*

"A Red is any son-of-a-bitch that wants thirty cents an hour when we're paying twenty-five!"

Unhappily, the AAA got off to a wobbly start. It was begun after much of the cotton crop for 1933 had been planted, and balky mules, trained otherwise, were forced to plow under countless young plants. Several million squealing pigs were purchased and slaughtered. Much of their meat was distributed to people on relief, but some of it was used for fertilizer. This "sinful" destruction of food, at a time when thousands of citizens were hungry, increased condemnation of the American economic system by many left-leaning voices.

"Subsidized scarcity" did have the effect of raising farm income, but the whole confused enterprise met with acid criticism. Farmers, food processors, consumers, and taxpayers were all to some degree unhappy. Paying the farmers not to farm actually increased unemployment, at a time when other New Deal agencies were striving to decrease it. When the Supreme Court finally killed the AAA in 1936 by declaring its regulatory taxation provisions unconstitutional, foes of the plow-under program rejoiced loudly.

Quickly recovering from this blow, the New Deal Congress hastened to pass the Soil Conservation and Domestic Allotment Act of 1936. The withdrawal of acreage from production was now achieved by paying farmers to plant soil-conserving crops, like soybeans, or to let their land lie fallow. With the emphasis thus on conservation, the Supreme Court placed the stamp of its approval on the revamped scheme.

The Second Agricultural Adjustment Act of 1938, passed two years later, was a more comprehensive substitute, although it continued conservation payments. If growers observed acreage restrictions on specified commodities like cotton and wheat, they would be eligible for parity payments. Other provisions of the new AAA were designed to give farmers not only a fairer price but a more substantial share of the national income. Both goals were partially achieved.

Dust Bowls and Black Blizzards

Nature meanwhile had been providing some unplanned scarcity. Late in 1933 a prolonged drought struck the states of the trans-Mississippi Great Plains. Rainless weeks were followed by furious, whining winds, while the sun was darkened by millions of

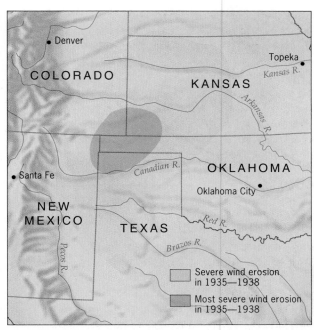

The Extent of Erosion in the 1930s   Note the extensive wind erosion in the western Oklahoma "panhandle" region, which was dubbed the "Dust Bowl" in the 1930s. Mechanized farmers had "busted" the sod of the southern plains so thoroughly that they literally broke the back of the land. Tons of dust blew out of the Dust Bowl in the 1930s and blotted the sun from the skies as far away as New York. A Kansas newspaperman reported in 1935 that in his dust-darkened town, "Lady Godiva could ride through streets without even the horse seeing her."

tons of powdery topsoil torn from homesteads in an area that stretched from eastern Colorado to western Missouri—soon to be dubbed the Dust Bowl. Despondent citizens sat on front porches with protective masks on their faces, watching their farms swirl by. A seven-year-old boy in Kansas suffocated. Overawed victims of the Dust Bowl disaster predicted the end of the world or the second coming of Christ.

Drought and wind triggered the dust storms, but they were not the only culprits. The human hand had also worked its mischief. High grain prices during World War I had enticed farmers to bring countless acres of marginal land under cultivation. Worse, dry-farming techniques and mechanization had revolutionized Great Plains agriculture. The steam tractor and the disk plow tore up infinitely more sod than a team of oxen ever could, leaving the powdery topsoil to be swept away at nature's whim.

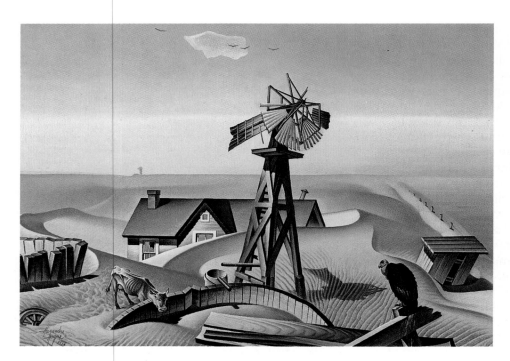

Drought-Stricken Area, by Alexandre Hogue
A combination of stingy nature and exploitative agricultural practices laid waste much of the southern Great Plains in the 1930s. Artist Alexandre Hogue rendered this grim depiction of the damage done by the desolating dust storms.

Burned and blown out of the Dust Bowl, tens of thousands of refugees fled their ruined acres (see "Makers of America: The Dust Bowl Migrants," pp. 792–793). In five years about 350,000 Oklahomans and Arkansans—"Okies" and "Arkies"—trekked to southern California in "junkyards on wheels." The dismal story of these human tumbleweeds was realistically portrayed in John Steinbeck's best-selling novel *The Grapes of Wrath* (1939), which proved to be the *Uncle Tom's Cabin* of the Dust Bowl.

Zealous New Dealers, sympathetic toward the soil-tillers, made various other efforts to relieve their burdens. The Frazier-Lemke Farm Bankruptcy Act, passed in 1934, made possible a suspension of mortgage foreclosures for five years, but it was voided the next year by the Supreme Court. A revised law, limiting the grace period to three years, was unanimously upheld. In 1935 the president set up the Resettlement Administration, charged with the task of removing near-farmless farmers to better land. And more than 200 million young trees were successfully planted on the bare prairies as windbreaks by the young men of the Civilian Conservation Corps, even though one governor jeered at trying to "grow hair on a bald head."

Native Americans also felt the far-reaching hand of New Deal reform. Commissioner of Indian Affairs John Collier ardently sought to reverse the forced-assimilation policies in place since the Dawes Act of 1887 (see p. 597). Inspired by a sojourn among the Pueblo Indians in Taos, New Mexico, Collier promoted the Indian Reorganization Act of 1934 (the "Indian New Deal"). The new law encouraged tribes to establish local self-government and to preserve their native crafts and traditions. The act also helped to stop the loss of Indian lands and revived tribes' interest in their identity and culture. Yet not all Indians applauded it. Some denounced the legislation as a "back-to-the-blanket" measure that sought to make museum pieces out of Native Americans. Seventy-seven tribes refused to organize under its provisions, though nearly two hundred others did establish tribal governments.

Battling Bankers and Big Business

Reformist New Dealers were determined from the outset to curb the "money changers" who had played fast and loose with gullible investors before the Wall Street crash of 1929. The Hundred Days Congress passed the "Truth in Securities Act" (Federal Securities Act), which required promoters to transmit to the investor sworn information regarding the soundness of their stocks and bonds. An old saying was thus reversed to read, "Let the seller beware," although the buyer might never read the fine print.

In 1934 Congress took further steps to protect the public against fraud, deception, and inside manipulation. It authorized the Securities and Exchange Commission (SEC), which was designed as a watchdog administrative agency. Stock markets henceforth were to operate more as trading marts and less as gambling casinos.

New Dealers likewise directed their fire at public utility holding companies, those supercorporations. Citizens had seen one of these incredible colossi collapse during the spring of 1932, when the Chicagoan Samuel Insull's multibillion-dollar financial empire crashed. Possibilities of controlling, with a minimum of capital, a half-dozen or so pyramided layers of big business suggested to Roosevelt "a ninety-six-inch dog being wagged by a four-inch tail." The Public Utility Holding Company Act of 1935 finally delivered a "death sentence" to this type of bloated growth, except where it might be deemed economically needful.

The TVA Harnesses the Tennessee River

Inevitably, the sprawling electric-power industry attracted the fire of New Deal reformers. Within a few decades, it had risen from nothingness to a behemoth with an investment of $13 billion. As a public utility, it reached directly and regularly into the pocketbooks of millions of consumers for vitally needed services. Ardent New Dealers accused it of gouging the public with excessive rates, especially since it owed its success to having secured, often for a song, priceless water-power sites from the public domain.

The tempestuous Tennessee River provided New Dealers with a rare opportunity. With its tributaries, the river drained a badly eroded area about the size of England, and one containing some 2.5 million of the most poverty-stricken people in America. The federal government already owned valuable properties at Muscle Shoals, where it had erected plants for needed nitrates in World War I. By developing the hydroelectric potential of the entire area, Washington could combine the immediate advantage of putting thousands of people to work with a long-term project for reforming the power monopoly.

An act creating the Tennessee Valley Authority (TVA) was passed in 1933 by the Hundred Days Congress. This far-ranging enterprise was largely a result of the steadfast vision and unflagging zeal of Senator George W. Norris of Nebraska, after whom one of the mighty dams was named. From the standpoint of "planned economy," the TVA was by far the most revolutionary of all the New Deal schemes.

This new agency was determined to discover precisely how much the production and distribution of electricity cost, so that a "yardstick" could be set up to test the fairness of rates charged by private companies. Utility corporations lashed back at this entering wedge of government control, charging that the low cost of TVA power was due to dishonest bookkeeping and the absence of taxes. Critics

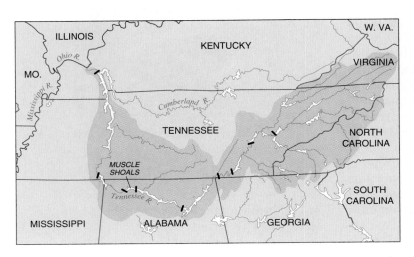

TVA Area Only the nine dams on the Tennessee River are shown here. More than twenty dams were constructed on the river's tributaries as part of a massive project to control flooding, generate hydroelectric power, and revitalize the Tennessee Valley region, while also creating jobs for the unemployed. The shaded area represents the area served by TVA electric power.

The Dust Bowl Migrants

Black dust clouds rolled across the southern Great Plains in the 1930s, darkening the skies above a landscape already desolated by the Great Depression. Its soil depleted by erosion, exhausted by over-intensive farming, and parched by drought, the prairie of eastern Colorado, northern Texas, Kansas, Oklahoma, Arkansas, and western Missouri became a dust bowl. The thirsty land offered up neither crops nor livelihood to the sturdy people whose forebears had staked out homesteads there. The desiccated earth exhaled only black dust and a dry wind that blew hundreds of thousands of people—the so-called Okies and Arkies—out of the Dust Bowl forever.

They headed mainly for California, piling aboard buses, hopping freight trains, or buying space in westbound cars. Most journeyed in their own autos, cramming their meager possessions into old jalopies and sputtering onto the highway. But unlike the aimless, isolated Joad family of John Steinbeck's classic novel *The Grapes of Wrath*, most Dust Bowl migrants knew where they were headed. Although many had lost everything in the depression, most knew relatives or friends who had migrated to California before the great crash and had sent back word about its abundant promise.

The earliest Okies had migrated under better circumstances in better times, and they often bragged of the good life in California. In the two decades preceding the Great Depression, more than a million people had left the states of Oklahoma, Texas, Arkansas, and Missouri. At least a quarter of them turned toward California, lured by advertisements that painted a life of leisure and plenty amid the palms.

Their ears so long filled with glowing reports from this earlier exodus, the Dust Bowl migrants refused to believe that the depression could sully the bright promise of California. Not even an ominous sign posted by the state of California on the highway just west of Tulsa deterred them. Indeed the billboard proclaimed its warning in vain—"NO JOBS in California . . . If YOU are looking for work—KEEP OUT."

Some Okies and Arkies made their way past the sign to California cities, but many of them favored the San Joaquin Valley, the southern part of central California's agricultural kingdom. The migrants chose it for its familiarity. The valley shared much in common with the southern plains—arid climate, cotton growing, newfound oil deposits, and abundant land.

During the 1930s the San Joaquin Valley also proved all too familiar in its poverty; in 1939 the median income for migrants from the southern

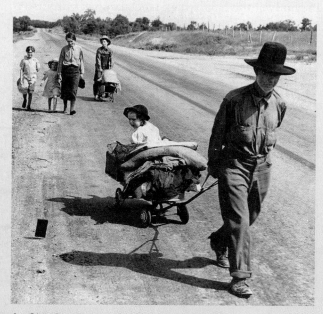

An Okie Family Hits the Road in the 1930s

plains hovered just below the official poverty line. Food, shelter, and clothing were scarce; the winter months, without work and without heat, proved nearly unendurable for the migrants. John Steinbeck, writing in a San Francisco newspaper, exposed the tribulations of the Dust Bowl refugees: "First the gasoline gives out. And without gasoline a man cannot go to a job even if he could get one. Then the food goes. And then in the rains, with insufficient food, the children develop colds. . . ."

Eventually the Farm Security Administration—a New Deal agency—set up camps to house the Okies. A fortunate few purchased land and erected makeshift homes, creating tiny "Okievilles" or "Little Oklahomas." During World War II, most Okies escaped the deprivation and uncertainty of seasonal farm labor, securing regular jobs in defense industries. But the "Okievilles" remained, to form the bedrock of a still-thriving subculture in California—one that has brought the Dust Bowl's country and western music, pecan pie, and evangelical religion to the Far West.

Factories in the Fields Many Okies became migrant farmworkers in the 1930s, drifting about the country to harvest different crops, like the pea pickers shown here.

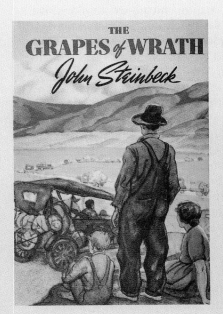

The Grapes of Wrath, 1939 Steinbeck's novel followed the Joad family on their epic trek from the drought-devastated farms of Oklahoma to the migrant labor camps of California. That so many Americans were forced to endure this misery aroused intense indignation among millions of readers.

A Dust Storm Envelops Baca County, Colorado, in the 1930s

> *In the early 1980s, Atlanta mayor Andrew Young (b. 1932) observed that the Tennessee Valley Authority created the economic structure for the later civil rights movement:*
>
> "It was the presence of the cheap electricity, lower interest rates, water projects, that laid the foundation for the New South."

complained that the whole dream was "creeping socialism in concrete."

But the New Dealers, shrugging off such outcries, pointed a prideful finger at the amazing achievements of the TVA. The gigantic project brought to the area not only full employment and the blessings of cheap electric power, but low-cost housing, abundant cheap nitrates, the restoration of eroded soil, reforestation, improved navigation, and flood control. Rivers ran blue instead of brown, and a once-poverty-cursed area was being transformed into one of the most flourishing regions in the United States. Foreigners were greatly impressed with the possibilities of similar schemes in their own lands, and exulting New Dealers agitated for parallel enterprises in the valleys of the Columbia, Colorado, and Missouri Rivers. Federally built dams one day would span all those waterways, impounding more than 30 percent of the total annual runoff from the "roof of America" in the Rocky Mountains. Hydroelectric power from those dams would drive the growth of the urban West, and the waters they diverted would nurture agriculture in the previously bone-dry western deserts. But conservative reaction against the "socialistic" New Deal would confine the TVA's brand of federally guided resource management and comprehensive regional development to the Tennessee Valley.

Housing Reform and Social Security

The New Deal had meanwhile framed sturdy new policies for housing construction. To speed recovery and better homes, Roosevelt set up the Federal Housing Administration (FHA) as early as 1934. The

building industry was to be stimulated by small loans to householders, both for improving their dwellings and for completing new ones. So popular did the FHA prove to be that it was one of the few "alphabetical agencies" to outlast the age of Roosevelt.

Congress bolstered the program in 1937 by authorizing the United States Housing Authority (USHA)—an agency designed to lend money to states or communities for low-cost construction. Although units for about 650,000 low-income people were started, new building fell tragically short of needs. New Deal efforts to expand the project collided with brick-wall opposition from real estate promoters, builders, and landlords ("slumlords"), to say nothing of anti–New Dealers who attacked what they considered down-the-rathole spending. Nonetheless, for the first time in a century, the slum areas in America ceased growing and even shrank.

Incomparably more important was the success of New Dealers in the field of unemployment insurance and old-age pensions. Their greatest victory was the epochal Social Security Act of 1935—one of the most complicated and far-reaching laws ever to pass Congress. To cushion future depressions, the measure provided for federal-state unemployment insurance. To provide security for old age, specified categories of retired workers were to receive regular payments from Washington. These payments ranged from $10 to $85 a month (later raised) and were financed by a payroll tax on both employers and employees. Provision was also made for the blind, the physically handicapped, delinquent children, and other dependents.

Republican opposition to the sweeping new legislation was bitter. "Social Security," insisted Hoover, "must be builded upon a cult of work, not a cult of leisure." The GOP national chairman falsely charged that every worker would have to wear a metal dog tag for life.

Social Security was largely inspired by the example of some of the more highly industrialized nations of Europe. In the agricultural America of an earlier day, there had always been farm chores for all ages, and the large family had cared for its own dependents. But in an urbanized economy, at the mercy of boom-or-bust cycles, the government was now recognizing its responsibility for the welfare of its citizens. By 1939 over 45 million people were eligible for Social Security benefits, and in subsequent years further categories of workers were added and the payments to them were periodically increased.

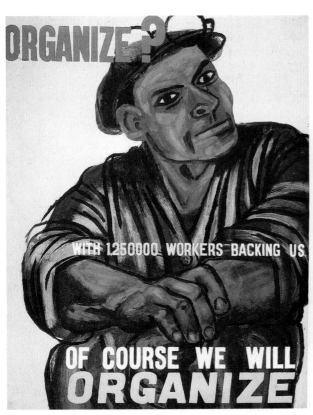

Labor Triumphant   After generations of struggle, organized labor made dramatic gains in membership and bargaining power during the New Deal years.

John L. Lewis (1880–1969) Inciting Textile Workers to Strike, 1937   A miner, Lewis worked his way up to the presidency of the United Mine Workers of America. He then founded the Committee for Industrial Organization, later reconstituted as the Congress of Industrial Organizations, in the mid-1930s to unite all industrial workers in a powerful bloc of "big labor" to stand up to "big business."

In contrast to Europe, where benefits generally were universal, American workers had to be employed to get coverage.

A New Deal for Unskilled Labor

The NRA blue eagles, with their call for collective bargaining, had been a godsend to organized labor. As New Deal expenditures brought some slackening of unemployment, labor began to feel more secure and hence more self-assertive. A rash of walkouts occurred in the summer of 1934, including a paralyzing general strike in San Francisco (following a "Bloody Thursday"), which was broken only when outraged citizens resorted to vigilante tactics.

When the Supreme Court axed the blue eagle, a Congress sympathetic to labor unions undertook to fill the vacuum. The fruit of its deliberations was the Wagner, or National Labor Relations, Act of 1935. This trailblazing law created a powerful new National Labor Relations Board for administrative purposes and reasserted the right of labor to engage

A worker at a Chevrolet plant in Flint, Michigan, wrote after the United Auto Workers–CIO victory in 1937,

"The inhuman high speed is *no more.* We now have a voice, and have slowed up the speed of the line. And [we] are now treated as human beings, and not as part of the machinery. The high pressure is taken off. . . . It proves clearly that united we stand, divided or alone we fall."

General Motors Sit-down Strikers, Flint, Michigan, 1937 Strikers like these sometimes kept their spirits up with the song "Sit Down":

When the boss won't talk
Don't take a walk;
Sit down, sit down.

in self-organization and to bargain collectively through representatives of its own choice. The Wagner Act proved to be one of the real milestones on the rocky road of the U.S. labor movement.

Under the encouragement of a highly sympathetic National Labor Relations Board, a host of unskilled workers began to organize themselves into effective unions. The leader of this drive was beetle-browed, domineering, and melodramatic John L. Lewis, boss of the United Mine Workers. In 1935 he succeeded in forming the Committee for Industrial Organization (CIO) within the ranks of the skilled-craft American Federation of Labor. But skilled workers, ever since the days of the ill-fated Knights of Labor in the 1880s, had shown only lukewarm sympathy for the cause of unskilled labor, especially blacks. In 1936, following inevitable friction with the CIO, the older federation suspended the upstart unions associated with the newer organization.

Undaunted, the rebellious CIO moved on a concerted scale into the huge automobile industry. Late in 1936 the workers resorted to a revolutionary technique (earlier used in both Europe and America) known as the sit-down strike: they refused to leave the factory building of General Motors at Flint,

Michigan, and thus prevented the importation of strikebreakers. Conservative respecters of private property were scandalized. The CIO finally won a resounding victory when its union, after heated negotiations, was recognized by General Motors as the sole bargaining agency for its employees.

Unskilled workers now pressed their advantage. The United States Steel Company, hitherto an impossible nut for labor to crack, averted a costly strike when it voluntarily granted rights of unionization to its CIO-organized employees. But the "little steel" companies fought back savagely. Citizens were shocked in 1937 by the Memorial Day massacre at the plant of the Republic Steel Company in South Chicago. In a bloody fracas, police fired upon pickets and workers, leaving the area strewn with several score dead and wounded.

A better deal for labor continued when Congress, in 1938, passed the memorable Fair Labor Standards Act (Wages and Hours Bill). Industries involved in interstate commerce were to set up minimum-wage and maximum-hour levels. The eventual goals were forty cents an hour (later raised) and a forty-hour week. Labor by children under sixteen (under eighteen if the occupation was dangerous) was forbidden. These reforms were bitterly

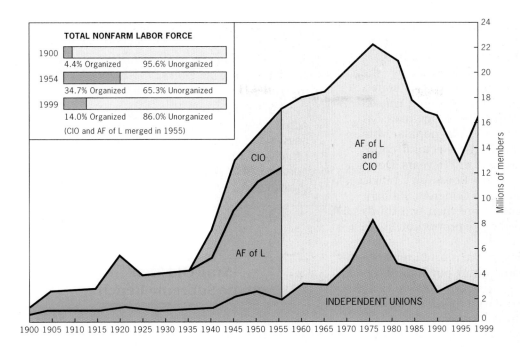

TOTAL NONFARM LABOR FORCE

1900 — 4.4% Organized   95.6% Unorganized

1954 — 34.7% Organized   65.3% Unorganized

1999 — 14.0% Organized   86.0% Unorganized

(CIO and AF of L merged in 1955)

CIO

AF of L

AF of L and CIO

INDEPENDENT UNIONS

Millions of members

1900 1905 1910 1915 1920 1925 1930 1935 1940 1945 1950 1955 1960 1965 1970 1975 1980 1985 1990 1995 1999

The Rise and Decline of Organized Labor, 1900–1999 The percentage of the total labor force that was organized increased until 1954, and it has declined ever since. (Source: Bureau of Labor Statistics.)

though futilely opposed by many industrialists, especially by those southern textile manufacturers who had profited from low-wage labor. But the exclusion of agricultural, service, and domestic workers meant that blacks, Mexican-Americans, and women—who were concentrated in these fields—did not benefit from the act.

In later New Deal days, labor unionization thrived; "Roosevelt wants you to join a union" was the rallying cry of professional organizers. The president received valuable support at ballot-box time from labor leaders and many appreciative working people. One mill worker remarked that Roosevelt was "the only man we ever had in the White House who would know that my boss is a s.o.b."

The CIO surged forward, breaking completely with the AF of L in 1938. On that occasion the *Committee* for Industrial Organization was formally reconstituted as the *Congress* of Industrial Organization*s* (the new CIO), under the high-handed presidency of John L. Lewis. By 1940 the CIO could claim about 4 million members in its constituent unions, including some 200,000 blacks. Nevertheless, bitter and annoying jurisdictional feuding involving strikes continued with the AF of L. At times labor seemed more bent on costly civil war than on its age-old war with management.

Landon Challenges "the Champ" in 1936

As the presidential campaign of 1936 neared, the New Dealers were on top of the world. They had achieved considerable progress, and millions of "reliefers" were grateful to their bountiful government. The exultant Democrats renominated Roosevelt on a platform squarely endorsing the New Deal.

The Republicans were hard-pressed to find someone to feed to "the Champ." They finally settled on the colorless but homespun and honest governor of the Sunflower State of Kansas, Alfred M. Landon. Landon himself was a moderate who accepted some New Deal reforms, although not the popular Social Security Act. But the Republican platform vigorously condemned the New Deal of Franklin "Deficit" Roosevelt for its radicalism, experimentation, confusion, and "frightful waste." Backing Landon, ex-president Hoover called for a "holy crusade for liberty," echoing the cry of the American Liberty League, a group of wealthy conservatives who had organized in 1934 to fight "socialistic" New Deal schemes.

Roosevelt gave as good as he got. Angry enough to stretch sheet iron, the president took to the stump and denounced the "economic royalists" who sought to "hide behind the flag and the Constitution." "I welcome their hatred," he proclaimed.

A landslide overwhelmed Landon, as the demoralized Republicans carried only two states, Maine and Vermont. This dismal showing caused political wiseacres to make the old adage read, "As Maine goes, so goes Vermont."* The popular vote was 27,752,869 to 16,674,665; the electoral count was 523 to 8—the most lopsided in 116 years. Democratic majorities, riding in on Roosevelt's magic coattails, were again returned to Congress. Jubilant Democrats could now claim more than two-thirds of the seats in the House and a like proportion in the Senate.

The battle of 1936, perhaps the most bitter since Bryan's defeat in 1896, partially bore out Republican charges of class warfare. Even more than in 1932, the needy economic groups were lined up against the so-called greedy economic groups. CIO units contributed generously to FDR's campaign chest. Many left-wingers turned to Roosevelt, as the customary third-party protest vote sharply declined. Blacks, several million of whom had also appreciated welcome relief checks, had by now largely shaken off their traditional allegiance to the Republican party. To them, Lincoln was "finally dead."

FDR won primarily because he appealed to the "forgotten man," whom he never forgot. Some of the president's support was only pocketbook-deep: "relievers" were not going to bite the hand that doled out the government checks. No one, as Al Smith remarked, "shoots at Santa Claus." But Roosevelt in fact had forged a powerful and enduring coalition of the South, blacks, urbanites, and the poor. He proved especially effective in marshaling the support of the multitudes of "New Immigrants"—mostly the Catholics and Jews who had swarmed into the great cities since the turn of the century. These once-scorned newcomers, with their now-numerous sons and daughters, had at last come politically of age. In the 1920s one out of every twenty-five federal judgeships went to a Catholic; Roosevelt appointed Catholics to one out of every four.

---

*Maine, which traditionally held its state elections in September, was long regarded as a political weathervane. Hence the expression, "As Maine goes, so goes the nation."

Three days before the 1936 election, Roosevelt took the moral high ground in his speech at New York's Madison Square Garden:

"I should like to have it said of my first Administration that in it the forces of selfishness and of lust for power met their match. I should like to have it said of my second Administration that in it these forces met their master."

Nine Old Men on the Supreme Bench

Bowing his head to the sleety blasts, Roosevelt took the presidential oath on January 20, 1937, instead of the traditional March 4. The Twentieth Amendment to the Constitution had been ratified in 1933. (See the Appendix.) It swept away the postelection lame duck session of Congress and shortened by six weeks the awkward period before inauguration.

Flushed with victory, Roosevelt interpreted his reelection as a mandate to continue New Deal reforms. But in his eyes, the cloistered old men on the supreme bench, like fossilized stumbling blocks, stood stubbornly in the pathway of progress. In nine major cases involving the New Deal, the Roosevelt administration had been thwarted seven times. The Court was ultraconservative, and six of the nine oldsters in black were over seventy. As luck would have it, not a single member had been appointed by FDR in his first term.

Roosevelt, his "Dutch up," viewed with mounting impatience what he regarded as the obstructive conservatism of the Court. Some of these Old Guard appointees were hanging on with a senile grip, partly because they felt it their patriotic duty to curb the "socialistic" tendencies of that radical in the White House. Roosevelt believed that the voters in three successive elections—the presidential elections of 1932 and 1936 and the midterm congressional elections of 1934—had returned a smashing verdict in favor of his program of reform. Democracy, in his view, meant rule by the people. If the American way of life was to be preserved, Roosevelt argued, the Supreme Court ought to get in line with the supreme court of public opinion.

Roosevelt finally hit upon a Court scheme that he regarded as "the answer to a maiden's prayer." In fact, it proved to be one of the most costly political misjudgments of his career. When he sprang his brainstorm on a shocked nation early in 1937, he caught the country and Congress completely by surprise. Roosevelt bluntly asked Congress for legislation to permit him to add a new justice to the Supreme Court for every member over seventy who would not retire. The maximum membership could then be fifteen. Roosevelt pointed to the necessity of injecting vigorous new blood, for the Court, he alleged, was far behind in its work. This charge, which turned out to be false, brought heated accusations of dishonesty. At best, Roosevelt was headstrong and not fully aware of the fact that the Court, in popular thinking, had become something of a sacred cow.

The Court Changes Course

Congress and the nation were promptly convulsed over the scheme to "pack" the Supreme Court with a "dictator bill," which one critic called "too damned slick." Franklin "Double-crossing" Roosevelt was vilified for attempting to break down the delicate checks and balances among the three branches of the government. He was accused of grooming himself as a dictator by trying to browbeat the judiciary. In the eyes of countless citizens, mostly Republicans but including many Democrats, basic liberties seemed to be in jeopardy. "God Bless the Supreme Court" was a fervent prayer.

The Court had meanwhile seen the ax hanging over its head. Whatever his motives, Justice Owen J. Roberts, formerly regarded as a conservative, began to vote on the side of his liberal colleagues. "A switch in time saves nine" was the classic witticism

The Response to Roosevelt's "Court Packing" Plan, 1937
Even the Democratic donkey kicked up a storm in opposition to President Roosevelt's plan to expand the Supreme Court to as many as fifteen judges.

ALL I SAID WAS "GIMME SIX MORE JUSTICES!"

inspired by this ideological change. By a five to four decision, the Court, in March 1937, upheld the principle of a state minimum wage for women, thereby reversing its stand on a different case a year earlier. In succeeding decisions a Court more sympathetic to the New Deal upheld the National Labor Relations Act (Wagner Act) and the Social Security Act. Roosevelt's "Court-packing" was further undermined when Congress voted full pay for justices over seventy who retired, whereupon one of the oldest conservative members resigned, to be replaced by a New Dealer, Justice Hugo Black.

Congress finally passed a court reform bill, but this watered-down version applied only to lower courts. Roosevelt, the master politician, thus suffered his first major legislative defeat at the hands of his own party in Congress. Americans have never viewed lightly a tampering with the Supreme Court by the president, no matter how popular their chief executive may be. Yet in losing this battle, Roosevelt incidentally won his campaign. The Court, as he had hoped, became markedly more friendly to New Deal reforms. Furthermore, a succession of deaths and resignations enabled him in time to make nine appointments to the tribunal—more than any of his predecessors since George Washington. The clock "unpacked" the Court.

Yet in a sense, FDR lost both the Court battle and the war. He so aroused conservatives of both parties in Congress that few New Deal reforms were passed after 1937, the year of the fight to "pack" the bench. With this catastrophic miscalculation, he squandered much of the political goodwill that had carried him to such a resounding victory in the 1936 election.

The Twilight of the New Deal

Roosevelt's first term, from 1933 to 1937, did not banish the depression from the land. Unemployment stubbornly persisted in 1936 at about 15 percent, down from the grim 25 percent of 1933 but still miserably high. Despite the inventiveness of New Deal programs and the billions of dollars in "pump priming," recovery had been dishearteningly modest, though the country seemed to be inching its way back to economic health.

Then in 1937 the economy took another sharp downturn, a surprisingly severe depression-within-the-depression that the president's critics quickly dubbed the "Roosevelt recession." In fact, government policies had caused the nosedive, as new Social Security taxes began to bite into payrolls and as the administration cut back on spending out of continuing reverence for the orthodox economic doctrine of the balanced budget.

Only at this late date did Roosevelt at last frankly and deliberately embrace the recommendations of the British economist John Maynard Keynes. The New Deal had run deficits for several years, but all of them had been rather small and

Millions

(Graph with years 1929–1942 on horizontal axis, millions 0–12 on vertical axis, with labels: STOCK CRASH, FDR'S ELECTION, NEW DEAL RECOVERY, RECESSION, WORLD WAR II BREAKS)

Unemployment, 1929–1942
These cold figures can only begin to suggest the widespread human misery caused by mass unemployment. One man wrote to a newspaper in 1932, "I am forty-eight; married twenty-one years; four children, three in school. For the last eight years I was employed as a Pullman conductor. Since September, 1930, they have given me seven months part-time work. Today I am an object of charity. . . . My small, weak, and frail wife and two small children are suffering and I have come to that terrible place where I could easily resort to violence in my desperation."

> *A basic objective of the New Deal was featured in Roosevelt's second inaugural address (1937):*
>
> "I see one-third of a nation ill-housed, ill-clad, ill-nourished. . . . The test of our progress is not whether we add more to the abundance of those who have much; it is whether we provide enough for those who have too little."

none was intended. Now, in April 1937, Roosevelt announced a bold program to stimulate the economy by planned deficit spending. Although the deficits were still undersized for the herculean task of conquering the depression, this abrupt policy reversal marked a major turning point in the government's relation to the economy. "Keynesianism" became the new economic orthodoxy and remained so for decades.

Roosevelt had meanwhile been pushing the remaining reform measures of the New Deal. Early in 1937 he urged Congress—a Congress growing more conservative—to authorize a sweeping reorganization of the national administration in the interests of streamlined efficiency. But the issue became tangled up with his presumed autocratic ambitions in regard to the Supreme Court, and he suffered another stinging defeat. Two years later, in 1939, Congress partially relented and in the Reorganization Act gave him limited powers for administrative reforms, including the key new Executive Office in the White House.

The New Dealers were accused of having the richest campaign chest in history, and in truth government relief checks had a curious habit of coming in bunches just before ballot time. To remedy such practices, which tended to make a farce of free elections, Congress adopted the much-heralded Hatch Act of 1939. This act barred federal administrative officials, except the highest policy-making officers, from active political campaigning and soliciting. It also forbade the use of government funds for political purposes as well as the collection of campaign contributions from people receiving relief payments. The Hatch Act was broadened in 1940 to place limits on campaign contributions and expenditures, but

Employment Agency, by Isaac Soyer, 1937 Millions of jobless Americans felt the despair Soyer captured in this painting, as depression-era unemployment reached levels never seen before or since in American history.

such clever ways of getting around it were found that on the whole the legislation proved disappointing.

By 1938 the New Deal had clearly lost most of its early momentum. Magician Roosevelt could find few dazzling new reform rabbits to pull out of his tall silk hat. In the congressional elections of 1938, the Republicans, for the first time, cut heavily into the New Deal majorities in Congress, though failing to gain control of either house. The international crisis that came to a boil in 1938–1939 shifted public attention away from domestic reform and no doubt helped save the political hide of the Roosevelt "spendocracy." The New Deal, for all practical purposes, had shot its bolt.

New Deal or Raw Deal?

Foes of the New Deal condemned its alleged waste, incompetence, confusion, contradictions, and cross-purposes, as well as the chiseling and graft in the alphabetical agencies—"alphabet soup," sneered Al Smith. Roosevelt had done nothing, cynics said, that an earthquake could not have done better. Critics deplored the employment of "crackpot" college professors, leftist "pinkos," and outright Communists. Such subversives, it was charged, were trying to make America over in the Bolshevik-Marxist image under "Rooseveltski." The Hearst newspapers lambasted,

> *The Red New Deal with a Soviet seal*
> *Endorsed by a Moscow hand,*
>   *The strange result of an alien cult*
> *In a liberty-loving land.*

Roosevelt was further accused by conservatives of being Jewish ("Rosenfield") and of tapping too many bright young Jewish leftists ("The Jew Deal") for his "Drain Trust."

Hardheaded businesspeople, who "had met a payroll," were shocked by the leap-before-you-look, try-anything-once spirit of Roosevelt, the jolly improviser. They accused him of confusing noise and movement with progress. Others appreciated the president's do-something approach. Humorist Will Rogers, the rope-twirling "poet lariat" of the era, remarked that if Roosevelt were to burn down the Capitol, people would say, "Well, we at least got a fire started, anyhow."

"Bureaucratic meddling" and "regimentation" were also bitter complaints of anti–New Dealers; in truth, bureaucracy did blossom. The federal government, with its hundreds of thousands of employees, became incomparably the largest single business in the country, as the states faded further into the background.

Promises of budget balancing, to say nothing of other promises, had flown out the window—so foes of the New Deal pointed out. The national debt had stood at the already enormous figure of $19,487,000,000 in 1932 and had skyrocketed to $40,440,000,000 by 1939. America was becoming, its critics charged, a "handout state" trying to squander itself into prosperity—*U.S.* stood for "unlimited spending." Such lavish benefactions were undermining the old virtues of thrift and initiative. Ordinary Americans, once self-reliant citizens, were getting a bad case of the "gimmies": their wishbones were becoming larger than their backbones. In the nineteenth century, hard-pressed workers went west; now they went on relief.

Business was bitter. Accusing the New Deal of fomenting class strife, conservatives insisted that the laborer and the farmer—especially the big operator—were being pampered. Why "soak the successful"? Countless businesspeople, especially Republicans, declared that they could pull themselves out of the depression if they could only get the federal government—an interventionist big government—off their backs. Private enterprise, they charged, was being stifled by "planned economy," "planned bankruptcy," "creeping socialism," and the philosophy "Washington can do it better," with a federal pill for every ill. States' rights were being ignored, while the government was competing in business with its own citizens, under a "dictatorship of do-gooders."

The aggressive leadership of Roosevelt—"one-man supergovernment"—also came in for denunciation. Heavy fire was especially directed at his attempts to browbeat the Supreme Court and to create a "dummy Congress." Roosevelt had even tried in the 1938 elections, with backfiring results, to "purge" members of Congress who would not lock-step with him. The three senators whom he publicly opposed were all triumphantly reelected.

The most damning indictment of the New Deal was that it had failed to cure the depression. Afloat in a sea of red ink, it had merely administered

Our Skipper This pro-FDR cartoon depicts a confident Roosevelt ignoring his critics while heading cheerily toward economic recovery. In fact, FDR's New Deal brought neither the recovery he promised nor the ruin his detractors prophesied. The depression dragged on with only periodic improvement for nearly eight years under his leadership, until the cataclysmic emergency of World War II finally banished unemployment from the land.

aspirin, sedatives, and Band-Aids. Many economists came to believe that better results would have been achieved by much greater deficit spending. Despite some $20 billion poured out in six years of deficit spending and lending, of leaf raking and pump priming, the gap was not closed between production and consumption. There were even more mountainous farm surpluses under Roosevelt than under Hoover. Millions of dispirited men and women were still unemployed in 1939, after six years of drain, strain, and pain. Not until World War II blazed forth in Europe was the unemployment headache solved. The sensational increase in the national debt was caused by World War II, not the New Deal. The national debt was only $40 billion in 1939 but $258 billion in 1945.

FDR's Balance Sheet

New Dealers staunchly defended their record. Admitting that there had been some waste, they pointed out that relief—not economy—had been the primary object of their multifront war on the depression. Conceding also that there had been some graft, they argued that it had been trivial in view of the immense sums spent and the obvious need for haste.

Apologists for Roosevelt further declared that the New Deal had relieved the worst of the crisis in 1933. It promoted the philosophy of "balancing the human budget" and accepted the principle that the federal government was morally bound to prevent mass hunger and starvation by "managing" the economy. The Washington regime was to be used, not feared. The collapse of America's economic system was averted, a fairer distribution of the national income was achieved, and the citizens were enabled

In his acceptance speech at the 1936 Democratic convention, Roosevelt stated,

"Governments can err; presidents do make mistakes, . . . but better the occasional faults of a Government that lives in a spirit of charity than the consistent omissions of a Government frozen in the ice of its own indifference."

to regain and retain their self-respect. "Nobody is going to starve" was Roosevelt's promise.

Though hated by business tycoons, FDR should have been their patron saint, so his admirers claimed. He deflected popular resentments against business and may have saved the American system of free enterprise. Roosevelt's quarrel was not with capitalism but with capitalists; he purged American capitalism of some of its worst abuses so that it might be saved from itself. He may even have headed off a more radical swing to the left by a mild dose of what was mistakenly reviled as "socialism." The head of the American Socialist party, when once asked if the New Deal had carried out the Socialist program, reportedly replied that it had indeed—on a stretcher.

Roosevelt, like Jefferson, provided bold reform without a bloody revolution—at a time in history when some foreign nations were suffering armed uprisings and when many Europeans were predicting either communism or fascism for America. He was upbraided by the left-wing radicals for not going far enough, by the right-wing radicals for going too far. Choosing the middle road, he has been called the greatest American conservative since Hamilton. He was in fact Hamiltonian in his espousal of big government, but Jeffersonian in his concern for the "forgotten man." Demonstrating anew the value of powerful presidential leadership, he exercised that power to relieve the erosion of the nation's greatest physical resource—its people. He helped preserve democracy in America in a time when democracies abroad were disappearing down the sinkhole of dictatorship. And in playing this role, he unwittingly girded the nation for its part in the titanic war that loomed on the horizon—a war in which democracy the world over would be at stake.

Chronology

1932 Roosevelt defeats Hoover for presidency	**1935** WPA established
	Wagner Act
1933 Bank holiday	Resettlement Administration
Emergency Banking Relief Act	Social Security Act
Beer and Wine Revenue Act	Public Utility Holding Company Act
The Hundred Days Congress enacts AAA,	*Schechter* "sick-chicken" case
TVA, HOLC, NRA, and PWA	CIO organized
Federal Securities Act	
Glass-Steagall Banking Reform Act	**1936** Soil Conservation and Domestic Allotment
CWA established	Act
Twentieth Amendment (changed calendar	Roosevelt defeats Landon for presidency
of congressional sessions and date of	
presidential inauguration)	**1937** USHA established
Twenty-first Amendment (prohibition repealed)	Roosevelt announces "Court-packing" plan
1934 Gold Reserve Act	**1938** Second AAA
Securities and Exchange Commission	Fair Labor Standards Act
authorized	
Indian Reorganization Act	**1939** Reorganization Act
FHA established	Hatch Act
Frazier-Lemke Farm Bankruptcy Act	

VARYING VIEWPOINTS

How Radical Was the New Deal?

The Great Depression was both a great calamity and a great opportunity. How effectively Franklin Roosevelt responded to the calamity and what use he made of the opportunity are the two great questions that have animated historical debate about the New Deal.

Some historians have actually denied that there was much of a connection between the depression and the New Deal. Arthur M. Schlesinger, Jr., for example, who believes in "cycles" of reform and reaction in American history, has written that "there would very likely have been some sort of New Deal in the 1930s even without the Depression." But most of the first generation of historians who wrote about the New Deal (in the 1940s, 1950s, and early 1960s) agreed with Carl Degler's judgment that the New Deal was "a revolutionary response to a revolutionary situation." In this view, though Roosevelt never found a means short of war to bring about economic recovery, he shrewdly utilized the stubborn economic crisis as a means to enact sweeping reforms. A handful of scholars, notably Edgar Eugene Robinson, condemned Roosevelt's record as a "socialistic" break with American traditions. But until the 1960s, the great majority of historians approved the political values of the new Deal and praised its accomplishments.

Some leftist scholars writing in the 1960s, however, notably Barton J. Bernstein, charged that the New Deal did not reach far enough. This criticism echoed the socialist complaint in the 1930s that the depression represented the total collapse of American capitalism, and that the New Deal had muffed the chance truly to remake American society. Roosevelt had the chance, these historians argue, to redistribute wealth, improve race relations, and bring the giant corporations to heel. Instead, say these critics, the New Deal simply represented a conservative holding action to shore up a sagging and corrupt capitalist order.

Those charges against the New Deal stimulated another generation of scholars in the 1970s, 1980s, and 1990s to look closely at the concrete institutional, attitudinal, and economic circumstances in which the New Deal unfolded. Historians such as James Patterson, Alan Brinkley, Kenneth Jackson, Harvard Sitkoff, and Lizabeth Cohen—sometimes loosely referred to as the "constraints school"—conclude that the New Deal offered just about as much reform as circumstances allowed and as the majority of Americans wanted. The findings of these historians are impressive: the system of checks and balances limited presidential power; the disproportionate influence of southern Democrats in Congress stalled attempts to move toward racial justice; the federal system, in fact, inhibited all efforts to initiate change from Washington. Most important, a majority of the American people at the time wanted to reform capitalism, not overthrow it. Industrial workers, for example, were not hapless pawns upon whom the New Deal was foisted, frustrating their yearning for more radical change. Instead they sought security and self-determination in ways quite compatible with the New Deal's programs for unemployment insurance, old-age pensions, and guarantees of labor's right to organize.

The best proof of the soundness of that conclusion is probably the durability of the political alliance that Roosevelt assembled. The great "New Deal coalition" that dominated American politics for nearly four decades after Roosevelt's election in 1932 represented a broad consensus in American society about the legitimate limits of government efforts to shape the social and economic order. William Leuchtenburg has offered the most balanced historical assessment in his description of the New Deal as a "half-way revolution," neither radical nor conservative, but accurately reflecting the American people's needs and desires in the 1930s—and for a long time thereafter.

For further reading, see page A23 of the Appendix. For web resources, go to **http://college.hmco.com.**

Franklin D. Roosevelt and the Shadow of War

~∾~

1933–1941

The epidemic of world lawlessness is spreading. When an epidemic of physical disease starts to spread, the community approves and joins in a quarantine of the patients in order to protect the health of the community against the spread of the disease. . . . There must be positive endeavors to preserve peace.

FRANKLIN D. ROOSEVELT, CHICAGO "QUARANTINE SPEECH," 1937

Americans in the 1930s tried to turn their backs on the world's problems. Their president at first seemed to share these views. The only battle Roosevelt sought was against the depression. America had its own burdens to shoulder, and the costs of foreign involvement, whether in blood or treasure, simply seemed too great.

But as the clouds of war gathered over Europe, Roosevelt eventually concluded that the United States could no longer remain aloof. Events gradually brought the American people around to his thinking: no nation was safe in an era of international anarchy, and the world could not remain half-enchained and half-free.

The London Conference

The sixty-six-nation London Economic Conference, meeting in the summer of 1933, revealed how thoroughly Roosevelt's early foreign policy was subordinated to his strategy for domestic economic recovery. The delegates to the London Conference hoped to organize a coordinated international attack on the global depression. They were particularly eager to stabilize the values of the various nations' currencies and the rates at which they could be exchanged. Exchange-rate stabilization was essential to the revival of world trade, which had all but evaporated by 1933.

Roosevelt at first agreed to send an American delegation to the conference, including Secretary of State Cordell Hull. But the president soon began to have second thoughts about the conference's agenda. He wanted to pursue his gold-juggling and other inflationary policies at home as a means of stimulating American recovery. An international agreement to maintain the value of the dollar in terms of other currencies might tie his hands, and at bottom Roosevelt was unwilling to sacrifice the possibility of domestic recovery for the sake of international cooperation. While vacationing on a yacht along the New England coast, he dashed off a radio message to London, scolding the conference for attempting to stabilize currencies and essentially declaring America's withdrawal from the negotiations.

Roosevelt's bombshell announcement yanked the rug from under the London Conference. The delegates adjourned empty-handed, amid cries of American bad faith. Whether the conference could have arrested the worldwide economic slide is debatable, but Roosevelt's every-man-for-himself attitude plunged the planet even deeper into economic crisis. The collapse of the London Conference also strengthened the global trend toward extreme nationalism, making international cooperation ever more difficult as the dangerous decade of the 1930s unfolded. Reflecting the powerful persistence of American isolationism, Roosevelt's action played directly into the hands of the power-mad dictators who were determined to shatter the peace of the world. Americans themselves would eventually pay a high price for the narrow-minded belief that the United States could go it alone in the modern world.

Freedom for (from?) the Filipinos and Recognition for the Russians

Roosevelt matched isolationism from Europe with withdrawal from Asia. The Great Depression burst the fragile bubble of President McKinley's imperialistic dream in the Far East. With the descent into hard times, American taxpayers were eager to throw overboard their expensive tropical liability in the Philippine Islands. Organized labor demanded the exclusion of low-wage Filipino workers, and American sugar producers clamored for the elimination of Philippine competition.

Just Another Customer, 1933 The United States recognizes the Soviet Union.

Remembering its earlier promises of freedom for the Philippines, Congress passed the Tydings-McDuffie Act in 1934. The act provided for the independence of the Philippines after a twelve-year period of economic and political tutelage—that is, by 1946. The United States agreed to relinquish its army bases, but naval bases were reserved for future discussion—and retention.

In truth, the American people were not so much giving freedom to the Philippines as they were freeing themselves *from* the Philippines. With a selfish eye to their own welfare, and with apparent disregard for the political situation in Asia, they proposed to leave the Philippines to their fate, while imposing upon the Filipinos economic terms so ungenerous as to threaten the islands with economic prostration. Once again, American isolationists rejoiced. Yet in Tokyo, Japanese militarists were calculating that they had little to fear from an inward-looking America that was abandoning its principal possession in Asia.

At the same time, Roosevelt made at least one internationalist gesture when he formally recognized the Soviet Union in 1933. Over the noisy protests of anticommunist conservatives, as well as Roman Catholics offended by the Kremlin's antireligious policies, Roosevelt extended the hand of diplomatic recognition to the sixteen-year-old Bolshevik regime. He was motivated in part by the hope for trade with Soviet Russia, as well as by the desire to bolster the Soviet Union as a friendly counterweight to the possible threat of German power in Europe and Japanese power in Asia.

Becoming a Good Neighbor

Closer to home, Roosevelt inaugurated a refreshing new era in relations with Latin America. He proclaimed in his inaugural address, "I would dedicate this nation to the policy of the Good Neighbor." Taken together, Roosevelt's noninvolvement in Europe and withdrawal from Asia, along with this brotherly embrace of his New World neighbors, suggested that the United States was giving up its ambition to be a world power and would content itself instead with being merely a regional power, its interests and activities confined exclusively to the Western Hemisphere.

Old-fashioned intervention by bayonet in the Caribbean had not paid off, except in an evil harvest of resentment, suspicion, and fear. The Great Depression had cooled off Yankee economic aggressiveness, as thousands of investors in Latin American securities became sackholders rather than stockholders. There were now fewer dollars to be protected by the rifles of the hated marines.

With war-thirsty dictators seizing power in Europe and Asia, Roosevelt was eager to line up the Latin Americans to help defend the Western Hemisphere. Embittered neighbors would be potential tools of transoceanic aggressors. President Roosevelt made clear at the outset that he was going to renounce armed intervention, particularly the vexatious corollary of the Monroe Doctrine devised by his cousin Theodore Roosevelt. Late in 1933, at the Seventh Pan-American Conference in Montevideo, Uruguay, the U.S. delegation formally endorsed nonintervention.

Deeds followed words. The last marines departed from Haiti in 1934. In the same year, res-

tive Cuba was released from the hobbles of the Platt Amendment, under which the United States had been free to intervene, although the naval base at Guantanamo was retained. The tiny country of Panama received a similar uplift in 1936, when Washington relaxed its grip on the isthmus nation.

The hope-inspiring Good Neighbor policy, with the accent on consultation and nonintervention, received its acid test in Mexico. When the Mexican government seized Yankee oil properties in 1938, American investors vehemently demanded armed intervention to repossess their confiscated businesses. But Roosevelt successfully resisted the badgering, and a settlement was finally threshed out in 1941, even though the oil companies lost much of their original stake.

Spectacular success crowned Roosevelt's Good Neighbor policy. His earnest attempts to usher in a new era of friendliness, though hurting some U.S. bondholders, paid rich dividends in goodwill among the peoples to the south. No other citizen of the United States has ever been held in such high esteem in Latin America during his lifetime. Roosevelt was cheered with tumultuous enthusiasm when, as a "traveling salesman for peace," he journeyed to the special Inter-American Conference at Buenos Aires, Argentina, in 1936. The Colossus of the North now seemed less a vulture and more an eagle.

Secretary Hull's Reciprocal Trade Agreements

Intimately associated with Good Neighborism, and also popular in Latin America, was the reciprocal trade policy of the New Dealers. Its chief architect was idealistic Secretary of State Hull, a high-minded Tennessean of the low-tariff school. Like Roosevelt, he believed that trade was a two-way street, that a nation can sell abroad only as it buys abroad, that tariff barriers choke off foreign trade, and that trade wars beget shooting wars.

Responding to the Hull-Roosevelt leadership, Congress passed the Reciprocal Trade Agreements Act in 1934. Designed in part to lift American export trade from the depression doldrums, this enlightened measure was aimed at both relief and recovery. At the same time, it activated the low-tariff policies of the New Dealers. (See the tariff chart in the Appendix.)

The Reciprocal Trade Agreements Act avoided the dangerous uncertainties of a wholesale tariff revision; it merely whittled down the most objectionable schedules of the Hawley-Smoot law by amending them. Roosevelt was empowered to lower existing rates by as much as 50 percent, provided that the other country involved was willing to respond with similar reductions. The resulting pacts, moreover, were to become effective without the formal approval of the Senate. This novel feature not only ensured speedier action but sidestepped the twin evils of high-stakes logrolling and high-pressure lobbying in Congress.

Secretary Hull, whose zeal for reciprocity was unflagging, succeeded in negotiating pacts with twenty-one countries by the end of 1939. During these same years, U.S. foreign trade increased appreciably, presumably in part as a result of the Hull-Roosevelt policies. Trade agreements undoubtedly bettered economic and political relations with Latin America and proved to be an influence for peace in a war-bent world.

The Reciprocal Trade Agreements Act was a landmark piece of legislation. It reversed the traditional high-protective-tariff policy that had persisted almost unbroken since Civil War days and that had so damaged the American and international economies following World War I. It paved the way for the American-led free-trade international economic system that took shape after World War II, a period that witnessed the most robust growth in the history of international trade.

Impulses Toward Storm-Cellar Isolationism

Post-1918 chaos in Europe, followed by the Great Depression, spawned the ominous spread of totalitarianism. The individual was nothing; the state was everything. The Communist USSR led the way, with the crafty and ruthless Joseph Stalin finally emerging as dictator. Blustery Benito Mussolini, a swaggering Fascist, seized the reins of power in Italy during 1922. And Adolf Hitler, a fanatic with a toothbrush mustache, plotted and harangued his way into control of Germany in 1933 with liberal use of the "big lie."

Hitler was the most dangerous of the dictators, because he combined tremendous power with impulsiveness. A frustrated Austrian painter, with hypnotic talents as an orator and a leader, he had secured control of the Nazi party by making political capital of the Treaty of Versailles and Germany's depression-spawned unemployment. He was thus a misbegotten child of the shortsighted postwar policies of the victorious Allies, including the United States. The desperate German people had fallen in behind the new Pied Piper, for they saw no other hope of escape from the plague of economic chaos and national disgrace. In 1936 the Nazi Hitler and the Fascist Mussolini allied themselves in the Rome-Berlin Axis.

International gangsterism was likewise spreading in the Far East, where imperial Japan was on the make. Like Germany and Italy, Japan was a so-called have-not power. Like them, it resented the ungenerous Treaty of Versailles. Like them, it demanded additional space for its teeming millions, cooped-up in their crowded island nation.

Japanese navalists were not to be denied. Determined to find a place in the Asiatic sun, Tokyo gave notice in 1934 of the termination of the twelve-year-old Washington Naval Treaty. A year later at London, the Japanese torpedoed all hope of effective naval

One of Our Quaint Ideas About Foreign Trade

The Wages of Despair   Disillusioned and desperate, millions of Germans in the 1930s looked to Adolf Hitler as their savior from the harsh terms of the Treaty of Versailles that concluded World War I. This Nazi poster reads, "Our Last Hope: Hitler."

The thirst of Benito Mussolini (1883–1945) for national glory in Ethiopia is indicated by his remark in 1940:

"To make a people great it is necessary to send them to battle even if you have to kick them in the pants." (The Italians were notoriously unwarlike.)

In 1934 Mussolini proclaimed in a public speech,

"We have buried the putrid corpse of liberty."

disarmament. Upon being denied complete parity, they walked out on the multipower conference and accelerated their construction of giant battleships.

Jut-jawed Mussolini, seeking both glory and empire in Africa, brutally attacked Ethiopia in 1935 with bombers and tanks. The brave defenders, armed with spears and ancient firearms, were speedily crushed. Members of the League of Nations could have caused Mussolini's war machine to creak to a halt—if they had only dared to embargo oil. But when the League quailed rather than risk global hostilities, it merely signed its own death warrant.

Isolationism, long festering in America, received a strong boost from these alarms abroad. Though disapproving of the dictators, Americans still believed that their encircling seas conferred a kind of mystic immunity. They were continuing to

suffer the disillusionment born of their participation in World War I, which they now regarded as a colossal blunder. They likewise nursed bitter memories of the ungrateful and defaulting debtors. As early as 1934, a spiteful Congress passed the Johnson Debt Default Act, which prevented debt-dodging nations from borrowing further in the United States. If attacked again by aggressors, these delinquents could "stew in their own juices."

Mired down in the Great Depression, Americans had no real appreciation of the revolutionary forces being harnessed by the dictators. The "have-not" powers were out to become "have" powers. Americans were not so much afraid that totalitarian aggression would cause trouble as they were fearful that they might be drawn into it. Strong nationwide sentiment welled up for a constitutional amendment to forbid a declaration of war by Congress—except in case of invasion—unless there was a favorable popular referendum. With a mixture of seriousness and frivolity, a group of Princeton University students began to agitate in 1936 for a bonus to be paid to the Veterans of Future Wars (VFW) while the prospective frontliners were still alive.

Congress Legislates Neutrality

As the gloomy 1930s lengthened, an avalanche of lurid articles and books condemning the munitions manufacturers as war-fomenting "merchants of death" poured from American presses. A Senate committee, headed by Senator Gerald Nye of North Dakota, was appointed in 1934 to investigate the "blood business." By sensationalizing evidence regarding America's entry into World War I, the senatorial probers tended to shift the blame away from the German submarines onto the American bankers and arms manufacturers. Because the munitions makers had obviously made money out of the war, many a naive citizen leaped to the illogical conclusion that these soulless scavengers had *caused* the war in order to make money. This kind of reasoning suggested that if the profits could only be removed from the arms traffic—"one hell of a business"—the country could steer clear of any world conflict that might erupt in the future.

Responding to overwhelming popular pressure, Congress made haste to legislate the nation out of war. Action was spurred by the danger that Mussolini's Ethiopian assault would plunge the world into a new bloodbath. The Neutrality Acts of 1935, 1936, and 1937, taken together, stipulated that *when the president proclaimed* the existence of a foreign war, certain restrictions would automatically go into effect. No American could legally sail on a belligerent ship, sell or transport munitions to a belligerent, or make loans to a belligerent.

This head-in-the-sand legislation in effect marked an abandonment of the traditional policy of freedom of the seas—a policy for which America had professedly fought two full-fledged wars and several undeclared wars. The Neutrality Acts were specifically tailored to keep the nation out of a conflict like World War I. If they had been in effect at that time, America probably would not have been sucked in—at least not in April 1917. Congress was one war too late with its legislation. What had seemed dishonorable to Wilson seemed honorable and desirable to a later disillusioned generation.

Storm-cellar neutrality proved to be tragically shortsighted. America falsely assumed that the decision for peace or war lay in its own hands, not in those of the satanic forces already unleashed in the world. Prisoner of its own fears, it failed to recognize that it might have used its enormous power to shape international events. Instead it remained at the mercy of events controlled by the dictators.

Statutory neutrality, though of undoubted legality, was of dubious morality. America served notice that it would make no distinction whatever between brutal aggressors and innocent victims. By striving to hold the scales even, it actually overbalanced them in favor of the dictators, who had armed themselves to the teeth. By declining to use its vast industrial strength to aid its democratic friends and defeat its totalitarian foes, it helped goad the aggressors along their blood-spattered path of conquest.

America Dooms Loyalist Spain

The Spanish Civil War of 1936–1939—a proving ground and dress rehearsal in miniature for World War II—was a painful object lesson in the folly of neutrality-by-legislation. Spanish rebels, who rose against the left-leaning republican government in Madrid, were headed by fascistic General Francisco Franco. Generously aided by his fellow conspirators Hitler and Mussolini, he undertook to overthrow the established Loyalist regime, which in turn was assisted on a smaller scale by the Soviet Union. This pipeline from communist Moscow chilled the natural sympathies of many Americans, especially Roman Catholics.

"The Only Way We Can Save Her," 1939
Even as war broke out in Europe, many Americans continued to insist on the morality of U.S. neutrality.

America's policy toward Spain "had been a grave mistake," Franklin D. Roosevelt (1882–1945) told his cabinet in early 1939:

"The policy we should have adopted was to forbid the transportation of munitions of war in American bottoms [ships]. This could have been done and Loyalist Spain would still have been able to come to us for what she needed to fight for her life against Franco—to fight for her life," Roosevelt concluded prophetically, "and for the lives of some of the rest of us as well, as events will very likely prove."

Washington continued official relations with the Loyalist government. In accordance with previous American practice, this regime should have been free to purchase desperately needed munitions from the United States. But Congress, with the encouragement of Roosevelt and with only one dissenting vote, amended the existing neutrality legislation so as to apply an arms embargo to both Loyalists and rebels. "Roosevelt," remarked dictator Franco, "behaved in the manner of a true gentleman." FDR later regretted being so gentlemanly.

Uncle Sam thus sat on the sidelines while Franco, abundantly supplied with arms and men by his fellow dictators, strangled the republican government of Spain. The democracies, including the United States, were so determined to stay out of war that they helped to condemn a fellow democracy to death. In so doing they further encouraged the dictators to take the dangerous road that led over the precipice to World War II.

Such peace-at-any-price-ism was further cursed with illogic. Although determined to stay out of war, America declined to build up its armed forces to a point where it could deter the aggressors. In fact, it allowed its navy to decline in relative strength. It had been led to believe that huge fleets caused huge wars; it was also trying to spare the complaining taxpayer during the grim days of the Great Depression. When President Roosevelt repeatedly called for preparedness, he was branded a warmonger. Not until 1938, the year before World War II exploded, did Congress come to grips with the problem when it passed a billion-dollar naval construction act. The calamitous story was repeated of too little, too late.

Appeasing Japan and Germany

Sulfurous war clouds had meanwhile been gathering in the tension-taut Far East. In 1937 the Japanese militarists, at the Marco Polo Bridge near Beijing (Peking), touched off the explosion that led to an all-out invasion of China. In a sense this attack was the curtain raiser of World War II.

Roosevelt shrewdly declined to invoke the recently passed neutrality legislation by refusing to call the China incident an officially declared *war.* If he had put the existing restrictions into effect, he would have cut off the trickle of munitions on which the Chinese were desperately dependent. The Japanese, of course, could continue to buy mountains of war supplies in the United States.

In Chicago—unofficial isolationist "capital" of America—President Roosevelt delivered his sensational "Quarantine Speech" in the autumn of 1937. Alarmed by the recent aggressions of Italy and Japan, he called for "positive endeavors" to "quarantine" the aggressors—presumably by economic embargoes.

The speech triggered a cyclone of protest from isolationists and other foes of involvement; they feared that a moral quarantine would lead to a shooting quarantine. Startled by this angry response, Roosevelt retreated and sought less direct means to curb the dictators.

America's isolationist mood intensified, especially in regard to China. In December 1937 Japanese aviators bombed and sank an American gunboat, the *Panay,* in Chinese waters, with a loss of two killed and thirty wounded. In the days of 1898, when the *Maine* went down, this outrage might have provoked war. But after Tokyo hastened to make the necessary apologies and pay a proper indemnity, Americans breathed a deep sigh of relief. Japanese militarists were thus encouraged to vent their anger against the "superior" white race by subjecting American civilians in China, both male and female, to humiliating slappings and strippings.

Adolf Hitler meanwhile grew louder and bolder in Europe. In 1935 he had openly flouted the Treaty of Versailles by introducing compulsory military service in Germany. The next year he brazenly marched into the demilitarized German Rhineland, likewise contrary to the detested treaty, while France and Britain looked on in an agony of indecision. Lashing his following to a frenzy, Hitler undertook to persecute and then exterminate the Jewish

What Next? 1938 The Western European democracies looked on helplessly as Nazi Germany swallowed up Austria and part of Czechoslovakia in 1938, and Hitler's juggernaut seemed unstoppable.

population in the areas under his control. In the end, he wiped out about 6 million innocent victims, mostly in gas chambers (see Makers of America: Refugees from the Holocaust, pp. 814–815). Calling upon his people to sacrifice butter for guns, he whipped the new German air force and mechanized ground divisions into the most devastating military machine the world had yet seen.

Suddenly, in March 1938, Hitler bloodlessly occupied German-speaking Austria, his birthplace. The democratic powers, wringing their hands in despair, prayed that this last grab would satisfy his passion for conquest.

But like a drunken reveler calling for madder music and stronger wine, Hitler could not stop. Intoxicated by his recent gains, he began to make bullying demands for the German-inhabited Sudetenland of neighboring Czechoslovakia. The leaders of Britain and France, eager to appease Hitler, sought frantically to bring the dispute to the conference table. President Roosevelt, also deeply alarmed, kept the wires hot with personal messages to both Hitler and Mussolini urging a peaceful settlement.

A conference was finally held in Munich, Germany, in September 1938. The Western European democracies, badly unprepared for war, betrayed Czechoslovakia to Germany when they consented to the shearing away of the Sudetenland. They hoped—and these hopes were shared by the American people—that the concessions at the conference table would slake Hitler's thirst for power and bring "peace in our time." Indeed Hitler publicly promised that the Sudetenland "is the last territorial claim I have to make in Europe."

"Appeasement" of the dictators, symbolized by the ugly word *Munich,* turned out to be merely surrender on the installment plan. It was like giving a cannibal a finger in the hope of saving an arm. In March 1939, scarcely six months later, Hitler suddenly erased the rest of Czechoslovakia from the map, contrary to his solemn vows. The democratic world was again stunned.

Hitler's Belligerency and U.S. Neutrality

Joseph Stalin, the sphinx of the Kremlin, was a key to the peace puzzle. In the summer of 1939, the British and French were busily negotiating with Moscow, hopeful of securing a mutual-defense treaty that would halt Hitler. But mutual suspicions proved insuperable. Then the Soviet Union astounded the world by signing, on August 23, 1939, a nonaggression treaty with the German dictator.

The notorious Hitler-Stalin pact meant that the Nazi German leader now had a green light to make war on Poland and the Western democracies, without fearing a stab in the back from the Soviet Union—his Communist arch-foe. Consternation struck those wishful thinkers in Western Europe who had fondly hoped that Hitler might be egged upon Stalin so that the twin menaces would bleed each other to death. It was as plain as the mustache on Stalin's face that the wily Soviet dictator was plotting to turn his German accomplice against the Western democracies. The two warring camps would then kill each other off—and leave Stalin bestriding Europe like a colossus.

With the signing of the Nazi-Soviet pact, World War II was only hours away. Hitler now demanded from neighboring Poland a return of the areas wrested from Germany after World War I. Failing to secure satisfaction, he sent his mechanized divisions crashing into Poland at dawn on September 1, 1939.

Refugees from the Holocaust

Fed by Adolf Hitler's genocidal delusions, anti-Semitism bared its fangs in the 1930s, spreading across Europe as Nazi Germany seized Austria and Czechoslovakia. Eluding the jackboots of Hitler's bloodthirsty SS (*Schutzstaffel*, an elite military and police force), Jews tried to flee from the Nazi juggernaut. Some succeeded, including the world's premier nuclear physicist, Albert Einstein, the Nobel laureate whose plea to Franklin Roosevelt helped initiate the top-secret atomic bomb project; the philosopher Hannah Arendt; the painter Marc Chagall; and the composer Kurt Weill. In all, some 150,000 Jews fled the Third Reich for America in the 1930s—a tiny fraction of the millions of Jews who eventually came under Hitler's heel. Why did America not make room for more?

For one thing, those exiled luminaries who managed to make it out of Germany found a divided Jewish community in America. Before the closing of unrestricted immigration in 1924, Jews had arrived in two stages—a trickle from Germany in the mid-nineteenth century, followed by a flood from Eastern Europe in the decades after 1890. Both groups had migrated as families and without a thought of return to the old country. But beyond that experience and their shared religious heritage, the two waves had relatively little in common, especially when it came to coping with the refugee crisis of the 1930s. The settled and prosperous German-Jewish community, organized in the American Jewish Committee, had fought hard to convince their fellow Americans of their loyalty, and many now feared that bold advocacy for refugees from Hitler's Germany would touch off an outburst of anti-Semitism in America. The notorious "Radio Priest," Father Charles Coughlin, was already preaching venomous pronouncements against the Jews, though his audience remained small—for the time being. The more numerous but less wealthy and influential Eastern

European Jews, organized in the American Jewish Congress, were intent on pressuring the Roosevelt administration to rescue Europe's Jews. This internal discord compromised the political effectiveness of the American Jewish community in the face of the refugee dilemma.

Other factors also helped to keep America's doors shut against Jews seeking refuge in the United

Nazi Anti-Semitism   This widely distributed German poster attacks "The Jew—Purveyor of War, Prolonger of War."

Hannah Arendt, 1933 A brilliant political theorist, she fled the Nazis and continued her career in the United States.

Albert Einstein Arriving in America, 1933 Sadly, the United States admitted only a trickle of refugees from Nazism, while some 6 million European Jews died.

States. The restrictive American immigration law of 1924 set rigid national quotas and made no provisions for seekers of asylum from racial, religious, or political persecution. The Great Depression made it impossible to provide employment for workers already in the United States, much less make room in the job line for newcomers. And opening America's gates to Germany's half-million Jews raised the daunting prospect that such action would unleash a deluge of millions more Jews from countries like Poland and Romania, which were advertising their eagerness to be rid of their Jewish populations. No one, of course, yet knew just how fiendish a destiny Hitler was preparing for Europe's Jews.

Many Jews and Gentiles alike, including Congressman Emmanuel Celler and Senator Robert Wagner, both of New York, nevertheless lobbied Roosevelt's government to extend a welcoming hand to Jews seeking asylum—to no avail. In 1941 Congress rejected a Wagner bill to bring twenty thousand German-Jewish children to the United States outside the quota restrictions. An even more desperate plan to settle refugees in Alaska also foundered.

Once the United States entered the war, the State Department went so far as to suppress early

A Survivor of the Holocaust A Polish Jew is reunited with his sister in the United States in 1946. He was lucky to have lived; most Polish Jews perished at Hitler's hands.

reports of Hitler's plan to exterminate all European Jewry. After the Führer's sordid final solution became known in America, the War Department rejected pleas to bomb the rail lines leading to the gas chambers. Military officials maintained that a raid on the death camps like Auschwitz would divert essential military resources and needlessly extend the war. Thus only a lucky few escaped the Nazi terror, while 6 million died in one of history's most ghastly testimonials to the human capacity for evil.

President Roosevelt was roused at 3 A.M. on September 1, 1939, by a telephone call from Ambassador William Bullitt (1891–1967) in Paris:

"Mr. President, several German divisions are deep in Polish territory. . . . There are reports of bombers over the city of Warsaw."

"Well, Bill," FDR replied, "it has come at last. God help us all."

Britain and France, honoring their commitments to Poland, promptly declared war. At long last they perceived the folly of continued appeasement. But they were powerless to aid Poland, which succumbed in three weeks to Hitler's smashing strategy of terror. Stalin, as prearranged secretly in his fateful pact with Hitler, came in on the kill for his share of old Russian Poland. Long-dreaded World War II was now fully launched, and the long truce of 1919–1939 had come to an end.

President Roosevelt speedily issued the routine proclamations of neutrality. Americans were overwhelmingly anti-Nazi and anti-Hitler; they fervently hoped that the democracies would win; they fondly believed that the forces of righteousness would triumph, as in 1918. But they were desperately determined to stay out: they were not going to be "suckers" again.

Neutrality promptly became a heated issue in the United States. Ill-prepared Britain and France urgently needed American airplanes and other weapons, but the Neutrality Act of 1937 raised a sternly forbidding hand. Roosevelt summoned Congress in special session, shortly after the invasion of Poland, to consider lifting the arms embargo. After six hectic weeks of debate, a makeshift law emerged.

The Neutrality Act of 1939 provided that henceforth the European democracies might buy American war materials, but only on a "cash-and-carry basis." This meant that they would have to transport the munitions in their own ships, after paying for them in cash. America would thus avoid loans, war debts, and the torpedoing of American arms-carriers. While Congress thus loosened former restrictions in response to interventionist cries, it added others in response to isolationist fears. Roo-

sevelt was now also authorized to proclaim danger zones into which American merchant ships would be forbidden to enter.

Despite its defects, this unneutral neutrality law clearly favored the democracies against the dictators—and was so intended. As the British and French navies controlled the Atlantic, the European aggressors could not send their ships to buy America's munitions. The United States not only improved its moral position but simultaneously helped its economic position. Overseas demand for war goods brought a sharp upswing from the recession of 1937–1938 and ultimately solved the decade-long unemployment crisis (see the chart on p. 800).

The Fall of France

The months following the collapse of Poland, while France and Britain marked time, were known as the "phony war." An ominous silence fell on Europe, as Hitler shifted his victorious divisions from Poland for a knockout blow at France. Inaction during this anxious period was relieved by the Soviets, who wantonly attacked neighboring Finland in an effort to secure strategic buffer territory. The debt-paying Finns, who had a host of admirers in America, were speedily granted $30 million by an isolationist Congress for *nonmilitary* supplies. But despite heroic resistance, Finland was finally flattened by the Soviet steamroller.

Adolf Hitler (1889–1945) promised to win his fellow Germans Lebensraum, *or "living space," and to win it by war if necessary. In his eyes, his nationalist and racist crusade justified every violent means at hand. As he told his commanders,*

"When you start a war, what matters is not who is right, but who wins. Close your hearts to pity. Act with brutality. Eighty million Germans must get what is their due. Their existence must be made secure. The stronger man is in the right."

An abrupt end to the "phony war" came in April 1940 when Hitler, again without warning, overran his weaker neighbors Denmark and Norway. Hardly pausing for breath, the next month he attacked the Netherlands and Belgium, followed by a paralyzing blow at France. By late June France was forced to surrender, but not until Mussolini had pounced on its rear for a jackal's share of the loot. In a pell-mell but successful evacuation from the French port of Dunkirk, the British managed to salvage the bulk of their shattered and partially disarmed army. The crisis providentially brought forth an inspired leader in Prime Minister Winston Churchill, the bulldog-jawed orator who nerved his people to fight off the fearful air bombings of their cities.

France's sudden collapse shocked Americans out of their daydreams. Stouthearted Britons, singing "There'll Always Be an England," were all that stood between Hitler and the death of constitutional government in Europe. If Britain went under, Hitler would have at his disposal the workshops, shipyards, and slave labor of Western Europe. He might even have the powerful British fleet as well. This frightening possibility, which seemed to pose a dire threat to American security, steeled the American people to a tremendous effort.

Roosevelt moved with electrifying energy and dispatch. He called upon an already debt-burdened nation to build huge airfleets and a two-ocean navy, which could also check Japan. Congress, jarred out of its apathy toward preparedness, within a year appropriated the astounding sum of $37 billion. This figure was more than the total cost of fighting World War I and about five times larger than any New Deal annual budget.

Congress also passed a conscription law, approved September 6, 1940. Under this measure—America's first peacetime draft—provision was made for training each year 1.2 million troops and 800,000 reserves. The act was later adapted to the requirements of a global war.

The Latin American bulwark likewise needed bracing. The Netherlands, Denmark, and France, all crushed under the German jackboot, had orphaned colonies in the New World. Would these fall into German hands? At the Havana Conference of 1940, the United States agreed to share with its twenty New World neighbors the responsibility of upholding the Monroe Doctrine. This ancient dictum, hitherto unilateral, had been a bludgeon brandished only in the hated Yankee fist. Now multilateral, it was to be wielded by twenty-one pairs of American hands—at least in theory.

Bolstering Britain with the Destroyer Deal (1940)

Before the fall of France in June 1940, Washington had generally observed a technical neutrality. But now, as Britain alone stood between Hitler and his dream of world domination, the wisdom of neutrality seemed increasingly questionable. Hitler launched air attacks against Britain in August 1940, preparatory to an invasion scheduled for September. For months the Battle of Britain raged in the air over the British Isles. The Royal Air Force's tenacious defense of its native islands eventually led Hitler to postpone his planned invasion indefinitely.

During the precarious months of the Battle of Britain, debate intensified in the United States over what foreign policy to embrace. Radio broadcasts

Just So There'll Be No Misunderstanding   Hitler and Mussolini are warned not to seize orphaned colonies in America.

from London brought the drama of the nightly German air raids directly into millions of American homes. Sympathy for Britain grew, but it was not yet sufficient to push the United States into war.

Roosevelt faced a historic decision: whether to hunker down in the Western Hemisphere, assume a "Fortress America" defensive posture, and let the rest of the world go it alone; or to bolster beleaguered Britain by all means short of war itself. Both sides had their advocates.

Supporters of aid to Britain formed propaganda groups, the most potent of which was the Committee to Defend America by Aiding the Allies. Its argument was double-barreled. To interventionists, it could appeal for direct succor to the British by such slogans as "Britain Is Fighting Our Fight." To the isolationists, it could appeal for assistance to the democracies by "All Methods Short of War," so that the terrible conflict would be kept in faraway Europe.

The isolationists, both numerous and sincere, were by no means silent. Determined to avoid American bloodshed at all costs, they organized the America First Committee and proclaimed, "England Will Fight to the Last American." They contended that America should concentrate what strength it had to defend its own shores, lest a victorious Hitler, after crushing Britain, plot a transoceanic assault. Their basic philosophy was "The Yanks Are Not Coming," and their most effective speechmaker was the famed aviator Colonel Charles A. Lindbergh, who, ironically, had narrowed the Atlantic in 1927.

Britain was in critical need of destroyers, for German submarines were again threatening to starve it out with attacks on shipping. Roosevelt moved boldly when, on September 2, 1940, he agreed to transfer to Great Britain fifty old-model, four-funnel destroyers left over from World War I. In return, the British promised to hand over to the United States eight valuable defensive base sites, stretching from Newfoundland to South America. These strategically located outposts were to remain under the Stars and Stripes for ninety-nine years.

Transferring fifty destroyers to a foreign navy was a highly questionable disposal of government property, despite a strained interpretation of existing legislation. The exchange was achieved by a simple presidential agreement, without so much as a "by your leave" to Congress. Applause burst from the aid-to-Britain advocates, many of whom had been urging such a step. But condemnation arose

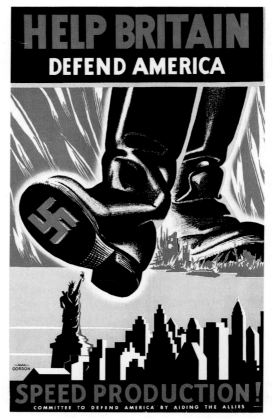

Pro-British Propaganda This patriotic poster was put out by the Committee to Defend America by Aiding the Allies.

from America Firsters and other isolationists, as well as from antiadministration Republicans. Some of them approved the transfer but decried Roosevelt's secretive and arbitrary methods. Yet so grave was the crisis that the president was unwilling to submit the scheme to the uncertainties and delays of a full-dress debate in the Congress.

Shifting warships from a neutral United States to a belligerent Britain was, beyond question, a flagrant violation of neutral obligations—at least neutral obligations that had existed before Hitler's barefaced aggressions rendered foolish such old-fashioned concepts of fair play. Public-opinion polls demonstrated that a majority of Americans were determined, even at the risk of armed hostilities, to provide the battered British with "all aid short of war."

FDR Shatters
the Two-Term Tradition (1940)

A distracting presidential election, as fate decreed, came in the midst of this crisis. The two leading Republican aspirants were round-faced and flat-voiced Senator Robert A. Taft of Ohio, son of the ex-president, and the energetic boy wonder, lawyer-prosecutor Thomas E. Dewey of New York. But in one of the miracles of American political history, the Philadelphia convention was swept off its feet by a colorful latecomer, Wendell L. Willkie, a German-descended son of Hoosier Indiana. This dynamic lawyer—tousled-headed, long-lipped, broad-faced, and large-framed—had until recently been a Democrat and the head of a huge public utilities corporation. A complete novice in politics, he had rocketed from political nothingness in a few short weeks. His great appeal lay in his personality, for he was magnetic, transparently trustful, and honest in a homespun, Lincolnesque way.

With the galleries in Philadelphia wildly chanting "We Want Willkie," the delegates finally accepted this political upstart as the only candidate who could possibly beat Roosevelt. The Republican platform condemned FDR's alleged dictatorship, as well as the costly and confusing zigzags of the New Deal. Willkie, an outspoken liberal, was opposed not so much to the New Deal as to its extravagances and inefficiencies. Democratic critics branded him "the rich man's Roosevelt" and "the simple barefoot Wall Street lawyer."

> *The old-line Republican bosses were not happy over having a recent Democrat head their ticket. A former senator reportedly told Willkie to his face,*
>
> "You have been a Democrat all your life. I don't mind the church converting a whore, but I don't like her to lead the choir the first night."

While the rumor pot boiled, Roosevelt delayed to the last minute the announcement of his decision to challenge the sacred two-term tradition. Despite what he described as his personal yearning for retirement, he avowed that in so grave a crisis he owed his experienced hand to the service of his country and humanity. The Democratic delegates in Chicago, realizing that only with "the Champ" could they defeat Willkie, drafted him by a technically unanimous vote. "Better a Third Term Than a Third-Rater" was the war cry of many Democrats.

Burning with sincerity and energy, Willkie launched out upon a whirlwind, Bryanesque campaign in which he delivered over five hundred speeches. At times his voice became a hoarse croak. The country was already badly split between interventionists and isolationists, and Willkie might have widened the breach dangerously by a violent attack

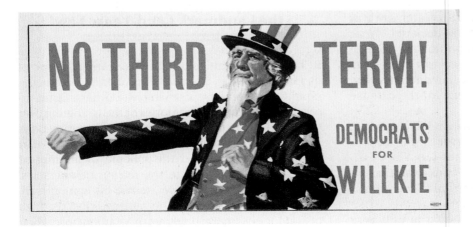

A Campaign Poster from the Election of 1940 Roosevelt emerged as the only president ever to break the two-term tradition.

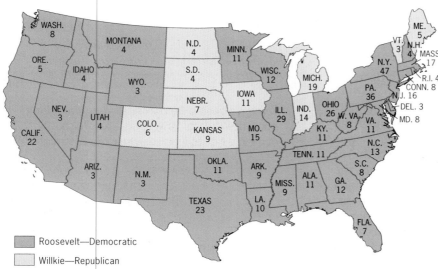

Presidential Election of 1940 (with electoral vote by state) Willkie referred to Roosevelt only as "the third-term candidate." On election eve FDR hinted that communists and fascists were among Willkie's supporters. Despite these campaign conflicts, the two men respected each other. FDR later asked Willkie to serve as his emissary abroad and even suggested that they run together on a coalition ticket in 1944.

on Roosevelt's aid-to-Britain policies. But seeing eye-to-eye with FDR on the necessity of bolstering the beleaguered democracies, he refrained from assailing the president's interventionism, though objecting to his methods.

In the realm of foreign affairs, there was not much to choose between the two candidates. Both promised to stay out of the war; both promised to strengthen the nation's defenses. Yet Willkie, with a mop of black hair in his eyes, hit hard at Rooseveltian "dictatorship" and the third term. His enthusiastic followers cried, "Win with Willkie," "No Fourth Term Either," and "There's No Indispensable Man."

Roosevelt, busy at his desk with mounting problems, made only a few speeches. Stung by taunts that he was leading the nation by the back door into the European slaughterhouse, he repeatedly denied any such intention. His most specific statement was at Boston, where he emphatically declared, "Your boys are not going to be sent into any foreign wars"—a pledge that later came back to plague him. He and his supporters vigorously defended the New Deal as well as all-out preparations for the defense of America and aid to the Allies.

Roosevelt triumphed, although Willkie ran a strong race. The popular total was 27,307,819 to 22,321,018, and the electoral count was 449 to 82. This contest was much less of a walkaway than in 1932 or 1936; Democratic majorities in Congress remained about the same.

Jubilant Democrats hailed their triumph as a mandate to abolish the two-term tradition. But the truth is that Roosevelt won in spite of the third-term handicap. Voters generally felt that should war come, the experienced hand of the tried leader was needed at the helm. Less appealing was the completely inexperienced hand of the well-intentioned Willkie, who had never held public office.

The time-honored argument that one should not change horses in the middle of a stream was strong, especially in an era of war-pumped prosperity. Roosevelt might not have won if there had not been a war crisis. On the other hand, he probably would not have run if foreign perils had not loomed so ominously. In a sense, his opponent was Adolf Hitler, not Willkie.

Congress Passes the Landmark Lend-Lease Law

By late 1940 embattled Britain was nearing the end of its financial tether; its credits in America were being rapidly consumed by insatiable war orders. But Roosevelt, who had bitter memories of the wrangling over the Allied debts of World War I, was determined, as he put it, to eliminate "the silly, foolish, old dollar sign." He finally hit on the scheme of lending or leasing American arms to the reeling democracies. When the shooting was over, to use his comparison, the guns and tanks could be returned, just as one's next-door neighbor would return a garden hose when a threatening fire was put out. But isolationist Senator

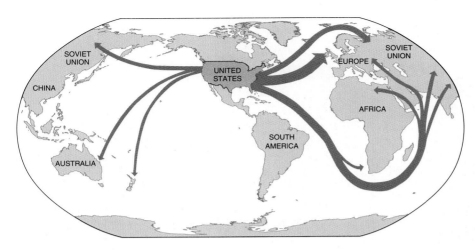

Main Flow of Lend-Lease Aid (width of arrows indicates relative amount) The proud but desperate British prime minister, Winston Churchill, declared in early 1941, "Give us the tools and we will finish the job." Lend-lease eventually provided the British and other Allies with $50 billion worth of "tools."

Taft (who was reputed to have the finest mind in Washington until he made it up) retorted that lending arms was like lending chewing gum: "You don't want it back." Who wants a chewed-up tank?

The Lend-Lease Bill, patriotically numbered 1776, was entitled "An Act Further to Promote the Defense of the United States." Sprung on the country after the election was safely over, it was praised by the administration as a device that would keep the nation out of the war rather than drag it in. The underlying concept was "Send guns, not sons" or "Billions, not bodies." America, so President Roosevelt promised, would be the "arsenal of democracy." It would send a limitless supply of arms to the victims of aggression, who in turn would finish the job and keep the war on their side of the Atlantic. Accounts would be settled by returning the used weapons or their equivalents to the United States when the war was ended.

Lend-lease was heatedly debated throughout the land and in Congress. Most of the opposition came, as might be expected, from isolationists and anti-Roosevelt Republicans. The scheme was assailed as "the blank-check bill" and, in the words of isolationist Senator Burton Wheeler, as "the new Triple-A [Agricultural Adjustment Act] bill"—a measure designed to "plow under every fourth American boy." Nevertheless, lend-lease was finally approved in March 1941 by sweeping majorities in both houses of Congress.

Lend-lease was one of the most momentous laws ever to pass Congress; it was a challenge hurled squarely into the teeth of the Axis dictators. America pledged itself, to the extent of its vast resources, to

bolster those nations that were indirectly defending it by fighting aggression. When the gigantic operation ended in 1945, America had sent about $50 billion worth of arms and equipment—much more than the cost to the country of World War I—to those nations fighting aggressors. The passing of lend-lease was in effect an economic declaration of war; now a shooting declaration could not be very far around the corner.

By its very nature, the Lend-Lease Bill marked the abandonment of any pretense of neutrality. It was no destroyer deal arranged privately by President Roosevelt. The bill was universally debated, over drugstore counters and cracker barrels, from California all the way to Maine, and the sovereign citizen at last spoke through convincing majorities in Congress. Most people probably realized that they were tossing the old concepts of neutrality out the window. But they also recognized that they would play a suicidal game if they bound themselves by the oxcart rules of the nineteenth century—especially while the Axis aggressors themselves openly spurned international obligations. Lend-lease would admittedly involve a grave risk of war, but most Americans were prepared to take that chance rather than see Britain collapse and then face the diabolical dictators alone.

Lend-lease had the somewhat incidental result of gearing U.S. factories for all-out war production. The enormously increased capacity thus achieved helped save America's own skin when, at long last, the shooting war burst around its head.

Hitler evidently recognized lend-lease as an unofficial declaration of war. Until then, Germany

No to Lend-Lease Members of the Massachusetts Woman's Political Club presented President Roosevelt with a petition protesting adoption of the Lend-Lease Bill and picketed the White House. They feared that America's increasing involvement with the Allied cause would eventually draw their sons into battle—as it did, despite the president's assurances to the contrary.

had avoided attacking U.S. ships; memories of America's decisive intervention in 1917–1918 were still fresh in German minds. But after the passing of lend-lease, there was less point in trying to curry favor with the United States. On May 21, 1941, the *Robin Moor,* an unarmed American merchantman, was torpedoed and destroyed by a German submarine in the South Atlantic, outside a war zone. The sinkings had started, but on a limited scale.

Hitler's Assault on the Soviet Union Spawns the Atlantic Charter

Two globe-shaking events marked the course of World War II before the assault on Pearl Harbor in December 1941. One was the fall of France in June 1940; the other was Hitler's invasion of the Soviet Union, almost exactly one year later, in June 1941.

The scheming dictators Hitler and Stalin had been uneasy yoke-fellows under the ill-begotten Nazi-Soviet pact of 1939. As masters of the double cross, neither trusted the other. They engaged in prolonged dickering in a secret attempt to divide potential territorial spoils between them, but Stalin balked at dominant German control of the Balkans.

Hitler thereupon decided to crush his coconspirator, seize the oil and other resources of the Soviet Union, and then have two free hands to snuff out Britain. He assumed that his invincible armies would subdue Stalin's "Mongol half-wits" in a few short weeks.

Out of a clear sky, on June 22, 1941, Hitler launched a devastating attack on his Soviet neighbor. This timely assault was an incredible stroke of good fortune for the democratic world—or so it seemed at the time. The two fiends could now slit each other's throats on the icy steppes of Russia. Or they would if the Soviets did not quickly collapse, as many military experts predicted.

Senator (later president) Harry S Truman (1884–1972) expressed a common reaction to Hitler's invasion of the Soviet Union in 1941:

"If we see that Germany is winning, we ought to help Russia, and if we see Russia is winning, we ought to help Germany, and that way let them kill as many as possible."

Sound American strategy seemed to dictate speedy aid to Moscow while it was still afloat. Roosevelt immediately promised assistance and backed up his words by making some military supplies available. Several months later, interpreting the lend-lease law to mean that the defense of the USSR was now essential for the defense of the United States, he extended $1 billion in lend-lease—the first installment on an ultimate total of $11 billion. Meanwhile, the valor of the red army, combined with the white paralysis of an early Russian winter, had halted Hitler's invaders at the gates of Moscow.

With the surrender of the Soviet Union still a dread possibility, the drama-charged Atlantic Conference was held in August 1941. British Prime Minister Winston Churchill, with cigar embedded in his cherubic face, secretly met with Roosevelt on a warship off the foggy coast of Newfoundland. This was the first of a series of history-making conferences between the two statesmen for the discussion of common problems, including the menace of Japan in the Far East.

The most memorable offspring of this get-together was the eight-point Atlantic Charter. It was

Unexpected Guest, 1941
Stalin joins the democracies, Britain and America.

formally accepted by Roosevelt and Churchill and endorsed by the Soviet Union later that year. Suggestive of Wilson's Fourteen Points, the new covenant outlined the aspirations of the democracies for a better world at war's end.

Surprisingly, the Atlantic Charter was rather specific. While opposing imperialistic annexations, it promised that there would be no territorial changes contrary to the wishes of the inhabitants (self-determination). It further affirmed the right of a people to choose their own form of government and, in particular, to regain the governments abolished by the dictators. Among various other goals, the charter declared for disarmament and a peace of security, pending a "permanent system of general security" (a new League of Nations).

Liberals the world over took heart from the Atlantic Charter, as they had taken heart from Wilson's comparable Fourteen Points. It was especially gratifying to subject populations, like the Poles, who were then ground under the iron heel of a conqueror. But the agreement was roundly condemned in the United States by isolationists and others hostile to Roosevelt. What right, they charged, had "neutral" America to confer with belligerent Britain on common policies? Such critics missed the point: the nation was in fact no longer neutral.

U.S. Destroyers and Hitler's U-boats Clash

Lend-lease shipments of arms to Britain on British ships were bound to be sunk by German wolf-pack submarines. If the intent was to get the munitions to England, not to dump them into the ocean, the freighters would have to be escorted by U.S. warships. Britain simply did not have enough destroyers. The dangerous possibility of being "convoyed into war" had been mentioned in Congress during the lengthy debate on lend-lease, but administration spokespeople had brushed the idea aside. Their strategy was to make only one commitment at a time.

Roosevelt made the fateful decision to convoy in July 1941. By virtue of his authority as commander in chief of the armed forces, the president issued orders to the navy to escort lend-lease shipments as far as Iceland. The British would then shepherd them the rest of the way.

Inevitable clashes with submarines ensued on the Iceland run, even though Hitler's orders were to strike at American warships only in self-defense. In September 1941 the U.S. destroyer *Greer*, provocatively trailing a German U-boat, was attacked by the undersea craft, without damage to either side. Roosevelt then proclaimed a shoot-on-sight policy. On October 17 the escorting destroyer *Kearny*, while engaged in a battle with U-boats, lost eleven men when it was crippled but not sent to the bottom. Two weeks later the destroyer *Reuben James* was torpedoed and sunk off southwestern Iceland, with the loss of more than a hundred officers and enlisted men.

Neutrality was still inscribed on the statute books, but not in American hearts. Congress, responding to public pressures and confronted with a shooting war, voted in mid-November 1941 to pull the teeth from the now-useless Neutrality Act of 1939. Merchant ships could henceforth be legally armed, and they could enter the combat zones with munitions for Britain. Americans braced themselves for wholesale attacks by Hitler's submarines.

Surprise Assault on Pearl Harbor

The blowup came not in the Atlantic, but in the faraway Pacific. This explosion should have surprised no close observer, for Japan, since September 1940, had been a formal military ally of Nazi Germany—America's shooting foe in the North Atlantic.

Japan's position in the Far East had grown more perilous by the hour. It was still mired down in the costly and exhausting "China incident," from which it could extract neither honor nor victory. Its war machine was fatally dependent on immense shipments of steel, scrap iron, oil, and aviation gasoline from the United States. Such assistance to the Japanese aggressor was highly unpopular in America. But Roosevelt had resolutely held off an embargo, lest he goad the Tokyo warlords into a descent upon the oil-rich but defense-poor Dutch East Indies.

Washington, late in 1940, finally imposed the first of its embargoes on Japan-bound supplies. This blow was followed in mid-1941 by a freezing of Japanese assets in the United States and a cessation of all shipments of gasoline and other sinews of war. As the oil gauge dropped, the squeeze on Japan grew steadily more nerve-racking. Japanese leaders were faced with two painful alternatives. They could either knuckle under to the Americans or break out of the embargo ring by a desperate attack on the oil supplies and other riches of Southeast Asia.

Final tense negotiations with Japan took place in Washington during November and early December of 1941. The State Department insisted that the Japanese clear out of China, but to sweeten the pill offered to renew trade relations on a limited basis. Japanese imperialists, after waging a bitter war against the Chinese for more than four years, were unwilling to lose face by withdrawing at the behest of the United States. Faced with capitulation or continued conquest, they chose the sword.

Officials in Washington, having "cracked" the top-secret code of the Japanese, knew that Tokyo's decision was for war. But the United States, as a democracy committed to public debate and action by Congress, could not shoot first. Roosevelt, misled by Japanese ship movements in the Far East, evidently expected the blow to fall on British Malaya or on the Philippines. No one in high authority in Washington seems to have believed that the Japanese were either strong enough or foolhardy enough to strike Hawaii.

But the paralyzing blow struck Pearl Harbor, while Tokyo was deliberately prolonging negotiations in Washington. Japanese bombers, winging in from distant aircraft carriers, attacked without warning on the "Black Sunday" morning of December 7, 1941. It was a date, as Roosevelt told Congress, "which will live in infamy." About three thousand casualties were inflicted on American personnel, many aircraft were destroyed, the battleship fleet was virtually wiped out when all eight of the craft were sunk or otherwise immobilized, and numerous small vessels were damaged or destroyed. Fortunately for America, the three priceless aircraft carriers happened to be outside the harbor.

An angered Congress the next day officially recognized the war that had been "thrust" upon the United States. The roll call in the Senate and House fell only one vote short of unanimity. Germany and Italy, allies of Japan, spared Congress the indecision of debate by declaring war on December 11, 1941. This challenge was formally accepted on the same day by a unanimous vote of both Senate and House. The unofficial war, already of many months' duration, was now official.

The Battleship *West Virginia,*
Wrecked at Pearl Harbor

America's Transformation from Bystander to Belligerent

Japan's hara-kiri gamble in Hawaii paid off only in the short run. True, the Pacific fleet was largely destroyed or immobilized, but the sneak attack aroused and united America as almost nothing else could have done. To the very day of the blowup, a strong majority of Americans still wanted to keep out of war. But the bombs that pulverized Pearl Harbor blasted the isolationists into silence. The only thing left to do, growled isolationist Senator Wheeler, was "to lick hell out of them."

But Pearl Harbor was not the full answer to the question of why the United States went to war. This treacherous attack was but the last explosion in a long chain reaction. Following the fall of France, Americans were confronted with a devil's dilemma. They desired above all to stay out of the conflict, yet they did not want Britain to be knocked out. They wished to halt Japan's conquests in the Far East— conquests that menaced not only American trade and security but international peace as well. To keep Britain from collapsing, the Roosevelt administration felt compelled to extend the unneutral aid that invited attacks from German submarines. To keep Japan from expanding, Washington undertook to cut off vital Japanese supplies with embargoes that invited possible retaliation. Rather than let democracy die and dictatorship rule supreme, most citizens were evidently determined to support a policy that might lead to war. It did.

Roosevelt's war message to Congress began with these famous words:

"Yesterday, December 7, 1941—a date which will live in infamy—the United States of America was suddenly and deliberately attacked by naval and air forces of the Empire of Japan."

Chronology

1933   FDR torpedoes the London Economic
Conference
United States recognizes the Soviet Union
FDR declares Good Neighbor policy toward
Latin America

1934   Tydings-McDuffie Act provides for
Philippine independence on July 4,
1946
Reciprocal Trade Agreements Act

1935   Mussolini invades Ethiopia
U.S. Neutrality Act of 1935

1936   U.S. Neutrality Act of 1936

**1936–
1939**   Spanish Civil War

1937   U.S. Neutrality Act of 1937
Panay incident
Japan invades China

1938   Hitler seizes Austria
Munich Conference

1939   Hitler seizes all of Czechoslovakia
Nazi-Soviet pact
World War II begins in Europe with Hitler's
invasion of Poland
U.S. Neutrality Act of 1939

1940   Fall of France
Hitler invades Denmark, Norway, the
Netherlands, and Belgium
United States invokes first peacetime draft
Havana Conference
Battle of Britain
Bases-for-destroyers deal with Britain
FDR defeats Willkie for presidency

1941   Lend-Lease Act
Hitler attacks the Soviet Union
Atlantic Charter
Japan attacks Pearl Harbor

For further reading, see page A24 of the Appendix. For web resources, go to **http://college.hmco.com.**

36

America in World War II

1941–1945

Never before have we had so little time in which to do so much.

FRANKLIN D. ROOSEVELT, 1942

The United States was plunged into the inferno of World War II with the most stupefying and humiliating military defeat in its history. In the dismal months that ensued, the democratic world teetered on the edge of disaster.

Japan's fanatics forgot that whoever stabs a king must stab to kill. A wounded but still potent American giant pulled itself out of the mud of Pearl Harbor, grimly determined to avenge the bloody treachery. "Get Japan first" was the cry that rose from millions of infuriated Americans, especially on the Pacific Coast. These outraged souls regarded America's share in the global conflict as a private war of vengeance in the Pacific, with the European front a kind of holding operation.

But Washington, in the so-called ABC-1 agreement with the British, had earlier and wisely adopted the grand strategy of "getting Germany first." If America diverted its main strength to the Pacific, Hitler might crush both the Soviet Union and Britain and then emerge unconquerable in Fortress Europe. But if Germany was knocked out first, the combined Allied forces could be concentrated on Japan, and its daring game of conquest would be up. Meanwhile, just enough American strength would be sent to the Pacific to prevent Japan from digging in too deeply.

The get-Germany-first strategy was the solid foundation on which all American military strategy was built. But it encountered much ignorant criticism from two-fisted Americans who thirsted for revenge against Japan. Aggrieved protests were also registered by shorthanded American commanders in the Pacific and by Chinese and Australian allies. But President Roosevelt, a competent strategist in his own right, wisely resisted these pressures.

Throwing in an Extra Charge, 1941   The Japanese attack on Pearl Harbor in 1941 excited virulent hatred of Japan among Americans, who called for a war of vengeance against the treacherous aggressor. Anti-Japanese sentiment remained stronger than anti-German sentiment throughout the war.

The Allies Trade Space for Time

Given time, the Allies seemed bound to triumph. But would they be given time? True, they had on their side the great mass of the world's population, but the wolf is never intimidated by the number of the sheep. The United States was the mightiest military power on earth—potentially. But wars are won with bullets, not blueprints. Indeed America came perilously close to losing the war to the well-armed aggressors before it could begin to throw its full weight onto the scales.

Time, in a sense, was the most needed munition. Expense was no limitation. The overpowering problem confronting America was to retool itself for all-out war production, while praying that the dictators would not meanwhile crush the democracies. Haste was all the more imperative because the highly skilled German scientists might turn up with unbeatable secret weapons, including rocket bombs and perhaps even atomic arms.

America's task was far more complex and back-breaking than during World War I. It had to feed, clothe, and arm itself, as well as transport its forces to regions as far separated as Britain and Burma. More than that, it had to send a vast amount of food and munitions to its hard-pressed allies, who stretched all the way from the USSR to Australia. Could the American people, reputedly "gone soft," measure up to this Herculean task? Was democracy "rotten" and "decadent," as the dictators sneeringly proclaimed?

The Shock of War

National unity was no worry, thanks to the electrifying blow by the Japanese at Pearl Harbor. American Communists had denounced the Anglo-French "imperialist" war before Hitler attacked Stalin in 1941, but they now clamored for an unmitigated assault on the Axis powers. The handful of strutting pro-Hitlerites in the United States melted away, while millions of Italian-Americans and German-Americans loyally supported the nation's war program. In contrast to World War I, when the patriotism of millions of immigrants was hotly questioned, World War II actually speeded the assimilation of many ethnic groups into American society. Immigration had been choked off for almost two decades before 1941, and America's ethnic communities were now composed of well-settled members, whose votes were crucial to Franklin Roosevelt's Democratic party. Consequently, there was virtually no government witch-hunting of minority groups, as had happened in World War I.

American song titles after Pearl Harbor combined nationalism with unabashed racism: "We Are the Sons of the Rising Guns," "Oh, You Little Son of an Oriental," "To Be Specific, It's Our Pacific," "The Sun Will Soon Be Setting on the Land of the Rising Sun," "The Japs Don't Stand a Chinaman's Chance," and "We're Gonna Find a Fellow Who Is Yellow and Beat Him Red, White, and Blue."

A painful exception was the plight of some 110,000 Japanese-Americans, concentrated on the Pacific Coast (see "Makers of America: The Japanese," pp. 830–831). The Washington top command, fearing that they might act as saboteurs for Japan in case of invasion, forcibly herded them together in concentration camps, though about two-thirds of them were American-born U.S. citizens. This brutal precaution was both unnecessary and unfair, as the loyalty and combat record of Japanese-Americans proved to be admirable. But a wave of post–Pearl Harbor hysteria, backed by the long historical swell of anti-Japanese prejudice on the West Coast, temporarily robbed many Americans of their good sense—and their sense of justice. The internment camps deprived these uprooted Americans of dignity and basic rights; the internees also lost hundreds of millions of dollars in property and foregone earnings. The wartime Supreme Court in 1944 upheld the constitutionality of the Japanese relocation in *Korematsu* v. *U.S.* But more than four decades later, in 1988, the U.S. government officially apologized for its actions and approved the payment of reparations of $20,000 to each camp survivor.

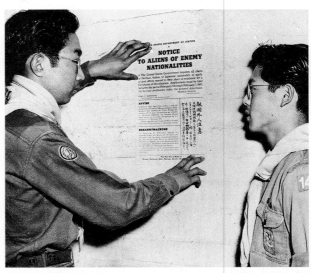

Enemy Aliens   When the United States suddenly found itself at war with Germany, Italy, and Japan in December 1941, noncitizen German, Italian, and Japanese immigrants became "enemy aliens" and were required to register with the authorities. Several hundred resident Germans and Italians were detained in internment camps, but the harshest treatment was meted out to the Japanese, some 110,000 of whom, noncitizens and citizens alike, were eventually interned. Ironically, the two Japanese-American Boy Scouts posting this notice in Los Angeles would soon be on their way to a government detention camp.

Monica Sone (b. 1919), a college-age Japanese-American woman in Seattle, recorded the shock she and her brother felt when they learned of Executive Order No. 9066, which authorized the War Department to remove Japanese—aliens and citizens alike—from their homes:

"In anger, Henry and I read and reread the Executive Order. Henry crumbled the newspaper in his hand and threw it against the wall. 'Doesn't my citizenship mean a single blessed thing to anyone? Why doesn't somebody make up my mind for me? First they want me in the army. Now they're going to slap an alien 4-C on me because of my ancestry. . . .' Once more I felt like a despised, pathetic two-headed freak, a Japanese and an American, neither of which seemed to be doing me any good."

The war prompted other changes in the American mood. Many programs of the once-popular New Deal—including the Civilian Conservation Corps, the Works Progress Administration, and the National Youth Administration—were wiped out by the conservative Congress elected in 1942. Roosevelt declared in 1943 that "Dr. New Deal" was going into retirement, to be replaced by "Dr. Win-the-War." His announcement acknowledged not only the urgency of the war effort but the power of the revitalized conservative forces in the country. The era of New Deal reform was over.

World War II was no idealistic crusade, as World War I had been. The Washington government did make some effort to propagandize at home and abroad with the Atlantic Charter, but the accent was on action. Opinion polls in 1942 revealed that nine out of ten Americans could cite no provisions of the Atlantic Charter. A majority then, and a near-majority two years later, confessed to having "no

MAKERS OF AMERICA

The Japanese

In 1853 the American commodore Matthew Perry sailed four gunboats into Japan's Uraga Bay and demanded that the nation open itself to diplomatic and commercial exchange with the United States. Perry's arrival ended two centuries of Japan's self-imposed isolation and eventually led to the overthrow of the last Japanese shogun (military ruler) and the restoration of the emperor. Within two decades of Perry's arrival, Japan's new "Meiji" government had launched the nation on an ambitious program of industrialization and militarization designed to make it the economic and political equal of the Western powers.

As Japan rapidly modernized, its citizens increasingly took ship for America. A steep land tax imposed by the Meiji government to pay for its reforms drove more than 300,000 Japanese farmers off their land. In 1884 the Meiji government permitted Hawaiian planters to recruit contract laborers from among this displaced population. By the 1890s many Japanese were sailing beyond Hawaii to the ports of Long Beach, San Francisco, and Seattle.

Between 1885 and 1924, roughly 200,000 Japanese migrated to Hawaii, and around 180,000 more ventured to the U.S. mainland. They were a select group: because the Meiji government saw overseas Japanese as representatives of their homeland, it strictly regulated emigration. Thus Japanese immigrants to America arrived with more money than their European counterparts. Also, because of Japan's system of compulsory education, Japanese immigrants on average were better educated and more literate than European immigrants.

Women as well as men migrated. The Japanese government, wanting to avoid the problems of an itinerant bachelor society that it observed among the Chinese in the United States, actively promoted women's migration. Although most Japanese immigrants were young men in their twenties and thirties, thousands of women also ventured to Hawaii

and the mainland as contract laborers or "picture brides," so called because their courtship had consisted exclusively of an exchange of photographs with their prospective husbands.

Like many Chinese and European immigrants, most Japanese who came to America expected to stay only temporarily. They planned to work hard for wages that were high by Japanese standards and then to return home and buy land. In Hawaii most Japanese labored on the vast sugar cane plantations. On the mainland they initially found migratory work on the railroads or in fish, fruit, or vegetable canneries. A separate Japanese economy of restaurants, stores, and boardinghouses soon sprang up in cities to serve the immigrants' needs.

From such humble beginnings, many Japanese—particularly those on the Pacific Coast—

Pledging in Vain   These Japanese-American school children in San Francisco were soon evacuated along with their parents.

830

Manzanar Internment Camp, 1943
This view of Manzanar is deceptively picturesque and tranquil. In reality, the six-thousand-acre camp on the barren flats of a dried-up lake in California's interior was enclosed in barbed wire, and the twenty-by-twenty uninsulated cabins were virtually uninhabitable. A riot in late 1942 against the government's use of informants within the camp resulted in the death of two and serious injury of eight internees.

Japanese-American Evacuees, 1942
After the U.S. Army's Western Defense Command ordered the forced evacuation of all Japanese and Japanese-Americans living on the Pacific Coast, families had no choice but to pack up whatever they could carry and move to the "relocation centers" hastily erected further inland.

quickly moved into farming. In the late nineteenth century, the spread of irrigation shifted California agriculture from grain to fruits and vegetables, and the invention of the refrigerated railcar opened hungry new markets in the East. The Japanese, with centuries of experience in intensive farming, arrived just in time to take advantage of these developments. As early as 1910, Japanese farmers produced 70 percent of California's strawberries, and by 1940 they grew 95 percent of the state's snap beans and more than half of its tomatoes. One Japanese farmer, known as the Potato King, sent his children to Harvard and Stanford Universities and died in 1926 with an estate valued at $15 million.

But the very success of the Japanese proved a lightning rod for trouble. On the West Coast, Japanese immigrants had long endured racist barbs and social segregation. Increasingly, white workers and farmers, jealous of Japanese success, pushed for immigration restrictions. Bowing to this pressure, President Theodore Roosevelt in 1908 negotiated the "Gentlemen's Agreement," under which the Japanese government voluntarily agreed to limit emigration. In 1913 the California legislature denied Japanese immigrants already living in the United States the right to own land.

Legally barred from becoming citizens, Japanese immigrants (the "Issei," from the Japanese word for *first*) became more determined than ever that their American-born children (the "Nissei," from the Japanese word for *second*) would reap the full benefits of their birthright. Japanese parents encouraged their children to learn English, to excel in school, and to get a college education. Many Nissei grew up in two worlds, a fact they often recognized by Americanizing their Japanese names. Although education and acculturation did not protect the Nissei from the hysteria of World War II, those assets did give them a springboard to success in the postwar era.

clear idea what the war is about." All Americans knew was that they had a dirty job on their hands and that the only way out was forward. They went about their bloody task with astonishing efficiency.

Building the War Machine

The war crisis caused the drooping American economy to snap to attention. Massive military orders—over $100 billion in 1942 alone—almost instantly soaked up the idle industrial capacity of the still-lingering Great Depression. Orchestrated by the War

The Four Freedoms, by Norman Rockwell   In his January 6, 1941, speech to Congress requesting lend-lease aid to the Allies, President Roosevelt spoke eloquently of the "four freedoms" then threatened by Nazi and Japanese aggression. They are here given pictorial representation by Norman Rockwell, probably the most popular and best-loved American artist of the time.

OURS...to fight for

Freedom of Speech

Freedom of Worship

Freedom from Want

Freedom from Fear

Production Board, American factories poured forth an avalanche of weaponry: 40 billion bullets, 300,000 aircraft, 76,000 ships, 86,000 tanks, and 2.6 million machine guns. Miracle-man shipbuilder Henry J. Kaiser was dubbed "Sir Launchalot" for his prodigies of ship construction; one of his ships was fully assembled in fourteen days, complete with life jackets and coat hangers.

The War Production Board halted the manufacture of nonessential items such as passenger cars. It assigned priorities for transportation and access to raw materials. When the Japanese invasion of British Malaya and the Dutch East Indies snapped America's lifeline of natural rubber, the government imposed a national speed limit and gasoline rationing in order to conserve rubber and built fifty-one synthetic-rubber plants. By war's end they were far outproducing the prewar supply.

Farmers, too, rolled up their sleeves and increased their output. The armed forces drained the farms of workers, but heavy new investment in agricultural machinery and improved fertilizers more than made up the difference. In 1944 and 1945, blue-jeaned farmers hauled in record-breaking billion-bushel wheat harvests.

These wonders of production also brought economic strains. Full employment and scarce consumer goods fueled a sharp inflationary surge in 1942. The Office of Price Administration eventually brought ascending prices under control with extensive regulations. Rationing held down the consumption of critical goods such as meat and butter, though some "black marketeers" and "meatleggers" cheated the system. The War Labor Board (WLB) imposed ceilings on wage increases.

Labor unions, whose membership grew from about 10 million to more than 13 million workers during the war, fiercely resented the government-dictated wage ceilings. Despite the no-strike pledges of most of the major unions, a rash of labor walkouts plagued the war effort. Prominent among the strikers were the United Mine Workers, who several times were called off the job by their crusty and iron-willed chieftain, John L. Lewis.

Threats of lost production through strikes became so worrisome that Congress, in June 1943, passed the Smith-Connally Anti-Strike Act. This act authorized the federal government to seize and operate tied-up industries. Strikes against any government-operated industry were made a criminal offense. Under the act, Washington took over the coal mines and, for a brief period, the railroads. Yet work stoppages, although dangerous, actually accounted for less than 1 percent of the total working hours of the United States' wartime laboring force—a record better than blockaded Britain's. American workers, on the whole, were commendably committed to the war effort.

Manpower and Womanpower

The armed services enlisted nearly 15 million men in World War II and some 216,000 women, who were employed for noncombat duties. Best known of these "women in arms" were the WAACs (army), WAVES (navy), and SPARs (Coast Guard). As the draft net was tightened after Pearl Harbor, millions of young men were plucked from their homes and clothed in "GI" (government issue) outfits. As the arsenal of democracy, the United States exempted certain key categories of industrial and agricultural workers from the draft, in order to keep its mighty industrial and food-producing machines humming.

Poster appeals and slogans urging women to enlist in the WAACs (Women's Army Auxiliary Corps) were "Speed Them Back, Join the WAAC," "I'd Rather Be with Them—Than Waiting for Them," "Back the Attack, Be a WAAC! For America Is Calling," and (a song throwback to World War I) "The WAACs and WAVES Will Win the War, Parlez Vous."

But even with these exemptions, the draft left the nation's farms and factories so short of personnel that new workers had to be found. An agreement with Mexico in 1942 brought thousands of Mexican agricultural workers, called *braceros,* across the border to harvest the fruit and grain crops of the West. The *bracero* program outlived the war by some twenty years, becoming a fixed feature of the agricultural economy in many western states.

War Workers   More than 6 million women—3 million of them homemakers who had never before worked for wages—entered the work force during World War II. In contrast to the experience of women workers in World War I, many of these newly employed women continued as wage workers after the war ended.

Even more dramatic was the march of women onto the factory floor. More than 6 million women took up jobs outside the home; over half of them had never before worked for wages. Many of them were mothers, and the government was obliged to set up some 3,000 day-care centers to care for "Rosie the Riveter's" children while she drilled the fuselage of a heavy bomber or joined the links of a tank track. When the war ended, Rosie and many of her sisters were in no hurry to put down their tools. They wanted to keep on working and often did. The war thus foreshadowed an eventual revolution in the roles of women in American society.

Yet the war's immediate impact on women's lives has frequently been exaggerated. The great majority of American women—especially those with husbands present in the home or with small children to care for—did not work for wages in the wartime economy but continued in their traditional roles. In both Britain and the Soviet Union, a far greater percentage of women, including mothers, were pressed into industrial employment as the gods of war laid a much heavier hand on those societies than they did on the United States. A poll in 1943 revealed that a majority of American women would not take a job in a war plant if it were offered.

At war's end, two-thirds of women war workers left the labor force. Many of these were forced out of their jobs by employers and unions eager to re-employ returning servicemen. But half of them told census takers that they quit their jobs voluntarily because of family obligations. The immediate postwar period witnessed not a permanent widening of women's employment opportunities, but a widespread rush into suburban domesticity and the mothering of the "baby boomers" who were born by the tens of millions in the decade and a half after 1945. America was destined to experience a thoroughgoing revolution in women's status later in the postwar period, but that epochal change was only beginning to gather momentum in the war years.

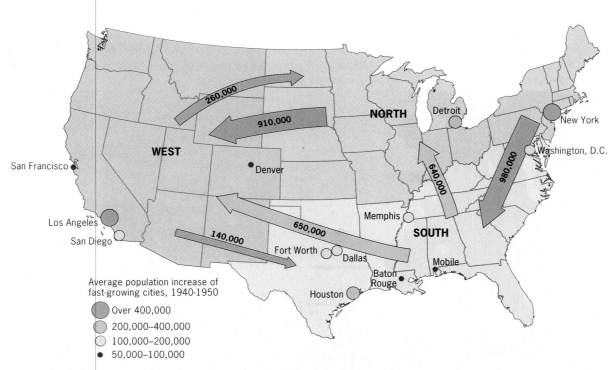

Internal Migration in the United States During World War II   Few events in American history have moved the American people about so massively as World War II. The West and the South boomed, and several war-industry cities grew explosively. A majority of migrants from the South were blacks; 1.6 million African-Americans left the region in the 1940s. (Source: United States Department of Labor, Bureau of Labor Statistics.)

Wartime Migrations

The war also proved to be a demographic cauldron, churning and shifting the American population. Many of the 15 million men and women in uniform, having seen new sights and glimpsed new horizons, chose not to go home again at war's end. War industries sucked people into boomtowns like Los Angeles, Detroit, Seattle, and Baton Rouge. California's population grew by nearly 2 million. The South experienced especially dramatic changes. Franklin Roosevelt had called the South "the nation's number one economic problem" in 1938; when war came, he seized the opportunity to accelerate the region's economic development. The states of the old Confederacy received a disproportionate share of defense contracts, including nearly $6 billion of federally financed industrial facilities. Here were the seeds of the postwar blossoming of the "Sunbelt."

Despite this economic stimulus in the South, some 1.6 million blacks left the land of their ancient enslavement to seek jobs in the war plants of the West and North. Forever after, race relations constituted a national, not a regional, issue. Explosive tensions developed over employment, housing, and segregated facilities. Black leader A. Philip Randolph, head of the Brotherhood of Sleeping Car Porters, threatened a massive "Negro March on

An African-American soldier angrily complained about segregation in the armed forces during World War II:

"Why is it we Negro soldiers who are as much a part of Uncle Sam's great military machine as any cannot be treated with equality and the respect due us? The same respect which white soldiers expect and demand from us? . . . There is great need for drastic change in this man's Army! How can we be trained to protect America, which is called a *free* nation, when all around us rears the ugly head of segregation?'"

Washington" in 1941 to demand equal opportunities for blacks in war jobs and in the armed forces. Roosevelt's response was to issue an executive order forbidding discrimination in defense industries. In addition, the president established the Fair Employment Practices Commission (FEPC) to monitor compliance with his edict. Blacks were also drafted into the armed forces, though they were still generally assigned to service branches rather than combat units and subjected to petty degradations such

Segregation in the Military
Lieutenant Colonel Benjamin Davis, standing on the wing, was the highest ranking black officer in the Army Air Corps, and the son of the highest ranked black officer in the regular army. Both father and son were educated at West Point to command segregated units, most of whom saw little combat. Lieutenant Colonel Davis, however, oversaw the elite 99th Fighter Pursuit Squadron, known as the "Tuskegee Airmen," an all-black bomber unit that trained at the Tuskegee Institute in Alabama founded by Booker T. Washington in 1881. Of the nearly 1,000 African-American pilots trained, 445 saw combat in Europe, North Africa, and the Mediterranean. In 1,600 missions, they never lost a bomber to enemy fighters.

The Mechanical Cotton Picker   The advent of this new machine in the 1940s deprived millions of southern blacks of their traditional meager employment in the cotton fields. Their massive displacement by the mechanical picker set off one of the greatest migrations in American history.

Navajo Code Talkers, 1943
One of the best-kept secrets of World War II was the use of the Navajo language in a Marine Corps code designed to confuse the Japanese. Two marines in the leatherneck unit, made up of Indians from Arizona and New Mexico, transmitted in code during the battle for Bougainville Island in the South Pacific in 1943.

as segregated blood banks for the wounded. But in general the war helped to embolden blacks in their long struggle for equality. They rallied behind the slogan "Double V"—victory over the dictators abroad and over racism at home. Membership in the National Association for the Advancement of Colored People (NAACP) shot up almost to the half-million mark, and a new militant organization, the Congress of Racial Equality (CORE), was founded in 1942.

The northward migration of African-Americans accelerated after the war, thanks to the advent of the mechanical cotton picker—an invention whose impact rivaled that of Eli Whitney's cotton gin. Introduced in 1944, this new mechanical marvel did the work of fifty people at about one-eighth the cost. Overnight, the Cotton South's historic need for cheap labor disappeared. Their muscle no longer required in Dixie, some 5 million black tenant farmers and sharecroppers headed north in the three decades after the war. Theirs was one of the great migrations in American history, comparable in size to the immigrant floods from Ireland, Italy, and Poland. Within a single generation, a near majority of African-Americans gave up their historic home-

land and their rural way of life. By 1970 half of all blacks lived outside of the South, and *urban* had become almost a synonym for *black*. The speed and scale of these changes jolted the migrants and sometimes convulsed the communities that received them.

The war also prompted an exodus of Native Americans from the reservations. Thousands of Indian men and women found war work in the major cities, and thousands more answered Uncle Sam's call to arms. More than 90 percent of Indians resided on reservations in 1940; six decades later more than half lived in cities, with a large concentration in southern California.

Some twenty-five thousand Native American men served in the armed forces. Comanches in Europe and Navajos in the Pacific made especially valuable contributions as "code talkers." They transmitted radio messages in their native languages, which were incomprehensible to the Germans and the Japanese.

The sudden rubbing against one another of unfamiliar peoples produced some distressingly violent friction. In 1943 young "zoot-suit"–clad Mexicans and Mexican-Americans in Los Angeles were viciously attacked by Anglo sailors who cruised the streets in taxicabs, searching for victims. Order was restored only after the Mexican ambassador made an emotional plea, pointing out that such outbreaks were grist for Nazi propaganda mills. At almost the same time, an even more brutal race riot that killed twenty-five blacks and nine whites erupted in Detroit.

Holding the Home Front

Despite these ugly episodes, Americans on the home front suffered little from the war, compared to the peoples of the other fighting nations. By war's end much of the planet was a smoking ruin. But in America the war invigorated the economy and lifted the country out of a decade-long depression. The gross national product vaulted from less than $100 billion in 1940 to more than $200 billion in 1945. Corporate profits rose from about $6 billion in 1940 to almost twice that amount four years later. ("If you are going to try to go to war in a capitalist country," said Secretary of War Henry Stimson, "you have to let business make money out of the process, or business won't work.") Despite wage ceilings, overtime pay fattened pay envelopes. Disposable personal income, even after payment of wartime taxes, more than doubled. On December 7, 1944, the third anniversary of Pearl Harbor, Macy's department store rang up the biggest sales day in its history. Americans had never had it so good—and they wanted it a lot better. When price controls were finally lifted in 1946, America's pent-up lust to consume pushed prices up 33 percent in less than two years. The rest of the world, meanwhile, was still clawing its way out from under the rubble of war.

The hand of government touched more American lives more intimately during the war than ever before. The war, perhaps even more than the New Deal, pointed the way to the post-1945 era of big-government interventionism. Every household felt the constraints of the rationing system. Millions of men and women worked for Uncle Sam in the armed forces. Millions more worked for him in the defense industries, where their employers and unions were monitored by the FEPC and the WLB, and their personal needs were cared for by government-sponsored housing projects, day-care facilities, and health plans. The Office of Scientific Research and Development channeled hundreds of millions of dollars into university-based scientific research, establishing the partnership between the government and universities that underwrote America's technological and economic leadership in the postwar era.

The flood of war dollars—not the relatively modest rivulet of New Deal spending—at last swept the plague of unemployment from the land. War, not enlightened social policy, cured the depression. As the postwar economy continued to depend dangerously on military spending for its health, many observers looked back to the years 1941–1945 as the origins of a "warfare-welfare state."

Billions of dollars

The National Debt, 1930–1950
Contrary to much popular mythology, it was World War II, not the New Deal, that first ballooned the national debt. The debt accumulated to still greater amounts in the 1980s and 1990s (see table, p. 986). (Source: *Historical Statistics of the United States.*)

The conflict was phenomenally expensive. The wartime bill amounted to more than $330 billion—ten times the direct cost of World War I and twice as much as *all* previous federal spending since 1776. Roosevelt would have preferred to follow a pay-as-you-go policy to finance the war, but the costs were simply too gigantic. The income-tax net was expanded to catch about four times as many people as before, and maximum tax rates rose as high as 90 percent. But despite such drastic measures, only about two-fifths of the war costs were paid from current revenues. The remainder was borrowed. The national debt skyrocketed from $49 billion in 1941 to $259 billion in 1945. When production finally slipped into high gear, the war was costing about $10 million an hour. This was the price of victory over such implacable enemies.

Corregidor and Bataan

The Rising Sun in the Pacific

Early successes of the efficient Japanese militarists were breathtaking: they realized that they would have to win quickly or lose slowly. Seldom, if ever, has so much territory been conquered so rapidly with so little loss.

Simultaneously with the assault on Pearl Harbor, the Japanese launched widespread and uniformly successful attacks on various Far Eastern bastions. These included the American outposts of Guam, Wake, and the Philippines. In a dismayingly short time, the Japanese invader seized not only the British-Chinese port of Hong Kong but also British Malaya, with its critically important supplies of rubber and tin.

Nor did the Japanese tide stop there. The over-ambitious soldiers of the emperor, plunging into the snake-infested jungles of Burma, cut the famed Burma Road. This was the route over which the United States had been trucking a trickle of munitions to the armies of the Chinese generalissimo Jiang Jieshi (Chiang Kai-shek), who was still resisting the Japanese invader in China. Thereafter, intrepid American aviators were forced to fly a handful of war supplies to Jiang "over the hump" of the towering Himalaya mountains from the India-Burma theater. Meanwhile, the Japanese had lunged southward against the oil-rich Dutch East Indies. The jungle-matted islands speedily fell to the assailants after the combined British, Australian, Dutch, and American naval and air forces had been smashed at an early date by their numerically superior foe.

Better news came from the Philippines, which succeeded dramatically in slowing down the mikado's warriors for five months. The Japanese promptly landed a small but effective army, and General Douglas MacArthur, the eloquent and egotistical American commander, withdrew to a strong defensive position at Bataan, not far from Manila. There about twenty thousand American troops, supported by a much larger force of ill-trained Filipinos, held off violent Japanese attacks until April 9, 1942. The defenders, reduced to eating mules and monkeys, heroically traded their lives for time in the face of hopeless odds. They grimly joked while vainly hoping for reinforcements:

We're the battling bastards of Bataan;
No Mamma, no Papa, no Uncle Sam. . . .

Before the inevitable American surrender, General MacArthur was ordered by Washington to depart secretly for Australia, there to head the resistance against the Japanese. Leaving by motorboat and airplane, he proclaimed, "I shall return." After the battered remnants of his army had hoisted the white flag, they were treated with vicious cruelty in the infamous eighty-mile Bataan Death March to prisoner-of-war camps. The island fortress of Corregidor, in Manila harbor, held out until May 6,

1942, when it too surrendered and left Japanese forces in complete control of the Philippine archipelago.

Japan's High Tide at Midway

The aggressive warriors from Japan, making hay while the Rising Sun shone, pushed relentlessly southward. They invaded the turtle-shaped island of New Guinea, north of Australia, and landed on the Solomon Islands, from which they threatened Australia itself. Their onrush was finally checked by a crucial naval battle fought in the Coral Sea, in May 1942. An American carrier task force, with Aus-tralian support, inflicted heavy losses on the victory-flushed Japanese. For the first time in history, the fighting was all done by carrier-based aircraft, and neither fleet saw or fired a shot directly at the other.

Japan next undertook to seize Midway Island, more than a thousand miles northwest of Honolulu. From this strategic base, it could launch devastating assaults on Pearl Harbor and perhaps force the weakened American Pacific fleet into destructive combat—possibly even compel the United States to negotiate a cease-fire in the Pacific. An epochal naval battle was fought near Midway on June 3–6, 1942. Admiral Chester W. Nimitz, a high-grade naval strategist, directed a smaller but skillfully maneuvered carrier force, under Admiral Raymond A. Spruance, against the powerful invading fleet. The fighting was all done by aircraft, and the Japanese broke off action after losing four vitally important carriers.

Midway was a pivotal victory. Combined with the Battle of the Coral Sea, the U.S. success at Midway halted Japan's juggernaut. But the thrust of the Japanese into the eastern Pacific did net them America's fog-girt islands of Kiska and Attu, in the Aleutian archipelago, off Alaska. This easy conquest aroused fear of an invasion of the United States from the northwest. Much American strength was consequently diverted to the defense of Alaska, including the construction of the "Alcan" Highway through Canada.

Yet the Japanese imperialists, overextended in 1942, suffered from "victory disease." Their appetites were bigger than their stomachs. If they had only dug in and consolidated their gains, they would have been much more difficult to dislodge once the tide turned.

Hell in the Pacific Assaulting Japanese island-fortresses in the Pacific was a bloody, costly business. These American soldiers perished as they stepped ashore at Buna beach in New Guinea in 1942. Their damaged landing craft wallows in the surf behind them.

American Leapfrogging Toward Tokyo

Following the heartening victory at Midway, the United States for the first time was able to seize the initiative in the Pacific. In August 1942 American ground forces gained a toehold on Guadalcanal Island, in the Solomons, in an effort to protect the lifeline from America to Australia through the Southwest Pacific. An early naval defeat inflicted by the Japanese shortened American supplies dangerously, and for weeks the U.S. troops held on to the malarial island only by their fingernails. After several desperate sea battles for naval control, the Japanese troops evacuated Guadalcanal in February 1943. Japanese losses were 20,000, compared to 1,700 for the Americans. That casualty ratio of more than ten to one, Japanese to American, persisted throughout the Pacific war.

American and Australian forces, under General MacArthur, meanwhile had been hanging on courageously to the southeastern tip of New Guinea, the last buffer protecting Australia. The scales of war gradually began to tip as the American navy, including submarines, inflicted lethal losses on Japanese supply ships and troop carriers. Conquest of the north coast of New Guinea was completed by August 1944, after General MacArthur had fought his way westward through tropical jungle hells. This hard-won victory was the first leg on his long return journey to the Philippines.

The U.S. Navy, with marines and army divisions doing the meat-grinder fighting, had meanwhile been "leapfrogging" the Japanese-held islands in the Pacific. Old-fashioned strategy dictated that the American forces, as they drove toward Tokyo, should reduce the fortified Japanese outposts on their flank. This course would have taken many blood-stained months, for the holed-in defenders were prepared to die to the last man in their caves. The new strategy of island hopping called for bypassing some of the most heavily fortified Japanese posts, capturing nearby islands, setting up airfields on them, and then neutralizing the enemy bases through heavy bombing. Deprived of essential supplies from the homeland, Japan's outposts would slowly wither on the vine—as they did.

Brilliant success crowned the American attacks on the Japanese island strongholds in the Pacific, where Admiral Nimitz skillfully coordinated the

United States Thrusts in the Pacific, 1942–1945 American strategists had to choose among four proposed plans for waging the war against Japan:
1. Defeating the Japanese in China by funneling supplies over the Himalayan "hump" from India.
2. Carrying the war into Southeast Asia (a proposal much favored by the British, who could thus regain Singapore).
3. Heavy bombing of Japan from Chinese air bases.
4. "Island hopping" from the South Pacific to within striking distance of the Japanese home islands. This strategy, favored by General Douglas MacArthur, was the one finally emphasized.

* Major battle sites
— Limit of Japanese conquest
▨ Japanese-held areas
◄— U.S. thrusts

efforts of naval, air, and ground units. In May and August of 1943, Attu and Kiska in the Aleutians were easily retaken. In November 1943 "bloody Tarawa" and Makin, both in the Gilbert Islands, fell after suicidal resistance. In January and February 1944, the key outposts of the Marshall Islands group succumbed after savage fighting.

Especially prized were the Marianas, including America's conquered Guam. From bases in the Marianas, the United States' new B-29 superbombers could carry out round-trip bombing raids on Japan's home islands. The assault on the Marianas opened on June 19, 1944, with what American pilots called the "Great Marianas Turkey Shoot." A combination of the combat superiority of the recently developed American "Hellcat" fighter plane and the new technology of the antiaircraft proximity fuse destroyed nearly 250 Japanese aircraft, with a loss of only 29 American planes. The following day, in the Battle of the Philippine Sea, U.S. naval forces sank several Japanese carriers. The Japanese navy never recovered from these massive losses of planes, pilots, and ships.

After fanatical resistance, including a mass suicide leap of surviving Japanese soldiers and civilians from "Suicide Cliff" on Saipan, the major islands of the Marianas fell to the U.S. attackers in July and August 1944. With these unsinkable aircraft carriers now available, virtual round-the-clock bombing of Japan began in November 1944.

The Allied Halting of Hitler

Early setbacks for America in the Pacific were paralleled in the Atlantic. Hitler had entered the war with a formidable fleet of ultramodern submarines, which ultimately operated in "wolf packs" with frightful effect, especially in the North Atlantic, the Caribbean, and the Gulf of Mexico. During ten months of 1942 more than 500 merchant ships were reported lost—111 in June alone—as ship destruction far outran construction.

The tide of subsea battle turned with agonizing slowness. Old techniques, such as escorting convoys of merchant vessels and dropping depth bombs from destroyers, were strengthened by air patrol, the newly invented technology of radar, and the bombing of submarine bases. "Keep 'Em Sailing" was the motto of oil-begrimed merchant seamen,

> *British prime minister Winston Churchill (1874–1965) observed in a speech (May 1943),*
>
> "The proud German Army has by its sudden collapse, sudden crumbling and breaking up . . . once again proved the truth of the saying, 'The Hun [German] is always either at your throat or at your feet.'"

hundreds of whom perished as unsung heroes in icy seas. Eventually Allied antisubmarine tactics improved substantially, thanks especially to British code-breakers, who had cracked the Germans' "Enigma" codes and could therefore pinpoint the locations of the U-boats lurking in the North Atlantic.

Not until the spring of 1943 did the Allies clearly have the upper hand against the U-boat. If they had not won the Battle of the Atlantic, Britain would have been forced under, and a second front could not have been launched from its island springboard. Victory over the undersea raiders was nerve-rackingly narrow. When the war ended, Hitler was about to mass-produce a fearsome new submarine —one that could remain underwater indefinitely and cruise at seventeen knots when submerged.

Meanwhile, the turning point of the land-air war against Hitler had come late in 1942. The British had launched a thousand-plane raid on Cologne in May. In August 1942 they were joined by the American air force and were cascading bombs on German cities. The Germans under Marshal Erwin Rommel—the "Desert Fox"—had driven eastward across the hot sands of North Africa into Egypt, perilously close to the Suez Canal. A breakthrough would have spelled disaster for the Allies. But late in October 1942, British general Bernard Montgomery delivered a withering attack at El Alamein, west of Cairo. With the aid of several hundred hastily shipped American Sherman tanks, he speedily drove the enemy back to Tunisia, more than a thousand miles away.

On the Soviet front, the unexpected successes of the red army gave a new lift to the Allied cause. In September 1942 the Russians stalled the German steamroller at rubble-strewn Stalingrad, graveyard of Hitler's hopes. More than a score of invading divisions, caught in an icy noose, later surrendered or were "mopped up." In November 1942 the resilient Russians unleashed a crushing counteroffensive, which was never seriously reversed. A year later Stalin had regained about two-thirds of the blood-soaked Soviet motherland wrested from him by the German invader.

A Second Front from North Africa to Rome

Soviet losses were already staggering in 1942: millions of soldiers and civilians lay dead, and Hitler's armies had overrun most of the western USSR. Anglo-American losses at this time could be counted only in the thousands. By war's end, the grave had closed over some 20 million Soviets, and a great swath of their country, equivalent in the United States to the area from Chicago to the Atlantic seaboard, had been laid waste. Small wonder that Kremlin leaders clamored for a second front to divert the German strength westward.

Many Americans, including FDR, were eager to begin a diversionary invasion of France in 1942 or 1943. They feared that the Soviets, unable to hold out forever against Germany, might make a separate peace as they had in 1918 and leave the Western Allies to face Hitler's fury alone.

But British military planners, remembering their appalling losses in 1914–1918, were not enthusiastic about a frontal assault on German-held France. It might end in disaster. They preferred to attack Hitler's Fortress Europe through the "soft underbelly" of the Mediterranean. Faced with British boot-dragging and a woeful lack of resources, the Americans reluctantly agreed to postpone a massive invasion of Europe.

An assault on French-held North Africa was a compromise second front. The highly secret attack, launched in November 1942, was headed by a gifted and easy-smiling American general, Dwight D. ("Ike") Eisenhower, a master of organization and conciliation. As a joint Allied operation ultimately involving some 400,000 men (British, Canadian, French, and chiefly American) and about 850 ships, the invasion was the mightiest waterborne effort up to that time in history. After savage fighting, the

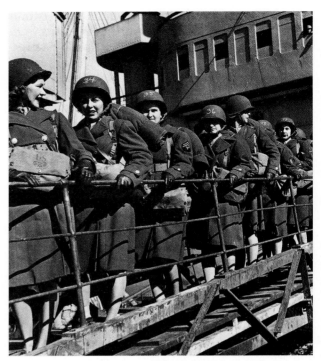

Women at War Members of the Women's Army Corps disembark in North Africa in 1944.

remnants of the German-Italian army were finally trapped in Tunisia and surrendered in May 1943.

New blows were now planned by the Allies. At Casablanca, in newly occupied French Morocco, President Roosevelt, who had boldly flown the Atlantic, met in a historic conference with Winston Churchill in January 1943. The Big Two agreed to step up the Pacific war, invade Sicily, increase pressure on Italy, and insist upon an "unconditional surrender" of the enemy, a phrase earlier popularized by General Ulysses S. Grant during the Civil War. Such an unyielding policy would presumably hearten the ultrasuspicious Soviets, who professed to fear separate Allied peace negotiations. It would also forestall charges of broken armistice terms, such as had come after 1918. Paradoxically, the tough-sounding unconditional surrender declaration was an admission of the weakness of the Western Allies. Still unable in 1943 to mount the kind of second front their Soviet partner desperately demanded, the British and the Americans had little but words to offer Stalin.

"Unconditional surrender" proved to be one of the most controversial moves of the war. The main criticism was that it steeled the enemy to fight to a last-bunker resistance, while discouraging antiwar groups in Germany from revolting. Although there was some truth in these charges, no one can prove that "unconditional surrender" either shortened or lengthened the war. But by helping to destroy the German government utterly, the harsh policy immensely complicated the problems of postwar reconstruction.

The Allied forces, victorious in Africa, now turned against the not-so-soft underbelly of Europe. Sicily fell in August 1943 after sporadic but sometimes bitter resistance. Shortly before the conquest of the island, Mussolini was deposed, and Italy surrendered unconditionally soon thereafter, in September 1943. President Roosevelt, referring to the three original Axis countries—Germany, Italy, and Japan—joked grimly that it was now one down and two to go.

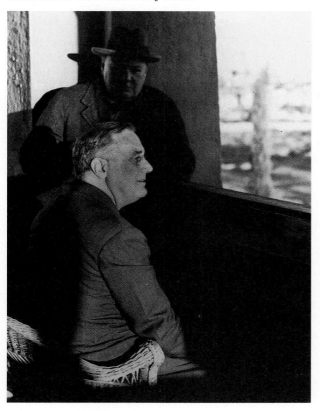

The Big Two British prime minister Winston Churchill and U.S. president Franklin D. Roosevelt meet at the Casablanca conference in Morocco, January 1943.

But if Italy dropped out of the war, the Germans did not drop out of Italy. Hitler's well-trained troops stubbornly resisted the Allied invaders now pouring into the toe of the Italian boot. They also unleashed their fury against the Italians, who had turned their coats and declared war on Germany in October 1943. "Sunny Italy" proceeded to belie its name, for in the snow-covered and mud-caked mountains of its elongated peninsula occurred some of the filthiest, bloodiest, and most frustrating fighting of the war.

For many months Italy appeared to be a dead end, as the Allied advance was halted by a seemingly impregnable German defense centered on the ancient monastery of Monte Cassino. After a touch-and-go assault on the Anzio beachhead, Rome was finally taken on June 4, 1944. The tremendous cross-channel invasion of France begun two days later turned Italy into a kind of sideshow, but the Allies, limited in manpower, continued to fight their way slowly and painfully into northern Italy. On May 2, 1945, only five days before Germany's official surrender, several hundred thousand Axis troops in Italy laid down their arms and became prisoners of war. While the Italian second front opened the Mediterranean and diverted some German divisions from the blazing Soviet and French battle lines, it also may have delayed the main Allied invasion of Europe, from England across the English Channel to France, by many months—allowing more time for the Soviet army to advance into Eastern Europe.

D-Day: June 6, 1944

The Soviets had never ceased their clamor for an all-out second front, and the time rapidly approached for Churchill, Roosevelt, and Stalin to meet in person to coordinate the promised effort. Marshal Joseph Stalin, with a careful eye on Soviet military operations, balked at leaving Moscow. President Roosevelt, who jauntily remarked in private, "I can handle that old buzzard," was eager to confer with him. The president seemed confident that Rooseveltian charm could woo the hardened conspirator of the Kremlin from his nasty communist ways.

Teheran, the capital of Iran (Persia), was finally chosen as the meeting place. To this ancient city Roosevelt riskily flew, after a stopover conference in

World War II in Europe and North Africa, 1939–1945

Cairo with Britain's Churchill and China's Jiang Jieshi regarding the war against Japan. At Teheran the discussions among Stalin, Roosevelt, and Churchill—from November 28 to December 1, 1943—progressed smoothly. Perhaps the most important achievement was agreement on broad plans, especially those for launching Soviet attacks on Germany from the east simultaneously with the prospective Allied assault from the west.

Preparations for the cross-channel invasion of France were gigantic. Britain's fast-anchored isle virtually groaned with munitions, supplies, and troops, as nearly 3 million fighting men were readied. Because the United States was to provide most of the Allied warriors, the overall command was entrusted to an American, General Eisenhower. He had already distinguished himself in the North African and Mediterranean Campaigns, not only for his military capacity but also for his gifts as a conciliator of clashing Allied interests.

French Normandy, less heavily defended than other parts of the European coast, was pinpointed for the invasion assault. On D-Day, June 6, 1944, the enormous operation, which involved some forty-six hundred vessels, unwound. Stiff resistance was encountered from the Germans, who had been misled by a feint into expecting the blow to fall farther north. The Allies had already achieved mastery of the air over France. They were thus able to block reinforcements by crippling the railroads, while worsening German fuel shortages by bombing gasoline-producing plants.

EXAMINING THE EVIDENCE

Franklin Roosevelt at Teheran, 1943   In late 1943 the "Big Three" wartime leaders—Britain's prime minister Winston Churchill, American president Franklin Roosevelt, and Soviet leader Marshal Joseph Stalin—gathered together for the first time. They met amidst growing Soviet frustration with the British and the Americans for their failure thus far to open a "second front" against Germany in western Europe, while the Soviets continued to suffer horrendous losses in the savage fighting in eastern Europe. American military planners were eager to open a second front as soon as possible, but the British, who would necessarily have to supply most of the troops until America was fully mobilized, balked. Tension among the three leaders over the second front plan—code-named OVERLORD, the operation that resulted in the Anglo-American invasion of Normandy on "D-Day," June 6, 1944—is evident in this transcript of

their discussions in the Iranian city of Teheran on November 28, 1943. The excerpts printed here are actually taken from two separate accounts: one composed by the American diplomat and Roosevelt's official translator Charles Bohlen, the other written by a military officer on behalf of the United States Joint Chiefs of Staff. Both versions are published in *Foreign Relations of the United States,* a compilation of American diplomatic records since 1861. The Soviets and the British also kept their own records of the Teheran meetings, giving historians remarkably rich sources with which to reconstruct the crucial negotiations and decisions that shaped wartime diplomacy. Why might the history of diplomacy be so lavishly documented? At this meeting, what were the principal objectives that each leader pursued? How did each man address his task? In what ways was the future of the war— and the post-war world—here foreshadowed?

FIRST PLENARY MEETING,
NOVEMBER 28, 1943, 4 P. M., CONFERENCE
ROOM, SOVIET EMBASSY

Bohlen Minutes

SECRET

THE PRESIDENT said as the youngest of the three present he ventured to welcome his elders. He said he wished to welcome the new members to the family circle and tell them that meetings of this character were conducted as between friends with complete frankness on all sides with nothing that was said to be made public. . . .

Chief of Staff Minutes

MARSHAL STALIN asked who will be the commander in this Operation Overlord. (THE PRESIDENT and PRIME MINISTER interpolated this was not yet decided.) MARSHAL STALIN continued, "Then nothing will come out of these operations." . . .

THE PRESIDENT said we again come back to the problem of the timing for OVERLORD. It was believed that it would be good for OVERLORD to take place about 1 May, or certainly not later than 15 May or 20 May, if possible.

THE PRIME MINISTER said that he could not agree to that. . . .

. . . He said he (the Prime Minister) was going to do everything in the power of His Majesty's Government to begin OVERLORD at the earliest possible moment. However, he did not think that the

many great possibilities in the Mediterranean should be ruthlessly cast aside as valueless merely on the question of a month's delay in OVERLORD.

MARSHAL STALIN said all the Mediterranean operations are diversions, . . .

THE PRESIDENT said he found that his staff places emphasis on OVERLORD. While on the other hand the Prime Minister and his staff also emphasize OVERLORD, nevertheless the United States does not feel that OVERLORD should be put off.

THE PRESIDENT questioned whether it would not be possible for the *ad hoc* committee to go ahead with their deliberations without any further directive and to produce an answer by tomorrow morning.

MARSHAL STALIN questioned, "What can such a committee do?" He said, "We Chiefs of State have more power and more authority than a committee. General Brooke cannot force our opinions and there are many questions which can be decided only by us." He said he would like to ask if the British are thinking seriously of OVERLORD only in order to satisfy the U.S.S.R.

THE PRIME MINISTER replied that if the conditions specified at Moscow regarding OVERLORD should exist, he firmly believed it would be England's duty to hurl every ounce of strength she had across the Channel at the Germans.

THE PRESIDENT observed that in an hour a very good dinner would be awaiting all and people would be very hungry. He suggested that the staffs should meet tomorrow morning and discuss the matter. . . .

Allies Landing in Normandy, June 6, 1944 Nine-foot ocean swells on invasion day made loading the assault landing craft, such as the one pictured here, treacherous business. Many men were injured or tossed into the sea as the bathtublike amphibious vessels bobbed wildly up and down alongside the troop transports. As the vulnerable boats churned toward the beach, some officers led their tense, grim-faced troops in prayer. One major, recalling the remarkable Battle of Agincourt in 1415, quoted from Shakespeare's *Henry V*: "He that outlives this day, and comes safe home / Will stand a tip-toe when this day is named."

The Allied beachhead, at first clung to with fingertips, was gradually enlarged, consolidated, and reinforced. After desperate fighting, the invaders finally broke out of the German iron ring that enclosed the Normandy landing zone. Most spectacular were the lunges across France by American armored divisions, brilliantly commanded by blustery and profane General George S. ("Blood 'n' Guts") Patton. The retreat of the German defenders was hastened when an American-French force landed in August 1944 on the southern coast of France and swept northward. With the assistance of the French "underground," Paris was liberated in August 1944, amid exuberant manifestations of joy and gratitude.

Allied forces rolled irresistibly toward Germany, and many of the Americans encountered places, like Château-Thierry, familiar to their fathers in 1918. "Lafayette, we are here again," quipped some of the American soldiers. The first important German city (Aachen) fell to the Americans in October 1944, and the days of Hitler's "thousand-year *Reich*" were numbered.

FDR: The Fourth-Termite of 1944

The presidential campaign of 1944, which was bound to divert energy from the war program, came most awkwardly as the awful conflict roared to its climax. But the normal electoral processes continued to function, despite some loose talk of suspending them "for the duration."

Victory-starved Republicans met in Chicago with hopeful enthusiasm. They quickly nominated

Liberating France
A G.I. from Des Moines, Iowa, receives a kiss of welcome from an elderly French couple after American troops liberated their town of St. Sauveur in August 1944.

the short, mustachioed, and dapper Thomas E. Dewey, popular vote-getting governor of New York. Regarded as a liberal, he had already made a national reputation as a prosecutor of grafters and racketeers in New York City. His shortness and youth—he was only forty-two—had caused one veteran New Dealer to sneer that the candidate had cast his diaper into the ring. To offset Dewey's mild internationalism, the convention nominated for the vice presidency a strong isolationist, handsome and white-maned Senator John W. Bricker of Ohio. Yet the platform called for an unstinted prosecution of the war and for the creation of a new international organization to maintain peace.

FDR, aging under the strain, was the "indispensable man" of the Democrats. No other major figure was available, and the war was apparently grinding to its finale. He was nominated at Chicago on the first ballot by acclamation. But in a sense he was the "forgotten man" of the convention, for in

view of his age, an unusual amount of attention was focused on the vice presidency.

The scramble for the vice-presidential plum turned into something of a free-for-all. Henry A. Wallace, onetime "plow 'em under" secretary of agriculture, had served four years as vice president and desired a renomination. But conservative Democrats distrusted him as an ill-balanced and unpredictable liberal. A "ditch Wallace" move developed tremendous momentum, despite the popularity of Wallace with large numbers of voters and many of the delegates. With Roosevelt's blessing, the vice-presidential nomination finally went to smiling and self-assured Senator Harry S Truman of Missouri ("the new Missouri Compromise"). Hitherto inconspicuous, he had recently attained national visibility as the efficient chairman of a Senate committee conducting an investigation of wasteful war expenditures. Nobody had much against him or on him.

Roosevelt Defeats Dewey

A dynamic Dewey took the offensive, for Roosevelt was too consumed with directing the war to spare much time for speechmaking. The vigorous young "crime buster," with his beautiful baritone voice and polished diction, denounced the tired and quarrelsome "old men" in Washington. He proclaimed repeatedly that after "twelve long years" of New Dealism, it was "time for a change." As for the war, Dewey would not alter the basic strategy but would fight it better—a type of "me-tooism" ridiculed by the Democrats. The fourth-term issue did not figure prominently, now that the ice had been broken by Roosevelt's third term. But "Dewey-eyed" Republicans half-humorously professed to fear fifth and sixth terms by the "lifer" in the White House.

In the closing weeks of the campaign, Roosevelt left his desk for the stump. He was stung by certain Republican charges, including criticism that he had sent a U.S. Navy destroyer to retrieve his pet Scottie dog, Fala. He was also eager to show himself, even in chilling rains, to spike well-founded rumors of failing health.

Substantial assistance came from the new political action committee of the CIO, which was organized to get around the law banning the direct use of union funds for political purposes. Zealous CIO members, branded as communists by the Republicans, rang countless doorbells and asked, with pointed reference to the recent depression, "What were you doing in 1932?" At times Roosevelt seemed to be running again against Hoover. As in every one of his previous three campaigns, FDR was opposed by a majority of the newspapers, which were owned chiefly by Republicans. Roosevelt, as customary, won a sweeping victory: 432 to 99 in the Electoral College; 25,606,585 to 22,014,745 in the popular vote. Elated, he quipped that "the first twelve years are the hardest."

Roosevelt won primarily because the war was going well. A winning pitcher is not ordinarily pulled from the game. Foreign policy was a decisive factor with untold thousands of voters, who concluded that Roosevelt's experienced hand was needed in fashioning a future organization for world peace. The dapper Dewey, cruelly dubbed "the little man on top of the wedding cake," had spoken smoothly of international cooperation, but his isolationist running mate, Bricker, had implanted serious doubts. The

During the bitter campaign of 1944, Roosevelt's pre–Pearl Harbor policies came under sharp attack from Congresswoman Clare Boothe Luce (1903–1987) (the "Blonde Bombshell"), who violently blasted Roosevelt:

"[He] lied us into war because he did not have the political courage to lead us into it."

Republican party was still suffering from the taint of isolationism fastened on it by the Hardingites.

The Last Days of Hitler

By mid-December 1944, the month after Roosevelt's fourth-term victory, Germany seemed to be wobbling on its last legs. The Soviet surge had penetrated eastern Germany. Allied aerial "blockbuster" bombs, making the "rubble bounce" with around-the-clock attacks, were falling like giant explosive hailstones on cities, factories, and transportation arteries. The German western front seemed about to buckle under the sledgehammer blows of the United States and its Allies.

Hitler then staked everything on one last throw of his reserves. Secretly concentrating a powerful force, he hurled it, on December 16, 1944, against the thinly held American lines in the heavily befogged and snow-shrouded Ardennes Forest. His objective was the Belgian port of Antwerp, key to the Allied supply operation. Caught off guard, the outmanned Americans were driven back, creating a deep "bulge" in the Allied line. The ten-day penetration was finally halted after the 101st Airborne Division had stood firm at the vital bastion of Bastogne. The commander, Brigadier General A. C. McAuliffe, defiantly answered the German demand for surrender with one word: "Nuts." Reinforcements were rushed up, and the last-gasp Hitlerian offensive was at length bloodily stemmed in the Battle of the Bulge.

In March 1945, forward-driving American troops reached Germany's Rhine River, where, by incredibly good luck, they found one strategic bridge undemolished. Pressing their advantage,

General Eisenhower's troops reached the Elbe River in April 1945. There, a short distance south of Berlin, American and Soviet advance guards dramatically clasped hands amid cries of *"Amerikanskie tovarishchi"* (American comrades). The conquering Americans were horrified to find blood-spattered and still-stinking concentration camps, where the German Nazis had engaged in scientific mass murder of "undesirables," including an estimated 6 million Jews. The Washington government had long been informed about Hitler's campaign of genocide against the Jews and had been reprehensibly slow to take steps against it. Roosevelt's administration had bolted the door against large numbers of Jewish refugees, and his military commanders declined even to bomb the rail lines that carried the victims to the camps. But until the war's end, the full dimensions of the "Holocaust" had not been known. When the details were revealed, the whole world was aghast.

The vengeful Soviets, clawing their way forward from the east, reached Berlin in April 1945. After desperate house-to-house fighting, followed by an

American and Soviet Soldiers Meet in Germany, 1945
Such friendly sights soon became rare as mutual suspicion deepened.

Battle of the Bulge,
December 1944–January 1945

orgy of pillage and rape, they captured the bomb-shattered city. Adolf Hitler, after a hasty marriage to his mistress, committed suicide in an underground bunker on April 30, 1945.

Tragedy had meanwhile struck the United States. President Roosevelt, while relaxing at Warm Springs, Georgia, suddenly died from a massive cerebral hemorrhage on April 12, 1945. The crushing burden of twelve depression and war years in the White House had finally taken its toll. Knots of confused, leaderless citizens gathered to discuss the future anxiously, as a bewildered, unbriefed Vice President Truman took the helm.

On May 7, 1945, what was left of the German government surrendered unconditionally. May 8 was officially proclaimed V-E (Victory in Europe) Day and was greeted with frenzied rejoicing in the Allied countries.

Japan Dies Hard

Japan's rickety bamboo empire meanwhile was tottering to its fall. American submarines—"the silent service"—were sending the Japanese merchant

A Nazi Death Camp These gaunt survivors of the Nazi concentration camp at Evensee, Austria, greeted their liberators from the U.S. 3rd Army on May 7, 1945. Scanty food and wretched sanitation claimed almost as many lives in the death camps as the horrid gas chambers. Although the world had some knowledge of these conditions before the war's end, the full revelation of Hitler's atrocities as the Allies overran Germany in the spring of 1945 stunned and sickened the invading troops.

marine to the bottom so fast they were running out of prey. All told, these undersea craft destroyed 1,042 ships, or about 50 percent of Japan's entire life-sustaining merchant fleet.

Giant bomber attacks were more spectacular. Launched from Saipan and other captured Mariana islands, they were reducing the enemy's fragile cities to cinders. The massive fire-bomb raid on Tokyo, March 9–10, 1945, was annihilating. It destroyed over 250,000 buildings, gutted a quarter of the city, and killed an estimated 83,000 people—a loss comparable to that later inflicted by atomic bombs.

General MacArthur was also on the move. Completing the conquest of jungle-draped New Guinea, he headed northwest for the Philippines, en route to Japan, with 600 ships and 250,000 men. In a scene well staged for the photographers, he splashed ashore at Leyte Island on October 20, 1944, with the summons, "People of the Philippines, I have returned. . . . Rally to me."

Japan's navy—still menacing—now made one last-chance effort to destroy MacArthur by wiping out his transports and supply ships. A gigantic clash at Leyte Gulf, fought on the sea and in the air, was actually three battles (October 23–26, 1944). The Americans won all of them, though the crucial engagement was almost lost when Admiral William F. ("Bull") Halsey was decoyed away by a feint.

Japan was through as a sea power: it had lost about sixty ships in the greatest naval battle of all time. American fleets, numbering more than four thousand vessels, now commanded the western Pacific. Several battleships, raised from the mud of Pearl Harbor, were exacting belated but sweet revenge.

Overrunning Leyte, MacArthur next landed on the main Philippine island of Luzon in January 1945. Manila was his major objective; the ravaged city fell in March, but the Philippines were not conquered until July. Victory was purchased only after bitter fighting against holed-in Japanese, who took a toll of over sixty thousand American casualties.

America's steel vise was tightening mercilessly around Japan. The tiny island of Iwo Jima, needed as a haven for damaged American bombers returning from Japan, was captured in March 1945. This desperate twenty-five-day assault cost over four thousand American dead.

Okinawa, a well-defended Japanese island, was next on the list: it was needed for closer bases from which to blast and burn enemy cities and industries. Fighting dragged on from April to June of 1945.

Japanese soldiers, fighting with incredible courage from their caves, finally sold Okinawa for fifty thousand American casualties, while suffering far heavier losses themselves.

The American navy, which covered the invasion of Okinawa, sustained severe damage. Japanese suicide pilots ("kamikazes") in an exhibition of mass hara-kiri for their god-emperor, crashed their bomb-laden planes onto the decks of the invading fleet. All told, the death squads sank over thirty ships and badly damaged scores more.

The Atomic Bombs

Strategists in Washington were meanwhile planning an all-out invasion of the main islands of Japan—an invasion that presumably would cost hundreds of thousands of American (and even more Japanese) casualties. Tokyo, recognizing imminent defeat, had secretly sent peace feelers to Moscow, which had not yet entered the Far Eastern war. The Americans, having broken the secret Japanese radio codes, knew of these feelers. But bomb-scorched Japan still showed no outward willingness to surrender *unconditionally* to the Allies.

The Potsdam conference, held near Berlin in July 1945, sounded the death knell of the Japanese. There President Truman, still new on his job, met in a seventeen-day parley with Joseph Stalin and the British leaders. The conferees issued a stern ultimatum to Japan: surrender or be destroyed. American bombers showered the dire warning on Japan in tens of thousands of leaflets, but no encouraging response was forthcoming.

America had a fantastic ace up its sleeve. Early in 1940, after Hitler's wanton assault on Poland, Roosevelt was persuaded by American and exiled scientists, notably German-born Albert Einstein, to push ahead with preparations for unlocking the secret of an atomic bomb. Congress, at Roosevelt's blank-check request, blindly made available nearly $2 billion. Many military minds were skeptical of this "damned professor's nonsense," but fears that the Germans might first acquire such an awesome weapon provided a powerful spur to action. Ironically, Germany eventually abandoned its own

The Flag Raising at Iwo Jima Atop Mount Suribachi, press photographer Joe Rosenthal snapped this dramatic picture, probably the most famous of the war.

atomic project as too costly. And as it happened, the war against Germany ended before the American weapon was ready. In a cruel twist of fate, Japan—not Germany, the original target—suffered the fate of being the first nation subjected to atomic bombardment.

The huge atomic project was pushed feverishly forward, as American know-how and industrial power were combined with the most advanced scientific knowledge. Much technical skill was provided by British and refugee scientists, who had fled to America to escape the torture chambers of the dictators. Finally, in the desert near Alamogordo, New Mexico, on July 16, 1945, the experts detonated the first awesome and devastating atomic device.

With Japan still refusing to surrender, the Potsdam threat was fulfilled. On August 6, 1945, a lone American bomber dropped one atomic bomb on the city of Hiroshima, Japan. In a blinding flash of death, followed by a funnel-shaped cloud, about 180,000 people were left killed, wounded, or missing. Some 70,000 of them died instantaneously. Sixty thousand more soon perished from burns and radiation disease.

Two days later, on August 8, Stalin entered the war against Japan, exactly on the deadline date pre-viously agreed upon with his allies. Soviet armies speedily overran the depleted Japanese defenses in Manchuria and Korea in a six-day "victory parade" that involved several thousand Russian casualties. Stalin was evidently determined to be in on the kill, lest he lose a voice in the final division of Japan's holdings.

Fanatically resisting Japanese, though facing atomization, still did not surrender. American aviators, on August 9, dropped a second atomic bomb on the city of Nagasaki. The explosion took a horrible toll of about eighty thousand people killed or missing.

The Japanese nation could endure no more. On August 10, 1945, Tokyo sued for peace on one condition: that Hirohito, the bespectacled Son of Heaven, be allowed to remain on his ancestral throne as nominal emperor. Despite their "unconditional surrender" policy, the Allies accepted this condition on August 14, 1945. The Japanese, though losing face, were able to save both their exalted ruler and what was left of their native land.

The formal end came, with dramatic force, on September 2, 1945. Official surrender ceremonies were conducted by General MacArthur on the battleship *Missouri* in Tokyo Bay. At the same time,

Hiroshima, Japan, August 1945   Two stunned survivors walk through the unbelievable destruction. The single atomic blast at Hiroshima killed an estimated 130,000 Japanese.

The Japanese Surrender Representatives of the Japanese government arrived to sign the surrender document on the deck of the battleship *Missouri* in Tokyo harbor, September 2, 1945. General Douglas MacArthur then made a conciliatory address, expressing hope "that from this solemn occasion a better world shall emerge . . . a world founded on faith and understanding." A Japanese diplomat attending wondered "whether it would have been possible for us, had we been victorious, to embrace the vanquished with a similar magnanimity." Soon thereafter, General MacArthur took up his duties as director of the U.S. occupation of Japan.

Americans at home hysterically celebrated V-J Day—Victory in Japan Day—after the most horrible war in history had ended in mushrooming atomic clouds.

The Allies Triumphant

World War II proved to be terribly costly. American forces suffered some 1 million casualties, about one-third of which were deaths. Compared with other wars, the proportion killed by wounds and disease was sharply reduced, owing in part to the use of blood plasma and "miracle" drugs, notably penicillin. Yet heavy though American losses were, the Soviet allies suffered casualties many times greater—perhaps 20 million people killed.

America was fortunate in emerging with its mainland virtually unscathed. Two Japanese submarines, using shells and bombers, had rather harmlessly attacked the California and Oregon coast, and a few balloons, incendiary and otherwise, had drifted across the Pacific. But that was about all.

Much of the rest of the world was utterly destroyed and destitute. America alone was untouched and healthy—oiled and muscled like a prize bull, standing astride the world's ruined landscape.

This complex conflict was the best-fought war in America's history. Though unprepared for it at the outset, the nation was better prepared than for the others, partly because it had begun to buckle on its armor about a year and a half before the war officially began. It was actually fighting German submarines in the Atlantic months before the explosion in the Pacific at Pearl Harbor. In the end the United States showed itself to be resourceful, tough, adaptable—able to accommodate itself to the tactics of an enemy who was relentless and ruthless.

American military leadership proved to be of the highest order. A new crop of war heroes emerged in brilliant generals like Eisenhower, MacArthur, and Marshall (chief of staff) and in imaginative admirals like Nimitz and Spruance. President Roosevelt and Prime Minister Churchill, as kindred spirits, collaborated closely in planning strategy. "It is fun to be in the same decade with you," FDR once cabled Churchill.

Industrial leaders were no less skilled, for marvels of production were performed almost daily. Assembly lines proved as important as battle lines, and victory went again to the side with the most smokestacks. The enemy was almost literally smothered by bayonets, bullets, bazookas, and bombs. Hitler and his Axis coconspirators had chosen to make war with machines, and the ingenious Yankees could ask for nothing better. They demonstrated again, as they had in World War I, that the American way of war was simply more—more men, more weapons, more machines, more technology, and more money than any enemy could hope to match. From 1940 to 1945, the output of American factories was simply phenomenal. As Winston Churchill remarked, "Nothing succeeds like excess."

Hermann Goering, a Nazi leader, had sneered, "The Americans can't build planes—only electric iceboxes and razor blades." Democracy had given its answer, as the dictators, despite long preparation, were overthrown and discredited. It is true that an unusual amount of direct control was exercised over the individual by the Washington authorities during the war emergency. But the American people preserved their precious liberties without serious impairment.

V-J Day: Crowds Cheering at Times Square, by Edward Dancig, 1947 Russian-born American artist Edward Dancig captured the feelings of triumph and relief that Americans felt at the end of World War II. His painting shows the V-J (Victory in Japan) Day celebration of August 15, 1945, in New York's Times Square.

Chronology

1941 United States declares war on Japan
Germany declares war on United States
Randolph plans black march on Washington
Fair Employment Practices Commission
  (FEPC) established

1942 Japanese-Americans sent to internment
  camps
Japan conquers the Philippines
Battle of the Coral Sea
Battle of Midway
United States invades North Africa
Congress of Racial Equality (CORE) founded

1943 Allies hold Casablanca conference
Allies invade Italy
Smith-Connally Anti-Strike Act
"Zoot-suit" riots in Los Angeles
Race riot in Detroit

1943 Japanese driven from Guadalcanal
Teheran conference

1944 *Korematsu* v. *U.S.*
D-Day invasion of France
Battle of Marianas
Roosevelt defeats Dewey for presidency

1944-
1945 Battle of the Bulge

1945 Roosevelt dies; Truman assumes presidency
Germany surrenders
Battles of Iwo Jima and Okinawa
Potsdam conference
Atomic bombs dropped on Hiroshima and
  Nagasaki
Japan surrenders

World War II: Triumph or Tragedy?

After World War II ended in 1945, many historians were convinced that the tragedy could have been averted if only the United States had awakened earlier from its isolationist illusions. These scholars condemned the policies and attitudes of the 1930s as a "retreat from responsibility." Much of the historical writing in the postwar period contained the strong flavor of medicine to ward off another infection by the isolationist virus.

This approach fell into disfavor during the Vietnam War in the 1960s, when many U.S. policymakers defended their actions in Southeast Asia by making dubious comparisons to the decade before World War II. Some scholars responded by arguing that the "lessons" of the 1930s—especially about the need to avoid "appeasement" and to take quick and decisive action against "aggressors"—could not properly be applied to any and all subsequent situations. Ho Chi Minh, they pointed out, was not Hitler, and Vietnam was not Nazi Germany. One controversial product of this line of thinking was Bruce Russett's *No Clear and Present Danger* (1972), which argued that the United States had no clearly defined national interests at stake in 1941, and that both the nation and the world might have been better off without U.S. intervention. This analysis paralleled "revisionist" commentaries written in the 1930s about U.S. participation in World World I.

Although few scholars fully accept Russett's conclusions, more recently writing on American entry into World War II has tended to avoid finding in that episode lessons for posterity. Attention has focused, rather, on the wisdom or folly of specific policies, such as Washington's hard line toward Tokyo throughout 1941, when the possibility of a negotiated settlement perhaps existed. P. W. Schroeder's *The Axis Alliance and Japanese-American Relations, 1941* (1958) makes that point with particular force. Other issues include Franklin Roosevelt's diplomatic role. Was the president a bold internationalist struggling heroically against an isolationist Congress and public opinion, or did he share much of the traditional isolationist credo? Robert Dallek's encyclopedic study of Roosevelt's foreign policy portrays Roosevelt as a shrewd and calculating internationalist, whereas Donald Cameron Watt's *How War Came* (1989) depicts him as a myopic and ill-informed leader who overestimated his own peacemaking abilities and, like most other Americans, only belatedly awakened to the menace of totalitarianism.

No decision of the war era has provoked sharper controversy than the atomic bombings of Japan in August 1945. Lingering moral questions about the nuclear incineration of Hiroshima and Nagasaki have long threatened to tarnish the crown of military victory. America is the only nation ever to have used an atomic weapon in war, and some critics have even claimed to find elements of racism in the fact that the bombs were dropped on people of a nonwhite race. The fact is, however, that Germany surrendered before the bombs were ready; had the war in Europe lasted just a few months longer, some German city would probably have suffered the fate of Hiroshima.

Some scholars, notably Gar Alperovitz, have further charged that the atomic holocausts at Hiroshima and Nagasaki were not the last shots of World War II, but the first salvos in the emerging Cold War. Alperovitz argues that the Japanese were already defeated in the summer of 1945 and were in fact attempting to arrange a *conditional* surrender. President Truman ignored those attempts and unleashed his horrible new weapons, so the argument goes, not simply to defeat Japan but to frighten the Soviets into submission to America's will, and to keep them out of the final stages of the war—and postwar reconstruction—in Asia.

Could the use of the atomic bombs have been avoided? As Martin J. Shewin's studies have shown, few policymakers at the time seriously asked that question. American leaders wanted to end the war as quickly as possible. Intimidating the Soviets might have been a "bonus" to using the bomb against Japan, but influencing Soviet behavior was never the *primary* reason for the fateful decision. American military strategists had always assumed the atomic bomb would be dropped as soon as it was available. That moment came on August 6, 1945. Yet misgivings and remorse about the atomic conclusion of World War II have plagued the American conscience ever since.

For further reading, see page A24 of the Appendix. For web resources, go to **http://college.hmco.com**.

PART SIX

MAKING MODERN AMERICA

—◆—

1945 to the Present

World War II broke the back of the Great Depression in the United States and also ended the century-and-a-half-old American tradition of isolationism in foreign affairs. Alone among the warring powers, the United States managed to emerge from the great conflict physically unscarred, economically healthy, and diplomatically strengthened. Yet if Americans faced a world full of promise at the war's end, it was also a world full of dangers, none more disconcerting than Soviet communism. These two themes of promise and menace mingled uneasily throughout the nearly five decades of the Cold War era, from the end of World War II in 1945 to the collapse of the Soviet Union in 1991.

At home unprecedented prosperity in the post-war quarter-century nourished a robust sense of national self-confidence and fed a revolution of ris-

ing expectations. Invigorated by the prospect of endlessly spreading affluence, Americans in the 1940s, 1950s, and 1960s had record numbers of babies, aspired to ever-higher standards of living, generously expanded the welfare state (especially for the elderly), widened opportunities for women, welcomed immigrants, and even found the will to grapple at long last with the nation's grossest legacy of injustice, its treatment of African-Americans. With the exception of Dwight Eisenhower's presidency in the 1950s, Americans elected liberal Democratic presidents (Harry Truman in 1948, John F. Kennedy in 1960, and Lyndon Johnson in 1964). The Democratic party, the party of the liberal New Deal at home and of an activist foreign policy abroad, comfortably remained the nation's majority party. Americans trusted their government and had faith in the American dream that their children would lead a

The Suburban Society
In the phenomenally affluent post–World War II years, newly prosperous Americans flocked to the freshly built suburbs.

richer life than their parents had done. Anything and everything seemed possible.

The rising curve of ascending expectations, propelled by exploding economic growth, bounded upward throughout the 1950s. It peaked in the 1960s, an exceptionally stormy decade during which faith in government, in the wisdom of American foreign policy, and in the American dream itself, began to sour. Lyndon Johnson's "Great Society" reforms, billed as the completion of the unfinished work of the New Deal, foundered on the rocks of fiscal limitations and stubborn racial resentments. Johnson, the most ambitious reformer in the White House since Franklin Roosevelt, eventually saw his presidency destroyed by the furies unleashed over the Vietnam War.

When economic growth flattened in the 1970s, the horizon of hopes for the future seemed to sink as well. The nation entered a frustrating period of stalled expectations, increasingly rancorous racial tensions, disillusion with government, and political stalemate, although in one important arena idealism survived. As "second-wave feminism" gathered steam, women burst through barriers that had long excluded them from male domains operating everywhere from the factory floor to the U.S. Army to the Ivy League. Not content with private victories, they also called on the government for help—to ensure women equal opportunity as workers, fair treatment as consumers, and the right to choose an abortion.

With the exceptions of Jimmy Carter in the 1970s and Bill Clinton in the 1990s, Americans after 1968 elected conservative Republicans to the White House (Richard Nixon in 1968 and 1972, Ronald Reagan in 1980 and 1984, George Bush in 1988), but continued to elect Democratic congresses. As the twenty-first century dawned, a newly invigorated conservative Republican party was bidding to achieve long-term majority status, while the Democratic party teetered on a tightrope between its liberal policies and the conservative demands of the day for tax cuts and welfare reform.

Abroad the fierce competition with the Soviet Union, and after 1949 with Communist China as well, colored most every aspect of America's foreign relations and shaped domestic life, too. Unreasoning fear of communists at home unleashed the destructive force of McCarthyism in the 1950s—a modern-day witch hunt in which careers were capsized and lives ruined by reckless accusations of communist sympathizing. The FBI encroached on sacred American liberties in its zeal to uncover communist "subversives."

The Cold War remained cold, in the sense that no shooting conflict broke out between the great power rivals. But the United States did fight two shooting wars, in Korea in the 1950s and Vietnam in the 1960s. Vietnam, the only foreign war in which the United States has ever been defeated, cruelly convulsed American society, ending not only Lyndon Johnson's presidency but the thirty-five year era of the Democratic party's political dominance as well. Vietnam also touched off the most vicious inflationary cycle in American history, and embittered and disillusioned an entire generation.

Uncle Sam in the Cold War era built a fearsome arsenal of nuclear weapons, great air and missile fleets to deliver them, a two-ocean navy, and, for a time, a large army raised by conscription. Whether the huge expenditures necessary to maintain that gigantic defense establishment stimulated or distorted the economy is a question that remains controversial. Either way, big reductions in defense spending after the end of the Cold War in 1989 helped reshape the American economy and its work force as the new century opened, as did burgeoning new information technologies like the personal computer and the Internet.

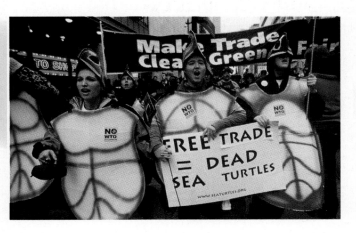

Politics in the Streets   The material prosperity that was the pride and glory of the immediate post–World War II years came in for criticism at the turn of the twenty-first century. American prominence in international trade after the end of the Cold War inspired thousands of activists—labor unionists, environmentalists, and human rights advocates—to decry the human costs of unfettered global capitalism. Demonstrators here protested at an international conference of the World Trade Organization in Seattle, November 1999.

The Cold War Begins

—⚬—

1945–1952

America stands at this moment at the summit of the world.

WINSTON CHURCHILL, 1945

The American people, 140 million strong, cheered their nation's victories in Europe and Asia at the conclusion of World War II. But when the shouting faded away, many Americans began to worry about their future. Four fiery years of global war had not entirely driven from their minds the painful memories of twelve desperate years of the Great Depression. Still more ominously, victory celebrations had barely ended before America's crumbling relations with its wartime ally, the Soviet Union, threatened a new and even more terrible international conflict.

Postwar Economic Anxieties

The decade of the 1930s had left deep scars. Joblessness and insecurity had pushed up the suicide rate and dampened the marriage rate. Babies went unborn as pinched budgets and sagging self-esteem wrought a sexual depression in American bedrooms. The war had banished the blight of depression, but would the respite last? Grim-faced observers were warning that the war had only temporarily lifted the pall of economic stagnation and that peace would bring the return of hard times. Homeward-bound GIs, so the gloomy predictions ran, would step out of the army's chow lines and back into the breadlines of the unemployed.

The faltering economy in the initial postwar years threatened to confirm the worst predictions of the doomsayers who foresaw another Great Depression. Real gross national product (GNP) slumped sickeningly in 1946 and 1947 from its wartime peak. With the removal of wartime price controls, prices giddily levitated by 33 percent in 1946–1947. An epidemic of strikes swept the country. During 1946 alone some 4.6 million laborers laid down their tools, fearful that soon they could barely afford the autos and other goods they were manufacturing.

The growing muscle of organized labor deeply annoyed many conservatives. They had their revenge against labor's New Deal gains in 1947, when a Republican-controlled Congress (the first in fourteen years) passed the Taft-Hartley Act over President Truman's vigorous veto. Labor leaders condemned the Taft-Hartley Act as a "slave-labor law." It outlawed the "closed" (all-union) shop, made unions liable for damages that resulted from jurisdictional disputes among themselves, and required union leaders to take a noncommunist oath.

Taft-Hartley was only one of several obstacles that slowed the growth of organized labor in the years after World War II. In the heady days of the New Deal, unions had spread swiftly in the industrialized Northeast, especially in huge manufacturing industries like steel and automobiles. But labor's postwar efforts to organize in the historically anti-union regions of the South and West proved frustrating. The CIO's "Operation Dixie," aimed at unionizing southern textile workers and steelworkers, failed miserably in 1948 to overcome lingering fears of racial mixing. And workers in the rapidly growing service sector of the economy—many of them middle-aged women, often working only part-time in small shops, widely separated from one another—proved much more difficult to organize than the thousands of assembly-line workers who in the 1930s had poured into the auto and steel unions.

Union membership would peak in the 1950s and then begin a long, unremitting decline.

The Democratic administration meanwhile took some steps of its own to forestall an economic downturn. It sold war factories and other government installations to private businesses at fire-sale prices. It secured passage in 1946 of the Employment Act, making it government policy "to promote maximum employment, production, and purchasing power." The act created a three-member Council of Economic Advisers to provide the president with the data and the recommendations to make that policy a reality.

Most dramatic was the passage of the Servicemen's Readjustment Act of 1944—better known as the GI Bill of Rights, or the GI Bill. Enacted partly out of fear that the employment markets would never be able to absorb 15 million returning veterans at war's end, the GI Bill made generous provisions for sending the former soldiers to school. In the postwar decade, some 8 million veterans advanced their education at Uncle Sam's expense. The majority attended technical and vocational schools, but colleges and universities were crowded to the blackboards as more than 2 million ex-GIs stormed the halls of higher learning. The total eventually spent for education was some $14.5 billion in taxpayer dollars. The act also enabled the Veterans Administration (VA) to guarantee about $16 billion in loans

The GI Bill   Financed by the federal government, thousands of World War II veterans crowded into college classrooms in the 1940s. Here a fresh crop of ex-soldier students lays in supplies for the new term.

for veterans to buy homes, farms, and small businesses. By raising educational levels and stimulating the construction industry, the GI Bill powerfully nurtured the robust and long-lived economic expansion that eventually took hold in the late 1940s and that profoundly shaped the entire history of the postwar era.

The Long Economic Boom, 1950–1970

Gross national product began to climb haltingly in 1948. Then, beginning about 1950, the American economy surged onto a dazzling plateau of sustained growth that was to last virtually uninterrupted for two decades. America's economic performance became the envy of the world. National income nearly doubled in the 1950s and almost doubled again in the 1960s, shooting

Coca-Colonizing the World American consumerism—and American products—flooded over the globe after World War II, as this 1950 cover from *Time* magazine illustrates.

through the trillion-dollar mark in 1973. Americans, some 6 percent of the world's people, were enjoying about 40 percent of the planet's wealth.

Nothing loomed larger in the history of the post–World War II era than this fantastic eruption of affluence. It did not enrich all Americans, and it did not touch all people evenly, but it transformed the lives of a majority of citizens and molded the agenda of politics and society for at least two generations. Prosperity underwrote social mobility; it paved the way for the eventual success of the civil rights movement; it funded vast new welfare programs, like Medicare; and it gave Americans the confidence to exercise unprecedented international leadership in the Cold War era.

As the gusher of postwar prosperity poured forth its riches, Americans drank deeply from the gilded goblet. Millions of depression-pinched souls sought to make up for the sufferings of the 1930s. They determined to "get theirs" while the getting was good. A people who had once considered a chicken in every pot the standard of comfort and security now hungered for two cars in every garage, swimming pools in their backyards, vacation homes, and gas-guzzling recreational vehicles. The size of the "middle class," defined as households earning between $3,000 and $10,000 a year, doubled from pre–Great Depression days and included 60 percent of the American people by the mid-1950s. By the end of that decade, the vast majority of American families owned their own car and washing machine, and nearly 90 percent owned a television set—a gadget invented in the 1920s but virtually unknown until the late 1940s. In another revolution of sweeping consequences, almost 60 percent of American families owned their own homes by 1960, compared with less than 40 percent in the 1920s.

Of all the beneficiaries of postwar prosperity, none reaped greater rewards than women. More than ever, urban offices and shops provided a bonanza of employment for female workers. The great majority of new jobs created in the postwar era went to women, as the service sector of the economy dramatically outgrew the old industrial and manufacturing sectors. Women accounted for a quarter of the American work force at the end of World War II and for nearly half the labor pool five decades later. Yet even as women continued their march into the workplace in the 1940s and 1950s, popular culture glorified the traditional feminine

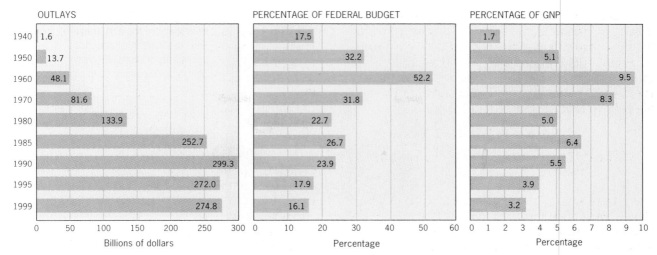

National Defense Budget, 1940–1999
(Sources: *Budget, Historical Tables,* and *Statistical Abstract of the United States,* relevant years.)

roles of homemaker and mother. The clash between the demands of suburban housewifery and the realities of employment eventually sparked a feminist revolt in the 1960s.

The Roots of Postwar Prosperity

What propelled this unprecedented economic explosion? The Second World War itself provided a powerful stimulus. While other countries had been ravaged by years of fighting, the United States had used the war crisis to fire up its smokeless factories and rebuild its depression-plagued economy. Invigorated by battle, America had almost effortlessly come to dominate the ruined global landscape of the postwar period.

Ominously, much of the glittering prosperity of the 1950s and 1960s rested on the underpinnings of colossal military budgets, leading some critics to speak of a "permanent war economy." The economic upturn of 1950 was fueled by massive appropriations for the Korean War, and defense spending accounted for some 10 percent of the GNP throughout the ensuing decade. Pentagon dollars primed the pumps of high-technology industries such as aerospace, plastics, and electronics—areas in which the United States reigned supreme over all foreign competitors. The military budget also financed much scientific research and development ("R and

D"—hence the name of one of the most famous "think tanks," the Rand Corporation). More than ever before, unlocking the secrets of nature was the key to unleashing economic growth.

Cheap energy also fed the economic boom. American and European companies controlled the flow of abundant petroleum from the sandy expanses of the Middle East, and they kept prices low. Americans doubled their consumption of inexpensive and seemingly inexhaustible oil in the quarter-century after the war. Anticipating a limitless future of low-cost fuels, they flung out endless ribbons of highways, installed air-conditioning in their homes, and engineered a sixfold increase in the country's electricity-generating capacity between 1945 and 1970. Spidery grids of electrical cables carried the pent-up power of oil, gas, coal, and falling water to activate the tools of workers on the factory floor.

With the forces of nature increasingly harnessed in their hands, workers chalked up spectacular gains in productivity—the amount of output per hour of work. In the two decades after the outbreak of the Korean War in 1950, productivity increased at an average rate of more than 3 percent per year. Gains in productivity were also enhanced by the rising educational level of the work force. By 1970 nearly 90 percent of the school-age population was enrolled in educational institutions—a dramatic contrast with the opening years of the century, when only half of this age group had attended

Agribusiness Expensive machinery of the sort shown here made most of American agriculture a capital-intensive, phenomenally productive big business by the 1990s—and sounded the death knell for many small-scale family farms.

school. Better educated and better equipped, American workers in 1970 could produce nearly twice as much in an hour's labor as they had in 1950. Productivity was the key to prosperity. Rising productivity in the 1950s and 1960s virtually doubled the average American's standard of living in the postwar quarter-century.

Also contributing to the vigor of the postwar economy were some momentous changes in the nation's basic economic structure. Conspicuous was the accelerating shift of the work force out of agriculture, which achieved productivity gains virtually unmatched by any other economic sector. The family farm nearly became an antique artifact as consolidation produced giant agribusinesses able to employ costly machinery. Thanks largely to mechanization and to rich new fertilizers—as well as to government subsidies and price supports—one farmworker by the century's end could produce food for over fifty people, compared with about fifteen people in the 1940s. Farmers whose forebears had busted sod with oxen or horses now plowed their fields in air-conditioned tractor cabs, listening on their stereophonic radios to weather forecasts or the latest Chicago commodities market quotations. Once the mighty backbone of the agricultural Republic, and still some 15 percent of the labor force at the end of World War II, farmers made up a slim 2 percent of the American population by the 1990s—yet they fed much of the world.

The Smiling Sunbelt

The convulsive economic changes of the post-1945 period shook and shifted the American people, amplifying the population redistribution set in motion by World War II. As immigrants and westward-trekking pioneers, Americans had always been a people on the move, but they were astonishingly footloose in the postwar years. For some three decades after 1945, an average of 30 million people changed residences every year. Families especially felt the strain, as distance divided parents from children, and brothers and sisters from one another. One sign of this sort of stress was the phenomenal popularity of advice books on child-rearing, especially Dr. Benjamin Spock's *The Common Sense Book of Baby and Child Care*. First published in 1945, it instructed millions of parents during the ensuing decades in the kind of homely wisdom that was once transmitted naturally from grandparent to parent, and from parent to child. In fluid postwar neighborhoods, friendships were also hard to sustain. Mobility could exact a high human cost in loneliness and isolation.

Especially striking was the growth of the "Sunbelt"—a fifteen-state area stretching in a smiling crescent from Virginia through Florida and Texas to Arizona and California. This region increased its population at a rate nearly double that of the old

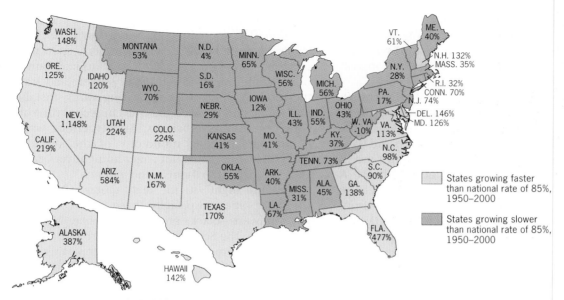

Population Increase, 1950–2000
States with figures higher than 85 percent were growing faster than the national average. Note that much of the growth was in the "Sunbelt," a loose geographical concept, as some Deep South states had very little population growth, whereas the mountain and Pacific states were booming. (Sources: *Statistical Abstract of the United States, Historical Abstract of the United States,* and *U.S. Census,* relevant years.)

industrial zones of the Northeast (the "Frostbelt"). In the 1950s California alone accounted for one-fifth of the entire nation's population growth and by 1963 had outdistanced New York as the most populous state—a position it still held at the start of the twenty-first century, with more than 30 million people, or one out of every eight Americans.

The South and Southwest were a new frontier for Americans after World War II. These modern pioneers came in search of jobs, a better climate, and lower

Sunbelt Prosperity
The old and new West are evident in this view of booming Dallas.

taxes. Jobs they found in abundance, especially in the California electronics industry, in the aerospace complexes in Florida and Texas, and in the huge military installations that powerful southern congressional representatives secured for their districts.

A Niagara of federal dollars accounted for much of the Sunbelt's prosperity, though, ironically, southern and western politicians led the cry against government spending. By the 1990s the South and West were annually receiving some $125 billion more in federal funds than the Northeast and Midwest. A new economic war between the states seemed to be shaping up. Northeasterners and their allies from the hard-hit heavy-industry region of the Ohio Valley (the "Rustbelt") tried to rally political support with the sarcastic slogan "The North shall rise again."

These dramatic shifts of population and wealth further broke the historic grip of the North on the nation's political life. Every elected occupant of the White House since 1964 has hailed from the Sunbelt, and the region's congressional representation rose as its population grew. With their frontier ethic of unbridled individualism and their devotion to unregulated economic growth, the Sunbelters were redrawing the Republic's political map.

The Rush to the Suburbs

In all regions America's modern migrants—if they were white—fled from the cities to the burgeoning new suburbs (see "Makers of America: The Suburbanites," pp. 868–869). Government policies encouraged this momentous movement. Federal Housing Administration (FHA) and Veterans Administration (VA) home-loan guarantees made it more economically attractive to own a home in the suburbs than to rent an apartment in the city. Tax deductions for interest payments on home mortgages provided additional financial incentive. And government-built highways that sped commuters from suburban homes to city jobs further facilitated this mass migration. By 1960 one of every four Americans dwelt in suburbia, and the same leafy neighborhoods held more than half the nation's population as the century neared its end.

The construction industry boomed in the 1950s and 1960s to satisfy this demand. Pioneered by innovators like the Levitt brothers, whose first "Levittown" sprouted on New York's Long Island in the 1940s, builders revolutionized the techniques of home construction. Erecting hundreds or even thousands of dwellings in a single project, specialized crews working from standardized plans laid foundations, while others raised factory-assembled framing modules, put on roofs, strung wires, installed plumbing, and finished the walls in record time and with cost-cutting efficiency. Snooty critics wailed about the aesthetic monotony of the suburban "tract" developments, but eager homebuyers nevertheless moved into them by the millions.

"White flight" to the leafy green suburbs left the inner cities—especially those in the Northeast and Midwest—black, brown, and broke. Migrating blacks from the South filled up the urban neighborhoods that were abandoned by the departing white middle class (see "Makers of America: The Great African-American Migration," pp. 892–893). In effect, the incoming blacks imported the grinding poverty of the rural South into the inner cores of northern cities. Taxpaying businesses fled with their affluent customers from downtown shops to suburban shopping malls (another post–World War II invention).

Government policies sometimes aggravated this spreading pattern of residential segregation. FHA administrators, citing the "risk" of making loans to blacks and other "unharmonious racial or nationality groups," often refused them mortgages for private home purchases, thus limiting black mobility out of the inner cities and driving many minorities into public housing projects. Even public housing programs frequently followed a so-called neighborhood composition rule, which effectively built housing for blacks in neighborhoods that were already identified as predominantly black—thus solidifying racial separation.

The Postwar Baby Boom

Of all the upheavals in postwar America, none was more dramatic than the "baby boom"—the huge leap in the birthrate in the decade and a half after 1945. Confident young men and women tied the nuptial knot in record numbers at war's end, and they began immediately to fill the nation's empty cradles. They thus touched off a demographic explosion that added more than 50 million bawling babies to the nation's population by the end of the 1950s. The soaring birthrate finally crested in 1957

EXAMINING THE EVIDENCE

Advertising Prosperity, 1956 This Ford advertisement in a popular magazine encouraged readers to buy a second car. By the mid-1950s, once manufacturers had met the demand for cars, homes, appliances, and other consumer goods that a decade and a half of depression and world war had pent up, they worried about how to keep expanding their markets. "Planned obsolescence"—changing design frequently enough to necessitate replacement purchasing—was one strategy. Altering expectations about what consumers needed was another. This advertisement suggests that the up-to-date family, living in its modern-style suburban home, had no choice but to own two cars, one for the male breadwinner's business, the other for the wife's "ferrying the family." What kinds of gender role prescriptions are reinforced in this advertisement? What assumptions has Ford made about prospective buyers of its cars? How much can mass advertising tell us about the actual values of Americans living at a particular time?

The only problem in posing this picture was getting the two Fords to stand still.

Seven good reasons for two FORDS

To free their family from one-car captivity the Bremers got two Fords: a Country Sedan and a Thunderbird—the car that inspired the styling and performance of all '56 Fords.

"We saw the need for a second car even before our first youngster arrived. If you're married you know why. The five children just made two Fords *more* necessary. I need a car for business. My wife needs one for ferrying the family.

"*Why are they Fords?* In the first place, you can't beat Ford's looks at *twice* the price. You get extra zip in a Ford V-8, too. That's why it's the world's best seller! It's a good investment, too. Nothing at the price keeps its value like a Ford. And, of course, you don't need children to appreciate the extra safety of Ford Lifeguard Design," says Mr. Bremer.

SEE YOUR LOCAL FORD DEALER

The Country Sedan, one of six Ford do-it-alls, has 4-doors, lots of room. And its 202-h.p. V-8 is the most powerful standard "8" in its field.

The Ford Thunderbird inspired the styling for *all* Fords. And you can have its own 225-h.p. Special V-8 in most of them.

Join the 300,000 TWO FORD families!

and was followed by a deepening birth dearth. By 1973 fertility rates had dropped below the point necessary to maintain existing population figures. If the downward trend persisted, only further immigration would lift the U.S. population above its 1996 level of some 264 million.

This boom-or-bust cycle of births begot a bulging wave along the American population curve. As the oversize postwar generation grew to maturity, it was destined—like the fabled pig passing through the python—to strain and distort many aspects of American life. Elementary-school enrollments, for example, swelled to nearly 34 million pupils in 1970. Then began a steady decline, as the onward-marching age group left in its wake closed schools and unemployed teachers.

The maturing babies of the postwar boom sent economic shock waves undulating through the decades. As tykes and toddlers in the 1940s and 1950s, they made up a lucrative market for manufacturers of canned food and other baby products. As teenagers in the 1960s, the same youngsters spent an estimated $20 billion a year for clothes and recorded rock music—and their sheer numbers laid the basis of the much-ballyhooed "youth culture" of that tumultuous decade. In the 1970s the consumer tastes of the aging baby boomers changed again, and the most popular jeans maker began marketing pants with a fuller cut for those former "kids" who could no longer squeeze into their size-thirty Levi's. In the 1980s the horde of baby boomers bumped and jostled one another in the job market, struggling to get a foothold on the crowded ladder of social mobility. In the 1990s the boom generation began to enter middle age, raising its own "secondary boom" of children—a faint demographic echo of the postwar population explosion. The impact of the huge postwar generation will continue to ripple through American society well into the twenty-first century, when its members pass eventually into retirement, placing enormous strains on the Social Security system.

Truman: The "Gutty" Man from Missouri

Presiding over the opening of the postwar period was an "accidental president"—Harry S Truman. "The moon, the stars, and all the planets" had fallen

What Next? 1946 This cartoon expresses the feeling of many Americans that their new president was overwhelmed, even bamboozled, by his job.

on him, he remarked when he was called upon to shoulder the dead Roosevelt's awesome burdens of leadership. Trim and owlishly bespectacled, with his graying hair and friendly, toothy grin, Truman was called "the average man's average man." Even his height—five feet eight inches—was average. The first president in many years without a college education, he had farmed, served as an artillery officer in France during World War I, and failed as a haberdasher. He then tried his hand at precinct-level Missouri politics, through which he rose from a judgeship to the U.S. Senate. Though a protégé of a notorious political machine in Kansas City, he had managed to keep his own hands clean.

The problems of the postwar period were staggering, and the suddenly burdened new president at first approached his tasks with humility. But gradually he evolved from a shrinking pipsqueak into a scrappy little cuss, gaining confidence to the point of cockiness. When the Soviet foreign minister complained, "I have never been talked to like that in my life," Truman shot back, "Carry out your agreements and you won't get talked to like that." Truman later boasted, "I gave him the one-two, right to the jaw."

A smallish man thrust suddenly into a giant job, Truman permitted designing old associates of the "Missouri gang" to gather around him and, like Grant, was stubbornly loyal to them when they were caught with cream on their whiskers. On occasion he would send critics hot-tempered and profane "s.o.b." letters. Most troubling, in trying to demonstrate to a skeptical public his decisiveness and power of command, he was inclined to go off half-cocked or stick mulishly to a wrongheaded notion. "To err is Truman," cynics gibed.

But if he was sometimes small in the small things, he was often big in the big things. He had down-home authenticity, few pretensions, rock-solid probity, and a lot of that old-fashioned character trait called moxie. Not one to dodge responsibility, he placed a sign on his White House desk that read, "The buck stops here." Among his favorite sayings was, "If you can't stand the heat, get out of the kitchen."

Yalta: Bargain or Betrayal?

Vast and silent, the Soviet Union continued to be the great enigma. The conference at Teheran in 1943, where Roosevelt had first met Stalin man to man, had done something to clear the air, but much had remained unresolved—especially questions about the postwar fates of Germany, Eastern Europe, and Asia.

A final fateful conference of the Big Three had taken place in February 1945 at Yalta. At this former tsarist resort on the relatively warm shores of the Black Sea, Stalin, Churchill, and the fast-failing Roosevelt reached momentous agreements, after pledging their faith with vodka. Final plans were laid for smashing the buckling German lines and shackling the beaten Axis foe. Stalin agreed that Poland, with revised boundaries, should have a representative government based on free elections—a pledge he soon broke. Bulgaria and Romania were likewise to have free elections—a promise also flouted. The Big Three further announced plans for fashioning a new international peacekeeping organization—the United Nations.

The Big Three From left to right, Churchill, Roosevelt, and Stalin take time out from their fateful meeting at Yalta in February 1945. Roosevelt was only weeks away from death.

The Suburbanites

Few images evoke more vividly the prosperity of the postwar era than aerial photographs of sprawling suburbs. Neat rows of look-alike tract houses, each with driveway and lawn and here and there a backyard swimming pool, came to symbolize the capacity of the economy to deliver the "American dream" to millions of families.

Suburbanization was hardly new. Well-off city dwellers had beaten paths to leafy outlying neighborhoods since the nineteenth century. But after 1945 the steady flow became a stampede. The baby boom, new highways, government guarantees for mortgage lending, and favorable tax policies all made suburbia blossom.

Who were the Americans racing to the new postwar suburbs? War veterans led the way in the late 1940s, aided by Veterans Administration mortgages that featured tiny down payments and low interest rates. The general public soon followed. The Federal Housing Administration (FHA) offered insured mortgages with low down payments and 2 to 3 percent interest rates on thirty-year loans. With deals like this, it was hardly surprising that American families flocked into "Levittowns," built by William and Alfred Levitt, and other similar suburban developments.

People of all kinds found their way to suburbia, heading for neighborhoods that varied from the posh to the plain. Yet for all this diversity, the overwhelming majority of suburbanites were white and middle-class. In 1967 sociologist Herbert Gans published *The Levittowners*, based on his own move to a Levitt-built community outside Philadelphia. He described suburban families in tract developments as predominantly third- or fourth-generation Americans with some college education and at least two children.

Men tended to work in either white-collar jobs or upper-level blue-collar positions such as foremen. Women usually worked in the home, so much so that suburbia came to symbolize the domestic confinement that feminists in the 1960s and 1970s decried in their campaign for women's rights.

The house itself became more important than ever as postwar suburbanites built their leisure lives around television, home improvement projects, and barbecues on the patio. The center of family life shifted to the fenced-in backyard, as neighborly city habits of visiting on the front stoop, gabbing on the sidewalk, and strolling to local stores disappeared.

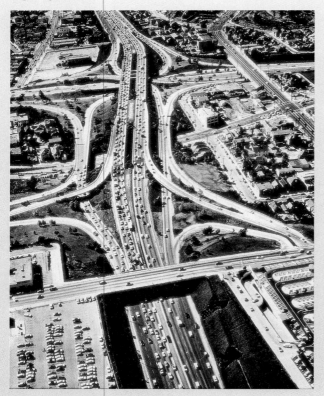

Aerial View of the On-Ramps to a Typical New Interstate Highway, 1950s

Institutions that had thrived as social centers in the city—churches, women's clubs, fraternal organizations, taverns—had a tougher time attracting patrons in the privatized world of postwar suburbia.

Life in the suburbs was a boon to the automobile, as parents jumped behind the wheel to shuttle children, groceries, and golf clubs to and fro. The second car, once an unheard-of luxury, became a practical "necessity" for suburban families constantly "on the go." A car culture sprang up with new destinations, like drive-thru restaurants and drive-in movies. Roadside shopping centers edged out downtowns as places to shop. Meanwhile, the new interstate highway system enabled breadwinners to live farther and farther from their jobs and still commute to work daily.

Many suburbanites continued to depend on cities for jobs, though by the 1980s the suburbs themselves became important sites of employment.

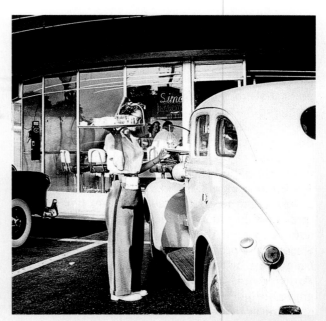

Drive-in Café in Los Angeles, the Mother and Model of all Suburbias

Moving to the Suburbs After World War II, Americans by the millions moved to suburban housing developments like this one. Although criticized for their architectural monotony and cultural barrenness, the suburbs provided inexpensive and spacious housing for growing families seeking to escape the crowded confines of the cities.

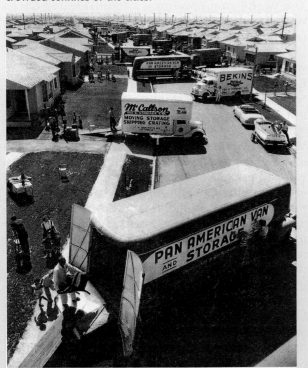

Wherever they worked, suburbanites turned their backs on the city and its problems. They fought to maintain their communities as secluded retreats, independent municipalities with their own taxes, schools, and zoning restrictions designed to keep out public housing and the poor. Even the naming of towns and streets reflected a pastoral ideal. Poplar Terrace and Mountainview Drive were popular street names; East Paterson, New Jersey, was renamed Elmwood Park in 1973. With a majority of Americans living in suburbs by the 1980s, cities lost their political clout. Bereft of state and federal aid, cities festered with worsening social problems: poverty, drug addiction, and crime.

Middle-class African-Americans began to move to the suburbs in substantial numbers by the 1980s, but even that migration failed to alter dramatically the racial divide of metropolitan America. Black suburbanites settled in towns like Rolling Oaks outside Miami or Brook Glen near Atlanta—black middle-class towns in white-majority counties. By the end of the twentieth century, suburbia as a whole was more racially diverse than at midcentury. But old patterns of urban "white flight" and residential segregation endured.

Of all the grave decisions at Yalta, the most controversial concerned the Far East. The atomic bomb had not yet been tested, and Washington strategists expected frightful American casualties in the projected assault on Japan. From Roosevelt's standpoint it seemed highly desirable that Stalin should enter the Asian war, pin down Japanese troops in Manchuria and Korea, and lighten American losses. But Soviet casualties had already been enormous, and Moscow presumably needed inducements to bring it into the Far Eastern conflagration.

Horse trader Stalin was in a position at Yalta to exact a high price. He agreed to attack Japan within three months after the collapse of Germany, and he later redeemed this pledge in full. In return, the Soviets were promised the southern half of Sakhalin Island, lost by Russia to Japan in 1905, and Japan's Kurile Islands as well. The Soviet Union was also granted joint control over the railroads of China's Manchuria and special privileges in the two key seaports of that area, Dairen and Port Arthur. These concessions evidently would give Stalin control over vital industrial centers of America's weakening Chinese ally.

As it turned out, Moscow's muscle was not necessary to knock out Japan. Critics charged that Roosevelt had sold Jiang Jieshi (Chiang Kai-shek) down the river when he conceded control of China's Manchuria to Stalin. The consequent undermining of Chinese morale, so the accusation ran, contributed powerfully to Jiang's overthrow by the communists four years later. The critics also assailed the "sellout" of Poland and other Eastern European countries.

Roosevelt's defenders countered that Stalin, with his mighty red army, could have secured much more of China if he wished and that the Yalta conference really set limits to his ambitions. Apologists for Roosevelt also contended that if Stalin had kept his promise to support free elections in Poland and the liberated Balkans, the sorry sequel would have been different. Actually, Soviet troops had then occupied much of Eastern Europe, and a war to throw them out was unthinkable.

The fact is that the Big Three at Yalta were not drafting a comprehensive peace settlement; at most they were sketching general intentions and testing one another's reactions. Later critics who howled about broken promises overlooked that fundamental point. In the case of Poland, Roosevelt admitted that the Yalta agreement was "so elastic that the Russians can stretch it all the way from Yalta to

Washington without ever technically breaking it." More specific understandings among the wartime allies—especially the two emerging superpowers, the United States and the Soviet Union—awaited the arrival of peace.

The United States and the Soviet Union

History provided little hope that the United States and the Soviet Union would reach cordial understandings about the shape of the postwar world. Mutual suspicions were ancient, abundant, and abiding. Communism and capitalism were historically hostile social philosophies. The United States had refused officially to recognize the Bolshevik revolutionary government in Moscow until it was sixteen years old, in 1933. Soviet skepticism toward the West was nourished by the British and American delays in opening up a second front against Germany, while the Soviet army paid a grisly price to roll the Nazi invaders back across Russia and Eastern Europe. Britain and America had also frozen their Soviet "ally" out of the project to develop atomic weapons, further feeding Stalin's mistrust. The Washington government rubbed salt in Soviet wounds when it abruptly terminated vital lend-lease aid to a battered USSR in 1945 and spurned Moscow's plea for a $6 billion reconstruction loan—while approving a similar loan of $3.75 billion to Britain in 1946.

Different visions of the postwar world also separated the two superpowers. Stalin aimed above all to guarantee the security of the Soviet Union. The USSR had twice in the twentieth century been stabbed in its heartland by attacks across the windswept plains of Eastern Europe. Stalin made it clear from the outset of the war that he was determined to have friendly governments along the Soviet western border, especially in Poland. By maintaining an extensive Soviet sphere of influence in Eastern and Central Europe, the USSR could protect itself and consolidate its revolutionary base as the world's leading communist country.

To many Americans, that "sphere of influence" looked like an ill-gained "empire." Doubting that Soviet goals were purely defensive, they remembered the earlier Bolshevik call for world revolution. Stalin's emphasis on "spheres" also clashed with

Franklin Roosevelt's Wilsonian dream of an "open world," decolonized, demilitarized, and democratized, with a strong international organization to oversee global peace.

Even the ways in which the United States and the Soviet Union resembled each other were troublesome. Both countries had been largely isolated from world affairs before World War II—the United States through choice, the Soviet Union through rejection by the other powers. Both nations also had a history of conducting a kind of "missionary" diplomacy—of trying to export to all the world the political doctrines precipitated out of their respective revolutionary origins.

Unaccustomed to their great-power roles, unfamiliar with or even antagonistic to each other, and each believing in the universal applicability of its own particular ideology, America and the USSR suddenly found themselves staring eyeball-to-eyeball over the prostrate body of battered Europe—a Europe that had been the traditional center of international affairs. In these circumstances some sort of confrontation was virtually unavoidable. The wartime "Grand Alliance" of the United States, the Soviet Union, and Britain had been a misbegotten child of necessity, kept alive only until the mutual enemy was crushed. When the hated Hitler fell, suspicion and rivalry between communistic, despotic Russia and capitalistic, democratic America were all but inevitable. In a fateful progression of events, marked often by misperceptions as well as by genuine conflicts of interest, the two powers provoked each other into a tense standoff known as the Cold War. Enduring four and a half decades, the Cold War not only shaped Soviet-American relations; it overshadowed the entire postwar international order in every corner of the globe. The Cold War also molded societies and economies and the lives of individual people all over the planet.

Shaping the Postwar World

Despite these obstacles, the United States did manage at war's end to erect some of the structures that would support Roosevelt's vision of an open world. Meeting at Bretton Woods, New Hampshire, in 1944, the Western Allies established the International Monetary Fund (IMF) to encourage world trade by regulating currency exchange rates. They also

In June 1946 Bernard Baruch (1870–1965), in presenting his plan for the control of atomic energy to the United Nations, said,

"We are here to make a choice between the quick and the dead. That is our business. Behind the black portent of the new atomic age lies a hope which, seized upon with faith, can work our salvation. If we fail, then we have damned every man to be the slave of fear. Let us not deceive ourselves; we must elect world peace or world destruction."

founded the International Bank for Reconstruction and Development (World Bank) to promote economic growth in war-ravaged and underdeveloped areas. In contrast to its behavior after World War I, the United States took the lead in creating these important international bodies and supplied most of their funding. The stubborn Soviets declined to participate.

As flags wept at half-mast, the United Nations Conference opened on schedule, April 25, 1945, despite Roosevelt's dismaying death thirteen days earlier. Unlike Woodrow Wilson, Roosevelt had displayed political tact by choosing both Republican and Democratic senators for the American delegation. Meeting at the San Francisco War Memorial Opera House, representatives from fifty nations fashioned the United Nations charter, which strongly resembled the old League of Nations Covenant. It featured the Security Council, dominated by the Big Five powers (the United States, Britain, the USSR, France, and China), each of whom had the right of veto, and the Assembly, which could be controlled by smaller countries. In contrast with the chilly American reception of the League in 1919, the Senate overwhelmingly approved the document on July 28, 1945, by a vote of 89 to 2.

The United Nations, setting up its permanent glass home in New York City, had some gratifying initial successes. It helped preserve peace in Iran, Kashmir, and other trouble spots. It played a large role in creating the new Jewish state of Israel. The U.N. Trusteeship Council guided former colonies to independence. Through such arms as UNESCO

(United Nations Educational, Scientific, and Cultural Organization), FAO (Food and Agricultural Organization), and WHO (World Health Organization), the U.N. brought benefits to peoples the world over.

Far less heartening was the failure of the United States to control the fearsome new technology of the atom. U.S. delegate Bernard Baruch called in 1946 for a U.N. agency, free from the great-power veto, with worldwide authority over atomic energy, weapons, and research. The Soviet delegate countered that the possession of nuclear weapons simply be outlawed by every nation. Both plans quickly collapsed. The Truman administration had no intention of giving up its bombs, and the Soviets flatly refused to give up their veto or to invite "capitalist spies" to inspect atomic facilities in the USSR. A priceless opportunity to tame the nuclear monster in its infancy was lost. The atomic clock ticked ominously on for the next forty-five years, shadowing all relations between the Soviet Union and the United States, and casting a pall over the future of the human race.

The Problem of Germany

Hitler's ruined Reich posed especially thorny problems for all the wartime Allies. They agreed only that the cancer of Nazism had to be cut out of the German body politic, which involved punishing Nazi leaders for war crimes. The Allies joined in trying twenty-two top culprits at Nuremberg, Germany, during 1945–1946. Accusations included committing crimes against the laws of war and humanity and plotting aggressions contrary to solemn treaty pledges.

Justice, Nuremberg-style, was harsh. Twelve of the accused Nazis swung from the gallows, and seven were sentenced to long jail terms. "Foxy Hermann" Goering, whose blubbery chest had once blazed with ribbons, cheated the hangman a few hours before his scheduled execution by swallowing a hidden cyanide capsule. The trials of several small-fry Nazis continued for years. Legal critics in America condemned these proceedings as judicial lynchings, because the victims were tried for offenses that had not been clear-cut crimes when the war began.

Beyond punishing the top Nazis, the Allies could agree on little about postwar Germany. Some

Opening Day at the Nuremberg War Crimes Trial, 1945 Twenty-two Nazi leaders faced charges of crimes against humanity in this German courtroom. On the second day of the trial, Reichsmarshal Hermann Goering, seated at the end of the first row of the prisoners' dock and leaning on the partition, would plead not guilty to the International Military Tribunal's indictment. The eleven-month trial brought the full scale of Nazi brutality to light.

American Hitler-haters, noting that an industrialized Germany had been a brutal aggressor, at first wanted to dismantle German factories and reduce the country to a potato patch. The Soviets, denied American economic assistance, were determined to rebuild their shattered land by extracting enormous reparations from the Germans. Both these desires clashed headlong with the reality that an industrial, healthy German economy was indispensable to the recovery of Europe. The Americans soon came to appreciate that fact. But the Soviets, deeply fearful of another blitzkrieg, resisted all efforts to revitalize Germany.

Former prime minister Winston Churchill (1874–1965), in a highly controversial speech at Fulton, Missouri (March 1946), warned of Soviet expansionism:

"From Stettin in the Baltic to Trieste in the Adriatic an iron curtain has descended across the Continent."

Along with Austria, Germany had been divided at war's end into four military occupation zones, each assigned to one of the Big Four powers (France, Britain, America, and the USSR). The Western Allies refused to allow Moscow to bleed their zones of the reparations that Stalin insisted he had been promised at Yalta. They also began to promote the idea of a reunited Germany. The communists responded by tightening their grip on their Eastern zone. Before long, it was apparent that Germany would remain indefinitely divided. West Germany eventually became an independent country, wedded to the West. East Germany, along with other Soviet-dominated Eastern European countries, such as Poland and Hungary, became nominally independent "satellite" states, bound to the Soviet Union. Eastern Europe virtually disappeared from Western sight behind the "iron curtain" of secrecy and isolation that Stalin clanged down across Europe from the Baltic to the Adriatic. The division of Europe would endure for more than four decades.

With Germany now split in two, there remained the problem of the rubble heap known as Berlin. Lying deep within the Soviet zone (see the map below), this beleaguered isle in a red sea had been broken, like Germany as a whole, into sectors occupied by troops of each of the four victorious powers. In 1948, following controversies over German currency reform and four-power control, the Soviets abruptly choked off all rail and highway access to Berlin. They evidently reasoned that the Allies would be starved out.

Berlin became a hugely symbolic issue for both sides. At stake was not only the fate of the city but a test of wills between Moscow and Washington. The Americans organized a gigantic airlift in the midst of hair-trigger tension. For nearly a year, flying some of the very aircraft that had recently dropped bombs on Berlin, American pilots ferried thousands of tons of supplies a day to the grateful Berliners, their former enemies. Western Europeans took heart from

Postwar Partition of Germany
Germany lost much of its territory in the east to Poland and the Soviet Union. The military occupation zones were the bases for the formation of two separate countries in 1949, when the British, French, and American zones became West Germany, and the Soviet zone became East Germany. (The two Germanies were reunited in 1990.) Berlin remained under joint four-power occupation from 1945 to 1990 and became a focus and symbol of Cold War tensions.

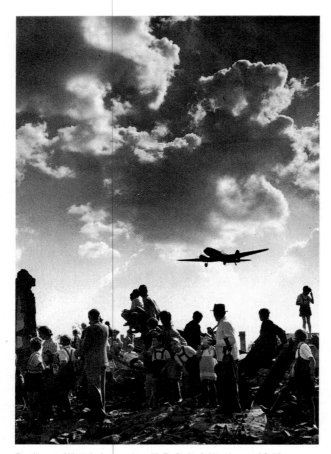

Berliners Watch Incoming U.S. Relief Airplane, 1948

this vivid demonstration of America's determination to honor its commitments in Europe. The Soviets, their bluff dramatically called, finally lifted their blockade in May 1949. In the same year, the governments of the two Germanies, East and West, were formally established. The Cold War had icily congealed.

Crystallizing the Cold War

A crafty Stalin also probed the West's resolve at other sensitive points, including oil-rich Iran. Seeking to secure oil concessions similar to those held by the British and Americans, Stalin in 1946 broke an agreement to remove his troops from Iran's northernmost province, which the USSR had occupied, with British and American approval, during World War II. Instead, he used the troops to aid a rebel movement. Truman sent off a stinging protest, and the Soviet dictator backed down.

Moscow's hard-line policies in Germany, Eastern Europe, and the Middle East wrought a psychological Pearl Harbor. The eyes of Americans were jarred wide open by the Kremlin's apparent unwillingness to continue the wartime partnership. Any remaining goodwill from the period of comradeship-in-arms evaporated in a cloud of dark distrust. "I'm tired of babying the Soviets," Truman remarked privately in 1946, as attitudes on both sides began to harden frostily.

Truman's piecemeal responses to various Soviet challenges took on intellectual coherence in 1947, with the formulation of the "containment doctrine." Crafted by a brilliant young diplomat and Soviet specialist, George F. Kennan, this concept held that Russia, whether tsarist or communist, was relentlessly expansionary. But the Kremlin was also cautious, Kennan argued, and the flow of Soviet power into "every nook and cranny available to it" could be stemmed by "firm and vigilant containment."

Truman embraced Kennan's advice when he formally and publicly adopted a "get-tough-with-Russia" policy in 1947. His first dramatic move was triggered by word that heavily burdened Britain could no longer bear the financial and military load of defending Greece against communist pressures. If Greece fell, Turkey would presumably collapse and the strategic eastern Mediterranean would pass into the Soviet orbit.

In a surprise appearance, the president went before Congress on March 12, 1947, and requested support for what came to be known as the Truman Doctrine. Specifically, he asked for $400 million to bolster Greece and Turkey, which Congress quickly granted. More generally, he declared that "it must be the policy of the United States to support free peoples who are resisting attempted subjugation by armed minorities or by outside pressures"—a sweeping and open-ended commitment of vast and worrisome proportions. Critics then and later charged that Truman had overreacted by promising unlimited support to any tinhorn despot who claimed to be resisting "Communist aggression." Critics also complained that the Truman Doctrine needlessly polarized the world into pro-Soviet and pro-American camps and unwisely construed the Soviet threat as primarily military in nature. Apologists for Truman have explained that it was Truman's fear of a revived isolationism that led him to exaggerate the Soviet threat and to cast his message in the charged language of a holy global war against godless communism—a description of the Cold War that straightjacketed future policymakers who would seek to tone down Soviet-American competition and animosity.

A threat of a different sort loomed in Western Europe—especially France, Italy, and Germany. These key nations were still suffering from the hunger and economic chaos spawned by war. They were in grave danger of being taken over from the inside by Communist parties that could exploit these hardships.

President Truman responded with a bold policy. In a commencement address at Harvard University on June 5, 1947, Secretary of State George C. Marshall invited the Europeans to get together and work out a *joint* plan for their economic recovery. If they did so, then the United States would provide substantial financial assistance. This forced cooperation constituted a powerful nudge on the road to the eventual creation of the European Community (EC).

The democratic nations of Europe rose enthusiastically to the life-giving bait of the so-called Marshall Plan. They met in Paris in July 1947 to thrash out the details. There Marshall offered the same aid to the Soviet Union and its allies, if they would make political reforms and accept certain outside controls. But nobody was surprised when the Soviets walked out, denouncing the "Martial Plan" as one more capitalist trick.

The Marshall Plan called for spending $12.5 billion over four years in sixteen cooperating countries. Congress at first balked at this mammoth sum. It looked even more huge when added to the nearly $2 billion the United States had already contributed to European relief through the United Nations Relief and Rehabilitation Administration (UNRRA) and the hefty American contributions to the United Nations, IMF, and World Bank. But a Soviet-sponsored communist coup in Czechoslovakia finally

Where To? 1947
A satirical view of the Truman Doctrine.

awakened the legislators to reality, and they voted the initial appropriations in April 1948. Congress evidently concluded that if Uncle Sam did not get the Europeans back on their feet, they would never get off his back.

Truman's Marshall Plan was a spectacular success. American dollars pumped reviving blood into the economic veins of the anemic Western European nations. Within a few years, most of them were exceeding their prewar outputs, as an "economic miracle" drenched Europe in prosperity. The Communist parties in Italy and France lost ground, and these two keystone countries were saved from the westward thrust of communism.

A resolute Truman made another fateful decision in 1948. Access to Middle Eastern oil was crucial to the European recovery program and, increasingly, to the health of the U.S. economy, as domestic American oil reserves dwindled. Yet the Arab oil countries adamantly opposed the creation

The Marshall Plan Turns Enemies into Friends The poster in this 1950 photograph in Berlin reads, "Berlin Rebuilt with Help from the Marshall Plan."

of the Jewish state of Israel in the British mandate territory of Palestine. Should Israel be born, a Saudi Arabian leader warned Truman, the Arabs "will lay siege to it until it dies of famine." Defying Arab wrath as well as the objections of his own State and Defense Departments and the European Allies, all of them afraid to antagonize the oil-endowed Arabs, Truman officially recognized the state of Israel on the day of its birth, May 14, 1948. Humanitarian sympathy for the Jewish survivors of the Holocaust ranked high among his reasons, as did his wishes to preempt Soviet influence in the Jewish state and to retain the support of American Jewish voters. Truman's policy of strong support for Israel would vastly complicate U.S. relations with the Arab world in the decades ahead.

United States Foreign Aid, Military and Economic, 1945–1954 Marshall Plan aid swelled the outlay for Europe. Note the emphasis on the "developed" world, with relatively little aid going to what are now called "Third World" countries.

American Motor of the Latest Type In this Russian view, the conquering Truman uses U.S. moneybags to induce dollar-hungry European nations to draw the U.S. capitalistic chariot.

America Begins to Rearm

The Cold War, the struggle to contain Soviet communism, was not war, yet it was not peace. The standoff with the Kremlin banished the dreams of tax-fatigued Americans that tanks could be beaten into automobiles.

The Soviet menace spurred the unification of the armed services as well as the creation of a huge new national security apparatus. Congress in 1947 passed the National Security Act, creating the Department of Defense. The department was to be housed in the sprawling Pentagon building on the banks of the Potomac and to be headed by a new cabinet officer, the secretary of defense. Under the secretary, but now without cabinet status, were the civilian secretaries of the navy, the army (replacing the old secretary of war), and the air force (a recognition of the rising importance of air power). The uniformed heads of each service were brought together as the Joint Chiefs of Staff.

The National Security Act also established the National Security Council (NSC) to advise the president on security matters and the Central Intelligence Agency (CIA) to coordinate the government's foreign fact-gathering. The "Voice of America," authorized by Congress in 1948, began beaming American radio broadcasts behind the iron curtain. In the same year, Congress resurrected the military draft, providing for the conscription of selected young men from nineteen to twenty-five years of age. The forbidding presence of the Selective Service System shaped millions of young people's educational, marital, and career plans in the following quarter-century. One shoe at a time, a war-weary America was reluctantly returning to a war footing.

The Soviet threat was also forcing the democracies of Western Europe into an unforeseen degree of unity. In 1948 Britain, France, Belgium, the Netherlands, and Luxembourg signed a path-breaking treaty of defensive alliance at Brussels. They then invited the United States to join them.

The proposal confronted the United States with a historic decision. America had traditionally avoided entangling alliances, especially in peacetime (if the Cold War could be considered peacetime). Yet American participation in the emerging coalition could serve many purposes: it would strengthen the policy of containing the Soviet Union; it would provide a framework for the reintegration of Germany into the European family; and it would reassure jittery Europeans that a traditionally isolationist Uncle Sam was not about to abandon them to the marauding Russian bear—or to a resurgent and domineering Germany.

The Truman administration decided to join the European pact, called the North Atlantic Treaty Organization in recognition of its transatlantic character. With white-tie pageantry, the NATO treaty was signed in Washington on April 4, 1949. The twelve original signatories pledged to regard an attack on one as an attack on all and promised to respond with "armed force" if necessary. Despite last-ditch howls from immovable isolationists, the Senate approved the treaty on July 21, 1949, by a vote of 82 to 13. Membership was boosted to fourteen in 1952 by the inclusion of Greece and Turkey, to fifteen in 1955 by the addition of West Germany.

The NATO pact was epochal. It marked a dramatic departure from American diplomatic convention, a gigantic boost for European unification, and a significant step in the militarization of the Cold War. NATO became the cornerstone of all Cold War

Reaching Across the Atlantic in Peacetime, 1948   When the United States joined with the Western European Powers in the North Atlantic Alliance, soon to be called the North Atlantic Treaty Organization, it overcame its historic isolationism in the wake of wars. By 1955, former enemy West Germany would be admitted to NATO to help defend Western Europe against Soviet Russian aggression.

American policy toward Europe. With good reason pundits summed up NATO's threefold purpose: "to keep the Russians out, the Germans down, and the Americans in."

Reconstruction and Revolution in Asia

Reconstruction in Japan was simpler than in Germany, primarily because it was largely a one-man show. The occupying American army, under the supreme Allied commander, five-star general Douglas MacArthur, sat in the driver's seat. In the teeth of violent protests from the Soviet officials, MacArthur went inflexibly ahead with his program for the democratization of Japan. Following the pattern in Germany, top Japanese "war criminals" were tried in Tokyo from 1946 to 1948. Eighteen of them were sentenced to prison terms, and seven were hanged.

General MacArthur, as a kind of Yankee mikado, enjoyed a stunning success. The Japanese cooperated to an astonishing degree. They saw that good behavior and the adoption of democracy would speed the end of the occupation—as it did. A MacArthur-dictated constitution was adopted in 1946. It renounced militarism and introduced Western-style democratic government—paving the way for a phenomenal economic recovery that within a few decades made Japan one of the world's mightiest industrial powers.

If Japan was a success story for American policymakers, the opposite was true in China, where a bitter civil war had raged for years between Nationalists and communists. Washington had half-heartedly supported the Nationalist government of Generalissimo Jiang Jieshi in his struggle with the communists under Mao Zedong (Mao Tse-tung). But ineptitude and corruption within the generalissimo's regime gradually began to corrode the confidence of his people. Communist armies swept south overwhelmingly, and late in 1949 Jiang was forced to flee with the remnants of his once-powerful force to the last-hope island of Formosa (Taiwan).

The collapse of Nationalist China was a depressing defeat for America and its allies in the Cold War—the worst to date. At one fell swoop, nearly one-fourth of the world's population—some 500 million people—was swept into the communist

In August 1949 Secretary of State Dean Acheson (1893–1971) explained publicly why America had "dumped" Jiang Jieshi:

"The unfortunate but inescapable fact is that the ominous result of the civil war in China was beyond the control of the government of the United States. Nothing that this country did or could have done within the reasonable limits of its capabilities could have changed that result; nothing that was left undone by this country has contributed to it. It was the product of internal Chinese forces, forces which this country tried to influence but could not."

Einstein, whose theories had helped give birth to the atomic age, declared that "annihilation of any life on earth has been brought within the range of technical possibilities." Not to be outdone, the Soviets exploded their first H-bomb in 1953, and the nuclear arms race entered a perilously competitive cycle. Nuclear "superiority" became a dangerous and delusive dream, as each side tried to outdo the other in the scramble to build more destructive weapons. If the Cold War should ever blaze into a hot war, there might be no world left for the communists to communize or the democracies to democratize—a chilling thought that constrained both camps. Peace through mutual terror brought a shaky stability to the superpower standoff.

Ferreting Out Alleged Communists

One of the most active Cold War fronts was at home, where a new antired chase was in full cry. Many nervous citizens feared that communist spies, paid with Moscow gold, were undermining the government and treacherously misdirecting foreign policy. In 1947 Truman launched a massive "loyalty" program. The attorney general drew up a list of ninety supposedly disloyal organizations, none of which was given the opportunity to prove its innocence. The Loyalty Review Board investigated more than 3 million federal employees, some 3,000 of whom either resigned or were dismissed, none under formal indictment.

Individual states likewise became intensely security-conscious. Loyalty oaths in increasing numbers were demanded of employees, especially teachers. The gnawing question for many earnest Americans was, Could the nation continue to enjoy traditional freedoms—especially freedom of speech, freedom of thought, and the right of political dissent—in a Cold War climate?

In 1949 eleven communists were brought before a New York jury for violating the Smith Act of 1940, the first peacetime antisedition law since 1798. Convicted of advocating the overthrow of the American government by force, the defendants were sent to prison. The Supreme Court upheld their convictions in *Dennis* v. *United States* (1951).

The House of Representatives in 1938 had established the Committee on Un-American Activities (popularly known as "HUAC") to investigate

camp. The so-called fall of China became a bitterly partisan issue in the United States. The Republicans, seeking "goats" who had "lost China," assailed President Truman and his bristly mustached, British-appearing secretary of state, Dean Acheson. They insisted that Democratic agencies, wormy with communists, had deliberately withheld aid from Jiang Jieshi so that he would fall. Democrats heatedly replied that when a regime has forfeited the support of its people, no amount of outside help will save it. Truman, the argument ran, did not "lose" China, because he never had China to lose. Jiang himself had never controlled all of China.

More bad news came in September 1949 when President Truman shocked the nation by announcing that the Soviets had exploded an atomic bomb—approximately three years earlier than many experts had thought possible. American strategists since 1945 had counted on keeping the Soviets in line by threats of a one-sided aerial attack with nuclear weapons. But atomic bombing was now a game that two could play.

To outpace the Soviets in nuclear weaponry, Truman ordered the development of the "H-bomb" (hydrogen bomb)—a city-smashing device many times more deadly than the atomic bomb. The United States exploded its first hydrogen device on a South Pacific atoll in 1952, despite warnings from some scientists that the H-bomb was so powerful that "it becomes a weapon which in practical effect is almost one of genocide." Famed physicist Albert

The Hydrogen Bomb, 1954
This test blast at Bikini Atoll in the Marshall Islands was so powerful that one Japanese fisherman was killed and all twenty-two of his crewmates were seriously injured by radioactive ash that fell on their vessel some eighty miles away. Fishing boats a thousand miles from Bikini later brought in radioactively contaminated catches.

"subversion." In 1948 committee member Richard M. Nixon, an ambitious red-catcher, led the chase after Alger Hiss, a prominent ex–New Dealer and a distinguished member of the "eastern establishment." Accused of being a communist agent in the 1930s, Hiss demanded the right to defend himself. He dramatically met his chief accuser before the Un-American Activities Committee in August 1948. Hiss denied everything but was caught in embarrassing falsehoods, convicted of perjury in 1950, and sentenced to five years in prison.

Was America really riddled with Soviet spies? It now seems unlikely. But for many ordinary Americans, the hunt for communists was not just about fending off the military threat of the Soviet Union. Unsettling dangers lurked closer to home. While men like Nixon and Senator Joseph McCarthy led the search for communists in Washington, conservative politicians at the state and local levels discovered that all manner of real or perceived social changes—including declining religious sentiment, increased sexual freedom, and agitation for civil rights—could be tarred with a red brush. Anticommunist crusaders ransacked school libraries for "subversive" textbooks and drove debtors, drinkers,

and homosexuals, all alleged to be security risks, from their jobs.

Some Americans, including President Truman, realized that the red hunt was turning into a witch hunt. In 1950 Truman vetoed the McCarran Internal Security Bill, which among other provisions authorized the president to arrest and detain suspicious people during an "internal security emergency." Critics protested that the bill smacked of police-state, concentration-camp tactics. But the congressional guardians of the Republic's liberties enacted the bill over Truman's veto.

The stunning success of the Soviet scientists in developing an atomic bomb was attributed by many to the cleverness of communist spies in stealing American secrets. Notorious among those who had allegedly "leaked" atomic data to Moscow were two American citizens, Julius and Ethel Rosenberg. They were convicted in 1951 of espionage and, after prolonged appeals, went to the electric chair in 1953—the only people in American history ever executed in peacetime for espionage. Their sensational trial and electrocution, combined with sympathy for their two orphaned children, began to sour some sober citizens on the excesses of the red-hunters.

Richard Nixon, Red-hunter Congressman Nixon examines the microfilm that figured as important evidence in Alger Hiss's conviction for perjury in 1950.

Atomic scientist Edward Condon (1902–1974) warned as early as 1946—three years before the Soviets exploded their own atomic bomb—that Americans' confidence in their nuclear monopoly was a dangerous delusion that could unleash vicious accusations and scapegoating:

"The laws of nature, some seem to think, are ours exclusively. . . . Having created an air of suspicion and distrust, there will be persons among us who think our nations can know nothing except what is learned by espionage. So, when other countries make atom bombs, these persons will cry 'treason' at our scientists, for they will find it inconceivable that another country could make a bomb in any other way."

Democratic Divisions in 1948

Attacking high prices and "High-Tax Harry" Truman, the Republicans had won control of Congress in the congressional elections of 1946. Their prospects had seldom looked rosier as they gathered in Philadelphia to choose their 1948 presidential candidate. They noisily renominated warmed-over New York governor Thomas E. Dewey, still as debonair as if he had stepped out of a bandbox.

Also gathering in Philadelphia, Democratic politicos looked without enthusiasm on their hand-me-down president and sang, "I'm Just Mild About Harry." But their "dump Truman" movement collapsed when war hero Dwight D. Eisenhower refused to be drafted. The peppery president, unwanted but undaunted, was then chosen in the face of vehement opposition by southern delegates. They were alienated by his strong stand in favor of civil rights for blacks, who now mustered many votes in the big-city ghettos of the North.

Truman's nomination split the party wide open. Embittered southern Democrats from thirteen states, like their fire-eating forebears of 1860, next met in their own convention, in Birmingham, Alabama, with Confederate flags brashly in evidence. Amid scenes of heated defiance, these "Dixiecrats" nominated Governor J. Strom Thurmond of South Carolina on a States' Rights party ticket.

To add to the confusion within Democratic ranks, former vice president Henry A. Wallace threw his hat into the ring. Having parted company with the administration over its get-tough-with-Russia policy, he was nominated at Philadelphia by the new Progressive party—a bizarre collection of disgruntled former New Dealers, starry-eyed pacifists, well-meaning liberals, and communist-fronters.

Wallace, a vigorous if misguided liberal, assailed Uncle Sam's "dollar imperialism" from the stump. This so-called Pied Piper of the Politburo took an apparently pro-Soviet line that earned him drenchings with rotten eggs in hostile cities. But to many Americans, Wallace raised the only hopeful voice in the deepening gloom of the Cold War.

With the Democrats ruptured three ways and the Republican congressional victory of 1946 just past, Dewey's victory seemed assured. Succumbing to overconfidence engendered by his massive lead in public-opinion polls, the cold, smug Dewey confined himself to dispensing soothing-syrup trivialities like "Our future lies before us."

The Harried Piano Player, 1948 Besieged by the left and right wings of his own party, and by a host of domestic and foreign problems, Truman was a long shot for reelection in 1948. But the scrappy president surprised his legions of critics by handily defeating his opponent, Thomas E. Dewey.

The seemingly doomed Truman, with little money and few active supporters, had to rely on his "gut-fighter" instincts and folksy personality. Traveling the country by train to deliver some three hundred "give 'em hell" speeches, he lashed out at the Taft-Hartley "slave labor" law and the "do-nothing" Republican Congress, while whipping up support for his program of civil rights, improved labor benefits, and health insurance. "Pour it on 'em, Harry!"

> *In his inaugural address, January 1949, President Harry S Truman (1884–1972) said,*
>
> "Communism is based on the belief that man is so weak and inadequate that he is unable to govern himself, and therefore requires the rule of strong masters. . . . Democracy is based on the conviction that man has the moral and intellectual capacity, as well as the inalienable right, to govern himself with reason and justice."

cried increasingly large and enthusiastic crowds, as the pugnacious president rained a barrage of verbal uppercuts on his opponent.

On election night the *Chicago Tribune* ran off an early edition with the headline "DEWEY DEFEATS TRUMAN." But in the morning, it turned out that "President" Dewey had embarrassingly snatched defeat from the jaws of victory. Truman had swept to a stunning triumph, to the complete bewilderment of politicians, pollsters, prophets, and pundits. Even though Thurmond took away 39 electoral votes in the South, Truman won 303 electoral votes, primarily from the South, Midwest, and West. Dewey's 189 electoral votes came principally from the East. The popular vote was 24,179,345 for Truman, 21,991,291 for Dewey, 1,176,125 for Thurmond, and 1,157,326 for Wallace. To make the victory sweeter, the Democrats regained control of Congress as well.

Truman's victory rested on farmers, workers, and blacks, all of whom were Republican-wary. Republican overconfidence and Truman's lone-wolf, never-say-die campaign also won him the support of many Americans who admired his "guts." No one wanted him, someone remarked, except the people. Dewey, in contrast, struck many voters as arrogant, evasive, and wooden. When Dewey took the platform to give a speech, said one commentator, "he comes out like a man who has been mounted on casters and given a tremendous shove from behind."

Smiling and self-assured, Truman sounded a clarion note in the fourth point of his inaugural

That Ain't the Way I Heard It! Truman wins.

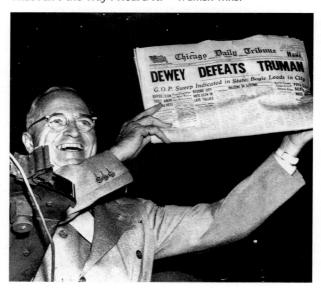

As Truman's Fair Deal was rebuffed by a hostile Congress, critics like the conservative New York Daily News *gloated that the odious New Deal was finally vanquished:*

"The New Deal is kaput like the Thirty Years' War or the Black Plague or other disasters. . . . [Its demise] is like coming out of the darkness into sunlight. Like feeling clean again after a long time in the muck."

address, when he called for a "bold new program" ("Point Four"). The plan was to lend U.S. money and technical aid to underdeveloped lands to help them help themselves. Truman wanted to spend millions to keep underprivileged peoples from becoming communists rather than spend billions to shoot them after they had become communists. This farseeing program was officially launched in 1950, and it brought badly needed assistance to impoverished countries, notably in Latin America, Africa, the Near East, and the Far East.

At home Truman outlined a sweeping "Fair Deal" program in his 1949 message to Congress. It called for improved housing, full employment, a higher minimum wage, better farm price supports, new TVAs, and an extension of Social Security. But most of the Fair Deal fell victim to congressional opposition from Republicans and southern Democrats. The only major successes came in raising the minimum wage, providing for public housing in the Housing Act of 1949, and extending old-age insurance to many more beneficiaries in the Social Security Act of 1950.

The Korean Volcano Erupts (1950)

Korea, the Land of the Morning Calm, heralded a new and more disturbing phase of the Cold War—a shooting phase—in June 1950. When Japan collapsed in 1945, Soviet troops had accepted the Japanese surrender north of the thirty-eighth parallel on the Korean peninsula, and American troops had done likewise south of that line. Both superpowers professed to want the reunification of Korea, but, as

in Germany, each helped to set up rival regimes above and below the parallel.

By 1949, when the Soviets and Americans had both withdrawn their forces, the entire peninsula was a bristling armed camp, with two hostile regimes eyeing each other suspiciously. Secretary of State Acheson seemed to wash his hands of the dispute early in 1950, when he declared in a memorable speech that Korea was outside the essential United States defense perimeter in the Pacific.

The explosion came on June 25, 1950. Spearheaded by Soviet-made tanks, North Korean army columns rumbled across the thirty-eighth parallel. Caught flat-footed, the South Korean forces were shoved back southward to a dangerously tiny defensive area around Pusan, their weary backs to the sea.

President Truman sprang quickly into the breach. The invasion seemed to provide devastating proof of a fundamental premise in the "containment doctrine" that shaped Washington's foreign policy: that even a slight relaxation of America's guard was an invitation to communist aggression somewhere.

The Korean invasion also provided the occasion for a vast expansion of the American military. Truman's National Security Council had recommended in a famous document of 1950 (known as National Security Council Memorandum Number 68, or NSC-68) that the United States should quadruple its defense spending. Buried at the time because it was considered politically impossible to implement, NSC-68 was resurrected by the Korean crisis. "Korea saved us," Secretary of State Acheson later commented. Truman now ordered a massive military buildup, well beyond what was necessary for the immediate purposes of the Korean War. Soon the United States had 3.5 million men under arms and was spending $50 billion per year on the defense budget—some 13 percent of the GNP.

NSC-68 was a key document of the Cold War period, not only because it marked a major step in the militarization of American foreign policy, but also because it vividly reflected the sense of almost limitless possibility that pervaded postwar American society. NSC-68 rested on the assumption that the enormous American economy could bear without strain the huge costs of a gigantic rearmament program. Said one NSC-68 planner, "There was practically nothing the country could not do if it wanted to do it."

Truman took full advantage of a temporary Soviet absence from the United Nations Security Council on June 25, 1950, to obtain a unanimous

June 25, 1950

Sept. 14, 1950

Nov. 25, 1950

July 27, 1953

The Shifting Front in Korea

condemnation of North Korea as an aggressor. (Why the Soviets were absent remains controversial. Scholars once believed that the Soviets were just as surprised as the Americans by the attack. It now appears that Stalin had given his reluctant approval to North Korea's strike plan but believed that the fighting would be brief and that the United States would take little interest in it.) The Council also called upon all U.N. members, including the United States, to "render every assistance" to restore peace. Two days later, without consulting Congress, Truman ordered American air and naval units to support South Korea. Before the week was out, he also ordered General Douglas MacArthur's Japan-based occupation troops into action alongside the beleaguered South Koreans.

Officially, the United States was simply participating in a United Nations "police action." But in fact, the United States made up the overwhelming bulk of the U.N. contingents, and General MacArthur, appointed U.N. commander of the entire operation, took his orders from Washington, not from the Security Council.

The Military Seesaw in Korea

Rather than fight his way out of the southern Pusan perimeter, MacArthur launched a daring amphibious landing behind the enemy's lines at Inchon.

This bold gamble on September 15, 1950, succeeded brilliantly; within two weeks the North Koreans had scrambled back behind the "sanctuary" of the thirty-eighth parallel. Truman's avowed intention was to restore South Korea to its former borders, but the pursuing South Koreans had already crossed the thirty-eighth parallel, and there seemed little point in permitting the North Koreans to regroup and come again. The U.N. Assembly tacitly authorized a crossing by MacArthur, whom President Truman ordered northward, provided that there was no intervention in force by the Chinese or Soviets.

The Americans thus raised the stakes in Korea, and in so doing they quickened the fears of another potential player in this dangerous game. The Chinese communists had publicly warned that they would not sit idly by and watch hostile troops approach the strategic Yalu River boundary between Korea and China. But MacArthur pooh-poohed all predictions of an effective intervention by the Chinese and reportedly boasted that he would "have the boys home by Christmas."

MacArthur erred badly. In November 1950 hordes of Chinese "volunteers" fell upon his rashly overextended lines and hurled the U.N. forces reeling back down the peninsula. The fighting now sank into a frostbitten stalemate on the icy terrain near the thirty-eighth parallel.

An imperious MacArthur, humiliated by this rout, pressed for drastic retaliation. He favored a blockade of the Chinese coast and bombardment of

Chinese bases in Manchuria. But Washington policy-makers, with anxious eyes on Moscow, refused to enlarge the already costly conflict. The chairman of the Joint Chiefs of Staff declared that a wider clash in Asia would be "the wrong war, at the wrong place, at the wrong time, and with the wrong enemy." Europe, not Asia, was the administration's first concern; and the USSR, not China, loomed as the more sinister foe.

Two-fisted General MacArthur felt that he was being asked to fight with one hand tied behind his back. He sneered at the concept of a "limited war" and insisted that "there is no substitute for victory." When the general began to take issue publicly with presidential policies, Truman had no choice but to remove the insubordinate MacArthur from command (April 11, 1951). MacArthur, a legend in his own mind, returned to an uproarious welcome, whereas Truman was condemned as a "pig," an "imbecile," a "Judas," and an appeaser of "Communist Russia and Communist China." In July 1951 truce discussions began in a rude field tent near the firing line but were almost immediately snagged on the issue of prisoner exchange. Talks dragged on unproductively for nearly two years while men continued to die.

Truman Takes the Heat

Chronology

1944	Servicemen's Readjustment Act (GI Bill) Bretton Woods economic conference
1945	Spock publishes *The Common Sense Book of Baby and Child Care* Yalta conference United States ends lend-lease to the USSR United Nations established
1945–1946	Nuremberg war crimes trials in Germany
1946	Employment Act creates Council of Economic Advisers Iran crisis
1946–1948	Tokyo war crimes trials
1947	Truman Doctrine Marshall Plan Taft-Hartley Act National Security Act creates Department of Defense, National Security Council (NSC), and Central Intelligence Agency (CIA)
1948	United States officially recognizes Israel "Voice of America" begins radio broadcasts behind iron curtain Hiss case begins Truman defeats Dewey for presidency
1948–1949	Berlin crisis
1949	NATO established Communists defeat Nationalists in China
1950	American economy begins postwar growth McCarthy red hunt begins McCarran Internal Security Bill passed by Congress over Truman's veto
1950–1953	Korean War
1951	Truman fires MacArthur Rosenbergs convicted of treason
1952	United States explodes first hydrogen bomb
1957	Postwar peak of U.S. birthrate
1973	U.S. birthrate falls below replacement level

Who Was to Blame for the Cold War?

Whose fault was the Cold War? (And, for that matter, who should get credit for ending it?) For two decades after World War II, American historians generally agreed that the aggressive Soviets were solely responsible. This "orthodox" or "official" appraisal squared with the traditional view of the United States as a virtuous, innocent land with an idealistic foreign policy. This point of view also justified America's Cold War containment policy, which cast the Soviet Union as the aggressor that must be confined by an ever-vigilant United States. America supposedly had only defensive intentions, with no expansionary ambitions of its own.

In the 1960s a vigorous revisionist interpretation flowered, powerfully influenced by disillusion over U.S. involvement in Vietnam. The revisionists stood the orthodox view on its head. The Soviets, they argued, had only defensive intentions at the end of World War II; it was the Americans who had behaved provocatively by brandishing their new atomic weaponry. Some of these critics pointed an accusing finger at President Truman, alleging that he abandoned Roosevelt's conciliatory approach to the Soviets and adopted a bullying attitude, emboldened by the American atomic monopoly.

More radical revisionists like Gabriel and Joyce Kolko even claimed to have found the roots of Truman's alleged belligerence in long-standing American policies of economic imperialism—policies that eventually resulted in the tragedy of Vietnam (see pp. 935–938). In this view the Vietnam War followed logically from America's insatiable "need" for overseas markets and raw materials. Vietnam itself may have been economically unimportant, but, so the argument ran, a communist Vietnam represented an intolerable challenge to American hegemony. Ironically, revisionists thus endorsed the so-called domino theory, which official apologists often cited in defense of America's Vietnam policy. According to the domino theory, if the United States declined to fight in Vietnam, other countries would lose their faith in America's will (or their fear of American power) and would tumble one after the other like "dominoes" into the Soviet camp. Revisionists stressed what they saw as the *economic necessity*

behind the domino theory: losing in Vietnam, they claimed, would unravel the American economy.

In the 1970s a "postrevisionist" interpretation emerged that is widely agreed upon today. Historians such as John Lewis Gaddis and Melvyn Leffler pooh-pooh the economic determinism of the revisionists, while frankly acknowledging that the United States did have vital security interests at stake in the post–World War II era. The postrevisionists analyze the ways in which inherited ideas (like isolationism) and the contentious nature of postwar domestic politics, as well as miscalculations by American leaders, led a nation in search of security into seeking not simply a sufficiency but a "preponderance" of power. The American *overreaction* to its security needs, these scholars suggest, exacerbated U.S.-Soviet relations and precipitated the four-decade-long nuclear arms race that formed the centerpiece of the Cold War.

In the case of Vietnam, the postrevisionist historians focus not on economic necessity, but on a failure of political intelligence, induced by the stressful conditions of the Cold War, that made the dubious domino theory seem plausible. Misunderstanding Vietnamese intentions, exaggerating Soviet ambitions, and fearing to appear "soft on communism" in the eyes of their domestic political rivals, American leaders plunged into Vietnam, sadly misguided by their own Cold War obsessions.

Most postrevisionists, however, still lay the lion's share of the blame for the Cold War on the Soviet Union. By the same token, they credit the Soviets with ending the Cold War—a view hotly disputed by Ronald Reagan's champions, who claim that it was his anti-Soviet policies in the 1980s that brought the Russians to their knees (see pp. 984–985). The great unknown, of course, is the precise nature of Soviet thinking in the Cold War years. Were Soviet aims predominantly defensive, or did the Kremlin incessantly plot world conquest? Was there an opportunity for reconciliation with the West following Stalin's death in 1953? Should Mikhail Gorbachev or Ronald Reagan be remembered as the leader who ended the Cold War? With the opening of Soviet archives, scholars are eagerly pursuing answers to such questions.

For further reading, see page A25 of the Appendix. For web resources, go to **http://college.hmco.com.**

38

The Eisenhower Era

1952–1960

Every warship launched, every rocket fired
signifies . . . a theft from those who hunger and are not fed,
those who are cold and are not clothed.

DWIGHT D. EISENHOWER, APRIL 16, 1953

In President Dwight D. Eisenhower, the man and the hour met. Americans yearned for a period of calm in which they could pursue without distraction their new visions of consumerist affluence. The nation sorely needed a respite from twenty years of depression and war. Yet the American people unexpectedly found themselves in the early 1950s dug into the frontlines of the Cold War abroad and dangerously divided at home over the explosive issues of communist subversion and civil rights. They longed for reassuring leadership. "Ike" seemed ready both to reassure and to lead.

The Advent of Eisenhower

Democratic prospects in the presidential election of 1952 were blighted by the military deadlock in Korea, Truman's clash with MacArthur, war-bred inflation, and whiffs of scandal from the White House. Dispirited Democrats, convening in Chicago, nominated a reluctant Adlai E. Stevenson, the witty, eloquent, and idealistic governor of Illinois. Republicans enthusiastically chose General Dwight D. Eisenhower on the first ballot. As a concession to the hard-line anticommunist wing of the party, the convention selected as "Ike's" running mate California senator Richard M. Nixon, who had distinguished himself as a relentless red-hunter.

Eisenhower was already the most popular American of his time, as "I Like Ike" buttons everywhere testified. His ruddy face, captivating grin, and glowing personality made him a perfect candidate in the dawning new age of television politics. He had an authentic hero's credentials as wartime supreme commander of the Allied forces in Europe, army chief of staff after the war, and the first supreme commander of NATO from 1950 to 1952. He had also been "civilianized" by a brief term as president of Columbia University from 1948 to 1950.

Striking a grandfatherly, nonpartisan pose, Eisenhower left the rough campaigning to Nixon, who relished pulling no punches. The vice-presidential candidate lambasted his opponents with charges that they had cultivated corruption, caved in on Korea, and coddled communists. He particularly blasted the intellectual ("egghead") Stevenson as "Adlai the appeaser," with a "Ph.D. from [Secretary of State] Dean Acheson's College of Cowardly Communist Containment."

Nixon himself faltered when reports surfaced of a secretly financed "slush fund" he had tapped while holding a seat in the Senate. Prodded by Republican party officials, Eisenhower seriously considered dropping him from the ticket, but a scared Nixon went on national television with a theatrical appeal filled with self-pity, during which he referred to the family cocker spaniel, Checkers. This heart-tugging "Checkers speech" saved him his place on the ticket.

The maudlin Checkers speech also demonstrated the awesome political potentialities of television—foreshadowed by FDR's mastery of the radio. Nixon had defied Republican party bosses and bent Eisenhower himself to his will by appealing directly to the American people in their living rooms. His performance illustrated the disturbing power of the new, vivid medium, which communicated with far more immediacy and effect than its electronic cousin, the radio, ever could.

Even Eisenhower reluctantly embraced the new technology of the black-and-white television screen. He allowed himself to be filmed in a New York TV studio giving extremely brief "answers" to a nonexistent audience, whose "questions" were taped later, then carefully spliced with Eisenhower's statements to give the illusion of a live discussion. "To think that an old soldier should come to this," Ike grumbled. These so-called "spots" foreshadowed the future of political advertising. They amounted, as one critic observed, to "selling the President like toothpaste." Devoid of substance, they vastly oversimplified complicated economic and social issues. "What about the high cost of living?" one spot asked. "My wife Mamie worries about the same thing," Ike answered. "I tell her it's my job to change that on November fourth."

In future years television made possible a kind of "plebiscitarian" politics, through which lone-wolf politicians could go straight to the voters without the mediating influence of parties or other institu-

The Republicans' Choice, 1952 Nominee Eisenhower and his vice-presidential running mate, Nixon, greet the delegates.

tions. The new medium thus stood revealed as a threat to the historic role of political parties, which traditionally had chosen candidates through complex internal bargaining and had educated and mobilized the electorate. And given television's origins in entertainment and advertising, political messages would be increasingly tuned to the standards of show business and commercialism. Gradually, as television spread to virtually every household in the land, those standards would rule politics with iron sway as ten-second television "sound bites" became the most common form of political communication.

The outcome of the presidential election of 1952 was never really in doubt. Given an extra prod by Eisenhower's last-minute pledge to go personally to Korea to end the war, the voters overwhelmingly declared for Ike. He garnered 33,936,234 votes to Stevenson's 27,314,992. He cracked the solid South wide open, ringing up 442 electoral votes to 89 for his opponent. Ike not only ran far ahead of his ticket but managed to pull enough Republicans into office on his military coattails to ensure GOP control of the new Congress by a paper-thin margin.

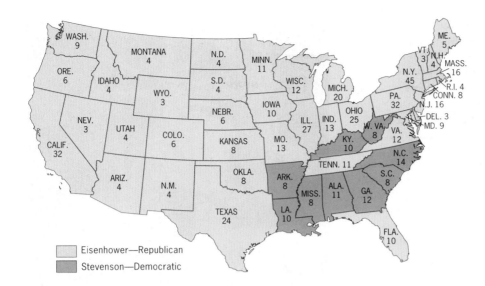

Presidential Election of 1952 (with electoral vote by state) A Democrat quipped that "if the voters liked the Republicans the way they liked Ike, the two-party system would be in bad shape." Fortunately for Democrats, Eisenhower scored a personal, not a party, victory. Republicans won minuscule majorities in Congress, majorities that disappeared in the congressional elections two years later.

Map legend:
- Eisenhower—Republican
- Stevenson—Democratic

"Ike" Takes Command

True to his campaign pledge, president-elect Eisenhower undertook a flying three-day visit to Korea in December 1952. But even a glamorous Ike could not immediately budge the peace negotiations off dead center. Seven long months later, after Eisenhower had threatened to use atomic weapons, an armistice was finally signed but was repeatedly violated in succeeding decades.

The brutal and futile fighting had lasted three years. About fifty-four thousand Americans lay dead, joined by perhaps more than a million Chinese, North Koreans, and South Koreans. Tens of billions of American dollars had been poured down the Asian sinkhole. Yet this terrible toll in blood and treasure bought only a return to the conditions of 1950: Korea remained divided at the thirty-eighth parallel. Americans took what little comfort they could from the fact that communism had been "contained" and that the bloodletting had been "limited" to something less than full-scale global war. The shooting had ended, but the Cold War still remained frigidly frozen.

As a military commander, Eisenhower had cultivated a leadership style that self-consciously projected an image of sincerity, fairness, and optimism. He had been widely perceived during the war as an "unmilitary" general, and in the White House he similarly struck the pose of an "unpolitical" president, serenely above the petty partisan fray. He also shrewdly knew that his greatest "asset" was his enjoyment of the "affection and respect of our citizenry," as he confided to his diary in 1949.

Ike thus seemed ideally suited to soothe the anxieties of troubled Americans, much as a distinguished and well-loved grandfather brings stability to his family. He played this role well as he presided over a decade of shaky peace and shining prosperity. Yet

Korean War Scene A grief-stricken American soldier whose buddy has been killed is being comforted, while a medical corpsman fills out casualty tags.

critics charged that he unwisely hoarded the "asset" of his immense popularity, rather than spend it for a good cause (especially civil rights), and that he cared more for social harmony than for social justice.

The Rise and Fall of Joseph McCarthy

One of the first problems Eisenhower faced was the swelling popularity and swaggering power of anti-communist crusader Senator Joseph R. McCarthy. Elected to the Senate on the basis of a trumped-up war-hero record, "Tailgunner Joe" was just an obscure junior senator from Wisconsin until he crashed into the limelight with the spectacular charge that scores of known communists worked in the State Department. In a February 1950 speech in Wheeling, West Virginia, McCarthy accused Secretary of State Dean Acheson of knowingly employing 205 Communist party members. Pressed to reveal the names, McCarthy later conceded that there were only 57 genuine communists and in the end failed to root out even one. But the speech won him national visibility, and McCarthy's Republican colleagues realized the usefulness of this kind of attack on the Democratic administration. The supposedly fair-minded Senator Robert Taft urged McCarthy, "If one case doesn't work, try another." Ohio's Senator John Bricker reportedly said, "Joe, you're a dirty s.o.b., but there are times when you've got to have an s.o.b. around, and this is one of them."

McCarthy's rhetoric grew bolder and his accusations spread more wildly after the Republican victory in 1952. McCarthy saw the red hand of Moscow everywhere. The Democrats, he charged, "bent to whispered pleas from the lips of traitors." Incredibly, he even denounced General George Marshall, former army chief of staff and ex–secretary of state, as "part of a conspiracy so immense and an infamy so black as to dwarf any previous venture in the history of man."

McCarthy flourished in the seething Cold War atmosphere of suspicion and fear. He was neither the first nor the most effective red-hunter, but he was surely the most ruthless, and he did the most damage to American traditions of fair play and free speech. The careers of countless officials, writers, and actors were ruined after "Low-Blow Joe" had "named" them, often unfairly, as communists or communist sympathizers. Politicians trembled in

Senator McCarthy Extinguishes the Torch of Liberty
While preaching patriotism, McCarthy irresponsibly menaced American traditions of civil liberties.

the face of such onslaughts, especially when opinion polls showed that a majority of the American people approved of McCarthy's crusade. His intervention in certain key senatorial elections brought resounding defeat for his enemies.

Eisenhower privately loathed McCarthy but publicly tried to stay out of his way, saying, "I will not get in the gutter with that guy." Trying to appease the brash demagogue from Wisconsin, Eisenhower allowed him, in effect, to control personnel policy at the State Department. One baleful result was severe damage to the morale and effectiveness of the professional foreign service. In particular, McCarthyite purges deprived the government of a number of Asian specialists who might have counseled a wiser course in Vietnam in the fateful decade that followed.

McCarthy finally bent the bow too far when he attacked the U.S. Army. The embattled military men fought back in thirty-five days of televised hearings in the spring of 1954. The political power of the new broadcast medium was again demonstrated as up to 20 million Americans at a time watched in fascination while a boorish, surly McCarthy publicly cut

In a moment of high drama during the Army-McCarthy hearings, attorney Joseph Welch (1890–1960) reproached McCarthy in front of a huge national television audience for threatening to slander a young lawyer on Welch's staff:

"Until this moment, Senator, I think I never really gauged your cruelty or your recklessness. Little did I dream you could be so cruel as to do an injury to that lad. . . . If it were in my power to forgive you for your reckless cruelty, I would do so. I like to think that I am a gentleman, but your forgiveness will have to come from someone other than me. . . . Have you no decency, sir, at long last? Have you left no sense of decency?"

his own throat by parading his essential meanness and irresponsibility. A few months later, the Senate formally condemned him for "conduct unbecoming a member." Three years later, unwept and unsung, McCarthy died of chronic alcoholism. But "McCarthyism" has passed into the English language as a label for the dangerous forces of unfairness and fear that a democratic society can unleash only at its peril.

Desegregating the South

America counted some 15 million black citizens in 1950, two-thirds of whom still made their homes in the South. There they lived bound by the iron folkways of a segregated society. A rigid set of antiquated rules known as Jim Crow laws governed all aspects of their existence, from the schoolroom to the restroom. Every day of their lives, southern blacks dealt with a bizarre array of separate social arrangements that kept them insulated from whites, economically inferior, and politically powerless. Later generations, black and white alike, would wonder at how their ancestors could have daily made their way through this anthropological museum of cruel and stifling customs.

Blacks everywhere in the South, for example, not only attended segregated schools but were compelled to use separate public toilets, drinking fountains, restaurants, and waiting rooms. Trains and buses had "whites only" and "colored only" seating. Because Alabama hotels were prohibited from serving blacks, the honeymooning Dr. Martin Luther King, Jr., and his wife, Coretta, spent their wedding night in 1953 in a blacks-only funeral parlor. Only about 20 percent of eligible southern blacks were registered to vote, and fewer than 5 percent were registered in some Deep South states like Mississippi and Alabama. As late as 1960, white southern sensibilities about segregation were so tender that television networks blotted out black speakers at the national political conventions for fear of offending southern stations.

Where the law proved insufficient to enforce this regime, vigilante violence did the job. Six black war veterans, claiming the rights for which they had fought overseas, were murdered in the summer of 1946. A Mississippi mob lynched black fourteen-year-old Emmett Till in 1955 for allegedly leering at a white woman. It is small wonder that a black clergyman declared that "everywhere I go in the South the Negro is forced to choose between his hide and his soul."

In his notable book of 1944, *An American Dilemma,* Swedish scholar Gunnar Myrdal had exposed the contradiction between America's professed belief that all men are created equal and its sordid treatment of black citizens. There had been token progress in race relations since the war—Jack Roosevelt ("Jackie") Robinson, for example, had cracked the racial barrier in big-league baseball when the Brooklyn Dodgers signed him in 1947. But for the most part, the national conscience still slumbered, and blacks still suffered.

Increasingly, however, African-Americans refused to suffer in silence. The war had generated a new militancy and restlessness among many members of the black community (see "Makers of America: The Great African-American Migration," pp. 892–893). The National Association for the Advancement of Colored People (NAACP) had for years pushed doggedly to dismantle the legal underpinnings of segregation and now enjoyed some success. In 1944 the Supreme Court ruled the "white primary" unconstitutional, thereby undermining the status of the Democratic party in the South as a white person's club. And in 1950 NAACP chief legal

The Great African-American Migration

The great social upheavals of World War II continued to transform America well after the guns had fallen silent in 1945. Among the groups most affected by the war's impact were African-Americans. Predominantly a rural, southern people before 1940, African-Americans were propelled by the war into the cities of the North and West, and by 1970 a majority lived outside the states of the old Confederacy. The results of that massive demographic shift were momentous, for African-Americans and for all of American society.

So many black southerners took to the roads during World War II that local officials lost track of their numbers. Black workers on the move crowded into boardinghouses, camped out in cars, and clustered in the juke joints of roadside America en route to their new lives.

Southern cotton fields and tobacco plantations had historically yielded slender sustenance to African-American farmers, most of whom struggled to make ends meet as tenants or sharecroppers. The Great Depression dealt black southerners yet another blow, for when New Deal farm programs paid growers to leave their land fallow, many landlords simply pocketed the money and evicted their tenants—white as well as black—from their now-idle fields. As the Depression deepened, dispossessed former tenants and sharecroppers toiled as seasonal farm workers or languished without jobs, without shelter, and without hope.

The spanking new munitions plants and bustling shipyards of the wartime South at first offered little solace to African-Americans. In 1940 and 1941, the labor-hungry war machine soaked up

The Migration of the Negro, by Jacob Lawrence, 1940–1941   Artist Jacob Lawrence depicted the migration of southern blacks to the North during and after World War II in a series of paintings. The first panel of the series bears the description, "During the World War there was a great migration north by southern Negroes."

The Home Front Though often fighting against prejudice and discrimination, many African-American migrants from the rural South during World War II found their first industrial jobs in wartime defense plants.

By war's end the great wartime exodus had scattered hundreds of thousands of African-Americans to new regions and new ways of life—a second black diaspora comparable in its scale and consequence to the original black dispersal out of Africa itself. In the post-war decades, blacks continued to pour out of the South in search of economic opportunity and political freedom. In western and northern cities, blacks now competed for housing and jobs, and they also voted—many of them for the first time in their lives.

As early as 1945, NAACP leader Walter White concluded that the war "immeasurably magnified the Negro's awareness of the disparity between the American profession and practice of democracy." After the war, he predicted, African-Americans would be "convinced that whatever betterment of their lot is achieved must come largely from their own efforts." The wartime migration thus set the stage for the success of the civil rights movement that began to stir in the 1950s. With their new political base outside the Old South, and with new support from the Democratic party, African-Americans eventually forced an end to the hated segregationist practices that had caused them to flee the South in the first place.

unemployed white workers but commonly denied jobs to blacks. When the Army constructed a training camp near Petersburg, Virginia, it imported white carpenters from all parts of the United States, rather than employ the hundreds of skilled black carpenters who lived nearby. Fed up with such injustices, many African-Americans headed for shipyards, factories, foundries, and fields on the Pacific Coast or north of the Mason-Dixon line, where their willing hands found waiting work in abundance.

Angered by the racism that was driving their people from the South, black leaders cajoled President Roosevelt into issuing an executive order in June 1941 declaring that "there shall be no discrimination in the employment of workers in defense industries or government because of race, creed, color, or national origin." Roosevelt's action was a tenuous, hesitant step. Yet in its way Executive Order 8802 amounted to a second Emancipation Proclamation, as the federal government for the first time since Reconstruction had committed itself to ensuring justice for African-Americans.

The entire nation was now forced to confront the evil of racism, as bloody wartime riots in Detroit, New York, Philadelphia, and other cities tragically demonstrated. But for the first time, large numbers of blacks had a foothold in the industrial economy, and they were not about to give it up.

Detroit Race Riot, 1943 A black passenger is dragged from a streetcar.

The Face of Segregation These women in the segregated South of the 1950s were compelled to enter the movie theater through the "Colored Entrance." Once inside, they were restricted to a separate seating section, usually in the rear of the theater.

A black woman described the day-in, day-out humiliations of life in a Jim Crow South:

"You could not go to a white restaurant; you sat in a special place at the movie house; and Lord knows, you sat in the back of the bus. It didn't make any difference if you were rich or poor, if you were black you were nothing. You might have a hundred dollars in your pocket, but if you went to the store you would wait at the side until all the clerks got through with all the white folks, no matter if they didn't have change for a dollar. Then the clerk would finally look at you and say, 'Oh, did you want something? I didn't see you there.'"

counsel Thurgood Marshall (later a Supreme Court justice), in the case of *Sweatt* v. *Painter,* wrung from the High Court a ruling that separate professional schools for blacks failed to meet the test of equality.

On a chilly day in December 1955, Rosa Parks, a college-educated black seamstress, made history in Montgomery, Alabama. She boarded a bus, took a seat in the "whites only" section, and refused to give it up. Her arrest for violating the city's Jim Crow statutes sparked a yearlong black boycott of the city buses and served notice throughout the South that blacks would no longer submit meekly to the absurdities and indignities of segregation.

The Montgomery bus boycott also catapulted to prominence a young pastor at Montgomery's Dexter Avenue Baptist Church, the Reverend Martin Luther King, Jr. Barely twenty-seven years old, King seemed an unlikely champion of the downtrodden and dis-

franchised. Raised in a prosperous black family in Atlanta and educated partly in the North, he had for most of his life been sheltered from the grossest cruelties of segregation. But his oratorical skill, his passionate devotion to biblical and constitutional conceptions of justice, and his devotion to the nonviolent principles of India's Mohandas Gandhi were destined to thrust him to the forefront of the black revolution that would soon pulse across the South and the rest of the nation.

Seeds of the Civil Rights Revolution

When President Harry Truman heard about the lynching of black war veterans in 1946, he exclaimed, "My God! I had no idea it was as terrible as that." The horrified Truman responded by commissioning a report titled "To Secure These Rights." Following the report's recommendations, Truman in 1948 ended segregation in federal civil service and ordered "equality of treatment and opportunity" in the armed forces. The military brass at first protested that "the army is not a sociological laboratory," but manpower shortages in Korea forced the integration of combat units, without the predicted loss of effectiveness. Yet Congress stubbornly resisted passing civil rights legislation, and Truman's successor, Dwight Eisenhower, showed no real signs of interest in the racial issue. Within the government that left only the judicial branch as an avenue of advancement for civil rights.

Breaking the path for civil rights progress was broad-jawed Chief Justice Earl Warren, former governor of California. Elevated to the supreme bench by Eisenhower, Warren shocked the president and other traditionalists with his active judicial intervention in previously taboo social issues. Publicly snubbed and privately scorned by President Eisenhower, Warren persisted in encouraging the Court to apply his straightforward populist principles. Critics assailed this "judicial activism," and "Impeach Earl Warren" signs blossomed along the nation's highways. But Warren's defenders argued that the Court was rightly stepping up to confront important social issues—especially civil rights for African-Americans—because the Congress had abdicated its responsibilities by refusing to deal with them. When it came to fundamental rights, Warren's allies claimed, "legislation by the judiciary" was better than no legislation at all.

The unanimous decision of the Warren Court in *Brown* v. *Board of Education of Topeka, Kansas* in May 1954 was epochal. In a forceful opinion, the learned justices ruled that segregation in the public schools was "inherently unequal" and thus unconstitutional. The uncompromising sweep of the deci-

---

Joseph E. Lowery (b. 1923), a Methodist minister and civil rights activist in Mobile, Alabama, reflected on the powerful message of the 1955 Montgomery bus boycott for blacks:

"You see, what the bus thing did was simply more than withholding patronage from the bus; it was restoring a sense of dignity to the patrons, as best expressed by an oft-quoted black woman in Montgomery who said, 'Since I've been walking, my feet are tired, but my soul's rested.' . . . [P]rior to the bus boycotts, the determination of our freedom rested with the courts. With the bus boycott, we determined it. . . . The court could say what it liked, we weren't gon' ride—in the back of the bus. We'd walk."

---

sion startled conservatives like an exploding time bomb, for it reversed the Court's earlier declaration of 1896 in *Plessy* v. *Ferguson* (see p. 511) that "separate but equal" facilities were allowable under the Constitution. That doctrine was now dead. Desegregation, the justices insisted, must go ahead with "all deliberate speed."

The Border States generally made reasonable efforts to comply with this ruling, but in the Deep South die-hards organized "massive resistance" against the Court's annulment of the sacred principle of "separate but equal." More than a hundred southern congressional representatives and senators signed the "Declaration of Constitutional Principles" in 1956, pledging their unyielding resistance to desegregation. Several states diverted public funds to hastily created "private" schools, for there the integration order was more difficult to apply. Throughout the South white citizens' councils, sometimes with fire and hemp, thwarted attempts to make integration a reality. Ten years after the Court's momentous ruling, fewer than 2 percent of the eligible blacks in the Deep South were sitting in classrooms with whites. The southern translation of "all deliberate speed" was apparently deliberately slow.

Crisis at Little Rock

President Eisenhower was little inclined toward promoting integration. He shied away from employing his vast popularity and the prestige of his office to educate white Americans about the need for racial justice. His personal attitudes may have helped to restrain him. He had grown up in an all-white town and spent his career in a segregated army. He had advised against integration of the armed forces in 1948 and had criticized Truman's call for a permanent Fair Employment Practices Commission. He complained that the Supreme Court's decision in *Brown* v. *Board of Education* had upset "the customs and convictions of at least two generations of Americans," and he steadfastly refused to issue a public statement endorsing the Court's conclusions. "I do not believe," he explained, "that prejudices, even palpably unjustifiable prejudices, will succumb to compulsion."

But in September 1957, Ike was forced to act. Orval Faubus, the governor of Arkansas, mobilized

Integration at Little Rock, 1957 While white mobs jeered at the first black students entering Central High School, federal troops, with bayonets fixed, enforced the law.

the National Guard to prevent nine black students from enrolling in Little Rock's Central High School. Confronted with a direct challenge to federal authority, Eisenhower sent troops to escort the children to their classes.

In the same year, Congress passed the first Civil Rights Act since Reconstruction days. Eisenhower characteristically reassured a southern senator that the legislation represented "the mildest civil rights

bill possible." It set up a permanent Civil Rights Commission to investigate violations of civil rights and authorized federal injunctions to protect voting rights.

Blacks meanwhile continued to take the civil rights movement into their own hands. Martin Luther King, Jr., formed the Southern Christian Leadership Conference (SCLC) in 1957. It aimed to mobilize the vast power of the black churches on

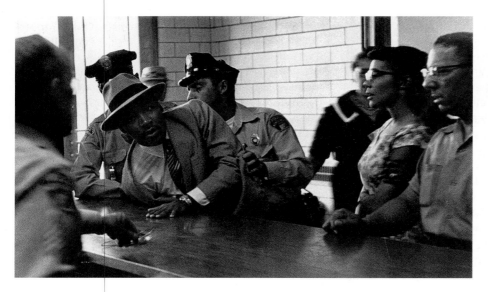

Martin Luther King, Jr., and His Wife, Coretta, Arrested King and his wife were arrested for the first time in Montgomery, Alabama, in 1955 while organizing the bus boycott.

behalf of black rights. This was an exceptionally shrewd strategy, because the churches were the largest and best-organized black institutions that had been allowed to flourish in a segregated society.

More spontaneous was the "sit-in" movement launched on February 1, 1960, by four black college freshmen in Greensboro, North Carolina. Without a detailed plan or institutional support, they demanded service at a whites-only Woolworth's lunch counter. Observing that "fellows like you make our race look bad," the black waitress refused to serve them. But they kept their seats and returned the next day with nineteen classmates. The following day, eighty-five students joined in; by the end of the week, a thousand. Like a prairie fire, the sit-in movement burned swiftly across the South, swelling into a wave of wade-ins, lie-ins, and pray-ins to compel equal treatment in restaurants, transportation, employment, housing, and voter registration. In April 1960 southern black students formed the Student Non-Violent Coordinating Committee (SNCC, pronounced "snick") to give more focus and force to these efforts. Young and impassioned, SNCC members would eventually lose patience with the more stately tactics of the SCLC and the even more deliberate legalisms of the NAACP.

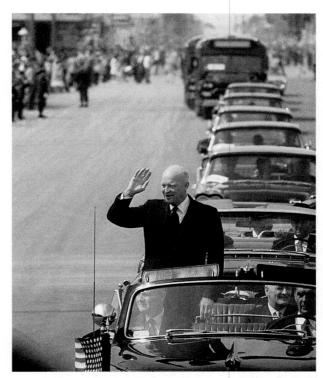

A Popular President   "Ike" exuded grandfatherly graciousness and goodwill.

Eisenhower Republicanism at Home

The balding, sixty-two-year-old General Eisenhower had entered the White House in 1953 pledging his administration to a philosophy of "dynamic conservatism." "In all those things which deal with people, be liberal, be human," he advised. But when it came to "people's money, or their economy, or their form of government, be conservative." This balanced, middle-of-the-road course harmonized with the depression-daunted and war-weary mood of the times. Some critics called Eisenhower's presidency a case of "the bland leading the bland."

Above all, Eisenhower strove to balance the federal budget and guard the Republic from what he called "creeping socialism." The former supreme allied commander put the brakes on Truman's enormous military buildup, though defense spending still soaked up some 10 percent of the GNP. True to his small-government philosophy, Eisenhower supported the transfer of control over offshore oil fields from the federal government to the states. Ike also tried to curb the TVA by encouraging a private power company to build a generating plant to compete with the massive public utility spawned by the New Deal. Speaking of the TVA, Eisenhower reportedly said, "By God, if ever we could do it, before we leave here, I'd like to see us *sell* the whole thing, but I suppose we can't go that far." Eisenhower's secretary of health, education, and welfare condemned the free distribution of the Salk antipolio vaccine as "socialized medicine."

Eisenhower responded to the Mexican government's worries that illegal Mexican immigration to the United States would undercut the *bracero* program of legally imported farmworkers inaugurated during World War II (see p. 833). In a massive roundup of illegal immigrants, dubbed Operation Wetback in reference to the migrants' watery route across the Rio Grande, as many as 1 million Mexicans were apprehended and returned to Mexico in 1954.

In yet another of the rude and arbitrary reversals that long have afflicted the government's relations with Native Americans, Eisenhower also sought to cancel the tribal preservation policies of the "Indian New Deal," in place since 1934 (see p. 790). He proposed to "terminate" the tribes as legal entities and to revert to the assimilationist goals of the Dawes Severalty Act of 1887 (see p. 597). A few tribes, notably the Klamaths of Oregon, were induced to terminate themselves. In return for cash payments, the Klamaths relinquished all claims on their land and agreed to their legal dissolution as a tribe. But most Indians resisted termination, and the policy was abandoned in 1961.

Eisenhower knew that he could not unscramble all the eggs that had been fried by New Dealers and Fair Dealers for twenty long years. He pragmatically accepted and thereby legitimated many New Dealish programs, stitching them permanently into the fabric of American society. As he told his brother, "Should any political party attempt to abolish Social Security, unemployment insurance, and eliminate labor and farm programs, you would not hear of that party again in our political history."

In some ways Eisenhower even did the New Deal one better. In a public works project that dwarfed anything the New Dealers had ever dreamed of, Ike backed the Interstate Highway Act of 1956, a $27 billion plan to build forty-two thousand miles of sleek, fast motorways. Laying down these modern, multilane roads created countless construction jobs and speeded the suburbanization of America. The Highway Act offered juicy benefits to the trucking, automobile, oil, and travel industries, while at the same time robbing the railroads, especially passenger trains, of business. The act also exacerbated problems of air quality and energy consumption, and had especially disastrous consequences for cities, whose once-vibrant downtowns withered away while shopping malls flourished in the far-flung suburbs. One critic carped that the most charitable assumption about the Interstate

Operation Wetback Thousands of illegal Mexican immigrants were forcibly repatriated to Mexico in the federal government's 1954 roundup operation, which was promoted in part by the Mexican government. The man in this photograph is being pulled across the border by a Mexican official, while an American spectator tries to pull him back into the United States.

Seldon E. Kirk, President of the Klamath Indian Tribal Council, 1959

Highway Act was that Congress "didn't have the faintest notion of what they were doing."

Despite his good intentions, Eisenhower managed to balance the budget only three times in his eight years in office, and in 1959 he incurred the biggest peacetime deficit thus far in American history. Yet critics blamed his fiscal timidity for aggravating several business recessions during the decade, especially the sharp downturn of 1957–1958, which left more than 5 million workers jobless. Economic troubles helped to revive the Democrats, who regained control of both houses of Congress in 1954. Unemployment jitters also helped to spark the merger of the AF of L and the CIO in 1955, ending two decades of bitter division in the house of labor.

A New Look in Foreign Policy

Mere containment of communism was condemned in the 1952 Republican platform as "negative, futile, and immoral." Incoming secretary of state John Foster Dulles—a pious churchgoer whose sanctimonious manner was lampooned by critics as "Dull, Duller, Dulles"—promised not merely to stem the red tide but to "roll back" its gains and "liberate captive peoples." At the same time, the new administration promised to balance the budget by cutting military spending.

How were these two contradictory goals to be reached? Dulles answered with a "policy of boldness" in early 1954. Eisenhower would relegate the army and the navy to the back seat and build up an air fleet of superbombers (called the Strategic Air Command, or SAC) equipped with city-flattening nuclear bombs. These fearsome weapons would inflict "massive retaliation" on the Soviets or the Chinese if they got out of hand. The advantages of this new policy were thought to be its paralyzing nuclear impact and its cheaper price tag when compared with conventional forces—"more bang for the buck." In 1955 Eisenhower actually threatened nuclear reprisal when Communist China shelled some small islands near the Nationalist Chinese stronghold of Taiwan.

At the same time, Eisenhower sought a thaw in the Cold War through negotiations with the new Soviet leaders who came to power after dictator Joseph Stalin's death in 1953. But the new Soviet premier, Nikita Khrushchev, rudely rejected Ike's heartfelt proposals for peace at the Geneva summit conference in 1955. When Ike called for "open skies" over both the Soviet Union and the United States to prevent either side from miscalculating the other's military intentions, Khrushchev replied, "This is a very transparent espionage device. . . . You could hardly expect us to take this seriously." Eisenhower went home empty-handed.

In the end, the touted "new look" in foreign policy proved illusory. In 1956 the Hungarians rose up against their Soviet masters and appealed in vain to the United States for aid, while Moscow reasserted its domination with the unmistakable language of force. Embittered Hungarian freedom fighters naturally accused Uncle Sam of "welshing" when the chips were down. The truth was that America's mighty nuclear sledgehammer was too heavy a weapon to wield in such a relatively minor crisis. The rigid futility of the "massive retaliation" doctrine was thus starkly exposed. To his dismay, Eisenhower also discovered that the aerial and atomic hardware necessary for "massive retaliation" was staggeringly expensive.

The Vietnam Nightmare

Europe, thanks to the Marshall Plan and NATO, seemed reasonably secure by the early 1950s, but East Asia was a different can of worms. Nationalist movements had sought for years to throw off the French colonial yoke in Indochina. The Vietnamese leader, goateed Ho Chi Minh, had tried to appeal personally to Woodrow Wilson in Paris as early as 1919 to support self-determination for the peoples of Southeast Asia. Franklin Roosevelt had likewise inspired hope among Asian nationalists.

Cold War events dampened the dreams of anticolonial Asian peoples. Their leaders—including Ho Chi Minh—became increasingly communist while the United States became increasingly anticommunist. By 1954 American taxpayers were financing nearly 80 percent of the costs of a bottomless French colonial war in Indochina. The United States' share amounted to about $1 billion a year.

Despite this massive aid, French forces continued to crumble under Viet Minh guerrilla

The Far East, 1955–1956

pressure. In March 1954 a key French garrison was trapped hopelessly in the fortress of Dienbienphu at the northwestern corner of Vietnam. The new "policy of boldness" was now put to the test. Secretary Dulles, Vice President Nixon, and the chairman of the Joint Chiefs of Staff favored intervention with American bombers to help bail out the beleaguered French. But Eisenhower, wary about another war in Asia so soon after Korea and correctly fearing British nonsupport, held back.

Dienbienphu fell to the nationalists, and a multination conference at Geneva roughly halved Vietnam at the seventeenth parallel (see map). The victorious Ho Chi Minh in the north consented to this arrangement on the assurance that Vietnam-wide elections would be held within two years. In the south a pro-Western government under Ngo Dinh Diem was soon entrenched at Saigon. The Vietnamese never held the promised elections, primarily because the communists seemed certain to win, and Vietnam remained a dangerously divided country.

Eisenhower promised economic and military aid to the autocratic Diem regime, provided that it undertook certain social reforms. Change came at a

snail's pace, but American aid continued, as communist guerrillas heated up their campaign against Diem. The Americans had evidently backed a losing horse but could see no easy way to call off their bet.

A False Lull in Europe

The United States had initially backed the French in Indochina in part to win French approval of a plan to rearm West Germany. Despite French fears, the Germans were finally welcomed into the NATO fold in 1955, with an expected contribution of half a million troops. In the same year, the Eastern European countries and the Soviets signed the Warsaw Pact, creating a red military counterweight to the newly bolstered NATO forces in the West.

Despite these hardening military lines, the Cold War seemed to be thawing a bit. Eisenhower earnestly endeavored to cage the nuclear demon by negotiating arms-control agreements with Moscow, and early signs were encouraging. In May 1955 the Soviets rather surprisingly agreed to end the occupation of Austria. A summit conference in July produced little progress on the burning issues, but it bred a conciliatory "spirit of Geneva" that caused a modest blush of optimism to pass over the face of the Western world. Hopes rose further the following year when Soviet Communist party boss Nikita Khrushchev, a burly ex–coal miner, publicly denounced the bloody excesses of Joseph Stalin, the dictator dead since 1953.

Violent events late in 1956 ended the post-Geneva lull. When the liberty-loving Hungarians struck for their freedom, they were ruthlessly overpowered by Soviet tanks. While the Western world looked on in horror, Budapest was turned into a slaughterhouse, and thousands of Hungarian refugees fled their country in panic for the Austrian border. The United States eventually altered its immigration laws to admit thirty thousand Hungarian fugitives.

Menaces in the Middle East

Increasing fears of Soviet penetration into the oil-rich Middle East prompted Washington to take audacious action. The government of Iran, suppos-

Egyptian President Gamal Abdel Nasser, 1954   Shown here greeting exuberant supporters after his election as the first president of the new Egyptian Republic, Nasser was long a thorn in the flesh of American and European policymakers anxious to protect the precious oil resources of the Middle East. By the time he died in 1970, however, his peacemaking efforts with Israel had made him a hero far beyond Egypt's borders.

edly influenced by the Kremlin, began to resist the power of the gigantic Western companies that controlled Iranian petroleum. In response, the American Central Intelligence Agency (CIA) engineered a coup in 1953 that installed the youthful shah of Iran, Mohammed Reza Pahlevi, as a kind of dictator. Though successful in the short run in securing Iranian oil for the West, the American intervention left a bitter legacy of resentment among many Iranians. More than two decades later, they took their revenge on the shah and his American allies (see p. 972).

The Suez crisis proved far messier than the swift stroke in Iran. President Nasser of Egypt, an ardent Arab nationalist, was seeking funds to build an immense dam on the upper Nile for urgently needed irrigation and power. America and Britain tentatively offered financial help, but when Nasser began to flirt openly with the communist camp, Secretary of State Dulles dramatically withdrew the dam offer. Nasser promptly regained face by nationalizing the Suez Canal, owned chiefly by British and French stockholders.

Nasser's action placed a razor's edge at the jugular vein of Western Europe's oil supply. Secretary Dulles labored strenuously to ward off armed intervention by the cornered European powers—as well as by the Soviets, who threatened to match any Western invasion by pouring "volunteers" into Egypt and perhaps by launching nuclear attacks on Paris and London. But the United States' apprehensive French and British allies, deliberately keeping Washington in the dark and coordinating their blow with one from Israel, staged a joint assault on Egypt late in October 1956.

For a breathless week, the world teetered on the edge of the abyss. The French and British, however, had made a fatal miscalculation—that the United States would supply them with oil while their Middle Eastern supplies were disrupted, as an oil-rich Uncle Sam had done in the two world wars. But to their unpleasant surprise, a furious President Eisenhower resolved to let them "boil in their own oil" and refused to release emergency supplies. The oilless allies resentfully withdrew their troops, and for the first time in history, a United Nations police force was sent to maintain order.

The Suez crisis also marked the last time in history that the United States could brandish its "oil weapon." As recently as 1940, the United States had produced two-thirds of the world's oil, while a scant 5 percent of the global supply flowed from the Middle East. But domestic American reserves had been rapidly depleted. In 1948 the United States had become a net oil importer. Its days as an "oil power" clearly were numbered as the economic and strategic importance of the Middle East oil region grew dramatically.

The U.S. president and Congress proclaimed the Eisenhower Doctrine in 1957, pledging U.S. military and economic aid to Middle Eastern nations threatened by communist aggression. The real threat to U.S. interests in the Middle East, however, was not communism but nationalism, as Nasser's wild popularity among the masses of all Arab countries demonstrated. The poor, sandy sheikdoms increasingly resolved to reap for themselves the lion's share of the enormous oil wealth that Western companies pumped out of the scorching Middle Eastern deserts. In a move with portentous implications, Saudi Arabia, Kuwait, Iraq, and Iran joined with Venezuela in 1960 to form the Organization of Petroleum Exporting Countries (OPEC). In the next two decades, OPEC's stranglehold on the Western economies would tighten to a degree that even Nasser could not have imagined.

Round Two for Ike

The election of 1956 was a replay of the 1952 contest, with President Eisenhower—no worse for wear after a heart attack in 1955 and major abdominal surgery in 1956—pitted once more against Adlai Stevenson. Democrats were hard-pressed to find an issue with which to attack the genial general in a time of prosperity and peace, and the voters made it clear that they still liked Ike. Eisenhower piled up an enormous majority of 35,590,472 popular votes to Stevenson's 26,022,752; in the electoral college, the count was even more unbalanced at 457 to 73. But despite the GOP national chairman's boast that "any jockey would look good riding Ike," in fact the general's coattails this time were not so stiff or broad. He failed to win for his party either house of Congress—the first time since Zachary Taylor's election in 1848 that a winning president had headed such a losing ticket.

In fragile health, Eisenhower began his second term as a part-time president. Critics charged that he kept his hands on his golf clubs, fly rod, and shotgun more often than on the levers of power. But in his last years in office, Ike rallied himself to do less golfing and more governing.

A key area in which the president bestirred himself was labor legislation. A drastic labor-reform bill in 1959 grew out of recurrent strikes in critical industries and scandalous revelations of gangsterism in unionist high echelons. In particular, fraud and brass-knuckle tactics tainted the Teamsters Union. The millionaire Teamster chief, "Dave" Beck, invoked the Fifth Amendment against self-incrimination 209 times before a Senate investigat-

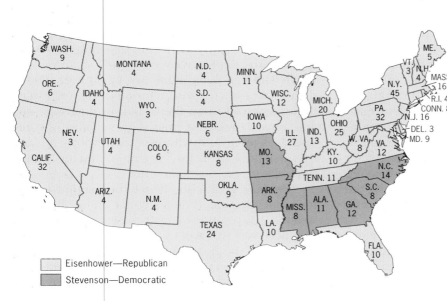

Presidential Election of 1956 (with electoral vote by state) Eisenhower made even deeper inroads into the traditional bastion of Democratic strength, the once-solid South, than he had in 1952. Louisiana went Republican for the first time since Reconstruction days, in 1876.

Competing with the Soviets **903**

ing committee in 1957 to avoid telling what he had done with $320,000. He was later sentenced to prison for embezzlement. When his union defiantly elected the tough-fisted James R. Hoffa as his successor, the AF of L–CIO expelled the Teamsters. The Senate committee reported that in fifteen years, union officials had stolen or misappropriated some $10 million. Hoffa later was jailed for jury tampering, served part of his sentence, and disappeared—evidently the victim of the gangsters whom he had apparently crossed.

Even labor's friends agreed that the house of labor needed a thorough housecleaning. Congress rallied to devise a tough labor-reform bill. Teamster boss Hoffa threatened to defeat for reelection congressional representatives who dared to vote for the proposed labor law. Eisenhower responded with a dramatic television appeal, and Congress in 1959

passed the Landrum-Griffin Act. It was designed to bring labor leaders to book for financial shenanigans and to prevent bullying tactics. Seizing the opportune moment, antilaborites also forced into the bill prohibitions against "secondary boycotts" and certain kinds of picketing.

The Race with the Soviets into Space

Soviet scientists astounded the world on October 4, 1957, by lofting into orbit around the globe a beep-beeping "baby moon" *(Sputnik I)* weighing 184 pounds. A month later they topped their own ace by sending aloft a larger satellite *(Sputnik II)* weighing 1,120 pounds and carrying a dog.

This amazing scientific breakthrough shattered American self-confidence. The Soviets had long been trying to convince the uncommitted nations that the shortcut to superior industrial production lay through communism, and the *Sputnik*s gave credence to their claim. America had seemingly taken a back seat in scientific achievement. Envious "backward" nations laughed at America's discomfiture, all the more so because the Soviets were occupying outer space while American troops were occupying the high school in Little Rock.

Military implications of these human-made satellites proved sobering. If the Soviets could fire heavy objects into outer space, they certainly could reach America with intercontinental ballistic missiles (ICBMs). Old-soldier Eisenhower, adopting a father-knows-best attitude toward the Soviet "gimmick," remarked that it should not cause "one iota" of concern. Others, chiefly Republicans, blamed the Truman administration for having spent more for supporting peanut propagation than for supporting a missile program. Agonizing soul-searching led to the conclusion that while the United States was well advanced on a broad scientific front, including color television, the Soviets had gone all out for rocketry. Experts testified that America's manned bombers were still a powerful deterrent, but heroic efforts were needed if the alleged "missile gap" was not to widen.

"Rocket fever" swept the nation. Eisenhower established the National Aeronautics and Space Administration (NASA) and directed billions of

The Helicopter Era, 1957 President Eisenhower was routinely criticized by liberals, as in this Herblock cartoon in the *Washington Post,* for his apparent indifference to many seething social problems of the day. His failure to employ his vast prestige on behalf of civil rights was especially conspicuous.

dollars to missile development. After humiliating and well-advertised failures—notably the Vanguard missle, which blew up on national television just a few feet above the ground in 1957—in February 1958 the United States managed to put into orbit a grapefruit-sized satellite weighing 2.5 pounds. By the end of the decade, several satellites had been launched, and the United States had successfully tested its own ICBMs.

The *Sputnik* success led to a critical comparison of the American educational system, which was already under fire as too easygoing, with that of the Soviet Union. A strong move now developed in the United States to replace "frills" with solid subjects—to substitute square roots for square dancing. Congress rejected demands for federal scholarships, but late in 1958 the National Defense and Education Act (NDEA) authorized $887 million in loans to needy college students and in grants for the improvement of teaching the sciences and languages.

The Continuing Cold War

The fantastic race toward nuclear annihilation continued unabated. Humanity-minded scientists urged that nuclear tests be stopped before the atmosphere became so polluted as to produce generations of deformed mutants. The Soviets, after completing an intensive series of exceptionally "dirty" tests, proclaimed a suspension in March 1958 and urged the Western world to follow. Beginning in October 1958, Washington did halt both underground and atmospheric testing. But attempts to regularize such suspensions by proper inspection sank on the reef of mutual mistrust.

Thermonuclear suicide seemed nearer in July 1958, when both Egyptian and communist plottings threatened to engulf Western-oriented Lebanon. After its president had called for aid under the Eisenhower Doctrine, the United States boldly landed several thousand troops and helped restore order without taking a single life.

The burly Khrushchev, seeking new propaganda laurels, was eager to meet with Eisenhower and pave the way for a "summit conference" with Western leaders. Despite grave misgivings as to any tangible results, the president invited him to America

What's So Funny? 1960
Premier Khrushchev gloats over Ike's spying discomfiture.

in 1959. Arriving in New York, Khrushchev appeared before the U.N. General Assembly and dramatically resurrected the ancient Soviet proposal of complete disarmament. But he offered no practical means of achieving this end.

A result of this tour was a meeting at Camp David, the presidential retreat in Maryland. Khrushchev emerged saying that his ultimatum for the evacuation of Berlin would be extended indefinitely. The relieved world gave prayerful but premature thanks for the "spirit of Camp David."

The Camp David spirit quickly evaporated when the follow-up Paris "summit conference," scheduled for May 1960, turned out to be an incredible fiasco. Both Moscow and Washington had publicly taken a firm stand on the burning Berlin issue, and neither could risk a public backdown. Then, on the eve of the conference, an American U-2 spy plane was shot down deep in the heart of Russia. After bungling bureaucratic denials in Washington, "honest Ike" took the unprecedented step of assuming personal responsibility. Khrushchev stormed into Paris filling the air with invective, and the conference collapsed before it could get off the ground. The concord of Camp David was replaced with the grapes of wrath.

Cuba's Castroism Spells Communism

Latin Americans bitterly resented Uncle Sam's lavishing of billions of dollars on Europe, while doling out only millions to the poor relations to the south. They also chafed at Washington's continuing habit of intervening in Latin American affairs—as in a CIA-directed coup that ousted a leftist government in Guatemala in 1954. On the other hand, Washington continued to support—even decorate—bloody dictators who claimed to be combating communists.

Most ominous of all was the communist beachhead in Cuba. The ironfisted dictator Fulgencio Batista had encouraged huge investments of American capital, and Washington in turn had given him some support. When black-bearded Dr. Fidel Castro engineered a revolution early in 1959, he denounced the Yankee imperialists and began to expropriate valuable American properties in pursuing a land-distribution program. Washington, finally losing patience, released Cuba from "imperialistic slavery" by cutting off the heavy U.S. imports of Cuban sugar. Castro retaliated with further wholesale confiscations of Yankee property and in effect made his left-wing dictatorship an economic and military satellite of Moscow. An exodus of anti-Castro Cubans headed for the United States, especially Florida. Nearly 1 million arrived between 1960 and 2000. Washington broke diplomatic relations with Cuba early in 1961.

Americans talked seriously of invoking the Monroe Doctrine before the Soviets set up a communist base only ninety miles from their shores. Khrushchev angrily proclaimed that the Monroe Doctrine was dead and indicated that he would shower missiles upon the United States if it attacked his good friend Castro.

The Cuban revolution, which Castro sought to "export" to his neighbors, brought other significant responses. At San Jose, Costa Rica, in August 1960, the United States induced the Organization of American States to condemn (unenthusiastically)

communist infiltration into the Americas. President Eisenhower, whom Castro dubbed "the senile White House golfer," hastily proposed a long-deferred "Marshall Plan" for Latin America. Congress responded to his recommendation with an initial authorization of $500 million. The Latin Americans had Castro to thank for attention that many of them regarded as too little and too late.

Kennedy Challenges Nixon for the Presidency

As Republicans approached the presidential campaign of 1960, Vice President Nixon was their heir apparent. To many he was a gifted party leader, to others a ruthless opportunist. The "old" Nixon had been a no-holds-barred campaigner, especially in assailing Democrats and left-wingers. The "new" Nixon was represented as a mature, seasoned statesman. More in the limelight than any earlier vice president, he had shouldered heavy responsibilities and had traveled globally as a "troubleshooter" in various capacities. He had vigorously defended American democracy in a famous "kitchen debate" with Khrushchev in Moscow in 1959. His supporters, flourishing a telling photograph of this finger-pointing episode, claimed that he alone knew how to "stand up to" the Soviets.

Nixon was nominated unanimously on the first ballot in Chicago. His running mate was the patrician Henry Cabot Lodge, Jr., of Massachusetts (grandson of Woodrow Wilson's arch-foe), who had served conspicuously for seven years as the U.S. representative to the United Nations.

By contrast, the Democratic race for the presidential nomination started as a free-for-all. John F. Kennedy—a tall, youthful, tooth-flashing millionaire senator from Massachusetts—won impressive victories in the primaries. He then scored a first-ballot triumph in Los Angeles over his closest rival, Senator Lyndon B. Johnson, the Senate majority leader from Texas. A disappointed South was not completely appeased when Johnson accepted second place on the ticket in an eleventh-hour marriage of convenience. Kennedy's challenging acceptance speech called upon the American people for sacrifices to achieve their potential greatness, which he hailed as the New Frontier.

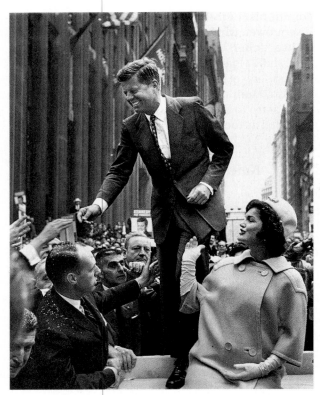

John F. Kennedy Campaigning for the Presidency, 1960
At right is his wife, Jacqueline Kennedy.

Candidate John F. Kennedy (1917–1963), in a speech to a Houston group of Protestant ministers (September 12, 1960), declared,

"I believe in an America where the separation of church and state is absolute—where no Catholic prelate would tell the President, should he be a Catholic, how to act, and no Protestant minister would tell his parishioners for whom to vote . . . and where no man is denied public office because his religion differs from the President who might appoint him or the people who might elect him."

The Presidential Issues of 1960

Bigotry inevitably showed its snarling face. Senator Kennedy was a Roman Catholic, the first to be nominated since Al Smith's ill-starred campaign in 1928. Smear artists revived the ancient charges about the Pope's controlling the White House. Kennedy pointed to his fourteen years of service in Congress, denied that he would be swayed by Rome, and asked if some 40 million Catholic Americans were to be condemned to second-class citizenship from birth.

Kennedy's Catholicism aroused misgivings in the Protestant, Bible Belt South, which was ordinarily Democratic. "I fear Catholicism more than I fear communism," declaimed one Baptist minister in North Carolina. But the religious issue largely canceled itself out. If many southern Democrats stayed away from the polls because of Kennedy's Catholicism, northern Democrats in unusually large numbers supported Kennedy because of the bitter attacks on their Catholic faith.

Kennedy charged that the Soviets, with their nuclear bombs and circling *Sputnik*s, had gained on America in prestige and power. Nixon, forced to defend the dying administration, insisted that the nation's prestige had not slipped, although Kennedy was causing it to do so by his unpatriotic talk.

Television may well have tipped the scales. Nixon agreed to meet Kennedy in four so-called debates. The contestants crossed words in millions of living rooms before audiences estimated at 60 million or more. Nobody "won" the debates. But Kennedy at least held his own and did not suffer by comparison with the more "experienced" Nixon. The debates demonstrated the importance of image in a television age. Many viewers found Kennedy's glamour and vitality far more appealing than Nixon's tired and pallid appearance.

Kennedy squeezed through by the rather comfortable margin of 303 electoral votes to 219,* but with the breathtakingly close popular margin of only 118,574 votes out of over 68 million cast. Like Franklin Roosevelt, Kennedy ran well in the large industrial centers, where he had strong support from workers, Catholics, and African-Americans. (He had solicitously telephoned the pregnant Coretta King, whose husband, Martin Luther King, Jr., was then imprisoned in Georgia for a sit-in.)

---

*Six Democratic electors in Alabama, all eight unpledged Democratic electors in Mississippi, and one Republican elector in Oklahoma voted for Senator Harry F. Byrd.

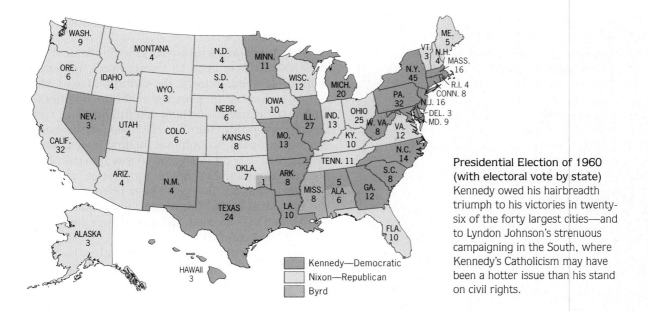

Presidential Election of 1960 (with electoral vote by state) Kennedy owed his hairbreadth triumph to his victories in twenty-six of the forty largest cities—and to Lyndon Johnson's strenuous campaigning in the South, where Kennedy's Catholicism may have been a hotter issue than his stand on civil rights.

Although losing a few seats, the Democrats swept both houses of Congress by wide margins. John Fitzgerald Kennedy—the youngest man to date and the first Catholic to be elected president—was free to set out for his New Frontier, provided that the die-hard conservatives in his party would join the wagon train.

An Old General Fades Away

President Eisenhower continued to enjoy extraordinary popularity to the final curtain. Despite Democratic jibes about "eight years of golfing and goofing," of "putting and puttering," Eisenhower was universally admired and respected for his dignity, decency, sincerity, goodwill, and moderation.

Pessimists had predicted that Eisenhower would be a seriously crippled "lame duck" during his second term, owing to the barrier against reelection erected by the Twenty-second Amendment, ratified in 1951. (See the Appendix.) In truth, he displayed more vigor, more political know-how, and more aggressive leadership during his last two years as president than ever before. For an unprecedented six years, from 1955 to 1961, Congress remained in Democratic hands, yet Eisenhower exerted unusual control over the legislative branch. He wielded the

veto 169 times, and only twice was his nay overridden by the required two-thirds vote.

America was fabulously prosperous in the Eisenhower years, despite pockets of poverty and unemployment, recurrent recessions, and perennial farm problems. "Old Glory" could now proudly display fifty stars. Alaska attained statehood in 1959, as did Hawaii. Alaska, though gigantic, was thinly populated and noncontiguous, but these objections were overcome in a Democratic Congress that expected Alaska to vote Democratic. Hawaii had ample population (largely of Asian descent), advanced democratic institutions, and more acreage than the mainland states of Rhode Island, Delaware, or Connecticut.

Though a crusading general, Eisenhower as president mounted no moral crusade for civil rights. This was perhaps his greatest failing. Yet he was no bigot, and he had done far more than grin away problems and tread water. As a Republican president, he had further woven the reforms of the Democratic New Deal and Fair Deal into the fabric of national life. As a former general, he had exercised wise restraint in his use of military power and had soberly guided foreign policy away from countless threats to peace. The old soldier left office crestfallen at his failure to end the arms race with the Soviets. Yet he had ended one war and avoided all others. As the decades lengthened, appreciation of him grew.

After campaigning with promises to reduce the defense budget, President Dwight Eisenhower (1890–1969) presided over unprecedented increases in military spending. In his Farewell Address on January 17, 1961, he sagely but ironically warned against the menace his own policies had nurtured:

"This conjunction of an immense military establishment and a large arms industry is new in the American experience. . . . In the councils of government, we must guard against the acquisition of unwarranted influence, whether sought or unsought, by the military-industrial complex."

Changing Economic Patterns

The continuing post–World War II economic boom wrought wondrous changes in American society in the 1950s. Prosperity triggered a fabulous surge in home construction, as a nation of renters became a nation of homeowners. One of every four homes standing in America in 1960 had been built during the 1950s, and 83 percent of those new homes were in suburbia.

More than ever, science and technology drove economic growth. The invention of the transistor in 1948 sparked a revolution in electronics, and especially in computers. The first electronic computers assembled in the 1940s were massive machines with hundreds of miles of wiring and thousands of fickle cathode ray tubes. Transistors and, later, printed circuits on silicon wafers made possible dramatic miniaturization and phenomenal computational speed. Computer giant International Business Machines (IBM) expanded robustly, becoming *the* prototype of the "high-tech" corporation in the dawning "information age." Eventually, personal computers and even inexpensive pocket calculators contained more computing power than room-size early models. Computers transformed age-old business practices like billing and inventory control and opened genuine new frontiers in areas

like airline scheduling, high-speed printing, and telecommunications.

Aerospace industries also grew fantastically in the 1950s, thanks both to Eisenhower's aggressive buildup of the Strategic Air Command and to a robustly expanding passenger airline business—and to the connections between military and civilian aircraft production. In 1957 the Seattle-based Boeing Company brought out the first large passenger jet, the "707." Its design owed much to the previous development of SAC's long-range strategic bomber, the B-52. Two years later Boeing delivered the first presidential jet, a specially modified 707. "Air Force One" dazzled President Eisenhower with its speed and comfort.

The nature of the work force was also changing. A sort of quiet revolution was marked in 1956 when "white-collar" workers for the first time outnumbered "blue-collar" workers, signaling the passage from an industrial to a postindustrial era. Keeping pace with that fundamental transformation, organized labor withered along with the smokestack industries that had been its sustenance. Union membership as a percentage of the labor force

An Early Computer, c. 1950 Just a few decades later, technological improvements would bring the computing power of this bulky behemoth to the user's desktop.

Occupational Distribution of Workingwomen, 1900–1998*

	1900	1920	1940	1960	1980	1998
Total white-collar workers[†]	17.8%	38.8%	44.9%	52.5%	65.6%	73.8%
Clerical workers	4.0	18.7	21.5	28.7	30.5	38.9
Manual workers	27.8	23.8	21.6	18.0	14.8	9.7
Farm workers	18.9	13.5	4.0	1.8	1.0	1.0
Service workers[‡]	35.5	23.9	29.4	21.9	18.1	15.4

*Major categories; percentage of all women workers, age fourteen and older, in each category.
[†]Includes clerical, sales, professional, and technical workers, managers and officials.
[‡]Includes domestic servants.
(Sources: *Historical Statistics of the United States* and *Statistical Abstract of the United States,* relevant years.)

peaked at about 35 percent in 1954 and then went into steady decline. Some observers concluded that the union movement had played out its historic role of empowering workers and ensuring economic justice, and that unions would eventually disappear altogether in the postindustrial era.

The surge in white-collar employment opened special opportunities for women. When World War II ended, most women, including those who had worked in war plants, returned to highly conventional female roles as wives and mothers—the remarkably prolific mothers of the huge "baby-boom" generation. A "cult of domesticity" emerged in popular culture to celebrate those eternal feminine functions. When 1950s television programs like "Ozzie and Harriet" or "Leave It to Beaver" depicted idyllic suburban families with a working husband, two children, and a wife who did not work outside the home, they did so without irony; much of middle-class America really did live that way. But as the 1950s progressed, another quiet revolution was gaining momentum that was destined to transform women's roles and even the character of the American family.

Of some 40 million new jobs created in the three decades after 1950, more than 30 million were in clerical and service work. Women filled the huge majority of these new positions. They were the principal employment beneficiaries of the postwar era, creating an extensive "pink-collar ghetto" of occupations that were dominated by women.

Exploding employment opportunities for women in the 1950s unleashed a groundswell of social and psychological shocks that mounted to tidal-wave proportions in the decades that followed. From one perspective, women's surge into the workplace was nothing new at all, but only a return to the days when the United States was an agricultural nation, and men and women alike toiled on the family farm. But the urban age was not the agricultural age, and women's new dual role as *both* workers *and* homemakers raised urgent questions about family life and about traditional definitions of gender differences.

Women in the Labor Force, 1900–2008 (est.)
(Sources: *Historical Statistics of the United States* and *Statistical Abstract of the United States*, relevant years.)

"Ozzie and Harriet" Throughout the 1950s, the storybook Nelson family triumphed weekly on their television program over the travails of parenting and adolescence. In real life, son Ricky (seated, left) later died in a possibly drug-related plane crash while touring with his rock band.

Feminist Betty Friedan gave focus and fuel to women's feelings in 1963 when she published *The Feminine Mystique,* a runaway best-seller and a classic of feminist protest literature that launched the modern women's movement. Friedan spoke in rousing accents to millions of able, educated women who applauded her indictment of the stifling boredom of suburban housewifery. Many of those women were already working for wages, but they were also struggling against the guilt and frustration of leading an "unfeminine" life as defined by the postwar "cult of domesticity."

The Booming Service Sector Services displaced manufacturing as the most dynamic area of the economy in the post–World War II era, and women made up a majority of new workers in the offices, classrooms, sales floors, and hospital wards of the booming service sector.

Consumer Culture in the Fifties

The 1950s witnessed a huge expansion of the middle class and the blossoming of a consumer culture. Diner's Club introduced the plastic credit card in 1950, and four years later the first McDonald's hamburger stand opened in San Bernardino, California. Also in 1955, Disneyland opened its doors in Anaheim, California. These innovations—easy credit, high-volume "fast-food" production, and new forms of recreation—were harbingers of an emerging new lifestyle of leisure and affluence that was in full flower by the decade's end.

Crucial to the development of that lifestyle was the rapid rise of the new technology of television. Only 6 TV stations were broadcasting in 1946; a decade later 442 stations were operating. TV sets were rich people's novelties in the 1940s, but 7 million sets were sold in 1951. By 1960 virtually every American home had one, in a stunning display of the speed with which new technologies can pervade and transform modern societies. Attendance at movies sank as the entertainment industry changed its focus from the silver screen to the picture tube. By the mid-1950s, advertisers annually spent $10 billion to hawk their wares on television, while critics fumed that the wildly popular new mass medium was degrading the public's aesthetic, social, moral, political, and educational standards. To the question, "Why is television called a medium?" pundits replied, "Because it's never rare or well done."

Even religion capitalized on the powerful new electronic pulpit. "Televangelists" like the Baptist Billy Graham, the Pentecostal Holiness preacher Oral Roberts, and the Roman Catholic Fulton J. Sheen took to the airwaves to spread the Christian gospel. Television also catalyzed the commercialization of professional sports, as viewing audiences that once numbered in the stadium-capacity thousands could now be counted in the couch-potato millions.

Sports also reflected the shift in population toward the West and South. In 1958 baseball's New

The Original McDonald's, 1955
Maurice and Richard McDonald's drive-in hamburger stand in San Bernardino, California, became the model for one of the largest franchised restaurant chains in the world.

The King   Rock star Elvis Presley revolutionized popular music in the 1950s.

York Giants moved to San Francisco and the Brooklyn Dodgers abandoned Flatbush for Los Angeles. Those moves touched off a new westward movement of sports franchises. Shifting population and spreading affluence led eventually to substantial expansion of the major baseball leagues and the principal football and basketball leagues as well.

Popular music was dramatically transformed in the fifties. The chief revolutionary was Elvis Presley, a white singer born in 1935 in Tupelo, Mississippi. Fusing black rhythm and blues with white bluegrass and country styles, Elvis created a new musical idiom known forever after as rock and roll. Rock was "crossover" music, carrying its heavy beat and driving rhythms across the cultural divide that separated black and white musical traditions. Listening and dancing to it became a kind of religious rite for the millions of baby boomers coming of age in the 1950s, and Presley—with his fleshy face, pouting lips, and antic, sexually suggestive gyrations—was its high priest. Bloated by fame, fortune, and drugs, he died in 1977 at the age of forty-two.

Traditionalists were repelled by Presley, and they found much more to upset them in the affluent fifties. Movie star Marilyn Monroe, with her ingenuous smile and mandolin-curved hips, helped to popularize—and commercialize—new standards of sensuous sexuality. So did *Playboy* magazine, first published in 1955. As the decade closed, Americans were well on their way to becoming free-spending consumers of mass-produced, standardized products, which were advertised on the electronic medium of television and often sold for their alleged sexual allure.

Many critics lamented the implications of this new consumerist lifestyle. Harvard sociologist David Riesman portrayed the postwar generation as a pack of conformists in *The Lonely Crowd* (1950), as did William H. Whyte, Jr., in *The Organization Man*. Novelist Sloan Wilson explored a similar theme in *The Man in the Gray Flannel Suit* (1955). Harvard economist John Kenneth Galbraith questioned the relation between private wealth and the public good in a series of books beginning with *The Affluent Society* (1958). The postwar explosion of prosperity, Galbraith claimed, had produced a troublesome combination of private opulence amid public squalor. Americans had televisions in their homes but garbage in their streets. They ate rich food but breathed foul air. Galbraith's call for social spending to match private purchasing proved highly influential in the 1960s. Sociologist Daniel Bell, in *The*

Coming of Post-Industrial Society (1973) and *The Cultural Contradictions of Capitalism* (1976), found even deeper paradoxes of prosperity. The hedonistic "consumer ethic" of modern capitalism, he argued, might undermine the older "work ethic" and thus destroy capitalism's very productive capacity. Collusion at the highest levels of the "military-industrial complex" was the subject of *The Power Elite* (1956), an influential piece of modern muckraking by radical sociologist C. Wright Mills, who became a hero to "New Left" student activists in the 1960s.

The Life of the Mind in Postwar America

America's affluence in the heady post–World War II decades was matched by a mother lode of literary gems. In fiction writing some of the prewar realists continued to ply their trade, notably Ernest Hemingway in *The Old Man and the Sea* (1952). A Nobel laureate in 1954, Hemingway was dead by his own duck gun in 1961. John Steinbeck, another prewar writer who persisted in graphic portrayals of American society, such as *East of Eden* (1952) and *Travels with Charley* (1962), received the Nobel Prize for literature in 1962, the seventh American to be so honored.

Curiously, World War II did not inspire the same kind of literary outpouring that World War I had. Searing realism, the trademark style of war writers in the 1920s, characterized the earliest novels that portrayed soldierly life in World War II, such as Norman Mailer's *The Naked and the Dead* (1948) and James Jones's *From Here to Eternity* (1951). But as time passed, realistic writing fell from favor. Authors tended increasingly to write about the war in fantastic and even psychedelic prose. Joseph Heller's *Catch-22* (1961) dealt with the improbable antics and anguish of American airmen in the wartime Mediterranean. A savage satire, it made readers hurt when they laughed. The supercharged imagination of Kurt Vonnegut, Jr., poured forth works of puzzling complexity in sometimes impenetrably inventive prose, including the dark comedy war tale *Slaughterhouse Five* (1969).

The dilemmas created by the new mobility and affluence of American life were explored by Pennsylvania-born John Updike in books like *Rabbit, Run* (1960) and *Couples* (1968), and by Massachusetts-bred John Cheever in *The Wapshot Chronicle* (1957) and *The Wapshot Scandal* (1964). Louis Auchincloss

John Steinbeck (1902–1968)   A college dropout (from Stanford University), Steinbeck wrote naturalistic works about Americans buffeted by forces beyond their control. His most famous work is *The Grapes of Wrath* (1939), a moving tale of the Joad family's migration out of the Oklahoma Dust Bowl to depression-era California.

wrote elegantly about upper-class New Yorkers. Gore Vidal penned a series of intriguing historical novels, as well as several impish and always iconoclastic works, including *Myra Breckinridge* (1968), about a reincarnated transsexual. Together, these writers constituted the rear guard of an older, WASP (white Angle-Saxon Protestant) elite that had long dominated American writing.

Poetry also flowered in the postwar era, though poets were often highly critical, even deeply despairing, about the character of American life. Older poets were still active, including cantankerous Ezra Pound, jailed after the war in a U.S. Army detention center near Pisa, Italy, for alleged collaboration with the Fascists. Connecticut insurance executive Wallace Stevens and New Jersey pediatrician William Carlos Williams continued after 1945 to pursue second careers as prolific poets of world-class stature. But younger poets were coming to the fore during the postwar period. Pacific northwesterner Theodore Roethke wrote lyrically about the

Death of a Salesman First performed in 1949, Arthur Miller's play probed the psychic costs of failure in a society that held out the promise of "success" to all. The play especially resonated with audiences in the booming 1950s, and quickly took its place as an American classic. This scene from the original Broadway production shows Arthur Kennedy as Biff Loman (left) confronting his father Willy, played by Lee J. Cobb (seated), while his brother Happy, performed by Cameron Mitchell, looks on. Not shown here is Willy's compassionate wife Linda, brilliantly acted by Mildred Dunnock.

land until his death by drowning in Puget Sound in 1963. Robert Lowell, descended from a long line of patrician New Englanders, sought to apply the wisdom of the Puritan past to the perplexing present in allegorical poems like *For the Union Dead* (1964). Troubled Sylvia Plath crafted the moving verses of *Ariel* (published posthumously in 1966) and a disturbing novel, *The Bell Jar* (1963), but her career was cut short when she took her own life in 1963. Anne Sexton produced brooding autobiographical poems until her death by apparent suicide in 1974. Another brilliant poet of the period, John Berryman, ended it all in 1972 by leaping from a Minneapolis bridge onto the frozen bank of the Mississippi River. Writing poetry seemed to be a dangerous pursuit in modern America. The life of the poet, it was said, began in sadness and ended in madness.

Playwrights were also active. Tennessee Williams wrote a series of searing dramas about psychological misfits struggling to hold themselves together amid the disintegrating forces of modern life. Noteworthy were *A Streetcar Named Desire* (1947) and *Cat on a Hot Tin Roof* (1955). Arthur Miller brought to the stage searching probes of American values, notably *Death of a Salesman*

(1949) and *The Crucible* (1953), which treated the Salem witch trials as a dark parable warning against the dangers of McCarthyism. Lorraine Hansberry offered an affecting portrait of African-American life in *A Raisin in the Sun* (1959). In the 1960s Edward Albee exposed the rapacious underside of middle-class life in *Who's Afraid of Virginia Woolf?* (1962).

Books by black authors also made the best-seller lists, beginning with Richard Wright's chilling portrait of a black Chicago killer in *Native Son* (1940). Ralph Ellison depicted the black individual's quest for personal identity in *Invisible Man* (1952), one of the most haunting novels of the postwar era. James Baldwin won plaudits as a novelist and essayist, particularly for his sensitive reflections on the racial question in *The Fire Next Time* (1963). Black nationalist LeRoi Jones, who changed his name to Imamu Amiri Baraka, crafted powerful plays like *Dutchman* (1964).

The South boasted a literary renaissance, led by veteran Mississippi author William Faulkner, who was a Nobel recipient in 1950. Fellow Mississippians Walker Percy and Eudora Welty grasped the falling torch from the failing Faulkner, who died in 1962. Tennessean Robert Penn Warren immortalized

Louisiana politico Huey Long in *All the King's Men* (1946). Flannery O'Connor wrote perceptively of her native Georgia, and Virginian William Styron confronted the harsh history of his home state in a controversial fictional representation of an 1831 slave rebellion, *The Confessions of Nat Turner* (1967).

Especially bountiful was the harvest of books by Jewish novelists. Some critics quipped that a knowledge of Yiddish was becoming necessary to understand much of the dialogue presented in modern American novels. J. D. Salinger painted an unforgettable portrait of a sensitive, upper-class, Anglo-Saxon adolescent in *Catcher in the Rye* (1951), but other Jewish writers found their favorite subject matter in the experience of lower- and middle-class Jewish immigrants. Bernard Malamud rendered a touching portrait of a family of New York Jewish storekeepers in *The Assistant* (1957). Malamud also explored the mythic qualities of the culture of base-

ball in *The Natural* (1952). Philip Roth wrote comically about young New Jersey suburbanites in *Goodbye, Columbus* (1959) and penned an uproarious account of a sexually obsessed middle-aged New Yorker in *Portnoy's Complaint* (1969). Chicagoan Saul Bellow contributed masterful sketches of Jewish urban and literary life in landmark books like *The Adventures of Augie March* (1953) and *Herzog* (1962). Bellow became the eighth American Nobel laureate for literature in 1977. Isaac Bashevis Singer immigrated to America from Poland in the 1930s and continued to write in Yiddish. He won the Nobel Prize for literature in 1978. E. L. Doctorow employed Old Testament themes in his fictional account of atomic spies Julius and Ethel Rosenberg, *The Book of Daniel* (1971), and later he imaginatively recast other modern historical materials in books like *Ragtime* (1975), *World's Fair* (1985), and *Billy Bathgate* (1989).

Chronology

1952 Eisenhower defeats Stevenson for presidency
Hemingway publishes *The Old Man and the Sea*

1953 CIA-engineered coup installs shah of Iran

1954 French defeated in Vietnam
Army-McCarthy hearings
Brown v. *Board of Education*
SEATO formed
First McDonald's hamburger stand opens
CIA-sponsored coup in Guatemala

1955 Montgomery bus boycott by blacks begins; emergence of Martin Luther King, Jr.
Geneva summit meeting
Warsaw Pact signed
AF of L merges with CIO
Tennessee Williams's *Cat on a Hot Tin Roof* first performed

1956 Soviets crush Hungarian revolt
Suez crisis
Eisenhower defeats Stevenson for presidency
Mills publishes *The Power Elite*

1957 Little Rock school desegregation crisis
Civil Rights Act passed
Southern Christian Leadership Conference (SCLC) formed
Eisenhower Doctrine
Soviet Union launches *Sputnik* satellites

1958 U.S. troops sent to Lebanon
NDEA authorizes loans and grants for science and language education
Galbraith publishes *The Affluent Society*

1958–
1959 Berlin crisis

1959 Castro leads Cuban revolution
Landrum-Griffin Act
Alaska and Hawaii attain statehood

1960 Sit-in movement for civil rights begins
U-2 incident sabotages Paris summit
OPEC formed
Kennedy defeats Nixon for presidency

For further reading, see page A26 of the Appendix. For web resources, go to **http://college.hmco.com**.

39

The Stormy Sixties

—◦⊱◦—

1960–1968

*Let the word go forth from this time and place, to friend
and foe alike, that the torch has been passed to a
new generation of Americans.*

JOHN F. KENNEDY, INAUGURAL 1961

C omplacent and comfortable as the 1950s closed, Americans elected in 1960 a young, vigorous president who pledged "to get the country moving again." Neither the nation nor the new president had any inkling as the new decade opened just how action-packed it would be, both at home and abroad. The 1960s would bring a sexual revolution, a civil rights revolution, the emergence of a "youth culture," a devastating war in Vietnam, and the beginnings, at least, of a feminist revolution. By the end of the stormy sixties, many Americans would yearn nostalgically for the comparative calm of the fifties.

Kennedy's "New Frontier" Spirit

Hatless and topcoatless in the twenty-two-degree chill, John F. Kennedy delivered a stirring inaugural address on January 20, 1961. Tall, elegantly handsome, speaking crisply and with staccato finger jabs at the air, Kennedy personified the glamour and vitality of the new administration. The youngest president ever elected, he assembled one of the youngest cabinets, including his thirty-five-year-old brother, Robert, as attorney general. "Bobby," the president quipped, would find "some legal experience" useful when he began to practice law. The new attorney general set out, among other reforms, to recast the priorities of the FBI. The bureau deployed nearly a thousand agents on "internal security" work but targeted only a dozen against organized crime and gave virtually no attention to civil rights violations. Robert Kennedy's efforts were stoutly resisted by J. Edgar Hoover, who had served as FBI director longer than the new attorney general had been alive. Business whiz Robert S. McNamara left the presidency of the Ford Motor Company to take over the Defense Department. Along with other youthful, talented advisers, these appointees made up an inner circle of "the best and the brightest" men around the president.

President John F. Kennedy and His Wife, Jacqueline Bouvier Kennedy
Shown here leaving the White House to attend a series of inaugural balls in January 1961, the young and vibrant first couple brought beauty, style, and grace to the presidency.

From the outset Kennedy inspired high expectations, especially among the young. His challenge of a "New Frontier" quickened patriotic pulses. He brought a warm heart to the Cold War when he proposed the Peace Corps, an army of idealistic and mostly youthful volunteers to bring American skills to underdeveloped countries. He summoned citizens to service with his clarion call to "ask not what your country can do for you: ask what you can do for your country."

Himself Harvard-educated, Kennedy and his Ivy League lieutenants (heavily from Harvard) radiated confidence in their abilities. The president's personal grace and wit won him the deep affection of many of his fellow citizens. A journalist called Kennedy "the most seductive man I've ever met. He exuded a sense of vibrant life and humor that seemed naturally to bubble up out of him." In an unprecedented gesture, he invited white-maned poet Robert Frost to speak at his inaugural ceremonies. The old Yankee versifier shrewdly took stock of the situation. "You're something of Irish and I suppose something of Harvard," he told Kennedy—and advised him to be more Irish than Harvard.

The New Frontier at Home

Kennedy came into office with fragile Democratic majorities in Congress. Southern Democrats threatened to team up with Republicans and ax New Frontier proposals such as medical assistance for the aged and increased federal aid to education. Kennedy won a first round in his campaign for a more cooperative Congress when he forced an expansion of the all-important House Rules Committee, dominated by conservatives who could have bottled up his entire legislative program. Despite this victory, the New Frontier did not expand swiftly. Key medical and education bills remained stalled in Congress.

Another vexing problem was the economy. Kennedy had campaigned on the theme of revitalizing the economy after the recessions of the Eisenhower years. While his advisers debated the best kind of economic medicine to apply, the president tried to hold the line against crippling inflation. His

Richard Goodwin (b. 1931), a young Peace Corps staffer, eloquently summed up the buoyantly optimistic mood of the early 1960s:

"For a moment, it seemed as if the entire country, the whole spinning globe, rested, malleable and receptive, in our beneficent hands."

On the Moon   (left) This moon's-eye view of the earth greeted the first men to land on the lunar surface. (right) Astronaut Edwin ("Buzz") Aldrin poses with a stretched U.S. flag on the windless moon. His companion, Neil Armstrong, said as he stepped from the spacecraft, "That's one small step for man; one giant leap for mankind."

administration helped negotiate a noninflationary wage agreement in the steel industry in early 1962. The assumption was that the companies, for their part, would keep the lid on prices.

Almost immediately, steel management announced significant price increases, thereby seemingly demonstrating bad faith. The president erupted in wrath, remarking that his father had once said that "all businessmen were sons of bitches." He called the "big steel" men onto the Oval Office carpet and unleashed his Irish temper. Overawed, the steel operators backed down, while displaying "S.O.B." buttons, meaning "Sons of Business" or "Save Our Business."

The steel episode provoked fiery attacks by big business on the New Frontier, but Kennedy soon appealed to believers in free enterprise when he announced his support of a general tax-cut bill. He rejected the advice of those who wished greater government spending and instead chose to stimulate the economy by slashing taxes and putting more money directly into private hands. When he announced his policy before a big business group, one observer called it "the most Republican speech since McKinley."

For economic stimulus, as well as for military strategy and scientific prestige, Kennedy also promoted a multibillion-dollar project to land an American on the moon. When skeptics objected that the money could best be spent elsewhere, Kennedy "answered" them in a speech at Rice University in Texas: "But why, some say, the moon? . . . And they may well ask, why climb the highest mountain? Why, thirty-five years ago, fly the Atlantic? Why does Rice play Texas?" Twenty-four billion dollars later, in 1969, two American astronauts triumphantly planted human footprints on the moon's dusty surface.

Rumblings in Europe

A few months after settling into the White House, the new president met Soviet premier Khrushchev at Vienna in June 1961. The tough-talking Soviet leader adopted a belligerent attitude, threatening to make a treaty with East Germany and cut off Western access to Berlin. Though visibly shaken, the president refused to be bullied.

The Soviets backed off from their most bellicose threats but suddenly began to construct the Berlin Wall in August 1961. A barbed-wire and concrete barrier, it was designed to plug the heavy population drain from East Germany to West Germany through the Berlin funnel. But to the free world, the "Wall of Shame" looked like a gigantic enclosure around a concentration camp. The Wall stood for almost three decades as an ugly scar symbolizing the post–World War II division of Europe into two hostile camps.

Kennedy meanwhile turned his attention to Western Europe, now miraculously prospering after the tonic of Marshall Plan aid and the growth of the American-encouraged Common Market, the free-trade area later called the European Union. He finally secured passage of the Trade Expansion Act in 1962, authorizing tariff cuts of up to 50 percent to promote trade with Common Market countries. This legislation led to the so-called Kennedy Round of tariff negotiations, concluded in 1967, and to a significant expansion of European-American trade.

But not all of Kennedy's ambitious designs for Europe were realized. American policymakers were dedicated to an economically and militarily united "Atlantic Community," with the United States the dominant partner. But they found their way blocked by towering, stiff-backed Charles de Gaulle, president of France. He was suspicious of American intentions in Europe and on fire to recapture the *gloire* of Napoleonic France. With a haughty *"non,"* he vetoed British application for Common Market membership in 1963, fearing that the British "special relationship" with the United States would make Britain a Trojan horse for deepening American control over European affairs. He likewise dashed cold water on a U.S. proposal to develop a multinational nuclear arm within NATO. De Gaulle deemed the Americans unreliable in a crisis, so he tried to preserve French freedom of action by developing his own small atomic force ("farce," scoffed his critics). Despite the perils of nuclear proliferation or Soviet domination, de Gaulle demanded an independent Europe, free of Yankee influence.

Foreign Flare-ups and "Flexible Response"

Special problems for U.S. foreign policy emerged from the worldwide decolonization of European overseas possessions after World War II. The African

The Berlin Wall, 1961–1989   The wall separating East and West Berlin stood for nearly thirty years as a hated symbol of the division of Europe into democratic and communist camps. Demonstrators celebrating the impending reunification of East and West Germany began to tear it down at last in 1989.

Congo received its independence from Belgium in 1960 and immediately exploded into violence. The United Nations sent in a peacekeeping force, to which Washington contributed much money but no manpower. The United States was picking up the tab for U.N. operations, while the organization itself was becoming dominated by the numerous nascent nations emerging in once-colonial Asia and Africa, which were often critical of U.S. foreign policy.

Sparsely populated Laos, freed of its French colonial overlords in 1954, was festering dangerously by the time Kennedy came into office. The Eisenhower administration had drenched this jungle kingdom with dollars but failed to cleanse the country of an aggressive communist element. A red Laos, many observers feared, would be a river on which the influence of Communist China would flood into all of Southeast Asia.

As the Laotian civil war raged, Kennedy's military advisers seriously considered sending in American troops. But the president found that he had insufficient forces to put out the fire in Asia and still honor his commitments in Europe. Kennedy thus sought a diplomatic escape hatch in the fourteen-power Geneva conference, which imposed a shaky peace on Laos in 1962.

These "brushfire wars" intensified the pressure for a shift away from Secretary Dulles's dubious doctrine of "massive retaliation." Kennedy felt hamstrung by the knowledge that in a crisis, he had the Devil's choice between humiliation and nuclear incineration. With Defense Secretary McNamara, he pushed the strategy of "flexible response"—that is, developing an array of military "options" that could be precisely matched to the gravity of the crisis at hand. To this end Kennedy increased spending on conventional military forces and bolstered the Special Forces (Green Berets). They were an elite antiguerrilla outfit trained to survive on snake meat and to kill with scientific finesse.

Stepping into the Vietnam Quagmire

The doctrine of "flexible response" seemed sane enough, but it contained lethal logic. It potentially lowered the level at which diplomacy would give way to shooting. It also provided a mechanism for a progressive, and possibly endless, stepping-up of

Backbone The United States supports South Vietnam.

the use of force. Vietnam soon presented grisly proof of these pitfalls.

The corrupt, right-wing Diem government in Saigon, despite a deluge of American dollars, had ruled shakily since the partition of Vietnam in 1954 (see p. 900). Anti-Diem agitators noisily threatened to topple the pro-American government from power. In a fateful decision late in 1961, Kennedy ordered a sharp increase in the number of "military advisers" (U.S. troops) in South Vietnam.

American forces had allegedly entered Vietnam to foster political stability—to help protect Diem from the communists long enough to allow him to enact basic social reforms favored by the Americans. But the Kennedy administration eventually despaired of the reactionary Diem and encouraged a successful coup against him in November 1963. Ironically, the United States thus contributed to a long process of political disintegration that its original policy had meant to prevent. Kennedy still told the South Vietnamese that it was "their war," but he had made dangerously deep political commit-

Vietnam and Southeast Asia, 1954–1975

ments. By the time of his death, he had ordered more than fifteen thousand American men into the far-off Asian slaughterpen. A graceful pullout was becoming increasingly difficult.

Cuban Confrontations

Although the United States regarded Latin America as its backyard, its southern neighbors feared and resented the powerful Colossus of the North. In 1961 Kennedy extended the hand of friendship with the Alliance for Progress *(Alianza para el Progreso)*, hailed as a Marshall Plan for Latin America. A primary goal was to help the Good Neighbors close the gap between the callous rich and the wretched poor,

and thus quiet communist agitation. But results were disappointing; there was little alliance and even less progress. American handouts had little positive impact on Latin America's immense social problems.

President Kennedy also struck below the border with the mailed fist. He had inherited from the Eisenhower administration a CIA-backed scheme to topple Fidel Castro from power by invading Cuba with anticommunist exiles. Trained and armed by Americans and supported by American air power, the invaders would trigger a popular uprising in Cuba and sweep to victory—or so the planners predicted.

On April 17, 1961, some twelve hundred exiles landed at Cuba's Bay of Pigs. Kennedy had decided from the outset against *direct* intervention, and the ancient aircraft of the anti-Castroites were no match

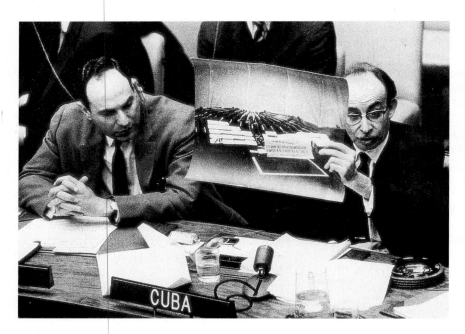

Failed Bay of Pigs Invasion, 1961 The Cuban Foreign Minister showed United Nations' delegates photographs of arms he said the United States had supplied for the Bay of Pigs invasion on April 17. The debacle was one of several unsuccessful American efforts to overthrow Cuban leader Fidel Castro.

for Castro's air force. In addition, no popular uprising greeted the invaders. With the invasion bogged down at the Bay of Pigs, Kennedy stood fast in his decision to keep hands off, and the bullet-riddled band of anti-Castroites surrendered. Most of the invaders rotted for two years in Cuban jails but were eventually "ransomed" for some $62 million worth of American pharmaceutical drugs and other humanitarian supplies. President Kennedy assumed full responsibility for the failure, remarking that "victory has a hundred fathers, and defeat is an orphan."

The Bay of Pigs blunder, along with continuing American covert efforts to assassinate Castro and overthrow his government, naturally pushed the Cuban leader even further into the Soviet embrace. Wily Chairman Khrushchev lost little time in taking full advantage of his Cuban comrade's position just ninety miles off Florida's coast. In October 1962 the aerial photographs of American spy planes revealed that the Soviets were secretly and speedily installing nuclear-tipped missiles in Cuba. The Soviets evidently intended to use these devastating weapons to shield Castro and to blackmail the United States into backing down in Berlin and other trouble spots.

Kennedy and Khrushchev now began a nerve-racking game of "nuclear chicken." The president flatly rejected air force proposals for a "surgical" bombing strike against the missile-launching sites. Instead, on October 22, 1962, he ordered a naval

"quarantine" of Cuba and demanded immediate removal of the threatening weaponry. He also served notice on Khrushchev that any attack on the United States from Cuba would be regarded as coming from the Soviet Union and would trigger nuclear retaliation against the Russian heartland.

For an anxious week, Americans waited while Soviet ships approached the patrol line established by the U.S. Navy off the island of Cuba. Seizing or sinking a Soviet vessel on the high seas would unquestionably be regarded by the Kremlin as an act of war. The world teetered breathlessly on the brink of global atomization. Only in 1991 did the full dimensions of this nuclear peril become known, when the Russians revealed that their ground forces in Cuba already had operational nuclear weapons at their disposal and were authorized to launch them if attacked.

In this tense eyeball-to-eyeball confrontation, Khrushchev finally flinched. On October 28 he agreed to a partially face-saving compromise, by which he would pull the missiles out of Cuba. The United States in return agreed to end the quarantine and not invade the island. The American government also quietly signaled that it would remove from Turkey some of its own missiles targeted on the Soviet Union.

Fallout from the Cuban missile crisis was considerable. A disgraced Khrushchev was ultimately hounded out of the Kremlin and became an "unperson." Hard-liners in Moscow, vowing never again to be humiliated in a nuclear face-off, launched an enormous program of military expansion. The Soviet buildup reached a crescendo in the next decade, stimulating, in turn, a vast American effort to "catch up with the Russians." The Democrats did better than expected in the midterm elections of November 1962—allegedly because the Republicans were "Cubanized." Kennedy, apparently sobered by the appalling risks he had just run, pushed harder for a nuclear test-ban treaty with the Soviet Union. After prolonged negotiations in Moscow, a pact prohibiting trial nuclear explosions in the atmosphere was signed in late 1963. Another barometer indicating a thaw in the Cold War was the installation (August 1963) of a Moscow-Washington "hot line," permitting immediate teletype communication in case of crisis.

Most significant was Kennedy's speech at American University, Washington, D.C., in June 1963. The president urged Americans to abandon a view of the Soviet Union as a Devil-ridden land filled with fanatics and instead to deal with the world "as it is, not as it might have been had the history of the last eighteen years been different." Kennedy thus tried to lay the foundations for a realistic policy of peaceful coexistence with the Soviet Union. Here were the modest origins of the policy that later came to be known as "détente" (French for "relaxation").

The Struggle for Civil Rights

Kennedy had campaigned with a strong appeal to black voters, but he proceeded gingerly to redeem his promises. Although he had pledged to eliminate racial discrimination in housing "with a stroke of the pen," it took him nearly two years to find the right pen. Civil rights groups meanwhile sent thousands of pens to the White House in an "Ink for Jack" protest against the president's slowness.

Political concerns stayed the president's hand on civil rights. Elected by a wafer-thin margin, and with shaky control over Congress, Kennedy needed the support of southern legislators to pass his economic and social legislation, especially his medical and educational bills. He believed, perhaps justifiably, that those measures would eventually benefit black Americans at least as much as specific legislation on civil rights. Bold moves for racial justice would have to wait.

But events soon scrambled these careful calculations. Following the wave of sit-ins that surged across the South in 1960, groups of Freedom Riders fanned out to end segregation in facilities serving interstate bus passengers. A white mob torched a Freedom Ride bus near Anniston, Alabama, in May 1961, and Attorney General Robert Kennedy's

Freedom Ride, 1961
Rampaging whites near Anniston, Alabama, burned this bus carrying an interracial group of Freedom Riders on May 14, 1961.

personal representative was beaten unconscious in another anti–Freedom Ride riot in Montgomery. When southern officials proved unwilling or unable to stem the violence, Washington dispatched federal marshals to protect the Freedom Riders.

Reluctantly but fatefully, the Kennedy administration had now joined hands with the civil rights movement. Because of that partnership, the Kennedys proved ultra-wary about the political associates of Martin Luther King, Jr. Fearful of embarrassing revelations that some of King's advisers had communist affiliations, Robert Kennedy ordered FBI director J. Edgar Hoover to wiretap King's phone in late 1963. But for the most part, the relationship between King and the Kennedys was a fruitful one. Encouraged by Robert Kennedy, and with financial backing from Kennedy-prodded private foundations, SNCC and other civil rights groups inaugurated a Voter Education Project to register the South's historically disfranchised blacks. Because of his support for civil rights, President Kennedy told a group of black leaders in 1963, "I may lose the next election . . . I don't care."

Integrating southern universities threatened to provoke wholesale slaughter. Some desegregated painlessly, but the University of Mississippi ("Ole Miss") became a volcano. A twenty-nine-year-old air force veteran, James Meredith, encountered violent opposition when he attempted to register in October 1962. In the end President Kennedy was

> *In his civil rights address of June 11, 1963, President John F. Kennedy (1917–1963) said,*
>
> "If an American, because his skin is dark, cannot eat lunch in a restaurant open to the public; if he cannot send his children to the best public school available; if he cannot vote for the public officials who represent him; if, in short, he cannot enjoy the full and free life which all of us want, then who among us would be content to have the color of his skin changed and stand in his place?"

forced to send in 400 federal marshals and 3,000 troops to enroll Meredith in his first class—in colonial American history. He ultimately graduated, with a sheepskin that cost the lives of 2 men, scores of injuries, and some 4 million taxpayer dollars.

In the spring of 1963, Martin Luther King, Jr., launched a campaign against discrimination in Birmingham, Alabama, the most segregated big city in America. Although blacks constituted nearly half of the city's population, they made up fewer than 15 percent of the city's voters. Previous attempts to crack the city's rigid racial barriers had produced more than fifty cross burnings and eighteen bomb

Hosing Down Civil Rights Demonstrators, Birmingham, Alabama, 1963

EXAMINING THE EVIDENCE

Conflicting Press Accounts of the "March on Washington," 1963 The day after the March on Washington of August 28, 1963 (see p. 926), newspapers all over the country carried reports of this historic assembly of more than 200,000 people to demand civil rights and equal job opportunities for African-Americans. Although the basic outlines of the story were the same in most papers, ancillary articles, photographs, and editorials revealed deep-seated biases in coverage. Shown here are continuations from the front page stories in *The New York Times*, a bastion of northeastern liberalism (below), and *The Atlanta Constitution*, a major southern newspaper (right). While the *Times* called the march "orderly" in its headline, the *Constitution*'s story in its right columns highlighted the potential for violence and the precautions taken by police. The article read: "There was such a force of uniformed officers on hand to cope with any possible trouble that one senator was prompted to comment: 'It almost looks like we had a military coup d'état during the night.'" In addition to stressing the march's potential for disruption, the *Constitution* ran an advertisement right below the March on Washington story for a National Ku Klux Klan Rally two days hence, featuring prominent speakers and a cross burning. This comparison of newspaper coverage of a controversial event serves as a reminder that press reporting must always be scrutinized for biases when it is used as historical evidence. What other differences in coverage separated these two newspapers? What factors contribute to press biases?

March a Big Boost for Bill, Kennedy Tells 10 Leaders

Continued From Page 1

PREDICTS PASSAGE

JUBILANT AT PEACE

SKIRT CAPITOL AREA

DIRKSEN UNYIELDING

ASSURED BY McCORMICK

Dr. King Names Ex-Red Cross Official as Aide

A former official of the American Red Cross has been appointed special assistant to Dr. Martin Luther King Jr., president of the Southern Christian Leadership Conference.

SCLC announced the appointment of Harry G. Boyte, 52, of Atlanta, who served 17 years with the Red Cross.

Boyte was born in Charlotte, N.C. He joined the Red Cross in 1942 and subsequently became administrative assistant chief of personnel.

(PAID ADVERTISEMENT)

(below) *The New York Times;* (right) *The Atlanta Constitution*

200,000 Join Orderly March in Capital for Civil Rights; Kennedy Sees Negro Gain

LEADERS OF RALLY URGE ACTION 'NOW'

Ask Laws Against Inequity —Picnic Air Prevails as Crowds Clap and Sing

Continued From Page 1, Col. 8

President Meets March Chiefs; Urges Bipartisan Aid on Rights

Continued From Page 1, Col. 7

[newspaper article text, partially legible]

Randolph Lauds Wilkins

LEADERS MEET WITH KENNEDY: From left Whitney M. Young Jr., of National Urban League; the Rev. Dr. Martin Luther King Jr., Southern Christian Leadership Conference; John Lewis, partly hidden, Student Nonviolent Coordinating Committee; Rabbi Joachim Prinz, American Jewish Congress; the Rev. Dr. Eugene Carson Blake, United Presbyterian Church in U.S.A.; A. Philip Randolph, Negro American Labor Council; the President; Walter P. Reuther, the United Automobile Workers; Vice President Johnson, almost hidden, and Roy Wilkins, N.A.A.C.P. Mr. Kennedy and Mr. Johnson met with leaders of the civil rights march at the White House after the ceremonies at the Lincoln Memorial.

Martin Luther King, Jr., Addresses the March on Washington, August 1963 This was the occasion of King's famous "I Have a Dream" speech, in which he declared, "When the architects of our great republic wrote the magnificent words of the Constitution and the Declaration of Independence, they were signing a promissory note to which every American was to fall heir. This note was a promise that all men, yes, black men as well as white men, would be guaranteed the inalienable rights of life, liberty, and the pursuit of happiness."

attacks since 1957. "Some of the people sitting here will not come back alive from this campaign," King advised his organizers. Events soon confirmed this grim prediction of violence. Watching developments on television screens, a horrified world saw peaceful civil rights marchers repeatedly repelled by police with attack dogs and electric cattle prods. Most fearsome of all were the high-pressure water hoses directed at the civil rights demonstrators. They delivered water with enough force to knock bricks loose from buildings or strip bark from trees at a distance of one hundred feet. Water from the hoses bowled little children down the street like tumbleweed.

Jolted by these vicious confrontations, President Kennedy delivered a memorable televised speech to the nation on June 11, 1963. In contrast to Eisenhower's cool aloofness from the racial question, Kennedy called the situation a "moral issue" and committed his personal and presidential prestige to finding a solution. Drawing on the same spiritual traditions as Martin Luther King, Jr., Kennedy declared that the principle at stake "is as old as the Scriptures and is as clear as the American Constitution." He called for new civil rights legislation to protect black citizens. In August King led 200,000 black and white demonstrators on a peaceful "March on Washington" in support of the proposed legislation. In an electrifying speech from the Lincoln Memorial, King declared, "I have a dream that my four little children will one day live in a nation where they will not be judged by the color of their skin, but by the content of their character."

Still the violence continued. On the very night of Kennedy's stirring television address, a white gunman shot down Medgar Evers, a black Mississippi civil rights worker. In September 1963 an explosion blasted a Baptist church in Birmingham, killing four black girls who had just finished their lesson called "The Love That Forgives." By the time of Kennedy's death, his civil rights bill was making little headway, and frustrated blacks were growing increasingly impatient.

The Killing of Kennedy

Violence haunted America in the mid-1960s, and it stalked onto center stage on November 22, 1963. While riding in an open limousine in downtown Dallas, Texas, President Kennedy was shot in the brain by a concealed rifleman and died within seconds. As a stunned nation grieved, the tragedy grew still more unbelievable. The alleged assassin, a furtive figure named Lee Harvey Oswald, was himself shot to death in front of television cameras by a self-appointed avenger, Jack Ruby. So bizarre were the events surrounding the two murders that even an elaborate official investigation conducted by Chief Justice Warren could not quiet all doubts and theories about what had really happened.

Vice President Johnson was promptly sworn in as president on a waiting airplane and flown back to Washington with Kennedy's body. Although he mistrusted "the Harvards," Johnson retained most of the bright Kennedy team. The new president managed a dignified and efficient transition, pledging continuity with his slain predecessor's policies.

For several days the nation was steeped in sorrow. Not until then did many Americans realize how fully their young, vibrant president and his captivating wife had cast a spell over them. Chopped down in his prime after only slightly more than a thousand days in the White House, Kennedy was acclaimed more for the ideals he had enunciated and the spirit he had kindled than for the concrete goals he had achieved. He had laid one myth to rest forever—that a Catholic could not be trusted with the presidency of the United States.

In later years revelations about Kennedy's womanizing and allegations about his involvement with organized crime figures tarnished his reputation. But despite those accusations, his vigor, charisma, and idealism made him an inspirational figure for the generation of Americans who came of age in the 1960s—including Bill Clinton, who as a boy had briefly met President Kennedy and would himself be elected president in 1992.

The LBJ Brand on the Presidency

The torch passed to craggy-faced Lyndon Baines Johnson, a Texan who towered six feet three inches. The new president hailed from the populist hill country of west Texas, whose people had first sent him to Washington as a twenty-nine-year-old congressman in 1937. Franklin D. Roosevelt was his political "Daddy," Johnson claimed, and he had supported New Deal measures down the line. But when LBJ lost a Senate race in 1941, he learned the sobering lesson that liberal political beliefs did not necessarily win elections in Texas. He trimmed his sails to the right and squeezed himself into a Senate seat in 1948 with a questionable eighty-seven-vote margin—hence the ironic nickname "Landslide Lyndon."

Entrenched in the Senate, Johnson developed into a masterful wheeler-dealer. He became the

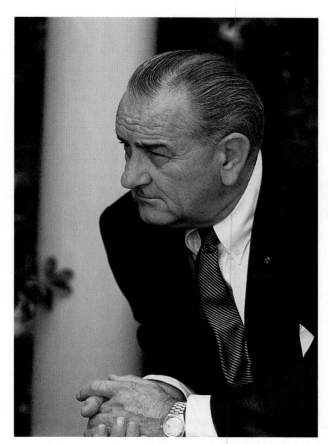

President Lyndon Baines Johnson (1908–1973)
Dedicated and hard-working, Johnson saw his presidency shattered by the trauma of Vietnam. By the end of his term, he was so unpopular that he could find nonheckling audiences only on military bases or navy ships.

Democratic majority leader in 1954, wielding power second only to that of Eisenhower in the White House. He could move mountains or checkmate opponents as the occasion demanded, using what came to be known as the "Johnson treatment"—a flashing display of backslapping, flesh-pressing, and arm-twisting that overbore friend and foe alike. His ego and vanity were legendary. On a visit to the Pope, Johnson was presented with a precious fourteenth-century painting from the Vatican art collection; in return, LBJ gave the Pope a bust—of LBJ!

As president, Johnson quickly shed the conservative coloration of his Senate years to reveal the latent liberal underneath. "No memorial oration or eulogy," Johnson declared to Congress, "could more eloquently honor President Kennedy's memory than the earliest possible passage of the Civil Rights Bill for which he fought so long." After a lengthy conservative filibuster, Congress at last passed the landmark Civil Rights Act of 1964. The act banned racial discrimination in most private facilities open to the public, including theaters, hospitals, and restaurants. It strengthened the federal government's power to end segregation in schools and other public places. It created the federal Equal Employment Opportunity Commission (EEOC) to eliminate discrimination in hiring. When conservatives tried to derail the legislation by adding a prohibition on *sexual,* as well as racial, discrimination, the tactic backfired. The bill's opponents cynically calculated that liberals would not be able to support a bill that threatened to wipe out laws that singled out women for special protection because of their sex. But the act's Title VII passed with the sexual clause intact. It soon proved to be a powerful instrument of federally enforced gender equality, as well as racial equality. Johnson struck another blow for women and minorities in 1965 when he issued an executive order requiring all federal contractors to take "affirmative action" against discrimination.

Johnson also rammed Kennedy's stalled tax bill through Congress and added proposals of his own

for a billion-dollar "War on Poverty." Johnson voiced special concern for Appalachia, where the sickness of the soft-coal industry had left tens of thousands of mountain folk on the human slag heap.

Johnson dubbed his domestic program the "Great Society"—a sweeping set of New Dealish economic and welfare measures aimed at transforming the American way of life. Public support for LBJ's antipoverty war was aroused by Michael Harrington's *The Other America* (1962), which revealed that in affluent America 20 percent of the population—and over 40 percent of the black population—suffered in poverty.

Johnson Battles Goldwater in 1964

Johnson's nomination by the Democrats in 1964 was a foregone conclusion; he was chosen by acclamation in Atlantic City as his birthday present. Thanks to the tall Texan, the Democrats stood foursquare on their most liberal platform since Truman's Fair Deal days. The Republicans, convening in San Francisco's Cow Palace, nominated box-jawed Senator Barry Goldwater of Arizona, a bronzed and bespectacled champion of rock-ribbed conservatism. The

Presidential Election of 1964 States are distorted according to the number of electoral votes indicated on each state. In New Orleans, toward the end of the campaign, a gutsy Johnson displayed his commitment to civil rights when he told a story about an old senator who once said of his Deep South constituents, "I would like to go back down there and make them just one more Democratic speech. . . . The poor old State, they haven't heard a Democratic speech in 30 years. All they hear at election time is Negro, Negro, Negro!" Johnson's open voicing of sentiments like this contributed heavily to his losses in the traditionally Democratic "solid South."

Johnson–Democratic
Goldwater–Republican

American stage was thus set for a historic clash of political principles.

Goldwater's forces had galloped out of the Southwest to ride roughshod over the moderate Republican "eastern establishment." Insisting that the GOP offer "a choice not an echo," Goldwater attacked the federal income tax, the Social Security system, the Tennessee Valley Authority, civil rights legislation, the nuclear test-ban treaty, and, most loudly, the Great Society. His fiercely dedicated followers proclaimed, "In Your Heart You Know He's Right," which prompted the Democratic response, "In Your Guts You Know He's Nuts." Goldwater warmed right-wing hearts when he announced that "extremism in the defense of liberty is no vice. And . . . moderation in the pursuit of justice is no virtue."

Democrats gleefully exploited the image of Goldwater as a trigger-happy cowboy who would "Barry us" in the debris of World War III. Johnson cultivated the contrasting image of a resolute statesman by seizing upon the Tonkin Gulf episode early in August 1964. Unbeknownst to the American public or Congress, U.S. Navy ships had been cooperating with South Vietnamese gunboats in provocative raids along the coast of North Vietnam. Two of these American destroyers were allegedly fired upon by the North Vietnamese on August 2 and 4, although exactly what happened still remains unclear. Later investigations strongly suggested that the North Vietnamese fired in self-defense on August 2 and that the "attack "of August 4 never happened. Johnson later reportedly wisecracked, "For all I know, the Navy was shooting at whales out there."

Johnson nevertheless promptly called the attack "unprovoked" and moved swiftly to make political hay out of this episode. He ordered a "limited" retaliatory air raid against the North Vietnamese bases, loudly proclaiming that he sought "no wider war"—thus implying that the truculent Goldwater did. Johnson also used the incident to spur congressional passage of the all-purpose Tonkin Gulf Resolution. With only two dissenting votes in both houses, the lawmakers virtually abdicated their war-declaring powers and handed the president a blank check to use further force in Southeast Asia. The Tonkin Gulf Resolution, Johnson boasted, was "like grandma's nightshirt—it covered everything."

The towering Texan rode to a spectacular victory in November 1964. The voters were herded into Johnson's column by fondness for the Kennedy legacy, faith in Great Society promises, and fear of Goldwater. A stampede of 43,129,566 Johnson votes trampled the Republican ticket with its 27,178,188 supporters. The tally in the Electoral College was 486 to 52. Goldwater carried only his native Arizona and five other states—all of them, significantly, in the racially restless South. This cracking of the once solidly Democratic South afforded the Republicans about the only faint light in an otherwise bleak political picture. Johnson's record-breaking 61 percent of the popular vote swept lopsided Democratic majorities into both houses of Congress.

The Great Society Congress

Johnson's huge victory temporarily smashed the conservative congressional coalition of southern Democrats and northern Republicans. A wide-open legislative road stretched before the Great Society programs, as the president skillfully ringmastered his two-to-one Democratic majorities. Congress poured out a flood of legislation, comparable only to the output of the New Dealers in the Hundred Days Congress of 1933. Johnson, confident that a growing economy gave him ample fiscal and political room for maneuver, delivered at last on long-deferred Democratic promises of social reform.

Escalating the War on Poverty, Congress doubled the appropriation of the Office of Economic Opportunity to $2 billion and granted more than $1 billion to redevelop the gutted hills and hollows of Appalachia. A tireless Johnson also prodded the Congress into creating two new cabinet offices: the Department of Transportation and the Department of Housing and Urban Development (HUD), to which he named the first black cabinet secretary in the nation's history, respected economist Robert C. Weaver. Other noteworthy laws established the National Endowments for the Arts and the Humanities, designed to lift the level of American cultural life.

Even more impressive were the Big Four legislative achievements that crowned LBJ's Great Society program: aid to education, medical care for the elderly and indigent, immigration reform, and a new voting rights bill.

Johnson neatly avoided the thorny question of separation of church and state by channeling educational aid to students, not schools, thus allowing funds to flow to hard-pressed parochial institutions.

Giving Thanks for Medicare
An elderly woman showed her gratitude to President Lyndon B. Johnson for his signing of the Medicare bill in April 1965, providing basic medical care for the aged. In tribute to former President Truman's unsuccessful effort to pass a national medical insurance program twenty years earlier, Johnson flew to Truman's Missouri home to sign the bill that he claimed would deliver "care for the sick and serenity for the fearful." No one acknowledged that Truman's earlier plan had been much more comprehensive or that Johnson, then a young Texas congressman, had opposed it.

(Catholic John F. Kennedy had not dared to touch this prickly issue.) With a keen eye for the dramatic, LBJ signed the education bill in the humble one-room Texas schoolhouse he had attended as a boy.

Medicare for the elderly, accompanied by Medicaid for the poor, became a reality in 1965. Although they were bitter pills for the American Medical Association to swallow, the new programs were welcomed by millions of older Americans who had no health insurance (half of those over the age of sixty-five in 1965) and by the poor who could not afford proper medical treatment. Like the New Deal's Social Security program, Medicare and Medicaid created "entitlements." That is, they conferred rights on certain categories of Americans virtually in perpetuity, without the need for repeated congressional approval. These programs were part of a spreading "rights revolution" that materially improved the lives of millions of Americans—but also eventually undermined the federal government's financial health.

Immigration reform was the third of Johnson's Big Four feats. The Immigration and Nationality Act of 1965 abolished at last the "national-origins" quota system that had been in place since 1921 (see p. 731). The act also doubled (to 290,000) the number of immigrants allowed to enter annually, while for the first time setting limits on immigrants from the Western Hemisphere (120,000). The new law fur-

ther provided for the admission of close relatives of United States citizens, outside those numerical limits. To the surprise of many of the act's architects, more than 100,000 persons per year took advantage of its "family unification" provisions in the decades after 1965, and the immigrant stream swelled beyond expectations. Even more surprising to the act's sponsors, the sources of immigration soon shifted heavily from Europe to Latin America and Asia, dramatically changing the racial and ethnic composition of the American population.

Great Society programs came in for rancorous political attack in later years. Conservatives charged that poverty could not be papered over with greenbacks and that the billions spent for "social engineering" had simply been flushed down the waste pipe. Yet the poverty rate declined measurably in the ensuing decade. Medicare made especially dramatic reductions in the incidence of poverty among America's elderly. Other antipoverty programs, among them Project Head Start, sharply improved the educational performance of underprivileged youth. Infant mortality rates also fell in minority communities as general health conditions improved. Lyndon Johnson was not fully victorious in the war against poverty, and he doubtless fought some costly and futile campaigns, but he did win several noteworthy battles.

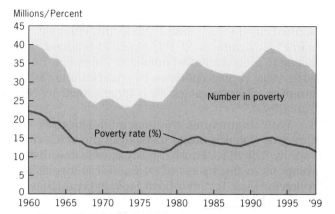

Millions/Percent

Poverty in the United States, 1960–1999
The poverty rate for 1999 (11.8%) was the lowest since 1979. These figures refer to the number of people who live in families whose total income is lower than a set "poverty threshold," which is tied to the Consumer Price Index, so it varies with inflation. The "poverty rate" means the percentage of all Americans living below that threshold. (Source: U.S. Bureau of the Census, Current Population Survey.)

Battling for Black Rights

With the last of his Big Four reforms, the Voting Rights Act of 1965, Johnson made heartening headway against one of the most persistent American evils, racial discrimination. In Johnson's native South, the walls of segregation were crumbling, but not fast enough for long-suffering African-Americans. The Civil Rights Act of 1964 gave the federal government more muscle to enforce school-desegregation orders and to prohibit racial discrimination in all kinds of public accommodations and employment. But the problem of voting rights remained. In Mississippi, which had the largest black minority of any state, only about 5 percent of eligible blacks were registered to vote. The lopsided pattern was similar throughout the South. Ballot-denying devices like the poll tax, literacy tests, and barefaced intimidation still barred black people from the political process. Mississippi law required the names of prospective black registrants to be published for two weeks in local newspapers—a device that virtually guaranteed economic reprisals, or worse.

Beginning in 1964, opening up the polling booths became the chief goal of the black movement in the South. The Twenty-fourth Amendment, ratified in January 1964, abolished the poll tax in federal elections. (See the Appendix.) Blacks joined hands with white civil rights workers—many of them student volunteers from the North—in a massive voter-registration drive in Mississippi during the "Freedom Summer" of 1964. Singing "We Shall Overcome," they zealously set out to soothe generations of white anxieties and black fears.

But events soon blighted bright hopes. In late June 1964, one black and two white civil rights workers disappeared in Mississippi. Their badly beaten bodies were later found buried beneath an earthen dam. FBI investigators eventually arrested twenty-one white Mississippians, including the local sheriff, in connection with the killings. But white juries refused to convict whites for these murders. In August an integrated "Mississippi Freedom Democratic party" delegation was denied its seat at the national Democratic convention. Only a handful of black Mississippians had succeeded in registering to vote.

Early in 1965 Martin Luther King, Jr., resumed the voter-registration campaign in Selma, Alabama, where blacks made up 50 percent of the population but only 1 percent of the voters. State troopers with tear gas and whips assaulted King's demonstrators as they marched peacefully to the state capital at Montgomery. A Boston Unitarian minister was killed, and a few days later a white Detroit woman was shotgunned to death by Klansmen on the highway near Selma.

As the nation recoiled in horror before these violent scenes, President Johnson, speaking in soft southern accents, delivered a compelling address on television. What happened in Selma, he insisted, concerned all Americans, "who must overcome the crippling legacy of bigotry and injustice." Then, in a stirring adaptation of the anthem of the civil rights movement, the president concluded, "And we shall overcome." Following words with deeds, Johnson speedily shepherded through Congress the landmark Voting Rights Act of 1965, signed into law on August 6. It outlawed literacy tests and sent federal voter registrars into several southern states.

The passage of the Voting Rights Act, exactly one hundred years after the conclusion of the Civil War, climaxed a century of awful abuse and robust resurgence for African-Americans in the South. "Give us the ballot," said Martin Luther King, Jr., "and the South will never be the same again." He was right. The act did not end discrimination and oppression overnight, but it placed an awesome lever for change in blacks' hands. Black southerners now had power and began to wield it without fear of reprisals. White southerners began to court black votes and business as never before. In the following decade, for the first time since emancipation, African-Americans began to migrate *into* the South.

Black Power

The Voting Rights Act of 1965 marked the end of an era in the history of the civil rights movement—the era of nonviolent demonstrations, focused on the South, led by peaceful moderates like Martin Luther King, Jr., and aimed at integrating blacks into American society. As if to symbolize the turn of events, just five days after President Johnson signed the landmark voting law, a bloody riot erupted in Watts, a black ghetto in Los Angeles. Blacks enraged by police brutality burned and looted their own neighborhoods for nearly a week. When the smoke finally cleared over the Los Angeles basin, thirty-one blacks and three whites lay dead, more than a thousand people had been injured, and hundreds of buildings stood charred and gutted. The Watts explosion heralded a new phase of the black struggle—increasingly marked by militant confrontation, focusing on northern and western cities, led by radical and sometimes violent spokespersons, and often aiming not at interracial cooperation but at black separatism.

The pious Christian moderation of Martin Luther King, Jr., came under heavy fire from this second wave of younger black leaders, who privately mocked the dignified Dr. King as "de Lawd." Deepening division among black leaders was highlighted by the career of Malcolm X. Born Malcolm Little, he was at first inspired by the militant black nationalists in the Nation of Islam. Like the Nation's founder, Elijah Muhammed (born Elijah Poole), Malcolm changed his surname to advertise his lost African identity in white America. A brilliant and charismatic preacher, Malcolm X trumpeted black separatism and inveighed against the "blue-eyed white devils." Eventually Malcolm distanced himself from Elijah Muhammed's separatist preachings and moved toward mainstream Islam. (By the 1990s Islam was among America's fastest-growing religions and counted some 2 million African-

American converts—or "reverts" as Muslims described it—in its ranks.) Malcolm changed his name yet again, to El Haj Malik El-Shabazz, and began to preach a more conciliatory message. But in early 1965, he was cut down by rival Nation of Islam gunmen while speaking to a large crowd in New York City.

With frightening frequency, violence or the threat of violence raised its head in the black community. The Black Panther party openly brandished weapons in the streets of Oakland, California. The following year Trinidad-born Stokely Carmichael, a leader of the Student Non-Violent Coordinating Committee (SNCC, pronounced "snick"), urged the abandonment of peaceful demonstrations and instead promoted "Black Power."

The very phrase "Black Power" unsettled many whites, and their fears increased when Carmichael was quoted as gloating that Black Power "will smash

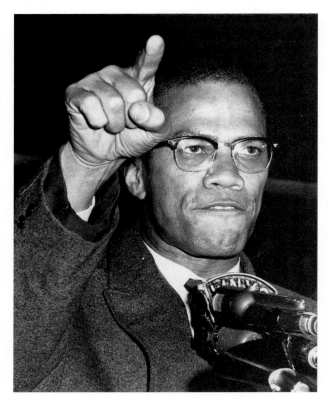

Malcolm X The charismatic black leader was a hypnotizing speaker who could rivet and arouse crowds with his call for black separatism. Yet at the end of his life, Malcolm began to temper his separatist creed.

emphasized African-American distinctiveness, promoted "Afro" hairstyles and dress, shed their "white" names for new African identities, and demanded black studies programs in schools and universities.

Ironically, just as the civil rights movement had achieved its greatest legal and political triumphs, more city-shaking riots erupted in the black ghettoes of several American cities. A bloody outburst in Newark, New Jersey, in the summer of 1967, took twenty-five lives. Federal troops restored order in Detroit, Michigan, after forty-three people died in the streets. As in Los Angeles, black rioters torched their own neighborhoods, attacking police officers and even firefighters, who had to battle both flames and mobs howling, "Burn, baby, burn."

These riotous outbursts angered many white Americans, who threatened to retaliate with their own "backlash" against ghetto arsonists and killers. Inner-city anarchy baffled many northerners, who had considered racial problems a purely "southern" question. But black concerns had moved north—as had nearly half the nation's black people. In the North the Black Power movement now focused less on civil rights and more on economic demands.

everything Western civilization has created." Some advocates of Black Power insisted that they simply intended the slogan to describe a broad-front effort to exercise the political and economic rights gained by the civil rights movement and to speed the integration of American society. But other African-Americans, recollecting previous black nationalist movements like that of Marcus Garvey earlier in the century (see p. 748), breathed a vibrant separatist meaning into the concept of Black Power. They

You Don't Understand Boy—You're Supposed to Just Shuffle Along

The Mechanized War
High technology and modern equipment, such as this helicopter, gave the Americans in Vietnam a huge military advantage. But unaccompanied by a clear political purpose and a national will to win, technological superiority was insufficient to achieve final victory.

Black unemployment, for example, was nearly double that for whites. These oppressive new problems seemed even less likely to be solved peaceably than the struggle for voting rights in the South.

Despair deepened when the magnetic and moderate voice of Martin Luther King, Jr., was forever silenced by a sniper's bullet in Memphis, Tennessee, on April 4, 1968. A martyr for justice, he had bled and died against the peculiarly American thorn of race. The killing of King cruelly robbed the American people of one of the most inspirational leaders in their history—at a time when they could least afford to lose him. This outrage triggered a nationwide orgy of ghetto-gutting and violence that cost over forty lives.

Rioters noisily made news, but thousands of other blacks quietly made history. Their voter registration in the South shot upward, and by the late 1960s several hundred blacks held elected office in the Old South. Cleveland, Ohio, and Gary, Indiana, elected black mayors. By 1972 nearly half of southern black children sat in integrated classrooms. Actually, more schools in the South were integrated than in the North. About a third of black families had risen economically into the ranks of the middle class—though an equal proportion remained below the "poverty line." King left a shining legacy of racial progress, but he was cut down when the job was far from completed.

Combating Communism in Two Hemispheres

Violence at home eclipsed Johnson's legislative triumphs, while foreign flare-ups threatened his political life. Discontented Dominicans rose in revolt against their military government in April 1965. Johnson speedily announced that the Dominican Republic was the target of a Castrolike coup by "Communist conspirators," and he dispatched American troops, ultimately some 25,000, to restore order. But the evidence of a communist takeover was fragmentary at best. Johnson was widely condemned, at home and in Latin America, for his temporary reversion to the officially abandoned "gunboat diplomacy." Critics charged that the two-fisted Texan was far too eager to back right-wing regimes with rifle-toting troops.

At about the same time, Johnson was floundering deeper into the monsoon mud of Vietnam. Viet Cong guerrillas attacked an American air base at Pleiku, South Vietnam, in February 1965. The president immediately ordered retaliatory bombing raids against military installations in North Vietnam and for the first time ordered attacking U.S. troops to land. By the middle of March 1965, the Americans had "Operation Rolling Thunder" in full swing—regular full-scale bombing attacks against North Vietnam. Before 1965 ended, some 184,000 American troops were involved, most of them slogging through the jungles and rice paddies of South Vietnam searching for guerrillas clad in black pajamas.

Johnson had now taken the first fateful steps down a slippery path. He and his advisers believed that a fine-tuned, step-by-step "escalation" of American force would drive the enemy to defeat with a minimum loss of life on both sides. But the president reckoned without due knowledge of the toughness, resiliency, and dedication of the Viet Cong guerrillas in South Vietnam and their North Vietnamese allies. Aerial bombardment actually strengthened the communists' will to resist. The enemy matched every increase in American firepower with more men and more wiliness in the art of guerrilla warfare.

The South Vietnamese themselves were meanwhile becoming spectators in their own war, as the fighting became increasingly Americanized. Corrupt and collapsible governments succeeded each other in Saigon with bewildering rapidity. Yet American officials continued to talk of defending a faithful democratic ally. Washington spokespeople also defended America's action as a test of Uncle Sam's "commitment" and of the reliability of his numerous treaty pledges to resist communist encroachment. If the United States were to cut and run from Vietnam, claimed prowar "hawks," other nations would doubt America's word and crumble under communist pressure (the so-called domino theory), which would ostensibly drive America's first line of defense back to Waikiki Beach, in Hawaii, or even to the coast of California. Persuaded by such panicky thinking, Johnson steadily raised the military stakes in Vietnam. By 1968 he had poured more than half a million troops into Southeast Asia, and the annual bill for the war was exceeding $30 billion. Yet the end was nowhere in sight.

Vietnam Vexations

America could not defeat the enemy in Vietnam, but it seemed to be defeating itself. World opinion grew increasingly hostile; the blasting of an underdeveloped country by a mighty superpower struck many critics as obscene. Several nations expelled American Peace Corps volunteers. Haughty Charles de Gaulle, ever suspicious of American intentions, ordered NATO off French soil in 1966.

Overcommitment in Southeast Asia also tied America's hands elsewhere. Capitalizing on American distractions in Vietnam, the Soviet Union expanded its influence in the Mediterranean area, especially in Egypt. Tiny Israel stunned the Soviet-backed Egyptians in a devastating Six-Day War in June 1967. When the smoke had cleared, Israel occupied new territories in the Sinai Peninsula, the Golan Heights, the Gaza Strip, and the West Bank of the Jordan River, including Jerusalem (see the map on p. 983). Although the Israelis eventually withdrew from the Sinai, they refused to relinquish the other areas and even introduced Jewish settlers into the heavily Arab district of the West Bank. The Arab Palestinians already living in the West Bank and their Arab allies elsewhere complained loudly about these Israeli policies, but to no avail. The Middle East was becoming an ever more dangerously packed powder keg that the war-plagued United States was powerless to defuse.

Domestic discontent festered as the Vietnamese entanglement dragged on. Antiwar demonstrations had begun on a small scale with campus "teach-ins" in 1965, and gradually these protests mounted to tidal-wave proportions. As the long arm of the military draft dragged more and more young men off to the Southeast Asian slaughterpen, resistance stiffened. Thousands of draft registrants fled to Canada; others publicly burned their draft cards. Hundreds of thousands of marchers filled the streets of New York, San Francisco, and other cities, chanting, "Hell no, we won't go" and "Hey, hey, LBJ, how many kids did you kill today?" Countless citizens felt the pinch of war-spawned inflation. Many Americans also felt pangs of conscience at the spectacle of their countrymen burning peasant huts and blistering civilians with ghastly napalm.

Opposition in Congress to the Vietnam involvement centered in the influential Senate Committee on Foreign Relations, headed by a former Rhodes scholar, Senator William Fulbright of Arkansas. A constant thorn in the side of the president, he staged a series of widely viewed televised hearings in 1966 and 1967, during which prominent personages aired their views, largely antiwar. Gradually the public came to feel that it had been deceived about the causes and "winnability" of the war. A yawning "credibility gap" opened between the government and the people. New flocks of antiwar "doves" were hatching daily.

Even within the administration, doubts were deepening about the wisdom of the war in Vietnam.

Antiwar Demonstration in California Public opinion gradually but inexorably turned against the war. In 1965 polls showed that only 15 percent of Americans favored withdrawal from Vietnam. But by 1969, 69 percent of those interviewed indicated that they considered the war a "mistake," and by 1970 a majority supported withdrawal of U.S. troops.

When Defense Secretary McNamara expressed increasing discomfiture at the course of events, he was quietly eased out of the cabinet. (Years later McNamara wrote that "we were wrong, terribly wrong," about Vietnam.) President Johnson did announce "bombing halts" in early 1966 and early 1967, supposedly to lure the enemy to the peace table. But Washington did not pursue its "peace offensive" with much energy, and the other side did not respond with any encouragement. Both sides used the bombing pauses to funnel more troops into South Vietnam.

By early 1968 the brutal and futile struggle had become the longest and most unpopular foreign war in the nation's history. The government had failed utterly to explain to the people what was supposed to be at stake in Vietnam. Many critics wondered if any objective could be worth the vast price, in blood and treasure, that America was paying. Casualties, killed and wounded, already exceeded 100,000. More bombs had been dropped on Vietnam than on all enemy territory in World War II.

The war was also ripping apart the fabric of American society and even threatening to shred the Constitution. In 1967 President Johnson ordered the CIA, in clear violation of its charter as a *foreign* intelligence agency, to spy on domestic antiwar activists. He also encouraged the FBI to turn its counterintelligence program, code-named "Cointelpro," against the peace movement. "Cointelpro" had been launched by J. Edgar Hoover in the 1950s to infiltrate communist organizations. Now under presidential directive, it sabotaged peace groups by conducting "black bag" break-ins. "Cointelpro" also subverted leading "doves" with false accusations

President Lyndon Johnson Haunted by Spectres of Vietnam, 1967

that they were communist sympathizers. These clandestine tactics made the FBI look like a totalitarian state's secret police rather than a guardian of American democracy.

As the war dragged on, evidence mounted that America had been entrapped in an Asian civil war, fighting against highly motivated rebels who were striving to overthrow an oppressive regime. Yet Johnson clung to his basic strategy of ratcheting up the pressure bit by bit. He stubbornly assured doubting Americans that he could see "the light at the end of the tunnel." But to growing numbers of Americans, it seemed that Johnson was bent on "saving" Vietnam by destroying it.

Vietnam Topples Johnson

Hawkish illusions that the struggle was about to be won were shattered by a blistering communist offensive launched in late January 1968, during Tet, the Vietnamese New Year. At a time when the Viet Cong were supposedly licking their wounds, they suddenly and simultaneously mounted savage attacks on twenty-seven key South Vietnamese cities, including the capital, Saigon. Although eventually beaten off with heavy losses, they demonstrated anew that victory could not be gained by Johnson's strategy of gradual escalation. The Tet offensive ended in a military defeat but a political victory for the Viet Cong. With an increasingly insistent voice, American public opinion demanded a speedy end to the war. Opposition grew so vehement that President Johnson could feel the very foundations of government shaking under his feet. He was also suffering through hells of personal agony over American casualties. He wept as he signed letters of condolence, and slipped off at night to pray with monks at a small Catholic church in Washington.

American military leaders responded to the Tet attacks with a request for 200,000 more troops. The largest single increment yet, this addition would have swollen American troop strength in Vietnam to about the three-quarter-million mark. The size of the request staggered many policymakers. Former secretary of state Dean Acheson reportedly advised the president that "the Joint Chiefs of Staff don't know what they're talking about." Johnson himself now began to doubt seriously the wisdom of continuing on his raise-the-stakes course.

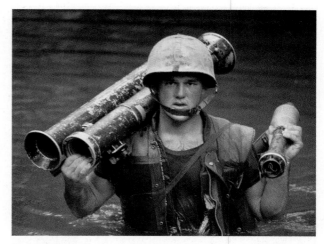

The Vietnam Quagmire　This soldier, carrying a rocket launcher across a stream in the ironically named "demilitarized zone" (DMZ) that separated North and South Vietnam, was killed in action just days after this photo was taken.

The president meanwhile was being sharply challenged from within his own party. Eugene McCarthy, a little-known Democratic senator from Minnesota, had emerged as a contender for the 1968 Democratic presidential nomination. The soft-spoken McCarthy, a sometime poet and devout Catholic, gathered a small army of antiwar college students as campaign workers. Going "clean for Gene," with shaven faces and shortened locks, these idealistic recruits of the "Children's Crusade" invaded the key presidential primary state of New Hampshire to ring doorbells. On March 12, 1968, their efforts gave McCarthy an incredible 42 percent of the Democratic votes and twenty of the twenty-four convention delegates. President Johnson was on the same ballot, but only as a write-in candidate. Four days later Senator Robert F. Kennedy of New York, the murdered president's younger brother and by now himself a "dove" on Vietnam, threw his hat into the ring. The charismatic Kennedy, heir to his fallen brother's mantle of leadership, stirred a passionate response among workers, African-Americans, Hispanics, and young people.

These startling events abroad and at home were not lost on LBJ. The country might explode in greater violence if he met the request of the generals for more troops. His own party was dangerously divided on the war issue. He might not even be able

Robert F. Kennedy Campaigning for the Presidency, 1968
Wrapped in the Kennedy family mystique and exuding his own
boyish charm, Kennedy excited partisan crowds to wildly
adulatory outpourings.

to win renomination after his relatively poor showing in New Hampshire. Yet he remained committed
to victory in Vietnam, even if the light at the end of
the tunnel was vanishing. How could he salvage his
blind-alley policy?

Johnson's answer came in a bombshell address
on March 31, 1968. He announced on nationwide
television that he would finally apply the brakes to
the escalating war. He would freeze American troop
levels and gradually shift more responsibility to the
South Vietnamese themselves. Aerial bombardment
of the enemy would be drastically scaled down.
Then, in a dramatic plea to unify a dangerously
divided nation, Johnson startled his vast audience
by firmly declaring that he would not be a candidate
for the presidency in 1968.

Johnson's "abdication" had the effect of preserving the military status quo. He had held the "hawks"
in check, while offering himself as a sacrifice to
the militant "doves." The United States could thus
maintain the maximum *acceptable* level of military
activity in Vietnam with one hand, while trying to
negotiate a settlement with the other.

North Vietnam responded somewhat encourag-
ingly three days later, when it expressed a willingness to talk about peace. After a month of haggling
over the site, the adversaries agreed to meet in Paris.
But progress was glacially slow, as prolonged bicker-
ing developed over the very shape of the conference
table.

The Presidential Sweepstakes of 1968

The summer of 1968 was one of the hottest political
seasons in the nation's history. Johnson's heir apparent for the Democratic nomination was his liberal
vice president, Hubert H. Humphrey, a former phar-
macist, college professor, mayor, and U.S. senator
from Minnesota. Loyally supporting LBJ's Vietnam
policies through thick and thin, he received the support of the party apparatus, dominated as it was by
the White House. Senators McCarthy and Kennedy
meanwhile dueled in several state primaries, with
Kennedy's bandwagon gathering ever-increasing
speed. But on June 5, 1968, the night of an exciting
victory in the California primary, Kennedy was shot
to death by a young Arab immigrant resentful of the
candidate's pro-Israel views.

Surrounded by bitterness and frustration, the
Democrats met in Chicago in late August 1968.
Angry antiwar zealots, deprived by an assassin's bullet of their leading candidate, streamed menacingly
into Chicago. Mayor Daley responded by arranging
for barbed-wire barricades around the convention
hall ("Fort Daley"), as well as thousands of police
and National Guard reinforcements. Many demonstrators baited the officers in blue by calling them
"pigs." Other militants, chanting "Ho, Ho, Ho Chi
Minh," shouted obscenities and hurled bags and
cans of excrement at the police lines. As people the
world over watched on television, the exasperated
"peace officers" broke into a "police riot," clubbing
and manhandling innocent and guilty alike. Acrid
tear gas fumes hung heavy over the city and even
drifted up to candidate Humphrey's hotel suite.
Hundreds of people were arrested and scores hospi-
talized, but there were no casualties—except, as
cynics said, the Democratic party and its candidate.

Humphrey steamrollered to the nomination on
the first ballot. The dovish McCarthyites failed even

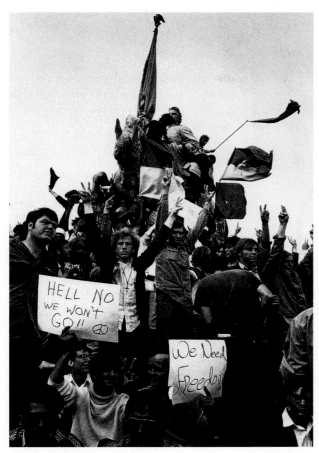

The Siege of Chicago, 1968
Antiwar protesters surrounded a monument to Civil War general John Logan during a week of demonstrations outside the Democratic National Convention in Chicago in August 1968. Confrontations with the Chicago police and National Guardsmen led to many injuries and the arrest of seven hundred people, and helped tarnish Democratic candidate Vice President Hubert Humphrey with responsibility for Lyndon Johnson's unpopular war. His Republican opponent, Richard Nixon, won the presidency with calls for "honorable peace" in Vietnam and "law and order" at home.

arose from his political grave to win the nomination. As a "hawk" on Vietnam and a right-leaning middle-of-the-roader on domestic policy, Nixon pleased the Goldwater conservatives and was acceptable to party moderates. He appealed to white southern voters and to the "law and order" element when he tapped as his vice-presidential running mate Maryland's Governor Spiro T. Agnew, noted for his tough stands against dissidents and black militants. The Republican platform called for victory in Vietnam and a strong anticrime policy.

A "spoiler" third-party ticket—the American Independent party—added color and confusion to the campaign. It was headed by a scrappy ex-pugilist, George C. Wallace, former governor of Alabama. In 1963 he had stood in the doorway to prevent two black students from entering the University of Alabama. "Segregation now! Segregation tomorrow! Segregation forever!" he shouted. Wallace jabbed repeatedly at "pointy-headed bureaucrats," and he taunted hecklers as "bums" in need of a bath. Speaking behind a bulletproof screen, he called for prodding the blacks into their place, with bayonets if necessary. He and his running mate, former air force general Curtis LeMay, also proposed smashing the North Vietnamese to smithereens by "bombing them back to the Stone Age."

Victory for Nixon

Vietnam proved a less crucial issue than expected. Between the positions of the Republicans and the Democrats, there was little choice. Both candidates were committed to carrying on the war until the enemy settled for an "honorable peace," which seemed to mean an "American victory." The millions of "doves" had no place to roost, and many refused to vote at all. Humphrey, scorched by the LBJ brand, went down to defeat as a loyal prisoner of his chief's policies, despite Johnson's last-minute effort to bail him out by announcing a *total* bombing halt.

Nixon, who had lost a cliffhanger to Kennedy in 1960, won one in 1968. He garnered 301 electoral votes, with 43.4 percent of the popular tally (31,785,480), as compared with 191 electoral votes and 42.7 percent of the popular votes (31,275,166) for Humphrey. Nixon was the first president-elect since 1848 not to bring in on his coattails at least

to secure an antiwar platform plank. Instead the Humphrey forces, echoing the president, hammered into place their own declaration that armed force would be relentlessly applied until the enemy showed more willingness to negotiate.

Scenting victory as the Democrats divided, the Republicans had jubilantly convened in plush Miami Beach, Florida, early in August 1968. Richard M. Nixon, the former vice president whom John F. Kennedy had narrowly defeated eight years earlier,

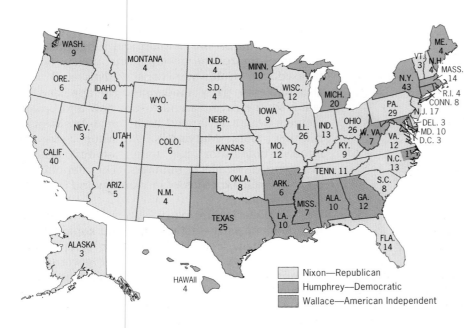

Presidential Election of 1968 (with electoral vote by state) George Wallace won in five states, and he denied a clear majority to either of the two major-party candidates in twenty-five other states. A shift of some fifty thousand votes might well have thrown the election into the House of Representatives, giving Wallace the strategic bargaining position he sought.

Nixon—Republican
Humphrey—Democratic
Wallace—American Independent

one house of Congress for his party in an initial presidential election. He carried not a single major city, thus attesting to the continuing urban strength of the Democrats, who also won about 95 percent of the black vote. Nixon had received no clear mandate to do anything. He was a minority president who owed his election to divisions over the war and protest against the unfair draft, crime, and rioting.

Wallace did worse than expected. Yet he won an impressive 9,906,473 popular votes and 46 electoral votes, all from five states of the Deep South, four of which the Republican Goldwater had carried in 1964. Wallace remained a formidable force, for he had amassed the largest third-party popular vote in American history. Wallace had also resoundingly demonstrated the continuing power of "populist" politics, which appealed to voters' fears and resentments rather than to the better angels of their nature. His candidacy foreshadowed a coarsening of American political life that would take deep root in the ensuing decades.

The Obituary of Lyndon Johnson

Talented but tragedy-struck Lyndon Johnson returned to his Texas ranch in January 1969 and died there four years later. His party was defeated, and

his "me-too" Hubert Humphrey was repudiated. Yet Johnson's legislative leadership for a time had been remarkable. No president since Lincoln had worked harder or done more for civil rights. None had shown more compassion for the poor, blacks, and the ill educated. LBJ seemed to suffer from an inferiority complex about his own arid cultural background, and he strove furiously to prove that he could be a great "people's president" in the image of his idol, Franklin Roosevelt. His legislative achievements in his first three years in office indeed invited comparison with those of the New Deal.

But by 1966 Johnson was already sinking into the Vietnam quicksands. The Republicans had made gains in Congress, and a white "backlash" had begun to form against the black movement. Great Society programs began to wither on the vine, as soaring war costs sucked tax dollars into the military machine. Johnson had promised both guns and butter but could not keep that promise. Ever-creeping inflation blighted the prospects of prosperity, and the War on Poverty met resistance that was as stubborn as the Viet Cong and eventually went down to defeat. Great want persisted alongside great wealth.

Johnson had crucified himself on the cross of Vietnam. The Southeast Asian quagmire engulfed his noblest intentions. Committed to some degree by his two predecessors, he had chosen to defend the American foothold and enlarge the conflict rather than be run out. He was evidently persuaded by his brightest advisers, both civilian and military, that a "cheap" victory was possible. It would be achieved by massive aerial bombing and large, though limited, troop commitments. His decision not to escalate the fighting further offended the "hawks," and his refusal to back off altogether antagonized the "doves." Like the Calvinists of colonial days, luckless Lyndon Johnson was damned if he did and damned if he did not.

The Cultural Upheaval of the 1960s

The struggles of the 1960s against racism, poverty, and the war in Vietnam had momentous cultural consequences. The decade came to be seen as a watershed dividing two distinct eras in terms of values, morals, and behavior.

Everywhere in 1960s America, a newly negative attitude toward all kinds of authority took hold. Disillusioned by the discovery that American society was not free of racism, sexism, imperialism, and oppression, many young people lost their traditional moral rudders. Neither families nor churches nor schools seemed to be able to define values and shape behavior with the certainty of shared purpose that many people believed had once existed. The upheaval even churned the tradition-bound Roman Catholic church, among the world's oldest and most conservative institutions. Clerics abandoned their Roman collars and Latin lingo, folk songs replaced Gregorian chants, and meatless Fridays became ancient history. No matter what the topic, conventional wisdom and inherited ideas came under fire. "Trust no one over thirty" was a popular sneer of rebellious youth.

Skepticism about authority had deep historical roots in American culture, and it had even bloomed in the supposedly complacent and conformist 1950s. "Beat" poets like Allen Ginsberg and iconoclastic novelists like Jack Kerouac had voiced dark disillusion with the materialistic pursuits and "establishment" arrogance of the Eisenhower era. In movies like *Rebel Without a Cause* (1955), the attractive young actor James Dean expressed the restless frustration of many young people.

The disaffection of the young reached crisis proportions in the tumultuous 1960s. One of the first organized protests against established authority broke out at the University of California at Berkeley in 1964, in the so-called Free Speech Movement. Leader Mario Savio, condemning the impersonal university "machine" more tied to corporate interests than humane values, urged his fellow students to "put your bodies upon the gears and upon the

The "Free Speech Movement," Berkeley, California, December 4, 1964 Student leader Mario Savio addresses a crowd at the University of California at Berkeley. The Free Speech Movement marked the first of the large-scale student mobilizations that would rock campuses across the country throughout the rest of the 1960s.

The Counterculture
Psychedelic buses carried hippies, seeking escape from conventional American living, to experimental communes and musical "happenings." Author Tom Wolfe inspired young people to hit the road with his chronicle of a wild bus tour in *The Electric Kool-Aid Acid Test*.

wheels, . . . and you've got to make it stop." But in only a few years, the clean-cut Berkeley activists and their sober-minded sit-ins would seem downright quaint. Fired by outrage against the war in Vietnam, some sons and daughters of the middle class became radical political rebels, while others turned to mind-bending drugs, tuned in to "acid rock," and dropped out of "straight" society. Others "did their own thing" in communes or "alternative" institutions. Patriotism became a dirty word. Beflowered women in trousers and long-haired men with earrings heralded the rise of a self-conscious "counterculture" blatantly opposed to traditional American ways.

The 1960s also witnessed a "sexual revolution," though its novelty and scale are often exaggerated. Without doubt, the introduction of the birth-control pill in 1960 made unwanted pregnancies much easier to avoid and sexual appetites easier to satisfy. But as early as 1948, Indiana University sexologist Dr. Alfred Kinsey had published sensational revelations about American sexual habits in *Sexual Behavior in the Human Male*, followed five years later by *Sexual*

The alternative newspaper The Village Voice *captured the momentousness of one aspect of the sexual revolution on the first anniversary of the Stonewall Rebellion in June 1969, the day when homosexuals had fought back against a police attack and thereby launched a new gay and lesbian liberation movement:*

"They stretched in a line, from Gimbels to Times Square, thousands and thousands and thousands, chanting, waving, screaming— the outrageous and the outraged, splendid in their flaming colors, splendid in their delirious up-front birthday celebration of liberation. . . . No one could quite believe it, eyes rolled back in heads, Sunday tourists traded incredulous looks, wondrous faces poked out of air-conditioned cars. My God, are those really homosexuals? Marching? Up Sixth Avenue?"

Behavior in the Human Female. Based on thousands of interviews, Kinsey's findings about the incidence of premarital sex and adultery caused a ruckus at the time and have been hotly debated ever since. Most controversial was Kinsey's estimate that 10 percent of American males were homosexuals. Whatever the exact number, by the 1960s gay men and lesbians were increasingly emerging from the closet and demanding sexual tolerance. The Mattachine Society, founded in Los Angeles in 1951, was a pioneering advocate for gay rights. A brutal attack on gay men by off-duty police officers at New York's Stonewall Inn in 1969 powerfully energized gay and lesbian militancy. Widening worries in the 1980s about sexually transmitted diseases like genital herpes and AIDS (acquired immunodeficiency syndrome) finally slowed, but did not reverse, the sexual revolution.

Launched in youthful idealism, many of the cultural "revolutions" of the 1960s sputtered out in violence and cynicism. Students for a Democratic Society (SDS), once at the forefront of the antipoverty and antiwar campaigns, had by decade's end spawned an underground terrorist group called the Weathermen. Peaceful civil rights demonstrations had given way to blockbusting urban riots. What started as apparently innocent experiments with drugs like marijuana and LSD had fried many youthful brains and spawned a loathsome underworld of drug lords and addicted users.

Straight-laced guardians of respectability denounced the self-indulgent romanticism of the "flower children" as the beginning of the end of modern civilization. Sympathetic observers hailed the "greening" of America—the replacement of materialism and imperialism by a new consciousness of human values. The upheavals of the 1960s could be largely attributed to three *P*s: the youthful population bulge, protest against racism and the Vietnam War, and the apparent permanence of prosperity. As the decade flowed into the 1970s, the flower children grew older and had children of their own, the civil rights movement fell silent, the war ended, and economic stagnation blighted the bloom of prosperity. Young people in the 1970s seemed more concerned with finding a job in the system than with tearing the system down. But if the "counterculture" had not managed fully to replace older values, it had weakened their grip, perhaps permanently.

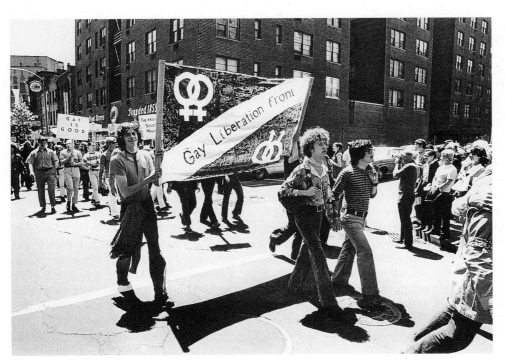

The First Gay Pride Parade, New York City, 1970 On the first anniversary of homosexuals' celebrated resistance to police harassment at the Stonewall Inn, on June 27, 1969, two hundred men and women marched from Greenwich Village to Central Park, initiating a tradition that now attracts thousands of paraders and onlookers, including prominent politicians.

Chronology

1961	Berlin crisis and construction of the Berlin Wall Alliance for Progress Bay of Pigs Kennedy sends "military advisers" to South Vietnam
1962	Pressure from Kennedy results in a rollback of steel prices Trade Expansion Act Laos neutralized Cuban missile crisis
1963	Anti-Diem coup in South Vietnam Civil rights march in Washington, D.C. Kennedy assassinated; Johnson assumes presidency
1964	Twenty-fourth Amendment (abolishing poll tax in federal elections) ratified "Freedom Summer" voter registration in the South Tonkin Gulf Resolution
1964	Johnson defeats Goldwater for presidency War on Poverty begins Civil Rights Act
1965	Great Society legislation Voting Rights Act U.S. troops occupy Dominican Republic
1965–1968	Race riots in U.S. cities Escalation of the Vietnam War
1967	Six-Day War between Israel and Egypt
1968	Tet offensive in Vietnam Martin Luther King, Jr., and Robert Kennedy assassinated Nixon defeats Humphrey and Wallace for presidency
1969	Astronauts land on moon

VARYING VIEWPOINTS

The Sixties: Constructive or Destructive?

The 1960s were convulsed by controversy, and they have remained controversial ever since. Conflicts raged in that turbulent decade between social classes, races, sexes, and generations. More than three decades later, the shock waves from the 1960s still reverberate through American society. The "Contract with America" that swept conservative Republicans to power in 1994 amounted to nothing less than a wholesale repudiation of the government activism that marked the sixties decade and a resounding reaffirmation of the "traditional values" that sixties culture supposedly trashed. Liberal Democrats, on the other hand, continue to press affirmative action for women and minorities, protection for the environment, an expanded welfare state, and sexual tolerance—all legacies of the stormy sixties.

Four issues dominate historical discussion of the 1960s: the struggle for civil rights, the Great Society's "War on Poverty," the Vietnam War and the antiwar movement, and the emergence of the "counterculture."

Although most scholars praise the civil rights achievements of the 1960s, they disagree over the civil rights movement's turn away from nonviolence and its embrace of separatism and Black Power. The Freedom Riders and Martin Luther King, Jr., find much more approval in most history books than do Malcolm X and the Black Panther party. But some scholars, notably William L. Van Deburg in *New Day in Babylon: The Black Power Movement and American Culture, 1965–1975* (1992), argue that the "flank effect" of radical Black Power advocates like Stokely Carmichael actually enhanced the bargaining position of moderates like Dr. King. Deburg also suggests that the enthusiasm of Black Power advocates for African-American cultural uniqueness reshaped both black self-consciousness and the broader culture, as it provided a model for the feminist and multiculturalist movements of the 1970s and later.

Johnson's War on Poverty has found its liberal defenders in scholars like Allen Matusow (*The Unraveling of America,* 1984) and John Schwarz (*America's Hidden Success,* 1988). Schwarz demonstrates, for example, that Medicare and Social Security reforms virtually eliminated poverty among America's elderly. But the Great Society has also provoked strong criticism from writers such as Charles Murray (*Losing Ground,* 1984) and Lawrence Meade (*Beyond Entitlements,* 1986). As those conservative critics see the poverty issue, to use a phrase popular in the 1960s, the Great Society was part of the problem, not part of the solution. In their view the War on Poverty did not simply fail to eradicate poverty among the so-called underclass; it actually deepened the dependency of the poor on the welfare state and even generated a multigenerational "cycle" of poverty. In this argument Johnson's Great Society stands indicted of creating, in effect, a permanent welfare class.

For many young people of the 1960s, the antiwar movement protesting America's policy in Vietnam provided their initiation into politics and their introduction to "movement culture," with its sense of community and shared purpose. But scholars disagree over the movement's real effectiveness in checking the war. Writers like John Lewis Gaddis (*Strategies of Containment,* 1982) explain America's eventual withdrawal from Vietnam essentially without reference to the protesters in the streets. Others, like Todd Gitlin (*The Sixties: Years of Hope, Days of Rage,* 1987), insist that mass protest was the force that finally pressed the war to a conclusion.

Debate over the counterculture not only pits liberals against conservatives but also pits liberals against radicals. A liberal historian like William O'Neill (*Coming Apart,* 1971) might sympathize with what he considers some of the worthy values pushed by student activists, such as racial justice, nonviolence, and the antiwar movement, but he also claims that much of the sixties "youth culture" degenerated into hedonism, arrogance, and social polarization. In contrast, younger historians such as Michael Kazin and Maurice Isserman argue that cultural radicalism and political radicalism were two sides of the same coin. Many young people in the sixties made little distinction between the personal and the political. As Sara Evans demonstrates in *Personal Politics* (1980), "the personal *was* the political" for many women. She finds the roots of modern feminism in the sexism women activists encountered in the civil rights and antiwar movements.

While critics may argue over the "good" versus the "bad" sixties, there is no denying the degree to which that tumultuous time, for better or worse, shaped the world in which we now live.

For further reading, see page A26 of the Appendix. For web resources, go to **http://college.hmco.com.**

The Stalemated Seventies

---◌◊◌---

1968–1980

*In all my years of public life, I have never obstructed justice. People
have got to know whether or not their President is a crook. Well, I'm
not a crook; I earned everything I've got.*

RICHARD NIXON, 1973

As the 1960s lurched to a close, the fantastic
quarter-century economic boom of the post–
World War II era also showed signs of petering out.
By increasing their productivity, American workers
had doubled their average standard of living in the
twenty-five years since the end of World War II. Now,
fatefully, productivity gains slowed to the vanishing
point. The entire decade of the 1970s did not witness a productivity advance equivalent to even one
year's progress in the preceding two decades. At the
new rate, it would take five hundred more years to
bring about another doubling of the average
worker's standard of living. The median income of
the average American family stagnated in the two
decades after 1970, and failed to decline only
because of the addition of working wives' wages to
the family income (see the chart on p. 947). The rising baby-boom generation now faced the depressing prospect of a living standard that would be lower
than that of their parents. As the postwar wave of
robust economic growth crested by the early 1970s,
at home and abroad the "can do" American spirit
gave way to an unaccustomed sense of limits.

Sources of Stagnation

What caused the sudden slump in productivity?
Some observers cited the increasing presence in the
work force of women and teenagers, who typically
had fewer skills than adult male workers and were
less likely to take the full-time, long-term jobs
where skills might be developed. Other commentators blamed declining investment in new machinery, the heavy costs of compliance with
government-imposed safety and health regulations,
and the general shift of the American economy from

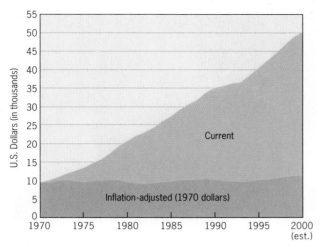

Median Family Income, 1970–2000
During the long post–World War II economic boom (from about 1950 to 1970), family incomes increased dramatically, but after 1970 "real," or inflation-adjusted, incomes stagnated. Prosperity at the end of the twentieth century has led to recent increases. (Sources: U.S. Census Bureau and Bureau of Labor Statistics.)

manufacturing to services, where productivity gains were allegedly more difficult to achieve and measure. Yet in the last analysis, much mystery attends the productivity slowdown, and economists have wrestled inconclusively with the puzzle.

The Vietnam War also precipitated painful economic distortions. The disastrous conflict in Southeast Asia drained tax dollars from needed improvements in education, deflected scientific skill and manufacturing capacity from the civilian sector, and touched off a sickening spiral of inflation. Sharply rising oil prices in the 1970s also fed inflation, but its deepest roots lay in government policies of the 1960s—especially Lyndon Johnson's insistence on simultaneously fighting the war in Vietnam and funding the Great Society programs at home, all without a tax increase to finance the added expenditures. Both military spending and welfare spending are inherently inflationary (in the absence of offsetting tax collections), because they put dollars in people's hands without adding to the supply of goods that those dollars can buy.

When too many dollars chase too few goods, prices rise—as they did astonishingly in the 1970s. The cost of living more than tripled in the dozen years following Richard Nixon's inauguration, in the longest and steepest inflationary cycle in American history.

Other weaknesses in the nation's economy were also laid bare by the abrupt reversal of America's financial fortunes in the 1970s. The competitive advantage of many major American businesses had

The Nixon Wave During Richard Nixon's presidency, Americans experienced the first serious inflation since the immediate post–World War II years. The inflationary surge grew to tidal-wave proportions by the late 1970s, when the consumer price index rose at an annual rate of more than 10 percent.

been so enormous after World War II that they had small incentive to modernize plants and seek more efficient methods of production. The defeated German and Japanese people had meanwhile clawed their way out of the ruins of war and built wholly new factories with the most up-to-date technology and management techniques. By the 1970s their efforts paid handsome rewards, as they came to dominate industries like steel, automobiles, and consumer electronics—fields in which the United States had once been unchallengeable.

The poor economic performance of the 1970s hung over the decade like a pall. It frustrated both policymakers and citizens who keenly remembered the growth and optimism of the quarter-century since World War II. The overachieving postwar generation had never met a problem it could not solve. But now a stalemated, unpopular war and a stagnant, unresponsive economy heralded the end of the self-confident postwar era. With it ended the liberal dream, vivid since New Deal days, that an affluent society could spend its way to social justice.

Nixon "Vietnamizes" the War

Inaugurated on January 20, 1969, Richard Nixon urged the American people, torn with dissension over Vietnam and race relations, to "stop shouting at one another." Yet the new president seemed an unlikely conciliator of the clashing forces that appeared to be ripping apart American society. Solitary and suspicious by nature, Nixon could be brittle and testy in the face of opposition. He also harbored bitter resentments against the "liberal establishment" that had cast him into the political darkness for much of the preceding decade. Yet Nixon brought one hugely valuable asset with him to the White House—his broad knowledge and thoughtful expertise in foreign affairs. With calculating shrewdness he applied himself to putting America's foreign-policy house in order.

The first burning need was to quiet the public uproar over Vietnam. President Nixon's announced policy, called "Vietnamization," was to withdraw the 540,000 U.S. troops in South Vietnam over an extended period. The South Vietnamese—with American money, weapons, training, and advice—could then gradually take over the burden of fighting their own war.

President Richard M. Nixon   Reversing Kennedy's inaugural plea to "bear any burden," Nixon told Congress in February 1970, "America cannot—and will not—conceive all the plans, design all the programs, execute all the decisions and undertake all the defense of the free nations of the world."

The so-called Nixon Doctrine thus evolved. It proclaimed that the United States would honor its existing defense commitments but that in the future, Asians and others would have to fight their own wars without the support of large bodies of American ground troops.

Nixon sought not to end the war, but to win it by other means, without the further spilling of American blood. But even this much involvement was distasteful to the American "doves," many of whom demanded a withdrawal that was prompt, complete, unconditional, and irreversible. Antiwar protesters staged a massive national Vietnam moratorium in October 1969, as nearly 100,000 people jammed the Boston Common and some 50,000 filed by the White House carrying lighted candles.

Undaunted, Nixon launched his own home-front counteroffensive. On November 3, 1969, he delivered a dramatic televised appeal to the great "silent majority," who presumably supported the war. Though ostensibly conciliatory, Nixon's appeal was in fact deeply divisive, as he sought to carve out a political constituency that would back his policies. His intentions soon became clear when he unleashed tough-talking Vice President Agnew to attack the "misleading" news media, as well as the "effete corps of impudent snobs" and the "nattering nabobs of negativism" who demanded quick withdrawal from Vietnam. Nixon himself in 1970 sneered at the student antiwar demonstrators as "bums."

By January 1970 the Vietnam conflict had become the longest in American history and, with 40,000 killed and over 250,000 wounded, the third most costly foreign war in the nation's experience. It had also become grotesquely unpopular, even among troops in the field. Because draft policies largely exempted college students and men with critical civilian skills, the armed forces in Vietnam were largely composed of the least privileged young Americans. Especially in the war's early stages, African-Americans were disproportionately represented in the army and accounted for a disproportionately high share of combat fatalities. Black and white soldiers alike fought not only against the Vietnamese enemy but also against the coiled fear of floundering through booby-trapped swamps and steaming jungles, often unable to distinguish friend from foe among the Vietnamese peasants. Drug abuse, mutiny, and sabotage dulled the army's fighting edge. Morale appeared to have plummeted to rock bottom when rumors filtered out of Vietnam that soldiers were "fragging" their own officers—murdering them with fragmentation grenades.

Domestic disgust with the war was further deepened in 1970 by revelations that in 1968 American troops had massacred innocent women and children in the village of My Lai. Increasingly desperate for a quick end to the demoralizing conflict,

Cold War? Not for Some

Nixon widened the war in 1970 by ordering an attack on Vietnam's neighbor, Cambodia.

Cambodianizing the Vietnam War

For several years the North Vietnamese and Viet Cong had been using Cambodia, bordering South Vietnam on the west, as a springboard for troops, weapons, and supplies. Suddenly, on April 29, 1970, without consulting Congress, Nixon ordered American forces to join with the South Vietnamese in cleaning out the enemy sanctuaries in officially neutral Cambodia.

Restless students nationwide responded to the Cambodian invasion with rock throwing, window smashing, and arson. At Kent State University in Ohio, jumpy members of the National Guard fired into a noisy crowd, killing four and wounding many more; at Jackson State College in Mississippi, the highway patrol discharged volleys at a student dormitory, killing two black students. The nation fell prey to turmoil as rioters and arsonists convulsed the land.

A Marine Corps officer expressed the disillusion that beset many American troops in Vietnam:

"For years we disposed of the enemy dead like so much garbage. We stuck cigarettes in the mouths of corpses, put *Playboy* magazines in their hands, cut off their ears to wear around our necks. We incinerated them with napalm, atomized them with B-52 strikes, shoved them out the doors of helicopters above the South China Sea. . . . All we did was count, count bodies. Count dead human beings. . . . That was our fundamental military strategy. Body count. And the count kept going up."

Nixon withdrew the American troops from Cambodia on June 29, 1970, after only two months. But in America the Cambodian invasion deepened the bitterness between "hawks" and "doves," as right-wing groups physically assaulted leftists. Disillusionment with "whitey's war" increased ominously among African-Americans in the armed forces. The Senate (though not the House) overwhelmingly repealed the Gulf of Tonkin blank check that Congress had given Johnson in 1964 and sought ways to restrain Nixon. The youth of America, still aroused, were only slightly mollified when the government reduced draft calls and shortened the period of draftability, on a lottery basis, from eight years to one year. They were similarly pleased, though not pacified, when the Twenty-sixth Amendment in 1971 lowered the voting age to eighteen (see the Appendix).

In the spring of 1971, mass rallies and marches once more erupted from coast to coast. New combustibles fueled the fires of antiwar discontent in June 1971, when *The New York Times* published a top-secret Pentagon study of America's involvement in the Vietnam War. These Pentagon Papers, "leaked" to the *Times* by former Pentagon official Daniel Ellsberg, laid bare the blunders and deceptions of the Kennedy and Johnson administrations,

The War at Home Antiwar students clash with police in Ann Arbor, Michigan, in 1970.

especially the provoking of the 1964 North Vietnamese attack in the Gulf of Tonkin.

Nixon's Détente with Beijing (Peking) and Moscow

As the antiwar firestorm flared ever higher, Nixon concluded that the road out of Vietnam ran through Beijing and Moscow. The two great communist powers, the Soviet Union and China, were clashing bitterly over their rival interpretations of Marxism. Nixon astutely perceived that the Chinese-Soviet tension afforded the United States an opportunity to play off one antagonist against the other and to enlist the aid of both in pressuring North Vietnam into peace.

Nixon's thinking was reinforced by his national security adviser, Dr. Henry A. Kissinger. Bespectacled and German-accented, Kissinger had reached America as a youth when his parents fled Hitler's anti-Jewish persecutions. In 1969 the former Harvard professor had begun meeting secretly on Nixon's behalf with North Vietnamese officials in Paris to negotiate an end to the war in Vietnam. He was meanwhile preparing the president's path to Beijing and Moscow.

Nixon, heretofore an uncompromising anti-communist, announced to a startled nation in July 1971 that he had accepted an invitation to visit China the following year. He made his historic journey in February 1972. Between glass-clinking toasts and walks on the fabled Great Wall of China, he paved the way for improved relations between Washington and Beijing.

Nixon next traveled to Moscow in May 1972 to play his "China card" in a game of high-stakes diplomacy in the Kremlin. The Soviets, hungry for American foodstuffs and alarmed over the possibility of intensified rivalry with an American-backed China, were ready to deal. Nixon's visits ushered in an era of *détente*, or relaxed tension, with the two communist powers. Détente resulted in several significant agreements. One product of eased relations was the great grain deal of 1972—a three-year arrangement by which the food-rich United States agreed to sell the Soviets at least $750 million worth of wheat, corn, and other cereals.

Far more important were steps to stem the dangerously frantic competition in nuclear arms. The

Some Chicken, Some Egg, 1975   This cartoon pokes fun at Henry Kissinger as a global statesman. Serving first as President Nixon's national security adviser and then as secretary of state in the Nixon and Ford administrations, the German-born Kissinger brought with him to Washington a sophisticated—some said cynical—view of the world honed during his nearly two decades as a political science professor at Harvard.

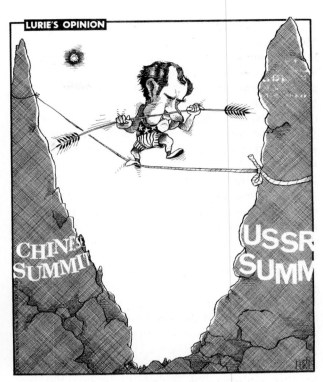

LURIE'S OPINION

CHINESE SUMMIT

USSR SUMM

Balancing Act   Nixon treads delicately between the two communist superpowers in 1973, holding some of the wheat with which he enticed both into détente.

first major achievement was an anti–ballistic missile (ABM) treaty, which limited each nation to two clusters of defensive missiles. The second significant pact was an agreement, known as SALT (Strategic Arms Limitation Talks), to freeze the numbers of long-range nuclear missiles for five years. These accords, both ratified in 1972, constituted a long-overdue first step toward slowing the arms race. Yet even though the ABM treaty forbade elaborate defensive systems, the United States forged ahead with the development of "MIRVs" (multiple independently targeted reentry vehicles), designed to overcome any defense by "saturating" it with large numbers of warheads, several to a rocket. Predictably, the Soviets proceeded to "MIRV" their own missiles, and the arms race ratcheted up to a still more perilous plateau, with over sixteen thousand nuclear warheads deployed by both sides by the end of the 1980s.

Nixon's détente diplomacy did, to some extent, deice the Cold War. Moreover, by checkmating and co-opting the two great communist powers, the president had cleverly set the stage for America's exit from Vietnam. But the concluding act in that wrenching tragedy still remained to be played.

A New Team on the Supreme Bench

Nixon had lashed out during the campaign at the "permissiveness" and "judicial activism" of the Supreme Court presided over by Chief Justice Earl Warren. Following his appointment in 1953, the jovial Warren had led the Court into a series of decisions that drastically affected sexual freedom, the rights of criminals, the practice of religion, civil rights, and the structure of political representation. The decisions of the Warren Court reflected its deep concern for the individual, no matter how lowly.

In *Griswold* v. *Connecticut* (1965), the Court struck down a state law that prohibited the use of contraceptives, even among married couples. The Court proclaimed (critics said "invented") a "right of privacy" that soon provided the basis for decisions protecting women's abortion rights.

In 1963 the Court held *(Gideon* v. *Wainwright)* that all defendants in serious criminal cases were entitled to legal counsel, even if they were too poor to afford it. More controversial were the rulings in two cases—*Escobedo* (1964) and *Miranda* (1966)—that ensured the right of the accused to remain silent and to enjoy other protections when accused of a crime. In this way safeguards were erected against confessions extorted under the rubber hose and other torture. Critics of these decisions were loud in their condemnation of "crook coddling" and demanded that the courts handcuff criminals, not the "cops."

Freedom of the press was also emphatically endorsed by the Warren Court in the case of *New York Times* v. *Sullivan* (1964). The Court ruled unanimously that public figures could sue for libel only if they could prove that "malice" had motivated their defamers. The decision opened a wide door for free-wheeling criticism of the public actions as well as the private lives of politicians and other officials.

Nor did the Court shy away from explosive religious issues. In two stunning decisions, *Engel* v. *Vitale* (1962) and *School District of Abington Township* v. *Schempp* (1963), it voted against required prayers and Bible reading in the public schools. These rulings were based on the First Amendment, which requires the separation of church and state, but to many religious believers they seemed to put the justices in the same bracket with atheistic communists. Cynics predicted that the "old goats in black coats" would soon be erasing "In God We Trust" from all coins.

Infuriating to many southerners was the determination of the Court, following the school-desegregation decision of 1954, to support black people in civil rights cases. Five southern state legislatures officially nullified the "sociological" Supreme Court decision, but they in turn were overruled by the high tribunal. In general, it held that the states could not deny to blacks the rights that were extended to whites. Conservatives maligned the Warren Court for not interpreting the Constitution but rewriting it, at the expense of states' rights and other constitutional guarantees. It was acting, they charged, too much like a legislature and not enough like a judicial body.

The Warren Court also struck at the overrepresentation in state legislatures of cow-pasture agricultural districts. Adopting the principle of one-man-one-vote, the Court in *Reynolds* v. *Sims* (1964) ruled that the state legislatures, both upper and lower houses, would have to be reapportioned according to the human population, irrespective of cows. States' righters and assorted right-wingers raised anew the battle cry "Impeach Earl Warren." But the legislatures grudgingly went ahead with reapportionment.

From 1954 on, the Court came under relentless criticism, the bitterest since New Deal days. Its foes made numerous but unsuccessful efforts to clip its wings through bills in Congress or through constitutional amendments. But for better or worse, the Court was grappling with stubborn social problems spawned by midcentury tensions, even—or especially—if duly elected legislatures failed to do so.

Fulfilling campaign promises, President Nixon undertook to change the Court's philosophical complexion. Taking advantage of several vacancies, he sought appointees who would strictly interpret the Constitution, cease "meddling" in social and political questions, and not coddle radicals or criminals. The Senate in 1969 speedily confirmed his nomination of white-maned Warren E. Burger of Minnesota to succeed the retiring Earl Warren as chief justice. Before the end of 1971, the Court counted four conservative Nixon appointments out of nine members.

Yet Nixon was to learn the ironic lesson that many presidents have learned about their Supreme Court appointees: once seated on the high bench, the justices are fully free to think and decide according to their own beliefs, not according to the president's expectations. The Burger Court that Nixon shaped proved reluctant to dismantle the "liberal" rulings of the Warren Court; it even produced the most controversial judicial opinion of modern times, the momentous *Roe* v. *Wade* decision in 1973, which legalized abortion (see p. 989).

Nixon on the Home Front

Surprisingly, Nixon presided over significant expansion of the welfare programs that conservative Republicans routinely denounced. He approved increased appropriations for entitlements like Food Stamps and Medicaid, as well as for the largest federal welfare program, Aid to Families with Dependent Children (AFDC), which especially targeted single mothers of young children. Nixon also implemented a new federal program, Supplemental Security Income (SSI), which gave generous benefits to the indigent aged, blind, and disabled. He signed legislation in 1972 that raised Social Security old-age pensions and provided for automatic increases when the cost of living rose more than 3 percent in any year. Ironically, though designed to protect the elderly against the ravages of inflation, this "indexing" actually helped to fuel the inflationary fires that raged out of control later in the decade. Yet in the short run, Nixon's generous expansion of Great Society programs—along with continuing economic growth—helped reduce the nation's poverty rate to 11 percent in 1973, its lowest level in modern history.

Amid much controversy, Nixon also did the Great Society one better in his attack on racial discrimination. His so-called Philadelphia Plan of 1969 required construction-trade unions working on federal contracts in Philadelphia to establish "goals and timetables" for the hiring of black apprentices. Nixon may have been motivated in part by a desire to weaken the forces of liberalism by driving a wedge between blacks and trade unions. But whatever his reasoning, the president's new policy had far-reaching implications. Soon extended to all federal contracts, the Philadelphia Plan in effect required thousands of employers to meet hiring quotas or to establish "set-asides" for minority subcontractors.

Nixon's Philadelphia Plan drastically altered the meaning of "affirmative action." Lyndon Johnson had intended affirmative action to protect *individuals* against discrimination. Nixon now transformed and escalated affirmative action into a program that conferred privileges on certain *groups*. The Supreme Court went along with Nixon's approach. In *Griggs* v. *Duke Power Co.* (1971), the black-robed justices prohibited intelligence tests or other devices that had the effect of excluding minorities or women from certain jobs. The Court's ruling strongly suggested that the only sure protection against charges of discrimination was to hire minority workers—or admit minority students—in proportion to their presence in the population.

Together the actions of Nixon and the Court opened broad employment and educational opportunities for minorities and women. They also opened a Pandora's box of protest. Critics assailed the new style of affirmative action as "reverse discrimination." They objected especially that such a sweeping policy had been created by executive order and judicial decision, not by democratically elected representatives in the legislature. Yet what other remedy was there, defenders asked, to offset centuries of prejudice and opportunity denied?

Among the other major legacies of the Nixon years was the creation in 1970 of the Environmental Protection Agency (EPA) and a companion body, the Occupational Health and Safety Administration (OSHA). Their births climaxed two decades of mounting concern for the environment, beginning with the establishment in Los Angeles of the Air Pollution Control Office in 1950. Author Rachel Carson gave the environmental movement a huge boost in 1962 when she published *Silent Spring*, an enormously effective piece of latter-day muckraking that exposed the poisonous effects of pesticides.

Author Rachel Carson   Some call her the mother of the modern conservation movement because of the impact of her 1962 book, *Silent Spring*.

Legislatively armed by the Clean Air Act of 1970, the Endangered Species Act of 1973, and similar laws, EPA and OSHA stood on the frontline of the battle for ecological sanity. They made notable progress in the ensuing decades on reducing automobile emissions and cleaning up befouled waterways and toxic waste sites. Impressed by the new environmentalist mood, Congress refused after 1972 to pay for any more of the huge irrigation projects that had watered—and ecologically transformed—much of the arid West over the preceding half century.

Worried about creeping inflation (then running at about 5 percent), Nixon overcame his distaste for economic controls and imposed a ninety-day wage and price freeze in 1971. To stimulate the nation's sagging exports, he next stunned the world by taking the United States off the gold standard and devaluing the dollar. These moves effectively ended the "Bretton Woods" system of international currency stabilization that had functioned for more that a quarter of a century after World War II.

Elected as a minority president, with only 43 percent of the vote in 1968, Nixon devised a clever but cynical plan—called the "southern strategy"—to achieve a solid majority in 1972. His Supreme Court nominations constituted an important part of his scheme. The southern strategy emphasized an appeal to white voters by soft-pedaling civil rights and openly opposing school busing to achieve racial balance. But as fate would have it, the southern strategy became superfluous as foreign policy dominated the presidential campaign of 1972.

The Nixon Landslide of 1972

Vietnam continued to be the burning issue. Nearly four years had passed since Nixon had promised, as a presidential candidate, to end the war and "win" the peace. Yet in the spring of 1972, the fighting escalated anew to alarming levels when the North Vietnamese, heavily equipped with foreign tanks, burst through the demilitarized zone (DMZ) separating the two Vietnams. Nixon reacted promptly by launching massive bombing attacks on strategic centers in North Vietnam, including Hanoi, the capital. Gambling heavily on foreign forbearance, he also ordered the dropping of contact mines to blockade the principal harbors of North Vietnam. Either Moscow or Beijing, or both, could have

responded explosively, but neither did, thanks to Nixon's shrewd diplomacy. The North Vietnamese offensive finally ground to a halt.

The continuing Vietnam conflict spurred the rise of South Dakota senator George McGovern to the 1972 Democratic nomination. McGovern's promise to pull the remaining American troops out of Vietnam in ninety days earned him the backing of the large antiwar element in the party. But his appeal to racial minorities, feminists, leftists, and youth alienated the traditional working-class backbone of his party. Moreover, the discovery shortly after the convention that McGovern's running mate, Missouri senator Thomas Eagleton, had undergone psychiatric care forced Eagleton's removal from the ticket and virtually doomed McGovern's candidacy.

Nixon's campaign emphasized that he had wound down the "Democratic war" in Vietnam from some 540,000 troops to about 30,000. His candidacy received an added boost just twelve days before the election when the high-flying Dr. Kissinger announced that "peace is at hand" in Vietnam and that an agreement would be settled in a few days.

Nixon won the election in a landslide. His lopsided victory encompassed every state except Massachusetts and the nonstate District of Columbia. He piled up 520 electoral votes to 17 for McGovern and a popular majority of 47,169,911 to 29,170,383 votes. McGovern had counted on a large number of young people's votes, but less than half the 18–21 age group even bothered to register to vote. Nixon's claim that the election gave him an unprecedented mandate for his policies was weakened by Republican election losses in both the House and Senate.

Bombing North Vietnam to the Peace Table

The dove of peace, "at hand" in Vietnam just before the balloting, took flight after the election, when Nixon refused to be stampeded into accepting terms pocked with obvious loopholes. After the fighting on both sides had again escalated, he launched a furious two-week bombing of North Vietnam in an ironhanded effort to force the North Vietnamese back to the conference table. This attack was the heaviest of the war and resulted in substantial losses of America's big B-52 bombers. But this merciless pounding drove the North Viet-

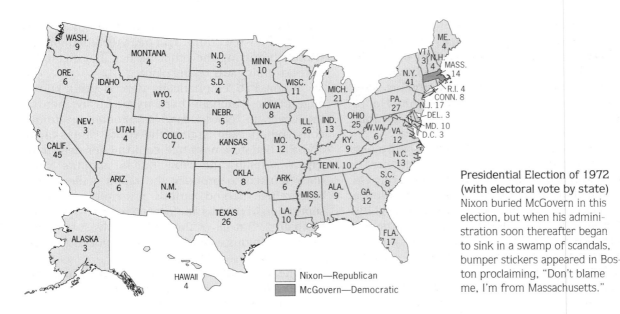

Presidential Election of 1972
(with electoral vote by state)
Nixon buried McGovern in this election, but when his administration soon thereafter began to sink in a swamp of scandals, bumper stickers appeared in Boston proclaiming, "Don't blame me, I'm from Massachusetts."

namese negotiators to agree to cease-fire arrangements on January 23, 1973, nearly three months after peace was prematurely proclaimed.

Nixon hailed the face-saving cease-fire agreements as "peace with honor," but the boast rang hollow. The United States was to withdraw its remaining 27,000 or so troops and could reclaim some 560 American prisoners of war. The government of South Vietnam would be permitted to continue receiving limited U.S. support but no more U.S. fighting forces. An election was eventually to be held to determine the future of the country. The North Vietnamese were allowed to keep some 145,000 troops in South Vietnam, where they could be used to spearhead a powerful new offensive when the time seemed ripe. Ominously, the North Vietnamese still occupied about 30 percent of South Vietnam. The shaky "peace" was in reality little more than a thinly disguised American retreat.

Watergate Woes

Nixon's electoral triumph was soon sullied by the so-called Watergate scandals. On June 17, 1972, some two months before his renomination, a bungled burglary had occurred in the Democratic headquarters, located in the Watergate apartment-office complex in Washington. Five men were arrested inside the building with electronic "bugging" equipment in their possession. They were working for the Republican Committee for the Re-election of the President—popularly known as CREEP—which had managed to raise tens of millions of dollars, often by secretive, unethical, or unlawful means. CREEP had also engaged in a "dirty tricks" campaign of espionage and sabotage, including faked documents, directed against Democratic candidates in the campaign of 1972.

The Watergate break-in was only the tip of an iceberg in a slimy sea of corruption that made the Grant and Harding scandals look almost respectable. Several prominently placed White House aides and advisers were forced to resign. Many were involved in the criminal obstruction of justice through tangled cover-ups or payments of hush money. By early 1974 twenty-nine people had been indicted, had pleaded guilty, or had been convicted of Watergate-related crimes.

The scandal in Washington also provoked the improper or illegal use of the Federal Bureau of Investigation and the Central Intelligence Agency. Even the Internal Revenue Service was called upon by Nixon's aides to audit or otherwise harass political opponents and others who had fallen into disfavor. A White House "enemies list" turned up that included innocent citizens who were to be hounded or prosecuted in various ways. In the name of national security, Nixon's aides had authorized a burglary of the files of Dr. Daniel Ellsberg's psychiatrist, so great was the determination to destroy the man who had "leaked" the Pentagon Papers. This was the most notorious exploit of the White House "plumbers unit," created to plug up leaks of confidential information.

A select Senate committee, headed by the aging Senator Sam Ervin of North Carolina, conducted a prolonged and widely televised series of hearings in 1973–1974. John Dean III, a former White House lawyer with a remarkable memory, testified glibly and at great length as to the involvement of the top echelons in the White House, including the president, in the cover-up of the Watergate break-in. Dean in effect accused Nixon of the crime of obstructing justice. But the committee then had only the unsupported word of Dean against weighty White House protestations of innocence.

The Great Tape Controversy

A bombshell exploded before Senator Ervin's committee in July 1973 when a former presidential aide reported the presence in the White House of "bugging" equipment, installed under the president's

authority. President Nixon's conversations, in person or on the telephone, had been recorded on tape without notifying the other parties that electronic eavesdropping was taking place.

Nixon had emphatically denied prior knowledge of the Watergate burglary or involvement in the cover-up. Now Dean's sensational testimony could be checked against the White House tapes, and the Senate committee could better determine who was telling the truth. But for months Nixon flatly refused to produce the taped evidence. He took refuge behind various principles, including separation of powers and executive privilege (confidentiality). But all of them were at least constitutionally dubious, especially when invoked to cover up crime or obstruct justice.

The anxieties of the White House deepened when Vice President Agnew was forced to resign in October 1973 for taking bribes or "kickbacks" from Maryland contractors while governor and also as vice president. President Nixon himself was now in danger of being removed by the impeachment route, so Congress invoked the Twenty-fifth Amendment (see the Appendix) to replace Agnew with a twelve-term congressman from Michigan, Gerald ("Jerry") Ford. His record in public life was politically respectable and his financial affairs proved to be above suspicion at a time when unquestioned honesty was in short supply.

John Dean Testifies at the Watergate Hearings When Dean's testimony was later corroborated by tape recordings of presidential conversations, President Richard Nixon was forced to resign. Behind Dean is his wife, Maureen.

Ten days after Agnew's resignation came the famous "Saturday Night Massacre" (October 20, 1973). Archibald Cox, a Harvard law professor appointed as a "special prosecutor" by Nixon in May, issued a subpoena for relevant tapes and other documents from the White House. A cornered Nixon thereupon ordered the firing of Cox and then accepted the resignations of the attorney general and the deputy attorney general because they refused to fire Cox.

The Secret Bombing of Cambodia and the War Powers Act

As if Watergate were not enough, the constitutionality of Nixon's continued aerial battering of Cambodia came under increasing fire. In July 1973 America was shocked to learn that the U.S. Air Force had already secretly conducted some thirty-five hundred bombing raids against North Vietnamese positions in Cambodia. They had begun in March 1969 and had continued for some fourteen months prior to the open American incursion in May 1970. The most disturbing feature of these sky forays was that while they were going on, American officials, including the president, were avowing that Cambodian neutrality was being respected. Countless Americans began to wonder what kind of representative government they had if the United States was fighting a war they knew nothing about.

Defiance followed secretiveness. After the Vietnam cease-fire in January 1973, Nixon openly carried on his large-scale bombing of communist forces in order to help the rightist Cambodian government. This stretching of presidential war-making powers met furious opposition from the public and from a clear majority in both houses of Congress, which repeatedly tried to stop the bombing by cutting off appropriations. But Nixon's vetoes of such legislation were always sustained by at least one-third-plus-one votes in the House. Finally, with appropriations running short, Nixon agreed to a compromise in June 1973 whereby he would end the Cambodian bombing six weeks later and seek congressional approval of any future action in that bomb-blasted country.

The years of bombing had inflicted grisly wounds on Cambodia. Incessant American air raids had blasted its people, shredded its economy, and revolutionized its politics. The long-suffering Cambodians soon groaned under the sadistic heel of Pol Pot, a murderous tyrant who dispatched as many as 2 million of his people to their graves. He was forced from power, ironically enough, only by a full-dress Vietnamese invasion in 1978, followed by a military occupation that dragged on for a decade.

Congressional opposition to the expansion of presidential war-making powers by Johnson and Nixon led to the War Powers Act in November 1973. Passed over Nixon's veto, it required the president to report to Congress within forty-eight hours after committing troops to a foreign conflict or "substantially" enlarging American combat units in a foreign

> *The* Washington Post *(July 19, 1973) carried this news item:*
>
> "American B-52 bombers dropped about 104,000 tons of explosives on Communist sanctuaries in neutralist Cambodia during a series of raids in 1969 and 1970. . . . The secret bombing was acknowledged by the Pentagon the Monday after a former Air Force major . . . described how he falsified reports on Cambodian air operations and destroyed records on the bombing missions actually flown."

country. Such a limited authorization would have to end within sixty days unless Congress extended it for thirty more days.

Compelling Nixon to end the bombing of Cambodia in August 1973 was but one manifestation of what came to be called the "New Isolationism." The draft had ended in January 1973, although it was retained on a standby basis. Future members of the armed forces were to be well-paid volunteers—a change that greatly eased tensions among youth. Insistent demands arose in Congress for reducing American armed forces abroad, especially because some 300,000 remained in Europe more than a quarter of a century after Hitler's downfall. The argument often heard was that the Western European countries, with more population than the Soviet Union, ought by now to be willing and able to provide for their own defense against the forces of communism. But President Nixon, fearful of a weakened hand in the high-stakes game of power politics, headed off all serious attempts at troop reduction.

The Arab Oil Embargo and the Energy Crisis

Adding to Nixon's problems, the long-rumbling Middle East erupted anew in October 1973, when the rearmed Syrians and Egyptians unleashed surprise attacks on Israel in an attempt to regain the territory they had lost in the Six-Day War of 1967. With the Israelis in desperate retreat, Kissinger, who had become secretary of state in September, hastily flew to Moscow in an effort to restrain the Soviets, who were

arming the attackers. Believing that the Kremlin was poised to fly combat troops to the Suez area, Nixon placed America's nuclear forces on alert and ordered a gigantic airlift of nearly $2 billion in war materials to the Israelis. This assistance helped save the day, as the Israelis aggressively turned the tide and had stormed to a stone's throw from Cairo when American diplomacy brought about an uneasy cease-fire.

America's policy of backing Israel against its oil-rich neighbors exacted a heavy penalty. Late in October 1973, the Arab nations suddenly clamped an embargo on oil for the United States and for other countries supporting Israel. Americans had to suffer through a long, cold winter of lowered thermostats and speedometers. Lines of automobiles at service stations lengthened as tempers shortened and a business recession deepened.

The "energy crisis" suddenly energized a number of long-deferred projects. Congress approved a costly Alaska pipeline and a national speed limit of fifty-five miles per hour to conserve fuel. Agitation mounted for heavier use of coal and nuclear power, despite the environmental threat they posed.

The five months of the Arab "blackmail" embargo in 1974 clearly signaled the end of an era—the era of cheap and abundant energy. A twenty-year surplus of world oil supplies had masked the fact that since 1948 the United States had been a net importer of oil. American oil production peaked in 1970 and then began an irreversible decline. Blissfully unaware of their dependence on foreign suppliers, Americans, like revelers on a binge, had more than tripled their oil consumption since the end of World War II. The number of automobiles increased 250 percent between 1949 and 1972, and Detroit's engineers gave nary a thought to building more fuel-efficient engines.

By 1974 America was oil addicted and extremely vulnerable to any interruption in supplies. That stark fact colored the diplomatic and economic history of the 1980s and 1990s. The Middle East loomed ever larger on the map of America's strategic interests, until the United States in 1990 at last found itself pulled into a shooting war with Iraq to protect its oil supplies.

The Middle Eastern sheiks, flexing their economic muscles through OPEC (Organization of Petroleum Exporting Countries), approximately quadrupled their price for crude oil after lifting the embargo in 1974. Huge new oil bills wildly disrupted the U.S. balance of international trade and added further fuel to the already raging fires of inflation.

The United States took the lead in forming the International Energy Agency in 1974 as a counterweight to OPEC, and various sectors of the economy, including Detroit's carmakers, began their slow, grudging adjustment to the rudely dawning age of energy dependency. But full reconciliation to that uncomfortable reality was a long time coming.

The Unmaking of a President

Political tribulations added to the nation's cup of woe in 1974. The continuing impeachment inquiry cast damning doubts on Nixon's integrity. Responding at last to the House Judiciary Committee's demand for the Watergate tapes, Nixon agreed in the spring of 1974 to the publication of "relevant" portions of the tapes, declaring that these would vindicate him. But substantial sections of the wanted tapes were missing, and Nixon's frequent obscenities were excised with the phrase "expletive deleted." Confronted with demands for the rest of the material, Nixon flatly refused. On July 24, 1974, the president suffered a disastrous setback when the Supreme Court unanimously ruled that "executive privilege" gave him no right to withhold from the special prosecutor portions of tapes relevant to criminal activity. Skating on thin ice over hot water, Nixon reluctantly complied.

The House Judiciary Committee pressed ahead with its articles of impeachment. The key vote came late in July 1974, when the committee adopted the first article, which charged obstruction of "the administration of justice," including Watergate-related crimes. Two other articles were later approved by the committee accusing Nixon of having abused the powers of his office and of having shown contempt of Congress by ignoring lawful subpoenas for relevant tapes and other evidence.

Seeking to soften the impact of inevitable disclosure, Nixon voluntarily took a step, on August 5, 1974, that had a devastating effect on what remained of his credibility. He now made public three subpoenaed tapes of conversations with his chief aide on June 23, 1972. One of them had him giving orders, six days after the Watergate break-in, to use the CIA to hold back an inquiry by the FBI. Now Nixon's own tape-recorded words convicted him of having been an active party to the attempted cover-up, in itself the crime of obstructing justice. More than that, he had solemnly told the American people on television that he had known nothing of the Watergate whitewash until about nine months later.

The public backlash proved to be overwhelming. Republican leaders in Congress concluded that the guilty and unpredictable Nixon was a loose cannon on the deck of the ship of state. They frankly informed the president that his impeachment by the full House and removal by the Senate were foregone conclusions. They made it clear that he would best serve his nation, his party, and himself by resigning with honor, or a semblance of it. If convicted by the Senate, he would lose all his normal retirement

Uncle Sam's Bed of Nails
The oil crises of the 1970s tortured the American economy.

Nixon, the Law-and-Order-Man

The First Unelected President

Gerald Rudolph Ford, the first man to be made president solely by a vote of Congress, entered the besmirched White House in August 1974 with serious handicaps. He was widely—and unfairly—suspected of being little more than a dim-witted former college football player. President Johnson had sneered that "Jerry" was so lacking in brainpower that he could not walk and chew gum at the same time. Worse, Ford had been selected, not elected, vice president, following Spiro Agnew's resignation in disgrace. The sour odor of illegitimacy hung about this president without precedent.

Then, out of a clear sky, Ford granted a complete pardon to Nixon for any crimes he may have committed as president, discovered or undiscovered. Democrats were outraged. They wanted iron-toothed justice, even vengeance. They heatedly charged, without persuasive evidence, that Ford was carrying out a "buddy deal" that had been cooked up when Nixon nominated him for the vice presidency. Ford explained that he only wanted to end Nixon's private agony, heal the festering wounds in the body

benefits; if he resigned he could retain them—more than $150,000 a year—and retire in royal splendor.

Left with no better choice, Nixon choked back his tears and announced his resignation in a dramatic television appearance on August 8, 1974. Few presidents had flown so high, and none had sunk so low. In his Farewell Address, Nixon admitted having made some "judgments" that "were wrong" but insisted that he had always acted "in what I believed at the time to be the best interests of the nation." Unconvinced, countless Americans would change the song "Hail to the Chief" to "Jail to the Chief."

The nation had survived a wrenching constitutional crisis, which proved that the impeachment machinery forged by the Founding Fathers could work when public opinion overwhelmingly demanded that it be implemented. The principles that no person is above the law and that presidents must be held to strict accountability for their acts were strengthened. The United States of America, on the eve of its two-hundredth birthday as a republic, had given an impressive demonstration of self-discipline and self-government to the rest of the world.

How Long Will Nixon Haunt the GOP? Doubts about Ford's pardon of Nixon clouded his brief presidency.

EXAMINING THE EVIDENCE

The "Smoking Gun" Tape, June 23, 1972, 10:04–11:39 A.M. The technological capability to record Oval Office conversations combined with Richard Nixon's obsession with documenting his presidency to give the public—and the Senate committee investigating his role in the break-in of the Democratic National Committee headquarters in the Watergate Office Tower—rare access to personal conversations between the president and his closest advisers. This tape, which undeniably exposed Nixon's central role in constructing a "cover-up" of the Watergate break-in, was made on Nixon's first day back in Washington after the botched burglary of June 17, 1972. In this conversation with White House Chief of Staff H. R. Haldeman, Nixon devised a plan to block a widening F.B.I. investigation by instructing the director of the C.I.A. to deflect any further F.B.I. snooping on the grounds that it would endanger sensitive C.I.A. operations. Nixon refused to turn over this and other tapes to Senate investigators until so ordered by the Supreme Court on July 24, 1974. Within four days of its release on August 5, Nixon was forced to resign. After eighteen months of protesting his innocence of the crime and his ignorance of any effort to obstruct justice, Nixon was finally undone by the evidence in this incriminating "smoking gun" tape. While tapes documented two straight years of Nixon's Oval Office conversations, other presidents, such as Franklin Roosevelt, John F. Kennedy, and Lyndon Baines Johnson, recorded important meetings and crisis deliberations. Since Watergate, however, it is unlikely that any president has permitted extensive tape recording, depriving historians of a unique insight into the inner-workings of the White House. Should taped White House discussions be part of the public record of a presidency, and if so, who should have access to them? What else might historians learn from a tape like this one, besides analyzing the Watergate cover-up?

Haldeman: . . . yesterday, they concluded it was not the White House, but are now convinced it is a CIA thing, so the CIA turn off would . . .

President: Well, not sure of their analysis, I'm not going to get that involved. I'm (unintelligible).

Haldeman: No, sir. We don't want you to.

President: You call them in.

President: Good. Good deal! Play it tough. That's the way they play it and that's the way we are going to play it.

Haldeman: O.K. We'll do it.

President: Yeah, when I saw that news summary item, I of course knew it was a bunch of crap, but I thought ah, well it's good to have them off on this wild hair thing because when they start bugging us, which they have, we'll know our little boys will not know how to handle it. I hope they will though. You never know. Maybe, you think about it. Good!

President: When you get in these people when you . . . get these people in, say: "Look, the problem is that this will open the whole, the whole Bay of Pigs thing, and the President just feels that" ah, without going into the details . . . don't, don't lie to them to the extent to say there is no involvement, but just say this is sort of a comedy of errors, bizarre, without getting into it, "the President believes that it is going to open the whole Bay of Pigs thing up again. And, ah because these people are plugging for, for keeps and that they should call the FBI in and say that we wish for the country, don't go any further into this case," period!

politic, and let the country get on with its business, undistracted by a possibly sensational trial. But lingering suspicions about the circumstances of the pardon cast a dark shadow over Ford's prospects of being elected president in his own right in 1976.

Ford at first sought to enhance the so-called détente with the Soviet Union that Nixon had crafted. In July 1975 President Ford joined leaders from thirty-four other nations in Helsinki, Finland, to sign several sets of historic accords. One group of agreements officially wrote an end to World War II by finally legitimizing the Soviet-dictated boundaries of Poland and other Eastern European countries. In return, the Soviets signed a "third basket" of agreements, guaranteeing more liberal exchanges of people and information between East and West and protecting certain basic "human rights." The Helsinki accords kindled small dissident movements in Eastern Europe and even in the USSR itself, but the Soviets soon poured ice water on these sputtering flames of freedom. Moscow's restrictions on Jewish emigration had already, in December 1974, prompted Congress to add punitive restrictions to a U.S.-Soviet trade bill.

Western Europeans, especially the West Germans, cheered the Helsinki conference as a milestone of détente. But in the United States, critics increasingly charged that détente was proving to be a one-way street. American grain and technology flowed across the Atlantic to the USSR, and little of comparable importance flowed back. And Soviet ships and planes continued to haul great quantities of arms and military technicians to procommunist forces around the globe.

Despite these difficulties, Ford at first clung stubbornly to détente. But the American public's fury over Moscow's double-dealing so steadily mounted that by the end of his term, the president was refusing even to pronounce the word *détente* in public. The thaw in the Cold War was threatening to prove chillingly brief.

Defeat in Vietnam

Early in 1975 the North Vietnamese gave full throttle to their long-expected drive southward. President Ford urged Congress to vote still more weapons for Vietnam, but his plea was in vain, and without the crutch of massive American aid, the South Vietnamese quickly and ingloriously collapsed.

The dam burst so rapidly that the remaining Americans had to be frantically evacuated by helicopter, the last of them on April 29, 1975. Also rescued were about 140,000 South Vietnamese, most of them so dangerously identified with the Americans that they feared a bloodbath by the victorious com-

Passing the Buck   A satirical view of where responsibility for the Vietnam debacle should be laid.

munists. Ford compassionately admitted these people to the United States, where they added further seasoning to the melting pot. Eventually some 500,000 arrived (see "Makers of America: The Vietnamese," pp. 964–965).

America's longest, most frustrating war thus ended not with a bang but a whimper. In a technical sense, the Americans had not lost the war; their client nation had. The United States had fought the North Vietnamese to a standstill and had then withdrawn its troops in 1973, leaving the South Vietnamese to fight their own war, with generous shipments of costly American aircraft, tanks, and other munitions. The estimated cost to America was $118 billion in current outlays, together with some 56,000 dead and 300,000 wounded. The people of the United States had in fact provided just about everything, except the will to win—and that could not be injected by outsiders.

Technicalities aside, America had lost more than a war. It had lost face in the eyes of foreigners, lost its own self-esteem, lost confidence in its military prowess, and lost much of the economic muscle that had made possible its global leadership since World War II. Americans reluctantly came to realize that their power as well as their pride had been deeply wounded in Vietnam and that recovery would be slow and painful.

Feminist Victories and Defeats

As the army limped home from Vietnam, there was little rejoicing on the college campuses, where demonstrators had once braved tear gas and billy clubs to denounce the war. The antiwar movement, like many of the other protest movements that convulsed the country in the 1960s, had long since splintered and stalled. One major exception to this pattern stood out: although they had their differences, American feminists showed vitality and momentum. They won legislative and judicial victories and provoked an intense rethinking of gender roles. (On the roots of this movement, see "Makers of America: The Feminists," pp. 968–969.)

Thousands of women marched in the Women's Stride for Equality on the fiftieth anniversary of woman suffrage in 1970. In 1972 Congress passed Title IX of the Education Amendments, prohibiting sex discrimination in any federally assisted educational program or activity. Perhaps this act's biggest impact was to create opportunities for girls' and women's athletics at schools and colleges, giving birth to a new "Title IX generation" that would reach maturity in the 1980s and 1990s and help professionalize women's sports as well. The Equal Rights Amendment (ERA) to the Constitution won congressional approval

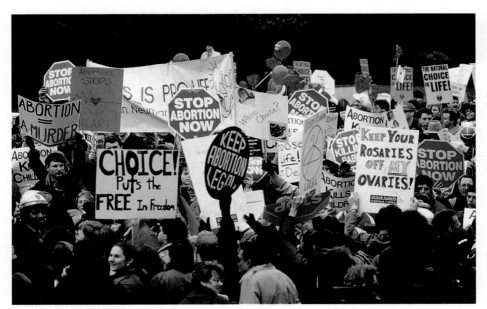

The Abortion Wars
Pro-choice and pro-life demonstrators brandish their beliefs. By the end of the twentieth century, the debate over abortion had become the most morally charged and divisive issue in American society since the struggle over slavery in the nineteenth century.

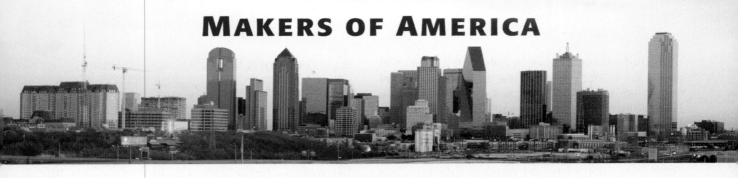

The Vietnamese

At first glance the towns of Westminster and Fountain Valley, California, seem to resemble other California communities nearby. Tract homes line residential streets; shopping centers flank the busy thoroughfares. But these are no ordinary American suburbs. Instead they make up "Little Saigons," vibrant outposts of Vietnamese culture in the contemporary United States. Shops offer exotic Asian merchandise; restaurants serve such delicacies as lemongrass chicken. These neighborhoods, living reminders of America's anguish in Vietnam, are a rarely acknowledged consequence of that sorrowful conflict.

Before South Vietnam fell in 1975, few Vietnamese ventured across the Pacific. Only in 1966 did U.S. immigration authorities even designate "Vietnamese" as a separate category of newcomers, and most early immigrants were the wives and children of U.S. servicemen. But as the communists closed in on Saigon, many Vietnamese, particularly those who had worked closely with American or South Vietnamese authorities, feared for their future. Gathering together as many of their extended-family members as they could assemble, thousands of Vietnamese fled for their lives. In a few hectic days in 1975, some 140,000 Vietnamese escaped before the approaching gunfire, a few dramatically clinging to the bottoms of departing helicopters. From Saigon they were conveyed to military bases in Guam and the Philippines. Another 60,000 less fortunate Vietnamese escaped at the same time over land and sea to Hong Kong and Thailand, where they waited nervously for permission to move on. To accommodate the refugees, the U.S. government set up camps across the nation. Arrivals were crowded into army barracks affording little room and less privacy. These were boot camps not for military service but for assimilation into American society. A rigorous program trained the Vietnamese in English, forbade children from speaking their native language in the classroom, and even immersed them in American slang. Many resented this attempt to mold them, to strip them of their culture.

Their discontent boiled over when authorities prepared to release the refugees from camps and board them with families around the nation. The resettlement officials had decided to find a sponsor for each Vietnamese family—an American family that would provide food, shelter, and assistance for the refugees until they could fend for themselves. But the Vietnamese people cherish their traditional extended families—grandparents, uncles, aunts, and cousins living communally with parents and children. Few American sponsors would accommodate a large extended family; fewer Vietnamese families would willingly separate.

The refugees were dispersed to Iowa, Illinois, Pennsylvania, New York, Washington, and Califor-

The Last Days of Saigon Violence often attended the frantic American evacuation from Vietnam in 1975.

nia. But the settlement sites, many of them tucked away in rural districts, offered scant economic opportunities. The immigrants, who had held mainly skilled or white-collar positions in Vietnam, bristled as they were herded into menial labor. As soon as they could, they relocated, hastening to established Vietnamese enclaves around San Francisco, Los Angeles, and Dallas.

Soon a second throng of Vietnamese immigrants pushed into these Little Saigons. Fleeing from the ravages of poverty and from the oppressive communist government, these stragglers had crammed themselves and their few possessions into little boats, hoping to reach Hong Kong or get picked up by ships. Eventually many of these "boat people" reached the United States. Usually less educated than the first arrivals and receiving far less resettlement aid from the U.S. government, they were, however, more willing to start at the bottom. Today these two groups total more than half a million people. Differing in experience and expectations, the Vietnamese share a new home in a strange land. Their uprooting is an immense, unreckoned consequence of America's longest war.

Boat People   Vietnamese refugees flee to freedom.

Preserving the Past
A Vietnamese-American boy learns classical calligraphy from his grandfather.

965

Anti-feminist Phyllis Schlafly (b. 1924) Phyllis Schlafly traveled the country promoting her "STOP ERA" campaign. She argued that ratification of the Equal Rights Amendment would undermine the American family by violating "the right of a wife to be supported by her husband," requiring women to serve in combat, and legalizing homosexual marriages.

in 1972. It declared, "Equality of rights under the law shall not be denied or abridged by the United States or by any State on account of sex." Twenty-eight states quickly ratified the amendment, first proposed by suffragists in 1923. Hopes rose that the ERA might soon become the law of the land.

Even the Supreme Court seemed to be on the movement's side. In *Reed* v. *Reed* (1971) and *Frontiero* v. *Richardson* (1973), the Court challenged sex discrimination in legislation and employment. And in the landmark case of *Roe* v. *Wade* (1973), the Court struck down laws prohibiting abortion, arguing that a woman's decision to terminate a pregnancy was protected by the constitutional right of privacy.

But the feminist movement soon faced a formidable backlash. In 1972 President Nixon vetoed a proposal to set up nationwide public day care, saying it would weaken the American family. Antifemi-

nists blamed the women's movement for the rising divorce rate, which tripled between 1960 and 1976. And the Catholic Church and the religious right organized a powerful grassroots movement to oppose the legalization of abortion.

For many feminists, the most bitter defeat was the death of the ERA. With ratification by thirty-eight state legislatures, the amendment would have become part of the Constitution. Conservative spokeswoman Phyllis Schlafly led the campaign to stop the ERA. Its advocates, she charged, were just "bitter women seeking a constitutional cure for their personal problems." In 1979 Congress extended the deadline for ratification, but ERA opponents dug in their heels. The amendment died in 1982, three states short of success.

The Seventies in Black and White

Although the civil rights movement had fractured, race remained an explosive issue in the 1970s. The Supreme Court in *Milliken* v. *Bradley* (1974) blindsided school integrationists when it ruled that desegregation plans could not require students to move across school-district lines. The decision effectively exempted suburban districts from shouldering any part of the burden of desegregating inner-city schools, thereby reinforcing "white flight" from cities to suburbs. By the same token, the decision distilled all the problems of desegregation into the least prosperous districts, often pitting the poorest, most disadvantaged elements of the white and black communities against one another. Boston and other cities were shaken to their foundations by attempts to implement school-desegregation plans under these painful conditions.

Affirmative action programs also remained highly controversial. White workers who were denied advancement and white students who were refused college admission continued to raise the cry of "reverse discrimination." They charged that their rights had been violated by employers and admissions officers who put more weight on racial or ethnic background than on ability or achievement.

One white Californian, Allan Bakke, made headlines in 1978 when the Supreme Court, by the narrowest of margins (five to four) upheld his claim that his application to medical school had been turned down because of an admissions program that partially favored minority applicants. In a tortured deci-

A Sad Day for Old Glory
In 1976 America's bicentennial year, anti-busing demonstrators convulsed Boston, the historic "cradle of liberty." White disillusionment with the race-based policies that were a legacy of Lyndon Johnson's "Great Society" programs of the 1960s helped to feed the conservative, antigovernment movement that elected Ronald Reagan in 1980.

sion, reflecting the troubling moral ambiguities and insoluble political complexities of this issue, the Court ordered the University of California at Davis medical school to admit Bakke, and declared that preference in admissions could not be given to members of any group, minority or majority, on the basis of ethnic or racial identity alone. Yet at the same time, the Court said that racial factors might be taken into account in a school's overall admissions policy. Among the dissenters on the sharply divided bench was the Court's only black justice, Thurgood Marshall. He warned in an impassioned opinion that the denial of racial preferences might sweep away years of progress by the civil rights movement. But many conservatives cheered the decision as affirming the principle that justice is colorblind.

One of the most remarkable developments of the 1970s was the resurgence of Native American political power. Inspired by the civil rights movement, American Indians learned to use the courts and well-planned acts of civil disobedience to advance their aims. But while blacks had fought against segregation, Indians used the tactics of the civil rights movement to assert their status as separate semisovereign peoples. Indian activists captured the nation's attention by seizing the island of Alcatraz in 1970 and the village of Wounded Knee, South Dakota, in 1972. A series of victories in the courts consolidated the decade's gains. In the case of *United States* v. *Wheeler* (1978), the Supreme

Court declared that Indian tribes possessed a "unique and limited" sovereignty, subject to the will of Congress but not to individual states.

The Bicentennial Campaign and the Carter Victory

America's two-hundredth birthday, in 1976, fell during a presidential election year—a fitting coincidence for a proud democracy. Gerald Ford energetically sought nomination for the presidency in his own right and won the Republican nod at the Kansas City convention.

The Democratic standard-bearer was fifty-one-year-old James Earl Carter, Jr., a dark-horse candidate who galloped out of obscurity during the long primary-election season. Carter, a peanut farmer from Plains, Georgia, had served as his state's governor from 1971 to 1975. Flashing a toothy smile and insisting on humble "Jimmy" as his first name, this born-again Baptist touched many people with his down-home sincerity. He ran against the memory of Nixon and Watergate as much as he ran against Ford. His most effective campaign pitch was his promise that "I'll never lie to you." Untainted by ties with a corrupt and cynical Washington, he attracted voters as an outsider who would clean the disorderly house of "big government."

The Feminists

A well-to-do housewife and mother of seven, Elizabeth Cady Stanton (1815–1902) was an unlikely revolutionary. Yet this founding mother of American feminism devoted seven decades of her life to the fight for women's rights.

Young Elizabeth Cady drew her inspiration from the fight against slavery. In 1840 she married fellow abolitionist Henry Stanton. Honeymooning in London, they attended the World Anti-Slavery Convention, where women were forced to sit in a screened-off balcony above the convention floor. This insult awakened Stanton to the cause that would occupy her life. With Lucretia Mott and other female abolitionists, Stanton went on to organize the Seneca Falls Convention in 1848. There she presented her Declaration of Sentiments, modeled on the Declaration of Independence and proclaiming that "all men *and women* are created equal." She demanded for women the right to own property, to enter the professions, and, most daring of all, to vote.

As visionaries of a radically different future for women, early feminists encountered a mountain of hostility and tasted bitter disappointment. Stanton failed in her struggle to have women included in the Fourteenth Amendment to the U.S. Constitution, which granted African-Americans equal citizenship. She died before seeing her dream of woman suffrage realized in the Nineteenth Amendment (1920). Yet by imagining women's emancipation as an expansion of America's founding principles of citizenship, Stanton

"All men and women are created equal," 1848 Elizabeth Cady Stanton delivered her Declaration of Sentiments at the first Woman's Rights Convention in Seneca Falls, New York, to an audience of about two hundred women and forty men who gathered on only two-weeks' notice.

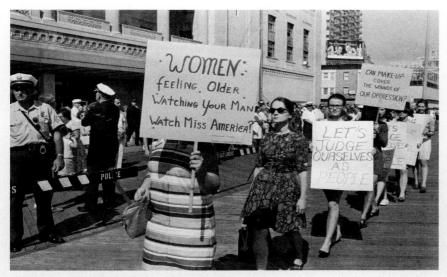

Protesters Picketing Miss America Pageant, 1968

the streets. Among these women was Robin Morgan (b. 1941). As a college student in the 1960s, Morgan was active in civil rights organizations like the Congress of Racial Equality (CORE) and the Student Non-Violent Coordinating Committee (SNCC). Civil rights activism provided Morgan with a model for crusading against social injustice. It also exposed her to the same sexism that plagued society at large. Women in the movement who protested against gender discrimination met ridicule, as in SNCC leader Stokely Carmichael's famous retort, "The only position for women in SNCC is prone." Morgan went on to found WITCH (Women's International Terrorist Conspiracy from Hell), made famous by its protest at the 1968 Miss America pageant in Atlantic City, New Jersey. There demonstrators crowned a sheep Miss America and threw symbols of women's oppression—bras, girdles, dishcloths—into trash cans. (Contrary to news stories, they did not burn the bras.)

charted a path that other feminists would follow a century later.

Historians use the terms "first wave" and "second wave" to distinguish the women's movement of the nineteenth century from that of the late twentieth century. The woman most often credited with launching the "second wave" is Betty Friedan (b. 1921). Growing up in Peoria, Illinois, Friedan had seen her mother grow bitter over sacrificing a journalism career to raise her family. Friedan, a suburban housewife, went on to write the 1963 best-seller *The Feminine Mystique*, exposing the quiet desperation of millions of housewives trapped in the "comfortable concentration camp" of the suburban home. The book struck a resonant chord and catapulted its author onto the national stage. In 1966 Friedan cofounded the National Organization for Women (NOW), the chief political arm of second-wave feminism.

Just as first-wave feminism grew out of abolitionism, the second wave drew ideas, leaders, and tactics from the civil rights movement of the 1960s. Civil rights workers and feminists alike focused on equal rights. NOW campaigned vigorously for an Equal Rights Amendment that in 1982 fell just three states short of ratification.

Second-wave feminism also had an avowedly radical wing, supported by younger women who were eager to challenge almost every traditional male and female gender role and to take the feminist cause to

As the contrast between WITCH and NOW suggests, second-wave feminism was a remarkably diverse movement. Feminists in the late twentieth century disagreed over many issues—from pornography and marriage to how much to expect from government, capitalism, and men. Some feminists placed a priority on gender equality, for example, full female service in the military. Others defended a feminism of gender difference—such as maternity leaves and other special protections for women in the workplace.

Still, beyond these differences feminists had much in common. Most advocated a woman's right to choose in the battle over abortion rights. Most regarded the law as the key weapon against gender discrimination. By century's end radical and moderate feminists alike could take pride in a host of achievements that had changed the landscape of gender relations beyond what most people could have imagined at midcentury. Yet, like Elizabeth Cady Stanton, second-wave feminists also shared the burden of understanding that the goals of genuine equality would take more than a lifetime to achieve.

Carter squeezed out a narrow victory on election day, with 51 percent of the popular vote. The electoral count stood at 297 to 240. The winner swept every state except Virginia in his native South. Especially important were the votes of African-Americans, 97 percent of whom cast their ballots for Carter.

Carter enjoyed hefty Democratic majorities in both houses of Congress. Hopes ran high that the stalemate of the Nixon-Ford years between a Republican White House and a Democratic Capitol Hill would now be ended. At first Carter enjoyed notable political success. Congress granted his request to create a new cabinet-level Department of Energy. Calling the American tax system "a disgrace to the human race," Carter also proposed tax reform and reduction. Congress eventually obliged him, in part, with an $18 billion tax cut in 1978. The new president's popularity remained exceptionally high during his first few months in office, even when he courted public disfavor by courageously keeping his campaign promise to pardon some ten thousand draft evaders of the Vietnam War era.

But Carter's honeymoon did not last long. An inexperienced outsider, he had campaigned against the Washington "establishment" and never quite made the transition to being an insider himself. He repeatedly rubbed congressional fur the wrong way, especially by failing to consult adequately with the leaders. Critics charged that he isolated himself in a shallow pool of fellow Georgians, whose ignorance of the ways of Washington compounded the problems of their greenhorn chief.

Carter's Humanitarian Diplomacy

As a committed Christian, President Carter displayed from the outset an overriding concern for "human rights" as the guiding principle of his foreign policy. In the African nations of Rhodesia (later Zimbabwe) and South Africa, Carter and his eloquent U.N. ambassador, Andrew Young, championed the oppressed black majority.

The president's most spectacular foreign-policy achievement came in September 1978 at Camp David, the woodsy presidential retreat in the Maryland highlands. Relations between Egypt and Israel had deteriorated so far that another blowup in the misery-drenched Middle East seemed imminent. So grave was the danger that Carter courageously risked humiliating failure by inviting President

Celebrating the Camp David Agreement, September 1978 Anwar Sadat of Egypt (left) and Menachem Begin of Israel (right) join U.S. president Jimmy Carter in confirming the historic accord that brought hopes of peace to the war-torn Middle East.

Historical Double Take Many Americans who looked back reverently to Theodore Roosevelt's "Rough Rider" diplomacy were outraged at the Panama "giveaway." But the Carter administration, looking to the future, argued persuasively that relinquishing control of the canal would be healthy for U.S.–Latin American relations.

Anwar Sadat of Egypt and Prime Minister Menachem Begin of Israel to a summit conference at Camp David.

Skillfully serving as go-between, Carter after thirteen days persuaded the two visitors to sign an accord (September 17, 1978) that held considerable promise of peace. Israel agreed in principle to withdraw from territory conquered in the 1967 war, and Egypt in return promised to respect Israel's borders. Both parties pledged themselves to sign a formal peace treaty within three months. The president crowned this diplomatic success by resuming full diplomatic relations with China in early 1979 after a nearly thirty-year interruption. Carter also successfully proposed two treaties turning over complete ownership and control of the Panama Canal to the Panamanians by the year 2000.

Despite these dramatic accomplishments, trouble stalked Carter's foreign policy. Overshadowing all international issues was the ominous reheating of the Cold War with the Soviet Union. Détente fell into disrepute as thousands of Cuban troops, assisted by Soviet advisers, appeared in Angola, Ethiopia, and elsewhere in Africa to support revolutionary factions. Arms control negotiations with Moscow stalled in the face of this Soviet military meddling.

Economic and Energy Woes

Adding to Carter's mushrooming troubles was the failing health of the economy. Prices had been rising feverishly, increasing at a rate of more than 10 percent a year by 1974 ("double-digit" inflation). Crippling oil-price hikes from OPEC in that same year dealt the reeling economy another body blow. A stinging recession during Gerald Ford's presidency brought the inflation rate down temporarily, but virtually from the moment of Carter's inauguration, prices resumed their dizzying ascent, driving the inflation rate well above 13 percent by 1979. The soaring bill for imported oil plunged America's balance of payments deeply into the red (an unprecedented $40 billion in 1978), as Americans paid more for foreign products than they were able to earn from selling their own goods overseas.

The "oil shocks" of the 1970s taught Americans a painful but necessary lesson: that they could never again seriously consider a policy of economic isolation, as they had tried to do in the decades between the two world wars. For most of its history, America's foreign trade had accounted for no more than 10 percent of gross national product (GNP). But huge foreign-oil bills drove that figure steadily upward in the 1970s and thereafter. By the century's end, some 27 percent of GNP depended on foreign trade. The nation's new economic interdependence meant that the United States could not dominate international trade and finance as easily as it had in the post–World War II decades. Americans, once happily insulated behind their ocean moats, would have to master foreign languages and study foreign cultures if they wanted to prosper in the rapidly globalizing economy.

Yawning deficits in the federal budget, reaching nearly $60 billion in 1980, further aggravated the U.S. ecomony's inflationary ailments. Americans living on fixed incomes—mostly elderly people or workers without a strong union to go to bat for them—suffered from the shrinking dollar. People with money to lend pushed interest rates ever higher, hoping to protect themselves from being repaid in badly depreciated dollars. The "prime rate" (the rate of interest that banks charge their very best customers) vaulted to an unheard-of 20 percent in early 1980. The high cost of borrowing money shoved small businesses to the wall and strangled the construction industry, heavily dependent on loans to finance new housing and other projects.

From the outset Carter diagnosed America's economic disease as stemming primarily from the nation's costly dependence on foreign oil. Accordingly, one of the first acts of his presidency was a dramatic appeal to embark on an energy crusade that he called "the moral equivalent of war." The president called for legislation to improve energy conservation, especially by curtailing the manufacture of large, gas-guzzling automobiles. But these proposals, in April 1977, ignited a blaze of indifference among the American people, who had already forgotten the long gasoline lines of 1973. Public apathy and congres-sional hostility smothered President Carter's hopes of quickly initiating an energetic energy program.

Events in Iran jolted Americans out of their complacency about energy supplies in 1979. The imperious Mohammed Reza Pahlevi, installed as shah of Iran with help from America's CIA in 1953, had long ruled his oil-rich land with a will of steel. His repressive regime was finally overthrown in January 1979. Violent revolution was spearheaded in Iran by Muslim fundamentalists who fiercely resented the shah's campaign to westernize and sec-ularize his country. Denouncing the United States as the "Great Satan" that had abetted the shah's efforts, these extremists engulfed Iran in chaos in the wake of his departure. The crippling upheavals soon spread to Iran's oil fields. As Iranian oil stopped flowing into the stream of world commerce, short-ages appeared, and OPEC again seized the opportu-nity to hike petroleum prices. Americans once more found themselves waiting impatiently in long lines at gas stations or buying gasoline only on specified days.

The History of the Consumer Price Index, 1967–2000 This graph shows both the annual percentage of inflation and the cumulative shrinkage in the dollar's value since 1967. (By 2000, it took more than five dollars to buy what one dollar purchased in 1967.) (Sources: Bureau of Labor Statistics and *Statistical Abstract of the United States*, relevant years.)

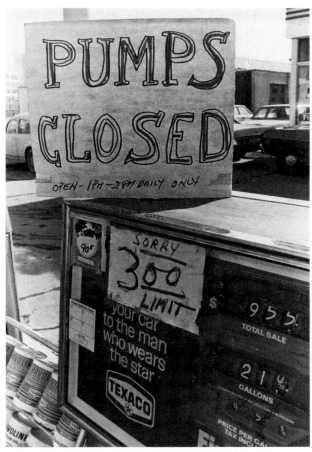

Coping with the Energy Crisis
A highly mobile people accustomed to limitless gasoline supplies, Americans were rudely reminded of their dependence on foreign-oil imports during the "oil shocks" of the 1970s.

As the oil crisis deepened, President Carter sensed the rising temperature of popular discontent. In July 1979 he retreated to the presidential mountain hideaway at Camp David, where he remained largely out of public view for ten days. Like a royal potentate of old, summoning the wise men of the realm for their counsel in a time of crisis, Carter called in over a hundred leaders from all walks of life to give him their views. Meanwhile, the nation waited anxiously for the results of these extraordinary deliberations.

Carter came down from the mountaintop on July 15, 1979. He revealed his thoughts to the American people in a remarkable television address, which amounted to a kind of old-fashioned "jere-

miad." He chided his fellow citizens for falling into a "moral and spiritual crisis" and for being too concerned with "material goods."

While Carter's address stunned and even perplexed the nation, he let drop another shoe a few days later. In a bureaucratic massacre of almost unprecedented proportions, he fired four cabinet secretaries. At the same time, he circled the wagons of his Georgian advisers more tightly about the White House by reorganizing and expanding the power of his personal staff. Critics began to wonder aloud whether Carter, the professed man of the people, was losing touch with the popular mood of the country.

Foreign Affairs and the Iranian Imbroglio

Hopes for a less dangerous world rose slightly in June 1979, when President Carter met with Soviet leader Leonid Brezhnev in Vienna to sign the long-stalled SALT II agreements, limiting the levels of

President Jimmy Carter (b. 1924) delivered what became known as his "malaise" speech (although he never used the word) on television in 1979. In time cultural conservatives would take up his theme to support their call for a return to "traditional values":

"In a nation that was proud of hard work, strong families, close-knit communities, and our faith in God, too many of us now tend to worship self-indulgence and consumption. Human identity is no longer defined by what one does, but by what one owns. But we've discovered that owning things and consuming things does not satisfy our longing for meaning. We've learned that piling up material goods cannot fill the emptiness of lives which have no confidence or purpose. . . . The symptoms of this crisis of the American spirit are all around us."

lethal strategic weapons in the Soviet and American arsenals. But conservative critics of the president's defense policies, still deeply suspicious of the Soviet Union, which they regarded as the Wicked Witch of the East, unsheathed their long knives to carve up the SALT II treaty when it came to the Senate for debate in the summer of 1979. Their hand was strengthened when news reports broke that a Soviet "combat brigade" was stationed in Castro's Cuba.

Political earthquakes in the petroleum-rich Persian Gulf region finally buried all hopes of ratifying the SALT II treaty. On November 4, 1979, a howling mob of rabidly anti-American Muslim militants stormed the United States embassy in Teheran, Iran, and took all of its occupants hostage. The captors then demanded that the American authorities ship back to Iran the exiled shah, who had arrived in the United States two weeks earlier for medical treatment. The shaky Iranian government, barely visible through the smoke of revolution and religious upheaval then rocking the country, refused to intervene against the militants. Ayatollah Ruhollah Khomeini, the white-bearded Muslim holy man who inspired the revolutionaries, even accused the United States of masterminding an attack on the sacred Muslim city of Mecca, in Saudi Arabia.

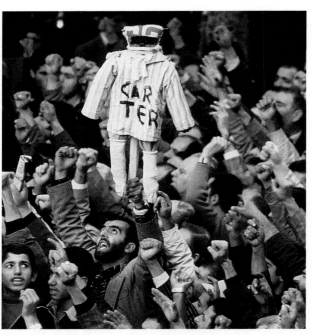

Iranians Denounce President Jimmy Carter, November 1979 Scenes like this one appeared almost nightly on American television during the 444 days of the Iranian hostage crisis, humiliating Carter and angering American citizens.

Two-Way SALT Talks The grim specter of nuclear holocaust haunted the SALT II talks between Carter and Soviet leader Leonid Brezhnev in Vienna in June 1979.

World opinion hotly condemned the diplomatic felony in Iran, while Americans agonized over both the fate of the hostages and the stability of the entire Persian Gulf region, so dangerously close to the Soviet Union. The Soviet army then aroused the West's worst fears on December 27, 1979, when it blitzed into the mountainous nation of Afghanistan, next door to Iran, and appeared to be poised for a thrust at the oil-jugular of the gulf.

President Carter reacted vigorously to these alarming events. He slapped an embargo on the export of grain and high-technology machinery to the USSR and called for a boycott of the upcoming Olympic Games in Moscow. He proposed the creation of a "Rapid Deployment Force" to respond to suddenly developing crises in faraway places and requested that young people (including women) be made to register for a possible military draft. The president proclaimed that the United States would "use any means necessary, including force," to protect the Persian Gulf against Soviet incursions. He grimly conceded that he had misjudged the Soviets, and the SALT II treaty became a dead letter in the Senate. Meanwhile, the Soviet army met unexpectedly stiff resistance in Afghanistan and bogged down in a nasty, decade-long guerrilla war that came to be called "Russia's Vietnam." But though the Soviets were stalled in Afghanistan, the crisis in Iran ground on.

The Iranian hostage episode was Carter's—and America's—bed of nails. The captured Americans languished in cruel captivity, while the nightly television news broadcasts in the United States showed humiliating scenes of Iranian mobs burning the American flag and spitting on effigies of Uncle Sam.

Carter at first tried to apply economic sanctions and the pressure of world public opinion against the Iranians, while waiting for the emergence of a stable government with which to negotiate. But the political turmoil in Iran rumbled on endlessly, and the

president's frustration grew. Carter at last ordered a daring rescue mission. A highly trained commando team penetrated deep into Iran's sandy interior. Their plan required ticktock-perfect timing to succeed, and when equipment failures prevented some members of the team from reaching their destination, the mission had to be scrapped. As the commandos withdrew in the dark desert night, two of their aircraft collided, killing eight of the would-be rescuers.

This disastrous failure of the rescue raid proved anguishing for Americans. The episode seemed to underscore the nation's helplessness and even incompetence in the face of a mortifying insult to the national honor. The stalemate with Iran dragged on throughout the rest of Carter's term, providing an embarrassing backdrop to the embattled president's struggle for reelection.

Chronology

1970	Nixon orders invasion of Cambodia Kent State and Jackson State incidents Environmental Protection Agency (EPA) created Clean Air Act
1971	Pentagon Papers published Twenty-sixth Amendment (lowering voting age to eighteen) passed
1972	Nixon visits China and the Soviet Union ABM and SALT I treaties ratified Nixon defeats McGovern for presidency Equal Rights Amendment passes Congress Title IX of Education Amendments passed
1973	Vietnam cease-fire and U.S. withdrawal Agnew resigns; Ford appointed vice president War Powers Act Arab-Israeli war and Arab oil embargo Endangered Species Act *Frontiero* v. *Richardson* *Roe* v. *Wade*

1973- 1974	Watergate hearings and investigations
1974	Nixon resigns; Ford assumes presidency First OPEC oil-price increase International Energy Agency formed *Milliken* v. *Bradley*
1975	Helsinki accords South Vietnam falls to communists
1976	Carter defeats Ford for presidency
1978	Egyptian-Israeli Camp David agreement *United States* v. *Wheeler*
1979	Iranian revolution and oil crisis SALT II agreements signed (never ratified by Senate) Soviet Union invades Afghanistan
1979- 1981	Iranian hostage crisis

For further reading, see page A27 of the Appendix. For web resources, go to **http://college.hmco.com.**

The Resurgence of Conservatism

1980–2000

It will be my intention to curb the size and influence of the federal establishment and to demand recognition of the distinction between the powers granted to the federal government and those reserved to the states or to the people.

RONALD REAGAN, INAUGURAL, 1981

"It's morning in America" was the slogan of Republican candidate Ronald Reagan in his 1980 presidential campaign. Certainly the 1980s were a new day for America's conservative right. Census figures confirmed that the average American was older than in the stormy sixties and much more likely to live in the South or West, the traditional bastions of the "Old Right," where many residents harbored suspicions of federal power. The conservative cause drew added strength from the emergence of a "New Right" movement, partly in response to the countercultural protests of the 1960s. Spearheading the New Right were evangelical Christian groups such as the Moral Majority, dedicated believers who enjoyed startling success as political fund-raisers and organizers.

Many New Right activists were far less agitated about economic questions than about cultural con-

In a speech to the National Association of Evangelicals on March 8, 1983, President Ronald Reagan (b. 1911) defined his stand on school prayer:

"The Declaration of Independence mentions the Supreme Being no less than four times. 'In God We Trust' is engraved on our coinage. The Supreme Court opens its proceedings with a religious invocation. And the Members of Congress open their sessions with a prayer. I just happen to believe the schoolchildren of the United States are entitled to the same privileges as Supreme Court Justices and Congressmen."

cerns—the so-called social issues. They denounced abortion, pornography, homosexuality, feminism, and especially affirmative action. They championed prayer in the schools and tougher penalties for criminals. Together, the Old and New Right added up to a powerful political combination, devoted to changing the very character of American society.

The Election of Ronald Reagan, 1980

Ronald Reagan was well suited to lead the gathering conservative crusade. Reared in a generation whose values were formed well before the upheavals of the 1960s, he naturally sided with the new right on social issues. In economic and social matters alike, he denounced the activist government and failed "social engineering" of the 1960s. He skillfully mobilized political resentments in a manner reminiscent of his early political hero, Franklin D. Roosevelt. Both Roosevelt and Reagan championed the "common man" against vast impersonal menaces that overshadowed the individual. But where the Democratic Roosevelt had branded big business the foe of the "forgotten man," the Republican Reagan depicted big government as the archvillain. He preached a "populist" political philosophy that condemned federal intervention in local affairs, favoritism for minorities, and the elitism of arrogant bureaucrats. He aimed especially to win over from the Democratic column working-class and lower-middle-class white voters by implying that the Democratic party had become the exclusive tool of its minority constituents.

Though Reagan was no intellectual, he drew on the ideas of a small but influential group of thinkers known as "neoconservatives." Their ranks included Norman Podhoretz, editor of *Commentary* magazine, and Irving Kristol, editor of *The Public Interest.* Reacting against what they saw as the excesses of 1960s liberalism, the neoconservatives championed free-market capitalism liberated from government restraints, and they took tough, harshly anti-Soviet positions in foreign policy. They also questioned liberal welfare programs and affirmative-action policies and called for reassertion of traditional values of individualism and the centrality of the family.

An actor-turned-politician, Reagan enjoyed enormous popularity with his crooked grin and aw-shucks manner. The son of a ne'er-do-well, impov-

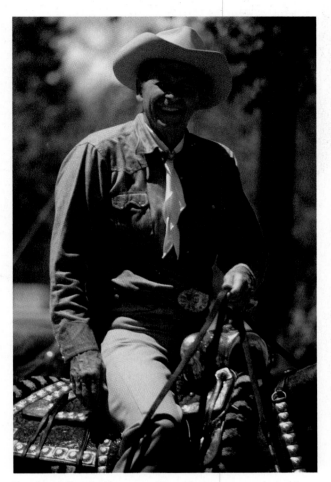

President Ronald Reagan   The oldest man ever elected to the presidency, Reagan displayed youthful vigor both on the campaign trail and in office.

erished Irish-American father with a fondness for the bottle, he had grown up in a small Illinois town. Reagan got his start in life in the depressed 1930s as a sports announcer for an Iowa radio station. Good looks and a way with words landed him acting jobs in Hollywood, where he became a B-grade star in the 1940s. He displayed a flair for politics as president of the Screen Actors Guild in the McCarthy era of the early 1950s, when he helped purge communists and other suspected "reds" from the film industry. In 1954 he became a spokesman for the General Electric Corporation at a salary of some $150,000 per year. In that position he began to abandon his New Dealish political views and increasingly to preach a conservative, antigovernment line. Reagan's huge visibility and growing skill

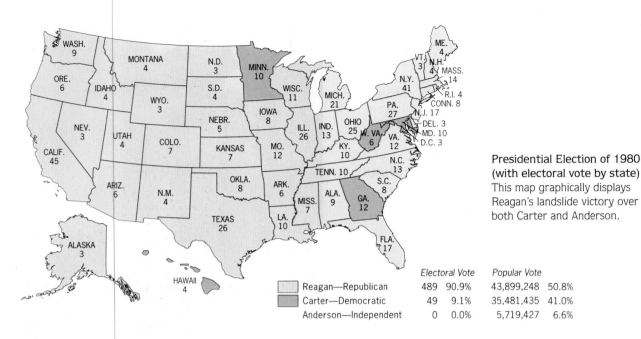

Presidential Election of 1980 (with electoral vote by state) This map graphically displays Reagan's landslide victory over both Carter and Anderson.

	Electoral Vote		Popular Vote	
Reagan—Republican	489	90.9%	43,899,248	50.8%
Carter—Democratic	49	9.1%	35,481,435	41.0%
Anderson—Independent	0	0.0%	5,719,427	6.6%

at promoting the conservative cause made him attractive to a group of wealthy California businessmen, who helped launch his political career as governor of California from 1966 to 1974.

By 1980 the Republican party was ready to challenge the Democrats' hold on the White House. Bedeviled abroad and becalmed at home, Jimmy Carter's administration struck many Americans as bungling and befuddled. Carter's inability to control double-digit inflation was especially damaging. Frustrated critics bellyached loudly about the Georgian's alleged mismanagement of the nation's affairs. Disaffection with Carter's apparent ineptitude ran deep even in his own Democratic party, where an "ABC" (Anybody but Carter) movement gathered steam. The liberal wing of the party found its champion in Senator Edward Kennedy of Massachusetts, the last survivor of the assassin-plagued Kennedy brothers. He and Carter slugged it out in a series of bruising primary elections, while delighted Republicans decorously proceeded to name Reagan their presidential nominee. In the end Kennedy's candidacy fell victim to the country's conservative mood and to lingering suspicions about a 1969 automobile accident on Chappaquiddick Island, Massachusetts, in which a young woman assistant was drowned when Kennedy's car plunged off a bridge. A badly battered Carter, his party divided and in disarray, was left to do battle with Reagan.

The Republican candidate proved to be a formidable campaigner. He used his professional acting skills to great advantage in a televised "debate" with the colorless Carter. Reagan attacked the incumbent's fumbling performance in foreign policy and blasted the "big-government" philosophy of the Democratic party (a philosophy that Carter did not fully embrace). Galloping inflation, sky-high interest rates, and a faltering economy also put the incumbent president on the defensive. Carter countered ineffectively with charges that Reagan was a trigger-happy cold warrior who might push the country into nuclear war.

Carter's spotty record in office was no defense against Reagan's popular appeal. On election day the Republican rang up a spectacular victory, bagging over 51 percent of the popular vote, while 41 percent went to Carter and 7 percent to moderate independent candidate John Anderson. The electoral count stood at 489 for Reagan and 49 for Carter. (Anderson failed to gain a single electoral vote.) Carter managed to win only six states and the District of Columbia, a defeat almost as crushing as George McGovern's loss to Richard Nixon in 1972. He was the first elected president to be unseated by the voters since Herbert Hoover was ejected from office in 1932. Equally startling, the Republicans gained control of the Senate for the first time in twenty-five years. Leading Democratic liberals who had been targeted for defeat by well-heeled new-right groups went down like dead timber in the conservative windstorm that swept the country.

Carter showed dignity in defeat, delivering a thoughtful Farewell Address that stressed his efforts to scale down the deadly arms race, to promote human rights, and to protect the environment. In one of his last acts in office, he signed a bill preserving some 100 million acres of Alaska land for national parks, forests, and wildlife refuges. An unusually intelligent, articulate, and well-meaning president, he had been hampered by his lack of managerial talent and had been badly buffeted by events beyond his control, such as the soaring price of oil, runaway inflation, and the galling insult of the continuing hostage crisis in Iran. If Carter was correct in believing that the country was suffering from a terrible "malaise," he never found the right medicine to cure the disease.

The Reagan Revolution

Reagan's arrival in Washington was triumphal. The Iranians contributed to the festive mood by releasing the hostages on Reagan's Inauguration Day, January 20, 1981, after 444 days of captivity.

Reagan assembled a conservative cabinet of the "best and the rightest" and relied on these and other advisers to make important decisions. The cabinet included a highly controversial Coloradan, James Watt, as secretary of the interior. Watt was a product of the "Sagebrush Rebellion," a fiercely anti-Washington movement that had sprung up to protest federal control over the rich mineral and timber resources in the western states. Environmentalists howled loudly about Watt's schemes to hobble the Environmental Protection Agency and to permit oil drilling in scenic places. After bitter protests they succeeded in halting Watt's plan to allow oil exploration off the California coastline. Watt blithely rebuffed critics by saying, "I make lots of mistakes because I make lots of decisions." He made one mistake too many in 1983, when he thoughtlessly told an offensive ethnic joke in public and was forced to resign.

The new president, a hale and hearty sixty-nine-year-old, was devoted to fiscal fitness. A major goal of Reagan's political career was to reduce the size of the government by shrinking the federal budget

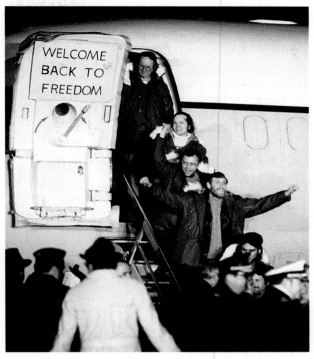

Coming Home   After more than a year in captivity in Iran, these hostages were released on the very day of Ronald Reagan's presidential inauguration.

and slashing taxes. He declared, "Government is not the solution to our problem. Government is the problem." Years of New Deal–style tax-and-spend programs, Reagan jested, had created a federal government that reminded him of the definition of a baby as a creature who was all appetite at one end, with no sense of responsibility at the other.

By the early 1980s, this antigovernment message found a receptive audience. In the two decades since 1960, federal spending had risen from about 18 percent of gross national product to nearly 23 percent. At the same time, the composition of the federal budget had been shifting from defense to entitlement programs, including Social Security and Medicare (see chart p. 1033). In 1973 the budget of the Department of Health, Education, and Welfare surpassed that of the Department of Defense. Citizens increasingly balked at paying the bills for further extension of government "benefits." After four decades of advancing New Deal and Great Society programs, a strong countercurrent took hold. Californians staged a "tax revolt" in 1978 (known by its official ballot title of Proposition 13) that slashed

The Triumph of the Right, 1980   Republican conservatives scored a double victory in 1980, winning control of both the White House and the Senate. Aided by conservative Democratic "boll weevils," they also dominated the House of Representatives, and a new era of conservatism dawned in the nation's capital.

property taxes and forced painful cuts in government services. The California "tax quake" jolted other state capitals and even rocked the pillars of Congress in faraway Washington, D.C. Ronald Reagan had ridden this political shock wave to presidential victory in 1980 and now proceeded to rattle the "welfare state" to its very foundations.

With near-religious zeal and remarkable effectiveness, Reagan set out to persuade Congress to legislate his smaller-government policies into law. He proposed a new federal budget that necessitated cuts of some $35 billion, mostly in social programs like food stamps and federally funded job-training centers. Reagan worked naturally in harness with the Republican majority in the Senate, but to get his way in the Democratic House, he undertook some old-fashioned politicking. He enterprisingly wooed a group of mostly southern conservative Democrats (dubbed "boll weevils"), who abandoned their own party's leadership to follow the president.

Then on March 6, 1981, a deranged gunman shot the president as he was leaving a Washington hotel. A .22-caliber bullet penetrated beneath Reagan's left arm and collapsed his left lung. With admirable courage and grace, and with impressive physical resilience for a man his age, Reagan seemed to recover rapidly from his violent ordeal. Twelve days after the attack, he walked out of the hospital and returned to work. When he appeared a few days later on national television to address the

Congress and the public on his budget, the outpouring of sympathy and support was enormous.

The Battle of the Budget

Swept along on a tide of presidential popularity, Congress swallowed Reagan's budget proposals, approving expenditures of some $695 billion, with a projected deficit of about $38 billion. To hit those financial targets, drastic surgery was required, and Congress plunged its scalpel deeply into Great Society–spawned social programs. Wounded Democrats wondered if the president's intention was to cut the budget or to gut the budget.

Reagan's triumph amazed political observers, especially defeated Democrats. The new president had descended upon Washington like an avenging angel of conservatism, kicking up a blinding whirlwind of political change. He sought nothing less than the dismantling of the welfare state and the reversal of the political evolution of the preceding half-century. His impressive performance demonstrated the power of the presidency with a skill not seen since Lyndon Johnson's day. Out the window went the textbooks that had concluded, largely on the basis of the stalemated 1970s, that this office had been eclipsed by a powerful, uncontrollable Congress.

Wallflowers   Reagan's budget cuts fell almost exclusively on social programs, whereas military outlays increased substantially.

Reagan hardly rested to savor the sweetness of his victory. The second part of his economic program called for deep tax cuts, amounting to 25 percent across-the-board reductions over a period of three years. Once again, Reagan displayed his skill as a performer and a persuader in a highly effective television address in July 1981, when he pleaded for congressional passage of the tax-cut bill. Democrats, he quipped, "had never met a tax they didn't hike." Thanks largely to the continued defection of the "boll weevils" from the Democratic camp, the president again had his way. In August 1981 Congress approved a set of far-reaching tax reforms that lowered individual tax rates, reduced federal estate taxes, and created new tax-free savings plans for small investors. Reagan's "supply-side" economic advisers assured him that the combination of budgetary discipline and tax reduction would stimulate new investment, boost productivity, foster dramatic economic growth, and reduce the federal deficit.

But at first "supply-side" economics seemed to be a beautiful theory mugged by a gang of brutal facts, as the economy slid into its deepest recession since the 1930s. Unemployment reached nearly 11 percent in 1982, businesses folded, and several bank failures jolted the nation's entire financial system. The automobile industry, once the brightest jewel in America's industrial crown, turned in its dimmest performance in history. Battling against Japanese imports, major automakers reported losses in the hundreds of millions of dollars. Fuming and frustrated Democrats angrily charged that the president's budget cuts slashed especially cruelly at the poor and the handicapped and that his tax cuts favored the well-to-do. They accused Reagan of trying to make those Americans with the frailest shoulders carry the heaviest burden in the fight for fiscal reform. In fact, the anti-inflationary "tight money" policies that precipitated the "Reagan recession" of 1982 had been initiated by the Federal Reserve Board in 1979, on Carter's watch.

Ignoring the yawping pack of Democratic critics, President Reagan and his economic advisers serenely waited for their supply-side economic policies ("Reaganomics") to produce the promised results. The supply-siders seemed to be vindicated when a healthy economic recovery finally got under way in 1983. Yet the economy of the 1980s was not uniformly sound. For the first time in the twentieth century, income gaps widened between the richest and the poorest Americans. The poor got poorer and

the very rich grew fabulously richer, while middle-class incomes largely stagnated. Symbolic of the new income stratification was the emergence of "yuppies," or young, urban professionals. Sporting Rolex watches and BMW sports cars, they made a near-religion out of conspicuous consumption. Though numbering only about 1.5 million people and being something of a stereotype, yuppies showcased the values of materialism and the pursuit of wealth that came to symbolize the high-rolling 1980s.

Some economists located the sources of the economic upturn neither in the president's budget cuts and tax reforms nor in the go-get-'em avarice of the yuppies. It was massive military expenditures, they argued, that constituted the real foundation of 1980s prosperity. Reagan cascaded nearly 2 trillion budget dollars onto the Pentagon in the 1980s, asserting the need to close a "window of vulnerability" in the armaments race with the Soviet Union. Ironically, this conservative president thereby plunged the government into a red-ink bath of deficit spending that made the New Deal look downright stingy. Federal budget deficits topped $100 billion in 1982, and the government's books were nearly $200 billion out of balance in every subsequent year of the 1980s. Massive government borrowing to cover those deficits kept interest rates high, and high interest rates in turn elevated the value of the dollar to record altitudes in the international money markets. The soaring dollar was good news for American tourists and buyers of foreign cars, but it dealt crippling blows to American exporters, as the American international trade deficit reached a record $152 billion in 1987. The masters of international commerce and finance for a generation after World War II, Americans suddenly became the world's heaviest borrowers in the global economy of the 1980s.

Reagan Renews the Cold War

Hard as nails toward the Soviet Union in his campaign speeches, Reagan saw no reason to soften up after he checked in at the White House. As the Soviets carried on their war in Afghanistan, Reagan continued to condemn the Kremlin. In one of his first presidential news conferences, he claimed that the Soviets were "prepared to commit any crime, to lie, to cheat," in pursuit of their goals of world conquest.

Star Wars Fantasies President Reagan's Strategic Defense Initiative (popularly known as Star Wars) evoked extravagant hopes for an impermeable defensive shield, but its daunting physical and engineering requirements also occasioned much ridicule in the scientific community.

In a later speech, he characterized the Soviet Union as the "focus of evil in the modern world."

Reagan believed in negotiating with the Soviets—but only from a position of overwhelming strength. Accordingly, his strategy for dealing with Moscow was simple: by enormously expanding U.S. military capabilities, he could threaten the Soviets with a fantastically expensive new round of the arms race. The American economy, theoretically, could better bear this new financial burden than could the creaking Soviet system. Desperate to avoid economic ruin, Kremlin leaders would come to the bargaining table and sing Reagan's tune.

This strategy resembled a riverboat gambler's ploy. It wagered the enormous sum of Reagan's defense budgets on the hope that the other side would not call Washington's bluff and initiate a new cycle of arms competition. Reagan played his trump card in this risky game in March 1983, when he announced his intention to pursue a high-technology missile-defense system called the Strategic Defense Initiative (SDI), popularly known as Star Wars. The plan called for orbiting battle stations in space that could fire laser beams or other forms of concentrated energy to vaporize intercontinental missiles on liftoff. Reagan described SDI as offering potential salvation from the nuclear nightmare by throwing an "astrodome" defense shield over American cities. Most scientists considered this an impossible goal. But the deeper logic of SDI lay in its fit with Reagan's overall Soviet strategy. By pitching the arms contest onto a stratospheric plane of high technology and astronomical expense, it would further force the Kremlin's hand.

By emphasizing defense rather than offense, SDI upset four decades of strategic thinking about nuclear weaponry. Many experts remained deeply skeptical about the plan. Those who did not dismiss it as ludicrous feared that Star Wars research might be ruinously costly, ultimately unworkable, and fatally destabilizing to the distasteful but effective "balance of terror" that had kept the nuclear peace since World War II. Scientific and strategic doubts combined to constrain congressional funding for SDI through the remainder of Reagan's term.

Relations with the Soviets further nose-dived in late 1981, when the government of Poland, needled for over a year by a popular movement of working-people organized into a massive union called "Solidarity," clamped martial law on the troubled country. Reagan saw the heavy fist of the Kremlin inside this Polish iron glove, and he imposed economic sanctions on Poland and the USSR alike. Notably absent from the mandated measures was a resumption of the grain embargo, which would have pinched the pocketbooks of too many American farmers.

Dealing with the Soviet Union was additionally complicated by the inertia and ill health of the aging oligarchs in the Kremlin, three of whom were swept away by death between late 1982 and early 1985. Relations grew even more tense when the Soviets, in September 1983, blasted from the skies a Korean passenger airliner that had inexplicably violated Soviet airspace. Hundreds of civilians, including many Americans, plummeted to their deaths in the frigid Sea of Okhotsk. By the end of 1983, all arms-control negotiations with the Soviets were broken off. The deepening chill of the Cold War was further felt in 1984, when, in response to the Western boycott of the 1980 Moscow Olympics, USSR and Soviet-bloc athletes boycotted the Los Angeles Olympic Games.

Troubles Abroad

The volatile Middle Eastern pot continued to boil ominously. Israel badly strained its bonds of friendship with the United States by continuing to allow new settlements to be established in the occupied territory of the Jordan River's West Bank. Israel further raised the stakes in the Middle East in June 1982

The Middle East A combination of political instability and precious petroleum resources has made the region from Egypt to Afghanistan an "arc of crisis."

when it invaded neighboring Lebanon, seeking to suppress once and for all the guerrilla bases from which Palestinian fighters harassed beleaguered Israel. The Palestinians were bloodily subdued, but Lebanon, already pulverized by years of episodic civil war, was plunged into armed chaos. President Reagan was obliged to send American troops to Lebanon in 1983 as part of an international peacekeeping force, but their presence did not bring peace. A suicide bomber crashed an explosives-laden truck into a United States Marine barracks on October 23, 1983, killing more than two hundred marines. President Reagan soon thereafter withdrew the remaining American troops, while miraculously

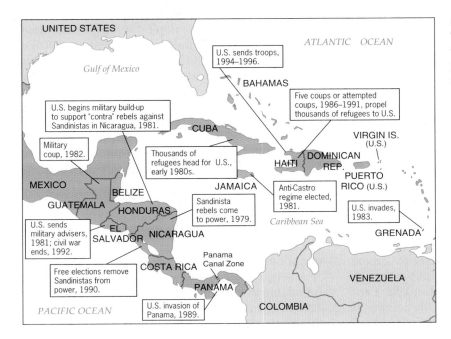

Central America and the Caribbean This region of historical importance to the United States experienced dramatic political upheavals in the 1970s, 1980s, and 1990s.

suffering no political damage from this horrifying and humiliating attack. His mystified Democratic opponents began to call him the "Teflon president," to whom nothing hurtful could stick.

Central America, in the United States' own back-yard, also rumbled menacingly. A leftist revolution had deposed the long-time dictator of Nicaragua in 1979. President Carter had tried to ignore the hotly anti-American rhetoric of the revolutionaries, known as "Sandinistas," and to establish good diplomatic relations with them. But cold warrior Reagan took their rhetoric at face value and hurled back at them some hot language of his own. He accused the Sandinistas of turning their country into a forward base for Soviet and Cuban military penetration of all of Central America. Brandishing photographs taken from high-flying spy planes, administration spokespeople claimed that Nicaraguan leftists were shipping weapons to revolutionary forces in tiny El Salvador, torn by violence since a coup in 1979.

Reagan sent military "advisers" to prop up the pro-American government of El Salvador. He also provided covert aid, including the CIA-engineered mining of harbors, to the "contra" rebels opposing the anti-American government of Nicaragua. Reagan flexed his military muscles elsewhere in the turbulent Caribbean. In a dramatic display of American might, in October 1983 he dispatched a heavy-fire-power invasion force to the island of Grenada, where a military coup had killed the prime minister and brought Marxists to power. Swiftly overrunning the tiny island and ousting the insurgents, American troops vividly demonstrated Reagan's determination to assert the dominance of the United States in the Caribbean, just as Theodore Roosevelt had done.

Round Two for Reagan

A confident Ronald Reagan, bolstered by a buoyant economy at home and by the popularity of his muscular posture abroad, handily won the Republican nomination in 1984 for a second White House term. His opponent was Democrat Walter Mondale, who made history by naming as his vice-presidential running mate Congresswoman Geraldine Ferraro of New York. She was the first woman ever to appear on a major-party presidential ticket. But even this dramatic gesture could not salvage Mondale's candidacy, which was fatally tainted by his service as vice president in the deeply discredited Carter administration. On election day Reagan walked away with 525 electoral votes to Mondale's 13, winning everywhere except in Mondale's home state of Minnesota and the District of Columbia. Reagan also overwhelmed Mondale in the popular vote—52,609,797 to 36,450,613.

Shrinking the federal government and reducing taxes had been the main objectives of Reagan's first term; foreign-policy issues dominated the news in his second term. The president soon found himself contending for the world's attention with a charismatic new Soviet leader, Mikhail Gorbachev, installed as chairman of the Soviet Communist party in March 1985. Gorbachev was personable, energetic, imaginative, and committed to radical reforms in the Soviet Union. He announced two policies with remarkable, even revolutionary, implications. *Glasnost,* or "openness," aimed to ventilate the secretive, repressive stuffiness of Soviet society by introducing free speech and a measure of political liberty. *Perestroika,* or "restructuring," was intended to revive the moribund Soviet economy by adopting many of the free-market practices—such as the profit motive and an end to subsidized prices—of the capitalist West.

Both *glasnost* and *perestroika* required that the Soviet Union shrink the size of its enormous military machine and redirect its energies to the dismal civilian economy. That requirement, in turn, necessitated an end to the Cold War. Gorbachev accordingly made warm overtures to the West, including an announcement in April 1985 that the Soviet Union would cease to deploy intermediate-range nuclear forces (INF) targeted on Western Europe, pending an agreement on their complete elimination. He pushed this goal when he met with Ronald Reagan at the first of four summit meetings, in Geneva in November 1985. A second summit meeting, in Reykjavik, Iceland, in October 1986 broke down in a stalemate. But at a third summit, in Washington, D.C., in December 1987, the two leaders at last signed the INF treaty, banning all intermediate-range nuclear missiles from Europe. This was a result long sought by both sides; it marked a victory for American policy, for Gorbachev's reform program, and for the peoples of Europe and indeed all the world, who now had at least one less nuclear weapons system to worry about.

Reagan and Gorbachev capped their new friendship in May 1988 at a final summit in Moscow. There Reagan, who had entered office condemning the "evil empire" of Soviet communism, warmly

East Meets West
President Reagan greets
Soviet leader Mikhail
Gorbachev at a summit
meeting in Moscow in
May 1988.

praised Gorbachev. Reagan, the consummate cold warrior, had been flexible and savvy enough to seize a historic opportunity to join with the Soviet chief to bring the Cold War to a kind of conclusion. For this, history would give both leaders high marks.

Reagan made other decisive moves in foreign policy. His administration provided strong backing in February 1986 for Corazon Aquino's ouster of dictator Ferdinand Marcos in the Philippines. Reagan ordered a lightning air raid against Libya in 1986, in retaliation for alleged Libyan sponsorship of terrorist attacks, including a bomb blast in a West Berlin discotheque that killed a U.S. serviceman. In the summer of 1987, U.S. naval vessels began escorting oil tankers through the Persian Gulf, inflamed by a long, brutal war between Iran and Iraq.

The Iran-Contra Imbroglio

Two foreign-policy problems seemed insoluble to Reagan: the continuing captivity of a number of American hostages, seized by Muslim extremist groups in bleeding, battered Lebanon; and the continuing grip on power of the left-wing Sandinista government in Nicaragua. The president repeatedly requested that Congress provide military aid to the contra rebels fighting against the Sandinista regime.

Congress repeatedly refused, and the administration grew increasingly frustrated, even obsessed, in its search for a means to help the contras.

Unknown to the American public, some Washington officials saw a possible linkage between the two thorny problems of the Middle Eastern hostages and the Central American Sandinistas. In 1985 American diplomats secretly arranged arms

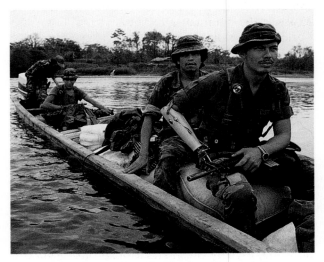

Contra Rebel Troops Head for Battle   These rebels were long-seasoned and battle-scarred veterans of Nicaragua's civil war by the time this photograph was taken in 1987.

On March 4, 1987, President Ronald Reagan somewhat confusingly tried to explain his role (or lack of role) in the arms-for-hostages deal with Iran:

"A few months ago I told the American people I did not trade arms for hostages. My heart and my best intentions still tell me that is true, but the facts and the evidence tell me it is not."

sales to the embattled Iranians in return for Iranian aid in obtaining the release of American hostages held by Middle Eastern terrorists. At least one hostage was eventually set free. Meanwhile, money from the payment for the arms was diverted to the

contras. These actions brazenly violated a congressional ban on military aid to the Nicaraguan rebels—not to mention Reagan's repeated vow that he would never negotiate with terrorists.

News of these secret dealings broke in November 1986 and ignited a firestorm of controversy. President Reagan claimed he was innocent of wrongdoing and ignorant about the activities of his subordinates, but a congressional committee condemned the "secrecy, deception, and disdain for the law" displayed by administration officials and concluded that "if the president did not know what his national security advisers were doing, he should have." Criminal indictments were later brought against several individuals tarred by the Iran-contra scandal, including marine colonel Oliver North; North's boss at the National Security Council, Admiral John Poindexter; and even Secretary of Defense Caspar Weinberger. North and Poindexter were both found guilty of criminal behavior, though all their convictions were eventually reversed on appeal.

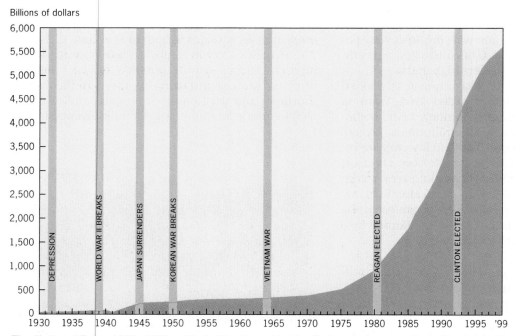

Billions of dollars

The National Debt, 1930–1999   World War II provided the first major boost to the national debt. But it was the policies of the Reagan and Bush administrations, 1981–1993, that explosively expanded the debt to the $4 trillion level. By the 1990s, 14 percent of federal revenues went to interest payments on the debt, though the budget surpluses created by the booming economy of the second Clinton administration raised the prospect that the debt might be paid off. (Sources: *Historical Statistics of the United States* and *Statistical Abstract of the United States,* relevant years; 1996 and 1997 figures from *Economic Indicators,* Council of Economic Advisors.)

Weinberger received a presidential pardon before he was formally tried.

The Iran-contra affair cast a dark shadow over the Reagan record in foreign policy, tending to obscure the president's outstanding achievement in establishing a new relationship with the Soviets. Out of the several Iran-contra investigations, a picture emerged of Reagan as a lazy, perhaps even senile, president who napped through meetings and paid little or no attention to the details of policy. Reagan's critics pounced on this portrait as proof that the movie-star-turned-politician was a mental lightweight who had merely acted his way through the role of the presidency without really understanding the script. But despite these damaging revelations, Reagan remained among the most popular and beloved presidents in modern American history.

Reagan's Economic Legacy

Ronald Reagan had taken office vowing to invigorate the American economy by rolling back government regulations, lowering taxes, and balancing the budget. He did ease many regulatory rules, and he pushed major tax reform bills through Congress in 1981 and 1986. But a balanced budget remained grotesquely out of reach. Supply-side economic theory had promised that lower taxes would actually *increase* government revenue because they would so stimulate the economy as a whole. But in fact the combination of tax reduction and huge increases in military spending opened a vast "revenue hole" of $200 billion annual deficits. In his eight years in office, President Reagan added nearly $2 trillion to the national debt—more than all of his predecessors combined, including those who had fought protracted global wars (see the chart on p. 986).

The staggering deficits of the Reagan years assuredly constituted a great economic failure. And because so much of the Reagan-era debt was financed by foreign lenders, especially the Japanese, the deficits virtually guaranteed that future generations of Americans would either have to work harder than their parents, lower their standard of living, or both, to pay their foreign creditors when the bills came due. The yawning deficits prompted Congress in 1986 to pass legislation mandating a balanced budget by 1991. Yet even this drastic measure proved pitifully inadequate to the task of closing the gap between the federal government's income and expenditures, and the national debt continued to grow.

But if the deficits represented an economic failure, they also constituted, strangely enough, a kind of political triumph. Among the paramount goals of Reagan's political life was his ambition to slow the growth of government, and especially to block or even repeal the social programs launched in the era of Lyndon Johnson's Great Society. By appearing to make new social spending both practically and politically impossible for the foreseeable future, the deficits served exactly that purpose. They achieved, in short, Reagan's highest political objective: the containment of the welfare state. Ronald Reagan thus ensured the long-term perpetuation of his dearest political values to a degree that few presidents have managed to achieve. For better or worse, the consequences of "Reaganomics" would be large and durable.

Yet another legacy of the 1980s was a sharp reversal of a long-term trend toward a more equitable distribution of income (see the chart on p. 988) and an increasing squeeze on the middle class. In the early 1990s, median household income (in 1993 dollars) actually declined, from about $33,500 in 1989 to about $31,000 in 1993. Whether that disturbing trend should be attributed to Reagan's policies or to more deeply running economic currents remained controversial.

Hollywood director Oliver Stone's (b. 1946) film Wall Street *both romanticized and vilified the business culture of the 1980s. The character of Gordon Gekko, inspired by real-life corporate raider Ivan Boesky, captured the spirit of the times:*

"Ladies and gentlemen, greed is good. Greed works, greed is right. . . . Greed for life, money, love, knowledge, has marked the upward surge of mankind—and greed, mark my words, will save the malfunctioning corporation called the U.S.A."

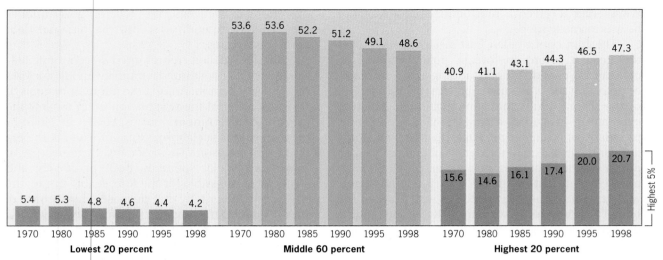

Share of Received Income by Families, by Quintile, 1970–1998   (Source: *Statistical Abstract of the United States,* 2000.)

The Religious Right

Religion pervaded American politics in the 1980s. Especially conspicuous was a coalition of conservative, evangelical Christians known as the religious right. In 1979 the Reverend Jerry Falwell, an evangelical minister from Lynchburg, Virginia, founded a political organization called the Moral Majority. Falwell preached with great success against sexual permissiveness, abortion, feminism, and the spread of gay rights. In its first two years, the Moral Majority registered between 2 million and 3 million voters. Using radio, direct-mail marketing, and cable TV, "tel-evangelists" reached huge audiences in the 1980s, collected millions of dollars, and became aggressive political advocates of conservative causes.

Members of the religious right were sometimes called "movement conservatives," a term that recalls the left-wing protest movements of the 1960s. In many ways the religious right of the 1980s was a reflection of, or answer to, sixties radicalism. Feminists in the 1960s declared that "the personal was political." The religious right did the same. What had in the past been personal matters—gender roles, homosexuality, and prayer—became the organizing ground for a powerful political movement. Like advocates of multiculturalism and affirmative action, the religious right practiced a form of "iden-tity politics." But rather than defining themselves as Hispanic voters or gay voters, they declared themselves Christian or pro-life voters. The New Right also mimicked the New Left in some of its tactics. If the left had consciousness-raising sessions, the right had prayer meetings. Adherents articulated their positions in a language of rights and entitlements, as in the "right-to-life" (or anti-abortion) movement. They even mirrored the tactics of civil disobedience. Protesters in the 1960s blocked entrances to draft offices; protesters in the 1980s blocked entrances to abortion clinics.

Several leaders of the religious right fell from grace in the latter part of the decade. One tearfully admitted to repeated trysts with prostitutes. Another went to prison following revelations of his own financial and sexual misconduct. But such scandals would not shake the faith of America's conservative Christians or diminish the new political clout of activist, evangelical religionists.

Conservatism in the Courts

If the budget was Reagan's chief weapon in the war against the welfare state, the courts became his principal instrument in the "cultural wars" demanded by the religious right. By the time he left office, Reagan had appointed a near-majority of all sitting judges. Equally important, he had named three conservative-minded justices to the U.S. Supreme Court. They included Sandra Day O'Connor, a brilliant, public-spirited Arizona judge. When she was sworn in on September 25, 1981, she became the first woman to ascend to the high bench in the Court's nearly two-hundred-year history.

Reaganism repudiated two great icons of the liberal political culture: affirmative action and abortion. The Court showed its newly conservative colors in 1984, when it decreed, in a case involving Memphis fire fighters, that union rules about job seniority could outweigh affirmative-action concerns in guiding promotion policies in the city's fire department. In two cases in 1989 *(Ward's Cove Packing v. Antonia and Martin v. Wilks),* the Court made it more difficult to prove that an employer practiced racial discrimination in hiring and made it easier for white males to argue that they were the victims of reverse discrimination by employers who followed affirmative-action practices. Congress passed legislation in 1991 that partially reversed the effects of those decisions.

The contentious issue of abortion also reached the Court in 1989. In the case of *Roe* v. *Wade* in 1973, the Supreme Court had prohibited states from making laws that interfered with a woman's right to an abortion during the early months of pregnancy. For nearly two decades, that decision had been the bedrock principle on which "pro-choice" advocates built their case for abortion rights. It had also provoked bitter criticism from Roman Catholics and various "right-to-life" groups, who wanted a virtually absolute ban on all abortions. In *Webster* v. *Reproductive Health Services,* the Court in July 1989 did not entirely overturn *Roe,* but it seriously compromised *Roe's* protection of abortion rights. By approving a Missouri law that imposed certain restrictions on abortion, the Court signaled that it was inviting the states to legislate in an area in which *Roe* had previously forbidden them to legislate. The Court renewed that invitation in *Planned Parenthood* v. *Casey* in 1992, when it ruled that states could restrict access to abortion as long as they did not place an "undue burden" on the woman. Using this standard, the Court held that Pennsylvania could not compel a wife to notify her husband about an abortion but could require a minor child to notify parents, as well as other restrictions.

Right-to-life advocates were at first delighted by the *Webster* decision. But the Court's ruling also gal-

Speaking to the National Association of Evangelicals, President Ronald Reagan said the following about abortion:

"More than a decade ago, a Supreme Court decision [*Roe* v. *Wade*, 1973] literally wiped off the books of fifty states statutes protecting the rights of unborn children. Abortion on demand now takes the lives of up to $1\frac{1}{2}$ million unborn children a year. Human life legislation ending this tragedy will some day pass the Congress, and you and I must never rest until it does. Unless and until it can be proven that the unborn child is not a living entity, then its right to life, liberty, and the pursuit of happiness must be protected."

vanized pro-choice organizations into a new militancy. Bruising, divisive battles loomed as state legislatures across the land confronted abortion. This painful cultural conflict over the unborn was also part of the Reagan era's bequest to the future.

Referendum on Reaganism in 1988

Republicans lost control of the Senate in the off-year elections of November 1986. Hopes rose among Democrats that the "Reagan Revolution" might be showing signs of political vulnerability at last. The newly Democratic majority in the Senate flexed its political muscle in 1987 when it rejected Robert Bork, Reagan's ultraconservative nominee for a Supreme Court vacancy.

Democrats also relished the prospect of making political hay out of both the Iran-contra scandal and the allegedly unethical behavior that tainted an unusually large number of Reagan's "official family." Top administrators of the Environmental Protection Agency resigned in disgrace over a misappropriation of funds. Reagan's secretary of labor stepped down in 1985 to stand trial on charges of fraud and larceny. (He was eventually acquitted.) The president's personal White House aide was convicted of perjury in 1988. The nation's chief law enforcement officer, Attorney General Edwin Meese, came under investigation by a federal special prosecutor on charges of influence-peddling. Reagan's secretary of housing and urban development was also investigated on charges of fraud and favoritism in the awarding of lucrative federal housing grants.

Disquieting signs of economic trouble also seemed to open political opportunities for Democrats. The "twin towers" of deficits—the federal budget deficit and international trade deficit—continued to mount ominously. Falling oil prices blighted the economy of the Southwest, slashing real estate values and undermining hundreds of savings-and-loans (S&L) institutions. The damage to the S&Ls was so massive that a federal rescue operation was eventually estimated to carry a price tag of well over $500 billion. Meanwhile, many American banks found themselves holding near-worthless loans they had unwisely foisted upon Third World countries, especially in Latin America. In 1984 it took federal assistance to save Continental Illinois Bank from a catastrophic failure. More banks and savings institutions were folding than at any time since the Great Depression of the 1930s. A wave of mergers, acquisitions, and leveraged buyouts washed over Wall Street, leaving many brokers and traders megarich and many companies saddled with megadebt. A cold spasm of fear struck the money markets on "Black Monday," October 19, 1987, when the leading stock-market index plunged 508 points—the largest one-day decline in history. This crash, said *Newsweek* magazine, heralded "the final collapse of the money culture . . . , the death knell of the 1980s." But as Mark Twain famously commented about his own obituary, this announcement proved premature.

Hoping to cash in on these ethical and economic anxieties, a pack of Democrats—dubbed the "Seven Dwarfs" by derisive Republicans—chased after their party's 1988 presidential nomination. But the Reaganites proved to have no monopoly on shady behavior. Ironically enough, the handsome and charismatic Democratic front-runner, former Colorado senator Gary Hart, was himself forced to drop out of the race in May 1987 after charges of sexual misconduct.

Black candidate Jesse Jackson, a rousing speechmaker who hoped to forge a "rainbow coalition" of minorities and the disadvantaged, campaigned energetically, but the Democratic nomination in the end went to the coolly cerebral governor of Massachusetts, Michael Dukakis. Republicans nominated

Bailing Out the Banks   Lax regulation and a booming real estate market imperiled hundreds of financial institutions in the 1980s, necessitating a massive taxpayer-funded bailout.

Reagan's vice president, George Bush, who ran largely on the Reagan record of tax cuts, strong defense policies, toughness on crime, opposition to abortion, and a long-running if hardly robust economic expansion. Dukakis made little headway exploiting the ethical and economic sorespots and came across to television viewers as almost supernaturally devoid of emotion. On election day the voters gave him just 41,016,000 votes to 47,946,000 for Bush. The Electoral College count was 111 to 426.

George Bush and the End of the Cold War

George Herbert Walker Bush was born with a silver spoon in his mouth. His father had served as a U.S. senator from Connecticut, and young George had enjoyed a first-rate education at Yale. After service in World War II, he had amassed a modest fortune of his own in the oil business in Texas. His deepest commitment, however, was to public service; he left the business world to serve briefly as a congressman and then held various posts in several Republican administrations, including emissary to China, ambassador to the United Nations, director of the Central Intelligence Agency, and vice president. He capped this long political career when he was inau-

George Bush (b. 1924), Forty-first President of the United States

Tiananmen Square, Beijing, China, June 1989   Before they were brutally suppressed by Chinese authorities, student demonstrators paraded a homemade Statue of Liberty to signify their passion for democracy.

gurated as president in January 1989, promising to work for "a kinder, gentler America."

In the first months of the Bush administration, the communist world commanded the planet's fascinated attention. Everywhere in the communist bloc, it seemed, astoundingly, that the season of democracy had arrived.

In China hundreds of thousands of prodemocracy demonstrators thronged through Beijing's Tiananmen Square in the spring of 1989. They proudly flourished a thirty-foot-high "Goddess of Democracy," modeled on the Statue of Liberty, as a symbol of their aspirations.

But in June of that year, China's aging and autocratic rulers brutally crushed the prodemocracy movement. Tanks rolled over the crowds, and machine-gunners killed hundreds of protesters. In the following weeks, scores of arrested demonstrators were publicly executed after perfunctory "trials."

World opinion roundly condemned the bloody suppression of the prodemocracy demonstrators. President Bush joined in the criticism. Yet despite angry demands in Congress for punitive restrictions on trade with China, the president insisted on maintaining normal relations with Beijing.

Stunning changes also shook Eastern Europe. Long oppressed by puppet regimes propped up by Soviet guns, the region was revolutionized in just a few startling months in 1989. The Solidarity movement in Poland led the way when it toppled Poland's communist government in August. With dizzying speed, communist regimes collapsed in Hungary, Czechoslovakia, East Germany, and even hyper-repressive Romania. In December 1989, jubilant Germans danced atop the hated Berlin Wall, symbol of the division of Germany and all of Europe into two armed and hostile camps. The Wall itself soon came down, heralding the imminent end of the forty-five-year-long Cold War. Chunks of the Wall's concrete became instant collectors' items—gray souvenirs of a grim episode in Europe's history. With the approval of the victorious Allied powers of World War II, the two Germanies, divided since 1945, were at last reunited in October 1990.

> *In his state of the union address on January 31, 1990, President George Bush (b. 1924) declared,*
>
> "The events of the year just ended, the revolution of '89, have been a chain reaction, changes so striking that it marks the beginning of a new era in the world's affairs."
>
> *Just six months later, speaking at Stanford University, Soviet president Mikhail Gorbachev (b. 1931) said,*
>
> "The Cold War is now behind us. Let us not wrangle over who won it. It is in the common interest of our two countries and nations not to fight this trend toward cooperation, but rather to promote it."

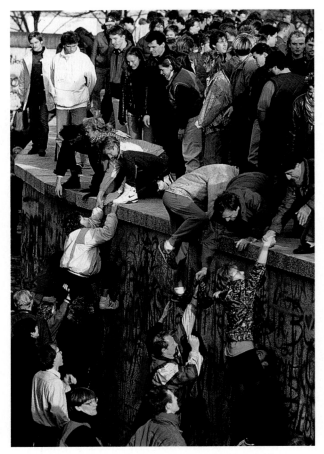

The End of the Post–World War II Era, 1989   Jubilant Berliners partied atop the hated Berlin Wall in December 1989, dramatically symbolizing the end of the Cold War division of Germany.

Most startling of all were the changes that rolled over the heartland of world communism, the Soviet Union itself. Mikhail Gorbachev's policies of *glasnost* and *perestroika* had set in motion a groundswell that surged out of his control. Old-guard hard-liners, in a last-gasp effort to preserve the tottering communist system, attempted to dislodge Gorbachev with a military coup in August 1991. With the support of Boris Yeltsin, president of the Russian Republic (one of the several republics that composed the Union of Soviet Socialist Republics, or USSR), Gorbachev foiled the plotters. But his days were numbered. In December 1991 Gorbachev resigned as Soviet president. He had become a leader without a country as the Soviet Union dissolved into its component parts, some fifteen republics loosely confederated in the Commonwealth of Independent States (CIS), with Russia the most powerful state and Yeltsin the dominant leader. To varying degrees, all the new governments in the CIS repudiated communism and embraced democratic reforms and free-market economies.

These developments astonished the "experts," who had long preached that the steely vise-grip of communist rule never could be peacefully broken. Yet suddenly and almost miraculously, the totalitarian tonnage of communist oppression had been rendered politically weightless. Most spectacularly, the demise of the Soviet Union wrote a definitive finish

to the Cold War era. More than four decades of nail-biting tension between two nuclear superpowers, the Soviet Union and the United States, evaporated when the USSR dismantled itself. With the Soviet Union swept into the dustbin of history and communism all but extinct, Bush spoke hopefully of a "new world order," where democracy would reign and diplomacy would supersede weaponry. Some observers even saw in these developments "the end of history," in the sense that democracy, victorious in its two-century-long struggle against foes on the left and right, had no ideological battles left to fight.

Exultant Americans joked that the USSR had become the "USS *were.*" But the disintegration of the Soviet Union was no laughing matter. Rankling questions remained. For example, who would honor arms-control agreements with the United States? Which of the successor states of the former Soviet Union would take command of the formidable Soviet nuclear arsenal? (A partial answer was provided in early 1993, when President Bush, in one of his last official acts, signed the START II accord with Russian president Boris Yeltsin, committing both powers to reduce their long-range nuclear arsenals by two-thirds within ten years.)

Throughout the former Soviet empire, waves of nationalistic fervor and long-suppressed ethnic and racial hatreds rolled across the vast land as communism's roots were wrenched out. A particularly nasty conflict erupted in the Russian Caucasus in 1991, when the Chechnyan minority tried to declare their independence from Russia, prompting President Yeltsin to send in Russian troops. Ethnic warfare flared in other disintegrating communist countries as well, notably in misery-drenched Yugoslavia, racked by vicious "ethnic cleansing" campaigns against various minorities.

The cruel and paradoxical truth stood revealed that the calcified communist regimes of Eastern Europe, whatever their sins, had at least bottled up the ancient ethnic antagonisms that were the region's peculiar curse and that now erupted in all their historical fury. Refugees from the strife-torn regions flooded into Western Europe. The sturdy German economy, the foundation of European prosperity, wobbled under the awesome burden of absorbing a technologically backward, physically decrepit communist East Germany. The stability of the entire European continent seemed at risk. The Western democracies, which for more than four decades had feared the military *strength* of the

The End of the Cold War Changes the Map of Europe

The Agony of Yugoslavia, 1992
These Bosnian refugees from the town of Jajce illustrate the plight of millions of Yugoslavians as their country slid into vicious interethnic battles in the wake of the Cold War's conclusion.

Eastern bloc, now ironically saw their well-being threatened by the social and economic *weakness* of the former communist lands.

The end of the Cold War also proved a mixed blessing for the United States. For nearly half a century, the containment of Soviet communism had been the paramount goal of U.S. foreign policy. Indeed the Cold War era had been the only lengthy period in American history when the United States had consistently pursued an internationalist foreign policy. With the Soviet threat now canceled, would the United States revert to its traditional isolationism? What principles would guide American diplomacy now that "anticommunism" had lost its relevance?

The Soviet-American rivalry, with its demands for high levels of military preparedness, had also deeply shaped and even invigorated the U.S. economy. Huge economic sectors such as aerospace were heavily sustained by military contracts. The economic cost of beating swords into plowshares became painfully apparent in 1991 when the Pentagon announced the closing of thirty-four military bases and canceled a $52 billion order for a navy attack plane. More closings and cancellations followed. Communities that had been drenched with Pentagon dollars now nearly dried up, especially in hard-hit southern California, where scores of defense plants shut their doors and unemployment soared. The problems of weaning the U.S. economy from its decades of dependence on defense spending tempered the euphoria of Americans as they welcomed the Cold War's long-awaited finale.

Elsewhere in the world, democracy marched triumphantly forward. The white regime in South Africa took a giant step toward liberating that troubled land from its racist past when in 1990 it freed African leader Nelson Mandela, who had served twenty-seven years in prison for conspiring to overthrow the government. Four years later Mandela was elected South Africa's president. Free elections in Nicaragua in February 1990 removed the leftist Sandinistas from power. Two years later, peace came at last to war-ravaged El Salvador.

The Persian Gulf Crisis

Sadly, the end of the Cold War did not mean the end of all wars. President Bush flexed the United States' still-intimidating military muscle in tiny Panama in December 1989, when he sent airborne troops to capture dictator and drug lord Manuel Noriega.

Still more ominous events in the summer of 1990 severely tested Bush's dream of a democratic and peaceful new world order. On August 2 Saddam Hussein, the brutal and ambitious ruler of Iraq, sent his armies to overrun Kuwait, a tiny, oil-rich desert sheikdom on Iraq's southern frontier.

Oil fueled Saddam's aggression. Financially exhausted by its eight-year war with Iran, which had ended in a stalemate in 1988, Iraq needed Kuwait's oil to pay its huge war bills. Saddam's larger design was ironfisted control over the entire Persian Gulf region. With his hand thus firmly clutching the world's economic jugular vein, he dreamed of dictating the terms of oil supplies to the industrial nations, and perhaps of totally extinguishing the Arabs' enemy, Israel.

Ironically the United States and its allies had helped supply Saddam with the tools of aggression. He was widely known to be a thug and assassin who intimidated his underlings by showing them the bodies of his executed adversaries hanging on meat hooks. But in the 1980s, American enmity for Islamic-fundamentalist Iran was intense, and Saddam was at war with Iran. Assuming that "the enemy of my enemy is my friend," American policymakers helped build Saddam's military machine into a formidable force.

On August 2, 1990, Saddam's army roared into Kuwait. The speed and audacity of the invasion was stunning, but the world responded just as swiftly. The United Nations Security Council unanimously condemned the invasion on August 3 and demanded the immediate and unconditional withdrawal of Iraq's troops. When an economic embargo failed to squeeze the Iraqis into compliance by November, the Security Council delivered an ultimatum to Saddam to leave Kuwait by January 15, 1991, or U.N. forces would "use all necessary means" to expel his troops. For perhaps the first time in the post–World War II era, the U.N. seemed to be fulfilling its founders' dreams that it could preserve international order by putting guns where its mouth was. It also put them where the world's critical oil supply was.

In a logistical operation of astonishing complexity, the United States spearheaded a massive international military deployment on the sandy Arabian peninsula. As the January 15 deadline approached, some 539,000 U.S. soldiers, sailors, and pilots—many of them women and all of them members of the new, post-Vietnam, all-volunteer American military—swarmed into the Persian Gulf region. They were joined by nearly 270,000 troops, pilots, and sailors from twenty-eight other countries in the coalition opposed to Iraq. When all diplomatic efforts to resolve the crisis failed, the U.S. Congress voted regretfully on January 12 to approve the use of

force. The time bomb of war now ticked off its final few beats.

Fighting "Operation Desert Storm"

On January 16, 1991, the United States and its U.N. allies unleashed a hellish air war against Iraq. For thirty-seven days, warplanes pummeled targets in occupied Kuwait and in Iraq itself. The air campaign constituted an awesome display of high-technology, precision-targeting modern warfare. Yet the Iraqis claimed, probably rightly, that civilians were killed.

Iraq responded to this pounding by launching several dozen "Scud" short-range ballistic missiles against military and civilian targets in Saudi Arabia and Israel. These missile attacks claimed several lives but did no significant military damage.

Yet if Iraq made but a feeble military response to the air campaign, the allied commander, the beefy and blunt American general Norman ("Stormin' Norman") Schwarzkopf, took nothing for granted. Saddam, who had threatened to wage "the mother of all battles," had the capacity to inflict awful damage. Iraq had stockpiled tons of chemical and biological weapons, including poison gas and the means to spread epidemics of anthrax. Saddam's tactics also included ecological warfare as he released a gigantic oil slick into the Persian Gulf to forestall amphibious assault and ignited hundreds of oil-well fires, whose smoky plumes shrouded the ground from aerial view. Faced with these horrifying tactics, Schwarzkopf's strategy was starkly simple: soften the Iraqis with relentless bombing, then suffocate them on the ground with a tidal-wave rush of troops and armor.

On February 23 the dreaded and long-awaited land war began. Dubbed "Operation Desert Storm," it lasted only four days—the "hundred-hour war." With lightning speed the U.N. forces penetrated deep into Iraq, outflanking the occupying forces in Kuwait and blocking the enemy's ability either to retreat or to reinforce. Allied casualties were amazingly light, whereas much of Iraq's remaining fighting force was quickly destroyed or captured. On February 27 Saddam accepted a cease-fire, and Kuwait was liberated.

Most Americans cheered the war's rapid and enormously successful conclusion. Some, remembering the antiwar movement of the 1960s, had protested against going to war. But the end had

Operation Desert Storm: The Ground War,
February 23–27, 1991

The war had nevertheless failed to dislodge Saddam from power. When the smoke cleared, he had survived to menace the world another day. The perpetually troubled Middle East knew scarcely less trouble after Desert Storm had ceased to thunder, and the United States, for better or worse, found itself even more deeply ensnared in the region's web of mortal hatreds and intractable conflicts.

Bush on the Home Front

In his inaugural address, George Bush pledged that he would work for a "kinder, gentler America." He redeemed that promise in part when he signed the Americans with Disabilities Act (ADA) in 1990, a landmark law prohibiting discrimination against the 43 million U.S. citizens with physical or mental disabilities. The president also signed a major water projects bill in 1992 that fundamentally reformed the distribution of subsidized federal water in the West. The bill put the interests of the environment ahead of agriculture, especially in California's heavily irrigated Central Valley, and made much more water available to the West's thirsty cities.

The new president continued to aggravate the explosive "social issues" that had so divided Americans throughout the 1980s, especially the nettlesome questions of affirmative action and abortion.

come so suddenly and decisively that antiwar sentiment on a large scale never crystallized. And unlike the forlorn veterans of Vietnam, who had straggled back to their embittered and disillusioned homeland, the troops from Operation Desert Storm returned home to enthusiastic heroes' welcomes.

The Hundred-Hour War
In what some have called a lightning victory, the U.N. allies' fighting men and women reduced Saddam's military machine, the fourth-largest army in the world, to wreckage and rubble.

Justice Clarence Thomas   Despite vivid allegations of sexual impropriety by law professor Anita Hill, Thomas was confirmed by the Senate in 1991 as the second African-American to serve on the Supreme Court (the other was former NAACP counsel Thurgood Marshall, who retired in 1991).

Professor Anita Hill Testifies Against Supreme Court Nominee Clarence Thomas, October 11, 1991   Her testimony failed to stop his confirmation but did sensitize the country to issues of sexual harassment.

In 1990 Bush's Department of Education challenged the legality of college scholarships targeted for racial minorities. Bush repeatedly threatened to veto civil rights legislation that would make it easier for employees to prove discrimination in hiring and promotion practices. (He grudgingly accepted a watered-down civil rights bill in 1991.)

Most provocatively, in 1991 Bush nominated for the Supreme Court the conservative African-American jurist Clarence Thomas. A stern critic of affirmative-action policies, Thomas was slated to fill a seat vacated by the retirement of Thurgood Marshall, the Court's lone black justice and an outspoken champion of civil rights.

Thomas's nomination was loudly opposed by liberal groups, including organized labor, the National Association for the Advancement of Colored People (NAACP), and the National Organization for Women (NOW), which objected to Thomas's presumed opposition to abortion rights—though the nominee studiously refrained from publicly commenting on the landmark abortion case of *Roe* v. *Wade,* claiming, incredibly, that he had never thought about it or discussed it.

Reflecting irreconcilable divisions over affirmative action and abortion, the Senate Judiciary Committee concluded its hearings on the nomination with a divided 7–7 vote and forwarded the matter to the full Senate without a recommendation. Then, just days before the Senate was scheduled to vote in early October 1991, a press leak revealed that Anita Hill, a law professor at the University of Oklahoma, had accused Thomas of sexual harassment. The public outcry at this allegation forced the Senate Judiciary Committee to reopen its hearings. For days a prurient American public sat glued to their television sets as Hill graphically detailed her charges of sexual improprieties and Thomas angrily responded. Although Hill passed a lie detector test, thirteen other female colleagues of Thomas testified that they had never witnessed any improper behavior. In the end, by a 52–48 vote, the Senate narrowly

Read My Nose When President Bush reneged on his 1988 campaign promise of "no new taxes," he inflicted mortal political damage on his reelection campaign in 1992.

confirmed Thomas as the second African-American ever to sit on the supreme bench. Hill's charges had failed to block Thomas's nomination, but many Americans hailed her as a heroine for her role in focusing the nation's attention on issues of sexual harassment. (Oregon's Republican senator Robert Packwood was among the most prominent officials to fall victim to the new sexual etiquette when he was forced to resign from the Senate in 1995 after charges that he had sexually harassed several women.) Thomas maintained that Hill's widely publicized, unproved allegations amounted to "a high-tech lynching for uppity blacks who in any way deign to think for themselves, to do for themselves."

The furor over Clarence Thomas's confirmation suggested that the social issues that had helped produce three Republican presidential victories in the 1980s were losing some of their electoral appeal. Many women, enraged by the all-male judiciary committee's behavior in the Clarence Thomas hearings, grew increasingly critical of the president's uncompromising stand on abortion. A "gender gap" opened between the two political parties, as pro-choice women grew increasingly cool toward the strong anti-abortion stand of the Republicans.

Still more damaging to President Bush's political health was the economy, which sputtered and stalled almost from the outset of his administration. By 1992 the unemployment rate exceeded 7 percent.

It approached 10 percent in the key state of California, ravaged by defense cutbacks. The federal budget deficit continued to mushroom cancerously, topping $250 billion in each of Bush's years as president. In a desperate attempt to stop the hemorrhage of red ink, Bush agreed in 1990 to a budget agreement with Congress that included $133 billion in new taxes.

Bush's 1990 tax and budget package added up to a political catastrophe. In his 1988 presidential campaign, Bush had belligerently declared, "Read my lips—no new taxes." Now he had flagrantly broken that campaign promise.

The intractable budgetary crisis and the stagnant economy congealed in a lump of disgust with all political incumbents. Disillusion thickened in 1991 when it was revealed that many members of the House of Representatives had written thousands of bad checks from their accounts in a private House "bank." Although no taxpayers' money was involved, the image of privileged politicians incompetently managing their private business affairs, with no penalty, even while they were grossly mismanaging the Republic's finances, further soured the voters. A movement to impose limits on the number of terms that elected officials could serve gained strength in many states. Sniffing this prevailing wind, unprecedented numbers of officeholders announced that they would not stand for reelection.

Bill Clinton: The First Baby-Boomer President

The slumbering economy, the widening gender gap, and the rising anti-incumbent spirit spelled opportunity for Democrats, frozen out of the White House for all but four years since 1968. In a bruising round of primary elections, Governor William Jefferson Clinton of Arkansas weathered blistering accusations of womanizing and draft evasion to emerge as his party's standard-bearer. Breaking with the tradition of a "balanced ticket," he selected a fellow fortysomething southern white male Protestant moderate, Senator Albert Gore of Tennessee, as his vice-presidential running mate.

Clinton claimed to be a "new" Democrat, chastened by the party's long exile in the political wilderness. Spurred especially by Walter Mondale's galling defeat at the hands of Ronald Reagan in 1984, Clinton and other centrist Democrats had formed the Democratic Leadership Council to point the party away from its traditional antibusiness, dovish, champion-of-the-underdog orientation and toward progrowth, strong defense, and anticrime policies. Clinton campaigned especially vigorously on promises to stimulate the economy, reform the welfare system, and overhaul the nation's health-care apparatus, which had grown into a scandalously

Presidential Campaign Debate, 1992   George Bush, Ross Perot, and Bill Clinton squared off at the University of Richmond (Virginia) on October 16, 1992. The telegenic Clinton handily dominated the television debates, especially in the "talk-show" format used on this occasion.

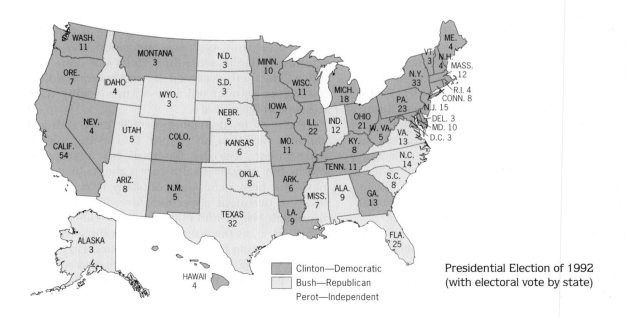

Clinton—Democratic
Bush—Republican
Perot—Independent

Presidential Election of 1992
(with electoral vote by state)

expensive contraption that failed to provide medical coverage to some 37 million Americans.

Trying to wring one more win out of the social issues that had underwritten two Reagan and one Bush presidential victories, the Republican convention in Houston in August 1992 dwelt stridently on "family values" and, as expected, nominated George Bush and Vice President J. Danforth Quayle for a second term. A tired and apparently dispirited Bush then took to the campaign trail. His listless performances and spaghetti sentences set him sharply apart from his youthful rival, the superenergetic, articulate Clinton. Bush halfheartedly attacked Clinton's character, contrasting the Arkansan's evasion of military service in the Vietnam War with his own heroic record as a navy flier in World War II. The president seemed to campaign more for vindication in the history books than for victory in the election. He tried to take credit for the end of the Cold War and trumpeted his leadership role in the Persian Gulf War.

But fear for the economic problems of the future swayed more voters than pride in the foreign policies of the past. The purchasing power of the average worker's paycheck had actually declined during Bush's presidency. At Clinton's campaign headquarters, a simple sign reminded staffers of his principal campaign theme: "It's the economy, stupid." Reflecting pervasive economic unease and the virulence of the throw-the-bums-out national mood, nearly 20 percent of voters cast their ballots for independent presidential candidate H. Ross Perot, a bantamweight, jug-eared Texas billionaire who harped incessantly on the problem of the federal deficit and made a boast of the fact that he had never held any public office.

Perot's colorful presence probably accounted for the record turnout on election day, when some 100 million voters—55 percent of those eligible—went to the polls. The final tallies gave Clinton 43,728,275 popular votes and 370 votes in the Electoral College. He was the first baby boomer to ascend to the White House, a distinction reflecting the electoral profile of the population, 70 percent of whom had been born after World War II. Bush polled some 38,167,416 popular and 168 electoral votes. Perot won no Electoral College votes but did gather 19,237,247 in the popular count—the strongest showing for an independent or third-party candidate since Theodore Roosevelt ran on the Bull Moose ticket in 1912. Democrats also racked up clear majorities in both houses of Congress, which

seated near-record numbers of new members, including thirty-nine African-Americans, nineteen Hispanic-Americans, seven Asian-Americans, one Native American, and forty-eight women. In Illinois Carol Moseley-Braun became the first African-American woman elected to the U.S. Senate, where she joined five other women in the largest female contingent ever in the upper chamber.

Women also figured prominently in President Clinton's cabinet, including the first female attorney general, Janet Reno, and former Wisconsin University president Donna Shalala, who became the secretary of health and human services. Vowing to shape a government that "looked like America," Clinton appointed several ethnic and racial minority members to his cabinet contingent, including former San Antonio mayor Henry Cisneros at Housing and Urban Development and an African-American, Ron Brown, as secretary of commerce. Clinton also seized the opportunity in 1993 to nominate Ruth Bader Ginsburg to the Supreme Court, where she joined Sandra Day O'Connor to make a pair of women justices.

A False Start for Reform

Badly overestimating his electoral mandate for liberal reform, the young president made a series of costly blunders upon entering the White House. In one of his first initiatives on taking office, he stirred a hornet's nest of controversy by advocating an end to the ban on gays and lesbians in the armed services. Faced with ferocious opposition, the president finally had to settle for a "don't ask, don't tell" policy that quietly accepted gay and lesbian soldiers and sailors without officially acknowledging their presence in the military.

Even more damaging to Clinton's political standing, and to his hopes for lasting liberal achievement, was the fiasco of his attempt to reform the nation's health-care system. In a dramatic but personally and politically risky innovation, the president appointed his wife, nationally prominent lawyer and child-advocate Hillary Rodham Clinton, as the director of a task force charged with redesigning the medical-service industry. After months of highly publicized hearings and scrappy planning sessions, the task force unveiled its stupefyingly complicated plan in October 1993. Critics

Bombing of Federal Building in Oklahoma City, 1995
Investigation into the truck bombing that destroyed this federal office building in downtown Oklahoma City led to the arrest and conviction for murder of Timothy McVeigh, an anti-government extremist.

immediately blasted the cumbersome, convoluted proposal, which was virtually dead on arrival in Congress, where it was finally buried one year later. As the reform plan's principal architect, the First Lady was doused with a torrent of abuse. She had entered the White House as a full political partner with her husband, sharing the national spotlight as no previous First Lady had done. But midway through his first term, she had become a political liability and sidestepped quietly to the shadows.

Clinton had better luck with a deficit-reduction bill in 1993, which combined with a moderately buoyant economy by 1996 to shrink the federal deficit to its lowest level in more than a decade. He also induced the Congress in 1993 to pass a gun-control law, the "Brady Bill," named for presidential aide James Brady, who had been wounded and disabled by gunfire in the assassination attempt on President Ronald Reagan in 1981. In July of 1994,

Clinton made further progress against the national plague of firearms when he persuaded Congress to pass a $30 billion anticrime bill, which contained a ban on several types of assault weapons.

With these measures the government struggled to hold the line against an epidemic of violence that rocked American society in the 1990s. A radical Muslim group bombed New York's World Trade Center in 1993, killing six people. A still larger blast destroyed a federal office building in Oklahoma City, Oklahoma, in 1995, taking 168 lives, presumably in retribution for a 1993 standoff in Waco, Texas, between federal agents and a fundamentalist sect known as the Branch Davidians. That showdown ended in the destruction of the sect's compound and the deaths of many Branch Davidians, including women and children. The last two episodes brought to light a lurid and secretive underground of paramilitary private "militias," composed of alienated citizens armed to the teeth and ultrasuspicious of all governments.

Even many law-abiding citizens shared to some degree in the antigovernment attitudes that drove the militia members to murderous extremes. Thanks largely to the disillusioning agony of the Vietnam War and the naked cynicism of Richard Nixon in the Watergate scandal, the confidence in government that had come naturally to the generation that licked the Great Depression and won the Second World War was in short supply by the century's end. Reflecting that pervasive disenchantment with politics and politicians, some twenty-three states had imposed restrictions on elected officials with term-limit laws by the mid-1990s, though the Supreme Court ruled in 1995 that such laws did not apply to federal officeholders.

The Politics of Distrust

Clinton's failed initiatives and widespread antigovernment sentiment offered conservative Republicans a golden opportunity in 1994, and they seized it aggressively. Led by outspoken Georgia representative Newt Gingrich, conservatives offered voters a "Contract with America" that promised an all-out assault on budget deficits and radical reductions in welfare programs. Liberal Democrats countered that the conservative pledge should be called a "Contract *on* America," but their protests were drowned in the right-wing tornado that roared across the land in the 1994 congressional elections. Every incumbent Republican gubernatorial, senatorial, and congressional candidate was reelected. Republicans also picked up eleven new governorships, eight seats in the Senate, and fifty-three seats in the House (where Gingrich became speaker), giving them control of both chambers of the federal Congress for the first time in forty years.

But if President Clinton had overplayed his mandate for liberal reform in 1993, the congressional Republicans now proceeded to overplay their mandate for conservative retrenchment. The new Republican majority did legislate one long-standing conservative goal when they restricted "unfunded mandates"—federal laws that imposed new obligations on state and local governments without providing new revenues. And in 1996 the new Congress

achieved a major conservative victory when it compelled a reluctant Clinton to sign the Welfare Reform Bill, which made deep cuts in welfare grants and required able-bodied welfare recipients to find employment. The new welfare law also tightly restricted welfare benefits for legal and illegal immigrants alike, reflecting a rising tide of anti-immigrant sentiment as the numbers of newcomers climbed toward an all-time high. Old-line liberal Democrats howled with pain at the president's alleged betrayal of his party's heritage, and some prominent administration members resigned in protest against his decision to sign the welfare bill. But Clinton's acceptance of the welfare reform package was part of his shrewd political strategy of accommodating the electorate's conservative mood by moving to his right.

President Clinton was at first stunned by the magnitude of the Republican congressional victory in 1994. For a time he was reduced to lamely reminding Congress that the president was still relevant to the political and policy-making process. But many Americans gradually came to feel that the Gingrich Republicans were bending their conservative bow too far, especially when the new speaker advocated provocative ideas like sending the children of welfare families to orphanages. In a tense confrontation between the Democratic president and the Republican Congress, the federal government actually had to shut down for several days at the end of 1995, until a budget package was agreed upon. These outlandishly partisan antics bred a backlash that helped President Clinton rebound from his condition as a political dead duck.

As the Republicans slugged it out in a noisy round of presidential primaries in 1996, Clinton's reelection campaign raised spectacular sums of money—some of it, investigations later revealed, from questionable sources. The eventual Republican standard-bearer was Kansas senator Robert Dole, a decorated World War II veteran who ran a listless campaign. Clinton, buoyed by a healthy economy and by his artful trimming to the conservative wind, breezed to an easy victory, with 45,628,667 popular votes to Dole's 37,869,435. The Reform party's egomaniacal leader, Ross Perot, ran a sorry third, picking up less than half the votes he had garnered in 1992. Clinton won 379 electoral votes, Dole only 159. But Republicans remained in control of Congress.

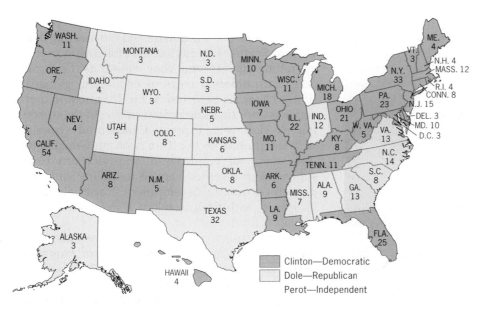

Presidential Election of 1996 (with electoral vote by state) The "solid South," once a safe Democratic stronghold, had by century's end largely become Republican territory.

Clinton Again

As Clinton began his second term—the first Democratic president since Franklin Delano Roosevelt to be reelected—he once again appointed a diversified cabinet, but the heady promises of far-reaching reform with which he had entered the White House four years earlier were no longer heard. Still facing Republican majorities in both houses of Congress, he proposed only modest legislative goals, even though soaring tax revenues generated by the prosperous economy produced in 1998 a balanced federal budget for the first time in three decades.

Clinton cleverly managed to put Republicans on the defensive by claiming the political middle ground. He now warmly embraced the landmark Welfare Reform Bill of 1996 that he had initially been slow to endorse. Juggling the political hot potato of affirmative action, Clinton pledged to "mend it, not end it." When voters in California in 1996 approved Proposition 209, prohibiting affirmative-action preferences in government and higher education, the number of minority students in the state's public universities temporarily plummeted. A federal appeals court decision, *Hopwood* v. *Texas*, had a

similar effect in Texas. Clinton criticized these broad assaults on affirmative action but stopped short of trying to reverse them, aware that public support for affirmative action, especially among white Americans, had diminished since the 1970s. In California and elsewhere, Clinton-style Democrats increasingly sought ways to aid the economically disadvantaged, including minorities, while avoiding the minefield of racial preferences.

Clinton's major political advantage continued to be the roaring economy, which by 2000 had sustained the longest period of growth in American history. While unemployment crept down to 4 percent and businesses scrambled madly for workers, inflationary pressure remained remarkably low. An economic crisis in late 1997 plunged Southeast Asia and South Korea into financial turmoil, arousing fears of a global economic meltdown. But despite volatility in the stock market, the United States surged ahead, driven by new Internet businesses and other high-tech and media companies. The economic "Asian flu" caused only a few sniffles for the robust American economy.

Prosperity did not make Clinton immune to controversy over trade policy. During his first term, Clinton had displayed political courage by

Federal Reserve Chairman Alan Greenspan (b. 1926)
Many observers credited the robust prosperity of Clinton's presidency to Alan Greenspan's skillful management of the economy. A Republican first appointed by Ronald Reagan, Greenspan led the Federal Reserve Board in carefully adjusting interest rates to control inflation while promoting economic growth.

supporting the North American Free Trade Agreement (NAFTA), creating in 1993 a free-trade zone encompassing Mexico, Canada, and the United States. In doing so, he reversed his own stand in the 1992 election campaign and bucked the opposition of protectionists in his own party, especially labor leaders fearful of losing jobs to low-wage Mexican workers. Clinton took another step in 1994 toward a global free-trade system when he vigorously promoted the creation of the World Trade Organization (WTO), the successor to the General Agreement on Tariffs and Trade (GATT) and a cherished goal of free-trade advocates since the end of the Second World War.

Simmering discontent over trade policy boiled over in 1999 when Clinton hosted the meeting of the WTO in Seattle. The city's streets filled with protesters railing against what they viewed as the human and environmental costs of economic "globalization." Clinton, eager to keep Democratic party activists and the trade unions in line in the upcoming election year, expressed measured sympathy with the protest, to the dismay of trade negotiators from the poor countries of the Southern Hemisphere, who resented Yankee meddling with their plans for economic development. Trade talks fizzled in Seattle, with Clinton taking a hefty share of the blame.

Money spurred controversy of another sort in the late 1990s. Campaign finance reform, long smoldering as a potential issue, suddenly flared up after the 1996 presidential campaign. Congressional investigators revealed that the Clinton campaign had received funds from many improper sources, including contributors who paid to stay overnight in the White House and foreigners who were legally prohibited from giving to American campaigns. But Republicans and Democrats alike had reason to avoid reform. Both parties had grown dependent on vast sums to finance television ads for their candidates. Clinton did little more than pay lip service to the cause of campaign finance reform. But within the ranks of both parties, a few mavericks proposed to eliminate the corrupting influence of big donors. Senator John McCain from Arizona made campaign finance reform a centerpiece of his surprisingly strong, though ulimately unsuccessful, bid for the Republican presidential nomination in the 2000 campaign.

Two domestic issues inspired Clinton to act boldly in his second term: the fights *against* big tobacco and *for* gun control. In 1998 the large tobacco companies and the attorneys general of several states worked their way toward a huge legal settlement. In return for restricting advertising targeted at young people and for giving the states $358 billion to offset the public-health costs of smoking, the tobacco firms would win immunity from further litigation, including at the federal level. When the deal came before Congress, Clinton weighed in heavily behind it, while big tobacco spent $40 million to snuff it out. The deal collapsed, but the tobacco wars continued. Months later eight states worked out a more limited settlement, and in 1999 the Clinton administration shifted its strategy to the courts, where it hoped lawsuits would eventually force the tobacco industry to reimburse the federal government the $20 million a year Clinton officials argued Uncle Sam had spent since the 1950s on smokers' health.

Clinton's focus on gun control had a tragic impetus. On an April morning in 1999, two students at Columbine High School in Littleton, Colorado, killed twelve fellow students and a teacher in the deadliest of a series of school shootings that shook the nation in the mid to late 1990s (see p. 1006). Debate flared over the origins of this epidemic of school violence. Some observers targeted the violence of movies, TV shows, and video games, others the failings of parents. But the culprit that attracted the most sustained political attention was guns— their abundance and accessibility, especially in suburban and rural communities, where most of the school shootings had occurred. Clinton engaged in a pugnacious debate with the progun National Rifle Association over the need to toughen gun laws. The "Million Mom March" in Washington in May 2000 demonstrated the growing public support for new antigun measures.

Problems Abroad

The end of the Cold War robbed the United States of the basic principles on which it had conducted foreign policy for nearly half a century, and Clinton groped for a diplomatic formula to replace anticommunism in the conduct of America's foreign affairs. The Cold War's finale also shook a number of skeletons loose from several government closets. Sensational revelations that Central Intelligence Agency double agents had sold secrets to the Soviets during the Cold War years, causing the execution of American agents abroad, demonstrated that the ghost of the Cold War still cast its frosty shadow over official Washington.

Absorbed by domestic issues, President Clinton at first seemed uncertain and even amateurish in his conduct of foreign policy. He followed his predecessor's lead in dispatching American troops as part of a peacekeeping mission to Somalia and reinforced the U.S. contingent after Somali rebels killed more than a dozen Americans in late 1993. But in March 1994, the president quietly withdrew the

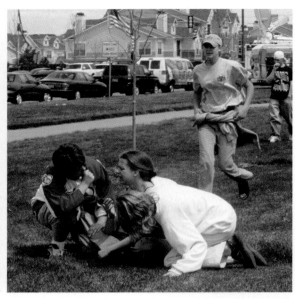

Aftermath of Columbine High School Shootings
Shocked and grieving friends rush to comfort each other after the shooting spree by two high-school gunmen in Littleton, Colorado, in April 1999.

American units, without having accomplished any clearly defined goal. Burned in Somalia, Washington stood on the sidelines in 1995 when catastrophic ethnic violence in the central African country of Rwanda resulted in the deaths of half a million people. A similar lack of clarity afflicted policy toward Haiti, where democratically elected president Jean-Bertrand Aristide had been deposed by a military coup in 1991. Clinton at last committed twenty thousand American troops to return Aristide to the Haitian presidency in 1994, after thousands of desperate Haitian refugees had sought asylum in the United States.

It took time, too, for Clinton to settle on an approach to China. Candidate Clinton had denounced George Bush in 1992 for not imposing economic sanctions on China as punishment for Beijing's wretched record of human rights abuses. But President Clinton learned what Bush had long known: China's economic importance to the United States did not permit Washington the luxury of taking the high road on human rights. Clinton soon soft-pedaled his criticism of the Beijing regime and instead began seeking improved trade relations with that rapidly industrializing country and poten-

tial market bonanza. By 2000 Clinton had become the country's leading crusader for a controversial China trade bill, passed by Congress in May 2000, which made the Asian giant a full-fledged trading partner of the United States.

Clinton's approach to the tormented Balkans in southeastern Europe showed a similar initial hesitation, followed eventually by his assumption of a leadership role. In the former Yugoslavia, as vicious ethnic conflict raged through Bosnia, the Washington government dithered until finally deciding to commit American troops to a NATO peacekeeping contingent in late 1995. Deadlines for removing the troops were postponed and then finally abandoned altogether as it became clear that they were the only force capable of preventing new hostilities. NATO's expansion to include the new member states of Poland, Hungary, and the Czech Republic in 1997, and its continuing presence in Bosnia, failed to pacify the Balkans completely. When Serbian president Slobodan Milošević in 1999 unleashed a new round of "ethnic cleansing" in the region, this time against ethnic Albanians in the province of Kosovo, U.S.-led NATO forces launched an air war against Serbia. The bombing campaign initially failed to stop ethnic terror, as refugees flooded into neighboring countries, but it eventually forced Milosević to accept a NATO peacekeeping force in Kosovo. With ethnic reconciliation still a distant dream in the Balkans, Washington accepted the reality that American forces had an enduring role as peacekeepers in the region.

The Middle East remained a major focus of American diplomacy right up to the end of Clinton's tenure. In 1993 Clinton presided over a historic meeting at the White House between Israeli premier Yitzhak Rabin and Palestine Liberation Organization (PLO) leader Yasir Arafat. They agreed in principle on self-rule for the Palestinians within Israel. But hopes flickered two years later when Rabin fell to an assassin's bullet. Clinton and his second-term secretary of state, Madeleine Albright, spent the rest of the 1990s struggling to broker the permanent settlement that continued to elude Israelis and Palestinians. In Iraq Saddam Hussein persisted in his game of hide-and-seek with U.N. inspectors monitoring the Iraqi weapons program. When the chief U.N. inspector reported in 1998 that Iraq was out of compliance with U.N. rules, America and Britain launched air strikes against Iraqi weapons factories and warehouses. That same year the United States also conducted missile attacks against alleged terrorist sites in Afghanistan and Sudan in retaliation for terrorist bombings that had killed more than two hundred people at the U.S. embassies in Kenya and Tanzania.

In his final year as president, Clinton stepped up his efforts to leave a legacy as an international peacemaker. Along with his work in the Middle East, he sought to bring peace to Northern Ireland and the Korean peninsula, and he traveled to India and Pakistan in hopes of reducing the rivalry between the two nuclear powers of southern Asia. Although the guiding principles of foreign policy in the post–Cold War era remained elusive, Clinton had become a stalwart opponent of the minority factions in both parties that yearned for a new isolationism.

Scandal and Impeachment

President Clinton had ample cause for concern about his lasting reputation, since scandal had dogged him from the beginning of his presidency. Allegations of flagrant wrongdoing, reaching back to his prepresidential days in Arkansas, included a failed real estate investment known as the Whitewater Land Corporation. The Clintons' role in that deal prompted the appointment of a federal special prosecutor to investigate. Suspicions were especially aroused by the apparent suicide in 1993 of White House counsel and close Clinton associate Vincent W. Foster, Jr., who had handled the Clintons' legal and financial affairs. The president's loose ethics and womanizing even found fictional expressions in a runaway 1996 best-seller, *Primary Colors,*

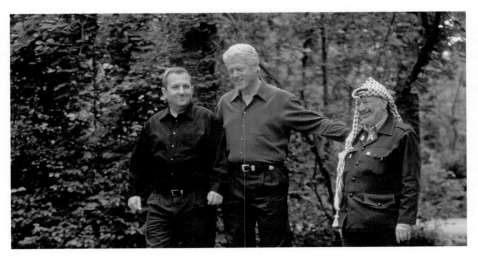

Clinton's Middle East Peace Initiatives In the last year of his presidency, President Clinton pushed hard for a resolution of the Palestinian-Israeli stalemate, hoping to deliver long-sought peace in the Middle East and secure his reputation as an international peacemaker. Despite extensive meetings with Palestinian leader Yasser Arafat and Israeli prime minister Ehud Barak, neither goal was accomplished, and tragically, tensions in the area only escalated.

though the actual Whitewater investigation never proved any Clinton wrongdoing.

But all the previous scandals were overshadowed when allegations broke in January 1998 that Clinton had engaged in a sexual affair with a young White House intern, Monica Lewinsky, and then lied about it when he testified under oath in a civil lawsuit. The lawsuit had been brought by an Arkansas woman, Paula Jones, who charged that then-governor Clinton had sexually harassed her when she was a state employee. The Supreme Court had unanimously agreed to permit the case to go forward in May 1997, ruling that being sued in a civil case would not "significantly distract" the president from his duties.

The accusation that Clinton had lied under oath in the Jones case presented a stunning windfall to the special prosecutor, Kenneth Starr, originally appointed to investigate the Whitewater deal. Like Captain Ahab pursuing the whale Moby Dick, Starr had relentlessly traced Clinton's steps for years, spending $40 million but never succeeding in finding evidence against the president himself. Clinton, now suddenly caught in a legal and political trap, delivered vehement public denials that he had engaged in "sexual relations" with "that woman." After maintaining his innocence for eight months, Clinton was finally forced to acknowledge an "inappropriate relationship." In September 1998 Starr presented to the House of Representatives a stinging report, including graphic sexual details, charging Clinton with eleven possible grounds for impeachment, all related to the Lewinsky matter.

Led by its fiercely anti-Clinton Republican majority, the House quickly cranked up the rusty machinery of impeachment. After a nasty partisan debate, the House Republicans in December 1998 eventually passed two articles of impeachment against the president: perjury before a grand jury and obstruction of justice. Crying foul, the Democratic minority charged that, however deplorable Clinton's personal misconduct, sexual transgressions did not rise to the level of "high crimes and misdemeanors" prescribed in the Constitution (see Art. II, Sec. IV in the Appendix). The House Republican managers (prosecutors) of impeachment for the Senate trial, led by Illinois congressman and House Judiciary Committee chairman Henry Hyde, claimed that perjury and obstruction were grave public issues and that nothing less than the "rule of law" was at stake.

As cries of "honor the Constitution" and "sexual McCarthyism" filled the air, the nation debated whether the president's peccadilloes amounted to high crimes or low follies. Most Americans apparently leaned toward the latter. In the 1998 midterm elections, voters reduced the House Republicans' majority, causing fiery House speaker Newt Gingrich to resign his post. Incredibly, Clinton's job approval rating remained high and even rose throughout the long impeachment ordeal. Although Americans held a low opinion of Clinton's slipshod personal morals, most liked the president's political and economic policies and wanted him to stay in office. Kenneth Starr's stock in public opinion fell accordingly.

In January and February 1999, for the first time in 130 years, the nation witnessed an impeachment proceeding in the U.S. Senate. Dusting off ancient precedents from Andrew Johnson's trial, the one hundred solemn senators heard arguments and evidence in the case, with Chief Justice William Rehnquist presiding. With the facts widely known and the two parties' political positions firmly locked in, the trial's outcome was a foregone conclusion. On the key obstruction of justice charge, five northeastern Republicans joined all forty-five Democratic senators in voting not guilty. The fifty Republican votes for conviction fell far short of the constitutionally required two-thirds majority. The vote on the perjury charge was forty-five guilty, fifty-five not guilty.

Clinton's Legacy

With the impeachment trial over, a weary nation yearned for Washington to move on to other business. Vowing to serve "until the last hour of the last day of my term," Clinton spent what remained of his presidency seeking to secure a legacy for himself as an effective leader and moderate reformer. He designated major swaths of undeveloped land as protected wilderness and won public support for health-care improvements in the form of a "patients' bill of rights." He took advantage of big federal budget surpluses to win congressional approval for hiring 100,000 more teachers and 50,000 more police officers. Budget surpluses brought out the enduring differences between Republicans and Democrats. The former urged big tax cuts, the latter a mixture of smaller cuts and new

Billions of dollars

Deficits into Surpluses
In 1998 the U.S. Budget deficit became a surplus for the first time in decades. (Sources: Office Management and Budget and Bureau of Labor Statistics.)

ways to shore up Medicare and Social Security—a conflict in aims that set the stage for the 2000 presidential campaign.

Beyond the obvious stain of impeachment, Clinton's legacy was bound to be a mixed one for his country and his party. He came to office in 1992 determined to make economic growth his first priority, and in this domain he surely succeeded. Benefiting from a global expansion he had done little to foster, he nonetheless made sound appointments to top economic posts and kept a steady eye on the federal budget. The country achieved nearly full employment by decade's end, poverty rates inched down, and median income reached new highs. From 1998 to 2000, the federal budgets resulted in surpluses rather than deficits. Yet by governing successfully as a "New Democrat" and avowed centrist, Clinton did more to consolidate than reverse the Reagan-Bush revolution against the New Deal liberalism that had for half a century provided the compass for the Democratic party and the nation. As a brilliant communicator, Clinton kept alive a vision of social justice and racial harmony. But as an executive, he discouraged people from expecting government to remedy all the nation's ills. By setting such a low standard for his personal conduct, he replenished the sad reservoir of public cynicism about politics that Vietnam and Watergate had created a generation before. In the last days of his presidency, Clinton negotiated a deal with the Special Prosecutor to win immunity from possible legal action over the Lewinsky scandal by agreeing to a fine and a five-year suspension of his law license.

Controversy trailed Clinton out the White House door when the departing president issued several executive pardons that gave at least the appearance of rewarding political backers and donors.

The Bush-Gore Presidential Battle

Like Dwight D. Eisenhower in the 1950s, Clinton regarded the election of his vice president as a further means of ensuring his own legacy. Clinton's loyal vice president, Al Gore, easily won the Democratic party's presidential nomination in 2000. A quarter-century in national government, as congressman, senator, and vice president, had made Gore a seasoned and savvy policy expert, but many Americans found his somewhat formal personal bearing to be off-putting, especially when contrasted with the winsome charm of his boss. Gore also faced the tricky challenge of somehow associating himself with Clinton-era prosperity while detaching himself from Clinton-era scandal. Trying to distance himself from Clinton's peccadilloes, he chose as his running mate Connecticut senator Joseph Lieberman, an outspoken critic of Clinton during the Lewinsky affair and the first Jew nominated to a national ticket by a major party. Meanwhile, consumer advocate Ralph Nader's Green party threatened to siphon off the ballots of environmentalists who might otherwise have voted for Gore, a long-time champion of vigorous pro-environmental policies.

The Republican nominee, George W. Bush, had catapulted to party prominence on the strength of his being the eldest son of former president George Bush and his popularity as a two-term governor of Texas. Though untested on the national stage, he inspired the loyalty of able lieutenants and organized a formidable campaign with a promise "to restore dignity to the White House"—a thinly veiled attack on Clinton's personal failings. Bush chose Dick Cheney, former secretary of defense in the elder Bush's administration and a key planner in the Persion Gulf War of 1991, as his vice-presidential running mate, lending the ticket a much-needed aura of experience. Styling himself a "compassionate conservative," "George W." (also "W," or sometimes "dubbya") promised to bridge the bitter division between moderates and die-hard conservatives within the Republican party.

Rosy estimates that the federal budget would produce a surplus of some $2 trillion over the coming decade set the stage for the presidential contest. Bush called for returning two-thirds of the surplus "to the people" in the form of a $1.3 trillion across-the-board tax cut. True to the Republican creed of smaller government, Bush championed private-sector initiatives, such as school vouchers, a reliance on "faith-based" institutions to serve the poor, and reforms to the Social Security system that would permit individual workers to invest part of their payroll taxes in private retirement accounts. Gore countered that Bush's tax plan would benefit the rich much more than the poor. Gore advocated a more modest tax cut targeted at the middle and lower classes and proposed using most of the surplus to reduce or even eliminate the national debt, shore up Social Security, and expand Medicare. In this post–Cold War era, foreign policy did not figure prominently in either candidate's campaign.

Pollsters and candidates alike predicted a close election, but they could not foresee that the result would be an epochal cliffhanger. Not since the Hayes-Tilden election of 1876 had the usual electoral mechanisms ground their gears so badly before yielding a definite conclusion. In the pivotal state of Florida (where the Republican candidate's brother Jeb Bush served as governor), the vote was so close that state law compelled a recount. When that second tally confirmed Bush's paper-thin margin of victory, Democrats called for further hand recounts in several counties where confusing ballots and faulty machines seemed to have denied Gore a legitimate majority. Crying foul, Republicans turned to the courts to block any more recounting. A bizarre judicial tussle ensued as battalions of Democratic lawyers challenged the legality of Florida's voting procedures and legions of Republican lawyers fought to stymie them.

When the Florida Supreme Court ordered a hand count of nearly sixty thousand ballots that the machines had failed to read, Republicans struck back on two fronts. The Republican-dominated

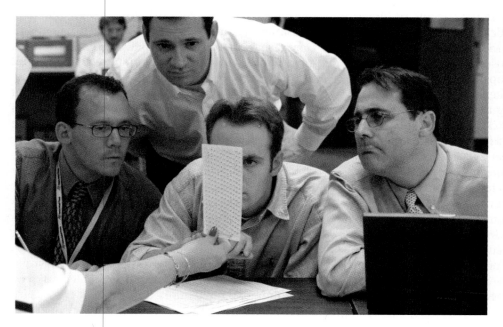

Counting Chads
With Bush and Gore neck-and-neck in Florida's presidential vote count, election officials in some counties like Broward examined by eye paper ballots disqualified by machine because the punched chads had not fully separated from the ballot. They hoped close scrutiny would reveal the voter's intention.

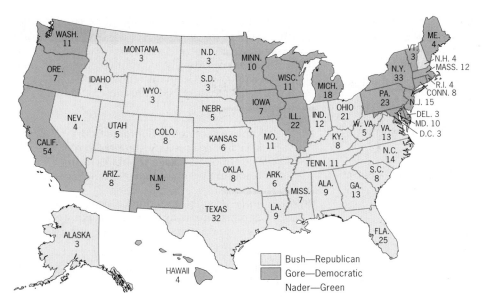

Presidential Election of 2000 (with electoral vote by state) Although Democratic vice president Albert Gore won the popular election for president by half a million votes, George W. Bush's contested five-hundred-vote advantage in Florida gave him a slight lead in the Electoral College. The 2.7 million popular votes won by Green party candidate and consumer activist Ralph Nader almost surely deprived Gore of victory, casting Nader in the role of spoiler. Bush's failure to win the popular vote inspired critics to protest at his inauguration with placards reading "Hail to the Thief."

Florida legislature moved to name a set of pro-Bush electors, regardless of the vote tabulating and retabulating then under way. The Bush campaign also took its case to the U.S. Supreme Court. There, with the eyes of an increasingly restive nation riveted on the proceedings, the nine justices broke into a bare-knuckle judicial brawl. Five bitterly divisive weeks after election day, the presidential campaign of 2000 finally ended when the high court's five most conservative members ruled in Bush's favor. They reasoned that since neither Florida's legislature nor its courts had established a uniform standard for evaluating disputed ballots, the hand counts amounted to an unconstitutional breach of the Fourteenth Amendment's "equal protection" clause. In a rare departure from high court decorum, the liberal minority excoriated the majority. Justice John Stevens wrote scathingly that the Court's decision jeopardized "the nation's confidence in the judge as an impartial guardian of the rule of law."

The Supreme Court ruling gave Bush the victory but also cast a cloud of illegitimacy over his presidency. Bush's final official margin of victory in Florida was only 537 votes of 6 million cast, and his national tally in the popular vote, 50,456,169 votes, fell short of Gore's 50,996,116. Bush also faced a Congress more evenly divided than any in history. For the first time, the Senate was split fifty-fifty between Democrats and Republicans, and the GOP's grip on the House dwindled to just a ten-vote majority.

The election featured other novelties besides its minuscule margins of victory. "W" became only the second son of a president, after John Quincy Adams, to win the White House. Hillary Rodham Clinton became the first First Lady to run for office, winning a U.S. Senate seat from New York.

The fiasco of the 2000 election severely tested American democracy, but in the end it earned a passing grade. The nation's two-century-old electoral machinery might have shown its age, but it managed to wheeze and clank its way to a peaceful resolution of one of the most ferociously contested presidential races ever. It could even be said that America's much-maligned political system managed to display a certain awkward dignity. Despite the fuss about unreadable ballots and all the partisan maneuvering, no credible charges of serious chicanery or outright corruption wafted up out of the election's cauldron of controversy. No really threatening riotous rabble filled the nation's streets. Both camps sought victory by calling out the lawyers, not the generals. No insoluble constitutional crisis emerged. And however unsettling the U.S. Supreme Court's intervention might have been, surely it was better to have the buck stop with the judges, not with a junta. The foresight of the Founders in crafting a system of elections and courts stood reaffirmed for the new century, although the imbroglio unquestionably demonstrated the need for modernized and nationally uniform balloting procedures. Some critics even called for the abolition of the Electoral College.

Chronology

1980	Reagan defeats Carter for presidency
1981	Iran releases American hostages "Reaganomics" spending and tax cuts passed Solidarity movement in Poland O'Connor appointed to Supreme Court (first woman justice)
1981–1991	United States aids antileftist forces in Central America
1982	Recession hits U.S. economy
1983	Reagan announces SDI plan (Star Wars) U.S. marines killed in Lebanon U.S. invasion of Grenada
1984	Reagan defeats Mondale for presidency
1985	Gorbachev comes to power in Soviet Union First Reagan-Gorbachev summit meeting, in Geneva
1986	Reagan administration backs Aquino in Philippines Iran-contra scandal revealed Second Reagan-Gorbachev summit meeting, in Reykjavik, Iceland
1987	Senate rejects Supreme Court nomination of Robert Bork U.S. naval escorts begin in Persian Gulf 508-point stock-market plunge Third Reagan-Gorbachev summit meeting, in Washington, D.C.; INF treaty signed
1988	Fourth Reagan-Gorbachev summit meeting, in Moscow Bush defeats Dukakis for the presidency
1989	Chinese government suppresses prodemocracy demonstrators *Webster* v. *Reproductive Health Services* Eastern Europe throws off communist regimes Berlin Wall torn down

1990	Iraq invades Kuwait East and West Germany reunite Americans with Disabilities Act (ADA)
1991	Persian Gulf War Thomas appointed to Supreme Court Gorbachev resigns as Soviet president Soviet Union dissolves; republics form Commonwealth of Independent States
1992	Twenty-seventh Amendment (prohibiting congressional pay raises from taking effect until an election seats a new session of Congress) ratified *Planned Parenthood* v. *Casey* Clinton defeats Bush and Perot for presidency
1993	NAFTA signed
1994	Republicans win majorities in both houses of Congress
1996	Welfare Reform Bill becomes law Clinton defeats Dole for presidency
1998	Clinton-Lewinsky scandal U.S. and Britain launch military strikes against Iraq House of Representatives impeaches Clinton
1999	Senate acquits Clinton on impeachment charges Kosovo crisis; NATO warfare with Serbia Protest in Seattle against World Trade Organization
2000	"Million Man March" against guns in Washington, D.C. U.S. normalizes trade relations with China George W. Bush wins presidency in Electoral College, although Albert Gore takes popular vote

Where Did Modern Conservatism Come From?

Ronald Reagan's election surprised many historians. Reflecting a liberal political outlook that is common among academic scholars, they were long accustomed to understanding American history as an inexorable, almost evolutionary, unfolding of liberal principles, including the quests for economic equality, social justice, and active government. That point of view animated the enormously popular writings of the so-called progressive historians, such as Charles and Mary Beard, earlier in the century (See Chapter 23, Varying Viewpoints: The Populists: Radicals or Reactionaries?). For the Beards, "conservatives" were the rich, privileged elites bent on preserving their wealth and power and determined to keep government impotent, but doomed in the end to give way to the forces of liberal democracy.

Even the "New Left" revisionists of the 1960s, while critical of the celebratory tone of their progressive forebears, were convinced that the deepest currents of American history flowed leftward. But whether they were liberal or revisionist, most scholars writing in the first three post–World War II decades dismissed conservatism as an obsolete political creed. The revisionists were much more interested in decrying liberalism's deficiencies than in analyzing conservatism's strengths. Liberals and revisionists alike abandoned the Beards' image of powerful conservative elites and offered instead a contemptuous portrait of conservatives as fringe wackos—paranoid McCarthyites or racist demagogues who, in the words of the liberal critic Lionel Trilling, trafficked only in "irritable mental gestures which seem to resemble ideas." Such an outlook is conspicuous in books like Daniel Bell, ed., *The Radical Right* (1963), and Richard Hofstadter, *The Paranoid Style in American Politics* (1965).

But what flowed out of the turbulent decade of the 1960s was not a strengthened liberalism, but a revived conservatism. Ronald Reagan's huge political success compelled a thorough reexamination of the tradition of American conservatism and the sources of its modern resurgence.

Historians including Leo Ribuffo and Alan Brinkley have argued that characters once dismissed as irrational crackpots or colorful irrelevancies—including religious fundamentalists and depression-era figures like Huey Long and Father Charles Coughlin—articulated values deeply rooted and widely shared in American culture. Those conservative spokespersons, whatever their peculiarities, offered a vision of free individuals, minimal government, and autonomous local communities that harked back to many of the themes of "civic republicanism" in the era of young nationhood.

But modern conservatism, however deep its roots, is also a product of the recent historical past. As scholars like Thomas Sugrue and Thomas Edsall have shown, the economic stagnation that set in after 1970 made many Americans insecure about their futures and receptive to new political doctrines. At the same time, as the commentator Kevin Phillips has stressed, "social issues," with little or no apparent economic content, became increasingly prominent, as movements for sexual liberation, abortion on demand, and women's rights sharply challenged traditional beliefs. Perhaps most important, the success of the civil rights movement thrust the perpetually agonizing question of race relations to the very center of American political life. Finally, the failure of government policies in Vietnam, runaway inflation in the 1970s, and the disillusioning Watergate episode cast doubt on the legitimacy, efficacy, and even the morality of "big government."

Many modern conservatives, including the pundit George Will, stress the deep historical roots of American conservatism. In their view, as Will once put it, it took sixteen years to count the ballots from the 1964 (Goldwater versus Johnson) election, and Goldwater won after all. But that argument is surely overstated. Goldwater ran against the legacy of the New Deal and was overwhelmingly defeated. Reagan ran against the consequences of the Great Society and won decisively. Many conservatives, in short, apparently acknowledge the legitimacy of the New Deal and the stake that many middle-class Americans feel they have in its programs of Social Security, home mortgage subsidies, farm price supports, and similar policies. But they reject the philosophy of the Great Society, with its more focused attack on urban poverty and its vigorous support of affirmative action. Modern conservatism springs less from a repudiation of government per se and more from a disapproval of the particular priorities and strategies of the Great Society. The different historical fates of the New Deal and the Great Society suggest the key to the rise of modern conservatism.

For further reading, see page A28 of the Appendix. For web resources, go to **http://college.hmco.com**.

42

The American People Face a New Century

⎯⎯ ✤ ⎯⎯

As our case is new, so we must think anew and act anew. We must disenthrall ourselves, and then we shall save our country.

ABRAHAM LINCOLN, 1862

More than two hundred years old as the twenty-first century began, the United States was both an old and a new nation. It boasted one of the longest uninterrupted traditions of democratic government of any country on earth. Indeed, it had pioneered the techniques of mass democracy and was, in that sense, the oldest modern polity. As one of the earliest countries to industrialize, America had also dwelt in the modern economic era longer than most nations.

But the Republic was in many ways still youthful as well. Innovation, entrepreneurship, and risk-taking—all characteristics of youth—were honored national values. The twenty-first century began much like the twentieth, with American society continuing to be rejuvenated by fresh waves of immigrants, full of energy and ambition. The U.S. economy, despite problems, was generating new jobs at a rate of some 2 million per year. American inventions—especially computer and communications technologies—were transforming the face of global society. The whole world seemed to worship the icons of American culture—downing soft drinks and donning blue jeans, watching Hollywood films, listening to rock or country and western music, even adopting indigenous American sports like baseball and basketball. In the realm of consumerism, American products appeared to have Coca-Colonized the globe.

The history of American society also seemed to have increased global significance as the third millennium of the Christian era opened. Americans were a pluralistic people who had struggled for centuries to provide opportunity and to achieve tolerance and justice for many different religious, ethnic, and racial groups. Their historical experience could offer valuable lessons to the rapidly internationalizing planetary society that was emerging at the dawn of the twenty-first century.

In politics, economics, and culture, the great social experiment of American democracy was far from completed as the United States faced its future. Much history remained to be made as the country entered its third century of nationhood. But men and women make history only within the framework bequeathed to them by earlier generations. For better or worse, they march forward along time's path bearing the burdens of the past. Knowing when they have come to a truly new turn in the road, when they can lay part of their burden down and when they cannot, or should not—all this constitutes the sort of wisdom that only historical study can engender.

Economic Revolutions

When the twentieth century opened, United States Steel Corporation was the flagship business of America's booming industrial revolution. U.S. Steel was a typical "heavy industry," cranking out the ingots and girders and sheet metal that built the nation's basic physical infrastructure. A generation later, General Motors, annually producing millions of automobiles, became the characteristic American corporation, signaling the historic shift to a mass consumer economy that began in the 1920s and flowered fully in the 1950s. Following World War II, the rise of International Business Machines (IBM) symbolized yet another momentous transformation, to the fast-paced "information age," when the storing, organizing, and processing of data became an industry in its own right.

The pace of the information age soon accelerated. By century's end, the rapid emergence of Microsoft Corporation and the phenomenal growth of the Internet heralded an explosive communications revolution. Americans now rocketed down the "information superhighway" toward the uncharted terrain of an electronic global village, where traditional geographic, social, and political boundaries could be vaulted with the tap of a keypad.

The communications revolution was full of both promise and peril. In the blink of an eye, ordinary citizens could gain access to information once available only to privileged elites with vast libraries or expert staffs at their disposal. Businesspeople instantaneously girdled the planet with transactions of prodigious scope and serpentine complexity. Japanese bankers might sell wheat contracts in Chicago and simultaneously direct the profits to buying oil

shipments from the Persian Gulf offered by a broker in Amsterdam. By the late 1990s, a "dot-com" explosion of new commercial ventures quickly expanded the market (and the stock-market stakes) for entrepreneurs leading the way in making the Internet a twenty-first-century electronic mall, library, and entertainment center rolled into one.

But the very speed and efficiency of the new communications tools threatened to wipe out entire occupational categories. Postal delivery people, travel agents, store clerks, bank tellers, stock brokers, and all kinds of other workers whose business it was to mediate between product and client, might find themselves rendered obsolete in the era of the Internet. And as the computer makes possible "classrooms without walls," where students can pursue learning largely on their own, even teachers, whose job is essentially to mediate between students and various bodies of knowledge, might well end up as roadkill on the information superhighway.

Increasingly, scientific research was the engine that drove the economy, and new scientific knowl-

The University Without Walls   Students getting their education from this facility at the Iowa Distance Learning Center need never enter a classroom.

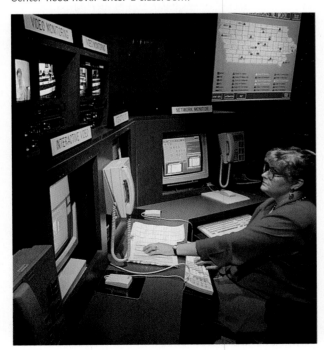

edge posed new social and moral dilemmas. When scientists first unlocked the secrets of molecular genetic structure in the 1950s, the road lay open to breeding new strains of high-yield, pest- and weather-resistant crops; to curing hereditary diseases; and also, unfortunately, to unleashing genetic mutations that might threaten the fragile ecological balance of the wondrous biosphere in which humankind was delicately suspended. As technical mastery of biological and medical techniques advanced, unprecedented ethical questions clamored for resolution. Should the human gene pool itself be "engineered"? What principles should govern the allocation of human organs for lifesaving transplants, or of scarce dialysis machines, or of artificial hearts? Was it wise in the first place to spend money on such costly devices rather than devote society's resources to improved sanitation, maternal and infant care, and nutritional and health education? Who was the rightful parent of a child born to a "surrogate mother" or conceived by artificial insemination? How, if at all, should society regulate the increasingly lengthy and often painful process of dying? What rules should guide efforts to clone human beings—or should such efforts even be attempted?

Affluence and Inequality

Americans were still an affluent people at the beginning of the twenty-first century. Median household income declined somewhat in the early 1990s but rebounded by 1998 to about $39,000. Yet even those Americans with incomes below the government's official poverty level (defined in 1998 as $16,600 for a family of four) enjoyed a standard of living higher than that of two-thirds of the rest of humankind.

Americans were no longer the world's wealthiest people in the 1990s, as they had been in the quarter-century after World War II. Citizens of several other countries enjoyed higher average per-capita incomes, and many nations boasted more equitable distributions of wealth. In an unsettling reversal of long-term trends in American society, during the last two decades of the twentieth century, the rich got much richer, while the poor got an ever-shrinking share of the pie. The richest 20 percent of Americans in the 1990s raked in nearly

half the nation's income, whereas the poorest 20 percent received less than 4 percent. The gap between rich and poor began to widen in the 1980s and widened further in the following decade. That trend was evident in many industrial societies, but it was most pronounced in the United States. Between 1968 and 1998, the share of the nation's income that flowed to the top 20 percent of its households swelled from 40 percent to more than 49 percent. Even more striking, in the same period the top 5 percent of income earners saw their share of the national income grow from about 15 percent to more than 20 percent. The Welfare Reform Bill of 1996, restricting access to social services and requiring able-bodied welfare recipients to find work, weakened the financial footing of many impoverished families still further.

Widening inequality could be measured in other ways as well: chief executives in the 1970s typically earned forty-one times the income of the average worker in their corporations; by the 1990s they earned 225 times as much. At the same time, some 34 million people, 12.7 percent of all Americans (8.2 percent of whites, 26.1 percent of African-Americans, and 25.6 percent of Latinos), remained mired in poverty—a depressing indictment of the inequities afflicting an affluent and allegedly egalitarian republic.

What caused the widening income gap? Some critics pointed to the tax and fiscal policies of the Reagan and Bush years, which favored the wealthy and penalized the poor. But deeper-running historical currents probably played a more powerful

White 10.5%
African–American 26.1%
Asian and Pacific Islander 12.5%
Latino origin (of any race) 25.6%

Poverty Rates of Americans by Race and Latino Origin, 1998 (Source: U.S. Bureau of the Census, March Current Population Survey.)

Two Nations? While decaying neighborhoods and the sad legions of the homeless blighted American urban life in the closing decades of the twentieth century, affluent Americans took refuge in gated communities like this one in the Brentwood section of Los Angeles.

Who Pays Federal Income Taxes?
(share of U.S. income tax, by income percentile)

Income Group (base income shown as of 1998)	1994	1998
Top 1% (above $269,496)	28.7%	34.8%
Top 5% (above $114,729)	47.4%	53.8%
Top 10% (above $83,220)	59.1%	65.0%
Top 25% (above $50,607)	79.5%	82.7%
Top 50% (above $25,491)	95.2%	95.8%
Bottom 50% (below $25,491)	4.8%	4.2%

Because the United States has long had a "progressive" income tax system, in which tax obligations are distributed according to ability to pay, widening income inequality was reflected in a redistribution of tax burdens. In the booming 1990s, the rich did indeed get richer—but they also paid an increasing fraction of the total federal tax take.
(Source: Internal Revenue Service data, Tax Foundation.)

role, as suggested by the similar experiences of other industrialized societies. Among the most conspicuous causes were intensifying global economic competition; the shrinkage in high-paying manufacturing jobs for semi-skilled and unskilled workers; the greater economic rewards commanded by educated workers in high-tech industries; the decline of unions; the growth of part-time and temporary work; the rising tide of relatively low-skill immigrants; and the increasing tendency of educated men and women to marry one another and both work, creating households with very high incomes.

Widening Income Inequality

Share of Aggregate Income	1980	1990	1999
Lowest fifth	4.3	3.9	3.6
Second fifth	10.3	9.6	8.9
Middle fifth	16.9	15.9	14.9
Fourth fifth	24.9	24.0	23.2
Highest fifth	43.7	46.6	49.4
Top 5%	15.8	18.6	21.5

During the last two decades of the twentieth century, the top fifth of the country's households made significant gains in income, while everyone else lost ground. (Source: U.S. Census.)

The Feminist Revolution

All Americans were caught up in the great economic changes of the late twentieth century, but no group was more profoundly affected than women. When the century opened, women made up about 20 percent of all workers. Over the next five decades, they increased their presence in the labor force at a fairly steady rate, except for a temporary spurt during World War II. Then, beginning in the 1950s, women's entry into the workplace accelerated dramatically. By the 1990s nearly half of all workers were women,

Women's World: Something Old, Something New   By the beginning of the twenty-first century, revolutionary changes in the economy and in social values had opened new career possibilities to women, while not fully relieving them of their traditional duties as mothers and homemakers. Dramatic changes in race relations and the redefinition of gender roles at the end of the twentieth century transformed even tradition-bound institutions like the U.S. Military Academy at West Point, New York, as this gathering of cadets suggests. Women's athletics came into their own in the wake of the feminist revolution. In 1999 the U.S. Women's World Cup Soccer Team brought home the trophy to a nation suddenly enthralled with women's soccer.

Percentage of Working Married Women with Children (husband present), 1950–1998

Year	Total Percentage	No Children Under 18	Children 6–17 Only	Children Under 6
1950	23.8	30.3	28.3	11.9
1960	30.5	34.7	39.0	18.6
1970	40.8	42.2	49.2	30.3
1980	50.1	46.0	61.7	45.1
1994	60.6	53.2	76.0	61.7
1998	61.8	70.6	76.8	63.7

(Source: *Statistical Abstract of the United States,* relevant years.)

"WELL, IT'S ABOUT TIME"

The Justice Is a Lady, 1981 Herblock hails Sandra Day O'Connor's appointment to the Supreme Court.

and the majority of working-age women held jobs outside the home. Most astonishing was the upsurge in employment among mothers. In 1950, 90 percent of mothers with children under the age of six did not work for pay. But by the 1990s, a majority of women with children as young as one year old were wage earners. Women now brought home the bacon and then cooked it, too.

Beginning in the 1960s, many all-male strongholds, including Yale, Princeton, West Point, Annapolis, the Air Force Academy, and even, grudgingly and belatedly, southern military academies like the Citadel and Virginia Military Institute, opened their doors to women. Women are now piloting commercial airliners and orbiting in outer space. They govern states and cities, write Supreme Court decisions, and debate the law of the land in both houses of Congress. In 1996 women cracked another gender barrier when they launched a professional basketball league of their own.

Yet despite these gains, many feminists remained frustrated. Women continued to receive lower wages—an average 76.5 cents on the dollar in 1999 compared with men doing the same full-time work—and they tended to concentrate in a few low-prestige, low-paying occupations (the "pink-collar ghetto"). Although they made up more than half the population, women in the 1990s accounted for only 25 percent of lawyers and judges (up from 5 percent in 1970) and 22 percent of physicians (up from 10 percent in 1970). Overt sexual discrimination explained some of this occupational segregation, but most of it seemed attributable to the greater burdens of parenthood on women than on men. Women were far more likely than men to interrupt their careers to bear and raise children, and even to

choose less demanding career paths to allow for fulfilling those traditional roles. Discrimination and a focus on children also helped account for the persistence of a "gender gap" in national elections. Women continued to vote in greater numbers than men for Democratic candidates, who were often perceived as being more willing to favor government support for health and child care, education, and job equality.

As the revolution in women's status rolled on in the 1990s, men's lives changed as well. A men's movement sprang up that sought to redefine male roles in a new age of increasing gender equality. Some employers provided paternity leave as well as maternity leave, in recognition of the shared obligations of the two-worker household. As traditional female responsibilities such as cooking, laundry, and child care spilled over to men, many corporations sponsored highly popular fatherhood seminars and husbands' support groups. Recognizing

The Modern Family Tree
High divorce rates and the increasing numbers of "blended families" in modern American society could often be confusing.

the new realities of the modern American household, Congress passed a Family Leave Bill in 1993, mandating job protection for working fathers as well as mothers who needed to take time off work for family-related reasons.

The Fading Family

The nuclear family, once prized as the foundation of society and the nursery of the Republic, suffered heavy blows in modern America. By the 1990s one out of every two marriages ended in divorce. Seven times more children were affected by divorce than at the beginning of the century. Kids who commuted between separated parents were commonplace. The 1950s ideal of a family with two parents, only one of whom worked, was now a virtually useless way to picture the typical American household.

Traditional families were not only falling apart at an alarming rate but were also increasingly slow to form in the first place. The proportion of adults living alone tripled in the four decades after 1950, and by the 1990s nearly one-third of women aged

twenty-five to twenty-nine had never married. In the 1960s, 5 percent of all births were to unmarried women, but three decades later one out of four white babies, one out of three Hispanic babies, and two out of three African-American babies were born to single mothers. Every fourth child in America was growing up in a household that lacked two parents. The collapse of the traditional family contributed heavily to the pauperization of many women and children, as single parents (usually mothers) strug-

> *In his inaugural address in January 1989, President George Bush (b. 1924) declared,*
>
> "My friends, we are not the sum of our possessions; they are not the measure of our lives. In our hearts we know what matters: . . . to be a loyal friend, a loving parent, a citizen who leaves his home, his neighborhood, and his town better than he found it."

gled to keep their households economically afloat and their families emotionally intact.

Child-rearing, the family's foremost function, was being increasingly assigned to "parent-substitutes" at day-care centers or schools—or to television, the modern age's "electronic baby-sitter." Estimates were that the average child by age sixteen had watched up to fifteen thousand hours of TV—more time than was spent in the classroom. Parental anxieties multiplied with the advent of the Internet—an electronic cornucopia where young-sters could "surf" through poetry and problem sets as well as pornography.

Born and raised without the family support enjoyed by their forebears, Americans were also increasingly likely to be lonely in their later years. Most elderly people in the 1990s depended on pen-sion plans and government Social Security pay-ments, not on their loved ones, for their daily bread. The great majority of them drew their last breath not in their own homes, but in hospitals and nurs-ing facilities. From youth to old age, the role of the family was dwindling.

The Aging of America

Old age was more and more likely to be a lengthy experience for Americans, who were living longer than ever before. A person born at the dawn of the century could expect to survive less than fifty years, but a white male born in the 1990s could anticipate a life span of more than seventy-six years. His white female counterpart would probably outlive him by seven years. (The figures were slightly lower for nonwhites, reflecting differences in living stan-dards, especially diet and health care.) The census of 1950 recorded that women for the first time made up a majority of Americans, thanks largely to greater female longevity. Miraculous medical advances lengthened and strengthened lives. Noteworthy were the development of antibiotics after 1940 and Dr. Jonas Salk's discovery in 1953 of a vaccine against a dreaded crippler, polio.

Longer lives spelled more older people. One American in eight was over sixty-five years of age in the 1990s, and projections were that one of every five people would be in the "sunset years" by 2050, as the median age rose toward forty. This aging of the population raised a host of political, social, and

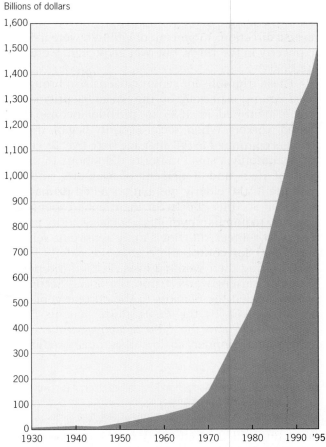

Billions of dollars

Government Expenditures for Social Welfare, 1930–1995
"Social welfare" includes unemployment and old-age insurance, medical insurance, and veterans' benefits. The skyrocketing costs from the mid-1960s onward reflect the increasing size (and political clout) of the elderly population, who were the main beneficiaries of Great Society programs like Medicare. The steep rise after 1970 is also explained by the galloping inflation of the 1970s.

economic questions. Elderly people formed a potent electoral bloc that aggressively lobbied for government favors and achieved real gains for senior citizens. The share of GNP spent on health care for people over sixty-five more than doubled in the three decades after the enactment of Medicare in 1965. This growth in medical payments for the old far outstripped the growth of educational expenditures for the young, with corresponding consequences for the social and economic situations of both populations. As late as the 1960s, nearly a quarter of Americans over the age of sixty-five lived in poverty; three decades later, only about one in ten did. The figures for young people moved in the reverse direction: 15 percent of children were living in poverty in the 1970s, but over 20 percent were in the 1990s.

These triumphs for senior citizens also brought fiscal strains, especially on the Social Security system, established in 1935 to provide income for retired workers. When Social Security began, most workers continued to toil after age sixty-five. By century's end only a small minority did (about 15 percent of men and 8 percent of women), and a majority of the elderly population relied primarily on Social Security checks for their living expenses. Contrary to popular mythology, Social Security payments to retirees did not simply represent reimbursement for contributions that the elderly had made during their working lives. In fact, the payments of current workers into the Social Security system funded the benefits to the current generation of retirees. By the 1990s, those benefits had risen so high, and the ratio of active workers to retirees had dropped so low, that drastic adjust-

Senior Power   Living longer and living healthier, older Americans coalesced into one of America's most politically powerful interest groups as the twentieth century drew to a close.

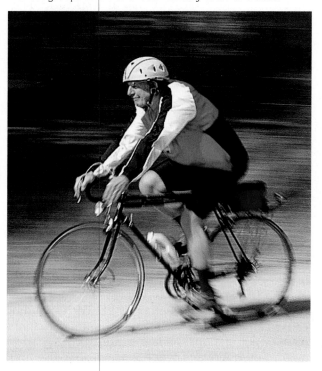

ments were necessary. The problem had intensified in the 1960s, when Medicare was added to the list of benefits for the elderly, and again in the 1970s, when a compassionate Congress dramatically increased retirement payments at a time when productivity growth was stalling. At the beginning of the new century, as the huge wave of post–World War II baby boomers approached retirement age, it seemed that the "unfunded liability"—the difference between what the government had promised to pay to the elderly and the taxes it expected to take in—might rise above $7 trillion, a sum that threatened to bankrupt the Republic unless drastic reforms were adopted. Yet because of the electoral power of older Americans, Social Security and Medicare reform remained the "third rail" of American politics, which politicians touched only at their peril.

Without substantial change, larger payments to retirees could only mean smaller paychecks for workers. Three-quarters of all employees in the 1990s already paid higher Social Security taxes than income taxes. (An individual paid a maximum of $5,829 in Social Security taxes in 2000, matched by an identical employer contribution.) A war between the generations loomed in the twenty-first century, as payments to the nonworking elderly threatened to soak up fully half the working population's income by about 2040.

The New Immigration

Newcomers continued to flow into modern America. They washed ashore in waves that numbered nearly 1 million persons per year in the 1980s and 1990s—the heaviest inflow of immigrants in America's experience. In striking contrast to the historic pattern of immigration, Europe contributed far fewer people than did the teeming countries of Asia and Latin America, especially Mexico.

What prompted this new migration to America? The truth is that the newest immigrants came for many of the same reasons as the old. They typically left countries where populations were growing rapidly and where agricultural and industrial revolutions were shaking people loose from old habits of life—conditions almost identical to those in nineteenth-century Europe. And they came to America, as previous immigrants had done, in search of jobs and economic opportunity.

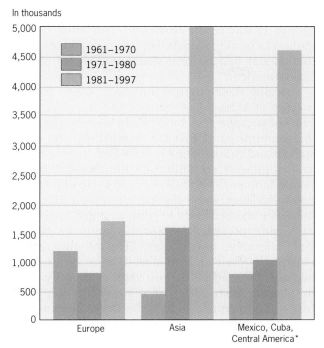

In thousands

- 1961–1970
- 1971–1980
- 1981–1997

Mexico represents approximately 75 percent of total.

Recent Legal Immigration by Area of Origin, 1961–1997

The Southwest, from Texas to California, felt the immigrant impact especially sharply, as Mexican migrants—by far the largest contingent of modern immigrants—concentrated heavily in that region. By the turn of the century, Latinos made up nearly one-third of the population in Texas, Arizona, and California, and almost half in New Mexico—a population shift that amounted to a demographic *reconquista* of the lands lost by Mexico in the war of 1846.

The size and geographic concentration of the Hispanic population in the Southwest had few precedents in the history of American immigration. Most previous groups had been so thinly scattered across the land that they had little choice but to learn English and make their way in the larger American society, however much they might have longed to preserve their native language and customs. But Mexican-Americans might succeed in creating a truly bicultural zone in the booming southwestern states, especially since their mother culture lies just next door and is easily accessible—another factor that differentiates this modern immigrant community from its nineteenth-century European and Asian antecedents.

Some old-stock Americans worried about the capacity of the modern United States to absorb these new immigrants. The Immigration Reform and Control Act of 1986 attempted to choke off illegal entry by penalizing employers of undocumented aliens and by granting amnesty to many of those already here. Anti-immigrant sentiment flared especially sharply in California in the wake of an economic recession in the early 1990s. California voters approved a ballot initiative that attempted to deny benefits, including education, to illegal immigrants, though courts blocked the effort. Congress in 1996 restricted access to some welfare benefits for *legal* immigrants who arrived after that year.

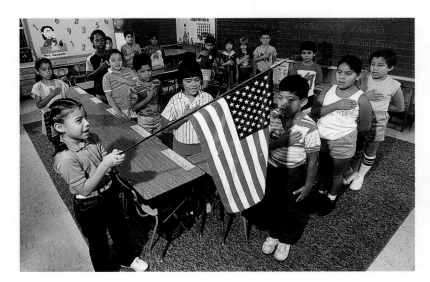

Changing Colors A second-grade bilingual class recites the Pledge of Allegiance (in both Spanish and English) in Austin, Texas. By the end of the twenty-first century, Americans who can trace their ancestry directly to Europe might well be a minority in the United States.

Yet the fact was that foreign-born people accounted for almost 10 percent of the American population by the end of the 1990s, a far smaller proportion than the historical high point of nearly 15 percent recorded in the census of 1910, but evidence nonetheless that American society continued to welcome—and need—newcomers. Somewhat inconsistently, critics charged both that immigrants robbed citizens of jobs and that they dumped themselves on the welfare rolls at the taxpayers' expense. But studies showed that immigrants took jobs scorned by Americans and that they paid more dollars in taxes (withholding and Social Security taxes, as well as sales taxes) than they claimed for welfare payments. A more urgent worry was that unscrupulous employers might take cruel advantage of alien workers, who often had scant knowledge of their legal rights.

Ethnic Pride

Thanks both to continued immigration and to their own high birthrate, Hispanic-Americans were becoming an increasingly important minority (see "Makers of America: The Latinos," pp. 1026–1027). The United States by the late 1990s was home to more than 31 million Hispanics. They included some 21 million Chicanos, or Mexican-Americans, mostly in the Southwest, as well as 3 million Puerto Ricans, chiefly in the Northeast, and more than 1 million Cubans in Florida (where it was jokingly said that Miami had become the most "Anglo" city in Latin America).

Flexing their political muscles, Latinos elected mayors of Miami, Denver, and San Antonio. After years of struggle, the United Farm Workers Organizing Committee (UFWOC), headed by the soft-spoken and charismatic César Chávez, succeeded in improving work conditions for the mostly Chicano "stoop laborers" who followed the cycle of planting and harvesting across the American West. Hispanic influence seemed likely to grow, as suggested by the increasing presence of Spanish-language ballots and television broadcasts. Hispanic-Americans, newly confident and organized, were destined to become the nation's largest ethnic minority, outnumbering even African-Americans, in the early twenty-first century. Indeed, by the first decade of the new century, the Chicano population of America's largest state, California, equaled the Anglo population, making the state a patchwork of minorities with no single ethnic majority.

Asian-Americans also made great strides. By the 1980s they were America's fastest-growing minority. Their numbers nearly doubled in that decade alone, thanks to heavy immigration, and continued to swell in the 1990s. Once feared and hated as the

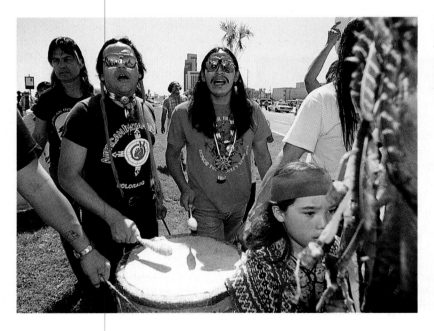

The Oldest Americans In 1992 Native Americans in Corpus Christi, Texas, protested against the five hundredth anniversary of Columbus's arrival in the New World.

"yellow peril" and relegated to the most menial and degrading jobs, citizens of Asian ancestry were now counted among the most prosperous and successful of Americans—a "model minority." The typical Asian-American household enjoyed an income nearly 20 percent greater than that of the typical white household. In 1996 the voters of Washington elected the first Asian-American to serve as governor of a mainland American state.

Indians, the original Americans, shared in the general awakening of ethnic and cultural pride. The 2000 census counted some 2.4 million Native Americans, half of whom had left their reservations to live in cities. Meanwhile, unemployment and alcoholism had blighted reservation life. Many tribes tried to take advantage of their special legal status as independent nations by opening bingo halls and gambling casinos for white patrons on reservation lands, but the cycle of discrimination and poverty proved hard to break.

Cities and Suburbs

America's "alabaster cities" of song and story grew more sooty and less safe in the closing decades of the twentieth century. Crime was the great scourge of urban life. The rate of violent crimes committed in cities reached an all-time high in the drug-infested 1980s and then leveled off in the early 1990s. The number of violent crimes even began to decline substantially in many areas after 1995. Nevertheless, murders, robberies, and rapes remained shockingly common not only in cities but also in suburbs and rural areas. America imprisoned a larger fraction of its citizens than almost any other country in the world, and some desperate citizens resorted to armed vigilante tactics to protect themselves.

Millions of Americans fled the cities altogether for the supposedly safer suburbs. So swift and massive was the exodus from the old urban neighborhoods that by the mid-1990s it ended the nation's rather brief "urban age," whose dawn had been heralded by the census of 1920, the first to show a majority of city dwellers.

A majority of Americans now lived in the suburbs, a historic phenomenon that many observers blamed for the spreading fragmentation and isolation of American life. Entire suburban neighborhoods, usually containing economically and racially

homogeneous populations, walled themselves off behind elaborate security systems in "gated communities." In these safe but segregated enclaves, the sense of a larger and inclusive national community might prove hard to sustain.

By the beginning of the twenty-first century, some major cities exhibited signs of renewal. Commercial redevelopment gained ground in cities such as New York, Boston, Chicago, and San Francisco. Well-to-do residents reclaimed once-fashionable neighborhoods and sent real estate values soaring. But these late-century urban homesteaders did little to make cities new centers of residential integration. Cities remained as divided by wealth and race as the suburban social landscape surrounding them.

Minority America

Racial and ethnic tensions also exacerbated the problems of American cities. These stresses were especially evident in Los Angeles, which, like New York a century earlier, was a magnet for minorities, especially immigrants from Asia and Latin America. When in 1992 a mostly white jury exonerated white Los Angeles police officers who had been videotaped ferociously beating a black suspect, the minority neighborhoods of South Central Los Angeles erupted in rage. Arson and looting laid waste entire city blocks, and scores of people were killed. In a sobering demonstration of the complexity of modern American racial rivalries, many black rioters vented their anger at the white police and the judicial system by attacking Asian shopkeepers, who in turn formed armed patrols to protect their property.

The Los Angeles riots vividly testified to black skepticism about the American system of justice. Just three years later, again in Los Angeles, the gaudy televised spectacle of former football star O. J. Simpson's murder trial fed white disillusionment with the state of race relations. After months of testimony that seemed to point to Simpson's guilt, the jury acquitted him, presumably because certain Los Angeles police officers involved in the case had been shown to harbor racist sentiments. In a later civil trial, another jury unanimously found Simpson liable for the "wrongful deaths" of his former wife and another victim. The reaction to the Simpson

MAKERS OF AMERICA

The Latinos

Today Mexican food is handed through fast-food drive-up windows in all fifty states, Spanish-language broadcasts fill the airwaves, and the Latino community has its own telephone book, the *Spanish Yellow Pages*. Latinos send representatives to Congress and mayors to city hall, record hit songs, paint murals, and teach history. Latinos, among the fastest-growing segments of the U.S. population, include Puerto Ricans, frequent voyagers between their native island and northeastern cities; Cubans, many of them refugees from the communist dictatorship of Fidel Castro, concentrated in Miami and southern Florida; and Central Americans, fleeing the ravages of civil war in Nicaragua and El Salvador.

But the most populous group of Latinos derives from Mexico. The first significant numbers of Mexicans began heading for *El Norte* ("the North") around 1910, when the upheavals of the Mexican

Revolution stirred and shuffled the Mexican population into more or less constant flux. Their northward passage was briefly interrupted during the Great Depression, when thousands of Mexican nationals were deported. But immigration resumed during World War II, and since then a steady flow of legal immigrants has passed through border checkpoints, joined by countless millions of their undocumented countrymen and countrywomen stealing across the frontier on moonless nights.

For the most part, these Mexicans came to work in the fields, following the ripening crops northward to Canada through the summer and autumn months. In winter many headed back to Mexico, but some gathered instead in the cities of the Southwest—El Paso, Los Angeles, Houston, and San Bernardino. There they found regular work, even if lack of skills and racial discrimination often confined them to

Cuban Refugees Arriving in the United States   These multi-racial exiles were among the many thousands of Cubans who fled to the United States in the years following Fidel Castro's seizure of power in Cuba in 1959. One such refugee, six-year-old Elian Gonzalez, caused a diplomatic tug-of-war in 2000 between the Cuban community in Miami, the Cuban government, and the U.S. Justice Department. Ultimately, Elian was returned to Cuba to live with his father over his Miami relatives' objections.

Chicana Pride A Mexican-American girl celebrates her cultural heritage at the Texas Folklife Festival in San Antonio.

Mexican-American Farm Workers Pitting Apricots in Fruit Groves near Los Angeles, 1924

manual labor. City jobs might pay less than farm labor, but the work was steady and offered the prospect of a stable home. Houses may have been shabby in the barrios, but these Mexican neighborhoods provided a sense of togetherness, a place to raise a family, and the chance to join a mutual-aid society. Such societies, or *Mutualistas*, sponsored baseball leagues, helped the sick and disabled, and defended their members against discrimination.

Mexican immigrants lived so close to the border that their native country acted like a powerful magnet, drawing them back time and time again. Mexicans frequently returned to see relatives or visit the homes of their youth, and relatively few became U.S. citizens. Indeed, in many Mexican-American communities, it was a badge of dishonor to apply for U.S. citizenship.

The Mexican government, likewise influenced by the proximity of the two countries, intervened in the daily lives of its nationals in America, further discouraging them from becoming citizens of their adopted country. As Anglo reformers attempted to Americanize the immigrants in the 1910s and 1920s, the Mexican consulate in Los Angeles launched a Mexicanization program. The consulate sponsored parades on *Cinco de Mayo* ("Fifth of May"), celebrating Mexico's defeat of a French army at the Battle of Puebla in 1892, and opened special Spanish-language schools for children. Since World War II, the Ameri-

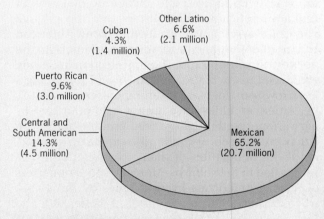

Sources of Latino Population in the United States, 1999

Cuban 4.3% (1.4 million)

Other Latino 6.6% (2.1 million)

Puerto Rican 9.6% (3.0 million)

Central and South American 14.3% (4.5 million)

Mexican 65.2% (20.7 million)

can-born generation has carried on the fight for political representation, economic opportunity, and cultural preservation.

Fresh arrivals from Mexico and from the other Latin American nations daily swell the Latino communities across America. The census of 2000 revealed that Latinos are now the largest minority group in the United States, surpassing African-Americans. As the United States heads into the twenty-first century, it is taking on a pronounced Spanish accent, although Latinos' reticence to vote in elections has retarded their influence on American politics.

> *In 1990 the African-American intellectual Shelby Steele (b. 1946) declared in his provocative book,* The Content of Our Character,
>
> "What is needed now is a new spirit of pragmatism in racial matters where blacks are seen simply as American citizens who deserve complete fairness and in some cases developmental assistance, but in no case special entitlements based on color. We need deracinated social policies that attack poverty rather than *black* poverty and that instill those values that make for self-reliance."

verdicts revealed the yawning chasm that separated white and black America, as most whites continued to believe Simpson guilty, while a majority of African-Americans told pollsters that the original not-guilty verdict was justified. African-American charges that they had been unlawfully kept from the polls during the 2000 presidential election in Florida convinced many blacks that they were still facing a Jim Crow South of black disenfranchisement.

American cities have always held an astonishing variety of ethnic and racial groups, but in the late twentieth century, minorities made up a majority of the population of many American cities, as whites fled to the suburbs. More than three-quarters of African-Americans lived in cities by the 1990s, whereas only about one-quarter of whites did. The most desperate black ghettos, housing a hapless "underclass" in the inner core of the old industrial cities, were especially problematic. Successful blacks who had benefited from the civil rights revolution of the 1950s and 1960s followed whites to the suburbs, leaving a residue of the poorest poor in the old ghettos. Without a middle class to sustain community institutions like schools and small businesses, the inner cities, plagued by unemployment and drug addiction, seemed bereft of leadership, cohesion, resources, and hope.

The friendless underclass, heavily composed of blacks and other minorities, represented a sorry—and dangerous—social failure that eluded any known remedy. But other segments of the African-American community had clearly prospered in the wake of the civil rights gains of the 1950s and 1960s, though they still had a long hill to climb before reaching full equality. By the 1990s about 40 percent of blacks were counted in the middle class (defined as enjoying family income greater than $25,000 per year). The number of black elected officials had risen above the seven thousand mark, including more than a thousand in the Old South, some two dozen members of Congress, and the mayors of several large cities. Voting tallies demonstrated that successful black politicians were moving beyond

Still Fighting to Vote This African-American father and daughter are participating in a rally in downtown Miami several weeks after the November 2000 election to demand a recount of dismissed presidential election ballots. Many Florida blacks complained that election officials had disproportionally disqualified their votes and unfairly turned them away from the polls, resurrecting the kind of obstacles that long had kept blacks from voting in the South.

EXAMINING THE EVIDENCE

A Country Politically Divided Between City and Country Computer mapping of election data has helped analysts identify patterns in Americans' political behavior. This county-level map of election-night returns from the November 2000 presidential election reveals a deadlock between urban Democrats and rural Republicans. Even though Democratic nominee Albert Gore won the popular vote, he prevailed in only 676 counties, fewer than half of what Bill Clinton had won four years earlier. Yet Gore took virtually all major cities and most of their surrounding suburbs, giving him the lead in the heavily populated coasts and most metropolitan areas in the interior. Bush, on the other hand, carried an impressive 2,477 counties, and virtually every small town on a straight line from Redding, California, to Springfield, Illinois. In the vast western plain of Republican red, cities like St. Louis,

Kansas City, Tulsa, and Las Vegas were rare outposts of Democratic blue. Gore's huge win in Portland was big enough to give him the state in the Electoral College, even though the rest of Oregon voted heavily for Bush. The division of this map into red and blue territory vividly portrays a deep cultural chasm between urban and rural America. While minorities, union members, and prospering white collar workers remained loyal to the party of Clinton, small-town white America experienced the Clinton years as an assault on their most cherished values concerning issues like abortion, gender roles, and gun ownership. What additional voting patterns does this election map reveal? How did other economic, social, and cultural issues separate Americans into these two camps? How else might computers be used for historical analysis?

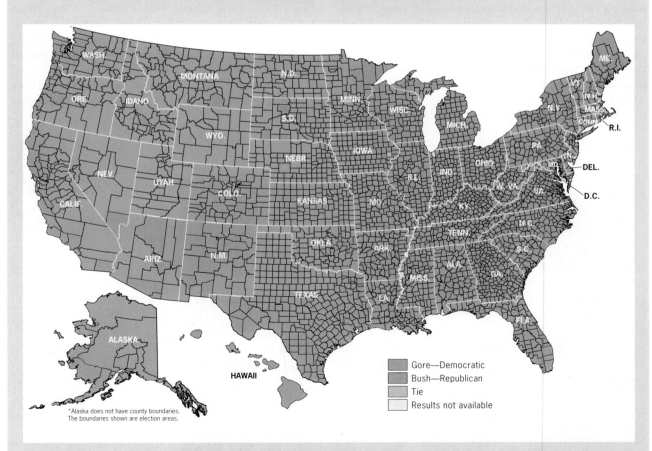

(Source: Adapted from VNS Graphic by Stanford Kay-Newsweek)

isolated racial constituencies and into the political mainstream by appealing to a wide variety of voters. In 1989 Virginians, only 15 percent of whom were black, chose L. Douglas Wilder as the first African-American elected to serve as a state governor. In 1994 voters in Illinois made Carol Moseley-Braun the first African-American woman elected to the U.S. Senate.

Single women headed over half of black families, almost three times the rate for whites. Many of those African-American women, husbandless and jobless, necessarily depended on welfare to feed their children. As social scientists increasingly emphasized the importance of the home environment for success in school, it became clear that many fatherless, impoverished African-American children seemed consigned to suffer from educational handicaps that were difficult to overcome. Black youths in the 1990s still had about one year less schooling than whites of the same age and were less than half as likely to earn college degrees. As the American economy became ever more driven by new applications of computers and biotechnology, these disadvantages were bound to widen the racial gap of employment opportunity. The political assault against affirmative action in California and elsewhere only compounded the obstacles to advanced training for many young African-Americans.

The Life of the Mind

Despite the mind-sapping chatter of the "boob tube," Americans in the late twentieth century read more, listened to more music, and were better educated than ever before. By the 1990s colleges were awarding nearly a million degrees a year, and one person in four in the twenty-five-to-thirty-four-year-old age group was a college graduate. This expanding mass of educated people lifted the economy to more advanced levels while creating consumers of "high culture." Americans annually made some 300 million visits to museums in the 1990s and patronized about a thousand opera companies and fifteen hundred symphony orchestras—as well as countless popular music groups, including the inventive performers known as Phish and the long-lived sixties survivors the Grateful Dead.

What Americans read said much about the state of American society at the dawn of the new century. Among the most striking development in American letters was the rise of authors from the once-marginal regions and ethnic groups now coming into their own. Reflecting the general population shift westward, the West became the subject of a particularly rich literary outpouring. Larry McMurtry wrote about the small-town West and

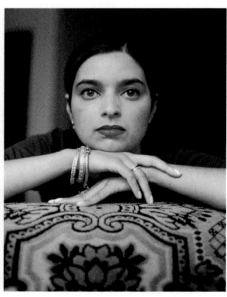

(left) Author Toni Morrison
(right) Author Jhumpa Lahiri

lovingly recollected the end of the cattle-drive era in *Lonesome Dove* (1985). Raymond Carver penned understated and powerful stories about working-class life in the Pacific Northwest. Annie Dillard, Ivan Doig, and Jim Harrison re-created the gritty frontier history of that same verdant region. David Guterson penned a moving tale of interracial anxiety and affection in the World War II–era Pacific Northwest in *Snow Falling on Cedars* (1994). Wallace Stegner, the acknowledged dean of western writers, produced several works that far transcended their regional themes, including *Angle of Repose* (1971) and *Crossing to Safety* (1987). Norman MacLean, a former English professor who turned to fiction writing in his retirement, left two unforgettable accounts of his boyhood in Montana: *A River Runs Through It* (1976) and *Young Men and Fire* (1992).

African-American authors and artists also increasingly made their mark. Playwright August Wilson retold the history of black Americans in the twentieth century, with special emphasis on the psychic costs of the northward migration (*Fences*, 1985; *Joe Turner's Come and Gone*, 1988; *Jitney*, 1998). In the usually lighthearted medium of the Broadway musical, George Wolfe sensitively explored sobering questions of black identity in *Jelly's Last Jam* (1992), the life story of the great New Orleans jazzman "Jelly Roll" Morton. Alice Walker gave fictional voice to the experiences of black women in her hugely popular *The Color Purple* (1982). Toni Morrison wove a bewitching portrait of maternal affection in *Beloved* (1987) and in 1993 became the first African-American woman to win the Nobel Prize for literature. Native-Americans, too, achieved literary recognition. Kiowa author N. Scott Momaday won a Pulitzer Prize for his portrayal of Indian life in *House Made of Dawn* (1968). James Welch wrote movingly about his Blackfoot ancestors in *Fools Crow* (1986).

Asian-American authors also flourished, among them playwright David Hwang and essayist Maxine Hong Kingston, whose *The Woman Warrior* (1976) and *China Men* (1980) imaginatively reconstructed the obscure lives of the earliest Chinese immigrants. Jhumpa Lahiri's *Interpreter of Maladies* (1999) explored the sometimes painful relationship between immigrant Indian parents and their American-born children. The older European migration continued to hold literary appeal as well, notably with Frank McCourt's memories of an Irish and American childhood, captured in *Angela's Ashes* (1996).

Women writers and women's themes forged to the fictional forefront as the feminist movement advanced. Jane Smiley modeled her touching narrative of a midwestern farm family, *A Thousand Acres* (1991), on Shakespeare's *King Lear* and followed up with a hilarious spoof of university life in *Moo* (1995). Ann Tyler penned memorable portraits of quirky characters, male as well as female, in *Dinner at the Homesick Restaurant* (1982) and *The Accidental Tourist* (1985). E. Annie Proulx won widespread acclaim with her comical yet tender portrayal of a struggling family in *The Shipping News* (1993). The rising interest in feminist and African-American themes revived the popularity of a 1930s writer, Zora Neale Hurston, especially her naturalistic novel *Their Eyes Were Watching God*, first published in 1937.

New York became the art capital of the world after World War II, as well-heeled Americans supported a large number of painters and sculptors. The Ford Foundation also became a major patron of the arts, as did the federal government after the creation of the tax-supported National Endowment for the Arts in 1965. The open and tradition-free American environment seemed especially congenial to the experimental mood of much modern art. Jackson Pollock pioneered abstract expressionism in

In her touching novel The Joy Luck Club, *Amy Tan explored the complex dilemmas of growing up as a Chinese-American:*

"'A girl is like a young tree,' [my mother] said. 'You must stand tall and listen to your mother standing next to you. That is the only way to grow strong and straight. But if you bend to listen to other people, you will grow crooked and weak. . . .' Over the years I learned to choose from the best opinions. Chinese people had Chinese opinions. American people had American opinions. And in almost every case, the American version was much better.

"It was only later that I discovered there was a serious flaw with the American version. There were too many choices, so it was easy to get confused and pick the wrong thing."

MECHA Mural, by Student Artists Directed by Sergio O'Cadiz, 1974   People have scribbled on walls since time immemorial, but in the 1960s and 1970s, mural painting emerged as a new form of American folk art. Drab buildings and bare fences, often in minority inner-city neighborhoods, were turned into huge canvases. This mural incorporates many Mexican-American and Mexican themes, including the United Farm Workers' bird symbol and a skeleton, a frequent motif in Mexican art.

the 1940s and 1950s, flinging paint on huge flats stretched on his studio floor. Realistic representation went out the window, as artists like Pollock and Willem de Kooning strove to create "action paintings" that expressed the painter's individuality and made the viewer a creative participant in defining the painting's meaning. Pop artists in the 1960s, notably Andy Warhol, canonized on canvas everyday items of consumer culture, such as soup cans. Robert Rauschenberg made elaborate collages out of objects like cardboard boxes and newspaper clippings. Claes Oldenburg tried to stun viewers into a new visual awareness with unfamiliar versions of familiar objects, such as giant plastic sculptures of pillow-soft telephones. The venerable Georgia O'Keeffe, whose first exhibit was in 1916, continued well into the post–World War II period to produce stunningly immaculate, vividly colored paintings of her beloved Southwest, and moved increasingly into abstract works as her career progressed.

On the stage, playwright David Mamet analyzed the barbarity of American capitalism in plays like *Glengarry Glen Ross* and *American Buffalo,* in which he crafted a kind of poetry from the sludge of American slang. Mamet also made savage sport of feminism and "political correctness" in *Oleanna,* a biting satire about a woman student and her professor. The AIDS epidemic inspired Tony Kushner's sensationally inventive *Angels in America,* a broad-ranging commentary, alternately hilarious and touching, about the condition of American life at century's end. Film, the most characteristic American art form, continued to flourish, especially as a wave of younger filmmakers like George Lucas, Steven Spielberg, Spike Lee, and the Coen brothers, as well as the innovative documentary artist Ken Burns, made their influence felt.

Architecture also benefited from the building boom of the postwar era. Old master Frank Lloyd Wright produced strikingly original designs, as in the round-walled Guggenheim Museum in New York. Louis Kahn employed stark geometric forms and basic building materials like brick and concrete to make beautiful, simple buildings. Eero Saarinen, the son of a Finnish immigrant, contributed a number of imaginative structures, including two Yale University residential colleges that evoked the atmosphere of an Italian hill town. Chinese-born I. M. Pei designed numerous graceful buildings on several college campuses, as well as the John F. Kennedy Library in Boston. Philip Johnson artfully rendered huge edifices intimate in structures like New York City's Seagram Building and the New York State Theater at Lincoln Center in Manhattan. "Postmodernists" such as Robert Venturi and Michael Graves, inspired by the decorative details of earlier historical styles, rejected the spare functionalism that had dominated modern architecture for much of the century.

The American Prospect in the Age of Terrorism

On September 11, 2001, America's good luck apparently ran out. Out of a crystal-clear sky, suicidal terrorists slammed two hijacked airliners, loaded with passengers and jet fuel, into the twin towers of New York City's World Trade Center. They flew a third plane into the military nerve-center of the Pentagon, near Washington, D.C., killing 189 people. Heroic passengers forced another hijacked aircraft to crash in rural Pennsylvania, killing all 44 aboard but depriving the terrorists of a fourth weapon of mass destruction. As the two giant New York skyscrapers thunderously collapsed, some three thousand innocent victims perished, including peoples of many races and faiths from more than sixty countries, as well as hundreds of New York's police- and fire-department rescue workers, A stunned nation blossomed with flags, as grieving and outraged Americans struggled to express their sorrow and solidarity in the face of catastrophic terrorism.

The murderous events of that late-summer morning reanimated American patriotism. They also dramatically ended an historical era. For nearly two centuries, the United States had been spared from foreign attack against its homeland. All but unique among modern peoples, that degree of national security had undergirded the values of openness and individual freedom that defined the distinctive character of American society. Now American security and American liberty alike were imperiled.

President Bush responded with a sober but stirring address to Congress nine days later. His solemn demeanor and the gravity of the situation helped to dissipate the cloud of illegitimacy that had shadowed his presidency since the disputed election of 2000. Warning that the struggle against terrorism would be long and messy, he pledged "we will not tire, we will not falter, and we will not fail" until "we bring our enemies to justice, or bring justice to our enemies." While emphasizing his respect for the Islamic religion and Muslim peoples, he identified the principal enemy as Osama bin Laden, head of a shadowy terrorist network known as Al Qaeda ("the base" in Arabic). A wealthy extremist exiled from his native Saudi Arabia, bin Laden was associated with earlier attacks on American embassies in East Africa and on a U.S. Naval vessel in Yemen. He had taken refuge in land-locked Afghanistan, ruled by Islamic fundamentalists called the Taliban. (Ironically, the United States had indirectly helped bring the Taliban to power, when it supported religious rebels resisting the Soviet invasion of Afghanistan in the 1980s). Bin Laden was known to harbor bitter resentments toward the United States for its economic embargo against Saddam Hussein's Iraq, its military presence on the sacred soil of the Arabian peninsula, and its support for Israel's hostility to Palestinian nationalism. Bin Laden also fed on world-wide resentment of America's enormous economic, military, and cultural power. Ironically, America's most conspicuous strengths had made it a conspicuous target.

When the Taliban refused to hand over bin Laden, Bush ordered a massive military campaign against Afghanistan. Within three months, American and Afghani rebel forces had overthrown the Taliban and were poised to flush bin Laden out of the fortified underground sanctuary where he was believed to have holed up.

The campaign in Afghanistan impressively demonstrated the wallop and sophistication of American air power and "smart," precision-guided munitions. But it remained an open question whether in the longer run America's high-tech arsenal would prove effective against foes so elusive, zealous, and determined—foes who sought not simply to destroy the United States but to demoralize it, perhaps to corrupt its very soul. Behind bin Laden lurked countless terrorist "cells" in several dozen countries, some of

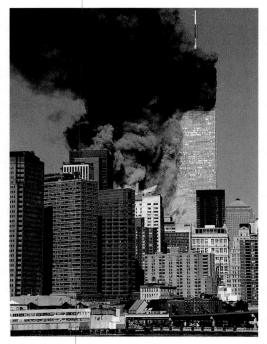

Chronology of Terror   The first hijacked plane hit the north World Trade Center tower at 8:45 a.m. New York time on September 11, 2001. Eighteen minutes later, a second plane hit the south tower, which collapsed at 10:05 a.m. (shown here). Twenty-three minutes later, the north tower also came down. In the frantic minutes after the first impact, thousands of people were evacuated from the two buildings by rescue workers, many of whom lost their own lives.

them possibly in possession of biochemical or even nuclear weapons. Some alarmed critics even warned that the events of September 11 heralded the onset of a protracted clash of civilizations, pitting millions of Muslims desperate to defend their traditional faith and culture against the relentlessly modernizing forces of the western world, spearheaded by the United States. Confronted with this unconventional, diffuse menace, anti-terrorism experts called for new tactics of "a-symmetrical warfare," employing not just traditional military muscle, but innovative intelligence-gathering, economic reprisals, infiltration of suspected organizations, and even assassinations. The new war against terror also compelled the Bush administration to back away from the unilateralist foreign policies it had pursued in its early months and seek anti-terrorist partners around the globe, as evidenced by the surprisingly warm relationship that

emerged after September 11 between the United States and its former adversary, Russia.

The terrorists' blows diabolically coincided with the onset of a recession. The already gathering economic downdraft worsened as edgy Americans shunned air travel and the tourist industry withered. Then, while the rubble in New York was still smoldering, a handful of Americans died after receiving letters contaminated with the deadly respiratory disease, anthrax. The gnawing fear spread that biological warfare would be the next threat facing the American people.

In this anxious atmosphere, Congress rammed through the USA-Patriot Act, permitting extensive telephone and e-mail surveillance, and authorizing the detention and deportation of immigrants suspected of terrorism. The Justice Department meanwhile rounded up hundreds of immigrants and held them without habeas corpus (formal charges in an open court). The Bush administration further called for trying suspected terrorists before military tribunals, where the usual rules of evidence and procedure did not apply. Public opinion polls showed Americans sharply divided on whether the terrorist threat fully warranted such drastic encroachments on America's ancient traditions of civil liberties.

Catastrophic terrorism posed an unprecedented challenge to the United States, but the world's oldest republic remained resilient and resourceful. Born as a revolutionary force in a world of conservatism, the United States had emerged in the twentieth century as a conservative force in a world of revolution. It held aloft the banner of liberal democracy in a world wracked by revolutions of the right and left, including fascism, Nazism, and communism. Yet through it all, much that was truly revolutionary also remained a part of America's liberal democratic heritage, as its people pioneered in revolutions against colonialism, racism, sexism, ignorance, and poverty.

The terrorist threat reminded Americans of the urgency of resolving the ethnic and cultural conflicts that continued to plague the planet after the Cold War's end—and of the urgency of making America's own character better understood around the world. Americans still aspired to live up to Lincoln's prediction that they and their heritage represented "the last best hope of earth"—but in the twenty-first century they would have to work harder than ever to prove it, to themselves as well as to others.

For further reading, see page A29 of the Appendix. For web resources, go to **http://college.hmco.com**.

APPENDIX

SUGGESTED READINGS

CHAPTER 22

PRIMARY SOURCE DOCUMENTS

Booker T. Washington's classic autobiography *Up from Slavery** (1901) records one freedman's experiences. Contemporary comments on Reconstruction include the laments of editor Edwin L. Godkin, *The Nation** (December 7, 1871, p. 364), and Frederick Douglass, *Life and Times of Frederick Douglass** (1882), as well as the debates in the *Congressional Globe** (1867–1868) between radicals such as Thaddeus Stevens and moderates like Lyman Trumbull.

SECONDARY SOURCES

Eric Foner, *Reconstruction: America's Unfinished Revolution, 1863–1877* (1988), is a superb synthesis of current scholarship. Overall accounts may be found in James G. Randall and David Donald, *The Civil War and Reconstruction* (rev. ed., 1969), and James McPherson, *Ordeal by Fire: The Civil War and Reconstruction* (1981), perhaps the best brief introduction. Lincoln's early efforts at Reconstruction are handled in Peyton McCrary, *Abraham Lincoln and Reconstruction* (1978), and Herman Belz, *Emancipation and Equal Rights* (1978). Willie Lee Rose engagingly describes a *Rehearsal for Reconstruction: The Port Royal Experiment* (1964). Dan Carter, *When the War Was Over: The Failure of Self-Reconstruction in the South, 1865–1867* (1985), charts the first years of the period. Following up the story of national politics is Eric L. McKitrick, *Andrew Johnson and Reconstruction: Principle and Prejudice, 1865–1866* (1963). Sympathetic to the radical Republicans are James M. McPherson, *The Struggle for Equality* (1964), and Hans L. Trefousse, *The Radical Republicans* (1969). See also David Montgomery, *Beyond Equality: Labor and the Radical Republicans, 1862–1872* (1967). Siding with the radicals in the impeachment fight are Michael L. Benedict, *The Impeachment and Trial of Andrew Johnson* (1973), and Hans L. Trefousse, *Impeachment of a President* (1975). Conditions in the South are analyzed in W. E. B. Du Bois's controversial classic *Black Reconstruction* (1935) and in Leon F. Litwack's brilliantly evocative *Been in the Storm So Long* (1979), a revealing study of the initial responses, by both blacks and whites, to emancipation. An excellent account of the Southern economy after the war is Gavin Wright, *Old South, New South: Revolutions in the Southern Economy Since the Civil War* (1986). It can be usefully supplemented by Roger Ransom and Richard L. Sutch, *One Kind of Freedom: The Economic Consequences of Emancipation* (1977). See also James Roark, *Masters Without Slaves: Southern Planters in the Civil War and Reconstruction* (1977), and Lawrence Powell, *New Masters: Northern Planters During the Civil War and Reconstruction* (1980). Barbara Fields looks at the border state of Maryland in *Slavery and Freedom on the Middle Ground* (1985). William McFeely offers an excellent biography of *Frederick Douglass* (1991). Roger Shugg, *Origins of Class Struggle in Louisiana* (1968); Dewey W. Grantham, *Life and Death of the Solid South*

(1988); Edward L. Ayers, *The Promise of a New South: Life After Reconstruction* (1992); Dwight Billings, *Planters and the Making of a "New South": Class, Politics and Development in North Carolina, 1865–1900* (1979); and Jonathan Wiener, *Social Origins of the New South: Alabama, 1860–1885* (1978), elucidate the political economy of the postbellum South. Joel Williamson offers a psychological portrait of race relations in *The Crucible of Race: Black-White Relations in the American South Since Emancipation* (1984). Consult also Thomas Holt, *Black over White: Negro Political Leadership in South Carolina During Reconstruction* (1977), and Martha Hodes, *White Women, Black Men: Illicit Sex in the Nineteenth-Century South* (1997). C. Vann Woodward, *The Strange Career of Jim Crow* (rev. ed., 1974), is a classic study of the origins of segregation. His views have drawn criticism in Harold O. Rabinowitz, *Race Relations in the Urban South, 1865–1890* (1977). See also Rabinowitz's *Southern Black Leaders of the Reconstruction Era* (1982). The Freedmen's Bureau has been the subject of several studies, including Peter Kolchin, *First Freedom* (1972); Claude Oubré, *Forty Acres and a Mule: The Freedmen's Bureau and Black Land Ownership* (1978); and Donald Nieman, *To Set the Law in Motion: The Freedmen's Bureau and the Legal Rights of Blacks, 1865–1868* (1979). Nell Irvin Painter follows African-Americans who chose to leave the South altogether in *Exodusters: Black Migration to Kansas After Reconstruction* (1976). Special studies of value are William P. Vaughn, *Schools for All* (1974); William C. Gillette, *The Right to Vote: Politics and the Passage of the 15th Amendment* (1965); Stanley I. Kutler, *Judicial Power and Reconstruction Politics* (1968); and Harold M. Hyman, *A More Perfect Union: The Impact of the Civil War and Reconstruction on the Constitution* (1973). Richard N. Current rehabilitates the maligned carpetbaggers in *Those Terrible Carpetbaggers* (1988). Provocative scholarship is presented in Kenneth M. Stampp and Leon Litwack, eds., *Reconstruction: An Anthology of Revisionist Writings* (1969), and Robert P. Swierenga, ed., *Beyond the Civil War Synthesis* (1975). J. Morgan Kousser and James M. McPherson, eds., *Region, Race, and Reconstruction: Essays in Honor of C. Vann Woodward* (1982), contains some intriguing essays. Eric Foner looks at emancipation in a comparative perspective in *Nothing but Freedom* (1983). A comprehensive study of the climax of this troubled period is William Gillette, *Retreat from Reconstruction, 1869–1879* (1979). Also see Michael Perman, *The Road to Redemption: Southern Politics, 1869–1879* (1984).

CHAPTER 23

PRIMARY SOURCE DOCUMENTS

Henry Adams penned some perceptive and sour observations on the era in his autobiographical *Education of Henry Adams* (1907) and in his novel *Democracy* (1880). See also the classic satire by Mark Twain and Charles Dudley Warner, *The Gilded Age* (1873).

SECONDARY SOURCES

The scandal-rocked Grant era is treated with brevity in James G. Randall and David Donald, *The Civil War and Reconstruction* (rev. ed., 1969), and at greater length in William Gillette, *Retreat from Reconstruction* (1979), and James M. McPherson, *Ordeal*

---

*An asterisk indicates that the document, or an excerpt from it, can be found in Thomas A. Bailey and David M. Kennedy, eds., *The American Spirit: United States History as Seen by Contemporaries*, 10th ed. (Boston: Houghton Mifflin, 2002).

by *Fire* (1981). On Hayes, see Ari Hoogenboom, *Rutherford B. Hayes: Warrior and President* (1995). A general look at corruption as a political issue is Mark W. Summers, *The Era of Good Stealings* (1993). Consult also William McFeely, *Grant* (1981). Southern politics is detailed in C. Vann Woodward's classic *Origins of the New South* (1951); Otto H. Olsen, *Reconstruction and Redemption in the South* (1980); Terry L. Seip, *The South Returns to Congress* (1983); Michael Perman, *The Road to Redemption* (1984); and J. Morgan Kousser, *The Shaping of Southern Politics* (1974). Barry A. Crouch, *The Freedmen's Bureau and Black Texans* (1992), describes the hopes and frustrations of freedom for blacks in post–Civil War Texas. Brenda Stevenson traces slavery's lingering impact on post–Civil War black life and race relations in *Life in Black and White: Family and Community Life in the Slave South* (1996). The origins of racial segregation are analyzed in C. Vann Woodward, *The Strange Career of Jim Crow* (rev. ed., 1974). William Gillette, *The Right to Vote* (1965); Dale Baum, *The Civil War Party System: The Case of Massachusetts, 1848–1876* (1984); and James C. Mohr, *The Radical Republicans and Reform in New York During Reconstruction* (1973), discuss the North. Mark W. Summers analyzes *Railroads, Reconstruction and the Gospel of Prosperity* (1984). Gary Brechin examines the West's largest city in *Imperial San Francisco: Urban Power, Earthly Ruin* (1999). On the party systems, see Paul Kleppner, *The Third Electoral System, 1835–1892* (1979); Morton Keller, *Affairs of State: Public Life in Nineteenth-Century America* (1977); Peter McCaffery, *When Bosses Ruled Philadelphia: The Emergence of the Republican Machine, 1867–1933* (1993); Samuel McSeveney, *The Politics of Depression: Political Behavior in the Northeast, 1893–1896* (1972); and Richard Jensen, *The Winning of the Mid-West* (1971). Jon Teaford defends the record of municipal governments in *The Unheralded Triumph: City Government in America, 1870–1900* (1984). Money questions are treated in Irwin Unger, *The Greenback Era* (1964); Walter T. K. Nugent, *Money and American Society, 1865–1880* (1968); and Allen Weinstein's account of the "Crime of '73," *Prelude to Populism* (1970). C. Vann Woodward sharply analyzes the Compromise of 1877 in *Reunion and Reaction* (rev. ed., 1956). California receives special attention in Alexander Saxton, *The Indispensable Enemy: Labor and the Anti-Chinese Movement in California* (1975). Labor issues are cogently and compellingly discussed in Paul Krause, *The Battle for Homestead, 1880–1892: Politics, Culture, and Steel* (1992). Charles Hoffman examines *The Depression of the Nineties* (1970), an issue given much attention in David P. Thelen, *The New Citizenship: Origins of Progressivism in Wisconsin, 1885–1900* (1972). Three intriguing cultural histories of the period are Alan Trachtenberg, *The Incorporation of America: Culture and Society in the Gilded Age* (1982); Richard Slotkin, *The Fatal Environment: The Myth of the Frontier in American History, 1800–1890* (1985); and Lawrence Levine, *Highbrow/Lowbrow: The Emergence of Cultural Hierarchy in America* (1988).

CHAPTER 24

PRIMARY SOURCE DOCUMENTS

Andrew Carnegie, "Wealth,"* *North American Review* (June 1889), gives the philosophy of the Gilded Age's greatest entre-

preneur. Henry Grady's Boston speech (1889), in Joel C. Harris, *Life of Henry W. Grady** (1890), dramatizes the plight of the South. Samuel Gompers penned his "Letter on Labor in Industrial Society," an open letter to Judge Peter Grossup, in 1894 (in Richard Hofstadter, *Great Issues in American History*). William Dean Howell's novel *The Rise of Silas Lapham* (1885) treats the moral impact of the new business culture on one New England businessman and his family.

SECONDARY SOURCES

A useful survey is Samuel P. Hays's penetrating study *The Response to Industrialism, 1885–1914* (1957). Stuart Bruchey puts the period in context in *The Growth of the Modern Economy* (1975). Business is the subject of Alfred D. Chandler, Jr., *The Visible Hand: The Managerial Revolution in American Business* (1978); Saul Engelbourg, *Power and Morality: American Business Ethics, 1840–1914* (1980); and Naomi R. Lamoreaux, *The Great Merger Movement in American Business, 1895–1904* (1985). Olivier Zunz surveys the development of corporate culture in *Making America Corporate, 1870–1920* (1990), while Scott M. Cutlip examines *The Unseen Power: Public Relations, a History* (1994). Thomas K. McCraw assesses government regulation in *Prophets of Regulation: Charles Francis Adams, Louis D. Brandeis, James M. Landis, Alfred E. Kahn* (1984). In *Control Through Communication: The Rise of System in American Management* (1989), Joanne Yates argues that big business was more efficient than Brandeis believed. The thought and attitudes characteristic of the new industrial age are examined in Richard Hofstadter, *Social Darwinism in American Thought* (rev. ed., 1955); Daniel T. Rodgers, *The Work Ethic in Industrial America, 1850–1920* (1978); and Alan Trachtenberg, *The Incorporation of America: Culture and Society in the Gilded Age* (1982). On the railroads, see George R. Taylor and Irene D. Neu, *The American Railroad Network, 1861–1890* (1956), and Robert Fogel's provocative *Railroads and American Economic Growth* (1964). An important new study is David H. Bain, *Empire Express: Building the First Transcontinental Railroad* (1999). C. Vann Woodward has provided a masterful analysis of *Origins of the New South, 1877–1913* (1951), which can be profitably supplemented by Jonathan M. Wiener, *Social Origins of the New South* (1978); Don H. Doyle, *New Men, New Cities, New South: Atlanta, Nashville, Charleston, Mobile, 1860–1910* (1980); and Edward Ayers, *The Promise of the New South: Life After Reconstruction* (1992). Also see Gaines M. Foster, *Ghosts of the Confederacy: Defeat, the Lost Cause and the Emergence of the New South, 1865–1913* (1987). For more on race relations in the post-Reconstruction South, see Joel Williamson, *The Crucible of Race* (1984); Howard Rabinowitz, *Race Relations in the Urban South, 1865–1890* (1978); and Neil R. McMillen, *Dark Journey: Black Mississippians in the Age of Jim Crow* (1989). Labor is the subject of Gerald Grob, *Workers and Utopia* (1961), and David Montgomery's innovative *The Fall of the House of Labor: The Workplace, the State, and American Labor Activism, 1865–1925* (1987). Paul Krause details *The Battle for Homestead, 1880–1892* (1992). Especially stimulating are two volumes by Herbert Gutman, *Work, Culture, and Society in Industrializing America* (1976) and *Power and Culture: Essays on the American Working Class* (1987). On women workers, see David Katzman, *Seven Days a Week: Women and Domestic Service in Industrializing America* (1978); Philip Foner, *Women and the American Labor*

Movement (1979); and Alice Kessler-Harris, *Out to Work: A History of Wage-Earning Women in the United States* (1982). For a discussion of labor and race, see Gerald David Jaynes, *Branches Without Roots: Genesis of the Black Working Class in the American South, 1862–1882* (1986), and Tera W. Hunter, *To 'Joy My Freedom: Southern Black Women's Lives and Labors After the Civil War* (1997).

CHAPTER 25

PRIMARY SOURCE DOCUMENTS

Jacob Riis, *How the Other Half Lives** (1890), is a vivid account of life in America's slums. In *A Hazard of New Fortunes* (1890), William Dean Howells penned one of the first "urban novels" in American literature. Frances Willard, *Glimpses of Fifty Years** (1880), is the memoir of a leading prohibitionist. Victoria Woodhull, *The Scarecrows of Sexual Slavery** (1874), provocatively illustrates some changing ideas about women's roles. Henry James's novel *The Bostonians* (1886) vividly portrays feminists and suffragists.

SECONDARY SOURCES

The Rise of the City, 1878–1898 (1933) is a classic study by Arthur M. Schlesinger. More recent are Gunther Barth, *City People: The Rise of Modern City Culture in Nineteenth-Century America* (1980); Howard Chudacoff, *The Evolution of American Urban Society* (1975); the opening chapters of Kenneth T. Jackson, *Crabgrass Frontier: The Suburbanization of America* (1985); and Eric H. Monkkonen, *America Becomes Urban: The Development of Cities and Towns, 1780–1980* (1988). Specific cities are discussed in Sam Bass Warner, Jr.'s *The Private City: Philadelphia in Three Periods of Its Growth* (1968) and in his study of Boston, *Streetcar Suburbs* (1962). See also Edward K. Spann, *The New Metropolis: New York City, 1840–1857* (1981), and Karen Sawislak's graceful and insightful *Smoldering City: Chicagoans and the Great Fire, 1871–1874* (1995). On architecture, see Robert Twombly, *Louis Sullivan: His Life and Work* (1986). On new urban spaces and their use by city dwellers, see Roy Rosenzweig and Elizabeth Blackmar, *The Park and The People: A History of Central Park* (1992); Kathy Peiss, *Cheap Amusements: Working Women and Leisure in Turn-of-the Century New York* (1986); and David Nasaw, *Going Out: The Rise and Fall of Public Amusements* (1993). Martin Melosi, *The Sanitary City: Urban Infrastructure in America from Colonial Times to the Present* (2000), and Joel Tarr, *The Search for the Ultimate Sink: Urban Pollution in Historical Perspective* (1996), argue that waste disposal has been a key force shaping urban politics in American history. Oscar Handlin pioneered the study of immigrant communities in American cities with his *Boston's Immigrants* (rev. ed., 1959). More recent studies of the same topic include John Bodnar, *The Transplanted: A History of Immigrants in Urban America* (1985); Jon Gjerde, *From Peasants to Farmers: The Migration from Norway to the Upper Middle West* (1985); Kerby A. Miller, *Emigrants and Exile: Ireland and the Irish Exodus to North America* (1985); Donna Gabaccia, *From the Other Side: Women, Gender, and*

Immigrant Life in the U.S., 1820–1990 (1994); Thomas Kessner, *The Golden Door: Italian and Jewish Mobility in New York City, 1880–1915* (1977); Stephan Thernstrom, *The Other Bostonians* (1973); Virginia Yans-McLaughlin, *Family and Community: Italian Immigrants in Buffalo, 1880–1930* (1975); Dino Cinel, *From Italy to San Francisco: The Immigrant Experience* (1982); Humbert Nelli, *Italians of Chicago, 1880–1920* (1970); Ronald Takaki, *Strangers from a Different Shore: A History of Asian Americans* (1989); and Irving Howe's monumental and moving account of Jewish immigration, *World of Our Fathers* (1976). Maldwyn Jones, *American Immigration* (1960), is a well-written introduction, as is Thomas J. Archdeacon, *Becoming American* (1983). Oscar Handlin, *The Uprooted* (1951), is an imaginative account of the immigrant experience. John Higham examines the "nativist" reaction in *Strangers in the Land* (1955). On medicine, consult Morris J. Vogel, *The Invention of the Modern Hospital: Boston, 1870–1930* (1980); Paul Starr, *The Social Transformation of American Medicine* (1982); and John Duffy, *The Sanitarians: A History of American Public Health* (1990). On education, see Lawrence Cremin, *The Transformation of the School* (1961), and Laurence Veysey, *The Emergence of the American University* (1965). Black thought for this period is illuminated by three studies: August Meier, *Negro Thought in America, 1880–1915* (1963); Louis R. Harlan, *Booker T. Washington: The Making of a Black Leader, 1865–1901* (1972); and David Levering Lewis's two-volume biography of *W. E. B. Du Bois* (1993 and 2000). For blacks in northern cities before World War I, see Allan H. Spear, *Black Chicago: The Making of a Negro Ghetto, 1890–1920* (1967), and James Borchert, *Alley Life in Washington: Family, Community, Religion, and Folklife in the City* (1980). On religion, see Susan Curtis, *A Consuming Faith: The Social Gospel and Modern American Culture* (1991). On women and the family, consult Carl Degler, *At Odds: Women and the Family from the Revolution to the Present* (1980); Steven Mintz, *A Prison of Expectations: The Family in Victorian Culture* (1983); Mari Jo Buhle, *Women and American Socialism, 1870–1920* (1981); Margaret W. Rossiter, *Women Scientists in America* (1982); Elisabeth Griffith, *In Her Own Right: The Life of Elizabeth Cady Stanton* (1984); Rosalind Rosenberg, *Beyond Separate Spheres* (1982) and *Divided Lives* (1992); Allen F. Davis, *American Heroine: The Life and Legend of Jane Addams* (1973); Elaine May, *Great Expectations: Marriage and Divorce in Post-Victorian America* (1980); Carroll Smith-Rosenberg, *Disorderly Conduct: Visions of Gender in Victorian America* (1985); and Estelle B. Freedman, *Their Sisters' Keepers: Women's Prison Reform in America, 1830–1930* (1981). John L. Thomas considers *Alternative America: Henry George, Edward Bellamy, Henry Demarest Lloyd, and the Adversary Tradition* (1983). Bruce Kuklick examines Harvard's star-studded philosophy department in *The Rise of American Philosophy* (1977). James Turner probes one aspect of the conflict between science and religion in *Without God, Without Creed: The Origins of Unbelief in America* (1985). Three fascinating studies document the rise of a "new" middle-class mentality: Burton J. Bledstein, *The Culture of Professionalism* (1976); Thomas Haskell, *The Emergence of Professional Social Science* (1977); and Stuart M. Blumin, *The Emergence of the Middle Class: Social Experience in the American City, 1760–1900* (1989). See also Alexandra Oleson and John Voss, eds., *The Organization of Knowledge in Modern America, 1860–1920* (1979).

CHAPTER 26

PRIMARY SOURCE DOCUMENTS

Black Elk Speaks, edited by John G. Neihardt (1932), is an eloquent Indian statement about the Sioux experience. Indian perspectives on the westward movement can be found in Jerome A. Greene, ed., *Lakota and Cheyenne: Indian Views of the Great Sioux Wars, 1876–1877** (1994). Theodore Roosevelt, *Hunting Trips of a Ranchman** (1885), offers the future president's views on the Indian question. Mary Lease's famous call to arms is recorded in William E. Connelley, ed., *History of Kansas, State and People** (1928). William H. Coin Harvey, *Coin's Financial School** (1894), expounded the silverite position. William Jennings Bryan's Cross of Gold speech* won him the Democratic nomination in 1896 and a hallowed place in the annals of American oratory.

SECONDARY SOURCES

Vivacious chapters appear in Ray A. Billington, *Westward Expansion* (5th ed., 1982). Walter Prescott Webb, *The Great Plains* (1931), is a classic. Robert V. Hine, *The American West* (2nd ed., 1984), is a useful survey. Patricia Nelson Limerick traces regional themes across time in *Legacy of Conquest: The Unbroken Past of the American West* (1987). Richard White's fresh account, *"It's Your Misfortune and None of My Own": A New History of the American West* (1991), emphasizes the role of the federal government, corporations, and the market economy in the region's development and pays special attention to the twentieth century, as do Donald Worster, *Rivers of Empire: Water, Aridity, and the Growth of the American West* (1986), and Donald J. Pisani, *To Reclaim a Divided West: Water, Law, and Policy, 1848–1902* (1992). Women in the West are discussed in Glenda Riley, *The Female Frontier: A Comparative View of Women on the Prairie and Plains* (1988), and Beverly Beeton, *Women Vote in the West: The Woman Suffrage Movement, 1869–1896* (1986). Native Americans are discussed in Robert Utley, *The Indian Frontier of the American West, 1846–1890* (1984), and in Dee Brown's *Bury My Heart at Wounded Knee: An Indian History of the American West* (1970). Consult also Francis P. Prucha, *The Great Father: The United States Government and the American Indians* (1984); Frederick E. Hoxie, *A Final Promise: The Campaign to Assimilate the Indians* (1984); Joe S. Sando, *Pueblo Nations: Eight Centuries of Pueblo Indian History* (1992); Thomas Berger's novel *Little Big Man* (1964); and Albert Hurtado, *Indian Survival on the California Frontier* (1988). The military history of the "Indian wars" is covered in S. L. A. Marshall, *Crimsoned Prairie* (1972). Two intriguing studies of cross-cultural perception are Robert F. Berkhofer, Jr., *The White Man's Indian* (1978), and Richard Drinnon, *Facing West: The Metaphysics of Indian Hating and Empire Building* (1980). A sweeping look at Chicano history is Juan Gómez-Quiñones, *Roots of Chicago Politics, 1600–1940* (1994). David Alan Johnson explores *Founding the Far West: California, Oregon, and Nevada, 1840–1890* (1992). William Cronon explores the relationship between Chicago and the development of the "Great West" in *Nature's Metropolis* (1991), a book nicely complemented by John C. Hudson, *Making the Corn Belt* (1994). Donald J. Pisani looks at western agriculture in *From the Family Farm to Agribusiness: The Irrigation Crusade in California and the West, 1850–1931* (1984). For beef see Philip Durham and Everett L. Jones, *The Negro Cowboys* (1965); Robert Dykstra, *The Cattle Town* (1968); and Gene M. Gressley, *Bankers and Cattlemen* (1966). See also David J. Weber, *The Spanish Frontier in North America* (1992). A powerful work on the farmers' protest is Lawrence Goodwyn, *Democratic Promise* (1976), abridged as *The Populist Moment* (1978). See also John D. Hicks's classic *The Populist Revolt* (1931); Walter T. K. Nugent, *The Tolerant Populists* (1963); Steven Hahn, *The Roots of Southern Populism* (1983); William A. Link, *The Paradox of Southern Progressivism, 1880–1930* (1992); and Bruce Palmer, *"Man over Money": The Southern Populist Critique of American Capitalism* (1980). Richard Hofstadter's stimulating *The Age of Reform* (1955) sparked a long-running debate among historians about the nature of Populism. A more recent study is Michael Kazin, *The Populist Persuasion: An American History* (1995). Paolo Coletta's biography of *William Jennings Bryan* (3 vols., 1964–1969) is rich in detail. The election of 1896 is examined in Robert F. Durden *The Climax of Populism: The Election of 1896* (1965), and Stanley Jones, *The Presidential Election of 1896* (1964). Also informative are Paul W. Glad, *McKinley, Bryan and the People* (1964), and H. Wayne Morgan, *William McKinley and His America* (1963). Kevin Starr probes the cultural history of California in both *Americans and the California Dream, 1850–1915* (1973) and *Inventing the Dream: California Through the Progressive Era* (1985). Henry Nash Smith, *Virgin Land: The American West as Symbol and Myth* (1950), is a landmark study of particular interest to students of literature.

CHAPTER 27

PRIMARY SOURCE DOCUMENTS

Examples of "yellow journalism" include Joseph Pulitzer's *New York World* and William R. Hearst's *New York Journal.* Particularly interesting is the editorial in the *World* of February 13, 1897,* and the article by Charles Duval in the *Journal* of October 10, 1897.* "McKinley's War Message,"* in James D. Richardson, ed., *Messages and Papers of the Presidents,* vol. 10 (1899), outlines the American rationale for intervention. The anti-imperialist answer can be found in Charles E. Norton's article in *Public Opinion** (June 23, 1898, pp. 775–776).

SECONDARY SOURCES

Main outlines are sketched in Thomas G. Paterson, *American Foreign Policy: A Brief History* (2nd ed., 1983). Two general (and quite contrasting) interpretations of modern American foreign policy are George F. Kennan, *American Diplomacy* (1951), and William Appleman Williams, *The Tragedy of American Diplomacy* (1959). Consult also Ernest R. May, *American Imperialism: A Speculative Essay* (1968), and Walter LaFeber, *The New Empire* (1963) and *Inevitable Revolutions* (1983). E. S. Rosenberg's *Spreading the American Dream* (1982) examines U.S. economic and cultural expansion from 1890 to 1945. Thoughtful perceptions can be found in Robert Seager II, *Alfred Thayer Mahan* (1977), and James L. Abrahamson, *America Arms for a New Century* (1981). On the Spanish-American War, see Frank Freidel,

The Splendid Little War (1958), and David F. Trask, The War with Spain in 1898 (1981). Fascinating reading is Hyman G. Rickover, How the Battleship Maine Was Destroyed (1976). Helpful studies of the opponents of expansion are Robert L. Beisner, Twelve Against Empire: The Anti-Imperialists, 1898–1900 (1968); E. Berkeley Tompkins, Anti-Imperialism in the United States: The Great Debates, 1890–1920 (1970); and Kendrick A. Clements, William Jennings Bryan: Missionary Isolationist (1983). Thomas McCormick sees a design for "informal" imperialism in The China Market (1967). David F. Healey examines The United States in Cuba, 1898–1902 (1963), and Leon Wolff paints a grim picture of American involvement in the Philippines in Little Brown Brother (1961). For more on the Philippine imbroglio, see Peter W. Stanley, A Nation in the Making: The Philippines and the United States, 1899–1921 (1975); H. W. Brands, Bound to Empire: The United States and the Philippines (1992); Richard E. Welch, Jr., Response to Imperialism: The United States and the Philippine-American War, 1899–1902 (1979); Stuart C. Miller, "Benevolent Assimilation": The American Conquest of the Philippines, 1899–1903 (1982); and Stanley Karnow, In Our Image: America's Empire in the Philippines (1989).

CHAPTER 28

PRIMARY SOURCE DOCUMENTS

Theodore Roosevelt's corollary* to the Monroe Doctrine, in A Compilation of the Messages and Papers of the Presidents, vol. 16, found its first expression in 1904. The Annual Report of the secretary of commerce and labor for 1908* contains the "Gentlemen's Agreement" with Japan. For the intrigue surrounding the independence of Panama and the building of the canal, see Foreign Relations of the United States* (1903) and Theodore Roosevelt to Albert Shaw, October 10, 1903,* in The Letters of Theodore Roosevelt, edited by Elting E. Morison vol. 3 (1951).

SECONDARY SOURCES

Howard K. Beale describes Theodore Roosevelt and the Rise of America to World Power (1956). See also the work of William Appleman Williams, cited in Chapter 29. Analytical and sympathetic is John M. Blum, The Republican Roosevelt (new ed., 1977). An outstanding single-volume biography of TR is William H. Harbaugh, Power and Responsibility (rev. ed., 1975). Lewis L. Gould focuses on The Presidency of Theodore Roosevelt (1991), while especially good on the youthful Roosevelt is David McCullough, Mornings on Horseback (1981). For the Open Door, consult Marilyn B. Young, The Rhetoric of Empire: America's China Policy, 1895–1901 (1968), and Jerry Israel, Progressivism and the Open Door: America and China 1905–1921 (1971). On relations with Japan, see Charles E. Neu, The Troubled Encounter: The United States and Japan (1975). Also valuable are two books by Akira Iriye, Across the Pacific (1967) and Pacific Estrangement: Japanese and American Expansion, 1897–1911 (1972). James Reed discusses The Missionary Mind and American East Asian Policy, 1911–1915 (1983). Also see William R. Hutchinson, Errand to the World: American Protestant Thought and Foreign Missions (1987). On the treatment of the Japanese in the United States, see Ronald Takaki, Strangers from a Different Shore (1989). The canal issue is analyzed in Walter LaFeber, The Panama Canal (1978), and Richard H. Collin, Theodore Roosevelt's Caribbean: The Panama Canal, the Monroe Doctrine, and the Latin American Context (1990). On race relations and foreign policy, see Alexander DeConde, Ethnicity, Race, and American Foreign Policy (1992). On gender and imperialism, see Gail Bederman, Manliness and Civilization (1995), and Kristen Hoganson, Fighting for American Manhood (1998).

CHAPTER 29

PRIMARY SOURCE DOCUMENTS

Lincoln Steffens, The Shame of the Cities* (1904), is an exemplary muckraking document, as is Upton Sinclair's notorious novel The Jungle (1906). For a less than gracious assessment of the muckrakers, see Theodore Roosevelt, "The Man with the Muckrake,"* Putnam's Monthly and The Critic (October 1906). A revealing account of municipal politics is George Washington Plunkitt, Plunkitt of Tammany Hall* (1905). See also the decision of the Supreme Court on state bakery regulations in Lochner v. New York, 198 U.S. 45 (1905). Oliver Wendell Holmes, Jr.'s thundering dissent in the Lochner case is reprinted in Richard Hofstadter, Great Issues in American History.

SECONDARY SOURCES

A brief introduction is John W. Chambers, The Tyranny of Change: America in the Progressive Era, 1900–1917 (1980). Perceptive interpretations are Samuel P. Hays, The Response to Industrialism, 1885–1914 (1957); Robert H. Wiebe, The Search for Order (1967); and Richard Hofstadter, The Age of Reform (1955). Valuable analyses of progressivism at the state level include Richard McCormick's exceptionally good From Realignment to Reform: Political Change in New York State, 1893–1910 (1981); David Thelen's study of Wisconsin, The New Citizenship (1972); and Dewey W. Grantham, Southern Progressivism (1983). Especially provocative are James Weinstein, The Corporate Ideal in the Liberal State (1968), and Gabriel Kolko, The Triumph of Conservatism (1963). Consult also Alfred D. Chandler, Jr., The Visible Hand (1977), and Morton Keller, Regulating a New Economy: Public Policy and Economic Change in America, 1900–1933 (1990). On pure food and drugs, see James Harvey Young, Pure Food: Securing the Federal Food and Drugs Act of 1906 (1989). Other social issues of importance are treated in James H. Timberlake, Prohibition and the Progressive Movement (1963); David J. Rothman, Conscience and Convenience: The Asylum and Its Alternatives in Progressive America (1980); Allen F. Davis, Spearheads for Reform: The Social Settlements and the Progressive Movement, 1890–1914 (1967); Mina Carson, Settlement Folk: Social Thought and the American Settlement Movement, 1885–1930 (1990); James Patterson, America's Struggle Against Poverty, 1900–1980 (1981); David B. Tyack, The One Best System: A History of American Urban Education (1974); and Lynn Gordon, Gender and Higher Education in the Progressive Era (1990). On religion, see Martin E. Marty, Modern American Religion: The Irony of It All, 1893–1919 (1986). T. J. Jackson Lears takes a different perspective in No Place of Grace: Antimodernism and the Transformation of American Culture (1981). Municipal reform is the subject of Martin J. Schiesl, The Politics of *Efficiency* (1977), and two useful anthologies, Bruce Stave, ed., *Urban Bosses, Machines and Progressive Reformers* (1972), and Blaine A. Brownell and Warren E. Stickle, eds., *Bosses and Reformers* (1973). On conservation, see Samuel P. Hays, *Conservation and the Gospel of Efficiency* (1959); Elmo Richardson, *The Politics of Conservation* (1962); and James Penick, Jr., *Progressive Politics and Conservation* (1968). Socialism is discussed in Nick Salvatore, *Eugene V. Debs: Citizen and Socialist* (1982); James Weinstein, *The Decline of Socialism in America, 1912–1925* (1967); and Mari Jo Buhle, *Women and American Socialism, 1897–1920* (1981). On women and progressivism, see Robyn Muncy, *Creating a Female Dominion in American Reform* (1991); Theda Skocpol, *Protecting Soldiers and Mothers* (1992); Ellen Fitzpatrick, *Endless Crusade: Women Social Scientists and Progressive Reform* (1990); and Rosalind Rosenberg, *Beyond Separate Spheres* (1982). Jacqueline Jones focuses on black women in *Labor of Love, Labor of Sorrow: Black Women, Work, and the Family from Slavery to the Present* (1985). The Taft era is summarized in Paolo Coletta, *The Presidency of William Howard Taft* (1973). See also Norman Wilensky, *Conservatives in the Progressive Era* (1965), and James Holt, *Congressional Insurgents and the Party System, 1909–1916* (1968). Otis Graham traces the progressive legacy in *Encore for Reform: The Old Progressives and the New Deal* (1967). Daniel T. Rodgers puts American Progressivism in an international perspective in his masterful *Atlantic Crossings: Social Politics in a Progressive Age* (1998).

CHAPTER 30

PRIMARY SOURCE DOCUMENTS

Theodore Roosevelt's "Acceptance Speech"* at the Progressive convention of 1912 and Woodrow Wilson's collection of campaign speeches, *The New Freedom** (1913), give the substance and flavor of the critical 1912 campaign. Louis D. Brandeis, *Other People's Money and How the Bankers Use It** (1914), expresses the philosophy of a key Wilson adviser. On the *Lusitania* incident, see *Foreign Relations of the United States*, 1915, Supplement.

SECONDARY SOURCES

See the titles by John W. Chambers, Samuel P. Hays, Richard Hofstadter, Robert H. Wiebe, and Daniel T. Rodgers cited in Chapter 29. Kendrick Clements, *The Presidency of Woodrow Wilson* (1992), in an elegant synthesis of the president and his age. John M. Cooper, Jr., *The Warrior and the Priest* (1983), deftly contrasts Wilson and Theodore Roosevelt. Biographies of Wilson include August Heckscher's voluminous *Woodrow Wilson: A Biography* (1991), Arthur Link's five-volume *Wilson* (1947–1965), and John M. Blum's *Woodrow Wilson and the Politics of Morality* (1956). Particularly interesting is Alexander and Juliette George's psychological study, *Woodrow Wilson and Colonel House* (1956). For a sharply contrasting view, see Edwin A. Weinstein, *Woodrow Wilson: A Medical and Psychological Biography* (1981). The road to World War I finds comprehensive treatment in Ernest May, *The World War and American Isolation, 1914–1917* (1959). Consult also Ross Gregory, *The Origins of American Intervention in the First World War* (1971), and

Patrick Devlin, *Too Proud to Fight: Woodrow Wilson's Neutrality* (1975). Mira Wilkins traces *The History of Foreign Investment in the United States to 1914* (1989). Superb biographies of prominent intellectuals include David Levy, *Herbert Croly of the New Republic: The Life and Thought of an American Progressive* (1985); Edward A. Stettner, *Shaping Modern Liberalism: Herbert Croly and Progressive Thought* (1993); and Philippa Strum, *Brandeis: Justice for the People* (1984). Special studies of value include Thomas A. Bailey and Paul B. Ryan, *The* Lusitania *Disaster* (1975); Jeffrey J. Safford, *Wilsonian Maritime Diplomacy* (1978); Ronald Radosh, *American Labor and Foreign Policy* (1969), and Burton I. Kaufman, *Efficiency and Expansion* (1974). For the European background, see Laurence Lafore, *The Long Fuse* (1965), and Fritz Fisher, *Germany's Aims in the First World War* (1967). Social and intellectual currents are described in Henry F. May, *The End of American Innocence: A Study of the First Years of Our Own Time, 1912–1917* (1959). Michael C. Adams, *The Great Adventure: Male Desire and the Coming of World War I* (1990), is a provocative work that tries to link Victorian gender ideology to the martial enthusiasms of the early twentieth century.

CHAPTER 31

PRIMARY SOURCE DOCUMENTS

John J. Pershing, *My Experiences in the World War** (1931), recounts American fighting tactics. Woodrow Wilson's "Fourteen Points Address" to Congress on January 8, 1918* (*Congressional Record*, 65th Cong., 2nd sess., 691), defined the nation's war aims. William E. Borah, "Speech on the League of Nations" (1919), in Richard Hofstadter, *Great Issues in American History*, reveals the isolationist position. Ernest Hemingway's *A Farewell to Arms* (1929) is an outstanding war novel.

SECONDARY SOURCES

The home front is emphasized in David M. Kennedy, *Over Here: The First World War and American Society* (1980). Economic mobilization is covered in Robert Cuff, *The War Industries Board* (1973), and Daniel R. Beaver, *Newton D. Baker and the American Financing of World War I* (1970). On labor, see Frank L. Grubbs, Jr., *The Struggle for Labor Loyalty* (1968); David Brody, *Labor in Crisis: The Steel Strike of 1919* (1965); and Michael Kazin, *Barons of Labor: The San Francisco Building Trades and Union Power in the Progressive Era* (1987). Politics is treated in Seward Livermore, *Politics Is Adjourned: Woodrow Wilson and the War Congress, 1916–1918* (1966). American propaganda efforts are colorfully portrayed in James R. Mock and Cedric Larson, *Words That Won the War* (1939), and Stephen L. Vaughn, *Holding Fast the Inner Lines: Democracy, Nationalism, and the Committee on Public Information* (1980). The abuse of civil liberties is analyzed in Harry N. Scheiber, *The Wilson Administration and Civil Liberties, 1917–1921* (1960), and Paul L. Murphy, *World War I and the Origin of Civil Liberties in the United States* (1979). Military matters are handled in Edward M. Coffman, *The War to End All Wars: The American Military Experience in World War I* (1968); Arthur E. Barbeau and Florette Henri, *Unknown Soldiers: Black American Troops in World War One* (1974); and John Whiteclay Chambers II, *To Raise an Army:*

The Draft Comes to Modern America (1987). The war experiences of women are captured in Maurine W. Greenwald, *Women, War, and Work* (1980). Gerd Hardach, *The First World War, 1914–1918* (1977), is a broad economic history. On Wilson's foreign economic policies, see Jeffrey J. Safford, *Wilsonian Maritime Diplomacy* (1978), and Burton I. Kaufman, *Efficiency and Expansion: Foreign Trade Organization in the Wilson Administration* (1974). The postwar international economic position of the United States is discussed in Carl Parrini, *Heir to Empire* (1969); Michael Hogan, *Informal Entente* (1977); and Joan Hoff Wilson, *American Business and Foreign Policy, 1920–1933* (1973). Paul P. Abrahams examines *The Foreign Expansion of American Finance and Its Relationship to the Foreign Economic Policies of the United States, 1907–1921* (1976). Works of cultural history include Stanley Cooperman, *World War I and the American Novel* (1966); Stuart Rochester, *American Liberal Disillusionment in the Wake of World War I* (1977); and Paul Fussell, *The Great War and Modern Memory* (1975). On the peace, see Arthur S. Link, *Woodrow Wilson: Revolution, War, and Peace* (1979), and two studies by Thomas A. Bailey, *Woodrow Wilson and the Lost Peace* (1944) and *Woodrow Wilson and the Great Betrayal* (1945). Lloyd E. Ambrosius updates the realist critique of Wilson in *Woodrow Wilson and Wilsonian Statecraft* (1991). Consult also N. Gordon Levin, Jr., *Woodrow Wilson and World Politics* (1968); Arno J. Mayer, *Politics and Diplomacy of Peacemaking* (1967); Thomas J. Knock, *To End All Wars: Woodrow Wilson and the Quest for a New World Order* (1992); Robert H. Ferrell, *Woodrow Wilson and World War I, 1917–1921* (1985); and Lloyd C. Gardner, *Safe for Democracy: The Anglo-American Response to Revolution, 1913–1923* (1984). Lodge is somewhat rehabilitated in John A. Garraty, *Henry Cabot Lodge* (1953), and especially in William C. Widenor, *Henry Cabot Lodge and the Search for an American Foreign Policy* (1980). The end of this troubled period is sketched in Burl Noggle, *Into the Twenties: The U.S. from Armistice to Normalcy* (1974).

CHAPTER 32

PRIMARY SOURCE DOCUMENTS

For the fallout from the red scare, see Walter Lippmann's eloquent plea for the lives of the Italian-American radicals Sacco and Vanzetti in the New York *World** (August 19, 1927). For caustic fictional versions of the decade's social conditions, see the novels of Sinclair Lewis: *Main Street* (1920), *Babbitt* (1922), and *Arrowsmith* (1925).

SECONDARY SOURCES

The best introduction to the 1920s is William Leuchtenburg, *The Perils of Prosperity, 1914–1932* (1958). Also strong is Michael E. Parrish, *Anxious Decades: America in Prosperity and Depression, 1920–1941* (1992). Frederick Lewis Allen, *Only Yesterday* (1931), is an evocative recollection of the texture of life in the decade. Equally informative are Robert S. Lynd and Helen M. Lynd's classic sociological studies, *Middletown* (1929) and *Middletown in Transition* (1937). Robert K. Murray, *Red Scare* (1955), is authoritative; on the same subject, see Stanley Coben, *A. Mitchell Palmer* (1963). Immigration restriction is dealt with

in John Higham, *Strangers in the Land* (1955). The standard work on the revived Klan is David M. Chalmers, *Hooded Americanism* (rev. ed., 1981). Also valuable is Nancy MacLean, *Behind the Mask of Chivalry: The Making of the Second KKK* (1993), and Kathleen Blee, *Women of the Klan: Racism and Gender in the 1920s* (1991). The changing experiences of women are discussed in Winnifred Wandersee, *Women's Work and Family Values, 1920–1940* (1981); Lois Scharf and Joan M. Jensen, eds., *Decades of Discontent: The Women's Movement, 1920–1940* (1983); Nancy F. Cott, *The Grounding of Modern Feminism* (1987); and Phyllis Palmer, *Domesticity and Dirt: Housewives and Domestic Servants in the United States, 1920–1945* (1990). Prohibition is handled in Norman H. Clark's highly readable *Deliver Us from Evil* (1976). On a related subject, see Humbert S. Nelli, *The Business of Crime* (1976). Revealing on the Scopes trial are Lawrence W. Levine's sensitive study of William Jennings Bryan, *Defender of the Faith* (1965), and Edward J. Larsen, *Summer for the Gods: The Scopes Trial and America's Continuing Debate over Science and Religion* (1997). On the economy, see Alfred D. Chandler, Jr., *Strategy and Structure: Chapters in the History of Industrial Enterprise* (1962); Irving Bernstein, *The Lean Years: A History of the American Worker, 1920–1933* (1960); and Daniel Nelson, *Frederick Winslow Taylor and the Rise of Scientific Management* (1980). On the culture of the 1920s, see Stanley Coben, *Rebellion Against Victorianism: The Impetus for Cultural Change in 1920s America* (1991), and Lynn Dumenil, *The Modern Temper: American Culture and Society in the 1920s* (1995). On advertising, consult Stuart Ewen, *Captains of Consciousness* (1976); Daniel Pope, *The Making of Modern Advertising* (1983); and Roland Marchand, *Advertising the American Dream: Making Way for Modernity* (1985). Susan Douglas, *Inventing American Broadcasting* (1987), and Susan Smulyan, *Selling Radio* (1994), describe the birth of a mass media. Movies are featured in Lary May, *Screening Out the Past: The Birth of Mass Culture and the Motion Picture Industry* (1980), and Robert Sklar, *Movie-Made America* (1975). The "youth culture" is the subject of Paula Fass, *The Damned and the Beautiful: American Youth in the 1920s* (1977). Changing sexual attitudes are analyzed in David M. Kennedy, *Birth Control in America: The Career of Margaret Sanger* (1970), and Linda Gordon, *Woman's Body, Woman's Right: A Social History of Birth Control in America* (1976). See also Ellen Chesler, *Woman of Valor: Margaret Sanger and the Birth Control Movement in America* (1992). Gilbert Osofsky describes the background of the Harlem Renaissance in *Harlem: The Making of a Ghetto, 1890–1930* (1966). See also David Lewis, *When Harlem Was in Vogue* (1981). William M. Tuttle, *Race Riot: Chicago in the Red Summer of 1919* (1970), describes the violent side of race relations in the 1920s. The "Great Migration" of blacks to the North is described in James R. Grossman's *Land of Hope: Chicago, Black Southerners, and the Great Migration* (1989). Judith Stein, *The World of Marcus Garvey* (1986), discusses the most popular black leader of the period. Richard W. Fox and T. J. Jackson Lears have edited a fascinating collection of essays on American culture, *The Culture of Consumption: Critical Essays in American History, 1880–1980* (1983). Also see William Leach, *Land of Desire: Merchants, Power and the Rise of a New American Culture* (1993), and Warren I. Susman, *Culture as History: The Transformation of American Society in the Twentieth Century* (1984). David M. Kennedy, *Over Here: The First World War and American Society*

(1980), pays special attention to the literature that emerged from the war experience.

CHAPTER 33

PRIMARY SOURCE DOCUMENTS

Herbert Hoover, *American Individualism* (1922), contains the philosophy of the man and his times. See also Hoover's "Rugged Individualism" speech (1928), in Richard Hofstadter, *Great Issues in American History*. As the Great Depression descended, Hoover fought to maintain his principles in a noteworthy speech at New York's Madison Square Garden*. (*New York Times*, November 1, 1932). On foreign affairs, see the "Stimson Doctrine" (1931), in Henry Steele Commager, ed., *Documents of American History*.

SECONDARY SOURCES

A lively introduction to the postwar decade is Burl Noggle, *Into the Twenties: The United States from Armistice to Normalcy* (1974). On Harding, see Robert K. Murray's balanced *The Harding Era* (1969); consult also his *Politics of Normalcy: Government Theory and Practice in the Harding-Coolidge Era* (1973). John D. Hicks presents the standard liberal interpretation of the decade in *Republican Ascendancy* (1960). Burl Noggle looks at the chief scandal of the period in *Teapot Dome* (1962). David M. Kennedy, *Over Here: The First World War and American Society* (1980), discusses postwar race relations and demobilization as well as the international economic aftermath of the war, a subject treated at greater length in Joan Hoff Wilson, *American Business and Foreign Policy, 1920–1933* (1971). Robert Cohen explores *When the Old Left Was Young: Student Radicals and America's First Mass Student Movement, 1929–1941* (1993). On labor, see Robert H. Zieger, *American Worker, American Unions, 1920–1985* (1986), for a concise summary. On the Washington disarmament conference, see Thomas H. Buckley, *The United States and the Washington Conference, 1921–1922* (1970). The Democratic party is analyzed in Douglas Craig, *After Wilson: The Struggle for the Democratic Party, 1920–1934* (1992), and David Burner, *The Politics of Provincialism* (1967). The complicated international financial tangle of the 1920s is deftly discussed in Herbert Feis, *The Diplomacy of the Dollar* (1950), and in the early chapters of Charles Kindleberger, *The World in Depression* (1973). The drama of the 1928 election is captured in Allan J. Lichtman, *Prejudice and the Old Politics: The Presidential Election of 1928* (1979), and Oscar Handlin, *Al Smith and His America* (1958). The election is placed in a larger context in Samuel Lubell's classic *The Future of American Politics* (1952) and Paul Kleppner's *Who Voted? The Dynamics of Electoral Turnout, 1870–1980* (1982). George H. Nash's multivolume biography, *The Life of Herbert Hoover* (1988), is detailed, while the best brief biography of Hoover is Joan Hoff Wilson, *Herbert Hoover, Forgotten Progressive* (1975). Brilliantly unsympathetic toward Hoover is Arthur M. Schlesinger, Jr., *The Crisis of the Old Order, 1919–1933* (1957). On the depression itself, consult John K. Galbraith's breezy *The Great Crash, 1929* (1955); Peter Temin's trenchant *Did Monetary Factors Cause the Great Depression?* (1976); Robert McElvaine's *The Great Depression* (1984); and

Lester V. Chandler's comprehensive *America's Greatest Depression* (1970).

CHAPTER 34

PRIMARY SOURCE DOCUMENTS

James Agee and Walker Evans, *Let Us Now Praise Famous Men* (1940), brilliantly evokes the misery of the depression in words and photographs. Franklin D. Roosevelt's dramatic "First Inaugural Address" (1933), in Henry Steele Commager, ed., *Documents of American History*, captured the imagination of the distressed nation. Less successful was Roosevelt's "Radio Address on Supreme Court Reform" (1937), in Richard Hofstadter, *Great Issues in American History* (1982). See also Dorothy Thompson's attack on the Court plan in the *Washington Star*, February 10, 1937.* Clifford Odets's play *Waiting for Lefty* (1935) and John Steinbeck's novel *The Grapes of Wrath* (1939) exemplify the literature stimulated by the Great Depression. Robert S. McElvaine has collected a compelling set of letters in *Down and Out in the Great Depression* (1983).

SECONDARY SOURCES

A masterly summation is William E. Leuchtenburg, *Franklin D. Roosevelt and the New Deal, 1932–1940* (1963). See also Leuchtenburg's *The Supreme Court Reborn: The Constitutional Revolution in the Age of Roosevelt* (1995). Briefer and more critical of the limitations of reform is Paul Conkin, *The New Deal* (rev. ed., 1975). A detailed biography is Frank Freidel, *Franklin D. Roosevelt* (4 vols., 1952–1973). Brilliantly pro-FDR are the three volumes of Arthur M. Schlesinger, Jr., *Age of Roosevelt: The Crisis of the Old Order* (1957), *The Coming of the New Deal* (1959), and *The Politics of Upheaval* (1960). John M. Blum, *From the Morgenthau Diaries* (3 vols., 1959–1967), gives the perspective of an important New Deal insider, as does T. H. Watkins, *Righteous Pilgrim: The Life and Times of Harold L. Ickes, 1874–1952* (1990). The views of other contemporaries may be found in Frances Perkins, *The Roosevelt I Knew* (1946); Rexford G. Tugwell, *In Search of Roosevelt* (1972); and Raymond Moley, *After Seven Years* (1939). A concise biography is Frank Freidel, *Franklin D. Roosevelt: Rendezvous with Destiny* (1990). The social impact of the depression is vividly etched in Studs Terkel, *Hard Times* (1970); Ann Banks, *First Person America* (1980); and James N. Gregory, *American Exodus: The Dust Bowl Migration and Okie Culture in California* (1989). For a comprehensive portrait of New Deal America, see David M. Kennedy's *Freedom from Fear: The American People in Depression and War* (1999). Two volumes by Lois Scharf are of interest: *To Work and to Wed: Female Employment, Feminism, and the Great Depression* (1980) and *Eleanor Roosevelt: First Lady of American Liberalism* (1987). Also see Susan Ware, *Beyond Suffrage: Women in the New Deal* (1981), and Blanche Wiesen Cook, *Eleanor Roosevelt: A Life* (1992). Alan Brinkley brilliantly chronicles *Voices of Protest: Huey Long, Father Coughlin, and the Great Depression* (1982). See also his treatment of the later New Deal in *The End of Reform* (1995). For a sharply critical portrayal, see William Ivy Hair, *The Kingfish and His Realm: The Life and Times of Huey P. Long* (1991). Greg Mitchell describes *The Campaign of the Century: Upton Sinclair's Race for*

Governor of California and the Birth of Media Politics (1992). Labor is dealt with in Irving Bernstein, *Turbulent Years* (1970), and Lizabeth Cohen, *Making a New Deal: Industrial Workers in Chicago, 1919–1939* (1990). Ellis Hawley, *The New Deal and the Problem of Monopoly* (1966), is a superb analysis of the conflicting currents of economic policy in the Roosevelt administration. W. Andrew Achenbaum examines one of the era's most important pieces of legislation in *Social Security: Visions and Revisions* (1986). On the TVA, see Erwin C. Hargrave, *Prisoners of Myth, The Leadership of the Tennessee Valley Authority, 1933–1990* (1994). A comprehensive assessment by several noted scholars is Harvard Sitkoff, ed., *Fifty Years Later: The New Deal Evaluated* (1985). James Patterson, *The New Deal and the States* (1969), examines the local impact of the Roosevelt measures, as does Charles H. Trout, *Boston, the Great Depression, and the New Deal* (1977). Indians receive special attention in Graham D. Taylor, *The New Deal and American Indian Tribalism* (1980), and Kenneth R. Philp, *John Collier's Crusade for Indian Reform* (1977). On blacks, see Nancy J. Weiss, *Farewell to the Party of Lincoln: Black Politics in the Age of FDR* (1983). Richard Lowitt analyzes *The New Deal and the West* (1984). On the impact of the Great Depression and the New Deal in the South, see Gavin Wright, *Old South, New South: Revolutions in the Southern Economy Since the Civil War* (1986); Bruce Schulman, *From Cotton Belt to Sunbelt* (1990); and James Cobb and Michael Namaroto, eds., *The New Deal and the South* (1984). Especially good on intellectual history is Richard H. Pells, *Radical Visions and American Dreams: Culture and Social Thought in the Depression Years* (1973). A trenchant appraisal of the New Deal legacy is Steven Fraser and Gary Gerstle, eds., *The Rise and Fall of the New Deal Order* (1989).

CHAPTER 35

PRIMARY SOURCE DOCUMENTS

For background on the date that will live in infamy, see *Pearl Harbor Attack: Hearings Before the Joint Committee on the Investigation of the Pearl Harbor Attack*, 79th Cong., 1st sess.* (1946). Franklin D. Roosevelt's "Quarantine the Aggressors Speech" (1937), in Richard Hofstadter, *Great Issues in American History* (1982), revealed what would become the goal of the president's foreign policy in succeeding years. See also Roosevelt's "Press Conference on Lend-Lease" (1940), in *The Public Papers and Addresses of Franklin D. Roosevelt, 1940 Volume* (1941). For opposition to lend-lease, see the speech of January 12, 1941, by Montana senator Burton K. Wheeler, *Congressional Record*, 77th Cong., 1st sess., Appendix, 178–179.* Charles A. Lindbergh elaborated the isolationist position in the *New York Times* (April 24, 1941).* Warren F. Kimball, ed., *Churchill and Roosevelt: The Complete Correspondence* (1984), is enlightening on many topics.

SECONDARY SOURCES

Indispensable and comprehensive is Robert Dallek, *Franklin D. Roosevelt and American Foreign Policy, 1932–1945* (rev. ed., 1995). Also strong is Kenneth S. Davis, *FDR: Into the Storm, 1937–1940; A History* (1993). A useful brief survey is John E. Wiltz, *From Isolation to War, 1931–1941* (1968). More special-

ized is Lloyd Gardner, *Economic Aspects of New Deal Diplomacy* (1964). Isolationism is ably handled in Manfred Jonas, *Isolationism in America, 1935–1941* (1966); Thomas Guinsburg, *The Pursuit of Isolationism in the United States Senate from Versailles to Pearl Harbor* (1982); and Robert A. Divine, *The Reluctant Belligerent* (1965). Sympathetic to the isolationists is Wayne S. Cole, *Roosevelt and the Isolationists, 1932–1945* (1983) and *Charles A. Lindbergh and the Battle Against American Intervention in World War II* (1974). On Good Neighborism, consult Irwin F. Gellman, *Good Neighbor Diplomacy* (1979). The Spanish Civil War is dealt with in Allen Guttmann, *The Wound in the Heart: America and the Spanish Civil War* (1962), and Douglas Little, *Malevolent Neutrality: The United States, Great Britain, and the Origins of the Spanish Civil War* (1985). On the Far East, see Dorothy Borg, *The United States and the Far Eastern Crisis of 1933–1938* (1964); P. W. Schroeder, *The Axis Alliance and Japanese-American Relations, 1941* (1958); Akira Iriye, *The Globalizing of America, 1913–1945* (1993); and Akira Iriye and Warren Cohen, eds., *American, Chinese, and Japanese Perspectives on Wartime Asia, 1931–49* (1990). Warren F. Kimball analyzes *The Most Unsordid Act: Lend Lease, 1939–1941* (1969). David L. Porter examines *The Seventy-Sixth Congress and World War II, 1939–1940* (1979). The Japanese attack on Pearl Harbor is considered in Gordon W. Prange, *At Dawn We Slept* (1981), and Michael Slackman, *Target: Pearl Harbor* (1990). A provocative analysis of the reasons (or lack thereof) for U.S. entry into the conflict is Bruce Russett, *No Clear and Present Danger* (1972). See also Donald Cameron Watt, *How War Came: The Immediate Origins of the Second World War, 1938–1939* (1989).

CHAPTER 36

PRIMARY SOURCE DOCUMENTS

Vivid portraits of the fighting are found in Ernie Pyle, *Here Is Your War* (1943) and *Brave Men* (1944). On the atomic bomb, consult the reactions of the *Nippon Times** (August 10, 1945), *The Christian Century** (August 29, 1945), and President Truman's justification of the bombing in *Memoirs of Harry S Truman** (1955).

SECONDARY SOURCES

See John M. Blum, *V Was for Victory: Politics and American Culture During World War II* (1976), and John W. Jeffries, *Wartime America: The World War II Home Front* (1996), for discussions of the home front. Consult also Doris Kearns Goodwin, *No Ordinary Time* (1994); William L. O'Neill, *A Democracy at War: America's Fight at Home and Abroad in World War II* (1993); Richard Polenberg, *War and Society: The United States, 1941–1945* (1972); and Harold G. Vatter, *The U.S. Economy in World War II* (1985). Studs Terkel has compiled an interesting oral history of the war experience in *The Good War* (1984). On women, see William H. Chafe, *The American Woman: Her Changing Social, Economic, and Political Roles, 1920–1970* (1972); Susan M. Hartmann, *The Home Front and Beyond* (1982); and D'Ann Campbell, *Women at War with America: Private Lives in a Patriotic Era* (1984). On the internment of the Japanese-Americans, consult Roger Daniels, *Prisoners Without Trial* (1993) and *Concentra-*

tion Camps U.S.A. (1971); Peter Irons, *Justice at War: The Story of the Japanese-American Internment Cases* (1983); and the oral histories provided in John Tateishi, ed., *And Justice for All* (1984). On blacks, see Neil A. Wynn, *The Afro-Americans and the Second World War* (1976), and Nicholas Lemann, *The Promised Land: The Great Black Migration and How It Changed America* (1991). Nelson Lichtenstein examines *Labor's War at Home: The CIO in World War II* (1983), and Gerald Nash describes *The American West Transformed: The Impact of the Second World War* (1985). The military history of the war is capably summarized in H. P. Willmott, *The Great Crusade: A New Complete History of the Second World War* (1990), and in Gerhard Weinberg's massively detailed *A World at Arms* (1994). See also Russell F. Weigley, *Eisenhower's Lieutenants: The Campaigns of France and Germany, 1944–1945* (1981); Eric Larrabee, *Commander in Chief: Franklin Delano Roosevelt, His Lieutenants, and Their War* (1987); and David Eisenhower, *Eisenhower at War: 1943–45* (1986). Ed Cray profiles *General of the Army: George C. Marshall, Soldier and Statesman* (1990). A good introduction to wartime diplomacy is Gaddis Smith, *American Diplomacy During the Second World War* (1965). More detailed are Herbert Feis's three volumes: *Churchill, Roosevelt, Stalin* (2nd ed., 1967), *Between War and Peace: The Potsdam Conference* (1960), and *The Atomic Bomb and the End of World War II* (1966). Also valuable are Robert Dallek's work, cited in Chapter 35; John L. Gaddis, *The United States and the Origins of the Cold War, 1941–1947* (1972); and two "revisionist" studies that are highly critical of American policy: Gabriel Kolko, *The Politics of War: The World and United States Foreign Policy, 1943–1945* (1968), and Lloyd Gardner, *Architects of Illusion: Men and Ideas in American Foreign Policy, 1941–1949* (1970). The war in Asia is covered in Ronald H. Spector's gracefully written *Eagle Against the Sun: The American War with Japan* (1985). John W. Dower explores the racial ideas that underlay the war against Japan in *War Without Mercy: Race and Power in the Pacific War* (1986) and the war's aftermath in his award-winning *Embracing Defeat: Japan in the Wake of World War II* (1999). Paul Fussell contrasts actual combat and wartime rhetoric in *Wartime: Understanding and Behavior in the Second World War* (1989). On the atomic bomb, the most comprehensive account is Richard Rhodes, *The Making of the Atomic Bomb* (1986). Also see Richard G. Hewlett and Oscar E. Anderson, Jr., *The New World* (1962); Martin J. Sherwin, *A World Destroyed: The Atomic Bomb and the Grand Alliance* (1975); and Gar Alperovitz's critiques of American nuclear strategy, *Atomic Diplomacy* (rev. ed., 1985) and *The Decision to Use the Atomic Bomb* (1995). Paul Boyer, *By the Bomb's Early Light* (1985), analyzes the bomb's impact on the American mind.

CHAPTER 37

PRIMARY SOURCE DOCUMENTS

George F. Kennan's "long telegram,"* in *Foreign Relations of the United States, 1946*, vol. 6 (1969), outlined the containment doctrine that would form the foundation of U.S. foreign policy in the Cold War era. Harry S Truman first applied the containment doctrine when he enunciated the Truman Doctrine,* *Congressional Record*, 80th Cong., 1st sess., 1981 (1947). On the changing postwar family, consult Dr. Benjamin Spock, *The Common Sense Book of Baby and Child Care** (1957).

SECONDARY SOURCES

Lucid overviews of the postwar years can be found in James Patterson, *Grand Expectations* (1996); William H. Chafe, *The Unfinished Journey: America Since World War II* (1986); John Patrick Diggins, *The Proud Decades: America in War and Peace, 1941–1960* (1988); and William O'Neill, *American High: The Years of Confidence, 1945–1960* (1986). Harold G. Vatter gives a valuable account of *The United States Economy in the 1950s* (1963). Edward Denison, in *The Sources of Economic Growth in the United States* (1962), argues that improved education was the key to economic growth. The southern economic boom is charted in two books by James C. Cobb: *The Selling of the South* (1982) and *Industrialization and Southern Society* (1984). The rise of the Sunbelt is dramatically portrayed in Kirkpatrick Sale, *Power Shift* (1975), and Kevin Phillips, *The Emerging Republican Majority* (1970). Suburbia is the subject of Herbert J. Gans, *The Levittowners* (1967); Zane Miller, *Suburb* (1981); Carol O'Connor, *A Sort of Utopia: Scarsdale, 1891–1981* (1983); and Kenneth T. Jackson's sweeping synthesis, *Crabgrass Frontier* (1986). On the baby boom and its implications, consult Landon Y. Jones, *Great Expectations: America and the Baby Boom Generation* (1980), and Michael X. Delli Carpini, *Stability and Change in American Politics: The Coming of Age of the Generation of the 1960s* (1986). Mark Silk chronicles the role of organized religion in America since the 1940s in *Spiritual Politics: Religion and America Since World War II* (1988). On the origins of the Cold War, see the titles cited in Chapter 36 by John L. Gaddis, Lloyd Gardner, Gar Alperovitz, Martin J. Sherwin, Herbert Feis, and Gabriel Kolko. Consult also Gaddis's *Strategies of Containment* (1982) and Joyce and Gabriel Kolko's *The Limits of Power: The World and United States Foreign Policy, 1945–1954* (1972), which roundly condemns Washington's actions. For an ambitious revisionist synthesis, see Thomas J. McCormick, *America's Half-Century: U.S. Foreign Policy in the Cold War* (1989). Useful surveys of the diplomatic history of the period, all of them in varying degrees critical of American policy, are Stephen Ambrose, *Rise to Globalism: American Foreign Policy since 1938* (rev. ed., 1983); Walter LaFeber, *America, Russia and the Cold War, 1945–1984* (8th ed., 1997); and Daniel Yergin, *Shattered Peace* (1977). Among the most comprehensive post-revisionist studies is Melvyn P. Leffler, *A Preponderance of Power: National Security, the Truman Administration, and the Cold War* (1992). On the first years of nuclear diplomacy, see Gregg Herken, *The Winning Weapon: The Atomic Bomb in the Cold War, 1945–1950* (1980). Broader accounts that include discussion of domestic events are David McCullough, *Truman* (1992), and Alonzo L. Hamby, *Beyond the New Deal: Harry S Truman and American Liberalism* (1973). The implications of the election of 1948 are examined in Samuel Lubell's perceptive *The Future of American Politics* (1952). Various aspects of foreign policy are analyzed in Timothy P. Ireland, *Creating the Entangling Alliance: The Origins of the North Atlantic Treaty Organization* (1981); Gordon Chang, *Friends and Enemies: The United States, China and the Soviet Union* (1990); Michael Schaller, *The American Occupation of Japan: The Origins of the Cold War in Asia* (1985); and Robert M. Blum, *Drawing the Line: The Origins of the American Containment Policy in East Asia* (1982). Korea is discussed in Callum A. MacDonald, *Korea: The War Before Vietnam* (1986); Bruce Cumings, ed., *Child of Conflict: The Korean-American Relationship, 1943–1953* (1983); and Bruce Cumings and Jon Halliday, *Korea: The Unknown War* (1988). On the "red scare" at home, see Richard Fried, *Nightmare in Red* (1990); Ellen Schrecker, *Many Are the Crimes* (1998); and David M. Oshinsky, *A Conspiracy So Immense: The World of Joe McCarthy* (1983). Daniel Bell, ed., *The Radical Right* (1963), places McCarthyism in a larger context. See also David W. Reinhard, *The Republican Right Since 1945* (1983). For more on J. Edgar Hoover, see Thomas Gid Powers, *Secrecy and Power: The Life of J. Edgar Hoover* (1987). Examinations of the impact of the Cold War on American culture include Nora Sayre, *Running Time: The Films of the Cold War* (1982); Ellen Schrecker, *No Ivory Tower: McCarthyism and the Universities* (1986); and Richard H. Pells, *The Liberal Mind in a Conservative Age* (1985). Valuable personal reflections by policymakers include Truman's own *Year of Decisions* (1955) and *Years of Trial and Hope* (1956); George F. Kennan, *Memoirs, 1925–1950* (1967); Dean Acheson, *Present at the Creation* (1969); and Charles Bohlen, *Witness to History* (1973).

CHAPTER 38

PRIMARY SOURCE DOCUMENTS

Earl Warren's decision in *Brown v. Board of Education of Topeka*, 347 U.S. 492–495* (1954), altered the course of race relations in the United States. It also sparked the opposition of 100 southern congressmen, *Congressional Record*, 84th Cong., 2nd sess., 4515–4516* (1956). Eisenhower's Farewell Address* (1961) warned of the dangers of the "military-industrial complex." John Kenneth Galbraith criticized the consumer culture in *The Affluent Society** (1958). Joe McCarthy's vitriol can be found in his *McCarthyism: The Fight for America** (1952).

SECONDARY SOURCES

The era is surveyed readably in several works, including those titles by James Patterson, William H. Chafe, John Patrick Diggins, and William O'Neill cited in Chapter 37. Eisenhower is the subject of Stephen Ambrose's two-volume biography, *Eisenhower: Soldier, General of the Army, President-Elect, 1890–1952* (1983) and *Eisenhower: The President* (1984). See also Jeff Broadwater, *Eisenhower and the Anti-Communist Crusade* (1992), and Chester Pach and Elmo Richardson, *The Presidency of Dwight D. Eisenhower* (1991). Fred I. Greenstein portrays Eisenhower as the master of *The Hidden Hand Presidency* (1982). Robert A. Divine, *Eisenhower and the Cold War* (1981), praises his diplomatic restraint. Various aspects of foreign policy are covered in Douglas Brinkley, *Dean Acheson: The Cold War Years, 1953–71* (1992); Richard Immerman, *The CIA in Guatemala: The Foreign Policy of Intervention* (1982); Walter Isaacson and Evan Thomas, *The Wise Men: Six Friends and the World They Made: Acheson, Bohlen, Harriman, Kennan, Lovett, McCloy* (1986); Richard E. Welch, Jr., *Response to Revolution: The United States and the Cuban Revolution, 1959–1961* (1985); Robert Schulzinger, *The Wise Men of Foreign Affairs: The History of the Council on Foreign Relations* (1984); and Herman Kahn's chilling *On Thermonuclear War* (1960). See also Gordon Chang's book cited in Chapter 37. For background and consequences of the Supreme Court's 1954 desegregation decision, see Richard Kluger, *Simple Justice: The History of Brown v. Board of Education* (1976); Raymond Wolters,

The Burden of Brown: Thirty Years of School Desegregation (1984); and Robert A. Margo, *Race and Schooling in the South, 1880–1950* (1990). Especially rich are Taylor Branch, *Parting the Waters: America in the King Years, 1954–1963* (1988), and David J. Garrow, *Bearing the Cross: Martin Luther King, Jr., and the Southern Christian Leadership Conference* (1986). The South before the civil rights movement is ably described in John Egerton, *Speak Now Against the Day: The Generation Before the Civil Rights Movement in the South* (1994), and Leon F. Litwack, *Trouble in Mind: Black Southerners in the Age of Jim Crow* (1998). For one man's experience of integration, see Jules Tygiel, *Baseball's Great Experiment: Jackie Robinson and His Legacy* (1983). Three excellent studies of race in northern cities are Thomas Sugrue, *Origins of the Urban Crisis* (1996); Arnold Hirsch, *Making the Second Ghetto: Race and Housing in Chicago, 1940–1960* (1983); and John T. McGreevy, *Parish Boundaries: The Catholic Encounter with Race in the Twentieth Century Urban North* (1996). Relevant memoirs and biographies include William O. Douglas, *The Court Years, 1939–1975* (1980); G. Edward White, *Earl Warren* (1982); John Bartlow Martin, *Adlai Stevenson* (2 vols., 1976–1977); and Townsend Hoopes, *The Devil and John Foster Dulles* (1973). On the election of 1960, see Theodore H. White's colorful *The Making of the President, 1960* (1961). For more on cultural developments during the 1950s, see Lary May, ed., *Recasting America: Culture and Politics in the Age of the Cold War* (1989); Elaine May, *Homeward Bound: American Families in the Cold War Era* (1988); Stephanie Coontz, *The Way We Never Were* (1992); Tino Balio, ed., *Hollywood in the Age of Television* (1990); David Halberstam, *The Fifties* (1993); Stephen J. Whitfield, *The Culture of the Cold War* (1991); Tom Engelhardt, *The End of Victory Culture* (1995); and Eugenia Kaledin, *Mothers and More: American Women in the 1950s* (1984). On postwar literature, see Tony Tanner, *City of Words* (1971), and Alfred Kazin, *Bright Book of Life* (1973). On the arts, consult Edward Lucie-Smith, *Late Modern: The Visual Arts Since 1945* (1969). On television, see David Marc, *Demographic Vistas: Television in American Culture* (1984), and Lynn Spigel, *Make Room for TV: Television and the Family Ideal in Postwar America* (1992).

CHAPTER 39

PRIMARY SOURCE DOCUMENTS

Norman Mailer paints vivid portraits of the 1968 conventions in *Miami and the Siege of Chicago* (1968) and of the antiwar March on Washington in *Armies of the Night* (1968). Martin Luther King, Jr.'s *Letter from Birmingham Jail** (1963) eloquently defends the civil rights movement. The progress of the war in Vietnam is chronicled in *The Pentagon Papers** (1971). Students for a Democratic Society (1962) and Young Americans for Freedom (1960) both issued manifestos* that suggest the political temper of the era. Stewart Alsop penned a notable editorial in *Newsweek** (1970) that reflects the "establishment's" disgust with the cultural upheavals of the decade.

SECONDARY SOURCES

The tumultuous decade of the 1960s is treated in William L. O'Neill, *Coming Apart: An Informal History of America in the*

1960s (1971); Howard Brink, *Age of Contradiction* (1998); and John Morton Blum, *Years of Discord* (1991), as well as in the surveys cited in Chapter 38. On Kennedy see Irving Bernstein, *Promises Kept: John F. Kennedy's New Frontier* (1991); Thomas Reeves, *A Question of Character: A Life of John F. Kennedy* (1991), Theodore C. Sorenson, *Kennedy* (1965); and Arthur M. Schlesinger, Jr., *A Thousand Days* (1965). More critical is Henry Fairlie, *The Kennedy Promise* (1973). Other useful biographies include Arthur M. Schlesinger, Jr., *Robert F. Kennedy and His Times* (1978), and Nigel Hamilton, *JFK: Reckless Youth* (1992). Seymour Harris is informative on *Economics of the Kennedy Years* (1964). Michael Beschloss details *The Crisis Years: Kennedy and Khrushchev, 1960–1963* (1991). The Cuban missile crisis is chronicled in Robert F. Kennedy, *Thirteen Days* (1969), and Graham Allison, *Essence of Decision* (1971). On the space program, consult Walter McDougall, *. . . the Heavens and the Earth* (1985), and Clayton Koppes, *JPL* [Jet Propulsion Laboratory] *and the American Space Program* (1982). Kennedy's assassination is scrutinized, not entirely satisfactorily, in *The Official Warren Commission Report* (1964). See also Gerald Posner, *Case Closed* (1993). On Johnson, a splendid short biography is Bruce J. Schulman, *Lyndon B. Johnson and American Liberalism* (1994). Eric Goldman, *The Tragedy of Lyndon Johnson* (1969), is a sympathetic yet critical account of the Johnson presidency. In the same vein, with a psychoanalytic touch, is Doris Kearns, *Lyndon B. Johnson and the American Dream* (1976). Johnson's own memoir, *The Vantage Point* (1971), is marred by excessive self-justification. Equally unbalanced antidotes are Robert Caro, *The Years of Lyndon Johnson: The Path to Power* (1982) and *Means of Ascent* (1990). More revealing is *Taking Charge: The Johnson White House Tapes, 1963–1964,* edited by Michael Beschloss. For a complex portrait, see Robert Dallek, *Lone Star Rising: Lyndon Johnson and His Times, 1908–1960* (1991). The conditions that called forth the Great Society programs are movingly described in Michael Harrington, *The Other America: Poverty in the United States* (1962). James Patterson summarizes *America's Struggle Against Poverty* (1981). Two superb chronicles of the civil rights movement focusing on Martin Luther King, Jr., are the books by Taylor Branch and David J. Garrow cited in Chapter 38. The racial upheavals of the decade are discussed in John Dittner, *Local People: The Struggle for Civil Rights in Mississippi* (1994); Harvard Sitkoff, *The Struggle for Black Equality, 1954–1992* (1993); Clayborne Carson, *In Struggle: SNCC* [Student Non-Violent Coordinating Committee] *and the Black Awakening of the 1960s* (1981); and William H. Chafe, *Civilities and Civil Rights: Greensboro, North Carolina, and the Black Struggle for Freedom* (1980). See also Alex Haley, ed., *The Autobiography of Malcolm X* (1966), and Eldridge Cleaver, *Soul on Ice* (1968). On the New Left, consult two volumes by Todd Gitlin, *The Sixties: Years of Hope, Days of Rage* (1987) and *The Whole World Is Watching: Mass Media in the Making and Unmaking of the New Left* (1980); James Miller, *"Democracy Is in the Streets": From Port Huron to the Sea of Chicago* (1987); Sara Evans, *Personal Politics* (1979); and Jerry Anderson *The Movement of the Sixties* (1995). On conservatism see Dan Carter, *The Politics of Rage: George Wallace, the Origins of the New Conservativism and the Transformation of American Politics* (1995). On Vietnam, consult Ronald Spector, *The United States Army in Vietnam* (1984); W. H. Brands, *Since Vietnam* (1996); and Stanley Karnow's encyclopedic *Vietnam: A History* (1983). Concise

accounts are George Herring, *America's Longest War* (1986), and Marilyn B. Young, *The Vietnam Wars, 1945–1990* (1991). George Q. Flynn looks at *The Draft, 1940–1973* (1993). See also Christian Appy, *Working-Class War* (1993). Neil Sheehan, *A Bright Shining Lie: John Paul Vann and America in Vietnam* (1988), is a gripping account of one unorthodox commander. Jeffrey P. Kimball, ed., *To Reason Why: The Debate About the Causes of U.S. Involvement in the Vietnam War* (1990), contains readings from academic and public-policy figures. Robert S. McNamara, *In Retrospect: The Tragedy and Lessons of Vietnam* (1995), is the sorrowful apology of one of the war's principal architects for the "mistake" of Vietnam. Two works by John Lewis Gaddis shrewdly analyze the Cold War context of the Vietnam conflict: *The Long Peace* (1987) and *The United States and the End of the Cold War* (1992). See also his *Strategies of Containment* (1982). Presidential elections are described in Theodore H. White's *The Making of the President, 1964* (1965) and *The Making of the President, 1968* (1969). The emergence of a "youth culture" in the 1960s is illuminated in three studies by Kenneth Keniston: *The Uncommitted* (1965), *Young Radicals* (1968), and *Youth and Dissent* (1971). Popular books indicating the mood of the 1960s include Theodore Roszak, *The Making of a Counter-Culture* (1969), and Charles Reich, *The Greening of America* (1970). In *American Genesis: A Century of Invention and Technological Enthusiasm* (1989), Thomas Hughes argues that the sixties marked the end of a century-long national love affair with technology. Also intriguing on the 1960s is Morris Dickstein, *The Gates of Eden: American Culture in the Sixties* (1977). A lucid survey of the intellectual history of the postwar era is Richard Pells, *The Liberal Mind in a Conservative Age* (1984). Changes in attitudes toward sex are scrutinized in Daniel Yankelovich, *The New Morality* (1974); Morton Hunt, *Sexual Behavior in the 1970s* (1974); and Paul Robinson, *The Modernization of Sex* (1976). A useful overview of the decade is Maurice Isserman and Michael Kazin, *America Divided: The Civil War of the 1960s* (2000).

CHAPTER 40

PRIMARY SOURCE DOCUMENTS

Richard Nixon's vision of the international order is delineated in his *RN: The Memoirs of Richard Nixon** (1978). The articles of impeachment reported against Nixon can be found in *House of Representatives Report No. 93-1305,* 93rd Cong., 2nd sess., 1–2* (1974). Opposing opinions on the Panama Canal treaty were voiced by Cyrus Vance and Ronald Reagan, *Hearings Before the Committee on Foreign Relations,* United States Senate, 95th Cong., 1st sess.,10–15, 96–103 (1977). An influential text of the feminist movement was Robin Morgan's anthology *Sisterhood Is Powerful* (1970).

SECONDARY SOURCES

The most comprehensive account of Nixon's early career is Stephen E. Ambrose, *Nixon: The Education of a Politician (1913–1962)* (1987). See also his *Nixon: The Triumph of a Politician, 1962–1972* (1989). Nixon's intriguing personality is examined in Gary Wills, *Nixon Agonistes: The Crisis of the Self-Made*

Man (1970). Theodore White continues his chronicle of presidential electioneering in *The Making of the President, 1972* (1973). Consult also Hunter S. Thompson's savagely masterful *Fear and Loathing on the Campaign Trail, 1972* (1973) and Timothy Crouse's insightful study of the political press, *The Boys on the Bus* (1973). A wide-ranging discussion of the home front is in Kim McQuaid, *The Anxious Years: America in the Vietnam-Watergate Era* (1989). Valuable background on U.S. foreign policy in the Nixon years can be found in David P. Calleo and Benjamin Rowland, *America and the World Political Economy* (1973). On multinational corporations, see Richard J. Barnet and Ronald E. Muller, *Global Reach* (1974). Retrospectives on Vietnam include George C. Herring, *America's Longest War* (1986); William Buckingham, *Operation Ranch Hand: The Air Force and Herbicides in Southeast Asia, 1961–1971* (1982); and William Shawcross's chilling account of U.S. involvement in Cambodia, *Sideshow* (2nd ed., 1981). Shawcross is vigorously rebutted in Henry Kissinger's rich memoirs, *White House Years* (1979) and *Years of Upheaval* (1982). A good biography of Nixon's secretary of state is Robert D. Schulzinger, *Henry Kissinger: Doctor of Diplomacy* (1989). The Middle East is the focus of William B. Quandt, *Decade of Decisions: American Policy Toward the Arab-Israeli Conflict, 1967–1976* (1977), and Wilbur C. Eveland, *Ropes of Sand* (1980). The background to the oil crisis is charted in Michael B. Stoff, *Oil, War and American Security* (1980). Arthur M. Schlesinger, Jr., traces the growth of *The Imperial Presidency* (1973). The Watergate crisis is vividly described in two books by Carl Bernstein and Robert Woodward, *All the President's Men* (1974) and *The Final Days* (1976), and in Stanley I. Kutler, *The Wars of Watergate* (1990). Jonathan Schell, *The Time of Illusion* (1976), assesses the impact of the crisis on the nation's spirit and institutions. Many of the fallen president's former men have written of their involvement in the Watergate affair, including Jeb Stuart Magruder, John Dean, John Erlichman, and H. R. Haldeman. Robert Woodward and Scott Armstrong provide a behind-the-scenes look at key decisions of the Burger Court in *The Brethren: Inside the Supreme Court* (1979). John Robert Greene describes the Nixon and Ford administrations in *The Limits of Power* (1992). "Jerry" Ford, the first appointed president, is analyzed by his former press secretary in J. F. ter Horst, *Gerald Ford and the Future of the Presidency* (1974). For a sharply critical view, see Clark Mollenhoff, *The Man Who Pardoned Nixon* (1976). Consult also Richard Reeves, *A Ford, Not a Lincoln* (1975), and Ford's own *A Time to Heal: The Autobiography of Gerald Ford* (1979). On the extremes of the women's movement in the 1970s, see Alice Echols, *Daring to Be Bad: Radical Feminism in America, 1967–1975* (1989), and Susan Hartman, *The Other Feminists: Activists in the Liberal Establishment* (1998). Jimmy Carter wrote his autobiography, *Why Not the Best?* (1975), as did his wife, Rosalynn Carter, *First Lady from Plains* (1984). They should be supplemented by Burton Kaufman *The Presidency of James Earl Carter* (1993), and John Dambrell, *The Carter Presidency* (1993). Sharply critical are Clark R. Mollenhoff, *The President Who Failed: Carter Out of Control* (1980), and Joseph A. Califano, Jr. (whom Carter fired from the cabinet), *Governing America: An Insider's Report from the White House and the Cabinet* (1981). Other useful memoirs are Carter's own *Keeping Faith* (1982) and National Security Adviser Zbigniew Brzezinski's *Power and Principle* (1983). Gaddis Smith, *Morality, Reason and Power* (1986), surveys Carter's

foreign policy. The debate on Panama spawned two noteworthy books: Walter LaFeber's prowithdrawal *The Panama Canal: The Crisis in Historical Perspective* (1978) and Paul B. Ryan's antiwithdrawal *The Panama Canal Controversy* (1977). On other aspects of Central American policy, see Richard Fagen, *The Nicaraguan Revolution* (1981), and Walter LaFeber's *Inevitable Revolutions: The United States in Central America* (1983). The catastrophe in Iran is described in James Bill, *The Eagle and the Lion: The Tragedy of Americans' Iranian Relations* (1987); Michael Ledeen and William Lewis, *Debacle: The American Failure in Iran* (1981); and Barry M. Rubin, *Paved with Good Intentions: The American Experience and Iran* (1980).

CHAPTER 41

PRIMARY SOURCE DOCUMENTS

The debate over "Reaganomics" can be followed in Reagan's nationally televised address of July 27, 1981, *Weekly Compilation of Presidential Documents,** vol. 17, no. 31, and in the critical response of the *New York Times** (August 2, 1981). See also the comments of Budget Director David Stockman in William Greider, *The Education of David Stockman and Other Americans* (1982). On arms control, see the pastoral letter of the National Council of Catholic Bishops and the reply of Albert Wohlstetter in Charles Kegley and Eugene Wittkopf, eds., *The Nuclear Reader* (1985). On Central American policy, see Reagan's remarkable speech of March 16, 1986.* The inside workings of the Iran-contra scandal can be studied in *The Tower Commission Report* (1987). President Bill Clinton's impeachment and trial can be followed in *The Impeachment and Trial of President Clinton: The Official Transcripts from the House Judiciary Committee Hearings to the Senate Trial*, ed. Merrill McLaughlin (1999).

SECONDARY SOURCES

Garry Wills, *Reagan's America: Innocents at Home* (1987), and Haynes Johnson, *Sleepwalking Through History: America in the Reagan Years* (1997), survey the Reagan era. Reagan is portrayed in Laurence Barrett, *Gambling with History* (1984); Fred Greenstein, *The Reagan Presidency* (1983); Michael Schaller, *Reckoning with Reagan* (1992); and Lou Cannon, *President Reagan: The Role of a Lifetime* (1992). Reagan's economic policies are discussed in Paul C. Roberts, *The Supply-Side Revolution* (1984), and are sharply criticized in David A. Stockman, *The Triumph of Politics: Why the Reagan Revolution Failed* (1986). Other views on the economy can be found in Lester Thurow, *The Zero-Sum Society* (1981), and Samuel Bowles et al., *Beyond the Wasteland* (1984). The debate over nuclear policy is covered in R. James Woolsey, *Nuclear Arms* (1984); Strobe Talbott, *The Russians and Reagan* (1984); and Charles Kegley and Eugene Wittkopf, eds., *The Nuclear Reader* (1985). The neoconservative movement is best elucidated by the writings of its leaders. See Norman Podhoretz, *Breaking Ranks* (1979), and Irving Kristol, *Reflections of a Neoconservative* (1983). For a critical view, consult Peter Steinfels, *The Neoconservatives* (1979). Issues of special concern to the neoconservatives are treated by Charles Murray, *Losing Ground* (1984), an indictment of federal government social programs. Its conclusions are sharply contested by John E. Schwartz, *America's Hidden Success* (rev. ed., 1988). This debate is put into historical perspective in James T. Patterson, *America's Struggle Against Poverty, 1900–1980* (1981). Two studies of affirmative action are Allan P. Sindler, *Bakke, DeFinis and Minority Admissions* (1978), and J. Harvie Wilkinson, *From Brown to Bakke* (1979). The presidential election of 1980 is chronicled by Jules Witcover and Jack Germond in *Blue Smoke and Mirrors* (1981) and put into historical perspective in Theodore H. White, *America in Search of Itself* (1982). For more on conservatism in the last decades of the twentieth century, see William C. Berman, *America's Right Turn: From Nixon to Bush* (1994). Kevin P. Phillips is also insightful about the implications of the conservative revival in *Post-Conservative America* (1982). Eugene Genovese explores *The Southern Tradition: The Achievement and Limitations of an American Conservatism* (1994). Useful books on the role of religion in modern politics include William Martin, *With God on Our Side: The Rise of the Religious Right in America* (1996); Garry Wills, *Under God: Religion and American Politics* (1990); Robert Wuthrow, *The New Christian Right* (1983); and Richard John Neuhaus, *The Naked Public Square: Religion and Democracy in America* (1984). On the Supreme Court, see Richard L. Pacelle, Jr., *The Transformation of the Supreme Court's Agenda: From the New Deal to the Reagan Administration* (1991). Critical of Reagan are William Leuchtenburg, *In the Shadow of FDR: From Harry Truman to Ronald Reagan* (1983); Paul D. Erickson, *Reagan Speaks: The Making of an American Myth* (1985); Ronnie Duggar, *On Reagan* (1983); June Mayer and Doyle McManus, *Landslide: The Unmaking of the President, 1984–88* (1988); and Richard Reeves, *The Reagan Detour* (1985). More balanced are two books by John L. Palmer, *The Reagan Record* (co-edited with Isabel V. Sawhill, 1984) and *Perspectives on the Reagan Years* (1986). Among the interesting memoirs by Reagan administration officials, in addition to David Stockman's book, are Martin Anderson's strongly pro-Reagan *Revolution* (1989); Secretary of State Alexander Haig's *Caveat* (1984); press secretary Larry Speakes's *Speaking Out* (1988); Michael Deaver's anecdotal *Behind the Scenes* (1987); Donald R. Regan's tattletale *For the Record* (1988); and speechwriter Peggy Noonan's somewhat bemused *What I Saw at the Revolution: A Political Life in the Reagan Era* (1990). Important topics in foreign policy are covered in John Ehrman, *The Rise of Neoconservatism: Intellectuals and Foreign Affairs, 1945–1994* (1995); Walter LaFeber, *Inevitable Revolutions* (2nd ed., 1984), which discusses Central America; Robert Pastor's more probing study, *Condemned to Repetition: The United States and Nicaragua* (1987); and Bob Woodward, *Veil: The Secret Wars of the CIA* (1987). Theodore Draper details the Iran-contra affair in *A Very Thin Line* (1991). In *The Devil We Knew: Americans and the Cold War* (1993), H. W. Brands attempts to calculate how much it cost the United States to win the Cold War. The legacy of the Reagan era is the subject of Kevin P. Phillips's devastating *The Politics of Rich and Poor: Wealth and the American Electorate in the Reagan Aftermath* (1990) and Barbara Ehrenreich's *The Worst Years of Our Lives: Irreverent Notes from a Decade of Greed* (1990). The Clarence Thomas/Anita Hill hearings of 1991 are discussed in Toni Morrison, ed., *Race-ing Justice, En-gendering Power* (1992). Bob Woodward, *The Agenda* (1994), and the same author's *The Choice* (1996) provide inside glimpses of politics in the Clinton

years. For insightful analysis by a historian, see James MacGregor Burns and Georgia J. Sorenson, *Dead Center: Clinton-Gore Leadership and the Perils of Moderation* (1999). On the precedent-shattering First Lady, see David Brock, *The Seduction of Hillary Rodham* (1996). James B. Stewart, *Blood Sport* (1996), is especially good on Clinton's complex relationship with the media. On Clinton's impeachment, see Richard Posner, *An Affair of State: The Investigation, Impeachment, and Trial of President Clinton* (1999).

CHAPTER 42

PRIMARY SOURCE DOCUMENTS

Up-to-date data on income and poverty can be found at the Census Bureau's web site, http://www.census.gov/hhes/income. The classic book that launched the modern women's movement is Betty Friedan, *The Feminine Mystique* (1963). For the views of a Christian conservative on the abortion issue, see Ralph Reed, "We Stand at a Crossroads," *Newsweek* (May 13, 1996). *Statistical Abstract of the United States* is an annual government publication with a wealth of information on a variety of topics, including immigration, Social Security funding, and the social and economic condition of minorities.

SECONDARY SOURCES

A useful overview of recent history is Paul Boyer, *Promises to Keep: The United States Since World War II* (1995). Growing income inequality is discussed in Barbara Ehrenreich, *Fear of Falling: The Inner Life of the Middle Class* (1989), and in Kevin P. Phillips, *The Politics of Rich and Poor: Wealth and the American Electorate in the Reagan Aftermath* (1990). The evolving social participation of women, and the dilemmas thereby created, are clearly spelled out in Rosalind Rosenberg, *Divided Lives* (1992), and in William H. Chafe, *The Paradox of Change: American Women in the 20th Century* (1991). See also Betty Friedan, *The Second Stage* (1981); Sylvia Ann Hewlett, *A Lesser Life: The Myth of Women's Liberation in America* (1986); Susanne M. Bianchi, *American Women in Transition* (1987); Marion Faux, *Roe vs. Wade* (1988); Jean E. Friedman, et al., eds., *Our American Sisters* (1987); and Susan Faludi's provocative best-seller, *Backlash: The Undeclared War Against American Women* (1991). George Masnick and Mary Jo Bane, *The Nation's Families: 1960–1990* (1980), is rich in statistical information. For a brilliant discussion of the same subject from an economic perspective, see Victor R. Fuchs, *How We Live* (1983), and also his *Women's Quest for Economic Equality* (1988). On the looming problems in the Social Security system, see Peter G. Peterson, *Will America Grow Up Before It Grows Old?* (1996); for a provocative analysis of the leading senior citizens' lobby, the American Association of Retired Persons, consult Charles R. Morris, *The AARP: America's Most Powerful Lobby and the Clash of Generations* (1996). George J. Borjas turns an economist's critical eye on recent immigration in *Friends or Strangers* (1990). America's newest immigrants are the subjects of David M. Reimers, *Still the Golden Door: The Third World Comes to America* (1986). On Mexican-Americans, see Carlos Munoz, Jr., *Youth, Identity, Power: The Chicano Movement* (1989); George J. Sanchez, *Becoming Mexican American* (1989);

and Richard Rodriguez's poignant memoir, *Hunger of Memory* (1982). Asian-Americans are discussed in Bill Ong Hing, *Making and Remaking Asian America Through Immigration Policy* (1993), and Ronald Takaki, *Strangers from a Different Shore* (1989). On blacks, see Andrew Hacker, *Two Nations: Black and White, Separate, Hostile, Unequal* (1992), and Gerald David Jaynes and Robin M. Williams, Jr., *A Common Destiny: Blacks and American Society* (1989). Oscar Lewis movingly depicts the problems of Puerto Ricans in *La Vida* (1966). Regarding Native Americans, consult Alvin M. Josephy, *Now That the Buffalo Have Gone: A Study of Today's American Indians* (1982). The problems of the cities are examined in Jon C. Teaford, *The Rough Road to Renaissance: Urban Revitalization in America, 1940–1985* (1990), and Larry Bennett, *Fragments of Cities: The New American Downtowns and Neighborhoods* (1990). Suburbs are the subject of Paul G. Lewis's *Shaping Suburbia* (1996). On crime, consult Elliott Currie, *Confronting Crime: An American Challenge* (1986). For penetrating analyses of the problems of the inner cities, consult three studies by William J. Wilson, *The Truly Disadvantaged: The Inner City, the Underclass, and Public Policy* (1987); *Poverty, Inequality, and the Future of Social Policy* (1995); and *When Work Disappears* (1996). A probing study of the job limitations of inner-city residents who do work is Katherine Newman's *No Shame in My Game: The Working Poor in the Inner City* (1999). Welfare reform is the subject of Mary Jo Bane, *Welfare Realities* (1994). Nicholas Lemann, *The Promised Land* (1991), provides a vivid account of the welfare system and the failed promises of Lyndon Johnson's "War on Poverty." The political implications of the debates over race and welfare policies are spelled out in Thomas Byrne Edsall and Mary D. Edsall, *Chain Reaction: The Impact of Race, Rights, and Taxes on American Politics* (1991). The broader cultural controversies of the era are examined in Arthur M. Schlesinger, Jr., *The Disuniting of America* (1992); Robert Hughes, *Culture of Complaint: The Fraying of America* (1993); and Henry Louis Gates, Jr., *Loose Canons: Notes on the Culture Wars* (1993). A sensitive and intriguing study of the values of modern Americans is Robert N. Bellah, *Habits of the Heart: Individualism and Commitment in American Life* (1985). See also Allan Bloom's conservative critique of modern higher education, *The Closing of the American Mind* (1987), and the rejoinder by Lawrence Levine, *The Opening of the American Mind* (1996).

DOCUMENTS

Declaration of Independence

In Congress, July 4, 1776

The Unanimous Declaration of the Thirteen United States of America

[Bracketed material in color has been inserted by the authors. For adoption background see pp. 146–148.]

When, in the course of human events, it becomes necessary for one people to dissolve the political bonds which have connected them with another, and to assume, among the powers of the earth, the separate and equal station to which the laws of nature and of nature's God entitle them, a decent respect to the opinions of mankind requires that they should declare the causes which impel them to the separation.

We hold these truths to be self-evident: That all men are created equal; that they are endowed by their Creator with certain unalienable rights; that among these are life, liberty, and the pursuit of happiness; that, to secure these rights, governments are instituted among men, deriving their just powers from the consent of the governed; that whenever any form of government becomes destructive of these ends, it is the right of the people to alter or to abolish it, and to institute new government, laying its foundation on such principles, and organizing its powers in such form, as to them shall seem most likely to effect their safety and happiness. Prudence, indeed, will dictate that governments long established should not be changed for light and transient causes; and accordingly all experience hath shown that mankind are more disposed to suffer, while evils are sufferable, than to right themselves by abolishing the forms to which they are accustomed. But when a long train of abuses and usurpations, pursuing invariably the same object, evinces a design to reduce them under absolute despotism, it is their right, it is their duty, to throw off such government, and to provide new guards for their future security. Such has been the patient sufferance of these colonies; and such is now the necessity which constrains them to alter their former systems of government. The history of the present King of Great Britain is a history of repeated injuries and usurpations, all having in direct object the establishment of an absolute tyranny over these states. To prove this, let facts be submitted to a candid world.

He has refused his assent to laws, the most wholesome and necessary for the public good. [See royal veto, p. 124.]

He has forbidden his governors to pass laws of immediate and pressing importance, unless suspended in their operation till his assent should be obtained; and, when so suspended, he has utterly neglected to attend to them.

He has refused to pass other laws for the accommodation of large districts of people [by establishing new countries], unless those people would relinquish the right of representation in the legislature, a right inestimable to them, and formidable to tyrants only.

He has called together legislative bodies at places unusual, uncomfortable, and distant from the depository of their public records, for the sole purpose of fatiguing them into compliance with his measures. [e.g., removal of Massachusetts Assembly to Salem, 1774.]

He has dissolved representative houses repeatedly, for opposing, with manly firmness, his invasions on the rights of the people. [e.g., Virginia Assembly, 1765.]

He has refused for a long time, after such dissolutions, to cause others to be elected; whereby the legislative powers, incapable of annihilation, have returned to the people at large for their exercise; the state remaining, in the mean time, exposed to all the dangers of invasions from without and convulsions within.

He has endeavored to prevent the population [populating] of these states; for that purpose obstructing the laws for naturalization of foreigners; refusing to pass others to encourage their migration hither, and raising the conditions of new appropriations of lands. [e.g., Proclamation of 1763, p. 121.]

He has obstructed the administration of justice, by refusing his assent to laws for establishing judiciary powers.

He has made judges dependent on his will alone, for the tenure of their offices, and the amount and payment of their salaries. [See Townshend Acts, p. 129.]

He has erected a multitude of new offices, and sent hither swarms of officers to harass our people and eat out their substance. [See enforcement of Navigation Laws, p. 130.]

He has kept among us, in times of peace, standing armies, without the consent of our legislatures. [See pp. 126, 130.]

He has affected to render the military independent of, and superior to, the civil power.

He has combined with others to subject us to a jurisdiction foreign to our constitution, and unacknowledged by our laws, giving his assent to their acts of pretended legislation:

For quartering large bodies of armed troops among us [See Boston Massacre, p. 130];

For protecting them, by a mock trial, from punishment for any murders which they should commit on the inhabitants of these states [See 1774 Acts, pp. 133–134];

For cutting off our trade with all parts of the world [See Boston Port Act, p. 133];

For imposing taxes on us without our consent [See Stamp Act, p. 126];

For depriving us, in many cases, of the benefits of trial by jury;

For transporting us beyond seas, to be tried for pretended offenses;

For abolishing the free system of English laws in a neighboring province [Quebec], establishing therein an arbitrary government, and enlarging its boundaries, so as to render it at once an example and fit instrument for introducing the same absolute rule into these colonies [Quebec Act, p. 134];

For taking away our charters, abolishing our most valuable laws, and altering fundamentally the forms of our governments [e.g., in Massachusetts, p. 133];

For suspending our own legislatures, and declaring themselves invested with power to legislate for us in all cases whatsoever [See Stamp Act repeal, p. 127.]

He has abdicated government here, by declaring us out of his protection and waging war against us. [Proclamation, p. 143.]

He has plundered our seas, ravaged our coasts, burned our towns, and destroyed the lives of our people. [e.g., the burning of Falmouth (Portland), p. 143.]

He is at this time transporting large armies of foreign mercenaries [Hessians, p. 143] to complete the works of death, desolation, and tyranny already begun with circumstances of cruelty and perfidy scarcely paralleled in the most barbarous ages, and totally unworthy the head of a civilized nation.

He has constrained our fellow-citizens, taken captive on the high seas [by impressment], to bear arms against their country, to become the executioners of their friends and brethren, or to fall themselves by their hands.

He has excited domestic insurrection among us [i.e., among slaves], and has endeavored to bring on the inhabitants of our frontiers the merciless Indian savages, whose known rule of warfare is an undistinguished destruction of all ages, sexes, and conditions.

In every stage of these oppressions we have petitioned for redress in the most humble terms; our repeated petitions have been answered only by repeated injury. [e.g., pp. 141–144.] A prince, whose character is thus marked by every act which may define a tyrant, is unfit to be the ruler of a free people.

Nor have we been wanting in our attentions to our British brethren. We have warned them, from time to time, of attempts by their legislature to extend an unwarrantable jurisdiction over us. We have reminded them of the circumstances of our emigration and settlement here. We have appealed to their native justice and magnanimity; and we have conjured them, by the ties of our common kindred, to disavow these usurpations, which would inevitably interrupt our connections and correspondence. They, too, have been deaf to the voice of justice and of consanguinity [blood relationship]. We must, therefore, acquiesce in the necessity which denounces [announces] our separation, and hold them, as we hold the rest of mankind, enemies in war, in peace friends.

We, therefore, the representatives of the United States of America, in General Congress assembled, appealing to the Supreme Judge of the world for the rectitude of our intentions, do, in the name and by the authority of the good people of these colonies, solemnly publish and declare, That these United Colonies are, and of right ought to be, FREE AND INDEPENDENT STATES; that they are absolved from all allegiance to the British crown, and that all political connection between them and the state of Great Britain is, and ought to be, totally dissolved; and that, as free and independent states, they have full power to levy war, conclude peace, contract alliances, establish commerce, and do all other acts and things which independent states may of right do. And for the support of this declaration, with a firm reliance on the protection of Divine Providence, we mutually pledge to each other our lives, our fortunes, and our sacred honor.

[Signed by]   JOHN HANCOCK [President]

[and fifty-five others]

Constitution of the
United States of America

[Boldface headings and bracketed explanatory matter and marginal comments (both in color) have been inserted for the reader's convenience. Passages that are no longer operative are printed in italic type.]

PREAMBLE

We the people of the United States, in order to form a more perfect union, establish justice, insure domestic tranquility, provide for the common defense, promote the general welfare, and secure the blessings of liberty to ourselves and our posterity, do ordain and establish this CONSTITUTION for the United States of America.

Article I. Legislative Department

SECTION I. Congress

Legislative power vested in a two-house Congress. All legislative powers herein granted shall be vested in a Congress of the United States, which shall consist of a Senate and a House of Representatives.

SECTION II. House of Representatives

1. The people elect representatives biennially. The House of Representatives shall be composed of members chosen every second year by the people of the several States, and the electors [voters] in each State shall have the qualifications requisite for electors of the most numerous branch of the State Legislature.

2. Who may be representatives. No person shall be a Representative who shall not have attained the age of twenty-five years, and been seven years a citizen of the United States, and who shall not, when elected, be an inhabitant of that State in which he shall be chosen.

See 1787 compromise, p. 179.

See 1787 compromise, p. 180.

3. Representation in the House based on population; census. Representatives and direct taxes[1] shall be apportioned among the several States which may be included within this Union, according to their respective numbers, *which shall be determined by adding to the whole number of free persons, including those bound to service for a term of years* [apprentices and indentured servants], *and excluding Indians not taxed, three-fifths of all other persons* [slaves].[2] The actual enumeration [census] shall be made within three years after the first meeting of the Congress of the United States, and within every subsequent term of ten years, in such manner as they shall by law direct. The number of Representatives shall not exceed one for every thirty thousand, but each State shall have at least one Representative; *and until such enumeration shall be made, the State of New Hampshire shall be entitled to choose three, Massachusetts eight, Rhode Island and Providence Plantations one, Connecticut five, New York six, New Jersey four, Pennsylvania eight, Delaware one, Maryland six, Virginia ten, North Carolina five, South Carolina five, and Georgia three.*

---

[1]Modified in 1913 by the Sixteenth Amendment re income taxes (see p. 691).

[2]The word *slave* appears nowhere in the original, unamended Constitution. The three-fifths rule ceased to be in force when the Thirteenth Amendment was adopted in 1865 (see p. 72 and amendments below).

4. Vacancies in the House are filled by election. When vacancies happen in the representation from any State, the Executive authority [governor] therefore shall issue writs of election [call a special election] to fill such vacancies.

See Chase and Johnson trials, pp. 219, 494; Nixon trial preliminaries, pp. 959–960; and discussion of Clinton's impeachment, pp. 1007–1008.

5. The House selects its Speaker; has sole power to vote impeachment charges (i.e., indictments). The House of Representatives shall choose their Speaker and other officers; and shall have the sole power of impeachment.

SECTION III.

Senate

1. Senators represent the states. The Senate of the United States shall be composed of two Senators from each State, *chosen by the legislature thereof,*[1] for six Years; and each Senator shall have one vote.

2. One-third of senators chosen every two years; vacancies. *Immediately after they shall be assembled in consequence of the first election, they shall be divided as equally as may be into three classes. The seats of the Senators of the first class shall be vacated at the expiration of the second year, of the second class at the expiration of the fourth year, and of the third class at the expiration of the sixth year,* so that one-third may be chosen every second year; *and if vacancies happen by resignation or otherwise, during the recess of the legislature of any State, the Executive* [governor] *thereof may make temporary appointments until the next meeting of the legislature, which shall then fill such vacancies.*[2]

3. Who may be senators. No person shall be a Senator who shall not have attained to the age of thirty years, and been nine years a citizen of the United States, and who shall not, when elected, be an inhabitant of that State for which he shall be chosen.

4. The vice president presides over the Senate. The Vice President of the United States shall be President of the Senate, but shall have no vote, unless they be equally divided [tied].

5. The Senate chooses its other officers. The Senate shall choose their other officers, and also a President *pro tempore,* in the absence of the Vice President, or when he shall exercise the office of the President of the United States.

See Chase and Johnson trials, pp. 219, 494; and discussion of Clinton's impeachment, pp. 1007–1008.

6. The Senate has sole power to try impeachments. The Senate shall have the sole power to try all impeachments. When sitting for that purpose, they shall be on oath or affirmation. When the President of the United States is tried, the Chief Justice shall preside[3]: and no person shall be convicted without the concurrence of two-thirds of the members present.

7. Penalties for impeachment conviction. Judgment in cases of impeachment shall not extend further than to removal from office, and disqualification to hold and enjoy any office of honor, trust or profit under the United States: but the party convicted shall nevertheless be liable and subject to indictment, trial, judgment and punishment, according to law.

SECTION IV.

Election and Meetings of Congress

1. Regulation of elections. The times, places and manner of holding elections for Senators and Representatives shall be prescribed in each State by the legislature thereof; but the Congress may at any time by law make or alter such regulations, except as to the places of choosing Senators.

2. Congress must meet once a year. The Congress shall assemble at least once in every year, and such meeting *shall be on the first Monday in December, unless they shall by law appoint a different day.*[4]

---

[1]Repealed in favor of popular election in 1913 by the Seventeenth Amendment.
[2]Changed in 1913 by the Seventeenth Amendment.
[3]The vice president, as next in line, would be an interested party.
[4]Changed in 1933 to January 3 by the Twentieth Amendment (see p. 798 and below).

SECTION V.   **Organization and Rules of the Houses**

1. Each house may reject members; quorums. Each house shall be the judge of the elections, returns and qualifications of its own members, and a majority of each shall constitute a quorum to do business; but a smaller number may adjourn from day to day, and may be authorized to compel the attendance of absent members, in such manner, and under such penalties, as each house may provide.

See "Bully" Brooks case, pp. 414–415.

2. Each house makes its own rules. Each house may determine the rules of its proceedings, punish its members for disorderly behavior, and with the concurrence of two-thirds, expel a member.

3. Each house must keep and publish a record of its proceedings. Each house shall keep a journal of its proceedings, and from time to time publish the same, excepting such parts as may in their judgment require secrecy; and the yeas and nays of the members of either house on any question shall, at the desire of one-fifth of those present, be entered on the journal.

4. Both houses must agree on adjournment. Neither house, during the session of Congress, shall, without the consent of the other, adjourn for more than three days, nor to any other place than that in which the two houses shall be sitting.

SECTION VI.   **Privileges of and Prohibitions upon Congressmen**

1. Congressional salaries; immunities. The Senators and Representatives shall receive a compensation for their services, to be ascertained by law and paid out of the treasury of the United States. They shall in all cases except treason, felony and breach of the peace, be privileged from arrest during their attendance at the session of their respective houses, and in going to and returning from the same; and for any speech or debate in either house, they shall not be questioned in any other place [i.e., they shall be immune from libel suits].

2. A congressman may not hold any other federal civil office. No Senator or Representative shall, during the time for which he was elected, be appointed to any civil office under the authority of the United States, which shall have been created, or the emoluments whereof shall have been increased, during such time; and no person holding any office under the United States shall be a member of either house during his continuance in office.

SECTION VII.   **Method of Making Laws**

See 1787 compromise, p. 179.

1. Money bills must originate in the House. All bills for raising revenue shall originate in the House of Representatives; but the Senate may propose or concur with amendments as on other bills.

Nixon, more than any predecessors, "impounded" billions of dollars voted by Congress for specific purposes, because he disapproved of them. The courts generally failed to sustain him, and his impeachment foes regarded wholesale impoundment as a violation of his oath to "faithfully execute" the laws.

2. The president's veto power; Congress may override. Every bill which shall have passed the House of Representatives and the Senate, shall, before it become a law, be presented to the President of the United States; if he approve he shall sign it, but if not he shall return it with his objections to that house in which it shall have originated, who shall enter the objections at large on their journal, and proceed to reconsider it. If after such reconsideration two-thirds of that house shall agree to pass the bill, it shall be sent, together with the objections, to the other house, by which it shall likewise be reconsidered, and, if approved by two-thirds of that house, it shall become a law. But in all such cases the votes of both houses shall be determined by yeas and nays, and the names of the persons voting for and against the bill shall be entered on the journal of each house respectively. If any bill shall not be returned by the President within ten days (Sundays excepted) after it shall have been presented to him, the same shall be a law, in like manner as if he had signed it, unless the Congress by their adjournment prevent its return, in which case it shall not be a law [this is the so-called pocket veto].

3. All measures requiring the agreement of both houses go to president for approval. Every order, resolution, or vote to which the concurrence of the Senate and House of Representatives may be necessary (except on a question of adjournment) shall be presented to the President of the United States; and before the same shall take effect, shall be approved by him, or being disapproved by him, shall be repassed by two-thirds of the Senate and House of Representatives, according to the rules and limitations prescribed in the case of a bill.

SECTION VIII.   **Powers Granted to Congress**

Congress has certain enumerated powers:

1. It may lay and collect taxes. The Congress shall have power to lay and collect taxes, duties, imposts, and excises, to pay the debts and provide for the common defense and general welfare of the United States; but all duties, imposts and excises shall be uniform throughout the United States;

2. It may borrow money. To borrow money on the credit of the United States;

3. It may regulate foreign and interstate trade. To regulate commerce with foreign nations, and among the several States, and with the Indian tribes;

For 1798 naturalization see p. 205.

4. It may pass naturalization and bankruptcy laws. To establish an uniform rule of naturalization, and uniform laws on the subject of bankruptcies throughout the United States;

5. It may coin money. To coin money, regulate the value thereof, and of foreign coin, and fix the standard of weights and measures;

6. It may punish counterfeiters. To provide for the punishment of counterfeiting the securities and current coin of the United States;

7. It may establish a postal service. To establish post offices and post roads;

8. It may issue patents and copyrights. To promote the progress of science and useful arts by securing for limited times to authors and inventors the exclusive right to their respective writings and discoveries;

9. It may establish inferior courts. To constitute tribunals inferior to the Supreme Court;

See Judiciary Act of 1789, p. 193.

10. It may punish crimes committed on the high seas. To define and punish piracies and felonies committed on the high seas [i.e., outside the three-mile limit] and offenses against the law of nations [international law];

11. It may declare war; authorize privateers. To declare war,[1] grant letters of marque and reprisal,[2] and make rules concerning captures on land and water;

12. It may maintain an army. To raise and support armies, but no appropriation of money to that use shall be for a longer term than two years;[3]

13. It may maintain a navy. To provide and maintain a navy;

14. It may regulate the army and navy. To make rules for the government and regulation of the land and naval forces;

See Whiskey Rebellion, p. 196.

15. It may call out the state militia. To provide for calling forth the militia to execute the laws of the Union, suppress insurrections, and repel invasions;

16. It shares with the states control of militia. To provide for organizing, arming, and disciplining the militia, and for governing such part of them as may be employed in the service of the United States, reserving to the States respectively the appointment of the officers, and the authority of training the militia according to the discipline prescribed by Congress;

---

[1]Note that presidents, though they can provoke war (see the case of Polk, p. 381) or wage it after it is declared, cannot declare it.

[2]Papers issued private citizens in wartime authorizing them to capture enemy ships.

[3]A reflection of fear of standing armies earlier expressed in the Declaration of Independence.

17. It makes laws for the District of Columbia and other federal areas. To exercise exclusive legislation in all cases whatsoever, over such district (not exceeding ten miles square) as may, by cession of particular States, and the acceptance of Congress, become the seat of government of the United States,[1] and to exercise like authority over all places purchased by the consent of the legislature of the State, in which the same shall be, for the erection of forts, magazines, arsenals, dock-yards, and other needful buildings;—and

Congress has certain implied powers:

This is the famous "elastic clause"; See p. 196.

18. It may make laws necessary for carrying out the enumerated powers. To make all laws which shall be necessary and proper for carrying into execution the foregoing powers, and all other powers vested by this Constitution in the government of the United States, or in any departure or officer thereof.

SECTION IX.   **Powers Denied to the Federal Government**

See 1787 slave compromise, p. 180.

1. Congressional control of slave trade postponed until 1808. *The migration or importation of such persons as any of the States now existing shall think proper to admit shall not be prohibited by the Congress prior to the year 1808; but a tax or duty may be imposed on such importation, not exceeding $10 for each person.*

See Lincoln's unlawful suspension, p. 445.

2. The writ of habeas corpus[2] may be suspended only in cases of rebellion or invasion. The privilege of the writ of habeas corpus shall not be suspended, unless when in cases of rebellion or invasion the public safety may require it.

3. Attainders[3] and ex post facto laws[4] forbidden. No bill of attainder or ex post facto law shall be passed.

4. Direct taxes must be apportioned according to population. No capitation [head or poll tax] or other direct, tax shall be laid, unless in proportion to the census or enumeration herein before directed to be taken.[5]

5. Export taxes forbidden. No tax or duty shall be laid on articles exported from any State.

6. Congress must not discriminate among states in regulating commerce. No preference shall be given by any regulation of commerce or revenue to the ports of one State over those of another; nor shall vessels bound to, or from, one State, be obliged to enter, clear, or pay duties in another.

See Lincoln's unlawful infraction, p. 445.

7. Public money may not be spent without congressional appropriation; accounting. No money shall be drawn from the treasury, but in consequence of appropriations made by law; and a regular statement and account of the receipts and expenditures of all public money shall be published from time to time.

8. Titles of nobility prohibited; foreign gifts. No title of nobility shall be granted by the United States; and no person holding office of profit or trust under them, shall, without the consent of Congress, accept of any present, emolument, office, or title, of any kind whatever, from any king, prince, or foreign state.

---

[1]The District of Columbia, ten miles square, was established in 1791 with a cession from Virginia (see p. 194).

[2]A writ of habeas corpus is a document that enables a person under arrest to obtain an immediate examination in court to ascertain whether he or she is being legally held.

[3]A bill of attainder is a special legislative act condemning and punishing an individual without a judicial trial.

[4]An ex post facto law is one that fixes punishments for acts committed before the law was passed.

[5]Modified in 1913 by the Sixteenth Amendment (see p. 691 and amendments below).

SECTION X. Powers Denied to the States

Absolute prohibitions on the states:

On contracts see Fletcher *v.* Peck, *p. 250.*

1. The states are forbidden to do certain things. No State shall enter into any treaty, alliance, or confederation; grant letters of marque and reprisal [i.e., authorize privateers]; coin money; emit bills of credit [issue paper money]; make anything but gold and silver coin a [legal] tender in payment of debts; pass any bill of attainder,[1] ex post facto,[1] or law impairing the obligation of contracts, or grant any title of nobility.

Conditional prohibitions on the states:

Cf. Confederation chaos, pp. 172–173.

2. The states may not levy duties without the consent of Congress. No State shall, without the consent of Congress, lay any imposts or duties on imports or exports, except what may be absolutely necessary for executing its inspection laws: and the net produce of all duties and imposts, laid by any State on imports or exports, shall be for the use of the treasury of the United States; and all such laws shall be subject to the revision and control of the Congress.

3. Certain other federal powers are forbidden the states except with the consent of Congress. No State shall, without the consent of Congress, lay any duty of tonnage [i.e., duty on ship tonnage], keep [nonmilitia] troops or ships of war in time of peace, enter into any agreement or compact with another State, or with a foreign power, or engage in war, unless actually invaded, or in such imminent danger as will not admit of delay.

Article II. *Executive Department*

SECTION I. President and Vice President

1. The president is the chief executive; term of office. The executive power shall be vested in a President of the United States of America. He shall hold his office during the term of four years,[2] and, together with the Vice President, chosen for the same term, be elected as follows:

See 1787 compromise, p. 180.

See 1876 Oregon case, p. 508.

2. The president is chosen by electors. Each State shall appoint, in such manner as the legislature thereof may direct, a number of electors, equal to the whole number of Senators and Representatives to which the State may be entitled in the Congress; but no Senator or Representative, or person holding an office of trust or profit under the United States, shall be appointed an elector.

See Burr-Jefferson disputed election of 1800, p. 214.

A majority of the electoral votes needed to elect a president. *The electors shall meet in their respective States, and vote by ballot for two persons, of whom one at least shall not be an inhabitant of the same State with themselves. And they shall make a list of all the persons voted for, and of the number of votes for each; which list they shall sign and certify, and transmit sealed to the seat of government of the United States, directed to the President of the Senate. The President of the Senate shall, in the presence of the Senate and House of Representatives, open all the certificates, and the votes shall be counted. The person having the greatest number of votes shall be the President, if such number be a majority of the whole number of electors appointed; and if there be more than one who have such majority, and have an equal number of votes, then the House of Representatives shall immediately choose by ballot one of them for President; and if no person have a majority, then from the five highest on the list the said house shall in like manner choose the President. But in choosing the President the votes shall be taken by States, the representation from each State*

---

[1]For definitions see footnotes 3 and 4 on preceding page.
[2]No reference to reelection; for anti–third term Twenty-second Amendment, see below.

having one vote; a quorum for this purpose shall consist of a member or members from two-thirds of the States, and a majority of all the States shall be necessary to a choice. In every case, after the choice of the President, the person having the greatest number of votes of the electors shall be the Vice President. But if there should remain two or more who have equal votes, the Senate shall choose from them by ballot the Vice President.[1]

See Jefferson as vice president in 1796, p. 202.

3. Congress decides time of meeting of Electoral College. The Congress may determine the time of choosing the electors and the day on which they shall give their votes; which day shall be the same throughout the United States.

To provide for foreign-born people, like Alexander Hamilton, born in the British West Indies.

4. Who may be president. No person except a natural-born citizen, *or a citizen of the United States at the time of the adoption of this Constitution,* shall be eligible to the office of President; neither shall any person be eligible to that office who shall not have attained to the age of thirty-five years, and been fourteen years a resident within the United States [i.e., a legal resident].

Modified by Twentieth and Twenty-fifth Amendments below.

5. Replacements for president. In case of the removal of the President from office or of his death, resignation, or inability to discharge the powers and duties of said office, the same shall devolve on the Vice President, and the Congress may by law provide for the case of removal, death, resignation, or inability, both of the President and Vice President, declaring what officer shall then act as President, and such officer shall act accordingly, until the disability be removed, or a President shall be elected.

6. The president's salary. The President shall, at stated times, receive for his services a compensation, which shall neither be increased or diminished during the period for which he shall have been elected, and he shall not receive within that period any other emolument from the United States, or any of them.

7. The president's oath of office. Before he enter on the execution of his office, he shall take the following oath or affirmation:—"I do solemnly swear (or affirm) that I will faithfully execute the office of the President of the United States, and will to the best of my ability preserve, protect and defend the Constitution of the United States."

Section II.   Powers of the President

See cabinet evolution, p. 191.

1. The president has important military and civil powers. The President shall be commander in chief of the army and navy of the United States, and of the militia of the several States, when called into the actual service of the United States; he may require the opinion, in writing, of the principal officer in each of the executive departments, upon any subject relating to the duties of their respective offices, and he shall have power to grant reprieves and pardons for offenses against the United States, except in cases of impeachment.[2]

For president's removal power, see p. 494.

2. The president may negotiate treaties and nominate federal officials. He shall have power, by and with the advice and consent of the Senate, to make treaties, provided two-thirds of the Senators present concur; and he shall nominate, and by and with the advice and consent of the Senate, shall appoint ambassadors, other public ministers and consuls, judges of the Supreme Court, and all other officers of the United States, whose appointments are not herein otherwise provided for, and which shall be established by law: but the Congress may by law vest the appointment of such inferior officers, as they think proper, in the President alone, in the courts of law, or in the heads of departments.

3. The president may fill vacancies during Senate recess. The President shall have power to fill up all vacancies that may happen during the recess of the Senate, by granting commissions which shall expire at the end of their next session.

---

[1]Repealed in 1804 by the Twelfth Amendment (for text see below).

[2]To prevent the president's pardoning himself or his close associates, as was feared in the case of Richard Nixon. See pp. 959–960.

SECTION III.   **Other Powers and Duties of the President**

For president's personal appearances, see p. 692.

Messages; extra sessions; receiving ambassadors; execution of the laws. He shall from time to time give to the Congress information of the state of the Union, and recommend to their consideration such measures as he shall judge necessary and expedient; he may, on extraordinary occasions, convene both houses, or either of them, and in case of disagreement between them, with respect to the time of adjournment, he may adjourn them to such time as he shall think proper; he shall receive ambassadors and other public ministers; he shall take care that the laws be faithfully executed, and shall commission all the officers of the United States.

SECTION IV.   **Impeachment**

See discussion of Presidents Johnson, p. 495; Nixon, pp. 959–960; and Clinton, pp. 1007–1008.

Civil officers may be removed by impeachment. The President, Vice President and all civil officers[1] of the United States shall be removed from office on impeachment for, and on conviction of, treason, bribery, and other high crimes and misdemeanors.

Article III.   *Judicial Department*

SECTION I.   **The Federal Courts**

See Judiciary Act of 1789, p. 193.

The judicial power belongs to the federal courts. The judicial power of the United States shall be vested in one Supreme Court, and in such inferior courts as the Congress may from time to time ordain and establish. The judges, both of the Supreme and inferior courts, shall hold their offices during good behavior, and shall, at stated times, receive for their services a compensation which shall not be diminished[2] during their continuance in office.

SECTION II.   **Jurisdiction of Federal Courts**

1. Kinds of cases that may be heard. The judicial power shall extend to all cases, in law and equity, arising under this Constitution, the laws of the United States, and treaties made, or which shall be made, under their authority;—to all cases affecting ambassadors, other public ministers and consuls;—to all cases of admiralty and maritime jurisdiction;—to controversies to which the United States shall be a party;—to controversies between two or more States;—*between a State and citizens of another State*[3];—between citizens of different States;—between citizens of the same State claiming lands under grants of different States, and between a State, or the citizens thereof, and foreign states, citizens or subjects.

2. Jurisdiction of the Supreme Court. In all cases affecting ambassadors, other public ministers and consuls, and those in which a State shall be a party, the Supreme Court shall have original jurisdiction.[4] In all the other cases before mentioned, the Supreme Court shall have appellate jurisdiction,[5] both as to law and fact, with such exceptions, and under such regulations, as the Congress shall make.

3. Trial for federal crime is by jury. The trial of all crimes, except in cases of impeachment, shall be by jury; and such trial shall be held in the State where the said crimes shall have been committed; but when not committed within any State, the trial shall be at such place or places as the Congress may by law have directed.

---

[1]i.e., all federal executive and judicial officers, but not members of Congress or military personnel.

[2]In 1978, in a case involving federal judges, the Supreme Court ruled that diminution of salaries by inflation was irrelevant.

[3]The Eleventh Amendment (see below) restricts this to suits by a state against citizens of another state.

[4]i.e., such cases must originate in the Supreme Court.

[5]i.e., it hears other cases only when they are appealed to it from a lower federal court or a state court.

SECTION III.   **Treason**

See Burr trial, p. 224.

1. Treason defined. Treason against the United States shall consist only in levying war against them, or in adhering to their enemies, giving them aid and comfort. No person shall be convicted of treason unless on the testimony of two witnesses to the same overt act, or on confession in open court.

2. Congress fixes punishment for treason. The Congress shall have power to declare the punishment of treason, but no attainder of treason shall work corruption of blood, or forfeiture except during the life of the person attained.[1]

Article IV.   ***Relations of the States to One Another***

SECTION I.   **Credit to Acts, Records, and Court Proceedings**

Each state must respect the public acts of the others. Full faith and credit shall be given in each State to the public acts, records, and judicial proceedings of every other State.[2] And the Congress may by general laws prescribe the manner in which such acts, records, and proceedings shall be proved [attested], and the effect thereof.

SECTION II.   **Duties of States to States**

1. Citizenship in one state is valid in all. The citizens of each State shall be entitled to all privileges and immunities of citizens in the several States.

This stipulation is sometimes openly flouted. In 1978 Governor Jerry Brown of California, acting on humanitarian grounds, refused to surrender to South Dakota an American Indian, Dennis Banks, who was charged with murder in an armed uprising.

Basis of fugitive-slave laws; see pp. 398–400.

2. Fugitives from justice must be surrendered by the state to which they have fled. A person charged in any State with treason, felony, or other crime, who shall flee from justice, and be found in another State, shall on demand of the executive authority [governor] of the State from which he fled, be delivered up, to be removed to the State having jurisdiction of the crime.

3. Slaves and apprentices must be returned. *No person held to service or labor in one State, under the laws thereof, escaping into another, shall, in consequence of any law or regulation therein, be discharged from such service or labor, but shall be delivered up on claim of the party to whom such service or labor may be due.*[3]

SECTION III.   **New States and Territories**

e.g., Maine (1820); see p. 245.

1. Congress may admit new states. New States may be admitted by the Congress into this Union; but no new State shall be formed or erected within the jurisdiction of any other State; nor any State be formed by the junction of two or more States, or parts of States, without the consent of the legislatures of the States concerned as well as of the Congress.[4]

2. Congress regulates federal territory and property. The Congress shall have power to dispose of and make all needful rules and regulations respecting the territory or other property belonging to the United States; and nothing in this Constitution shall be so construed as to prejudice any claims of the United States, or of any particular State.

SECTION IV.   **Protection to the States**

See Cleveland and the Pullman strike, p. 614.

United States guarantees to states representative government and protection against invasion and rebellion. The United States shall guarantee to every State in this Union a

---

[1] i.e., punishment only for the offender; none for his or her heirs.

[2] e.g., a marriage in one is valid in all.

[3] Invalidated in 1865 by the Thirteenth Amendment (for text see below).

[4] Loyal West Virginia was formed by Lincoln in 1862 from seceded Virginia. This act was of dubious constitutionality and was justified in part by the wartime powers of the president. See p. 436.

republican form of government, and shall protect each of them against invasion; and on application of the legislature, or of the executive [governor] (when the legislature cannot be convened), against domestic violence.

Article V. *The Process of Amendment*

The Constitution may be amended in four ways. The Congress, whenever two-thirds of both houses shall deem it necessary, shall propose amendments to this Constitution, or, on the application of the legislature of two-thirds of the several States, shall call a convention for proposing amendments, which, in either case, shall be valid to all intents and purposes, as part of this Constitution, when ratified by the legislatures of three-fourths of the several States, or by conventions in three-fourths thereof, as the one or the other mode of ratification may be proposed by the Congress; provided *that no amendments which may be made prior to the year one thousand eight hundred and eight shall in any manner affect the first and fourth clauses in the ninth section of the first article;*[1] and that no State, without its consent, shall be deprived of its equal suffrage in the Senate.

Article VI. *General Provisions*

This pledge honored by Hamilton, pp. 193–194.

1. The debts of the Confederation are taken over. All debts contracted and engagements entered into, before the adoption of this Constitution, shall be as valid against the United States under this Constitution, as under the Confederation.

2. The Constitution, federal laws, and treaties are the supreme law of the land. This Constitution, and the laws of the United States which shall be made in pursuance thereof; and all treaties made, or which shall be made, under the authority of the United States, shall be the supreme law of the land; and the judges in every State shall be bound thereby, anything in the Constitution or laws of any State to the contrary notwithstanding.

3. Federal and state officers bound by oath to support the Constitution. The Senators and Representatives before mentioned, and the members of the several State legislatures, and all executive and judicial officers, both of the United States and of the several States, shall be bound by oath or affirmation to support this Constitution; but no religious test shall ever be required as a qualification to any office or public trust under the United States.

Article VII. *Ratification of the Constitution*

See 1787 irregularity, pp. 181–183.

The Constitution effective when ratified by conventions in nine states. The ratification of the conventions of nine States shall be sufficient for the establishment of this Constitution between the States so ratifying the same.

Done in Convention by the unanimous consent of the States present, the seventeenth day of September in the year of our Lord one thousand seven hundred and eighty-seven and of the Independence of the United States of America the twelfth. In witness whereof we have hereunto subscribed our names.

[Signed by]

Gº WASHINGTON

Presidt and Deputy from Virginia

[and thirty-eight others]

---

[1]This clause, re slave trade and direct taxes, became inoperative in 1808

AMENDMENTS TO THE CONSTITUTION

Amendment I.   *Religious and Political Freedom*

For background of Bill of Rights, see pp. 192–193.

Congress must not interfere with freedom of religion, speech or press, assembly, and petition. Congress shall make no law respecting an establishment of religion,[1] or prohibiting the free exercise thereof; or abridging the freedom of speech, or of the press; or the right of the people peaceably to assemble, and to petition the government for a redress of grievances.

Amendment II.   *Right to Bear Arms*

The people may bear arms. A well-regulated militia being necessary to the security of a free State, the right of the people to keep and bear arms [i.e., for military purposes] shall not be infringed.[2]

Amendment III.   *Quartering of Troops*

See Declaration of Independence and British quartering above.

Soldiers may not be arbitrarily quartered on the people. No soldier shall, in time of peace, be quartered in any house without the consent of the owner, nor in time of war, but in a manner to be prescribed by law.

Amendment IV.   *Searches and Seizures*

A reflection of colonial grievances against the crown.

Unreasonable searches are forbidden. The right of the people to be secure in their persons, houses, papers, and effects, against unreasonable searches and seizures, shall not be violated, and no [search] warrants shall issue but upon probable cause, supported by oath or affirmation, and particularly describing the place to be searched, and the persons or things to be seized.

Amendment V.   *Right to Life, Liberty, and Property*

When witnesses refuse to answer questions in court, they routinely "take the Fifth Amendment."

The individual is guaranteed certain rights when on trial and the right to life, liberty, and property. No person shall be held to answer for a capital, or otherwise infamous crime, unless on a presentment [formal charge] or indictment of a grand jury, except in cases arising in the naval forces, or in the militia, when in actual service in time of war or public danger; nor shall any person be subject for the same offense to be twice put in jeopardy of life or limb; nor shall be compelled in any criminal case to be a witness against himself, nor be deprived of life, liberty, or property, without due process of law; nor shall private property be taken for public use [i.e., by eminent domain] without just compensation.

Amendment VI.   *Protection in Criminal Trials*

See Declaration of Independence above.

An accused person has important rights. In all criminal prosecutions, the accused shall enjoy the right to a speedy and public trial, by an impartial jury of the State and district

---

[1] In 1787 "an establishment of religion" referred to an "established church," or one supported by all taxpayers, whether members or not. But the courts have often acted under this article to keep religion, including prayers, out of the public schools.

[2] The courts, with "militia" in mind, have consistently held that the "right" to bear arms is a limited one.

wherein the crime shall have been committed, which district shall have been previously ascertained by law, and to be informed of the nature and cause of the accusation; to be confronted with the witnesses against him; to have compulsory process [subpoena] for obtaining witnesses in his favor, and to have the assistance of counsel for his defense.

Amendment VII.   *Suits at Common Law*

The rules of common law are recognized. In suits at common law, where the value in controversy shall exceed twenty dollars, the right of trial by jury shall be preserved, and no fact tried by a jury shall be otherwise re-examined in any court of the United States, than according to the rules of the common law.

Amendment VIII.   *Bail and Punishments*

Excessive fines and unusual punishments are forbidden. Excessive bail shall not be required, nor excessive fines imposed, nor cruel and unusual punishment inflicted.

Amendment IX.   *Concerning Rights Not Enumerated*

The Ninth and Tenth Amendments were bulwarks of southern states' rights before the Civil War.

The people retain rights not here enumerated. The enumeration in the Constitution, of certain rights, shall not be construed to deny or disparage others retained by the people.

Amendment X.   *Powers Reserved to the States and to the People*

A concession to states' rights, p. 195.

Powers not delegated to the federal government are reserved to the states and the people. The powers not delegated to the United States by the Constitution, nor prohibited by it to the States, are reserved to the States respectively, or to the people.

Amendment XI.   *Suits Against a State*

The federal courts have no authority in suits by citizens against a state. The judicial power of the United States shall not be construed to extend to any suit in law or equity, commenced or prosecuted against one of the United States by citizens of another State, or by citizens or subjects of any foreign state. [Adopted 1798.]

Amendment XII.   *Election of President and Vice President*

Forestalls repetition of 1800 electoral dispute, p. 214.

See 1876 disputed election. p. 519.

See 1824 election, pp. 257–259.

1. Changes in manner of electing president and vice president; procedure when no presidential candidate receives electoral majority. The electors shall meet in their respective States, and vote by ballot for President and Vice President, one of whom, at least, shall not be an inhabitant of the same state with themselves; they shall name in their ballots the person voted for as President, and in distinct ballots the person voted for as Vice President, and they shall make distinct lists of all persons voted for as President, and of all persons voted for as Vice President, and of the number of votes for each, which lists they shall sign and certify, and transmit sealed to the seat of government of the United States, directed to the President of the Senate;—the President of the Senate shall, in the presence of the Senate and House of Representatives, open all the certificates and the votes shall be counted;—the person having the greatest number of votes for President shall be the President, if such number be a majority of the whole number of electors appointed; and if no person have such majority, then from the persons having the highest numbers not exceeding three on the list of those voted for as President, the House of Representatives shall choose immediately, by ballot, the President. But in choosing the President, the votes shall be taken by States, the representation from each State having one vote; a quorum for this purpose shall consist of a member or members from two-thirds of the States, and a majority of all the States shall be necessary to a choice. And if the House of Representatives shall not choose a President whenever the right of choice shall devolve upon them, before *the fourth day of March*[1] next following, then the Vice President shall act as President, as in the case of the death or other constitutional disability of the President.

2. Procedure when no vice presidential candidate receives electoral majority. The person having the greatest number of votes as Vice President, shall be the Vice President, if such number be a majority of the whole number of electors appointed; and if no person have a majority, then from the two highest numbers on the list the Senate shall choose the Vice President; a quorum for the purpose shall consist of two-thirds of the whole number of Senators, and a majority of the whole number shall be necessary to a choice. But no person constitutionally ineligible to the office of President shall be eligible to that of Vice President of the United States. [Adopted 1804.]

Amendment XIII.   *Slavery Prohibited*

For background see pp. 458–460.

Slavery forbidden. 1. Neither slavery[2] nor involuntary servitude, except as a punishment for crime whereof the party shall have been duly convicted, shall exist within the United States, or any place subject to their jurisdiction.

2. Congress shall have power to enforce this article by appropriate legislation. [Adopted 1865.]

Amendment XIV.   *Civil Rights for Ex-slaves,[3] etc.*

For background see pp. 485–486.

For corporations as "persons," see pp. 542–543.

Abolishes three-fifths rule for slaves, Art. I., Sec. II, para. 3.

1. Ex-slaves made citizens; U.S. citizenship primary. All persons born or naturalized in the United States, and subject to the jurisdiction thereof, are citizens of the United States and of the State wherein they reside. No State shall make or enforce any law which shall abridge the privileges or immunities of citizens of the United States; nor shall any State deprive any person of life, liberty, or property, without due process of law; nor deny to any person within its jurisdiction the equal protection of the laws.

2. When a state denies citizens the vote, its representation shall be reduced. Representatives shall be apportioned among the several States according to their respective numbers, counting the whole number of persons in each State, excluding Indians not taxed. But when the right to vote at any election for the choice of Electors for President and Vice President of the United States, Representatives in Congress, the executive and judicial officers of a State, or the members of the legislature thereof, is denied to any of the male inhabitants of such State, being twenty-one years of age and citizens of the United States, or in any way abridged, except for participation in rebellion, or other crime, the basis of representation therein shall be reduced in the proportion which the number of such make citizens shall bear to the whole number of male citizens twenty-one years of age in such State.[4]

Leading ex-Confederates denied office. See p. 486.

3. Certain persons who have been in rebellion are ineligible for federal and state office. No person shall be a Senator or Representative in Congress, or Elector of President and Vice President, or hold any office, civil or military, under the United States, or under any State, who, having previously taken an oath, as a member of Congress, or as an officer

---

[1]Changed to January 20 by the Twentieth Amendment (for text see below).

[2]The only explicit mention of slavery in the Constitution.

[3]Occasionally an offender is prosecuted under the Thirteenth Amendment for keeping an employee or other person under conditions approximating slavery.

[4]The provisions concerning "male" inhabitants were modified by the Nineteenth Amendment, which enfranchised women. The legal voting age was changed from twenty-one to eighteen by the Twenty-sixth Amendment.

of the United States, or as a member of any State legislature, or as an executive or judicial officer of any State, to support the Constitution of the United States, shall have engaged in insurrection or rebellion against the same, or given aid or comfort to the enemies thereof. But Congress may, by a vote of two-thirds of each house, remove such disability.

The ex-Confederates were thus forced to repudiate their debts and pay pensions to their own veterans, plus taxes for the pensions of Union veterans, their conquerors.

4. Debts incurred in aid of rebellion are void. The validity of the public debt of the United States, authorizing by law, including debts incurred for payment of pensions and bounties for services in suppressing insurrection or rebellion, shall not be questioned. But neither the United States nor any State shall assume or pay any debt or obligation incurred in aid of insurrection or rebellion against the United States, or any claim for the loss or emancipation of any slave; but all such debts, obligations, and claims shall be held illegal and void.

5. Enforcement. The Congress shall have power to enforce, by appropriate legislation, the provisions of this article. [Adopted 1868.]

Amendment XV.   *Suffrage for Blacks*

For background see p. 489.

Black males are made voters. 1. The right of the citizens of the United States to vote shall not be denied or abridged by the United States or by any State on account of race, color, or previous condition of servitude.

2. The Congress shall have power to enforce this article by appropriate legislation. [Adopted 1870.]

Amendment XVI.   *Income Taxes*

For background see p. 691.

Congress has power to lay and collect income taxes. The Congress shall have power to lay and collect taxes on incomes, from whatever source derived, without apportionment among the several States, and without regard to any census or enumeration. [Adopted 1913.]

Amendment XVII.   *Direct Election of Senators*

Senators shall be elected by popular vote. 1. The Senate of the United States shall be composed of two Senators from each State, elected by the people thereof, for six years; and each Senator shall have one vote. The electors in each State shall have the qualifications requisite for electors of [voters for] the most numerous branch of the State legislatures.

2. When vacancies happen in the representation of any State in the Senate, the executive authority of such State shall issue writs of election to fill such vacancies: Provided, that the Legislature of any State may empower the executive thereof to make temporary appointments until the people fill the vacancies by election as the Legislature may direct.

3. This amendment shall not be so construed as to affect the election or term of any Senator chosen before it becomes valid as part of the Constitution. [Adopted 1913.]

Amendment XVIII.   *National Prohibition*

For background see p. 732.

The sale or manufacture of intoxicating liquors is forbidden. 1. *After one year from the ratification of this article the manufacture, sale, or transportation of intoxicating liquors within, the importation thereof into, or the exportation thereof from the United States and all territory subject to the jurisdiction thereof, for beverage purposes, is hereby prohibited.*

2. *The Congress and the several States shall have concurrent power to enforce this article by appropriate legislation.*

3. *This article shall be inoperative unless it shall have been ratified as an amendment to the Constitution by the legislatures of the several States, as provided by the Constitution,* *within seven years from the date of the submission thereof to the States by the Congress.* [Adopted 1919; repealed 1933 by Twenty-first Amendment.]

Amendment XIX.   *Woman Suffrage*

For background see p. 712.

Women guaranteed the right to vote. 1. The right of citizens of the United States to vote shall not be denied or abridged by the United States or by any State on account of sex.

2. Congress shall have power to enforce this article by appropriate legislation. [Adopted 1920.]

Amendment XX.   *Presidential and Congressional Terms*

Shortens lame duck periods by modifying Art. I, Sec. IV, para. 2.

1. Presidential, vice presidential, and congressional terms of office begin in January. The terms of the President and Vice President shall end at noon on the 20th day of January, and the terms of Senators and Representatives at noon on the 3d day of January, of the years in which such terms would have ended if this article had not been ratified; and the terms of their successors shall then begin.

2. New meeting date for Congress. The Congress shall assemble at least once in every year, and such meeting shall begin at noon on the 3d day of January, unless they shall by law appoint a different day.

3. Emergency presidential and vice presidential succession. If, at the time fixed for the beginning of the term of the President, the President-elect shall have died, the Vice President–elect shall become President. If a President shall not have been chosen before the time fixed for the beginning of his term, or if the President-elect shall have failed to qualify, then the Vice President–elect shall act as President until a President shall have qualified; and the Congress may by law provide for the case wherein neither a President-elect nor a Vice President–elect shall have qualified, declaring who shall then act as President, or the manner in which one who is to act shall be selected, and such persons shall act accordingly until a President or Vice President shall have qualified.

4. The Congress may by law provide for the case of the death of any of the persons from whom the House of Representatives may choose a President whenever the right of choice shall have devolved upon them, and for the case of the death of any of the persons from whom the Senate may choose a Vice President whenever the right of choice shall have devolved upon them.

5. Sections 1 and 2 shall take effect on the 15th day of October following the ratification of this article.

6. This article shall be inoperative unless it shall have been ratified as an amendment to the Constitution by the Legislatures of three-fourths of the several States within seven years from the date of its submission. [Adopted 1993.]

Amendment XXI.   *Prohibition Repealed*

For background see p. 788.

1. Eighteenth Amendment repealed. The eighteenth article of amendment to the Constitution of the United States is hereby repealed.

2. Local laws honored. The transportation or importation into any State, Territory, or Possession of the United States for delivery or use therein of intoxicating liquors, in violation of the laws thereof, is hereby prohibited.

3. This article shall be inoperative unless it shall have been ratified as an amendment to the Constitution by conventions in the several States, as provided in the Constitution, within seven years from the date of the submission thereof to the States by the Congress. [Adopted 1933.]

Amendment XXII.

Sometimes referred to as the anti–Franklin Roosevelt amendment.

Anti–Third Term Amendment

1. Presidential term is limited. No person shall be elected to the office of President more than twice, and no person who has held the office of President, or acted as President, for more than two years of a term to which some other person was elected President shall be elected to the office of President more than once. But this article shall not apply to any person holding the office of President when this article was proposed by the Congress [i.e., Truman], and shall not prevent any person who may be holding the office of President, during the term within which this article becomes operative [i.e., Truman] from holding the office of President or acting as President during the remainder of such term.

2. This article shall be inoperative unless it shall have been ratified as an amendment to the Constitution by the legislatures of three-fourths of the several States within seven years from the date of its submission to the States by the Congress. [Adopted 1951.]

Amendment XXIII.

Designed to give the District of Columbia three electoral votes and to quiet the century-old cry of "No taxation without representation." Yet the District of Columbia still has only one nonvoting member of Congress.

District of Columbia Vote

1. Presidential electors for the District of Columbia. The District, constituting the seat of government of the United States, shall appoint in such manner as the Congress shall direct:

A number of electors of President and Vice President equal to the whole number of Senators and Representatives in Congress to which the District would be entitled if it were a State, but in no event more than the least populous State; they shall be in addition to those appointed by the States, but they shall be considered for the purposes of the election of President and Vice President, to be electors appointed by a State; and they shall meet in the District and perform such duties as provided by the twelfth article of amendment.

2. Enforcement. The Congress shall have the power to enforce this article by appropriate legislation. [Adopted 1961.]

Amendment XXIV.

Designed to end discrimination against poor people, including southern blacks who were often denied the vote through inability to pay poll taxes. See p. 931.

Poll Tax

1. Payment of poll tax or other taxes not to be prerequisite for voting in federal elections. The right of citizens of the United States to vote in any primary or other election for President or Vice President, for electors for President or Vice President, or for Senator or Representative in Congress, shall not be denied or abridged by the United States or any State by reason of failure to pay any poll tax or other tax.

2. Enforcement. The Congress shall have the power to enforce this article by appropriate legislation. [Adopted 1964.]

Amendment XXV.

Gerald Ford was the first "appointed president." See pp. 956, 960.

Presidential Succession and Disability

1. Vice president to become president. In case of the removal of the President from office or of his death or resignation, the Vice President shall become President.[1]

2. Successor to vice president provided. Whenever there is a vacancy in the office of the Vice President, the President shall nominate a Vice President who shall take office upon confirmation by a majority vote of both Houses of Congress.

---

[1]The original Constitution (Art. II, Sec. I, para. 5) was vague on this point, stipulating that "the powers and duties" of the president, but not necessarily the title, should "devolve" on the vice president. President Tyler, the first "accidental president," assumed not only the powers and duties but the title as well.

3. Vice president to serve for disabled president. Whenever the President transmits to the President pro tempore of the Senate and the Speaker of the House of Representatives his written declaration that he is unable to discharge the powers and duties of his office, and until he transmits to them a written declaration to the contrary, such powers and duties shall be discharged by the Vice President as Acting President.

4. Procedure for disqualifying or requalifying president. Whenever the Vice President and a majority of either the principal officers of the executive departments or of such other body as Congress may by law provide, transmit to the President pro tempore of the Senate and the Speaker of the House of Representatives their written declaration that the President is unable to discharge the powers and duties of his office, the Vice President shall immediately assume the powers and duties of the office as Acting President.

Thereafter, when the President transmits to the President pro tempore of the Senate and the Speaker of the House of Representatives his written declaration that no inability exists, he shall resume the powers and duties of his office unless the Vice President and a majority of either the principal officers of the executive department[s] or of such other body as Congress may by law provide, transmit within four days to the President pro tempore of the Senate and the Speaker of the House of Representatives their written declaration that the President is unable to discharge the powers and duties of his office. Thereupon Congress shall decide the issue, assembling within forty-eight hours for that purpose if not in session. If the Congress, within twenty-one days after receipt of the latter written declaration, or, if Congress is not in session, within twenty-one days after Congress is required to assemble, determines by two-thirds vote of both Houses that the President is unable to discharge the powers and duties of his office, the Vice President shall continue to discharge the same as Acting President; otherwise, the President shall resume the powers and duties of his office. [Adopted 1967.]

Amendment XXVI.   *Lowering Voting Age*

A response to the current revolt of youth. See p. 950.

1. Ballot for eighteen-year-olds. The right of citizens of the United States, who are eighteen years of age or older, to vote shall not be denied or abridged by the United States or any state on account of age.

2. Enforcement. The Congress shall have the power to enforce this article by appropriate legislation. [Adopted 1971.]

Amendment XXVII.   *Restricting Congressional Pay Raises*

Reflects anti-incumbent sentiment of early 1990s. First proposed by James Madison in 1789; took 203 years to be ratified.

Congress not allowed to increase its current pay. No law varying the compensation for the services of the Senators and Representatives shall take effect, until an election of Representatives shall have intervened. [Adopted 1992.]

*An American Profile:
The United States
and Its People*

Population, Percentage Change, and Racial Composition for the United States, 1790–2000

Census	Population of United States	Increase over Preceding Census Number	Increase over Preceding Census Percentage	Racial Composition, Percent Distribution* White	Black	Latino	Asian
1790	3,929,214			80.7	19.3	NA	NA
1800	5,308,483	1,379,269	35.1	81.1	18.9	NA	NA
1810	7,239,881	1,931,398	36.4	81.0	19.0	NA	NA
1820	9,638,453	2,398,572	33.1	81.6	18.4	NA	NA
1830	12,866,020	3,227,567	33.5	81.9	18.1	NA	NA
1840	17,069,453	4,203,433	32.7	83.2	16.8	NA	NA
1850	23,191,876	6,122,423	35.9	84.3	15.7	NA	NA
1860	31,433,321	8,251,445	35.6	85.6	14.1	NA	NA
1870	39,818,449	8,375,128	26.6	86.2	13.5	NA	NA
1880	50,155,783	10,337,334	26.0	86.5	13.1	NA	NA
1890	62,947,714	12,791,931	25.5	87.5	11.9	NA	NA
1900	75,994,575	13,046,861	20.7	87.9	11.6	NA	0.3
1910	91,972,266	15,997,691	21.0	88.9	10.7	NA	0.3
1920	105,710,620	13,738,354	14.9	89.7	9.9	NA	0.3
1930	122,775,046	17,064,426	16.1	89.8	9.7	NA	0.4
1940	131,669,275	8,894,229	7.2	89.8	9.8	NA	0.4
1950	150,697,361	19,028,086	14.5	89.5	10.0	NA	0.4
1960†	179,323,175	28,625,814	19.0	88.6	10.5	NA	0.5
1970	203,235,298	23,912,123	13.3	87.6	11.1	NA	0.7
1980	226,504,825	23,269,527	11.4	85.9	11.8	6.4	1.5
1990	248,709,873	22,205,048	9.8	83.9	12.3	9.0	2.9
2000	281,421,906	32,712,033	13.2	82.2	12.2	11.7	3.8

*Not every racial group included (e.g., no Native Americans). Persons of Latino origin may be of any race. Data for 1980, 1990, 2000 add up to more than 100% because those who identify themselves as "Latino" could still be counted as "White."
†First year for which figures include Alaska and Hawaii.
(Source: Census Bureau, *Historical Statistics of the United States*, updated by relevant *Statistical Abstract of the United States*.)

Population Density and Distribution, 1790–2000

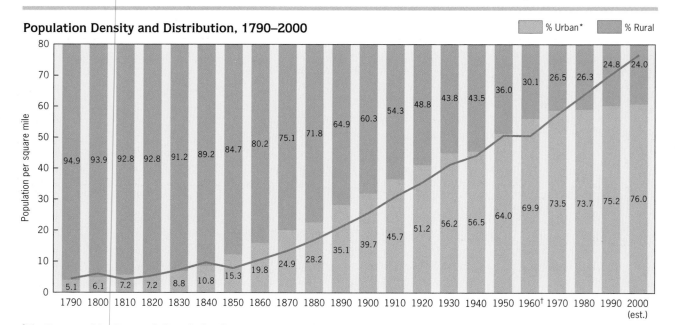

*The Bureau of the Census defines "urban" as communities of 2,500 or more inhabitants.
†First year for which figures include Alaska and Hawaii.
(Source: Census Bureau, *Historical Statistics of the United States*, updated by relevant *Statistical Abstract of the United States*.)

Changing Characteristics of the U.S. Population

Birthrates per thousand women ages 15–44

Life expectancy at birth

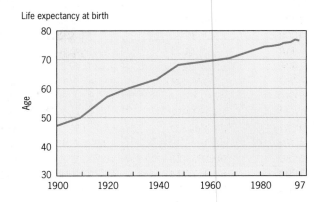

Median age of population (years)

Infant mortality

Household size

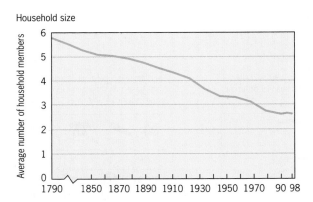

Median age at first marriage

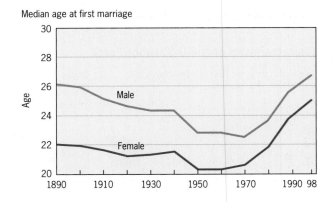

(Sources: *Historical Statistics of the United States* and *Statistical Abstract of the United States,* relevant years.)

Changing Lifestyles in Modern America

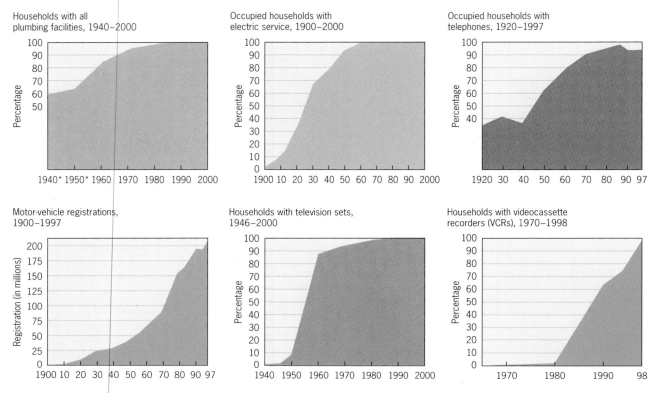

Households with all plumbing facilities, 1940–2000

Occupied households with electric service, 1900–2000

Occupied households with telephones, 1920–1997

Motor-vehicle registrations, 1900–1997

Households with television sets, 1946–2000

Households with videocassette recorders (VCRs), 1970–1998

*Except for 1940 and 1950, figures for "all plumbing facilities" (not detailed in source). For 1940, figure is for flush toilet, inside structure, private use (64.7 percent had flush toilet and private and/or shared inside structure, and 60.9 percent had installed bath or shower). For 1950, figure designates units with private toilet and bath and hot running water (flush toilet, private or shared inside structure is 74.3 percent; installed bathtub or shower, 72.9 percent).
(Sources: *Historical Statistics of the United States* and *Statistical Abstract of the United States*, relevant years.)

Characteristics of the U.S. Labor Force

Total labor force (age 16 or over, employed and unemployed seeking work)

Gender composition of labor force, 1900–2006 (percentage of men and women in civilian labor force)

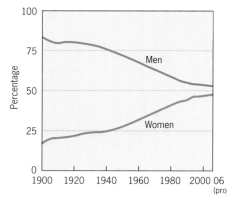

Top three occupational categories (rank based on total numbers) for workers age 14 and older

	farm	manual*	white collar†	service
Rank	1	2	3	
1900	farm	manual	white collar	
1920	manual	farm	white collar	
1940	manual	white collar	farm	
1960	white collar	manual	service	
1990	white collar	manual	service	
1998	white collar	manual	service	

*Manual workers = operators, fabricators, and laborers plus precision production, craft, and repair.
†White-collar workers = managerial and professional plus technical, sales, and administrative support.
(Sources: *Historical Statistics of the United States* and *Statistical Abstract of the United States*, relevant years, and Department of Labor, Bureau of Labor Statistics, *Handbook of Labor Statistics*, relevant years.)

Leading Economic Sectors (various years)

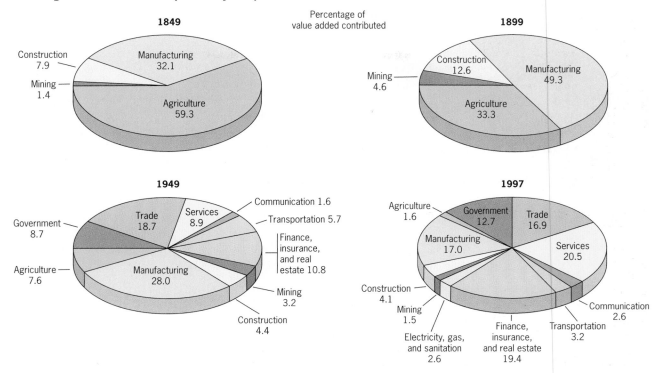

Percentage of value added contributed

1849

- Construction 7.9
- Mining 1.4
- Manufacturing 32.1
- Agriculture 59.3

1899

- Construction 12.6
- Mining 4.6
- Manufacturing 49.3
- Agriculture 33.3

1949

- Government 8.7
- Trade 18.7
- Services 8.9
- Communication 1.6
- Transportation 5.7
- Finance, insurance, and real estate 10.8
- Agriculture 7.6
- Manufacturing 28.0
- Mining 3.2
- Construction 4.4

1997

- Agriculture 1.6
- Government 12.7
- Trade 16.9
- Manufacturing 17.0
- Services 20.5
- Construction 4.1
- Mining 1.5
- Electricity, gas, and sanitation 2.6
- Finance, insurance, and real estate 19.4
- Transportation 3.2
- Communication 2.6

(Sources: *Historical Statistics of the United States* and *Statistical Abstract of the United States,* relevant years.)

Per Capita Disposable Personal Income in Constant (1987) Dollars, 1940–1998

1987 Dollars

Comparative Tax Burdens (percentage of gross domestic product paid as taxes in major industrial countries, 1998)

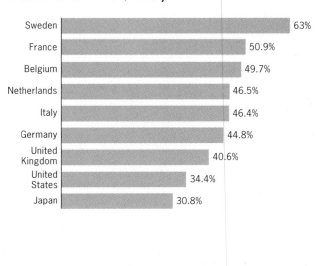

- Sweden 63%
- France 50.9%
- Belgium 49.7%
- Netherlands 46.5%
- Italy 46.4%
- Germany 44.8%
- United Kingdom 40.6%
- United States 34.4%
- Japan 30.8%

(Source for both graphs: *Statistical Abstract of the United States.*)

The Federal Budget Dollar and How It Is Spent, by Major Category

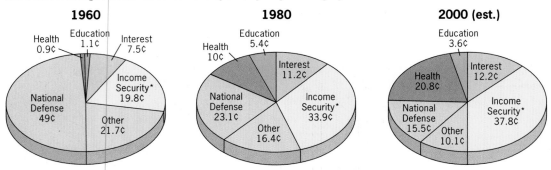

*Includes Social Security payments to the elderly and disabled, unemployment compensation, and welfare. Note the shifting emphasis in the budget from defense spending to health and income security, and to interest payments on the national debt.

The U.S. Balance of Trade, 1900–1998

Billions of dollars

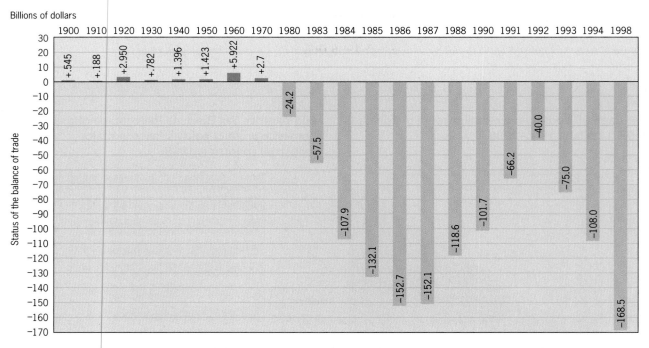

Status of the balance of trade

(Sources: *Historical Statistics of the United States* and *Statistical Abstract of the United States,* relevant years.)

Tariff Levies on Dutiable Imports, 1821–1996 (ratio of duties to value of dutiable imports)

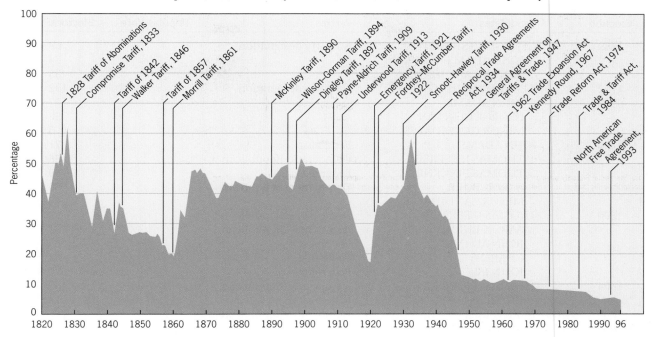

(Sources: *Historical Statistics of the United States* and *Statistical Abstract of the United States,* relevant years.)

Gross Domestic Product in Current and Constant 1995 Dollars*

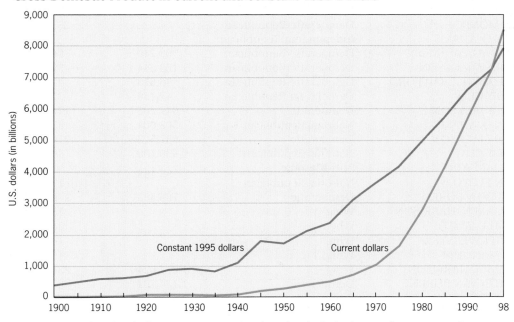

*Gross *national* product before 1960. Gross national product includes income from overseas investment and excludes profits generated in the United States but accruing to foreign accounts. Gross *domestic* product excludes overseas profits owed to American accounts but includes the value of all items originating in the United States, regardless of the ultimate destination of the profits. Until recent years, those factors made for negligible differences in the calculation of *national* and *domestic* product, but most economists now prefer the latter methodology.

Presidential Elections*

Election	Candidates	Parties	Popular Vote	Electoral Vote
1789	GEORGE WASHINGTON	No party designation		69
	JOHN ADAMS			34
	MINOR CANDIDATES			35
1792	GEORGE WASHINGTON	No party designation		132
	JOHN ADAMS			77
	GEORGE CLINTON			50
	MINOR CANDIDATES			5
1796	JOHN ADAMS	Federalist		71
	THOMAS JEFFERSON	Democratic-Republican		68
	THOMAS PINCKNEY	Federalist		59
	AARON BURR	Democratic-Republican		30
	MINOR CANDIDATES			48
1800	THOMAS JEFFERSON	Democratic-Republican		73
	AARON BURR	Democratic-Republican		73
	JOHN ADAMS	Federalist		65
	CHARLES C. PINCKNEY	Federalist		64
	JOHN JAY	Federalist		1
1804	THOMAS JEFFERSON	Democratic-Republican		162
	CHARLES C. PINCKNEY	Federalist		14
1808	JAMES MADISON	Democratic-Republican		122
	CHARLES C. PINCKNEY	Federalist		47
	GEORGE CLINTON	Democratic-Republican		6
1812	JAMES MADISON	Democratic-Republican		128
	DEWITT CLINTON	Federalist		89
1816	JAMES MONROE	Democratic-Republican		183
	RUFUS KING	Federalist		34
1820	JAMES MONROE	Democratic-Republican		231
	JOHN Q. ADAMS	Independent Republican		1
1824	JOHN Q. ADAMS (Min.)†	Democratic-Republican	108,740	84
	ANDREW JACKSON	Democratic-Republican	153,544	99
	WILLIAM H. CRAWFORD	Democratic-Republican	46,618	41
	HENRY CLAY	Democratic-Republican	47,136	37
1828	ANDREW JACKSON	Democratic	647,286	178
	JOHN Q. ADAMS	National Republican	508,064	83
1832	ANDREW JACKSON	Democratic	687,502	219
	HENRY CLAY	National Republican	530,189	49
	WILLIAM WIRT	Anti-Masonic ⎫	33,108	7
	JOHN FLOYD	National Republican ⎬		11
1836	MARTIN VAN BUREN	Democratic	765,483	170
	WILLIAM H. HARRISON	Whig ⎫		73
	HUGH L. WHITE	Whig ⎪	739,795	26
	DANIEL WEBSTER	Whig ⎬		14
	W. P. MANGUM	Whig ⎭		11
1840	WILLIAM H. HARRISON	Whig	1,274,624	234
	MARTIN VAN BUREN	Democratic	1,127,781	60
1844	JAMES K. POLK (Min.)†	Democratic	1,338,464	170
	HENRY CLAY	Whig	1,300,097	105
	JAMES G. BIRNEY	Liberty	62,300	

* Candidates receiving less than 1 percent of the popular vote are omitted. Before the Twelfth Amendment (1804), the Electoral College voted for two presidential candidates, and the runner-up became vice president. Basic figures are taken primarily from *Historical Statistics of the United States, Colonial Times to 1970* (1975), pp. 1073–1074, and *Statistical Abstract of the United States,* relevant years.

†"Min." indicates minority president—one receiving less than 50 percent of all popular votes.

Presidential Elections (continued)

Election	Candidates	Parties	Popular Vote	Electoral Vote
1848	ZACHARY TAYLOR	Whig	1,360,967	163
	LEWIS CASS	Democratic	1,222,342	127
	MARTIN VAN BUREN	Free Soil	291,263	
1852	FRANKLIN PIERCE	Democratic	1,601,117	254
	WINFIELD SCOTT	Whig	1,385,453	42
	JOHN P. HALE	Free Soil	155,825	
1856	JAMES BUCHANAN (Min.)*	Democratic	1,832,955	174
	JOHN C. FRÉMONT	Republican	1,339,932	114
	MILLARD FILLMORE	American	871,731	8
1860	ABRAHAM LINCOLN (Min.)*	Republican	1,865,593	180
	STEPHEN A. DOUGLAS	Democratic	1,382,713	12
	JOHN C. BRECKINRIDGE	Democratic	848,356	72
	JOHN BELL	Constitutional Union	592,906	39
1864	ABRAHAM LINCOLN	Union	2,206,938	212
	GEORGE B. MC CLELLAN	Democratic	1,803,787	21
1868	ULYSSES S. GRANT	Republican	3,013,421	214
	HORATIO SEYMOUR	Democratic	2,706,829	80
1872	ULYSSES S. GRANT	Republican	3,596,745	286
	HORACE GREELEY	Democratic Liberal Republican	2,843,446	66
1876	RUTHERFORD B. HAYES (Min.)*	Republican	4,036,572	185
	SAMUEL J. TILDEN	Democratic	4,284,020	184
1880	JAMES A. GARFIELD (Min.)*	Republican	4,453,295	214
	WINFIELD S. HANCOCK	Democratic	4,414,082	155
	JAMES B. WEAVER	Greenback-Labor	308,578	
1884	GROVER CLEVELAND (Min.)*	Democratic	4,879,507	219
	JAMES G. BLAINE	Republican	4,850,293	182
	BENJAMIN F. BUTLER	Greenback-Labor	175,370	
	JOHN P. ST. JOHN	Prohibition	150,369	
1888	BENJAMIN HARRISON (Min.)*	Republican	5,447,129	233
	GROVER CLEVELAND	Democratic	5,537,857	168
	CLINTON B. FISK	Prohibition	249,506	
	ANSON J. STREETER	Union Labor	146,935	
1892	GROVER CLEVELAND (Min.)*	Democratic	5,555,426	277
	BENJAMIN HARRISON	Republican	5,182,690	145
	JAMES B. WEAVER	People's	1,029,846	22
	JOHN BIDWELL	Prohibition	264,133	
1896	WILLIAM MC KINLEY	Republican	7,102,246	271
	WILLIAM J. BRYAN	Democratic	6,492,559	176
1900	WILLIAM MC KINLEY	Republican	7,218,491	292
	WILLIAM J. BRYAN	Democratic; Populist	6,356,734	155
	JOHN C. WOOLLEY	Prohibition	208,914	
1904	THEODORE ROOSEVELT	Republican	7,628,461	336
	ALTON B. PARKER	Democratic	5,084,223	140
	EUGENE V. DEBS	Socialist	402,283	
	SILAS C. SWALLOW	Prohibition	258,536	
1908	WILLIAM H. TAFT	Republican	7,675,320	321
	WILLIAM J. BRYAN	Democratic	6,412,294	162
	EUGENE V. DEBS	Socialist	420,793	
	EUGENE W. CHAFIN	Prohibition	253,840	

* "Min." indicates minority president—one receiving less than 50 percent of all popular votes.

Presidential Elections (continued)

Election	Candidates	Parties	Popular Vote	Electoral Vote
1912	WOODROW WILSON (Min.)*	Democratic	6,296,547	435
	THEODORE ROOSEVELT	Progressive	4,118,571	88
	WILLIAM H. TAFT	Republican	3,486,720	8
	EUGENE V. DEBS	Socialist	900,672	
	EUGENE W. CHAFIN	Prohibition	206,275	
1916	WOODROW WILSON (Min.)*	Democratic	9,127,695	277
	CHARLES E. HUGHES	Republican	8,533,507	254
	A. L. BENSON	Socialist	585,113	
	J. F. HANLY	Prohibition	220,506	
1920	WARREN G. HARDING	Republican	16,143,407	404
	JAMES M. COX	Democratic	9,130,328	127
	EUGENE V. DEBS	Socialist	919,799	
	P. P. CHRISTENSEN	Farmer-Labor	265,411	
1924	CALVIN COOLIDGE	Republican	15,718,211	382
	JOHN W. DAVIS	Democratic	8,385,283	136
	ROBERT M. LA FOLLETTE	Progressive	4,831,289	13
1928	HERBERT C. HOOVER	Republican	21,391,993	444
	ALFRED E. SMITH	Democratic	15,016,169	87
1932	FRANKLIN D. ROOSEVELT	Democratic	22,809,638	472
	HERBERT C. HOOVER	Republican	15,758,901	59
	NORMAN THOMAS	Socialist	881,951	
1936	FRANKLIN D. ROOSEVELT	Democratic	27,752,869	523
	ALFRED M. LANDON	Republican	16,674,665	8
	WILLIAM LEMKE	Union	882,479	
1940	FRANKLIN D. ROOSEVELT	Democratic	27,307,819	449
	WENDELL L. WILLKIE	Republican	22,321,018	82
1944	FRANKLIN D. ROOSEVELT	Democratic	25,606,585	432
	THOMAS E. DEWEY	Republican	22,014,745	99
1948	HARRY S TRUMAN (Min.)*	Democratic	24,179,345	303
	THOMAS E. DEWEY	Republican	21,991,291	189
	J. STROM THURMOND	States' Rights Democratic	1,176,125	39
	HENRY A. WALLACE	Progressive	1,157,326	
1952	DWIGHT D. EISENHOWER	Republican	33,936,234	442
	ADLAI E. STEVENSON	Democratic	27,314,992	89
1956	DWIGHT D. EISENHOWER	Republican	35,590,472	457
	ADLAI E. STEVENSON	Democratic	26,022,752	73
1960	JOHN F. KENNEDY (Min.)*†	Democratic	34,226,731	303
	RICHARD M. NIXON	Republican	34,108,157	219
1964	LYNDON B. JOHNSON	Democratic	43,129,566	486
	BARRY M. GOLDWATER	Republican	27,178,188	52
1968	RICHARD M. NIXON (Min.)*	Republican	31,785,480	301
	HUBERT H. HUMPHREY, JR.	Democratic	31,275,166	191
	GEORGE C. WALLACE	American Independent	9,906,473	46
1972	RICHARD M. NIXON	Republican	47,169,911	520
	GEORGE S. MC GOVERN	Democratic	29,170,383	17
1976	JIMMY CARTER	Democratic	40,828,657	297
	GERALD R. FORD	Republican	39,145,520	240

* "Min." indicates minority president—one receiving less than 50 percent of all popular votes.
†Six Democratic electors in Alabama, all eight unpledged Democratic electors in Mississippi, and one Republican elector in Oklahoma voted for Senator Harry F. Byrd.

Presidential Elections (continued)

Election	Candidates	Parties	Popular Vote	Electoral Vote
1980	RONALD W. REAGAN	Republican	43,899,248	489
	JIMMY CARTER	Democratic	35,481,435	49
	JOHN B. ANDERSON	Independent	5,719,437	0
1984	RONALD W. REAGAN	Republican	52,609,797	525
	WALTER MONDALE	Democratic	36,450,613	13
1988	GEORGE BUSH	Republican	47,946,422	426
	MICHAEL DUKAKIS	Democratic	41,016,429	111
1992	WILLIAM CLINTON (Min.)*	Democratic	43,728,275	370
	GEORGE BUSH	Republican	38,167,416	168
	H. ROSS PEROT	Independent	19,237,247	
1996	WILLIAM CLINTON (Min.)*	Democratic	45,628,667	379
	ROBERT DOLE	Republican	37,869,435	159
	H. ROSS PEROT	Reform	7,874,283	
2000	GEORGE W. BUSH (Min.)*	Republican	50,456,169	271
	ALBERT GORE, JR.	Democratic	50,996,116	267
	RALPH NADER	Green	2,783,728	0

* "Min." indicates minority president—one receiving less than 50 percent of all popular votes.

Presidents and Vice Presidents

Term	President	Vice President
1789–1793	George Washington	John Adams
1793–1797	George Washington	John Adams
1797–1801	John Adams	Thomas Jefferson
1801–1805	Thomas Jefferson	Aaron Burr
1805–1809	Thomas Jefferson	George Clinton
1809–1813	James Madison	George Clinton (d. 1812)
1813–1817	James Madison	Elbridge Gerry (d. 1814)
1817–1821	James Monroe	Daniel D. Tompkins
1821–1825	James Monroe	Daniel D. Tompkins
1825–1829	John Quincy Adams	John C. Calhoun
1829–1833	Andrew Jackson	John C. Calhoun (resigned 1832)
1833–1837	Andrew Jackson	Martin Van Buren
1837–1841	Martin Van Buren	Richard M. Johnson
1841–1845	William H. Harrison (d. 1841) John Tyler	John Tyler
1845–1849	James K. Polk	George M. Dallas
1849–1853	Zachary Taylor (d. 1850) Millard Fillmore	Millard Fillmore
1853–1857	Franklin Pierce	William R. D. King (d. 1853)
1857–1861	James Buchanan	John C. Breckinridge
1861–1865	Abraham Lincoln	Hannibal Hamlin
1865–1869	Abraham Lincoln (d. 1865) Andrew Johnson	Andrew Johnson

Presidents and Vice Presidents (continued)

Term	President	Vice President
1869–1873	Ulysses S. Grant	Schuyler Colfax
1873–1877	Ulysses S. Grant	Henry Wilson (d. 1875)
1877–1881	Rutherford B. Hayes	William A. Wheeler
1881–1885	James A. Garfield (d. 1881) Chester A. Arthur	Chester A. Arthur
1885–1889	Grover Cleveland	Thomas A. Hendricks (d. 1885)
1889–1893	Benjamin Harrison	Levi P. Morton
1893–1897	Grover Cleveland	Adlai E. Stevenson
1897–1901	William McKinley	Garret A. Hobart (d. 1899)
1901–1905	William McKinley (d. 1901) Theodore Roosevelt	Theodore Roosevelt
1905–1909	Theodore Roosevelt	Charles W. Fairbanks
1909–1913	William H. Taft	James S. Sherman (d. 1912)
1913–1917	Woodrow Wilson	Thomas R. Marshall
1917–1921	Woodrow Wilson	Thomas R. Marshall
1921–1925	Warren G. Harding (d. 1923) Calvin Coolidge	Calvin Coolidge
1925–1929	Calvin Coolidge	Charles G. Dawes
1929–1933	Herbert Hoover	Charles Curtis
1933–1937	Franklin D. Roosevelt	John N. Garner
1937–1941	Franklin D. Roosevelt	John N. Garner
1941–1945	Franklin D. Roosevelt	Henry A. Wallace
1945–1949	Franklin D. Roosevelt (d. 1945) Harry S Truman	Harry S Truman
1949–1953	Harry S Truman	Alben W. Barkley
1953–1957	Dwight D. Eisenhower	Richard M. Nixon
1957–1961	Dwight D. Eisenhower	Richard M. Nixon
1961–1965	John F. Kennedy (d. 1963) Lyndon B. Johnson	Lyndon B. Johnson
1965–1969	Lyndon B. Johnson	Hubert H. Humphrey, Jr.
1969–1974	Richard M. Nixon	Spiro T. Agnew (resigned 1973); Gerald R. Ford
1974–1977	Gerald R. Ford	Nelson A. Rockefeller
1977–1981	Jimmy Carter	Walter F. Mondale
1981–1985	Ronald Reagan	George Bush
1985–1989	Ronald Reagan	George Bush
1989–1993	George Bush	J. Danforth Quayle III
1993–2001	William Clinton	Albert Gore, Jr.
2001–	George W. Bush	Richard Cheney

Admission of States

(See p. 182 for order in which the original thirteen entered the Union.)

Order of Admission	State	Date of Admission	Order of Admission	State	Date of Admission
14	Vermont	Mar. 4, 1791	33	Oregon	Feb. 14, 1859
15	Kentucky	June 1, 1792	34	Kansas	Jan. 29, 1861
16	Tennessee	June 1, 1796	35	W. Virginia	June 20, 1863
17	Ohio	Mar. 1, 1803	36	Nevada	Oct. 31, 1864
18	Louisiana	April 30, 1812	37	Nebraska	Mar. 1, 1867
19	Indiana	Dec. 11, 1816	38	Colorado	Aug. 1, 1876
20	Mississippi	Dec. 10, 1817	39	N. Dakota	Nov. 2, 1889
21	Illinois	Dec. 3, 1818	40	S. Dakota	Nov. 2, 1889
22	Alabama	Dec. 14, 1819	41	Montana	Nov. 8, 1889
23	Maine	Mar. 15, 1820	42	Washington	Nov. 11, 1889
24	Missouri	Aug. 10, 1821	43	Idaho	July 3, 1890
25	Arkansas	June 15, 1836	44	Wyoming	July 10, 1890
26	Michigan	Jan. 26, 1837	45	Utah	Jan. 4, 1896
27	Florida	Mar. 3, 1845	46	Oklahoma	Nov. 16, 1907
28	Texas	Dec. 29, 1845	47	New Mexico	Jan. 6, 1912
29	Iowa	Dec. 28, 1846	48	Arizona	Feb. 14, 1912
30	Wisconsin	May 29, 1848	49	Alaska	Jan. 3, 1959
31	California	Sept. 9, 1850	50	Hawaii	Aug. 21, 1959
32	Minnesota	May 11, 1858			

Estimates of Total Costs and Number of Battle Deaths of Major U.S. Wars*

War	Total Costs[†] (millions of dollars)	Original Costs (millions of dollars)	Number of Battle Deaths
Vietnam Conflict	$352,000	$140,600	47,355[‡]
Korean Conflict	164,000	54,000	33,629
World War II	664,000	288,000	291,557
World War I	112,000	26,000	53,402
Spanish-American War	6,460	400	385
Civil War { Union only	12,952	3,200	140,414
Civil War { Confederacy (est.)	N.A.	1,000	94,000
Mexican War	147	73	1,733
War of 1812	158	93	2,260
American Revolution	190	100	6,824

* Deaths from disease and other causes are not shown. In earlier wars especially, owing to poor medical and sanitary practices, nonbattle deaths substantially exceeded combat casualties.
[†] The difference between total costs and original costs is attributable to continuing postwar payments for items such as veterans' benefits, interest on war debts, and so on.
[‡] 1957–1990
(Sources: *Historical Statistics of the United States, Statistical Abstract of the United States*, relevant years, and *The World Almanac and Book of Facts, 1986*.)

PHOTOGRAPH CREDITS

INDEX

CANADA

WASHINGTON

Columbia R.

OREGON COUNTRY
(By Agreement
with Britain, 1846)

OREGON

49° N

MONTANA

Missouri R.

NORTH DAKOTA

SOUTH DAKOTA

IDAHO

42° N

WYOMING

NEVADA

Great
Salt
Lake

MEXICAN CESSION
(1848)

UTAH

NEBRASKA

LOUISIANA
PURCHASE
(From France,
1803)

COLORADO

KANSAS

Colorado R.

CALIFORNIA

PACIFIC
OCEAN

ARIZONA

OKLAHOM

NEW MEXICO

GADSDEN PURCHASE
(From Mexico, 1853)

TEXAS
(Independent Republic,
Annexed 1845)

TEXAS

Rio Grande

Nueces R.

MEXICO

PACIFIC OCEAN

HAWAII
(Annexed 1898)

HAWAII

RUSSIA

ALASKA

CANADA

0   100   200 Miles
0   100   200 Kilometers

ALASKA PURCHASE
(From Russia, 1867)

PACIFIC OCEAN

0   200   400 Miles
0   200   400 Kilometers

GULF OF
ST. LAWRENCE

Lake Superior

WISCONSIN

MAINE

VT.

N.H.

MASS.

CONN.

R.I.

MICHIGAN

Lake Michigan

Lake Huron

Lake Erie

Lake Ontario

NEW YORK

SOTA

IOWA

ILLINOIS

INDIANA

OHIO

PENNSYLVANIA

NEW
JERSEY

DELAWARE

MASON-DIXON
LINE

MARYLAND

WEST
VIRGINIA

Ohio R.

KENTUCKY

VIRGINIA

MISSOURI

**THE ORIGINAL
UNITED STATES**
(By Treaty with Britain, 1783)

THE ORIGINAL THIRTEEN COLONIES

36°30′N

TENNESSEE

NORTH
CAROLINA

ARKANSAS

Mississippi R.

MISSISSIPPI

ALABAMA

SOUTH
CAROLINA

GEORGIA

ATLANTIC
OCEAN

LOUISIANA

**(Seized from Spain,
1810, 1813)**

FLORIDA
**(By Treaty with
Spain, 1819)**

Territorial Growth
of the
United States

GULF OF MEXICO

FLORIDA

BAHAMAS

PUERTO RICO
(Acquired from
Spain, 1898)

VIRGIN IS.
(Acquired from
Denmark, 1916-1917)

PUERTO RICO

VIRGIN ISLANDS

0   50   100 Miles

0   50   100 Kilometers

CUBA

DOMINICAN
REPUBLIC

0   200   400 Miles

0   200   400 Kilometers

Albers Equal-Area Projection

HAITI

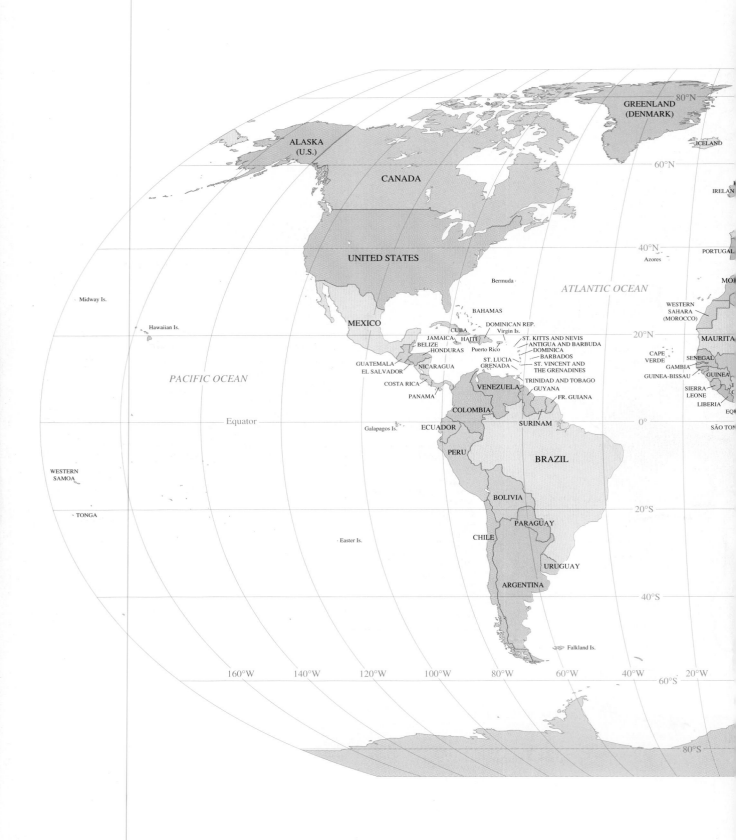

GREENLAND
(DENMARK)

ICELAND

ALASKA
(U.S.)

60°N

CANADA

IRELAN

40°N

PORTUGAL

UNITED STATES

Azores

MO

Bermuda ·

ATLANTIC OCEAN

WESTERN
SAHARA
(MOROCCO)

20°N

MEXICO

BAHAMAS

DOMINICAN REP.

CUBA

Virgin Is.

HAITI

ST. KITTS AND NEVIS

MAURITA

JAMAICA

ANTIGUA AND BARBUDA

BELIZE

DOMINICA

CAPE
VERDE

SENEGAL

HONDURAS

Puerto Rico

BARBADOS

GAMBIA

GUATEMALA

NICARAGUA

ST. LUCIA

ST. VINCENT AND

GUINEA-BISSAU

GUINEA

EL SALVADOR

GRENADA

THE GRENADINES

COSTA RICA

TRINIDAD AND TOBAGO

SIERRA

PACIFIC OCEAN

PANAMA

VENEZUELA

GUYANA

LEONE

FR. GUIANA

LIBERIA

COLOMBIA

SURINAM

EQ

Equator

Galapagos Is.

ECUADOR

0°

SÃO TON

PERU

BRAZIL

WESTERN
SAMOA

BOLIVIA

TONGA

20°S

PARAGUAY

Easter Is.

CHILE

URUGUAY

40°S

ARGENTINA

160°W   140°W   120°W   100°W   80°W   60°W   40°W   20°W

Falkland Is.

60°S

80°S

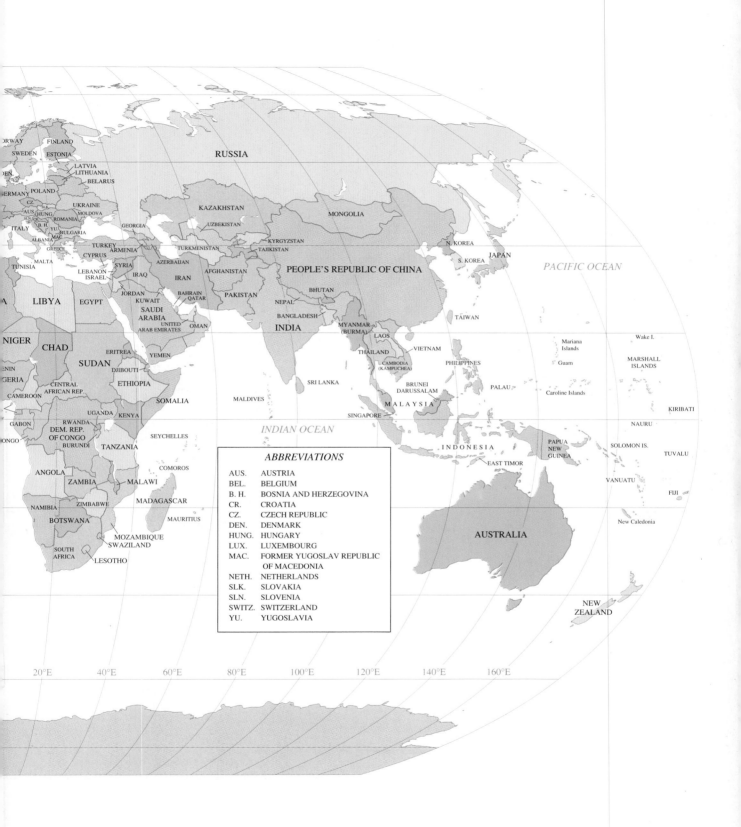

RUSSIA

NORWAY
FINLAND
SWEDEN
ESTONIA
LATVIA
LITHUANIA
DEN.
BELARUS
GERMANY POLAND
UKRAINE
KAZAKHSTAN
MONGOLIA
CZ.
SLK.
HUNG.
ROMANIA
MOLDOVA
UZBEKISTAN
AUS.
SLN.
ITALY
B.H.
YU.
BULGARIA
GEORGIA
KYRGYZSTAN
N. KOREA
ALBANIA
MAC.
GREECE
TURKEY
ARMENIA
TAJIKISTAN
S. KOREA
JAPAN
PACIFIC OCEAN
CYPRUS
AZERBAIJAN
TURKMENISTAN
TUNISIA
MALTA
SYRIA
IRAN
AFGHANISTAN
PEOPLE'S REPUBLIC OF CHINA
LEBANON
IRAQ
ISRAEL
LIBYA
EGYPT
JORDAN
KUWAIT
BAHRAIN
PAKISTAN
BHUTAN
QATAR
SAUDI
NEPAL
TAIWAN
ARABIA
UNITED
ARAB EMIRATES
OMAN
BANGLADESH
MYANMAR
NIGER
CHAD
ERITREA
YEMEN
INDIA
(BURMA)
LAOS
Wake I.
SUDAN
DJIBOUTI
THAILAND
VIETNAM
Mariana
Islands
NIGERIA
CENTRAL
AFRICAN REP.
ETHIOPIA
CAMBODIA
(KAMPUCHEA)
PHILIPPINES
Guam
MARSHALL
ISLANDS
CAMEROON
SOMALIA
SRI LANKA
BRUNEI
DARUSSALAM
PALAU
Caroline Islands
MALDIVES
UGANDA
KENYA
MALAYSIA
KIRIBATI
GABON
RWANDA
SINGAPORE
NAURU
CONGO
DEM. REP.
OF CONGO
BURUNDI
TANZANIA
SEYCHELLES
INDIAN OCEAN
INDONESIA
PAPUA
NEW
GUINEA
SOLOMON IS.
TUVALU
ANGOLA
COMOROS
EAST TIMOR
VANUATU
ZAMBIA
MALAWI
FIJI
NAMIBIA
ZIMBABWE
MADAGASCAR
MAURITIUS
BOTSWANA
New Caledonia
AUSTRALIA
MOZAMBIQUE
SWAZILAND
SOUTH
AFRICA
LESOTHO
NEW
ZEALAND

ABBREVIATIONS

AUS.	AUSTRIA
BEL.	BELGIUM
B. H.	BOSNIA AND HERZEGOVINA
CR.	CROATIA
CZ.	CZECH REPUBLIC
DEN.	DENMARK
HUNG.	HUNGARY
LUX.	LUXEMBOURG
MAC.	FORMER YUGOSLAV REPUBLIC OF MACEDONIA
NETH.	NETHERLANDS
SLK.	SLOVAKIA
SLN.	SLOVENIA
SWITZ.	SWITZERLAND
YU.	YUGOSLAVIA

20°E   40°E   60°E   80°E   100°E   120°E   140°E   160°E